Annotated

Laboratory Manual

PRENTICE HALL
Chemistry
Connections to Our Changing World

PRENTICE HALL
Upper Saddle River, New Jersey
Needham, Massachusetts

Annotated Teacher's Edition
Laboratory Manual

PRENTICE HALL Chemistry
Connections to Our Changing World

Contributing Writers

Bette Bridges
Chemistry Teacher
Bridgewater-Raynham High School
Bridgewater, Massachusetts

John C. Hugo
Chemistry Teacher
Carman-Ainsworth High School
Flint, Michigan

George E. Hussey
Chemistry Teacher
Falmouth High School
Falmouth, Massachusetts

Cristina Kerekes
Chemistry Teacher
Phillips Academy
Andover, Massachusetts

Kenneth Lyle
Chemistry Teacher
St. John's School
Houston, Texas

Joseph W. MacQuade, Jr.
Former Science Program Administrator
Marblehead High School
Marblehead, Massachusetts

Thomas L. Messer
Former Chemistry Teacher
The American School in Japan
Tokyo, Japan

Karen M. Robblee
Chemistry Teacher
Millbrook High School
Raleigh, North Carolina

Pamala Schupp
Chemistry Teacher
Kelly Walsh High School
Casper, Wyoming

Patricia Soghigian
Chemistry Teacher
Beverly High School
Beverly, Massachusetts

Clarice Wenz
Chemistry Teacher
Goose Creek High School
Goose Creek, South Carolina

Safety Expert
James A. Kaufman
Director
Laboratory Safety Workshop
Natick, Massachusetts

© 1996 by Prentice-Hall, Inc., a Simon & Schuster Company, Upper Saddle River, NJ 07458. All rights reserved. No part of this book may be reproduced or transmitted in any form or by any means, electronic or mechanical, including photocopying, recording, or by any information storage and retrieval system, without permission in writing from the publisher. Printed in the United States of America.

ISBN 0-13-837691-3

2 3 4 5 6 7 8 9 10   99 98 97 96 95

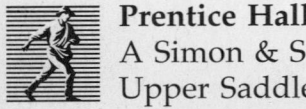
Prentice Hall
A Simon & Schuster Company
Upper Saddle River, NJ 07458

CONTENTS

To the Teacher T5

Correlation to Student Textbook T7

Small-Scale Chemistry T8

Guidelines for Laboratory Safety T12

Injury/Incident Report T17

Storage and Disposal of Chemicals T18

Selected Bibliography T23

Materials Inventory T24

Laboratory Suppliers T28

Preparation of Solutions T29

Guidelines for Disposal of Laboratory Wastes T31

To the Teacher

Laboratory investigations are a fundamental component of a comprehensive chemistry program. Laboratory work enables students to receive hands-on experience that complements the learning that takes place in the classroom. These firsthand observations allow students to develop and sharpen their manipulative, process, and critical-thinking skills, while giving them experience with a variety of techniques used in laboratory chemistry. The laboratory manual for *Chemistry: Connections to Our Changing World* was developed with these objectives in mind.

In this manual, you will find 80 investigations, designed to provide a range of laboratory experiences. For most chapters, there are three investigations that explore and reinforce concepts. One investigation per chapter is an application lab, which uses everyday materials or addresses a real-world problem. Additionally, about 40 percent of the investigations use a small-scale approach, thereby introducing students to lab techniques frequently used by working scientists and technicians. In every investigation, students will have opportunities to learn and practice the following laboratory skills:

- manipulating materials
- taking measurements
- making observations
- organizing data
- reporting data
- analyzing and interpreting data
- drawing conclusions
- following safe lab practices

Many labs also involve the use of graphing and calculating skills in the analysis and interpretation of quantitative data.

Each laboratory investigation has been designed to suit the varied needs of both students and teachers. The basic format of each lab is easy to follow and is flexible enough to accommodate differing student ability levels. The Pre-Lab Discussion, for example, helps students focus on the concepts related to the investigation and the procedures to be followed. Students who wish to expand their understanding of particular concepts can be encouraged to pursue the Going Further section of the investigations. Other features of this manual are designed to accommodate the needs of the teacher. The detailed teacher's notes, sample data, chapter correlations, and safety guidelines are included to facilitate your planning and teaching activities. Special consideration has been given to the disposal of hazardous wastes.

Using This Teacher's Edition

The teacher's notes that accompany each investigation are designed to help you implement the lab activity safely and smoothly. Each section of the notes provides specific information. As you familiarize yourself with this manual, you may find the following guide to the teacher's annotations helpful.

Materials: The Materials list is organized for a class of 30 students, usually working in pairs. The list identifies, by order of use in the Procedure, the total amount of chemicals and equipment needed for one class.

Time Required: An estimate is provided of how much lab time the investigation requires. While most labs can be completed in one period, some investigations require observations or multiple procedures that will entail two or more periods. Time constraints may be a critical factor for some teachers, and this consideration is reflected in the suggestions for shortening the required time.

Advance Preparation: This section helps you maximize the use of prep periods and lab time by identifying the materials that must be acquired or prepared before the investigation begins. You also will find specific instructions for mixing solutions and setting up equipment. When working with chemicals, be sure to follow the safety precautions that appear in the preparation instructions and elsewhere in this manual.

Introduction: In this section, you will find suggestions for demonstrations, discussions, and other approaches that provide ways of engaging the students' interest in the topic prior to the actual lab work. Background information to supplement the student Introduction also may appear.

Safety: Your teacher's notes complement the student safety information by alerting you to some specific hazards and the precautions that should be followed. They also supply reminders about standard procedures.

Teaching Tips: This section provides hints, strategies, notes on the Procedure, and other information that will help you to help your students conduct the investigation successfully. In these tips, you will find suggestions for refining student lab technique, handling equipment, facilitating the collection of data, and generating additional discussions.

Waste Disposal: Although most of the investigations in this manual avoid the use of highly hazardous chemicals, some labs include chemicals and other materials that necessitate specific disposal measures. These notes provide information for the safe disposal of all materials used in each investigation. Because regulations vary from one community, municipality, or state to another, be sure to check with your local authorities about specific requirements.

Cooperative Learning: Although most of the investigations are designed for students working in pairs, many of the labs lend themselves to situations where students can work in cooperative groups of three or four, or where students pool and analyze their data as a class. Suggestions for implementing cooperative learning activities appear in this section.

Sample Observations and Calculations: Sample data are provided in every lab as a guide to the observations and data students are expected to collect. Actual data, of course, will vary with the materials and techniques used by the students. Sample calculations appear in those labs where quantitative analysis of data is required.

Answers to Questions: These are sample responses to the questions in the Pre-Lab Discussion and Critical Thinking sections. In many cases, additional insights are provided for the teacher. Notes to aid discussion of some responses may also appear in the Teaching Tips.

Going Further: This section is designed to provide enrichment activities for motivated students and to give you an opportunity to expand the concepts of the investigation with students. The teacher's notes supply resource information, explanations, and background notes. If you choose to have students do the follow-up laboratory activities, be sure their experimental designs are logical and complete, and include a safety plan. Never let students work in the laboratory without supervision.

Correlation to Student Textbook

Each laboratory investigation that appears in this manual correlates to a specific chapter and section of *Chemistry: Connections to Our Changing World*. The following chart shows how you can match your lab program to your teaching plan.

Lab	Textbook Section	Lab	Textbook Section	Lab	Textbook Section	Lab	Textbook Section
1	1–5	21	7–2	41	14–4	61	21–1
2	1–6	22	8–2	42	14–4	62	21–2
3	1–6	23	8–2	43	15–1	63	21–4
4	2–2	24	8–2	44	15–4	64	22–1
5	2–3	25	9–2	45	15–4	65	22–3
6	2–5	26	9–2	46	16–1	66	22–3
7	3–2	27	9–3	47	16–3	67	23–2
8	3–2	28	10–2	48	16–3	68	23–3
9	3–3	29	10–2	49	17–1	69	23–3
10	4–3	30	10–3	50	17–2	70	24–1
11	4–3	31	11–1	51	17–2	71	24–2
12	4–5	32	11–2	52	18–1	72	25–2
13	5–1	33	11–3	53	18–2	73	25–3
14	5–2	34	12–2	54	18–3	74	25–5
15	5–2	35	12–2	55	19–1	75	26–2
16	6–1	36	12–4	56	19–1	76	26–2
17	6–4	37	13–3	57	19–3	77	26–4
18	6–5	38	13–4	58	20–1	78	27–2
19	7–1	39	13–5	59	20–1	79	27–4
20	7–2	40	14–2	60	20–2	80	27–4

Small-Scale Chemistry

Why Do Small-Scale Investigations?

If you have been in the chemistry classroom recently, you know how challenging it is to manage a chemistry laboratory. Safety and liability are a constant concern. Time is limited. The cost of chemicals and equipment is increasing rapidly. The problems associated with waste disposal are becoming more and more complex.

These trends have caused many chemistry teachers to reevaluate traditional laboratory activities. The small-scale movement is one response to these challenges. Small-scale experiments utilize a set of equipment and techniques that were originally developed for medical and clinical chemistry, then modified for high school laboratories. Much of the equipment used in small-scale experiments was first designed for genetics and biochemical research, such as research on recombinant DNA.

As their name implies, small-scale experiments require smaller amounts of chemicals than traditional labs. A student or team of students often uses no more than 1 or 2 milliliters of reagents during an experiment. Small-scale experiments also use lower concentrations of reagents than traditional labs. In many cases, solutions of reagents are no more concentrated than 1 M.

Because small-scale experiments use only a fraction of the materials necessary for traditional experiments, they have many advantages:

- The cost of chemicals is reduced.
- Risk of injury from spillage is greatly reduced.
- Fire and explosion hazards are almost entirely eliminated.
- Air quality is improved.
- Less waste is produced.
- Because they use significantly less reagents than traditional labs do, small-scale activities conserve resources and protect the environment by reducing toxic wastes at their source.
- Small-scale experiments normally can be completed in a shorter period of time than traditional labs. Because of the short duration of a small-scale experiment, there is usually time for pre-lab discussion and analysis of results as well as for the lab work itself. There may even be time to repeat an experiment in order to verify results.

If you choose to use small-scale labs, remember that they are not simply miniature versions of traditional labs. In many cases, they use new procedures and require slightly different lab skills. Often the experiments are qualitative rather than quantitative in nature.

Students need to learn different techniques when using small-scale equipment. For example, students may be asked to measure a reagent by counting drops from a micropipet rather than by reading the meniscus on a graduated cylinder. Students may need to practice these techniques before beginning an experiment, but in general the equipment is quite simple to use. In fact, small-scale labs are often easier for students to understand than traditional labs, where the focus may be on developing lab techniques rather than on chemical principles.

Small-scale activities may require a different approach than the more traditional methods, but they also provide students with a safe and inexpensive opportunity for hands-on exploration of chemical properties and transformations. Teachers who have used these techniques have enthusiastically endorsed them as an effective way to help students learn the principles of chemistry.

Small-Scale Equipment

Small-scale experiments use very different equipment than the apparatus used in traditional chemistry labs. In place of glass and metal equipment such as beakers, test tubes, and graduated cylinders, small-scale labs use simple plastic equipment. Most small-scale equipment is made of plastics such as polyethylene or polystyrene. These plastics have nonwettable—or hydrophobic—surfaces. This property of the plastics makes it easy to transfer and store aqueous solutions. It also makes the equipment easy to clean.

The equipment used in small-scale experiments gives these activities a number of advantages over traditional labs:

- Small-scale equipment is inexpensive and often reusable.
- In most cases, small-scale equipment is easier to manipulate than traditional lab equipment.
- The use of plastic equipment eliminates the hazards of working with breakable glass.
- The equipment can be set up and taken down in a short period of time.
- Most of the small-scale equipment and materials can be stored in a shoe box or other container that is easily transportable.

The two kinds of equipment used most frequently in small-scale activities are micropipets and well plates. Micropipets can be used for measuring and dispensing solutions, as well as for storing reagents. Figure 1 shows some of the micropipets that are commonly used in small-scale experiments. The Materials lists in most investigations do not specify the size of the bulb or the stem of the pipets, allowing the teacher to select the micropipets that are most appropriate for class needs and to adapt them as desired.

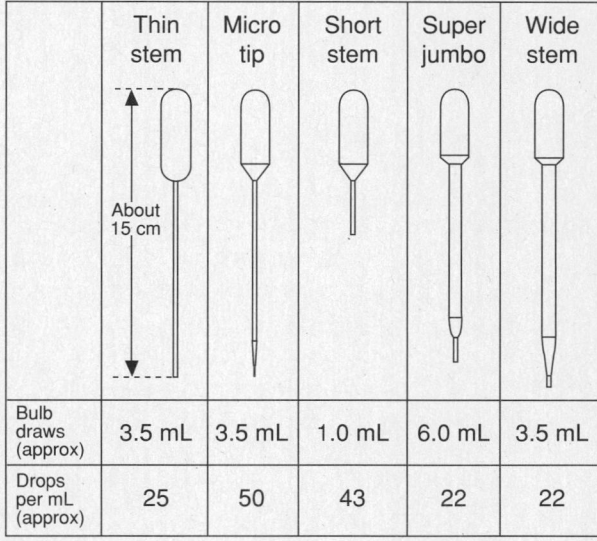

Figure 1

Instead of large test tubes in test-tube racks, small-scale experiments use the shallow wells of a well plate to observe chemical phenomena. Depending on the experimental procedure, a lab may use well plates with 6, 24, or 96 wells. Figure 2 shows a plate with 24 wells. Because well plates are made of clear polystyrene, they can also be used to demonstrate chemical phenomena on the overhead projector. Well plates usually come from the manufacturer with labels designating the rows and columns or the individual wells. Sometimes these labels are difficult to read. At other times, students may need additional information in the labels. If marking the wells is impractical, you can have students create the appropriate template on a sheet of white paper and place the well plate over the template for the duration of the procedure.

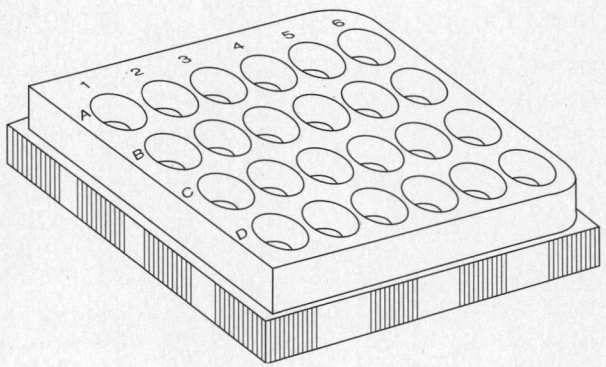

Figure 2

If you wish to implement small-scale procedures but do not have access to well plates or spot plates and micropipets, the following approach will work when the volumes of reactants are very small (one or two drops): Have students create a labeled template for the procedure on a sheet of white paper and lay a piece of clear plastic wrap over the template. Students then can add reagents to the appropriate areas on the plastic wrap and observe the reactions. Make sure students space their template labels far enough apart to prevent the samples from touching each other. Dropper bottles can be substituted for micropipets.

Small-Scale Techniques

Drawing Out a Thin-Stem Micropipet Stretching a thin-stem micropipet decreases the diameter of the stem opening. A smaller stem opening provides a more uniform drop size and decreases the likelihood of accidental spillage. To stretch the thin stem of a micropipet, hold the bulb end of the pipet in one hand with your thumb and index finger at the point where you want the drawn portion of the stem to start. With the other hand, wrap the rest of the stem around your index finger. Gently pull until you feel the stem beginning to lengthen. Allow the stem to stretch about 2 to 4 centimeters beyond its normal length.

Cutting the Stem of a Stretched Thin-Stem Pipet Using a knife, cut the stretched stem to the desired length. Cut the stem to a 1-cm length if you want to use the pipet for dropping solutions into the wells of a well plate. Make the stem length a little longer than the depth of the well if you plan to use the pipet for transferring a solution from one well to another or for removing a solution from a well. Because many well plates have wells that are a little less than 2 cm deep, a stem with a 2-cm length usually works best. You can use the short clipped-off pieces of stem as caps for filled micropipets. The tips of longer pieces can be heat-sealed and used for small-scale stirring rods.

Using a Micropipet Whenever a drawn-out thin-stem micropipet is used to dispense liquids, the pipet should be held vertically at a 90° angle to the desktop in order to ensure that each drop has the same size. You may want your students to practice this technique before beginning an experiment. After use, micropipets containing stock solutions may be retained for the following year. If micropipets contain hazardous wastes, empty their contents into appropriately labeled containers and refer to the guidelines in this manual for instructions on how to safely discard the chemicals and the contaminated pipets.

Labeling a Micropipet Label micropipets with an extra-fine permanent marker, or use adhesive labels covered by transparent tape. If you use a well plate as a holder for micropipets, label the pipets so that students can read the labels when the pipets sit upside down within the well plate. Micropipets also may be stored upside down in a beaker or in plastic audio-cassette cases.

Preparing a Plastic Funnel To make a small-scale plastic funnel for either liquids or solids, cut off both ends of a wide-stem micropipet using a knife. To make a filter for the small-scale funnel, fold some filter paper in half two times and cut to about the size of a quarter. You can also filter material with a small amount of cotton inserted into the funnel.

Cleaning Well Plates Fill the wells with tap water and then turn the well plate over in the sink area and shake. Rinse once more with distilled or deionized water (obtainable from the supermarket), and shake and tap on a paper towel to remove the water. If solid residues remain in the wells, clean the wells with a cotton swab and clean-rinsing detergent solution. Then rinse as described above. Avoid using test-tube brushes, as they tend to scratch the surface of the wells. If the well plate contains a material that requires special waste disposal methods, a dropper should be used to remove the material from the well plate. Then the material should be disposed of as directed in the guidelines for safe disposal of chemicals as described on pages T31–T32.

Guidelines for Laboratory Safety

This section on laboratory safety is included as a resource for the teacher. Rather than providing definitive rules and regulations, the information is intended to be the basis for the establishment of safe laboratory practice. Prentice-Hall, Inc., and its consultants make no claims as to the completeness of this material. Not all the precautions necessitated by the use, storage, and disposal of chemicals are covered here. Additional steps and safeguards may be required.

Responsibilities of the Teacher and the School

Over the past decade, chemistry teachers have become increasingly aware of the potential health risks involved in performing demonstrations and experiments as a part of high school chemistry classes. At the same time, teachers are aware of the importance of providing students with opportunities for hands-on experience with chemicals and their transformations. How can the educational objectives of active involvement in the laboratory be balanced with the need to control risks?

Laboratory safety is a shared responsibility. Both the school and the teacher need to be sure that all educational activities protect and promote the health and safety of students, school employees, and the environment. Society expects that schools and teachers will protect the safety of students. To do this, teachers need to understand the hazards, precautions, and emergency procedures associated with laboratory activities. When schools or teachers fail to live up to this responsibility, their behavior may be considered negligent. As a result, they may be liable for resulting injuries.

The best way to avoid being considered negligent is to ask yourself four simple questions:

1. What are the hazards?
2. What are the worst things that could happen?
3. What do I need to do if they do happen?
4. What are the prudent practices, protective facilities, and protective equipment needed to minimize the risk?

Be sure that you can answer all four of these questions before starting any science activity or demonstration.

Risk is part of all of our lives. Chemistry labs are no different. Safety is a judgment about the acceptability of risk. By understanding hazards, by using proper methods of protection, and by preparing for emergencies, the risks can be reduced to an acceptable level. This is the level where the pedagogical benefits of the activity outweigh the risks.

General Safety Guidelines

The safety and well-being of the participants in a chemistry laboratory are the responsibility of all those involved, but especially the teacher. Teachers should promote a "safety first" philosophy to avoid health hazards and injuries, while maintaining a stimulating learning environment. This can be accomplished by personal example and by the careful planning and implementation of safety strategies. It is equally important to make health and safety an integral part of the chemistry curriculum.

The following recommendations should be helpful in the pursuit of a safe laboratory.

1. Set up a laboratory safety committee made up of both teachers and administrators. Arrange to meet regularly to set safety policy for the school, discuss any safety problems that might arise, and organize periodic inspections of laboratories.

2. Establish a safety and health reference shelf in the science department office.

3. Develop detailed plans explaining what to do in case of emergency; review the procedures periodically throughout the school year.

4. Inform students of these emergency plans and carry out unannounced drills.

5. Keep up to date in first aid and CPR (cardiopulmonary resuscitation) training.

6. Post emergency phone numbers for ambulance, fire, police, hospital, and the poison control center next to the laboratory telephone.

7. Read the Material Safety Data Sheets (MSDS) furnished by chemical manufacturing companies for each chemical used, noting any possible hazards as well as directions for proper handling. These sheets are now required by law to be provided with every chemical purchased. Upon request, companies will provide you with MSDSs for chemicals purchased before the law went into effect.

8. Perform laboratory investigations before assigning them to students. Take note of any potential hazards; devise plans for dealing with any possible mishaps or emergencies.

9. Emphasize safety considerations in pre-laboratory discussions. Hang posters dealing with safety issues in both the classroom and the laboratory as reminders.

10. Be sure that your laboratory room has at least two exits.

11. Keep laboratory aisles and exits clear from obstruction.

12. Insist on serious, proper conduct in the lab.
- No horseplay.
- No smoking, eating, or drinking.
- No unauthorized experiments.

13. Do not allow students to work without supervision.

14. Require proper clothing at all times. Insist that long hair, dangling jewelry, and loose clothing be restrained; do not allow students to wear open shoes.

15. Require proper eye protection at all times. Request that students wear eyeglasses instead of contact lenses. Contacts, particularly soft lenses, may be a hazard in the event of a chemical splash into the eye. If a student does not have eyeglasses to replace contact lenses in the lab, parents should be notified about the possible additional risk. Always require students to wear goggles over contact lenses.

16. Encourage students to keep lab benches neat and clear of extraneous objects, such as books and jackets.

17. Make sure that investigations utilizing toxic, fuming, or flammable materials are performed under the fume hood.

18. Keep the fume hood clear of unnecessary chemicals and equipment. Have the fume hood checked periodically to ensure that it is operating safely and efficiently.

19. Demonstrate to students the proper handling of glass materials, such as tubing, pipets, and cylinders.

20. Only wastepaper should be discarded in wastepaper receptacles. Keep a separate container for broken glass.

21. Emphasize that suction bulbs are to be used with pipets—students should never use their mouths to create suction.

22. Consider the use of dispensing devices for liquids. They help prevent spills, skin contact with chemicals, and waste.

23. Use hot plates in place of open flames whenever possible. Never use open flames or hot plates when flammables are present in the room.

24. Whenever possible, use nonmercury thermometers in investigations that call for the measurement of temperature.

25. When inserting glass tubing or thermometers into rubber stoppers, use safety stoppers, which have holes with bevelled edges and are easier to use. Use glycerin or water to lubricate the glass.

26. Require the use of safety shields during experiments in which there is a chance of explosion or implosion.

27. Do not leave equipment running unattended.

28. Wear all safety equipment required of students.

29. Actively supervise students whenever lab activities are being conducted.

30. Report in writing all unsafe conditions to the department head, maintenance director, and principal.

31. Have clearly defined penalties for violations of safety rules. Have these penalties approved and supported by the principal.

32. Document safety training, rules violations, and penalties in your records.

33. Develop clear written guidelines for dealing with common emergency situations such as fires, spills, poisoning, burns, cuts, electric shock, medical problems, and explosions.

34. Require students to sign a rules agreement. Also ask their parents to sign this agreement to indicate that they understand what is expected of their daughter or son.

Emergency Equipment

Laboratory emergency equipment includes a telephone or intercom, fire extinguishers, a safety shower, fire blankets, spill kits, an eye wash, and a first-aid kit. Teachers and students should know how to use this equipment and be aware of its location in the room. When installing or storing this equipment, be sure to consider the special needs of any disabled students in your classes.

1. Post emergency phone numbers and instructions on every phone and intercom. Do not allow this information to become hidden by other materials.

2. Train your students how to summon assistance in an emergency.

3. Emergency equipment should be up to date and maintained in good working order. Be sure that this equipment is easily accessible to all of your students.

4. Install smoke alarms and fire detectors, especially if there is no water sprinkler system.

5. Fire extinguishers should be tested annually and kept in good working order.

6. The eye wash should be plumbed into the building (not portable) and should be able to provide a continuous stream of water at body temperature for 15 minutes. Proper use consists of holding the eyelids back and rolling the eyeballs to allow a thorough flushing of both eyes for at least 15 minutes.

7. Spill kits can be purchased from supply companies. They can also be made from sand or kitty litter, although the homemade kits do not absorb gases as do the commercially prepared kits.

8. The safety shower should have a lever action valve that remains on until it is pushed to the off position. The shower should deliver 30 gallons per minute.

Safety Equipment

1. All students should wear eye protection in the laboratory. They should also wear lab aprons or lab coats and, when appropriate, gloves.

2. Supply students with chemical splash goggles whenever an investigation involves liquid reagents or products. Chemical splash goggles have shielded air vents on the sides that protect against the entry of liquids while allowing for ventilation. When no liquid chemicals are involved, safety goggles with unshielded vents are adequate. Students should never use eye protection that does not enclose the eyes.

3. Students should use tongs, test-tube holders, and similar equipment whenever appropriate.

4. Teachers should demonstrate and practice the proper use of all safety equipment.

Safety Incident Record

It is extremely important to maintain a record of any injury that may occur in the laboratory, no matter how minor it may seem. All injuries and incidents (close calls) should be documented and reported to the appropriate school officials. These officials may include the science department head, the principal, and a designated safety officer. All reports should be thoroughly discussed at a department meeting to avoid recurrence of the incident.

Safety Inspections and Audits

Regular inspections of laboratories are essential. They help to identify unsafe conditions and unsafe practices. Laboratories and storage areas should be inspected quarterly by members of the science department. Audits should include an inspection of the laboratory facilities, the chemical storeroom, emergency equipment, and waste disposal procedures.

Checklists to help you conduct an inspection are available from several sources. One such checklist is available from The Laboratory Safety Workshop, 101 Oak Street, Wellesley, MA 02181-4723.

OSHA Laboratory Standard

The United States Occupational Safety and Health Administration (OSHA) has developed a set of regulations for laboratory safety called the OSHA Laboratory Standard, or "Occupational Exposure to Hazardous Chemicals in Laboratories." At present, the regulations in this standard apply to all private schools and public schools in 26 states. It is likely that OSHA reform legislation will make this law mandatory for all schools by 1997.

The OSHA Laboratory Standard requires schools to appoint a chemical hygiene officer and to create a written chemical hygiene plan. A chemical hygiene plan outlines practices that, if followed, will prevent exposure to harmful chemicals at levels believed to be unhealthful. The chemical hygiene officer for the school should assist in the development and implementation of the chemical hygiene plan.

Model chemical hygiene plans are available from many state departments of education and school chemical suppliers. OSHA has included their model plan in Appendix A of the Laboratory Standard.

Injury/Incident Report

STUDENT'S NAME: _____ DATE OF REPORT: _____

STUDENT'S HOME ADDRESS: _____
_____

NAME OF SCHOOL'S INSURANCE COMPANY: _____
_____

NAME OF SUPERVISING EMPLOYEE: _____

NAME OF WITNESS(ES): _____
_____

LOCATION, DATE, AND TIME OF INCIDENT: _____
_____
_____

DESCRIPTION OF INCIDENT: _____
_____
_____
_____
_____
_____

DESCRIPTION OF MEDICAL CARE PROVIDED: _____
_____
_____
_____
_____

NAME OF DOCTOR AND HOSPITAL: _____
_____

SUGGESTIONS FOR PREVENTION OF FUTURE RECURRENCE: _____
_____
_____

NAME OF PERSON COMPLETING THIS FORM: _____

© Prentice-Hall, Inc.   *Guidelines for Laboratory Safety*

Storage and Disposal of Chemicals

Proper storage and disposal of chemicals is an essential part of an overall laboratory safety program. With a well-planned and implemented storage system, most safety hazards and injuries can be avoided. The following are recommendations for safe chemical storage in a high school.

The Storeroom

Chemicals should not be stored in the classroom or laboratory. Instead, they should be kept in a separate room designated solely for that purpose. Access to this room should be restricted.

The storeroom should be well ventilated. There should be two means of exit from the storeroom; a window will suffice as one exit if the room is on a floor that is low enough.

The storeroom should be equipped with a fire alarm system that can be heard outside the room. Emergency equipment, such as a first-aid kit, spill kit, fire extinguisher, eye wash, and shower, should be readily available to the storeroom. There should be a telephone near the storeroom with emergency numbers for ambulance, fire, police, hospital, and the poison control center posted next to it. A circuit breaker for the storeroom should be easily accessible in case of emergency.

The shelving structures in the storeroom should be arranged so that there are no blind alleys and it is easy to exit the room. Make sure that the shelves are stable, with no chance of collapse. In areas where earthquake risk is significant, shelves should have a no-roll lip on their edges.

Storing Reagents

Many chemical companies provide information about the hazards, storage, and safety of reagents on the container label. Examine these labels carefully for pertinent information. More detailed information may be obtained from the Material Safety Data Sheets provided with the chemicals. A good source of additional information is the "Fire Protection Guide on Hazardous Materials" from the National Fire Protection Association, Quincy, MA.

Flammable and toxic materials should be stored in fireproof cabinets. If such cabinets are not available, these chemicals should be stored in safety cans. If you are storing chemicals that need to be refrigerated, use only an explosion-proof refrigerator. Do not use a kitchen refrigerator for chemical storage, and never store food in the same refrigerator.

It is wise to store particularly hazardous substances, such as corrosive liquids or volatile toxins, in bottles that are coated with plastic. The plastic coating prevents spillage in case the bottle is cracked or broken. Coated bottles are available from chemical supply houses.

Chemicals should be arranged on shelves according to compatible chemical families. Several chemical supply companies have devised systems of compatible chemical families, complete with color-coded reagent labels that make it easy to arrange the chemicals on the shelves in compatible groups. In general, store oxidizing agents away from organic chemicals. Do not arrange chemicals alphabetically, because this arrangement often places incompatible chemicals close together. The table on page T21 identifies some examples of incompatible chemicals.

Do not overload shelves. Store bottles no more than two deep, and leave adequate space between them. Avoid using the floor or shelves above eye level for storage. Place large containers on lower shelves and put trays under them to catch leaks.

Keep only the minimum amount of chemicals necessary on hand. Remember this goal when placing chemical orders. When new chemicals are purchased, label the container with the date received and the expected shelf life.

Perform an inventory of the storeroom periodically and dispose of any chemicals that are old or unlikely to be used. Check the labels on containers annually to make sure they are secure.

Disposing of Chemicals

The disposal of chemical wastes is governed by a variety of federal and state regulations. The Resource Conservation and Recovery Act of 1976 (RCRA), as administered by the U.S. Environmental Protection Agency (EPA), addresses the disposal of hazardous solid wastes. Some individual states have regulations for waste disposal that are even more stringent than those required by this act, however. Check with your local environmental agencies to obtain more complete and current information on this issue. The addresses of the EPA Regional Offices are provided on page T22.

RCRA defines a hazardous waste as an ignitable, corrosive, reactive, toxic, and/or acutely hazardous substance that is of no value, i.e., of no further use. Schools have several options for disposing of substances that cannot be reused or recycled. Disposal contractors can be hired to pack up, label, and deliver hazardous wastes to EPA-sanctioned disposal sites; these contractors must then certify that these measures have been taken. Schools should establish routine budgeting for this option just as they do for nonhazardous wastes. In some cases, the school itself may pack the wastes in Department of Transportation–approved steel drums, containing absorbent material, which can then be hauled away by an EPA-approved contractor.

The American Chemical Society suggests several other alternatives for chemical disposal. Schools may perform simple neutralization reactions for acidic or basic wastes and then use drain disposal, but only if the resulting products are themselves not regulated as hazardous wastes. Additional steps may be added to existing lab procedures to produce less hazardous or nonhazardous products.

When laboratory sink drains are connected to publicly operated treatment works, it may be permissible to pour certain wastes down the drain. In this case, drain disposal is regulated by the Clean Water Act and the Safe Drinking Water Act. The science department should contact the municipal water treatment facility and discuss the identity, quantity, and concentration of such materials. Proceed only with written permission obtained in response to a written request.

On the following page, you will find broad recommendations for the safe disposal of chemical wastes. See pages T31–T32 for additional information.

- In general, consult the reagent's Material Safety Data Sheet (MSDS) for handling, disposal, and emergency instructions. However, you may need to review chemical disposal procedures published by certain supply houses. These procedures may not comply sufficiently with RCRA regulations.

- Before each investigation, instruct your students concerning where and how they are to dispose of chemicals that are used or produced during the investigation.

- Keep each excess or used chemical in a separate container; do not mix them. This allows for possible recycling or reuse. It also eliminates unexpected reactions or the need for expensive separation by a contractor if the wastes must be disposed of professionally.

- Limit the quantity of wastes by using minimal amounts of reagents in experiments. Small-scale experiments are very helpful in this regard.

- Reduce wastes by substituting less hazardous chemicals for more hazardous ones and by maintaining a current inventory to avoid purchasing unneeded materials.

- Keep drainage lines for the laboratory sinks separate from sanitary lines.

- Only nonflammable, neutral, nontoxic, nonreactive, and water-soluble chemicals should be flushed down the drain.

- Provide special, properly labeled disposal containers for hazardous wastes. Water-insoluble liquids that are denser than water may clog the drain. If liquids are volatile, the container should be kept in the fume hood. Lids on waste containers must be kept closed except when waste is being poured into the container. Do not allow flammable or toxic solvents to evaporate.

- Contact other local schools, colleges, and universities to find out how they deal with waste disposal. When schools work together, they obtain cost savings on waste disposal.

- Each school must have an EPA hazardous waste generator identification number. Contact your regional EPA office or state agency to get a notification form.

- Keep a permanent record of waste material that is removed from your school. Your copy of the EPA-required manifest will serve this purpose. It will show the identity of the chemicals, their amount, the date they were labeled "hazardous waste," the date of disposal, the disposal contractor, and the disposal site. Your school is liable for these materials even after they have been removed from the school. For this reason, it is essential to hire only reputable, EPA-licensed contractors who dispose of wastes at EPA-licensed sites.

- For further information about RCRA and EPA, call 1-800-424-9346.

Table of Incompatible Chemicals

The selected chemicals on the left should be stored as far away as possible from those on the right.

acetic acid	chromic acid, ethylene glycol, hydroxyl compounds, nitric acid, perchloric acid, permanganates, peroxides
acetone	concentrated nitric and sulfuric acid solutions
alkali and alkaline earth metals (Ca, Li, Na, K, and Mg), and powdered Al	carbon dioxide, carbon tetrachloride (and other chlorinated hydrocarbons), halogens, water
ammonia	calcium hypochlorite, halogens, hydrofluoric acid, mercury
carbon (activated)	calcium hypochlorite, oxidizing agents
carbon tetrachloride	sodium
copper	acetylene, hydrogen peroxide, nitric acid
flammable liquids	ammonium nitrate, chromic acid, halogens, hydrogen peroxide, nitric acid, sodium peroxide
hydrocarbons	bromine, chlorine, chromic acid, fluorine, sodium peroxide
hydrogen peroxide	acetone, alcohols, aniline, chromium, combustible materials, copper, iron, organic materials, most metals or their salts
iodine	acetylene, ammonia, hydrogen
nitrates	sulfuric acid
nitric acid	acetic acid, chromic acid, copper, flammable liquids or gases, heavy metals, hydrocyanic acid, hydrogen sulfide
nitrites	acids
oxygen	flammable liquids/solids/gases, grease, hydrogen, oils
phosphorus (white)	air, alkalis, oxygen, reducing agents
silver	acetylene, ammonium compounds, oxalic acid, tartaric acid
sulfides	acids
sulfuric acid	chlorates, perchlorates, and permanganates of light metals

This table is adapted from: *Safety in Academic Chemistry Laboratories,* American Chemical Society, 1985.

U.S. Environmental Protection Agency Regional Offices

EPA Region I
Waste Regulation Section
90 Canal Street
Boston, Massachusetts 02203
(617) 573-5740

Connecticut, Massachusetts, Maine, New Hampshire, Rhode Island, Vermont

EPA Region II
Air and Waste Management Division
26 Federal Plaza
New York, New York 10278
(212) 264-5175

New Jersey, New York, Puerto Rico, Virgin Islands

EPA Region III
Waste Management Branch
841 Chestnut Street
Philadelphia, Pennsylvania 19107
(215) 597-3200

Delaware, Maryland, Pennsylvania, Virginia, West Virginia, District of Columbia

EPA Region IV
Hazardous Waste Management Division
345 Courtland Street, N.E.
Atlanta, Georgia 30365
(404) 347-3016

Alabama, Florida, Georgia, Kentucky, Mississippi, North Carolina, South Carolina, Tennessee

EPA Region V
Resource Conservation and Recovery Act Branch
77 West Jackson Boulevard
Chicago, Illinois 60604
(312) 886-7435

Illinois, Indiana, Michigan, Minnesota, Ohio, Wisconsin

EPA Region VI
Hazardous Waste Management Division
1445 Ross Avenue (6H)
Dallas, Texas 75202-2733
(214) 665-6700

Arkansas, Louisiana, New Mexico, Oklahoma, Texas

EPA Region VII
Resource Conservation and Recovery Act Branch
726 Minnesota Avenue
Kansas City, Kansas 66101
(913) 551-7051

Iowa, Kansas, Missouri, Nebraska

EPA Region VIII
Waste Management Division
999 18th Street, Suite 500 (HWM-WM)
Denver, Colorado 80202-2405
(303) 294-1361

Colorado, Montana, North Dakota, South Dakota, Utah, Wyoming

EPA Region IX
Air and Toxics Division
75 Hawthorne Street
San Francisco, California 94105
(415) 744-1219

Arizona, California, Hawaii, Nevada, American Samoa, Guam, Trust Territories of the Pacific

EPA Region X
Waste Management Branch
1200 Sixth Avenue (WD-134)
Seattle, Washington 98101
(206) 553-1213

Alaska, Idaho, Oregon, Washington

Selected Bibliography

Benedict, R. *New Chemicals for Old*. Minnesota Department of Education, 1987.

Bretherick, L. *Hazards in the Chemical Laboratory*, 4th ed. Royal Society of Chemistry, 1986.

Committee on Chemical Safety. *Safety in Academic Chemistry Laboratories*, 5th ed. American Chemical Society, 1990.

Committee on Hazardous Substances in the Laboratory, Assembly of Mathematical and Physical Sciences, National Research Council. *Prudent Practices for Handling Chemicals in Laboratories*. National Academy Press, 1981.

Committee on Hazardous Substances in the Laboratory, Commission on Physical Sciences, Mathematics, and Resources, National Research Council. *Prudent Practices for Disposal of Chemicals from Laboratories*. National Academy Press, 1983.

Council of State Science Supervisors. *School Science Laboratories—A Guide to Some Hazardous Substances*, 1984.

Department of Government Relations and Science Policy. *Less Is Better—Laboratory Management for Waste Reduction*. American Chemical Society, 1985.

Environmental Protection Agency. *Understanding the Small Quantity Generator Hazardous Waste Rules*, 1986.

Furr, K. *Handbook of Laboratory Safety*, 3rd ed. CRC Press, 1990.

Gerlovich, J. A., et al. *School Science Safety*. Flinn Scientific, Inc., 1984.

Kaufman, J. A. *Waste Disposal in Academic Institutions*. Lewis Publishers, 1990.

Lefevre, M. J. *First Aid Manual for Chemical Accidents*, 2nd ed. Van Nostrand Reinhold, 1989.

National Fire Protection Association. *Fire Protection for Laboratories Using Chemicals*, Code 45-91, 1991.

National Fire Protection Association, *Fire Protection Guide on Hazardous Materials*, HAZ-94, 1994.

National Institute of Environmental Health Sciences. *Annual Report on Carcinogens*, 7th ed. U.S. Department of Health and Human Services, 1994.

National Institute for Occupational Safety and Health. *Safety in the School Science Laboratory*, 1980.

National Institute for Occupational Safety and Health. *Manual of Safety and Health Hazards in the School Science Laboratory*, 1980.

Office of Curriculum and Program Development. *Planning A Safe and Effective Science Learning Environment*. Texas Education Agency, 1989.

Pipitone, D. A., ed. *Safe Storage of Laboratory Chemicals*, 2nd ed. Wiley-Interscience, 1990.

Task Force on RCRA, Department of Government Relations and Science Policy. *The Waste Management Manual for Laboratory Personnel*. American Chemical Society, 1990.

Wahl, G. H. Jr., ed. *Reduction of Hazardous Waste from High School Chemistry Laboratories*. Kaufman & Associates, 1994.

Woods, C. *Safety in Science Laboratories*. Kaufman & Associates, 1994.

Young, J. A., Editor, *Improving Safety in the Chemical Laboratory: A Practical Guide*, 2nd ed. Wiley-Interscience, 1991.

Materials Inventory

CHEMICALS

Substance	Quantity*	Investigation	Disposal Method*	Substance	Quantity	Investigation	Disposal Method
2-propanol	1.5 L	43	3 or 8	dry ice, 10 × 10 cm	15 pieces	70	
acetic acid (17 M)	25 mL	6, 52, 53, 74	2	EDTA	1 g	51	8
aluminum foil	0.5 × 4 cm	16	1	ethanol	2.5 L	2, 8, 20, 23, 77	(D001) 3 or 8
aluminum oxide	15 g	16	1	ethylene glycol	100 mL	2, 23	3
ammonia (18 M)	250 mL	6, 39, 48	2	FRH chemical samples	8	35	4
ammonia, household	1.5 L	21, 57	2	galvanized iron, 2 × 5 cm	15 pieces	32	1
ammonium carbonate	15 g	25	1	glycerin	1 L	20, 23, 25	8
ammonium chloride	200 g	34, 51	1	hydrochloric acid (12 M)	2 L	5, 10, 18, 21, 25, 28, 32, 38, 39, 46, 47, 52, 53, 54, 65, 66, 67, 68	(D002) 2
ammonium hydroxide (15 M)	125 mL	17, 51, 56	(D001) 2				
ammonium nitrate	900 g	4	4	hydrogen peroxide, 3%	150 mL	25	8
barium nitrate	10 g	10, 13	4	hydrogen peroxide, 6%	1.5 L	79	8
benzoic acid	10 g	41	1	ice	50 kg	1, 28, 31, 45, 47, 56, 65, 66, 69	
bleach, household	100 mL	17, 21	4 or 8				
borax	5 g	21	1	iodine	100 g	20	4 or 7
bromcresol green	30 mL	56	8	iodine solution	100 mL	80	7
bromthymol blue	2 g	46, 56, 61	8	iron filings	150 g	5, 35, 52	1
buffer capsules	11	55	1	iron powder	100 g	35	1
butane refill cylinders	15	29	4	iron strips, 0.5 × 3 cm	15 strips	58	1
butanol	75 mL	6	(D001) 3 or 8	iron sulfate heptahydrate	150 g	24, 58, 59, 60	1 or 8
calcium carbide	50 g	73	4	iron(III) chloride	5 g	79	1 or 8
calcium carbonate	5 g	51	1 or 8	iron(III) nitrate	10 g	27, 77	8
calcium chloride	350 g	26, 34	1 or 8	isopropyl alcohol	350 mL	2, 63, 70	(D001) 3 or 8
calcium hydroxide	25 g	21, 25, 52	2	lauric acid	225 g	40	2
calcium metal turnings	5 g	16	6	lead metal	15 cm	62	(D008) 1
calcium nitrate	25 g	10, 13, 17	1	lead nitrate	50 g	13, 19, 62	(D008) 9
calcium sulfate dihydrate	75 g	30	1 or 8	lithium carbonate	2.5 g	13	1 or 8
calmagite indicator	15 mL	51	8	lithium nitrate	2 g	10	1 or 8
camphor	100 g	20	1	litmus paper, blue	45 pieces	52	1
cobalt chloride	25 g	47	1	litmus paper, red	45 pieces	52	1
cobalt chloride paper	30 pieces	25	1	magnesium carbonate	15 g	53	1 or 8
copper carbonate	45 g	25	1	magnesium chloride	2.5 g	50	1 or 8
copper foil, 25 × 30 cm	2 pieces	14, 25, 58, 62, 63	1	magnesium nitrate	20 g	14, 62	1 or 8
copper wire, 18–22 gauge	5 m	31, 63, 52, 38	1	magnesium oxide	15 g	67	1 or 8
copper(II) nitrate	25 g	10, 14, 27, 62	1	magnesium ribbon	2 m	5, 14, 16, 25, 28, 35, 38, 52, 58, 67	1
copper(II) sulfate	125 g	5, 30	1				
copper(II) sulfate pentahydrate	150 g	5, 30, 46, 50, 58	1	magnesium sulfate	100 g	30, 58	1 or 8
				malachite green powder	2 g	24	1
distilled water	50 L	1, 16, 19, 21, 34, 44, 45, 46, 47, 50, 51, 54, 53, 56, 57, 60, 61, 62, 64, 65, 68, 74, 77, 80		manganese dioxide	10 g	25, 79	1
				manganese sulfate monohydrate	75 g	30	1
				methanol	75 mL	2, 6	(D001) 3 or 8

*See page T28.

Substance	Quantity	Investigation	Disposal Method	Substance	Quantity	Investigation	Disposal Method
methyl orange powder	5 g	24, 53	1	sodium carbonate	100 g	13, 30, 42, 50	1 or 8
molasses and yeast fermentation mixture	1 L	75	1	sodium chloride	1.5 kg	5, 10, 13, 17, 20, 21, 27, 35, 42, 45, 46, 59, 78	1 or 8
naphthalene	10 g	41	(U165) 4	sodium fluoride	2 g	17	1 or 8
nitric acid (16 M)	400 mL	13, 31, 63	(D002) 2	sodium hydrogen carbonate	125 g	21, 25, 56	2
orange IV indicator	100 mL	53	1	sodium hydrogen sulfite	1 g	64	1 or 8
oxalic acid dihydrate	50 g	57	4	sodium hydroxide	400 g	21, 27, 31, 34, 46, 52, 54, 57, 59, 66, 68, 80	2
pH paper, wide range	15 rolls	31, 52	1				
phenol red indicator	50 mL	26	4	sodium iodide	125 g	13, 17, 19, 20	1 or 8
phenolphthalein	250 mL	13, 16, 35, 52, 55, 57, 59, 73, 80	8	sodium nitrate	2 g	50	1 or 8
				sodium phosphate	5 g	27	2
polyvinyl alcohol	25 g	76	8	sodium sulfate	25 g	13, 24, 27, 61	1 or 8
potassium carbonate	7.5 g	13	1 or 8	sodium sulfite	6 g	48	1 or 8
potassium chloride	100 g	20	1 or 8	sodium thiosulfate	200 g	17, 34, 65	1 or 8
potassium ferricyanide	2 g	59	4	soluble starch	10 g	17, 80	1
				strontium nitrate	20 g	10, 13	1 or 8
potassium iodate	2.5 g	64	4	sucrose	300 g	21, 41, 69	1
potassium iodide	15 g	25	1 or 8	sulfur	20 g	5, 41	1
potassium nitrate	400 g	10, 49, 62	8	sulfuric acid (18 M)	300 mL	24, 31, 48, 56, 58, 60	(D002) 2
potassium nitrite	5 g	56	4	universal indicator	30 mL	56	8
potassium permanganate	10 g	60	4	urea	40 g	44	1
				vinegar	125 mL	21	1
potassium phosphate	5 g	50	1 or 8	wide-range pH paper	2 rolls	78	1
propylene glycol	50 mL	23	8	zinc electrodes, 3 × 10 cm	30	8	1
radioactive sources	15	70	4	zinc granules, 18–22 mesh	250 g	18, 31	1
salicylic acid solution	50 mL	77	2	zinc nitrate	75 g	14, 62, 63	1 or 8
				zinc ribbon	2 m	14, 58, 62	1
silver metal	15 cm	62	1	zinc strips, 2.5 × 15 cm	5 strips	63	1
silver nitrate	40 g	5, 14, 17, 27, 47, 50, 54, 58, 62	9	zinc sulfate	5 g	58	1 or 8
				zinc sulfate dihydrate	75 g	30	1 or 8
sodium borate	10 g	76	1 or 8	zinc sulfate septahydrate	1 kg	8	1 or 8
sodium bromide	10 g	13, 17	8	zinc, mossy	15 g	52	1

EQUIPMENT

Item	Quantity	Investigation
ammeters	15	8
barometer	1	28
beaker tongs	15	41
beaker, 1000-mL	1	32
beakers, 50-mL	90	10, 35, 53, 77, 80
beakers, 100-mL	60	3, 6, 12, 15, 39, 41, 42, 45, 57, 74, 80
beakers, 250-mL	30	8, 21, 31, 32, 36, 47, 54, 63, 72
beakers, 400-mL	30	28, 35, 38, 40, 49, 54
beakers, 500-mL	15	1, 8, 23, 73
beakers, 600-mL	30	18, 31, 45, 46, 65, 79
Boyle's law apparatuses	15	37
buret brushes	15	60
buret clamps	15	57, 60
burets	30	57, 60
capillary tubes	210	23, 41
chemical splash goggles	30	2, 3, 4, 5, 6, 8, 10, 13, 14, 16, 17, 18, 19, 20, 21, 23, 24, 25, 26, 27, 28, 30, 31, 32, 34, 35, 36, 38, 39, 40, 41, 42, 43, 44, 45, 46, 47, 48, 49, 50, 51, 52, 53, 54, 55, 56, 57, 58, 59, 60, 61, 62, 63, 64, 65, 66, 67, 68, 69, 70, 72, 73, 74, 75, 76, 77, 78, 79, 80
clamps, utility	15	41
crucibles with covers	15	30
dropper bottles, brown	38	10
droppers	30	1, 2, 14, 17, 27, 43, 45
evaporating dishes	15	31
filter paper	30	6, 12, 62, 74
flame-test loops	15	54
flasks, 50-mL	15	75
flasks, 125-mL	30	60
flasks, 250-mL	15	57
flasks, 500-mL	15	29
fluorescent light source	1	11
forceps	15	16, 20, 35, 54, 62, 68, 73
funnels	15	15, 74
gas-collecting bottles, 500-mL	15	66
glass elbows	15	25, 52
glass squares	15	5, 29, 66
graduated cylinders, 10-mL	30	1, 2, 3, 5, 6, 20, 28, 38, 42, 45, 49, 51, 65, 80
graduated cylinders, 100-mL	15	1, 4, 14, 26, 31, 34, 35, 36, 44, 45, 46, 53, 54, 60, 67, 68, 76, 77, 80
hot plates	15	1, 6, 24, 31, 36, 40, 46, 47, 49, 54, 74, 75, 79
incandescent light source	1	11
insulating pads	15	5, 30
iron rings	15	30, 41, 42, 44, 74
lab burners	15	5, 10, 16, 25, 30, 41, 44, 54, 72
laboratory aprons	30	all
laboratory balances	15	1, 2, 4, 5, 8, 9, 15, 20, 26, 30, 31, 32, 34, 36, 44, 45, 46, 49, 54, 57, 67, 68, 80
latex gloves	750 pairs	5, 10, 14, 17, 19, 24, 27, 31, 32, 34, 38, 39, 41, 47, 50, 54, 58, 60, 62, 68, 70, 74, 76
marking pens	15	8, 10, 12, 13, 14, 15, 16, 19, 20, 23, 27, 35, 39, 46, 47, 49, 50, 51, 53, 54, 58, 64, 65, 66, 77, 79
matches	15	3, 5, 10, 16, 18, 25, 30, 41, 44, 52, 54, 72, 73
melting point tubes	15	72
micropipets, graduated	30	73
micropipets	2000	2, 5, 6, 13, 14, 17, 18, 19, 23, 27, 28, 35, 38, 39, 42, 46, 47, 48, 51, 52, 53, 54, 55, 56, 57, 58, 59, 62, 64, 65, 73, 77, 80
microscope-slide cover slips	15	61
microspatulas	15	5, 16, 20, 35, 32
mortars and pestles	15	5, 35, 44, 66, 77
multimeters with leads	15	62
nichrome wire loops	15	10
petri dishes	15	6, 16, 35, 39, 46, 47, 48, 56, 61, 62, 70
pipe-stem triangles	15	30
plastic tubing	3 m	75
platinum electrodes	30	61
pneumatic troughs	15	29
ring stands	15	30, 37, 41, 44, 49, 57, 60, 72, 74
rubber tubing	10 m	25, 29
safety goggles	30	1, 7, 9, 11, 12, 15, 22, 29, 37
scalpels	15	74
scoopulas	15	26, 54, 69
spatulas	15	4, 25, 30, 35, 41, 72
spectrometers	15	11
spectrum tube power supply	1	11
spectrum tubes	4 gases	11
stirring rods	15	4, 5, 6, 13, 31, 34, 36, 44, 45, 49, 53, 54, 68, 77, 80
stoppers, cork and rubber–various sizes	90	18, 20, 25, 38, 41, 44, 46, 52, 73, 75
test tubes, assorted sizes	135	5, 6, 13, 19, 20, 25, 40, 44, 45, 46, 47, 49, 52, 61, 73, 75, 79
test-tube clamps	15	5, 25, 40, 44, 49
test-tube racks	15	5, 6, 12, 18, 20, 25, 46, 49, 52, 54, 79
thermometers	40	1, 2, 4, 34, 35, 36, 38, 40, 41, 44, 45, 49, 65, 66, 67, 68, 72, 75
thermometer clamps	15	72
tongs, crucible	15	6, 16, 25, 31, 30
tripod ring stands	15	12
utility clamps	15	37, 49
wash bottles	30	10, 16, 21, 38, 39, 48, 51, 54, 56, 57, 70
watch glasses	15	5, 6, 25, 31, 54, 75
water tubs	15	75
well plates	15	6, 10, 14, 17, 19, 23, 27, 47, 50, 51, 52, 53, 58, 59, 64, 65, 77, 80
wire gauze	15	16, 41, 44, 76
wire leads with alligator clips	45	8, 63

MISCELLANEOUS

Item	Quantity	Investigation
adhesive tape, clear	2 rolls	39, 73
Alka-Seltzer tablets	165	26, 66
aluminum pie pans	15	3
antacid	1 tablet	21
antifreeze, permanent	600 mL	45
apple	1	79
aspirin	50 g	21, 72, 77
baby-food jars with covers	30	69
ball-and-stick model sets	15	22
banana	1	79
batteries, 9V	15	61
batteries, D-type	60	8
batteries, lantern	5	63
birthday candles	30	5, 73
black felt	15 pieces	70
boiling stones	200	1, 44
bowls, mixing	15	78
boxes (approx. 20 × 30 × 5 cm)	15	7
brass masses	15	1
bright light sources	15	70
cabbage, red	3 kg	48, 78
carbonated soft drink	1 can	21
cardboard covers for cups	15	67
clear acrylic spray paint	1 can	63
clear plastic straws	30	39
clock with a second hand	1	4, 8, 40, 64, 65, 66, 67, 75
club soda	1 can	66
coffee	125 mL	21
commercial radon test kit	4	71
compasses, geometric	15	12
conductivity testers	15	21
cotton swabs	100	39, 48, 63
cotton T-shirts, white	30	43
cutting boards	15	78
dishwasher detergent	1 bottle	21
dried peas	450 g	12
eggs	4	69
fabric strips	30	24
felt-tip pens, permanent, multiple colors	150	43
files	15	25
flowers, assorted	30	48
food coloring	1 package	76
fresh pineapple	1	79
fruit juices	several flavors	21, 80
gloves, heat-proof	15 pairs	1, 70
glue	15 tubes	70
glue stick	1	7
glue, white (containing polyvinyl acetate)	200 mL	76
half-and-half	1 L	69
hammers	8	35, 63
hot pads	15	41
instant pudding	1 box	69
index cards	15	33
iron slabs, 20 × 10 × 2 cm	8	35
kidney beans	600 g	15
kitchen scales	15	78
knives	15	78
large coffee cans with lids	30	43, 69
large plastic bags	30	43
lead sinkers, 50-g	15	36
lima beans	1200 g	15
liver, fresh	1	79
magnets, bar or horseshoe	15	5
magnets, donut-type	15	7
masking tape	15 rolls	3, 7, 63, 70
medicine-dose cups	30	74, 76
mineral oil	1.5 L	41
miscellaneous solid objects	30	1
motor oil	300 mL	3
nail, iron	1	63
natural straw	1 L	3
navy beans	200 g	15
newspapers	20	3, 12
paper, black	30 pieces	39, 56
paper, white	150 pieces	27, 48, 51, 56, 57, 59, 64, 65, 77
paper cups	60	15
paper towels	10 rolls	3, 6, 23, 24, 32, 42, 45, 47, 48, 56, 63, 65, 67, 68, 70, 75
pennies, minted after 1982	240	9, 42
pennies, minted before 1982	60	9, 42
pins, straight	15	28
pint jars with lids	15	78
pinto beans	400 g	15
plastic bags, resealable	30	9, 26
plastic basins	15	1, 28, 66
plastic containers	15	12
plastic foam cups	30	4, 34, 36, 67, 68
plastic wrap	1 roll	28
pliers	8 pairs	35
pot holders	30	69
potato	1	79
rock salt	5 kg	69
rubber bands	60	28, 41, 43, 72
rulers, common metric	30	6, 7, 12, 19, 32, 38, 61
sand	400 mL	3
scissors	15	5, 6, 12, 18, 28, 39, 48, 53, 62, 67, 70, 73
skim milk	300 mL	74
single-hole paper punches	15	48
single-edge razors	15	63
small candies with colored coatings	60	6
soap	1 bar	21, 24, 60
soft foam (approx. 2500 cm^2)	1	7
sponge, 2 cm × 2 cm	30	61
spoons, kitchen table	15	78
steel balls (0.5–1.0 cm diameter)	15	7
steel plates	15	59
steel wool	100 pieces	8, 16, 35, 58, 59, 62, 63, 67
stopwatches	15	8, 40, 64, 65, 66, 67, 75

Materials Inventory **T27**

Item	Quantity	Investigation
straws	15	56
string	10 m	3, 36
sugar-free gelatin mix	15 12-g packages	74
textbooks	75	37
tin snips	1 pair	63
tissues	15	39
toothpicks, wooden	4 boxes	6, 17, 80
toothpicks, plastic	50	47, 51
vanilla	2 mL	69
vegetable oil	3 L	2, 20, 21, 72
vitamin C tablets	20	80
whole milk	1 L	69
white wool yarn	1 skein	6
wooden splints	200	3, 18, 25, 52, 74, 76

*This inventory includes approximate total quantities for one class of 30 students (usually working in pairs), and the experiments in which the materials are used. The Disposal Method column keys each chemical to the disposal methods outlined in the Guidelines for Disposal of Laboratory Wastes on pages T31–T32.

Laboratory Suppliers

Carolina Biological Supply Company
2700 York Road
Burlington, NC 27215
(800) 227-1150, (910) 584-0381

Central Scientific Company
3300 Cenco Parkway
Franklin Park, IL 60131
(800) 262-3626, (708) 451-0150

Connecticut Valley Biological Supply Company, Inc.
P.O. Box 326
82 Valley Road
Southampton, MA 01073
(800) 628-7748, (413) 527-4030

Fisher Scientific Company
Educational Materials Division
485 South Frontage Road
Burr Ridge, IL 60521
(800) 955-7999, (312) 378-7770

Flinn Scientific, Inc.
P.O. Box 219
131 Flinn Street
Batavia, IL 60510
(800) 452-1261, (708) 879-6900

Frey Scientific Company
P.O. Box 8101
905 Hickory Lane
Mansfield, OH 44901-8101
(800) 225-3739, (419) 589-1900

Lab-Aids, Inc.
17 Colt Court
Ronkonkoma, NY 11779
(516) 737-1133, FAX (516) 737-1286

Nasco
901 Janesville Avenue
Fort Atkinson, WI 53538
(800) 558-9595, (414) 563-2446

Parco Scientific Company
P.O. Box 189
316 Youngstown-Kingsville Road
Vienna, OH 44473
(800) 247-2726, (216) 394-1100

Sargent-Welch Scientific Company
911 Commerce Court
Buffalo Grove, IL 60089-2362
(800) 727-4368, (708) 677-0600

Science Kit and Boreal Labs
777 East Park Drive
Tonawanda, NY 14150
(800) 828-7777, (716) 874-6020

Ward's Natural Science Establishment, Inc.
5100 West Henrietta Road
P.O. Box 92912
Rochester, NY 14692-9012
(800) 962-2660, (716) 359-2502

Preparation of Solutions

NOTE: Unless otherwise indicated, quantities PER LITER OF SOLUTION are given. The Disposal Method column keys each solution to the disposal methods outlined on pages T31–T32.

Solution	Concentration:	Preparation Method	Disposal Method
Acetic acid	6 M:	353 mL of 17 M $HC_2H_3O_2$	2
	1 M:	59 mL of 17 M $HC_2H_3O_2$	
	0.1 M:	6 mL of 17 M $HC_2H_3O_2$	
Ammonia (*aq*)	3 M:	200 mL concentrated $NH_3(aq)$	2
	1 M:	66.7 mL concentrated $NH_3(aq)$	2
Ammonium acetate	0.1 M:	7.7 g $NH_4C_2H_3O_2$	1 or 8
Ammonium sulfate	0.1 M:	13 g $(NH_4)_2SO_4$	1 or 8
Barium nitrate	0.1 M:	26 g $Ba(NO_3)_2$	4
Calcium chloride	1 M:	111 g $CaCl_2$	1 or 8
	0.1 M:	11.1 g $CaCl_2$	
Calcium hydroxide	saturated:	Add solid $Ca(OH)_2$ to distilled water until no more dissolves. Filter off solid.	2
Calcium nitrate	0.5 M:	82 g $Ca(NO_3)_2$ or 118 g $Ca(NO_3)_2 \cdot 4H_2O$	1 or 8
	0.1 M:	16.4 g $Ca(NO_3)_2$ or 24 g $Ca(NO_3)_2 \cdot 4H_2O$	
Copper(II) nitrate	0.5 M:	148 g $Cu(NO_3)_2 \cdot 6H_2O$ or 121 g $Cu(NO_3)_2 \cdot 3H_2O$	1 or 8
	0.1 M:	30 g $Cu(NO_3)_2 \cdot 6H_2O$ or 24 g $Cu(NO_3)_2 \cdot 3H_2O$	
Copper(II) sulfate	1 M:	160 g $CuSO_4$ or 250 g $CuSO_4 \cdot 5H_2O$	1 or 8
	0.01 M:	1.6 g $CuSO_4$ or 2.5 g $CuSO_4 \cdot 5H_2O$	
Hydrochloric acid	6 M:	Mix equal parts 12 M HCl and distilled water.	2
	3 M:	Mix 1 part 12 M HCl to 3 parts distilled water.	
	1 M:	83 mL 12 M HCl per liter of solution	
	0.5 M:	42 mL 12 M HCl per liter of solution	
	0.1 M:	8.4 mL 12 M HCl per liter of solution	
Iron(III) chloride	0.1 M:	16 g $FeCl_3$ or dissolve 27 g $FeCl_3 \cdot 6H_2O$ in 50 mL 6 M HCl. Dilute to 1 L.	1 or 8
Iron(III) nitrate	0.1 M:	24 g $Fe(NO_3)_3$ or 40 g $Fe(NO_3)_3 \cdot 9H_2O$	1 or 8
Lead(III) nitrate	0.5 M:	166 g $Pb(NO_3)_2$	9
	0.1 M:	33 g $Pb(NO_3)_2$	
	0.01 M:	3.3 g $Pb(NO_3)_2$	
Lithium nitrate	0.5 M:	35 g $LiNO_3$	1 or 8

Solution	Concentration: Preparation Method		Disposal Method
Magnesium bromide	0.1 M:	18 g $MgBr_2$ or 29 g $MgBr_2 \cdot 6H_2O$	1 or 8
Magnesium chloride	0.1 M:	9.4 g $MgCl_2$	1 or 8
Magnesium hydroxide	saturated:	Add solid $Mg(OH)_2$ to distilled water until no more dissolves. Filter off solid.	2
Potassium bromide	0.1 M:	12 g KBr	1 or 8
Potassium carbonate	0.1 M:	14 g K_2CO_3	1 or 8
Potassium chloride	0.1 M:	7 g KCl	1 or 8
Potassium ferricyanide	0.1 M:	33 g $K_3Fe(CN)_6$	4
Potassium iodate	0.02 M:	4.3 g KIO_3	8
Potassium iodide	0.5 M:	83 g KI	1 or 8
	0.02 M:	3.3 g KI	
Potassium nitrate	0.5 M:	56 g KNO_3	8
Potassium phosphate	0.1 M:	21 g K_3PO_4	1 or 8
Potassium thiocyanate	0.1 M:	10 g KSCN	1 or 8
Silver nitrate	0.1 M:	17 g $AgNO_3$	9
Sodium acetate	0.1 M:	8 g $NaC_2H_3O_2$	2
Sodium bromide	0.1 M:	10 g NaBr	8
Sodium carbonate	1 M:	106 g Na_2CO_3 or 124 g $Na_2CO_3 \cdot H_2O$	1 or 8
	0.1 M:	10.6 g Na_2CO_3 or 12.4 g $Na_2CO_3 \cdot H_2O$	
Sodium chloride	0.1 M:	5.85 g NaCl	1 or 8
Sodium fluoride	0.1 M:	4.2 g NaF	1 or 8
Sodium hydroxide	0.1 M:	4 g NaOH	2
	1 M:	40 g NaOH	
	0.5 M:	20 g NaOH	
	0.2 M:	8 g NaOH	
Sodium iodide	0.1 M:	15 g NaI	1 or 8
Sodium nitrate	0.5 M:	43 g $NaNO_3$	1 or 8
Sodium phosphate tribasic	0.1 M:	38 g $Na_3PO_4 \cdot 12H_2O$	2
Sodium sulfate	1 M:	142 g Na_2SO_4	1 or 8
Sodium sulfide	0.1 M:	7.8 g Na_2S or 24 g $Na_2S \cdot 9H_2O$	1
Sodium sulfite	1 M:	126 g Na_2SO_3	1 or 8
Strontium nitrate	0.1 M:	21 g $Sr(NO_3)_2$	1 or 8
Sulfuric acid	1 M:	56 mL 18 M H_2SO_4	2
Zinc acetate	0.1 M:	22 g $Zn(C_2H_3O_2)_2 \cdot 2H_2O$	1 or 8
Zinc nitrate	0.5 M:	95 g $Zn(NO_3)_2$	1 or 8
	0.1 M:	19 g $Zn(NO_3)_2$	
Zinc sulfate	1 M:	288 g $ZnSO_4 \cdot 7H_2O$	1 or 8

INDICATORS

Methyl orange: 0.1 g per 100 mL 50% ethanol	1 or 8
Orange IV: 0.1 g per 100 mL 50% ethanol	1 or 8
Phenolphthalein, 1%: Can be purchased commercially or 1 g per 100 mL 50% ethanol.	8

Guidelines for Safe Disposal of Laboratory Wastes

Every effort should be made to recover, recycle, and reuse chemicals and other materials used in the laboratory. When disposal is required, however, specific procedures should be followed in order to ensure that your school complies with local, state, and federal regulations. To this end, pages T8–T20 of this teacher's manual provide you with some background information and general guidelines for initiating a disposal plan. In addition to the recommendations listed on those pages, your plan also should include the following general guidelines:

- Discard only dry paper into ordinary wastebaskets.
- Discard broken glass into a separate container clearly marked "For Broken Glass Only."
- Equip the laboratory with plainly marked safety collection containers, spill buckets, mercury-absorbent sponges (if your school is permitted to use mercury or if you have mercury thermometers in use), and chemicals needed for neutralizing other substances. These products are available from chemical supply houses.
- Acidic or basic solutions can be flushed down the drain only after they have been neutralized.
- Have your fume hood checked periodically to make certain that it is operating in a safe, efficient manner.
- If you are permitted to use small quantities of mildly noxious liquids in your classroom, they can be disposed of by evaporating them in the fume hood. (Large quantities of toxic substances should not be allowed in the school.)
- Use the fume hood when conducting experiments that use or produce noxious gases or noxious nongaseous substances that have high vapor pressures. Good ventilation should be a high priority in the laboratory at all times.
- Keep abreast of your field in terms of the proper disposal of waste. Many chemicals are currently being investigated. Some of this research may reveal hazards that are unknown at the present time.

Methods of Disposal of Chemical Wastes

The information that follows is intended as a guide for the safe disposal of specific chemicals that are commonly used in the chemistry laboratory. These methods complement the information provided in the Waste Disposal section of the Teacher's Notes of each investigation. Additionally, the item number of each method corresponds to those listed in the Chemicals section of the Materials Inventory and in Preparation of Solutions. These procedures should be reviewed to ensure that they are permitted under local regulations.

Be sure to have all necessary safety equipment and materials on hand before beginning a disposal procedure. Wear chemical splash goggles, gloves, and a lab apron or coat. Use a face shield when working with explosive or highly corrosive or caustic chemicals, and work in a fume hood when necessary.

1. This material can be disposed of in the local landfill.

2. Neutralize the material and dispose of it by flushing down the drain. Use large amounts of water. Hold containers with heat-resistant gloves because reactions may be exothermic.

3. This material is flammable and can be incinerated or used as a fuel supplement. If it is water soluble, check with your municipal water treatment facility to determine if it may be flushed down the drain. Otherwise, see method 4.

4. Store separately for commercial disposal or shipment to a secure landfill.

5. Acidify dilute solutions with sulfuric acid to a pH less than 3, and react with 50% excess of sodium hydrogen sulfite. The products can be flushed down the drain.

6. Use the procedure described in Investigation 16. The resulting solutions can be neutralized and flushed down the drain.

7. React by adding to 50% sodium thiosulfate solution and then acidify with 3 M sulfuric acid. After several hours, the reduction is completed, and the products can be neutralized and flushed down the drain with large quantities of water.

8. If water soluble, small quantities can be flushed directly down the drain. Use large quantities of water.

9. Precipitate the cation with 1 M sodium hydroxide or excess sodium chloride solution. Filter the product mixture. Use method 4 for the dried precipitate and method 2 for the filtrate.

Laboratory Manual

PRENTICE HALL
Chemistry
Connections to Our Changing World

PRENTICE HALL
Upper Saddle River, New Jersey
Needham, Massachusetts

Laboratory Manual

PRENTICE HALL
Chemistry
Connections to Our Changing World

Contributing Writers

Bette Bridges
Chemistry Teacher
Bridgewater-Raynham High School
Bridgewater, Massachusetts

John C. Hugo
Chemistry Teacher
Carman-Ainsworth High School
Flint, Michigan

George E. Hussey
Chemistry Teacher
Falmouth High School
Falmouth, Massachusetts

Cristina Kerekes
Chemistry Teacher
Phillips Academy
Andover, Massachusetts

Kenneth Lyle
Chemistry Teacher
St. John's School
Houston, Texas

Joseph W. MacQuade, Jr.
Former Science Program Administrator
Marblehead High School
Marblehead, Massachusetts

Thomas L. Messer
Former Chemistry Teacher
The American School in Japan
Tokyo, Japan

Karen M. Robblee
Chemistry Teacher
Millbrook High School
Raleigh, North Carolina

Pamala Schupp
Chemistry Teacher
Kelly Walsh High School
Casper, Wyoming

Patricia Soghigian
Chemistry Teacher
Beverly High School
Beverly, Massachusetts

Clarice Wenz
Chemistry Teacher
Goose Creek High School
Goose Creek, South Carolina

Safety Expert
James A. Kaufman
Director
Laboratory Safety Workshop
Natick, Massachusetts

© 1996 by Prentice-Hall, Inc., a Simon & Schuster Company, Upper Saddle River, NJ 07458. All rights reserved. No part of this book may be reproduced or transmitted in any form or by any means, electronic or mechanical, including photocopying, recording, or by any information storage and retrieval system, without permission in writing from the publisher. Printed in the United States of America.

ISBN 0-13-837329-9

2 3 4 5 6 7 8 9 10   99 98 97 96 95

Prentice Hall
A Simon & Schuster Company
Upper Saddle River, NJ 07458

CONTENTS

Safety in the Chemistry Laboratory vii
First Aid ix
Safety Symbols xi
Safety Contract xii
Using This Laboratory Manual xiii
Common Laboratory Equipment xiv
    Using a Laboratory Balance xvi
    Using a Burner xviii
Working with Chemicals xix

The symbol 🔍 denotes small-scale investigations.

CHAPTER 1   Chemistry and You

    1. Uncertainty and Measurement 1
    2. Density of Liquids 11
    3. APPLICATION: Cleaning Up an Oil Spill 17

CHAPTER 2   Energy and Matter

    4. APPLICATION: Simulating a Cold Pack 23
    5. Physical and Chemical Changes 29
    6. APPLICATION: Candy Coatings: Compounds or Mixtures? 35

CHAPTER 3   Atomic Structure

    7. Rutherford's Experiment 41
    8. Finding the Charge of an Electron 45
    9. APPLICATION: Isotopes of "Pennium" 51

CHAPTER 4   Electron Configurations

    10. Flame Tests 55
    11. APPLICATION: Spectral Analysis of Fluorescent Lights 61
    12. Electron Distribution Using Peas 67

CHAPTER 5   The Periodic Table

    13. Mendeleev for a Day 73
    14. Chemical Activity of Metals 77
    15. APPLICATION: Relative Mass with Beans 81

CHAPTER 6 Groups of Elements
16. Reactivity of Alkaline Earth Metals 87
17. Exploring the Halides 93
18. APPLICATION: Making Micro-*Hindenburgs* 99

CHAPTER 7 Chemical Formulas and Bonding
19. Formula of Lead Iodide 103
20. Solubility and Bond Type 109
21. APPLICATION: Conductivity of Molecular and Ionic Compounds 113

CHAPTER 8 Molecular Shape
22. Models of Molecular Compounds 117
23. Capillary Action and Polarity of Molecules 121
24. APPLICATION: Exploring Dyes 127

CHAPTER 9 Chemical Reactions and Equations
25. Equation Writing and Predicting Products 131
26. APPLICATION: Bags of Reactions 137
27. Double Replacement Reactions 141

CHAPTER 10 The Mole
28. Molar Volume of Hydrogen Gas 145
29. APPLICATION: Molar Mass of Butane 151
30. Water in a Hydrate 157

CHAPTER 11 The Mathematics of Chemical Equations
31. Stoichiometry Using Copper 163
32. APPLICATION: Zinc Thickness in Galvanized Iron 169
33. APPLICATION: Limiting Reactants in Brownies 173

CHAPTER 12 Heat in Chemical Reactions
34. Heat of Solution 177
35. APPLICATION: Simulating the Flameless Ration Heater 183
36. APPLICATION: Determining Heat Capacity 191

CHAPTER 13 Gases

37. Boyle's Law by the Book.....................197
38. The Ideal Gas Constant.....................203
39. APPLICATION: Diffusion of Two Gases.....................209

CHAPTER 14 Liquids and Solids

40. APPLICATION: How Many Drops Can You Pile on a Penny?.....................217
41. Changes of State.....................223
42. Melting Points of Common Substances.....................229

CHAPTER 15 Solutions

43. APPLICATION: T-Shirt Chromatography.....................235
44. Boiling Points of Solutions.....................239
45. APPLICATION: Freezing Point Depression with Antifreeze.....................245

CHAPTER 16 Chemical Equilibrium

46. Observing Chemical Equilibrium.....................251
47. Le Chatelier's Principle.....................255
48. APPLICATION: Shifting Equilibria in Plant Tissues.....................261

CHAPTER 17 Solubility and Precipitation

49. Solubility Curve of KNO_3.....................267
50. Precipitates and Solubility Rules.....................273
51. APPLICATION: Investigating Hardness of Water.....................277

CHAPTER 18 Acids, Bases, and Salts

52. Properties of Acids and Bases.....................283
53. Comparing Acid Strengths.....................289
54. APPLICATION: Making Table Salt.....................295

CHAPTER 19 Reactions of Acids and Bases

55. Determining the pH of an Unknown.....................301
56. APPLICATION: An Indicator for Acid Rain.....................305
57. Titration with Oxalic Acid.....................313

CHAPTER 20   Oxidation and Reduction

58. Activity Series..321
59. APPLICATION: Rust Marches On..325
60. Quantitative Redox Titration.......................................329

CHAPTER 21   Electrochemistry

61. Electrolysis of Water..333
62. Small-Scale Voltaic Cells..339
63. APPLICATION: Zinc Plating of Ornaments.............................347

CHAPTER 22   Rates of Reaction

64. Reaction Kinetics..353
65. Concentration and Reaction Order...................................359
66. APPLICATION: Rates of an Antacid Reaction..........................367

CHAPTER 23   Thermodynamics

67. Hess's Law...373
68. Entropy and Enthalpy Changes.......................................379
69. APPLICATION: Thermodynamics of Homemade Ice Cream..................385

CHAPTER 24   Applications of Nuclear Chemistry

70. Making a Cloud Chamber...389
71. APPLICATION: Using a Radon Test Kit................................395

CHAPTER 25   Carbon and Its Compounds

72. Melting Point of an Organic Compound...............................399
73. Properties of an Alkyne..403
74. APPLICATION: Playing with Polymers.................................409

CHAPTER 26   Classes of Organic Compounds

75. APPLICATION: Observing Fermentation................................415
76. APPLICATION: Making Slime..419
77. APPLICATION: Analyzing Commercial Aspirin..........................423

CHAPTER 27   The Chemistry of Life

78. APPLICATION: Making Sauerkraut.....................................429
79. Organic and Inorganic Catalysts....................................433
80. APPLICATION: Analysis of Commercial Vitamin C......................439

Safety in the Chemistry Laboratory

In the laboratory, you will be working with equipment and materials that can cause injury if they are not handled properly. Accidents happen because of carelessness, haste, and disregard of safety rules and practices. The laboratory can be a safe place to work, however, and accidents can be avoided if you know what risks are present and take steps to reduce them.

Safety rules for the laboratory are listed below. Before beginning any lab work, read these rules and learn them. When working in the lab, follow them carefully. If you have any questions about these rules, ask your teacher before starting lab work.

General Precautions

1. Be prepared to work when you arrive at the laboratory. Familiarize yourself with the lab procedures before beginning the lab.
2. Carefully follow all written and oral instructions. Perform only those activities assigned by your teacher. Never do anything in the laboratory that is not called for in the lab procedure or by your teacher.
3. Notify your teacher if you have any medical problems that might be affected by lab work, such as allergies or asthma.
4. Never work in the laboratory without supervision.
5. Never eat or drink in the laboratory.
6. Never smoke in the laboratory.
7. Keep work areas clean and tidy at all times. Only notebooks and lab manuals or written lab procedures should be brought to the work area. All other items, such as books, purses, and backpacks, should be left at your desk or in a designated storage area.
8. Wear appropriate clothing for working in the laboratory. Remove jackets, ties, and other loose garments. Roll up or secure long sleeves. Remove jewelry, such as dangling necklaces, chains, and bracelets, that might present a hazard in the lab.
9. Tie back or cover long hair, especially in the vicinity of an open flame.
10. Never wear open shoes or sandals in the laboratory.
11. Wear goggles and a lab coat or apron at all times during an investigation.
12. Avoid wearing contact lenses in the lab. Change to glasses, if possible, or notify your teacher.
13. Do not engage in horseplay.
14. Set up apparatus as described in the written laboratory procedures or by your teacher. Never use makeshift arrangements.
15. Always use the prescribed instrument, such as tongs, test-tube holder, or forceps, for handling apparatus.
16. Keep all combustible materials away from open flames.
17. Never put your face near the mouth of a container that holds chemicals. Never smell any chemical directly. When testing for odors, use a wafting motion to direct the odors to your nose.

18. Conduct any experiment involving poisonous vapors in a fume hood.
19. Dispose of waste materials as instructed by your teacher.
20. Clean and wipe dry all work surfaces at the end of class. Wash your hands thoroughly.
21. Know the location of emergency equipment, such as the first-aid kit, eye-wash station, fire extinguisher, fire shower, and fire blanket, and how to use them.
22. In case of chemical spills, notify your teacher immediately.
23. Report all injuries to your teacher immediately.

Handling Chemicals

24. Read and double-check labels on chemical bottles before removing any chemical from a container. Take only as much as you need.
25. To avoid contamination, do not return unused chemicals to stock bottles.
26. When transferring chemicals from one container to another, hold the containers away from your body.
27. Avoid touching chemicals with your hands. If chemicals do come in contact with your hands, wash them immediately.
28. Wear latex gloves when handling concentrated acids and bases.
29. When mixing an acid and water, always add the acid to the water.

Handling Glassware

30. Carry glass tubing, especially long pieces, in a vertical position to minimize the likelihood of breakage and to avoid stabbing anyone.
31. Always wear heavy gloves when inserting a piece of glassware, such as tubing or a thermometer, into a stopper. Before inserting glassware into a stopper, lubricate the glassware with water or glycerin. Use a twisting motion when inserting or removing glassware from a stopper—never apply force. If a piece of glassware becomes stuck in a stopper, take it to your teacher.
32. Do not place hot glassware directly on a table. Always use some type of insulating pad.
33. Allow plenty of time for hot glass to cool before touching it. Remember: Hot glass *looks* cool but can cause painful burns.
34. Never handle broken glass with your bare hands. Use a brush and dustpan to clean up. Dispose of the glass as directed by your teacher.

Heating Substances

35. Use extreme caution with gas burners. Keep your head and clothing away from the flame.
36. Always turn off burners and hot plates when not in use.
37. Do not bring any substance into contact with a flame unless instructed to do so.
38. Never heat anything unless instructed to do so. Never leave unattended anything that is being heated or is visibly reacting.

39. When heating a substance in a test tube, make sure that the mouth of the tube is not pointed at you or anyone else. Never look into a container that is being heated.
40. Never heat a closed container.

In Case of an Injury

41. If an injury should occur, it is important to remain calm.
42. Notify your instructor immediately.
43. Be familiar with the first-aid practices that are to be followed.
44. Know how to use the emergency equipment.
45. Know how to summon assistance.

First Aid

Accidents do not often happen in well-equipped chemistry laboratories if students understand safe laboratory procedures and are careful to follow them. When an occasional accident does occur, it is likely to be a minor one.

In many schools, the nurse is responsible for treating injuries. For some types of injuries, though, you must take action immediately, before the nurse takes over. Find out what your school's emergency procedures are and make sure that they are posted in the laboratory. Always notify your teacher if there is an injury in the classroom, no matter how minor it may seem.

Bleeding from a Cut

Most cuts that occur in the chemistry laboratory are minor. For minor cuts, apply pressure to the wound with a clean, absorbent cloth. If blood begins to soak through, add more layers of cloth. If possible, keep a sheet of plastic over the topmost layer or wear latex or plastic gloves. Take the victim to the nurse.

If the victim is bleeding badly, raise the bleeding part, if possible, and apply pressure to the wound with a clean, absorbent cloth. While first aid is being given, send someone to notify the school nurse.

Acid or Base Spilled on the Skin

Remove all clothing that has the chemical on it and flush the skin with water for at least 15 minutes. Take the victim to the school nurse.

Chemicals in the Eyes

Getting any kind of chemical in the eyes is undesirable, but certain chemicals are especially harmful. They can destroy eyesight in a matter of seconds. Because you will be wearing safety goggles at all times during investigations, the likelihood of this kind of accident is remote. However, if it does happen, go to the nearest eyewash station and begin flushing the eyes with water immediately. It is important to flush with water for at least 15 minutes. While flushing continues, send someone to inform the school nurse. Do NOT attempt to go to the nurse's office before flushing your eyes.

Chemicals in the Mouth

Many chemicals are poisonous to varying degrees. Any chemical taken into the mouth should be spat out and the mouth rinsed thoroughly with water. Tell the victim NOT to swallow the water. Note the name of the chemical and notify the nurse immediately.

If the victim swallows a chemical, note the name of the chemical and notify the nurse immediately. Do NOT give the victim anything to drink.

If necessary, the nurse will contact the Poison Control Center, a hospital emergency room, or a physician for instructions.

Clothing or Hair on Fire

A person whose clothing or hair catches on fire will often run around frantically in an unsuccessful effort to get away from the fire. This action only provides the fire with more oxygen and makes it burn faster. If your clothing catches fire, drop to the floor and roll around to extinguish the flames. If you are helping another person whose clothing is on fire, smother the flames by rolling the person on the floor, in a fire blanket, or in a heavy coat. For hair fires, use a fire blanket to smother the flames. Send someone to notify the nurse immediately.

Breathing Smoke or Chemical Fumes

Inhalation of smoke or chemical fumes is unlikely if all experiments that give off smoke or noxious gases are conducted in a well-ventilated fume hood.

If smoke or chemical fumes are present in the laboratory, all persons—even those who do not feel ill—should leave the laboratory immediately. Since smoke rises, crawl along the floor while evacuating a smoke-filled room. Close all doors to the laboratory after the last person has left. Notify the nurse immediately. Make sure the room is thoroughly ventilated before anyone returns.

Shock

People who are suffering from any severe injury (for example, a bad burn or major loss of blood) may be in a state of shock. A person in shock is usually pale and faint. The person may be sweating, and have cold, moist skin and a weak, rapid pulse.

Shock is a serious medical condition. Do NOT allow a person in shock to walk anywhere—even to the nurse's office. Call for emergency help immediately. While emergency help is being summoned, loosen any tightly fitting clothing and keep the person comfortable.

Safety Symbols

SAFETY CLOTHING
This symbol is to remind you to wear a laboratory apron over your street clothes to protect your skin and clothing from spills.

SAFETY GOGGLES
This symbol is to remind you that safety goggles are to be worn *at all times* when working in the laboratory. For some activities, your teacher may also instruct you to wear protective gloves.

GLOVES
This symbol is to remind you to wear gloves to protect your hands from contact with corrosive substances, broken glass, or hot objects.

HEATING
This symbol indicates that you should be careful not to touch hot objects with your bare hands. Use either tongs or heat-proof gloves to pick up hot objects.

FIRE
This symbol indicates the presence of an open flame. Loose hair should be tied back or covered, and bulky or loose clothing should be secured in some manner. This symbol also alerts you to the hazard of working with a flammable liquid.

CORROSIVE SUBSTANCE
This symbol indicates a caustic or corrosive substance—most frequently an acid. Avoid contact with skin, eyes, and clothing. Do not inhale vapors.

BREAKAGE
This symbol indicates an activity in which the likelihood of breakage is greater than usual, such as working with glass tubing, funnels, and so forth.

DANGEROUS VAPORS
This symbol indicates the presence of or production of poisonous or noxious vapors. *Use the fume hood* when directed to do so. Care should be taken not to inhale vapors directly. When testing an odor, use a wafting motion to direct the vapor toward your nose.

EXPLOSION
This symbol indicates that the potential for an explosive situation is present. When you see this symbol, read the instructions carefully and *follow them exactly*.

POISON
This symbol indicates the presence of a poisonous substance. Do not let such a substance come in contact with your skin and do not inhale its vapors.

ELECTRICAL SHOCK
This symbol indicates that the potential for an electrical shock exists. Read all instructions carefully. Disconnect all apparatus when not in use.

RADIATION
This symbol indicates a radioactive substance. Follow your teacher's instructions as to proper handling of such substances.

DISPOSAL
This symbol indicates that a chemical should be disposed of in a special way. Dispose of these chemicals only as directed by your teacher.

HYGIENE
This symbol is to remind you always to wash your hands thoroughly after completing a laboratory investigation. Never touch your face or eyes during a laboratory investigation.

Safety Contract

After you have read all the safety information on pages *vii–xi* in this laboratory manual and are sure you understand all the rules, fill out the Safety Contract that follows. Signing this contract tells your teacher that you are aware of the rules of the laboratory. The signature of your parent or guardian indicates an awareness of the need for adult supervision if you work on laboratory assignments at home. Return your signed contract to your teacher.

Safety Contract

I, _____, have read the section *Safety in the Chemistry Laboratory* on pages *vii–xi* of this laboratory manual. I understand its contents completely and agree to comply with all the safety rules and guidelines that have been established in each of the following categories:

(please check)

- _____ General Precautions
- _____ Handling Chemicals
- _____ Handling Glassware
- _____ Heating Substances
- _____ First Aid
- _____ Safety Symbols

Certain laboratory investigations, such as those involving the preparation of food, may need to be performed at home. If so, I agree to follow all established safety rules and to work only under the supervision of an adult.

Signature _____ Date _____
(student)

Signature _____ Date _____
(parent or guardian)

Using This Laboratory Manual

The laboratory investigations in this manual provide an opportunity for you to observe chemical principles in action and to become familiar with the techniques used by chemists. Each investigation follows a standard outline that will help you tackle the stated problem in a systematic manner. The sections of each investigation are described below.

Introduction The Introduction provides background information and ties the investigation to specific concepts discussed in your textbook.

Pre-Lab Discussion The Pre-Lab Discussion asks questions that will prepare you to carry out the investigation. These questions help ensure that you understand the purpose and plan of the investigation.

Problem This section presents a problem in the form of a question. Your job during the investigation is to solve the problem based on your observations.

Materials A list of all the materials you will need to conduct the investigation appears at the beginning of each investigation.

Safety This section warns you of potential hazards and tells you about precautions you should take to decrease the risk of accident. The safety symbols that are relevant to the investigation appear next to the title of the Safety section. They also appear next to certain steps of the Procedure. A chart explaining these symbols is found on page *xi*.

Procedure This section tells how to conduct the investigation. Make sure you read the entire Procedure carefully before you begin the investigation. Diagrams are included where necessary to explain a technique or to show an experimental setup. If safety symbols appear next to a certain step, follow the corresponding safety precaution for that step and all subsequent steps. CAUTION statements within the Procedure warn of possible hazards.

Observations As you carry out the investigation, you need to record your observations. You may be asked to describe your observations in words (qualitatively) or you may be required to record quantitative data such as measurements of mass, temperature, and volume. Be sure to record your observations as they occur—do not rely on your memory.

Calculations Once you have recorded your observations, further calculations may be required in order to reach a conclusion. If no further processing of data is necessary, the Calculations section is omitted.

Critical Thinking: Analysis and Conclusions Two steps of the traditional scientific method—analyzing data and forming a conclusion—are represented in this section. Using data gathered during the investigation and knowledge gained from your textbook and the Introduction, you are asked to analyze and interpret your experimental results. You will need to support your analysis and conclusions with the data you collected during the investigation.

Critical Thinking: Applications This section challenges you to apply the concepts learned in the investigation to other scientific and real-world situations.

Going Further This section suggests additional activities for you to pursue on your own. Some of these are brief extensions of the investigation. Others involve library or other types of research. Still others suggest experiments you might perform with your teacher's permission.

Common Laboratory Equipment

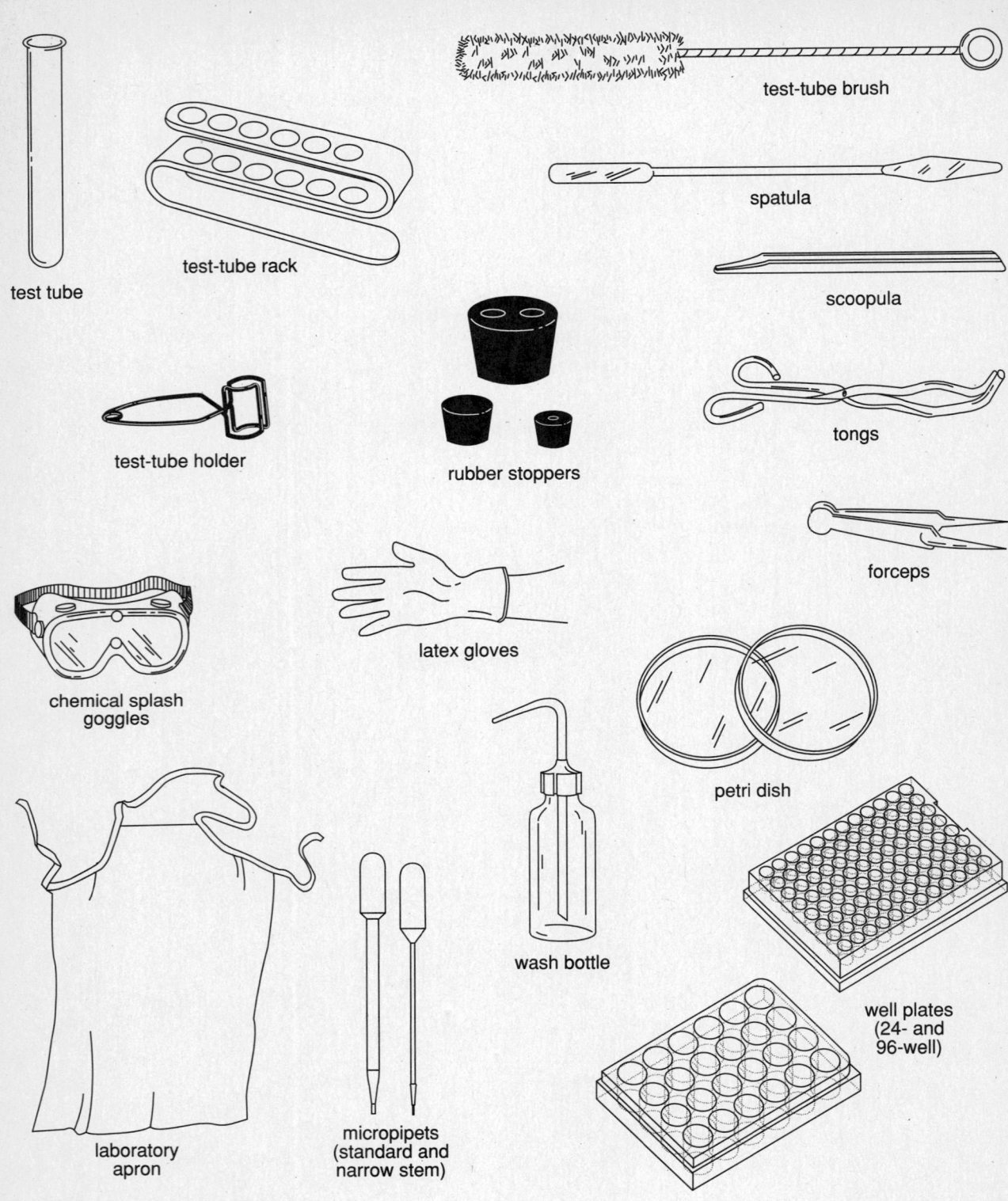

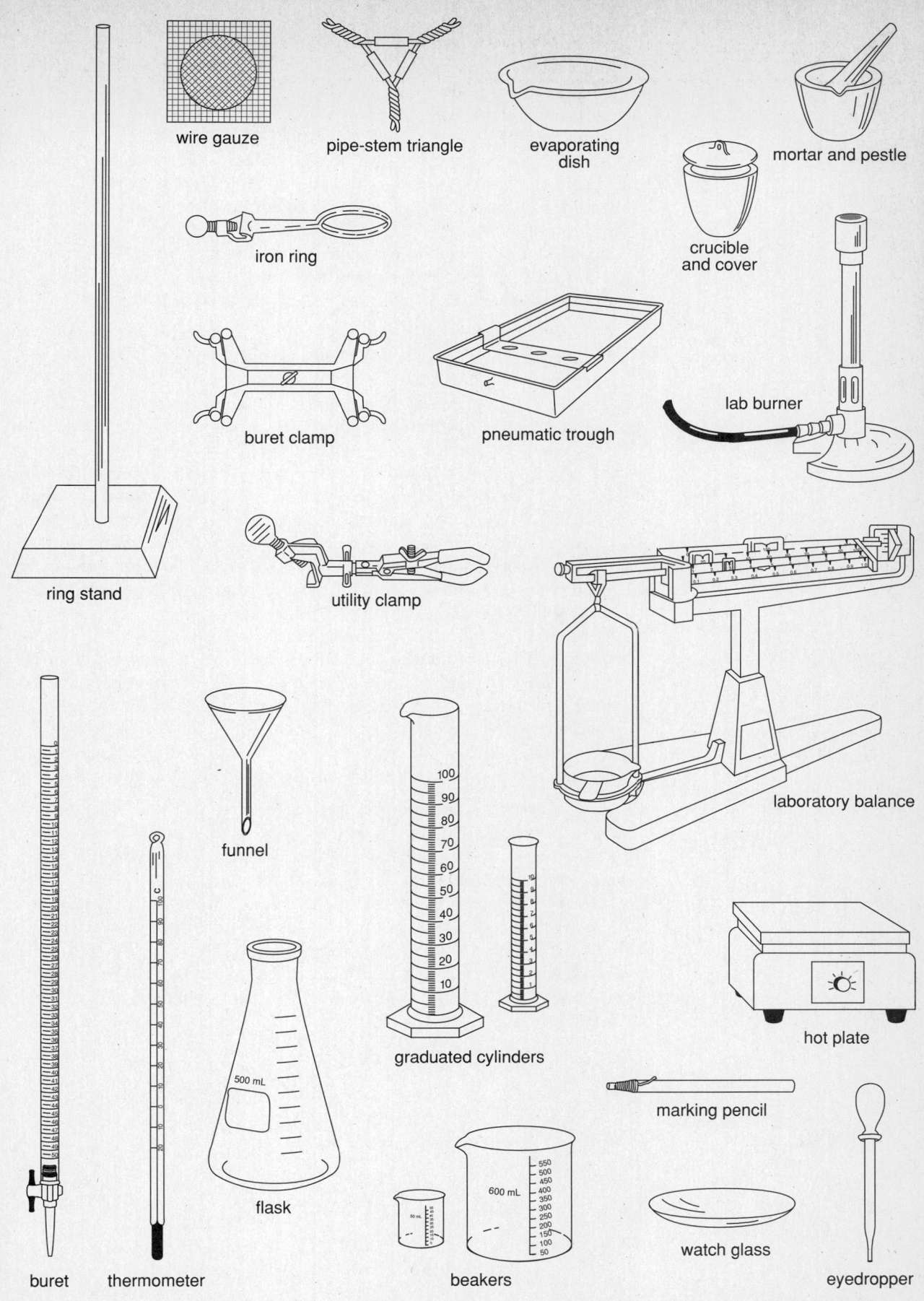

Common Laboratory Equipment

Using a Laboratory Balance

In chemistry investigations, you will frequently use a laboratory balance to measure mass. Although balances vary somewhat in style, and you may use more than one type of balance in your class, they all work on the same principle. One common balance is shown in Figure 1 on the next page. Note that it consists of a suspended pan for holding material and a set of calibrated beams with riders. An object to be measured is placed on the pan, and the riders are moved until the pointer is centered. Then the mass is read.

The balance is a sensitive instrument and must be handled properly. Read the following steps for using a balance, and practice a few times with familiar objects until you become comfortable with the procedure.

1. Carry the balance with two hands. Place it on a level surface.
2. Set all the riders to zero and remove any material from the balance pan.
3. Calibrate the balance by turning the adjustment screw until the pointer on the end of the beam swings equally on either side of the midpoint. See Figure 1.
4. A single solid object, such as a nail or a coin, can be placed directly on the balance pan. Liquids or loose solids, such as salt or sugar, should be placed in a premeasured container or on a weighing paper.
5. Move the largest rider along the beam one notch at a time until the pointer drops. Then move the rider back one notch. Repeat this procedure with the next smaller rider. Continue in the same manner until you are using the smallest rider.
6. The beam on which the smallest rider moves does not have any notches. Slowly slide the rider along until the pointer on the end of the beam is swinging equally on either side of the midpoint. You may prefer to use a pencil to move the rider in order to minimize disturbance to the balance.
7. The mass of the object on the pan is the sum of the masses shown on the beams. Be sure to subtract the mass of the container, if any.

A balance is a graduated measuring device. As such, the precision of any measurement depends on the smallest division of the scale. In the case of the quadruple-beam balance, the smallest division is 0.01 g. A value can be estimated to one place smaller than the smallest division. For example, the mass indicated by the balance in the figure is 123.456 g.

Electronic balances are more accurate and easier to use than conventional balances. Simply place a container or weighing paper on the pan, press the zero (sometimes called tare) button, and add the material you wish to measure. The balance will give the mass of the material indicated as a digital readout.

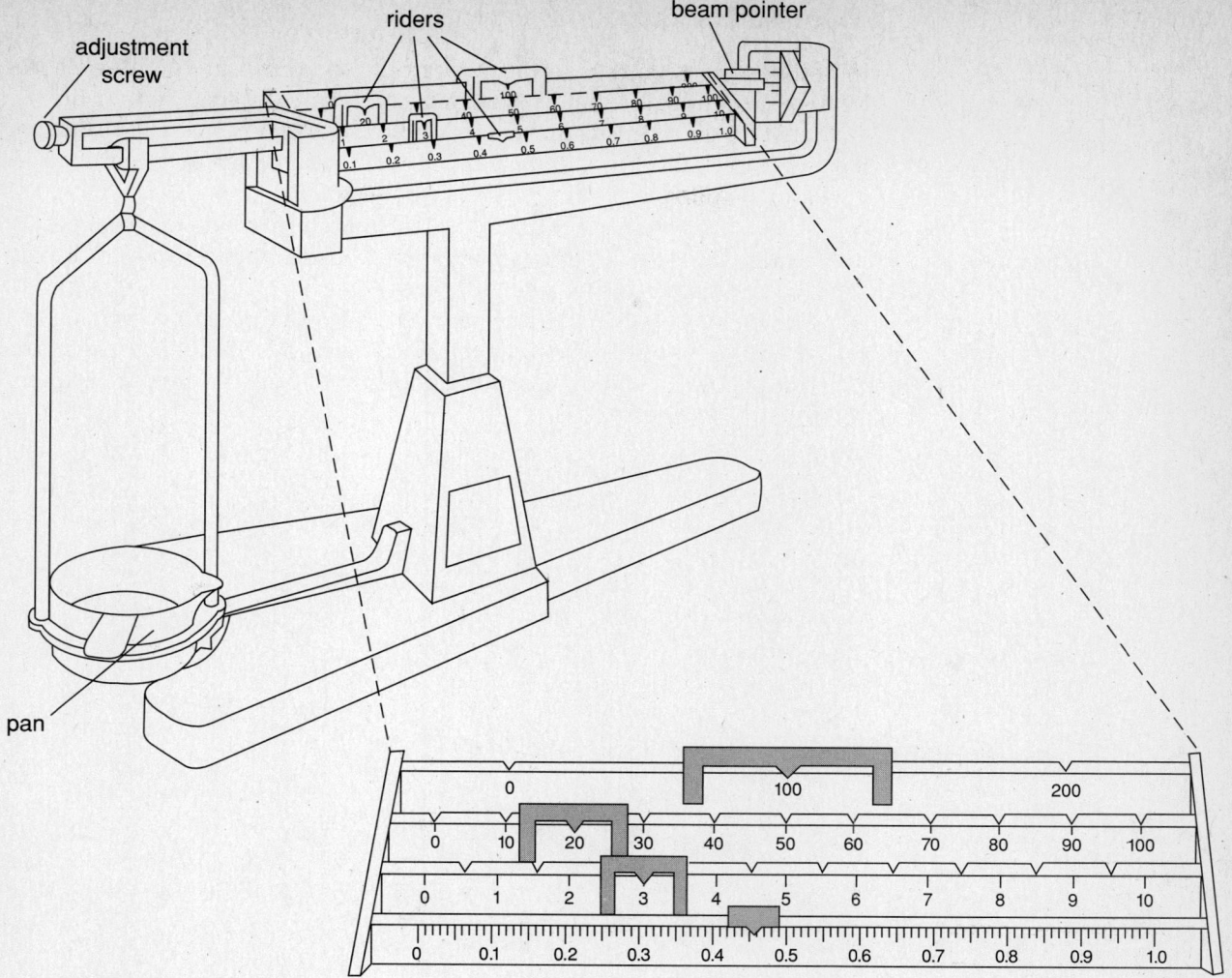

Figure 1

Using a Laboratory Balance **xvii**

Using a Burner

When heating materials in the laboratory, you most often will use a hot plate. There are times, however, when a burner is specified. A burner is fueled by gas and supplies an open flame. As such, it is important for you to know how to operate a burner safely in order to minimize risk of injury or fire.

Learn the following directions for operating a burner. Make sure you understand them before attempting to use a burner, and work only under the supervision of your teacher.

1. Tie back any loose hair or clothing. Put on your safety goggles.
2. Examine the burner to familiarize yourself with its construction. Operate the air intake control and, if present, the fine adjustment valve. See Figure 2.

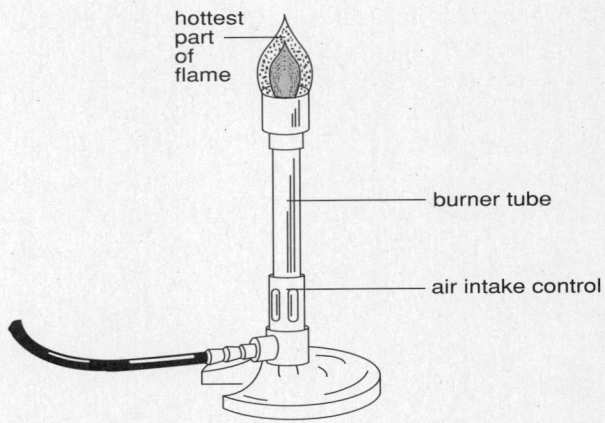

Figure 2

3. Make sure that the opening of the burner tube is clean and free from debris.
4. Push one end of the rubber tubing onto the burner inlet pipe. Push the other end onto the gas valve. The tubing should be securely in place before you go on to the next step.
5. Make sure the burner is level and on a flat surface. There should be no flammable material near the burner.
6. Light a match and hold it against the side of the burner tube about 2 cm below the top. Turn on the gas slowly and move the match up until the gas ignites.
7. Adjust the flame by manipulating the air intake control. A good burner flame gives off little light and has two distinct cones, as shown in Figure 2. Adjust the flame as follows:
   - If the flame is too large, slowly turn down the gas.
   - If the flame is yellow and/or smoky, adjust the air intake control.
   - If there is a gap between the top of the tube and the base of the flame, slowly turn down the gas.
   - If the flame disappears down the tube, turn off the gas, decrease the air intake, and relight the burner.
8. Turn off the burner as soon as you no longer need it.
9. NEVER leave a lighted burner unattended.

Working with Chemicals

Success in laboratory chemistry depends on many factors, one of which is your confidence in handling the materials that you must work with during investigations. Knowing how to safely dispense and transfer chemicals, to use equipment, and to protect yourself helps to create a productive working environment for you and your classmates. In other sections of this book you will find general safety guidelines and specific instructions for using a laboratory balance and burner. The information that follows will help you become acquainted with some of the other standard procedures you will use throughout this course.

Measuring Liquids

When you need an approximate volume of liquid, you can measure it simply by pouring the liquid into a beaker or flask that is imprinted with volume calibrations. If you need a more exact volume, use a graduated cylinder or micropipet. Choose the size of the graduated cylinder that best matches the volume you need to measure. A micropipet may be used to measure volumes of 1 to 6 milliliters or to add drops of liquid to a precise mark in a 10-milliliter graduated cylinder.

In graduated cylinders made of glass, liquids will form a meniscus, or curved surface, with the sides of the cylinder. For most liquids, you should read the volume indicated by the bottom of the meniscus, as shown in Figure 1–1 on page 4 of Investigation 1.

Transferring Liquids

Most high school students are unfamiliar with the techniques for safely transferring liquids. The first thing you need to know is how to get the liquid out of the reagent bottle and into another container without contaminating the class supply. With your palm facing upward, grasp the stopper between your first two fingers, as shown in Figure 3A, and remove it. Hold the stopper while you pick up the reagent bottle with the same hand. Pour out the amount of liquid you need and replace the stopper. In this way, the stopper never touches another surface, preventing contamination of the stopper and the work area.

To minimize splashing when you pour a liquid into a wide-mouth container, such as a beaker, place a stirring rod in the container and

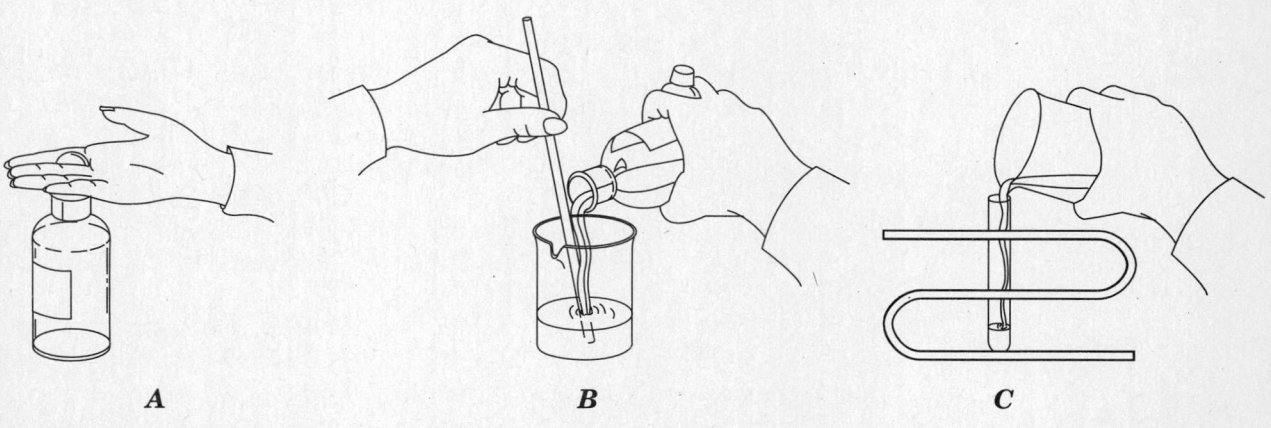

Figure 3

pour the liquid down the rod, as shown in Figure 3B. When pouring liquid into a small-mouth container, such as a test tube, place the liquid into a beaker first. You then will have more control over the liquid when pouring it from the beaker's spout. By placing the test tube in a test-tube rack, as shown in Figure 3C, you protect your fingers from spills.

Transferring Solids

If you want to transfer a solid chemical to a wide-mouth container, tilt the supply bottle toward the container and slowly rotate your wrist back and forth as you tap the side of the bottle so that the solid falls gently from the mouth. (See Figure 4.) If you are transferring a solid into a small-mouth container, such as a test tube, first pour the solid onto a piece of paper into which you have folded a crease. Then pour the solid out of the crease.

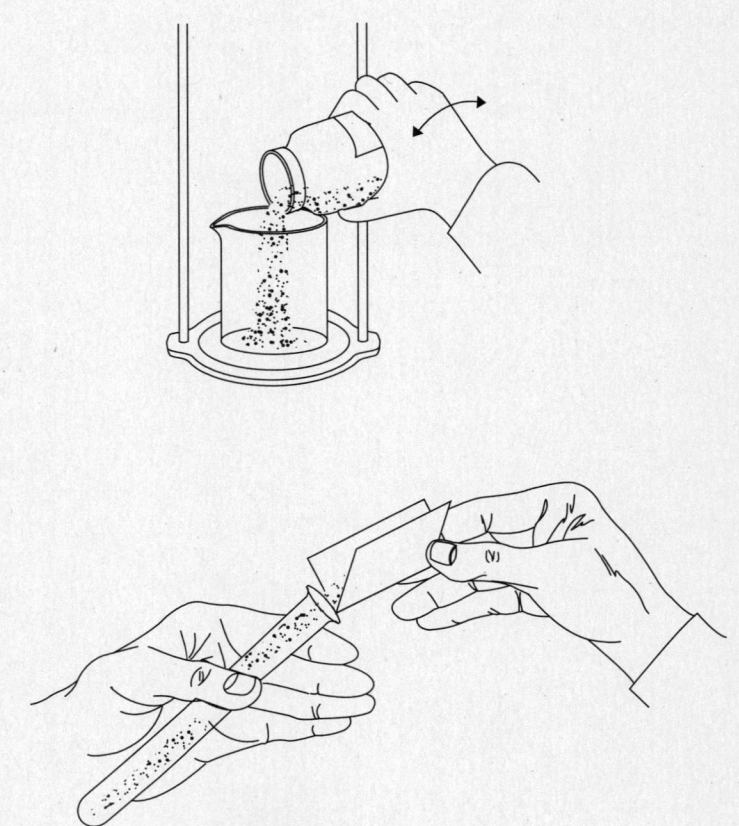

Figure 4

Mixing Materials

Be sure you use a container large enough to hold all the chemicals with room to spare. Never use a thermometer to stir mixtures. Use a stirring rod or wooden splint instead.

If the contents of a test tube must be shaken, put a stopper into the tube and shake it up and down, holding the tube so that its mouth points away from you and others. Remove the stopper slowly in case mixing has caused pressure to build up inside the tube.

Heating Materials

Whenever possible, use a hot plate instead of a laboratory burner to heat chemicals. The absence of a flame reduces the risk of fire. If you are boiling a liquid, place two or three boiling stones or a stirring rod in the container to reduce the amount of bumping and allow the boiling to proceed smoothly. Never add boiling stones to a hot liquid because large amounts of vapor may form and cause splashes. Never heat a closed container, and be sure that open test tubes point away from you and others while being heated.

If you must use a lab burner, follow the safety instructions described elsewhere in this book. Never heat flammable material or leave the flame unattended. Be sure to adjust the burner as described on page *xviii* to use the minimum flame necessary.

Materials that are heated become too hot to touch with bare hands. Be sure to use a test-tube holder to handle glass test tubes. Hold porcelain crucibles and evaporating dishes with tongs as shown in Figure 5. Allow containers to cool before touching them directly.

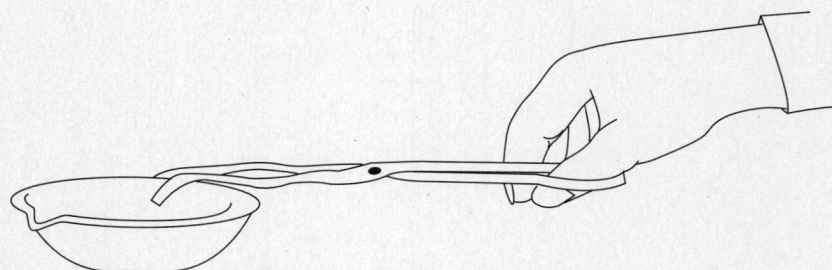

Carrying an evaporating dish

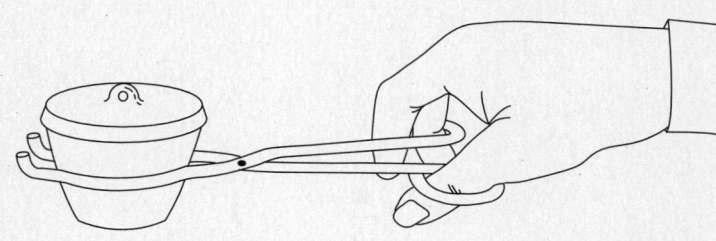

Carrying a crucible

Figure 5

Filtering Mixtures

A mixture of an insoluble solid and a liquid can be separated by pouring the mixture through a filter. To prepare a filter, fold a round piece of filter paper in half and then in quarters as shown in Figure 6. Tear off a small corner from the fold and open the paper to form a cone as shown. Note the position of the torn corner, which allows the paper to lie flat against the funnel.

Place the filter paper into a funnel and set the funnel in an iron ring attached to a ring stand. Place a container under the funnel to catch the

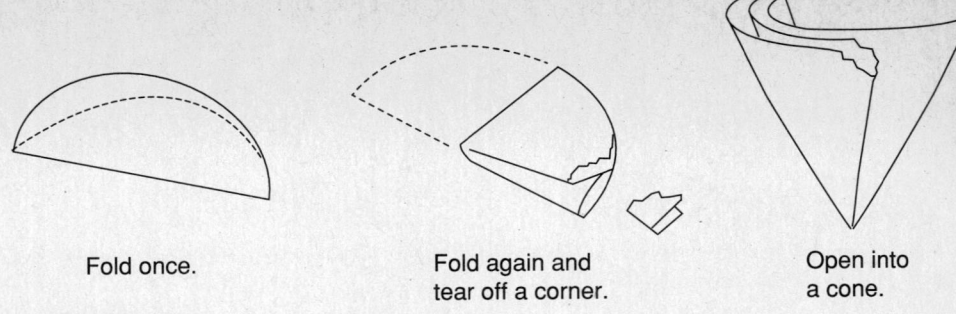

Figure 6

filtered liquid, or filtrate. You will have to wet the filter paper to make it stick to the funnel. Press out air bubbles that might slow the filtration, and pour the mixture into the funnel, taking care not to let the mixture overflow. Use a stirring rod, as mentioned earlier, to guide the liquid into the funnel and reduce spillage.

Uncertainty and Measurement

Lab 1

Text reference: Chapter 1

Introduction

Suppose you have a summer job monitoring the pollution in a local lake. You are instructed to collect three 100-mL water samples at certain locations at set times each day. To each sample, you add 5 mL of a coloring agent that reacts and changes color intensity in proportion to the amount of pollutant in the water. You then check each sample with an instrument that detects color intensity and gives a quantitative, or numerical, measure of the amount of pollutant in each sample. Unfortunately, your measurements of similar samples vary by 10 to 20 percent. How could you increase the accuracy and precision of your measurements?

Every measurement has an uncertainty, or a built-in error. This error is due to limitations in the measurement scale, the manufacturing process, and the ability of the human eye to detect small differences. For example, when measuring volume with a graduated cylinder, the width of the scale lines, variations in glass thickness, and slight changes in the angle of sight when reading the scale are some of the factors that cause uncertainty. Because of this uncertainty, no measurement should be thought of as an exact value, but rather as a value within a range that varies with the uncertainty. For example, the uncertainty of a volume measurement made with a 100-mL graduated cylinder may be ± 0.5 mL. Thus, if you measured 100.0 mL of water, the actual volume would be 100.0 ± 0.5 mL, or within a range of 99.5 mL to 100.5 mL. Although ± 0.5 mL represents only a $\pm 0.5\%$ error for a 100.0 mL measurement, it becomes a much larger error of $\pm 10\%$ when you measure a smaller quantity, such as 5.0 mL.

There are two important lessons you should learn about making measurements. First, you should familiarize yourself with the scale of each piece of lab equipment and learn to read each scale as accurately as possible. Second, you should know the uncertainty of your measurements, because your results cannot be more accurate than the built-in error allows.

In this laboratory investigation, you will become familiar with the measurement scale of a balance, graduated cylinders, and a thermometer. Then you will determine the uncertainty of measurements made with this equipment. If you really do get a job monitoring water pollution, you will know how to increase the accuracy and precision of your measurements so that they are scientifically useful.

Pre-Lab Discussion

Read the entire laboratory investigation and the relevant pages of your textbook. Then answer the questions that follow.

Materials (class of 30 in pairs)
30 pairs safety goggles
30 laboratory aprons
15 laboratory balances
15 standard masses, brass
unknown object #1
unknown object #2
15 graduated cylinders, 10-mL
15 graduated cylinders, 100-mL
2 L distilled water
15 droppers
15 Celsius thermometers
15 pairs heat-proof gloves
beaker, 500-mL
2 boiling stones
tap water
hot plate
plastic tub
package of ice

Time Required
50–90 minutes. To save time, have students do only Parts A and B, or assign Parts A, B, and C to different student groups. Discuss the results of all groups when the investigation is over.

Advance Preparation
At the start of the lab period, bring a large beaker of distilled water to a steady boil on a hot plate. Add 2 boiling stones to the beaker to prevent superheating. Obtain a tub of ice and add a minimum amount of water shortly before students use it. Select cylinders, balances, and thermometers that are of the same accuracy and style, if possible. Set up a labeled data bank for the collection of student data. If your lab has a computer, the data can be pooled and manipulated on the computer.

Lab 1

Introduction
Discuss how accuracy and precision in measurement are important in everyday activities; for example, carpentry, sewing, cooking, and monitoring home water and air quality. Accuracy and precision are also extremely important in the cosmetics and pharmaceutical industries. Correct medical diagnosis frequently depends on accurate, precise analysis of substances in the body.

Create a colorful demonstration to show how a small difference in volume can create a big difference in results. Use the acid/base indicator phenolphthalein in a beaker of dilute acid. Prepare the mixture so that adding a measured volume of concentrated base to the swirling acid leaves it clear after briefly turning pink. Then add one additional drop of base to create a sudden, colorful change.

Safety
Make sure students wear their goggles and lab aprons at all times during the investigation. Point out the beaker of boiling water and caution students not to touch any hot surfaces and to be conscious of the danger of splashing boiling water. ■

Teaching Tips
Students often want to know how many decimal places to include in the measurements they make. The object here is to have students discover how accurately instruments will allow measurements to be made and to report all measurements to this degree of accuracy.

To help illustrate the importance of measuring accurately, you may wish to use the following example: suppose you estimate that each side of a square room is roughly 20 feet long. Because you did not use a

---

Name _____

1. Why is it important to wear eye protection at all times in the chemistry laboratory, even when you are not using an open flame or dangerous chemicals? Without protection, eyes are susceptible to damage from many hazards, including splintered glass or splashed boiling water. For these reasons, goggles should always be worn in the laboratory.

2. In the diagram of the graduated cylinder shown in Figure 1–1, what fraction of a mL does each division, or increment, between the 1-mL markings represent? Each increment represents one fifth or 0.2 mL.

3. What is the volume of the liquid shown in Figure 1–1? (Hint: Read the volume measurement at the bottom of the curved meniscus.) The volume of the liquid shown in Figure 1–1 is 7.4 mL.

4. Which do you think will have a more predictable impact on the measurements you make in the laboratory, human error or uncertainty in the measurement scales of the lab equipment? Explain. The uncertainty that is built into equipment usually can be quantified and is, therefore, relatively predictable. Human error is harder to quantify or predict.

Problem
How large are the uncertainties in measurements made with common lab equipment?

Materials
safety goggles
laboratory apron
laboratory balance
standard masses
2 objects of unknown mass
graduated cylinder, 10-mL
graduated cylinder, 100-mL

distilled water (at 20°C)
dropper
Celsius thermometer
heat-proof gloves
beaker containing boiling water
plastic tub
ice

Safety

Wear your goggles and lab apron at all times during the investigation. Your eyes are fragile, and you should always protect them from potential laboratory hazards such as shattering glass or splashing boiling water. Note the caution alert symbols here and with certain steps of the Procedure. Refer to page *xi* for the specific precautions associated with each symbol.

Lab 1

Procedure

Part A: Estimating the Uncertainty of a Balance

1. Put on your goggles and lab apron. Obtain a laboratory balance and use the zeroing adjustment so the scale reads zero with no mass on the pan. Gently disturb the pan by touching it, and check to make sure that the balance returns to zero with no visible deviation.

2. Study the balance scale that has the smallest counterweight. Determine the mass increment size (in grams) represented by any one of the smallest scale divisions (between two adjacent marks), and record this value. Once you know this value, determine the mass represented by one half and one fifth of this scale increment. Record these values. (Note: If you are using an electronic balance, skip this step.)

3. Obtain a standard mass and place it on the balance pan. Adjust the counterweights to find its mass. The mass should be equal or very close to the standard's given value. Once the exact balance point is found, record the mass as accurately as the smallest scale increment allows (e.g., 10.00 g).

4. Shift the smallest counterweight just slightly until you observe the slightest deviation from the zero point. The shift may be less than one scale division. Do the same for a shift in the opposite direction. These slightly higher and lower mass readings represent the apparent uncertainty range. Record the masses for the upper and lower ends, or limits, of the range. (Note: If you are using an electronic balance, the apparent uncertainty is represented by the range between the higher and lower masses that may flicker on the display.)

5. As exactly as possible, measure and record the mass of each of the two objects of unknown mass. Contribute your measurements to the class data bank for later use. While waiting for your turn with the two unknowns, you can proceed with Part B of this investigation.

Part B: Estimating the Uncertainty of Graduated Cylinders

6. Using the laboratory balance, measure and record the mass of a dry 10-mL graduated cylinder and a dry 100-mL graduated cylinder. **CAUTION:** *If glass cylinders are being used, take care not to knock them over and break them. If a cylinder does shatter, do not pick up the broken pieces with your bare hands.*

7. Record the volume represented by the smallest volume increment on each of the cylinders. Also determine and record the volume represented by one half and one fifth of the smallest volume increment.

8. Use a dropper to add 10.0 mL of distilled water to each cylinder. Add the last few drops to each cylinder carefully so that the bottom curve of the meniscus (observed in glass cylinders only) is on the 10.0-mL mark. Figure 1–1 shows you where to position your sight line so that you obtain an accurate reading.

---

tape measure, the uncertainty of your measurement is probably plus or minus 1 foot. If you wanted to order an expensive floor covering, what difference would this uncertainty make in the total cost of the floor covering, assuming the floor covering costs $50 per square yard? Answer: The difference between 21^2 and 20^2 is about 40 square feet or 5 square yards. Therefore the inaccuracy of your original measurement would cost you an additional $250.

Some students may benefit from a discussion about the density of water (and the relationship between the mass and volume of water) before they work on Step 2b in the calculations for Part B.

Cooperative Learning Strategy

After the lab, set aside time for the class as a group to discuss and evaluate the data bank as directed in the calculations.

Lab 1

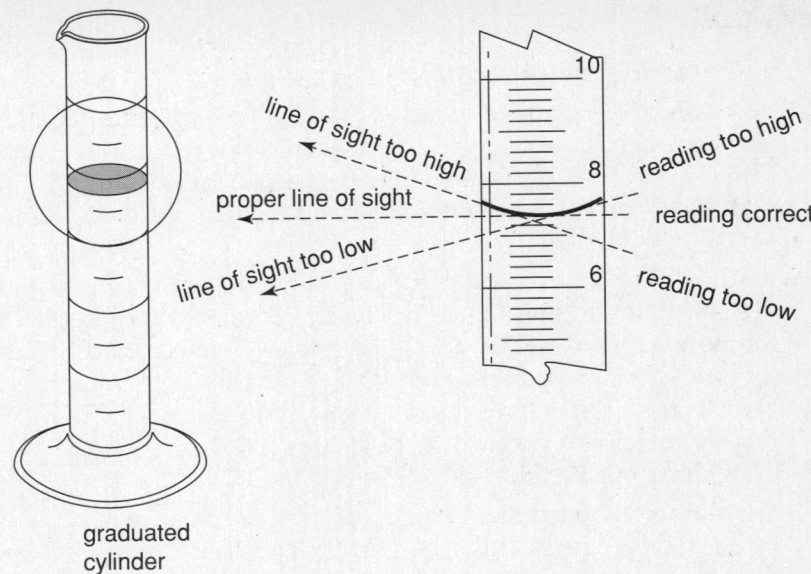

Figure 1-1

 9. With the laboratory balance, measure and record the mass of each cylinder containing 10.0 mL of water. **CAUTION:** *If glass cylinders are being used, take care not to knock them over and break them.* Subtract the mass of the empty cylinder to find the mass of water in the 10-mL and 100-mL cylinders. Record and contribute your measurements to the class data bank for later use. Pour the water into the sink and return all your lab equipment to the supply area. Then proceed with Part C.

Part C: Estimating the Uncertainty of a Thermometer

 10. Obtain a Celsius thermometer. Determine and record the temperature represented by the smallest scale increment. Also determine and record the temperature represented by one half and one fifth of the smallest scale increment. **CAUTION:** *Thermometers are fragile. Handle with care.*

 11. Put on a pair of heat-proof gloves and place the thermometer in the beaker of boiling water provided by your teacher. For 1 to 2 minutes, hold the thermometer in the boiling water so that the tip is not touching the beaker bottom. Remove the thermometer from the boiling water and quickly read it. Record the temperature, estimating to tenths of a degree. Contribute your measurement to the class data bank. **CAUTION:** *Do not touch the beaker or hot plate with your bare hands.*

12. Turn off the hot plate. Allow the thermometer to cool to room temperature. Then place it in a tub of ice water provided by your teacher. Leave the thermometer in the ice bath for 1 to 2 minutes. Record the temperature and contribute your measurement of the freezing point of water to the class data bank.

13. Return all equipment to the supply area. Clean up your work area and wash your hands before leaving the laboratory.

Name _____

Lab 1

Observations (sample data)

Part A: Laboratory Balance

Smallest mass scale increment	0.01 g
One half of smallest mass scale increment	0.005 g
One fifth of smallest mass scale increment	0.002 g
Mass of standard weight	10.00 g

Highest limit __10.01 g__   Lowest limit __9.99 g__

Mass of unknown #1	10.51 g
Mass of unknown #2	3.12 g

Part B: Graduated Cylinders

	10-mL	100-mL
Smallest volume scale increment	0.2 mL	1 mL
One half of smallest volume scale increment	0.1 mL	0.5 mL
One fifth of smallest volume scale increment	0.04 mL	0.2 mL
Mass of empty cylinder	9.11 g	84.15 g
Mass of cylinder with 10.0 mL of water	18.94 g	94.78 g
Mass of 10.0 mL of water	9.83 g	10.63 g

Part C: Thermometer

Smallest temperature scale increment	1.0°C
One half of smallest temperature scale increment	0.5°C
One fifth of smallest temperature scale increment	0.2°C
Temperature of boiling water	99.5°C
Temperature of freezing water	0.0°C

Calculations (based on sample data)

Part A: Uncertainty for Laboratory Balance

1. Use your data for the mass of the standard weight to find the apparent uncertainty of your balance. Subtract the lower limit mass of the standard weight from the higher limit and divide this difference by 2. Round to one significant digit to get the apparent uncertainty (e.g., 0.0125 g rounds off to 0.01 g). Write the mass of the standard weight followed by the uncertainty (e.g., 10.00 g ± 0.01 g).

$$\text{apparent uncertainty} = \frac{(10.01 \text{ g} - 9.99 \text{ g})}{2} = 0.01 \text{ g}$$

mass __10.00 g ± 0.01 g__

2. With classmates, evaluate the class measurements of the masses of the unknowns. Discard any values that are much greater or much

© Prentice-Hall, Inc.

Uncertainty and Measurement

smaller than the majority of values. List and average the remaining masses for each unknown to find an average mass for each.

Class Data Bank: Masses of Unknowns (g)

Unknown #1

10.50 10.51 10.47 10.53 10.50
10.49 10.50 10.48 10.51 10.48

Unknown #2

3.15 3.12 3.17 3.14 3.15
3.13 3.16 3.14 3.13 3.16

Average mass __10.494 g__   Average mass __3.149 g__

3. Determine the practical uncertainty for the lab balance by doing the following steps:
   a. To find the deviation in mass measurements for each unknown, compute the difference (absolute value) between the average mass value (see answer to Question 2) and each of the mass measurements in the data list for Question 2.

Deviations from Average Mass (g)

Unknown #1

0.006 0.016 0.024 0.036 0.006
0.004 0.006 0.014 0.016 0.014

Unknown #2

0.001 0.029 0.021 0.009 0.001
0.019 0.011 0.009 0.019 0.011

   b. Average the list of mass deviations for each unknown and round to one significant figure (e.g., 0.0125 g rounds off to 0.01 g). This is the practical uncertainty.

   Average deviation (uncertainty)   Unknown #1 __0.01 g__

   Unknown #2 __0.01 g__

   c. Report the average mass of each unknown followed by its uncertainty (e.g., 5.25 ± 0.01 g).

   Average mass with uncertainty   Unknown #1 __10.49 ± 0.01 g__

   Unknown #2 __3.15 ± 0.01 g__

Part B: Uncertainty for Graduated Cylinders

1. With classmates, evaluate the class measurements of the masses of 10 mL of water. Discard any values that are much greater or much smaller than the majority of measurements. List the remaining measurements and compute an average mass for the water in each cylinder.

Name _____

Lab 1

Class Data Bank: Mass of 10 mL of Water (g)

10-mL cylinder	100-mL cylinder
10.15 9.83 10.27 10.20 9.50	10.50 9.50 9.75 10.25 11.00
10.00 10.15 9.78 9.96 9.85	9.25 10.35 9.55 10.63 9.45

Average mass __9.995 g__   Average mass __10.023 g__

2. Determine the practical uncertainty of the mass measurements made in the 10-mL and the 100-mL graduated cylinders by doing the following steps:

   a. Take the difference (absolute value) between the average mass of water and each individual mass of water in the data list for the 10-mL graduated cylinder. This gives a list of data deviations. Do the same for the 100-mL cylinder.

   Deviations from Average Mass (g)

10-mL cylinder	100-mL cylinder
0.155 0.165 0.275 0.205 0.095	0.477 0.523 0.273 0.227 0.977
0.005 0.155 0.215 0.035 0.145	0.773 0.327 0.473 0.607 0.573

   b. Average the deviations for each cylinder and round to one significant digit (e.g., 0.133 g rounds off to 0.1 g). This practical uncertainty of the mass measurement is equivalent to the practical uncertainty of the cylinder volume because 1.00 g of water at 20°C has a volume of 1.00 mL.

   Average deviation (uncertainty) 10-mL cylinder __0.1 mL__

   100-mL cylinder __0.5 mL__

   c. Report the volume of water (10.0 mL) in each cylinder, followed by the calculated uncertainty for each cylinder from Part B.

   Average volume with uncertainty 10-mL cylinder __10.0 ± 0.1 mL__

   100-mL cylinder __10.0 ± 0.5 mL__

Part C: Uncertainty of a Celsius Thermometer

1. With classmates, evaluate the class measurements of the boiling points and freezing points of water. Discard any values that are much higher or lower than the majority of temperatures in each list. List the remaining temperatures and compute an average boiling point temperature and an average freezing point temperature.

Lab 1

Name _____

Class Data Bank: Water Temperature (°C)

Boiling point					Freezing point				
101.0	99.5	99.0	100.0	100.5	0.2	−0.5	0.0	0.0	0.5
98.5	101.0	100.0	99.5	100.0	−0.8	0.5	−0.4	−0.8	1.0

Average boiling point __99.9°C__ Average freezing point __−0.03°C__

2. Determine the practical uncertainty of the thermometers by doing the following steps:
   a. Take the difference (absolute value) between the average boiling point and each boiling point in the data list. This gives a list of data deviations. Do the same with the average freezing point data.

Deviations from Average Temperature (°C)

Boiling point					Freezing point				
1.1	0.4	0.9	0.1	0.6	0.23	0.47	0.03	0.03	0.53
1.4	1.1	0.1	0.4	0.1	0.77	0.53	0.37	0.77	1.03

   b. Average the deviations for the boiling points and the freezing points and round to one significant figure (e.g., 0.455°C rounds off to 0.5°C). These are the practical uncertainties for the thermometers.

   Average deviation (uncertainty) Boiling point __0.6°C__

   Freezing point __0.5°C__

   c. Report the average boiling point and freezing point of water followed by the calculated uncertainty of each.

   Average boiling point with uncertainty __99.9°C ± 0.6°C__

   Average freezing point with uncertainty __−0.03°C ± 0.5°C__

Critical Thinking: Analysis and Conclusions

1. Why do students measuring the mass of the same object on similar balances report slightly different masses? *(Drawing conclusions)* __The mass values differ because they represent ranges of values measured on balances, each of which has a different uncertainty.__

2. Which did you find to have a smaller uncertainty, the 10-mL or 100-mL graduated cylinder? Give a reason why one has a smaller uncertainty. *(Interpreting data)* __The 10-mL graduated cylinder has a smaller uncertainty because the scale divisions are smaller.__

Name _____

Lab 1

3. Based on your uncertainty determinations, tell whether balances or graduated cylinders appear to be more accurate measuring devices. Explain your answer. *(Making comparisons)* Balances are more accurate because the uncertainty is smaller than the tenths position.

4. Assuming that the equipment was functioning properly, explain the probable source of error in data values that were discarded because of their large deviations. *(Making inferences)* Values with large deviations result from human error.

5. Do the uncertainties you calculated for each type of lab equipment more closely match the size of the smallest scale division, one-half division, or one-fifth division? *(Interpreting data)* The uncertainties should match one half the smallest scale division.

6. Based on your answer to Question 5, what uncertainty would you assign to each type of equipment used? *(Evaluating)*

   Balance ___±0.005 g___   10-mL graduated cylinder ___±0.1 mL___
   Thermometer ___±0.5°C___   100-mL graduated cylinder ___±0.5 mL___

Critical Thinking: Applications

1. If the uncertainty of a balance is ±0.005 g, how many significant figures would you use to report a scale reading when the counterweights lie exactly on the 8-gram mark? Explain your answer. *(Applying concepts)* Use 8.000 g ±0.005 g because its last significant digit is in the same decimal position as the reported uncertainty.

2. Suppose a student asks your advice about how to measure 9 mL of a liquid as accurately as possible using a graduated cylinder. Would you recommend a 10-mL or a 100-mL graduated cylinder? Support your answer using the results of this investigation. *(Making judgments)* Use the 10-mL graduated cylinder because the uncertainty is smaller and the volume to be measured is small enough to fit in the 10-mL graduate.

3. What procedural change would you recommend to increase the accuracy and precision of the measurements discussed in the Introduction to this lab? *(Evaluating)* Use a smaller graduated cylinder (which has a smaller uncertainty) to measure the 5 mL of coloring agent.

Going Further

1. Determine the uncertainty of a carpenter's tape measure, a tape measure used for sewing, or a measuring cup used for cooking. To make this determination, use methods similar to those used in this investigation. Present your findings to your class.

Going Further

1. The school industrial arts and domestic arts areas may be willing to provide tape measures and measuring cups.

Name _____ Date _____ Class _____

Density of Liquids

Small Scale Lab 2

Text reference: **Chapter 1**

Introduction

Have you ever wondered why the oil in bottled salad dressing settles on top of the water-and-vinegar mixture? The answer has to do with the different densities of the liquids in the dressing. Oil has a lower density than the water-and-vinegar mixture. When two liquids of different densities are mixed, the liquid that is less dense, in this case the oil, floats above the other liquid.

Density is the mass of a substance per unit of volume. The density of any substance is a ratio and may be calculated by dividing the mass of the sample by its volume.

$$\text{density} = \frac{\text{mass}}{\text{volume}}$$

The most common units of measurement for density that you will encounter in this course are g/mL and g/cm^3.

When measured at the same temperature and pressure, all samples of a particular substance have the same density regardless of the quantity or shape of the sample. Thus, density is a characteristic property of matter that is often used by chemists to identify a substance.

In this investigation, you will first determine the density of tap water by finding the density of three separate samples and calculating an average. You will then repeat this procedure for an unknown liquid. Finally, you will compare your measured values with the accepted values for the densities of these liquids and compute the percent error for your results.

Pre-Lab Discussion

Read the entire laboratory investigation and the relevant pages of your textbook. Then answer the questions that follow.

1. Define *density* in your own words and give two everyday examples of substances that differ in density. <u>Density is a measure of the amount of a substance's mass in a unit of volume. Examples will vary, but may include oil and water, helium and air, wood and iron.</u>

2. How can the density of an unknown substance help you identify it? <u>The accepted densities of many substances may be obtained from reference books. If the density of an unknown is measured and compared with the known densities of substances having similar properties, the identity of the unknown becomes easier to determine.</u>

Materials (class of 30 in pairs)
30 pairs chemical splash goggles
30 laboratory aprons
90 plastic micropipets
tap water
15 laboratory balances
15 graduated cylinders, 10-mL
50 mL unknown liquid (ethanol, isopropyl alcohol, methanol, corn oil, or ethylene glycol)

Time Required
30 minutes. Allow more time if students work individually.

Advance Preparation
Stretch and cut the micropipets if necessary. Refer to the instructions at the front of this teacher's edition for an explanation of how to stretch micropipets.
Have available one or more of the following suggested liquids for use as the unknown: ethanol, isopropyl alcohol, methanol, corn oil, or ethylene glycol. You may wish to supply different groups with different unknowns. Have containers ready in which to collect the liquids for reuse or disposal.

Introduction
Have on display a container of layered liquids, such as water, vegetable oil, corn syrup, and isopropyl alcohol. You can make it more fun by adding food coloring to the water and alcohol. Ask students why it is possible to create the display. Discuss how the densities of the liquids compare based on the order of the liquids in the column.

© Prentice-Hall, Inc.

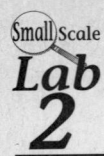

Small Scale Lab 2

Name _____

Before doing the investigation, discuss other physical properties that can aid in the identification of substances, such as melting point, boiling point, and index of refraction (the ratio of the speed of light in a vacuum to the speed of light in a substance).

Safety

Make sure students wear their goggles and lab aprons at all times during the investigation. Remind students to exercise care in handling the unknowns because they do not know if the liquids are hazardous. Students should avoid contact of their skin and clothing with the liquids or inhalation of their vapors. Some of the unknowns are flammable. Be sure all burner flames are extinguished before the unknowns are used. ■

Teaching Tips

The investigation can be done with balances that measure masses to 0.1 g, but better results are obtained with more sensitive balances.

Data for the entire class can be pooled and averaged to increase precision.

When students are ready to answer Question 3 in Analysis and Conclusions, provide them with the density of water at 20°C (0.998 g/mL) and the densities of their unknowns.

If you discuss the Application questions in class, tell students that in general, density increases with decreasing temperature. Water is unusual, however, because it is more dense at 4°C than at 0°C.

3. Why is the accuracy of the laboratory balance that you use in this investigation important? What effect would a less accurate balance have on your results? _The amounts used in this investigation are small and, therefore, must be measured as accurately as possible. A less accurate balance would increase the deviation from the accepted values._

4. What is the advantage in taking three sets of measurements instead of just one or two when determining the density of each liquid? _The calculated values will be more reliable if they are based on a greater number of trials._

5. Why should you avoid skin contact with the unknown solution? _Because the liquid is unknown, the potential hazards are unknown. The liquid may be toxic, flammable, or hazardous in some other way._

6. Do you expect your measured values for the density of water and the unknown to differ from the accepted values? Explain your answer. _Students should expect variations as a result of the small quantities in use and some inaccuracy of measurement. Also, the temperature of the liquids may vary from 20°C, which is the temperature on which Table 3 is based._

Problem

What is the density of tap water and how can a property such as density be used to identify an unknown substance?

Materials

chemical splash goggles
laboratory apron
6 plastic micropipets
tap water

laboratory balance
graduated cylinder, 10-mL
unknown liquid

Safety

Wear your goggles and lab apron at all times during the investigation. Handle the unknown liquid with care. It may be toxic, flammable, or it may give off hazardous vapors. Avoid spills and contact with your skin or clothing. Do not inhale the vapors. If contact occurs, flush with water. Do not bring an open flame into the laboratory.

Note the caution alert symbols here and with certain steps of the Procedure. Refer to page xi for the specific precautions associated with each symbol.

Name _____

Small Scale Lab 2

Procedure

1. Put on your goggles and lab apron. Obtain six micropipets and number them 1, 2, 3, 4, 5, and 6. Make sure each micropipet is dry and clean.
2. Place micropipet #1 on the laboratory balance. Measure its mass to the nearest 0.01 g and record this value in Data Table 1.
3. Fill the micropipet with tap water as completely as possible. Place it on the balance and measure its mass to the nearest 0.01 g. Record the mass in Data Table 1.
4. Completely transfer the water in the micropipet into a *dry* graduated cylinder. Measure and record the volume of the water to the nearest 0.1 mL. (Note: If the graduated cylinder is made of glass, your eye must be at the same level as the bottom of the meniscus to measure the volume accurately. See Figure 2–1.)

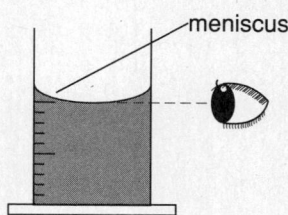

Figure 2–1

5. Using micropipets #2 and #3, repeat Steps 2–4 so that you have three sets of mass and volume data for water.

6. Obtain 50 mL of an unknown liquid from your teacher. Use micropipets #4, #5, and #6 and the preceding procedure to measure the mass and volume of three samples of the unknown. Record your measurements in Data Table 2. **CAUTION:** *The unknown solutions may be flammable or toxic, or they may give off hazardous vapors. Avoid skin contact and inhaling their vapors. Do not work near a burner flame.*

7. Dispose of all chemicals according to your teacher's instructions. Clean up your work area and wash your hands before leaving the laboratory.

Waste Disposal
If the flammable liquids used in the investigation cannot be reused, collect them in a single container for non-halogenated organic solvents. Dispose of them commercially, or get a local permit for drain disposal. ■

Observations (sample data)
DATA TABLE 1 Water

	Trial 1	Trial 2	Trial 3
mass of empty micropipet (g)	0.75	0.76	0.75
mass of filled micropipet (g)	4.66	4.71	4.05
mass of water (g)	3.91	3.95	3.30
volume of water (mL)	3.9	4.0	3.5
density of water (g/mL)	1.0	0.99	0.94

© Prentice-Hall, Inc.

Density of Liquids 13

Small Scale Lab 2

Name _____

DATA TABLE 2 Unknown (sample data for ethanol)

	Trial 1	Trial 2	Trial 3
mass of empty micropipet (g)	0.84	0.79	0.82
mass of filled micropipet (g)	3.80	3.99	3.84
mass of unknown (g)	2.96	3.20	3.02
volume of unknown (mL)	3.8	4.2	4.0
density of unknown (g/mL)	0.78	0.76	0.76

Calculations (based on sample data)

1. Calculate the mass of each water sample by subtracting the mass of the empty micropipet from the mass of the water-filled micropipet. Record this value in Data Table 1.

$$4.66 \text{ g} - 0.75 \text{ g} = 3.91 \text{ g}$$

2. Calculate the density of each water sample at room temperature in grams per milliliter (g/mL). Enter this value in Data Table 1.

$$\frac{3.91 \text{ g}}{3.9 \text{ mL}} = 1.0 \text{ g/mL}$$

3. Find the average density of water based on the results of the three trials.

$$(1.0 \text{ g/mL} + 0.99 \text{ g/mL} + 0.94 \text{ g/mL})/3 = 0.98 \text{ g/mL}$$

Average density of water __0.98 g/mL__

4. Similarly calculate the mass and density of each sample of unknown and record these values in Data Table 2. Then find the average density of the unknown.

Average density of unknown __0.77 g/mL__

Critical Thinking: Analysis and Conclusions

1. Based on your data, which of the liquids in the table on the next page could be your unknown? Explain. *(Drawing conclusions)*

Name _____

Small Scale Lab 2

TABLE 3 Densities of Some Liquids

Liquid	Density (g/mL)
ethanol	0.789
isopropyl alcohol	0.786
methanol	0.791
corn oil	0.921–0.928
water	0.998
ethylene glycol	1.114
glycerine	1.261

Answers will vary. Students should select one or more liquids from the table above that have densities closest to the average density of their unknowns.

2. Could your unknown be a liquid that is not listed in the table in Question 1? Explain. *(Making comparisons)* Yes. If the density of the unknown does not match any liquids in the table, there may be other liquids that have the same density as the unknown.

3. Using the formula below, calculate the percent error for the average density of water that you determined in the investigation. Do the same for the average density of the unknown liquid. Your teacher will provide you with the accepted value for the density of each liquid. *(Interpreting data)*

$$\text{percent error} = \frac{|\text{measured value} - \text{accepted value}|}{\text{accepted value}} \times 100\%$$

$$\text{percent error (water)} = \frac{|0.98 \text{ g/mL} - 0.998 \text{ g/mL}|}{0.99 \text{ g/mL}} \times 100\% = 2\%$$

$$\text{percent error (ethanol)} = \frac{|0.77 \text{ g/mL} - 0.789 \text{ g/mL}|}{0.789 \text{ g/mL}} \times 100\% = 2\%$$

Percent error for density of water __2%__

Percent error for density of unknown __2%__

4. Why do you think your measured values differ from the accepted density values for water and the unknown liquid? *(Evaluating)* Measurements taken with the balance and graduated cylinder are not exact. Calculations made using these measurements can be no more certain than the least certain measurement. Another possible source of uncertainty is the failure to remove all the liquid from the pipet.

Name _____

5. What changes could you make in the procedure to increase the accuracy of your results? *(Designing experiments)* Use equipment with smaller ranges of error; use a larger sample; measure the mass of the liquid directly in the graduated cylinder to eliminate possible loss of liquid during transfer from the micropipet.

Critical Thinking: Applications

1. Look again at Table 3. If your unknown had a density of 0.79 g/mL and you knew that it was one of the three substances listed in the table having a density close to your value, how would you go about determining which liquid was your unknown? *(Designing experiments)* Look for another property, such as boiling point, that is different for each of the liquids. For example, ethanol boils at 78.5°C at standard pressure, whereas methanol boils at 64.7°C.

2. Ice floats on water. Is ice more or less dense than water? How do you think the density of ice affects the survival of water-dwelling organisms in environments where temperatures fall below the freezing point? *(Developing hypotheses)* Because ice floats on water, it must be less dense than water. As a result, ice forms first at the surface of water rather than from the bottom up. Water-dwelling organisms can survive below the ice during freezing conditions.

3. When stating the density of a liquid, why is it necessary to state the temperature? *(Applying concepts)* The density of a liquid changes with temperature.

4. The density of petroleum oil is less than the density of sea water. How would this property affect methods used to clean up an oil spill in the ocean? *(Making predictions)* Because of its lower density, the oil will float on top of the sea water and spread out over a large area. Clean-up methods should include ways to contain the oil on the surface of the water.

Going Further

1. Under your teacher's supervision, design and conduct an experiment to determine how the density of tap water compares to the density of salt water that contains a large amount of dissolved salt.
2. Describe the procedures you would use to measure the densities of a solid and a gas. Explain how these procedures would differ from those used to determine the density of a liquid.

Name _____ Date _____ Class _____

Cleaning Up an Oil Spill

Lab 3 APPLICATION

Text reference: **Chapter 1**

Introduction

Have you ever considered the difficulty of cleaning up an oil spill? You may have read about the *Exxon Valdez* oil spill in Prince William Sound off the coast of Alaska. It was one of the largest oil spills in North American history. Many scientists in chemistry, marine biology, wildlife physiology, and shoreline ecology worked together to clean up the spill and to save as much wildlife as they could. The cleanup was a very time-consuming and difficult operation. Scientists continue to monitor the long-term effects of the spill on the environment.

As you probably know, oil is less dense than water. It not only floats on top of the water, but also spreads rapidly on the water's surface. The first step that scientists take in cleaning up an oil spill is to contain the oil if possible. Because cleanup crews need time to reach a spill site, however, some oil is carried away before containment procedures can be employed. Also, waves and currents in the ocean make containment difficult over an extended time period. Thus, other methods must be employed to clean up the spill.

Natural processes, such as evaporation, wave action, and the biological breakdown of oil by bacteria, begin the process of cleaning up an oil spill immediately, but they often occur too slowly to save the organisms whose habitats have been polluted or destroyed. A big factor in the cleanup of the Prince William Sound oil spill was bioremediation—introducing large numbers of oil-eating bacteria to remove oil. Unfortunately, this process is long and slow. Scientists are searching for faster methods to clean up spills in order to save more wildlife.

In this investigation, you will evaluate some physical and chemical techniques that can be used to clean up an oil spill. As you do the investigation, keep in mind that your goal is to remove as much of the oil as fast as possible and with the minimum amount of damage to your model environment.

Pre-Lab Discussion

Read the entire laboratory activity and the relevant pages of your textbook. Then answer the questions that follow.

1. Why is containment alone not a satisfactory answer to the oil spill problem? <u>Some oil will be swept away before containment can begin. Also, containment is a temporary measure and cannot withstand winds and strong ocean currents.</u>

Materials (class of 30 in pairs)
30 pairs chemical splash goggles
30 laboratory aprons
newspapers
masking tape
15 aluminum pie pans
tap water
motor oil, 300 mL
15 containers to hold the oil
30 droppers
string, 4 m
30 beakers, 150-mL
15 graduated cylinders, 10-mL
30 wooden splints
15 small boxes of matches
sand, 400 mL
natural straw, 1L
liquid detergent, 25 mL
paper towels

Time Required
30 minutes.

Advance Preparation
Pour 20 mL of oil into a container for each group. Cut the 25-cm lengths of string. Have a bucket or similar container available for disposal of oil and oil-water-sand mixtures. Have another container available for disposal of oil-contaminated paper towels, newspapers, straw, and pie tins.

Introduction
Before beginning this lab, discuss what students know about the difference in the densities of oil and water. Remind them that the density of water is about 1 g/mL. You may wish to tell them the density of motor oil (about 0.8 g/mL).
  Discuss the types of environmental damage that

Cleaning Up an Oil Spill 17

Lab 3
APPLICATION

Name _____

result from oil spills, such as fouling of coastlines and poisoning of marine life.

Emphasize that all students should dispose properly of the materials used in the lab, and caution students not to pour any oil down the drain.

There is an excellent video put out by Exxon entitled *Scientists and the Alaska Oil Spill* that could be used to introduce this investigation.

2. Of the methods you will be using in this investigation, which do you predict will be the best for cleaning up an oil spill and minimizing further damage to the environment? Explain your reasoning. <u>Answers will vary with the students' prior knowledge of environmental issues. The best method overall probably is absorption by straw because it removes most of the oil, although the disposal of the contaminated straw also must be considered.</u>

3. In Step 5 of the Procedure, why are you told to tie back long hair and loose clothing? <u>To avoid creating a fire hazard while working with the match and burning splint.</u>

4. What effect do you think the sand will have on the oil? <u>The oil may stick to and sink with the sand when it is added to the water.</u>

Problem

What are some effective, environmentally safe methods for cleaning up an oil spill?

Materials

chemical splash goggles
laboratory apron
newspapers
masking tape
aluminum pie pan
tap water
motor oil
container
2 droppers

string, 25-cm piece
2 beakers, 150-mL
graduated cylinder, 10-mL
2 wooden splints
matches
sand
natural straw
liquid detergent
paper towels

Safety
Make sure students wear their goggles and lab aprons at all times during the investigation. Show students how to ignite their splints with matches. Remind them to be sure the match is extinguished and to keep their faces away from the oil when they attempt to ignite it.

This investigation has the potential to be quite messy. Caution students to clean up any oil spills on the tabletops or floors immediately due to the potential hazard and to dispose of waste materials as soon as a procedural step is finished. Point out the appropriate disposal containers the students should use. ∎

Safety

Wear your goggles and lab apron at all times during the investigation. Tie back long hair and secure loose clothing to avoid any fire hazard while working with the matches and burning splints. Clean up any spilled oil immediately to avoid the potential hazard of slipping on the floor or ruining clothing from oily work areas. If a spill occurs, tell your teacher immediately.

Dispose of excess oil, waste oil-and-water mixtures, and oil-soaked sand and straw in the containers provided by your teacher. Do not pour any oil down the drain.

Note the caution alert symbols here and with certain steps of the Procedure. Refer to page *xi* for the specific precautions associated with each symbol.

Name _____

Lab 3
APPLICATION

Procedure

1. Put on your goggles and lab apron. Cover your work area with sheets of newspaper, secured with masking tape.

2. Fill the pie pan with water to a depth of about 2 cm. Add two drops of oil to the center of the water. Tie the ends of the string together and gently place the circle of string around the oil on the water's surface.

3. Carefully add another 2 mL of oil inside the string. Try using the string to pull the oil to one side of the pan. Record your observations in the Data Table.

4. Using one of the droppers, try to suction the oil from the containment area. Place the oil from your dropper in one of the beakers and dispose of it in the container provided by your teacher. **CAUTION:** *Do not pour any oil down the drain.* Record your observations.

5. Remove the string from the pan and dispose of it in the container provided by your teacher. Using a graduated cylinder, measure 5 mL of oil and add it to the water. Fill a clean 150-mL beaker with tap water. Ignite a wooden splint with a match. Using the burning split, ignite the oil on the water in the pie pan. Extinguish the splint by placing it in the beaker of tap water. **CAUTION:** *Avoid contact with the flame from the match and the burning splint. Tie back hair and loose clothing.* Record your observations of the ignited oil.

6. If you were able to remove all the oil in Step 5, add another 5 mL of oil to the pan. If the oil was not cleaned up in Step 5, proceed using the oil already in your pan. Spread a handful of sand lightly over the surface of the oil. Wait one or two minutes. Record your observations.

7. If all the oily sand from Step 6 is below water level, add another 5 mL of oil to the pan. If the sand is above water level, dispose of the contents of the pan in the container provided by your teacher. Then add a fresh supply of water to a depth of about 2 cm and add 5 mL of oil to the water. Sprinkle a handful of straw on the surface of the oil. Record your observations until no further changes occur.

8. Dispose of the contents of the pan in the container provided by your teacher, and rinse and wipe your pan. Again, fill the pan with water to a depth of 2 cm and add one drop of oil. Now add one drop of liquid detergent to the oil and stir the two together using a clean wooden splint. Record your observations.

9. Dispose of the contents of the pan in the container provided by your teacher. Clean up your work area and wash your hands before leaving the laboratory.

Teaching Tips

After completing the investigation you may wish to have a class discussion concerning which method worked best to clean up the oil spill. Have students identify the various environmental issues that must be considered.

If the oil seems to spread too much, you may wish to use a heavier weight oil or decrease the amount of oil called for in the investigation.

Waste Disposal

The remaining motor oil and all oil-contaminated materials are considered hazardous waste. Contact the local public works department or a business that services cars and find out the disposal procedure in your area. ■

Lab 3 APPLICATION

Name _____

Observations (sample data)

DATA TABLE

Cleanup Procedure	Observations
containment with string	Oil should stay inside the circle of string. If too much oil is added, it will overflow the string.
suction with dropper	Most of the oil will be recovered. Students should notice that the reclaimed oil is mixed with water.
burning the oil	The oil should not ignite.
sand	Most of the oil should sink with the sand. After sinking, however, oil may escape and rise to the surface.
straw	The straw should absorb all the oil.
detergent	A milky-white suspension should form.

Critical Thinking: Analysis and Conclusions

1. The string used in Steps 1–3 of the procedure shows how a boom works to contain oil spills. Were you able to contain your oil with the string provided? Why or why not? *(Drawing conclusions)* Yes. The string works because the less dense oil floats on the water's surface. If the string becomes waterlogged and sinks, however, the oil is not contained. If there is too much oil for the string to contain, the oil overflows into the rest of the pan.

2. Do you think it would be possible to use a suction device—like the dropper used in this investigation—to remove a large oil spill? Explain. *(Drawing conclusions)* It will work only if the oil is thick and there is little turbulence in the water. More likely, a mixture of oil and water will be recovered and still will have to be separated to reclaim the oil.

3. Why did the sand cause the oil to sink? *(Making inferences)* The oil coated the sand particles and, because sand is more dense than water, the sand sank, carrying the oil with it.

4. Does sinking the oil with sand appear to be an effective method of cleaning up an oil spill? Explain your answer. *(Drawing conclusions)* No, because some oil can break away from the sand and escape to the surface. Also, the oil-coated sand that sinks would damage bottom-dwelling organisms.

5. Why did the straw not cause the oil to sink? *(Making inferences)* The straw is less dense than water.

6. What effect did the detergent have on the oil? Would this effect aid in cleaning up an oil spill? *(Interpreting data)* The detergent broke the oil into small droplets and dispersed it in the water. The tiny droplets would be harder to remove and would still be harmful to wildlife, but they might allow natural processes to operate more quickly.

Critical Thinking: Applications

1. If the oil could be ignited, would you consider this an effective and safe way to clean up an oil spill? Explain. *(Making judgments)* No, because burning oil would cause air pollution, resulting in a different type of environmental damage.

2. Based on your results, which method of cleanup tested in this investigation do you think is the most effective? Defend your answer. *(Evaluating)* The use of straw seems most effective because it absorbs the oil and then may be removed from the water without causing further damage.

3. If scientists are able to reclaim oil by removing it from the water's surface, what problems would they encounter in trying to make the oil suitable for reuse? *(Applying concepts)* The oil still would have to be separated from the water that would be picked up in the recovery effort. Organisms, debris, and other contaminants would have to be removed.

4. If you had to develop a plan to be used in cleaning up an oil spill, taking into consideration factors such as speed of removal, damage to the environment, and cost, what strategies would you include? *(Developing models)* Answers will vary, but should include a combination of methods shown to be the most feasible in this investigation, as well as suggestions for bioremediation and other ideas students may have.

Going Further

1. Research the most recent major oil spills around the world. Prepare a report describing the cleanup methods used and their effectiveness.
2. Research the use of bioremediation in cleaning up oil spills. Discuss the advantages and disadvantages of using this technology.
3. Research the way that oil is transported. Find out if other, more environmentally safe methods exist for transporting oil. If they do, discuss why you think some of these methods have not been put to use.

Going Further
You may wish to show the video from the Discovery Channel, Fall 1992, that describes the invention of elastol (polyisobutylene), a substance considered very effective in cleaning up an oil spill.

Name _____ Date _____ Class _____

Simulating a Cold Pack

Lab 4
APPLICATION

Text reference: **Chapter 2**

Introduction

Suppose you are on a hike and you sprain your ankle. The immediate application of a cold pack would be a wise first-aid practice. Injuries such as a sprained ankle are accompanied by an increase in blood flow to the affected area, which brings excess heat and contributes to swelling. A cold pack is much colder than your injured ankle, so it removes some of the heat, causes blood vessels to constrict, and reduces swelling, inflammation, and pain.

How exactly does a cold pack work? An instant cold pack, shown in Figure 4–1, usually consists of a tough plastic bag with two compounds inside: water and a salt such as ammonium nitrate (NH_4NO_3), a common lawn fertilizer. The water is sealed inside a fragile inner bag to keep it separated from the ammonium nitrate.

Materials (class of 30 in pairs)
30 pairs chemical s...
  goggles
30 laboratory apron...
tap water
15 graduated cylinders,
  100-mL
15 plastic foam cups
15 laboratory balances
60 pieces of weighing paper
15 spatulas
900 g ammonium nitrate
  (NH_4NO_3)
15 thermometers
15 stirring rods
clock

Time Required
55 minutes. If your lab periods are shorter, have students prepare their four 15.0-g portions of ammonium nitrate the day before and store them in stoppered test tubes.

Advance Preparation
Inexpensive 50-lb bags of ammonium nitrate are usually available at a local farming or gardening supply store. (Ammonium nitrate is commonly used as a lawn fertilizer with the analysis of 34-0-0. If the store doesn't have it in stock, it can be ordered.) Do not substitute ammonium sulfate (($NH_4)_2SO_4$) fertilizer as it will not give the same results. If you need to purchase ammonium nitrate through a supply house, the cheapest grade will suffice, but avoid a fertilizer that has herbicides added to it. If your supply of ammonium nitrate is limited, the lab may be scaled down by using 25.0 ml of water and 8.0-g portions of ammonium nitrate.

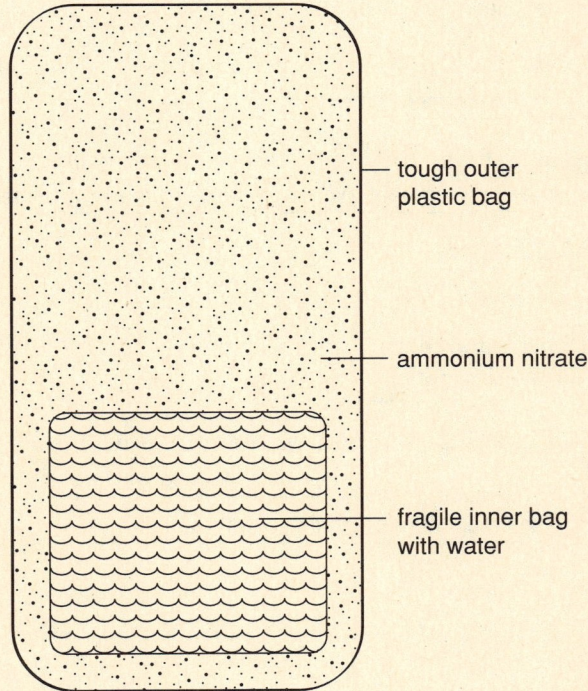

Figure 4–1

When the cold pack is needed, the ammonium nitrate is brought into contact with the water by squeezing the pack until the fragile inner container pops open. As the ammonium nitrate dissolves in the water, a subtle chemical change occurs. The water breaks the solid ammonium nitrate into positively and negatively charged particles (ions).

© Prentice-Hall, Inc.

Lab 4
APPLICATION

Introduction

Bring in a commercial cold pack to show the class. You may be able to get one from a coach or teacher in the athletic department, or you can purchase one at any local drug store. Cut open the outer plastic bag with scissors to show students the contents. Reseal the bag between class demonstrations since ammonium nitrate is hygroscopic. You also may wish to show students a bag of ammonium nitrate fertilizer and read them a description of the product along with the instructions and warning for its use as a fertilizer.

The classification of a dissolving reaction as a chemical or physical change is tricky, and you may wish to discuss some aspects of the process in class. The dissolving of sugar in water, for example, is a physical change. The sugar molecules are not disrupted, and the sugar is easily recoverable through evaporation. A salt such as sodium chloride or ammonium nitrate, however, becomes ionized. It can conduct electricity in solution, but not as a solid. Chemical bonds have been broken, and an energy change occurs. Yet the salt, like the sugar, is recoverable through evaporation.

In discussing the energy changes that accompany chemical reactions, you might mention that some reactions have a net change of zero even though energy may be absorbed at one point and given off at another.

Safety

Make sure students wear their goggles and lab aprons at all times during the investigation. Ammonium nitrate is flammable when dry and can explode if enclosed in a container that is heated above 250°C. Warn students

Chemical changes always involve changes in energy. Often, heat is released, which may be detected as an increase in temperature. Other times, heat energy is absorbed, which results in a decrease in temperature.

In this investigation, you will experiment with the materials that make up an instant cold pack. You will combine water and ammonium nitrate in an insulated cup. The cup will prevent any heat exchange with the environment while the dissolving process removes heat from the water. In order to have a useful cold pack, there must be more than enough solid ammonium nitrate present to reduce the temperature of the liquid in the bag to near zero and keep it cold for an additional 10 to 15 minutes. You will determine the amount of ammonium nitrate solid necessary to lower the temperature to that of melting ice or below and to maintain that temperature for at least 10 minutes.

Pre-Lab Discussion

Read the entire laboratory investigation and the relevant pages of your textbook. Then answer the questions that follow.

1. Define *heat*. Heat is a form of kinetic energy, caused by the internal motion of particles of matter.

2. Define *temperature*. Temperature is a measure of heat and, therefore, a measure of the kinetic energy of a substance.

3. In your experience, in what direction does heat exchange occur? Heat moves from a warmer object to a cooler object.

4. Why are plastic foam cups used in this investigation? The cups are insulated, so they prevent heat exchange between the environment and the materials in the cup.

5. Why should ammonium nitrate not be exposed to an open flame or to temperatures above 250°C? Ammonium nitrate will burn or explode at temperatures above 250°C.

6. Why should clothing splashed with ammonium nitrate solution be rinsed immediately with water? The clothing will become quite flammable if the ammonium nitrate solution is left to dry.

Problem

How can an effective cold pack be made from ammonium nitrate and water?

Materials

chemical splash goggles
laboratory apron
graduated cylinder, 100-mL
tap water
plastic foam cup
4 large pieces weighing paper

laboratory balance
spatula
ammonium nitrate (NH_4NO_3)
thermometer
stirring rod
clock

Name _____

Lab 4
APPLICATION

Safety

Wear your goggles and lab apron at all times during the investigation. Ammonium nitrate is poisonous and can burn or explode when dry or if it is exposed to temperatures above 250°C. Do not expose ammonium nitrate to fire or store in a hot environment. Clothing splashed with ammonium nitrate solution becomes flammable when dried. If ammonium nitrate accidentally comes in contact with your skin or clothing, rinse it off with large quantities of water and inform your teacher immediately. Dispose of the ammonium nitrate solution as instructed by your teacher.

Note the caution alert symbols here and with certain steps of the Procedure. Refer to page *xi* for the specific precautions associated with each symbol.

Procedure

1. Put on your goggles and lab apron. Fill the graduated cylinder with 50 mL of tap water that is at room temperature, and pour the water into the plastic foam cup.

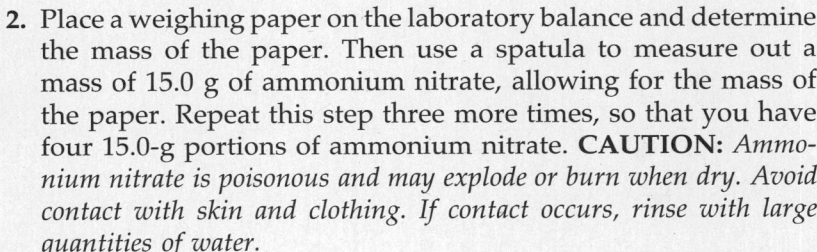
2. Place a weighing paper on the laboratory balance and determine the mass of the paper. Then use a spatula to measure out a mass of 15.0 g of ammonium nitrate, allowing for the mass of the paper. Repeat this step three more times, so that you have four 15.0-g portions of ammonium nitrate. **CAUTION:** *Ammonium nitrate is poisonous and may explode or burn when dry. Avoid contact with skin and clothing. If contact occurs, rinse with large quantities of water.*

3. Using the thermometer, measure the temperature of the water and record this value in the data table.

4. Add one of the 15.0-g portions of ammonium nitrate to the cup and stir it slowly with the stirring rod until it is dissolved. Measure and record the temperature of the water. Also record your observations, such as how much time it takes for the ammonium nitrate to dissolve and how quickly the temperature of the solution changes.

5. Repeat Step 4 with each of the remaining 15.0-g portions of ammonium nitrate until enough of the compound is present to maintain the temperature of the water at 0°C or below for at least 10 minutes.

6. Dispose of the ammonium nitrate solution according to your teacher's instructions. Clean up your work area and wash your hands before leaving the laboratory.

not to use burners for any reason during this lab. If ammonium nitrate contacts skin or clothing, it should be rinsed off with plenty of water. Do not use powdered ammonium nitrate. Granular ammonium nitrate (as it is sold in bags of fertilizer) is preferred. Since ammonium nitrate is hygroscopic, students should clean their work area with a wet cloth and wash their hands when they are finished. ■

Teaching Tips

Students are surprised at the large amount of solid ammonium nitrate present in a commercial cold pack and the small amount of liquid available to dissolve it. They also may be surprised at the solubility of the ammonium nitrate when they carry out the procedure. Students often stop adding portions of ammonium nitrate once they have attained temperatures near zero. Stress the importance of having excess ammonium nitrate present to maintain the cold temperature for 10 minutes. Finally, remind students that the dissolving processes for other substances do not necessarily absorb energy, but may release it instead.

Some students may wonder why there aren't equal drops in temperature with each 15.0 g of ammonium nitrate. You may wish to explain that the dissolving capacity of water changes as it cools and approaches saturation.

Waste Disposal

If the school's sewer system is connected to a sewage treatment plant, the ammonium nitrate can be flushed down the drain with plenty of water. If not, the concentrated solution can be stored in a sealed container for disposal in a hazardous waste landfill. ■

Simulating a Cold Pack

Lab 4

APPLICATION

Cooperative Learning Strategy

This investigation works especially well if you divide the class into groups of four. Designate one member to be the coordinator, one member to find the mass of the ammonium nitrate portions, one member to gather the equipment and dissolve the portions while observing the temperatures, and the final member to be the scribe (recorder). The scribe should record all data and observations in the data table. These data should be made available for all of the students to record before class is finished. The coordinator should be responsible for maintaining safety, assisting in the measuring process, and monitoring the assigned roles in the group.

Name _____

Observations (sample data)

Data Table

Mass of NH_4NO_3 in Solution (g)	Temp. (°C)	Change in Temp. (°C)	Observations
0.0	26.0	0.0	
15.0	10.0	−16.0	solid dissolves quickly
30.0	−1.0	−11.0	solid dissolves more slowly
45.0	−5.0	−4.0	solid dissolves in 5 minutes; temperature begins to rise
60.0	−6.0	−1.0	excess solid remains; temperature stabilizes

Calculations

1. Calculate the change in temperature that occurs after each 15.0-g portion of ammonium nitrate is added to the water, and write these values in the Data Table.

Critical Thinking: Analysis and Conclusions

1. At what point did the largest change in temperature occur? How can this observation be explained? *(Interpreting data)* The largest drop in temperature occurred when the first sample was added. There was no ammonium nitrate in solution, so the first sample dissolved very quickly, causing the temperature to drop quickly.

2. Identify any patterns that you observed as the portions of ammonium nitrate were added to the water. *(Making comparisons)* The more NH_4NO_3 already in solution, the longer it took for additional NH_4NO_3 to dissolve and the more slowly the temperature decreased.

3. What do you think would happen if you tried to dissolve another 15.0 g of ammonium nitrate in the water? Explain your reasoning. *(Drawing conclusions)* It would not dissolve. Excess solid already remained after 60.0 g were added, so the addition of more ammonium nitrate would make no difference

Critical Thinking: Applications

1. In this investigation, the insulated cup prevents the cold solution from being warmed by the outside environment. Would you expect a commercial cold pack to remain as cold for the same length of time if it was applied to an injured ankle? Explain. *(Applying concepts)* No. The uninsulated cold pack will become warmer as heat is absorbed from a warm injured body part and the environment.

Name _____

Lab 4
APPLICATION

2. Predict what happens to any undissolved ammonium nitrate in the cold pack as heat is absorbed. *(Making predictions)* As the cold pack absorbs heat, more ammonium nitrate dissolves, keeping the temperature from rising quickly. When the solid ammonium nitrate has completely dissolved, the temperature will rise more quickly.

3. One of the dangers of using a cold pack made of ice—especially one taken from a freezer—is frostbite. In light of the temperatures reached by the addition of the final portions of ammonium nitrate, would you expect the danger of frostbite to exist with a cold pack made from ammonium nitrate? Explain. *(Making judgments)* Yes, temporarily. The temperature in the cup falls to $-6.0°C$. Prolonged exposure to this temperature can cause frostbite, but because the cold pack begins to warm more quickly than an ice pack would, the danger of frostbite diminishes.

Going Further

1. Describe how you would design an instant cold pack from common household items, ammonium nitrate, and water. Include a list of the materials needed, directions for using the cold pack, and the appropriate safety warnings. Make a sketch of your design. (Note: You can calculate the ratio of the mass of ammonium nitrate per gram of water used in the investigation, and use the ratio to specify the amount of each compound needed in your design.)

2. Ammonium nitrate is commonly used as a fertilizer. You might think that it could be disposed of simply by adding it to soil or water. Consult an environmentalist or do library research to determine what problems might be created by dumping large amounts of ammonium nitrate into the environment.

Going Further
2. Ammonium nitrate would have a similar polluting effect to phosphates in detergents when they are released into the environment. If your school has access to a media center, students may search there for documentation of the problems posed by agricultural pollution.

Simulating a Cold Pack

Name _____ Date _____ Class _____

Physical and Chemical Changes

Lab 5

Text reference: **Chapter 2**

Introduction

As you read this, it is probably fall. Summer flowers are fading and dying. Leaves are changing from green to red, yellow, and orange. All these changes involve chemistry.

As you have learned, chemistry is the study of matter and the changes that it undergoes. These changes can be classified as either physical or chemical. When a physical change occurs, the physical properties of a substance—such as its size, shape, density, or state—are altered, but its chemical composition remains the same. Examples of physical changes include melting ice, crushing gravel, tearing paper, grinding pepper, and boiling water. No new substances are formed as a result of these changes.

Chemical changes, also known as chemical reactions, result in the formation of one or more new substances with different chemical properties and compositions from the original material. Examples of chemical changes include plants dying, leaves changing color, paper burning, bananas ripening, bread baking, or iron rusting. Some signs of chemical changes include a change in color, the formation of a precipitate (a new solid substance that settles out of solution), the production and release of gas, or a change in temperature.

It is important that you distinguish between pure substances and mixtures as you observe physical and chemical changes in matter. Remember that pure substances—such as elements or compounds—are made up of one type of matter. Mixtures are two or more pure substances that are combined physically. Mixtures can be separated into their components by physical means, such as evaporation, filtration, or distillation.

In this investigation, you will conduct tests on several substances and then use your data to determine whether the resulting changes are chemical or physical. As you observe each change, remember to ask yourself, "Has the change altered the identity of the substances?"

Pre-Lab Discussion

Read the entire laboratory investigation and the relevant pages of your textbook. Then answer the questions that follow.

1. Identify the following as either a chemical or a physical change:

    a. burning wood _____chemical_____

    b. dry ice (solid) changing into a gas _____physical_____

    c. freezing water _____physical_____

    d. ripening fruit _____chemical_____

    e. sugar dissolving in water _____physical_____

Materials (class of 30 in pairs)
30 pairs chemical splash goggles
30 laboratory aprons
30 pairs latex gloves
15 birthday candles
75 test tubes
15 pairs test-tube tongs
15 laboratory burners
15 test-tube racks
4 boxes of matches
15 glass squares
15 pieces of paper, 2 cm × 2 cm
15 watch glasses
15 insulating pads
tap water
15 graduated cylinders, 10-mL
15 microspatulas
30 g sodium chloride (NaCl)
15 glass stirring rods
30 micropipets
50 mL silver nitrate ($AgNO_3$), 0.1 M
75 cm Mg ribbon
15 pairs scissors
30 mL hydrochloric acid (HCl), 6.0 M
30 g copper sulfate pentahydrate crystals ($CuSO_4 \cdot 5H_2O$)
15 mortars and pestles
15 laboratory balances
5 g iron filings (Fe)
5 g powdered sulfur (S)
15 magnets

Time Required
50–60 minutes. To shorten the required time, do Steps 7 and 8 as a demonstration.

Advance Preparation
Mix equal parts 12.0 M HCl and distilled water to make 6.0 M HCl. Be sure to add acid to water.
Add 0.85 g $AgNO_3$ to enough water to make 50 mL of 0.1 M $AgNO_3$ solution.

© Prentice-Hall, Inc.

Physical and Chemical Changes **29**

Lab 5

Provide containers for disposal of silver solutions and HCl.

Introduction
Make sure that students can differentiate between physical and chemical properties and changes by having students give examples. Discuss the difference between a mixture, an element, and a compound. You may want to have students read through the list of materials to see if they can distinguish between the elements and compounds on the list.

Demonstrate the techniques for heating a test tube, using a micropipet, and grinding substances with a mortar and pestle. Make sure students are able to use the laboratory balance correctly.

Safety
Make sure students discuss fire safety and the correct method of heating test tubes. Remind students that when they heat the contents of a test tube, the opening of the test tube should never be directed toward anyone. The test tubes must be allowed to cool sufficiently before being touched. Remind students to wear gloves and exercise caution when handling acids and silver nitrate solutions. Explain the procedure for cleaning up a spilled acid.

If you do not have hood space for everyone, do Steps 7 and 8 as a demonstration. ■

Teaching Tips
Briefly discuss terms, such as *precipitate* and *hydrate*, that students may not be aware of yet. When explaining the meaning of *hydrate*, write the formula for copper sulfate pentahydrate on the chalkboard and explain that the dot means that five water molecules are chemically combined with each formula unit of copper

Name _____

2. What are some observable signs that indicate a chemical change is taking place? <u>Change in color, formation of a precipitate, gas formation, or a change in temperature.</u>

3. Why are you instructed to feel the outside of the test tube after two chemicals are mixed, as in Steps 5 and 6 of this investigation? <u>To observe a temperature change, which indicates a chemical change.</u>

4. What are the safety cautions that you need to observe during this investigation? <u>Wear goggles and a laboratory apron. Wear gloves when handling hydrochloric acid and silver nitrate solutions. Observe safety cautions that apply to fire, corrosive substances, vapors, disposal, heating, and hygiene.</u>

Problem
How can you recognize and differentiate between physical and chemical changes in matter?

Materials
chemical splash goggles
laboratory apron
latex gloves
birthday candle
5 test tubes
test-tube tongs
laboratory burner
test-tube rack, wood or metal
matches
glass square
piece of paper, 2 cm × 2 cm
watch glass
insulating pad
tap water
graduated cylinder, 10-mL
microspatula

sodium chloride (NaCl)
glass stirring rod
micropipet with silver nitrate ($AgNO_3$), 0.1 M
magnesium (Mg) ribbon
scissors
micropipet with hydrochloric acid (HCl), 6.0 M
copper sulfate pentahydrate ($CuSO_4 \cdot 5H_2O$)
mortar and pestle
laboratory balance
iron filings (Fe)
powdered sulfur (S)
magnet

Safety

Wear your goggles and lab apron at all times during the investigation. Tie back loose hair and clothing to avoid any fire hazard. Always point the open end of a test tube away from yourself and others when heating a substance. Since glass retains heat without looking hot, heated glassware should be given ample time to cool before it is handled.

Name_____

Lab 5

Use extreme caution when dealing with 6.0 M hydrochloric acid. It can cause severe burns if allowed to come into contact with the skin. Any spills should be reported to your instructor and cleaned up with cold water and sodium bicarbonate ($NaHCO_3$). Silver nitrate solution will stain skin and clothing. Wear gloves and avoid spills and splashes. Heat iron and sulfur in a fume hood. Note the caution alert symbols here and with certain steps of the Procedure. Refer to page xi for the specific precautions associated with each symbol.

sulfate. You also may wish to explain that M is the symbol for molarity, and discuss briefly the concept of concentration of a solution.

Copper sulfate pentahydrate turns a lighter color when it is ground. This is because the smaller crystals increase the scattering of light. When sodium chloride dissolves in water, there is a chemical change (the ionization of sodium and chlorine). However, students may be aware that if they were to evaporate the water off, they would get back sodium chloride. This would indicate that there was no chemical change. Use these ideas as a basis for discussion, especially with Question 1 in Analysis and Conclusions.

Procedure

1. Put on your goggles and lab apron. Break off a small amount of wax from the bottom of a birthday candle, and place it into a test tube. Holding the test tube with tongs, heat it gently over a burner flame until the wax melts completely. Place the test tube in the test-tube rack and let it cool for ten minutes. Record your observations in the Data Table. **CAUTION:** *Keep loose hair tied back or covered. Hold the tube away from you and others while heating it. Use tongs to hold the hot test tube.*

2. With the matches, light the candle. Secure the candle to the glass square by dripping wax onto the square and then holding the base of the candle in the molten wax until the wax hardens. Allow the candle to burn until it goes out. Record your observations in the Data Table.

3. Tear a small piece of paper into tiny pieces, and place the pieces in a watch glass. Place the watch glass on an insulating pad and ignite the paper with the matches. **CAUTION:** *Keep all other flammable material away from the burning paper.* Allow the paper to burn completely. Record your observations in the Data Table.

4. Measure 5 mL of water in the graduated cylinder. Pour the water into a test tube and add a microspatula of sodium chloride (NaCl). Stir the contents to mix. Put on latex gloves. Using the micropipet, add 10 drops of silver nitrate (0.1 M $AgNO_3$) to the NaCl-water mixture. **CAUTION:** *Silver nitrate is toxic and can stain your skin and clothing, so avoid direct contact with it.* Record your observations in the Data Table. Dispose of the solutions containing silver according to your teacher's instructions.

5. Obtain a 5-cm piece of magnesium (Mg) ribbon and use scissors to cut it into 1-cm pieces. Place two of the pieces into a test tube and, using the micropipet, add a few drops of hydrochloric acid (6.0 M HCl). **CAUTION:** *The 6.0 M hydrochloric acid is highly corrosive. Do not let any get on your skin or clothing. Wear latex gloves.* Touch the outside of the test tube with your fingertip. Record your observations in the Data Table. Dispose of the solution according to your teacher's instructions.

6. Grind several crystals of copper sulfate pentahydrate ($CuSO_4 \cdot 5H_2O$) with the mortar and pestle. Place a microspatula of the powder into a test tube. Heat gently over a burner flame for 2 minutes. Allow to cool for 5 minutes; then add a few drops of

Physical and Chemical Changes

water. Touch the bottom of the test tube with your fingertip. Record your observations in the Data Table.

7. Fold two pieces of weighing paper by folding them in half, and then again in quarters. Using a balance, measure out 0.20 g of iron (Fe) filings and 0.20 g of powdered sulfur (S) on the papers. Test each sample with a magnet by running the magnet along the underside of the paper. As you do this, keep the samples near the well formed by the folds of the paper so that they do not spill. Mix the two samples thoroughly in a test tube. Run the magnet along the bottom and sides of the test tube. Record your observations in the Data Table.

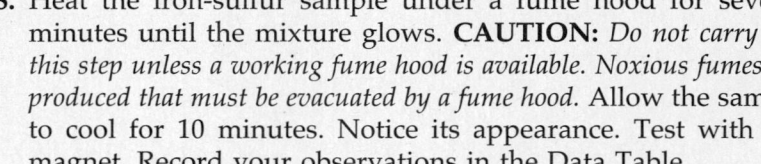

8. Heat the iron-sulfur sample under a fume hood for several minutes until the mixture glows. **CAUTION:** *Do not carry out this step unless a working fume hood is available. Noxious fumes are produced that must be evacuated by a fume hood.* Allow the sample to cool for 10 minutes. Notice its appearance. Test with the magnet. Record your observations in the Data Table.

9. Clean up your work area and wash your hands before leaving the laboratory.

Waste Disposal

The micropipets with $AgNO_3$ and HCl can be saved and reused. Neutralize the excess 6.0 *M* HCl and flush it down the drain with large amounts of water. Precipitate the silver from the excess $AgNO_3$ by mixing it with 1 *M* NaOH. Filter the product mixture. Store the precipitate separately for commercial disposal or shipment to a secure landfill. The filtrate may be disposed of by flushing down the drain with large amounts of water.

All other materials may be disposed of as solid waste.

Observations (sample data)
DATA TABLE

Step	Observations
1	Wax liquified when heated and solidified when cooled.
2	When burned, the candle changed into gaseous substances, leaving a charred wick and a bit of wax.
3	When torn, the paper changed only in size. When burned, the paper turned into black ash.
4	NaCl dissolved in the water. When $AgNO_3$ was added, a cloudy white precipitate formed and settled to the bottom.
5	Small pieces of Mg were the same as larger pieces except for size. With HCl, bubbles were produced and heat was given off. Mg was used up. Clear liquid remained.
6	The ground crystals seemed lighter colored. When heated, a liquid was given off and the crystals turned white. When water was added, the powder turned blue again. The test tube was warm to the touch.
7	Iron was attracted to the magnet; sulfur was not. When mixed, the iron remained magnetic and could be separated from the sulfur with the magnet.
8	When heated, a yellow gas was given off. After cooling, a hard, shiny, black substance was observed. The new substance was no longer attracted by a magnet.

Name _____

Lab 5

Critical Thinking: Analysis and Conclusions

1. Indicate whether the following changes are physical or chemical. Support your conclusions. *(Classifying)*

   a. melting candle wax Physical; only the state changed from solid to liquid and back to solid.

   b. burning candle wax Chemical; the substances at the end are different. Evolution of heat is a sign of chemical change.

   c. tearing paper Physical; only the size has changed.

   d. burning paper Chemical; a new substance is formed.

   e. dissolving NaCl Student answers may vary because the data are inconclusive.

   f. mixing NaCl and $AgNO_3$ Chemical; a new substance is formed. Formation of precipitate is sign of chemical change.

   g. cutting Mg ribbon Physical; only the size has changed.

   h. adding HCl to Mg Chemical; evolution of heat and gas and the disappearance of Mg are signs of chemical change.

   i. grinding $CuSO_4 \cdot 5\ H_2O$ Physical; crushing is a physical change.

   j. heating $CuSO_4 \cdot 5\ H_2O$ Chemical; formation of liquid drops and white powder indicates a new substance has been formed.

   k. mixing Fe and S Physical; no new substance is formed. Iron is still magnetic.

   l. heating Fe and S Chemical; a new substance is formed that is not magnetic.

2. Name two possible indications that a chemical change has occurred, using examples from this investigation. *(Giving an example)* Indications of a chemical change could be the color changes in Steps 2 and 3; the formation of a precipitate in Step 4; the formation of a gas or the change in temperature in Step 5.

3. A change in color does not always indicate chemical change. Explain why it could be the result of a physical change. *(Interpreting data)* The physical change of grinding the copper sulfate pentahydrate produced a lighter color powder than the original crystals.

4. Answer the following questions using examples from this investigation to support your answers. *(Drawing conclusions)*

   a. How can substances in a mixture be separated?
   Mixtures can be separated by physical means. The iron-sulfur mixture was separated by means of the magnet.

   b. How can substances in a compound be separated?
   Compounds can be separated by chemical means. The water in the copper sulfate pentahydrate was separated by heating.

Critical Thinking: Applications

1. Sodium chloride dissolves in water, leaving a clear homogenous mixture with no physical evidence of the crystals with which you started. Design an experiment that you could perform to separate the sodium chloride from the water. *(Designing experiments)* Procedures will vary, but should include evaporating the water to recover the sodium chloride.

2. How would the experiment you designed in response to Question 1 differ if some sand was mixed in with the sodium chloride before it was added to the water? *(Developing hypotheses)* Same as above, but the solution must be filtered before the water is evaporated and the sodium chloride recovered.

Going Further

1. Based on what you have learned in this investigation, write a story in which you include as many physical and chemical changes as possible. When you finish the story underline the physical changes and circle the chemical changes.
2. Cooking involves both physical and chemical changes. Give examples that support this statement.

Name _____ Date _____ Class _____

Candy Coatings: Compounds or Mixtures?

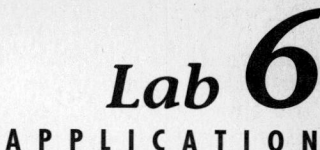

Lab 6
APPLICATION

Text reference: **Chapter 2**

Introduction

Perhaps you are familiar with the small, round, candy-coated chocolates whose manufacturer once claimed: "Melts in your mouth, not in your hand." The manufacturer could make such a claim because each candy is covered with a hard coating. Although the candy doesn't necessarily melt right away, the dyes in the coatings eventually do dissolve, making one's hands turn different colors.

In this investigation, you will use two separation techniques to determine whether the dyes in candy coatings are compounds or mixtures. In the first part of the investigation, you will use wool yarn in a series of chemical reactions to separate the dyes from the sugar, chocolate, and other nondye substances in the candies.

In the second part of the investigation, you will explore the makeup of the dye by using a separation technique called paper chromatography. In this technique, a liquid medium, or solvent, is used to dissolve the dyes and carry them along a piece of paper. Different chemicals will have different rates of travel. The results will show whether the dye is a compound or a mixture of compounds.

Pre-Lab Discussion

Read the entire laboratory investigation and the relevant pages of your textbook. Then answer the questions that follow.

1. What is the chemical definition of a compound? A mixture? <u>A compound is a pure substance that contains two or more elements chemically combined in a fixed proportion. A mixture is a blend of two or more pure substances in any proportion.</u>

2. Why should you wear chemical splash goggles and a safety apron throughout this investigation? <u>These safety precautions prevent damage to eyes or clothes when hazardous chemicals are in use.</u>

3. Why would it be inappropriate to eat the candy? <u>It could be contaminated with chemicals. Also the student's hands could be contaminated. Food should never be eaten in the laboratory.</u>

4. What does it mean "to decant" the liquid with the dissolved dye in it? <u>"To decant" means to carefully pour off the liquid portion of a mixture leaving any solid parts behind.</u>

Materials (class of 30 in pairs)
Part A
30 pairs chemical splash goggles
30 laboratory aprons
15 large test tubes, 18 × 150 mm
60 small candies (such as M&M's or Skittles)
15 test-tube racks
15 graduated cylinders, 10-mL
120 mL distilled water
10 mL acetic acid, ($HC_2H_3O_2$), 3 M, in dropper bottles or micropipets
30 small test tubes, 13 × 100 mm
1 skein of white wool yarn
15 hot plates
15 beakers, 150-mL
tap water
15 pairs tongs
15 stirring rods
15 paper towels
100 mL ammonia water (NH_3), 1%
15 watch glasses

Part B
15 micropipets
15 pieces of filter paper, 11-cm diameter
15 pairs scissors
15 well plates
box of toothpicks
15 graduated cylinders, 10-mL
100 mL developing solution
15 petri dishes
15 rulers

Time Required
90 minutes. Part A and Part B can be done on two separate days.

Advance Preparation
To make 100 mL of developing solvent, mix 57 mL butanol, 29 mL 2 M ammonia, and 14 mL

© Prentice-Hall, Inc.   *Candy Coatings: Compounds or Mixtures?* **35**

Lab 6 APPLICATION

methanol. Store in containers with screw caps. Do not work near any heat sources. To make 1% ammonia, either dilute 3.6 mL concentrated (28%) ammonia solution with water to a total volume of 100 mL or dilute 10 mL household (10%) ammonia with water to a total volume of 100 mL. Prepare 300 mL of 3 M acetic acid by adding 51.6 mL of glacial (17 M) acetic acid to enough water to make 300 mL of solution.

Try to obtain natural wool yarn that has no dyes added. If this is not possible, boil the yarn for 5 minutes in 1% acetic acid to remove any fluorescent dyes that may be present. Dry the yarn before the students use it. Make sure that every color of candy is tested by someone.

Introduction
To introduce this lab, you may wish to demonstrate how household food colorings separate during chromatography. Water can be used as a solvent. You also may wish to discuss with students the concepts of solutions, solutes, and solvents.

Safety
Make sure students wear their goggles and lab aprons at all times during the investigation. Concentrated acetic acid (glacial) is irritating to skin and other tissues and has a flash point of 39°C. Keep the solvents capped at all times when not in use, and store them away from heat.

Emphasize to students that all hot plates must be turned off before they begin Part B. Remind students not to eat the candies. ■

Teaching Tips
Have available separate containers to collect the waste acetic acid solution and developing solution.

Name _____

5. What is the purpose of the paper wick? <u>The wick allows the developing solution to travel at a steady rate through the filter paper.</u>

Problem
Are the dyes found in candy coatings one compound or many?

Materials

Part A
chemical splash goggles
laboratory apron
hot plate
20 cm wool yarn
beaker, 150-mL
tap water
4 small candies, same color
large test tube, 18 × 150 mm
test tube rack

graduated cylinder, 10-mL
distilled water
acetic acid, 3 M
2 small test tubes, 13 × 100 mm
tongs
stirring rod
paper towel
ammonia water (NH_3), 1%
watch glass

Part B
micropipet
filter paper, 11-cm diameter
scissors
well plate
toothpick

graduated cylinder, 10-mL
developing solution
petri dish
ruler

Safety

Wear your goggles and lab apron at all times during the investigation. Never eat any foodstuffs in the laboratory. Acetic acid and ammonia can irritate or burn your skin. Do not rub your eyes or touch your skin without first washing your hands. If these solutions contact your skin or clothing, wash the area with large amounts of water and notify your teacher.

The solutions used in Part B are extremely flammable. Be sure there are no burner flames in the laboratory. Turn off the hot plate during Part B. Note the caution alert symbols here and with certain steps of the Procedure. Refer to page *xi* for the specific precautions associated with each symbol.

Procedure

Part A

1. Put on your goggles and lab apron. Fill a 150-mL beaker one-third full of water, and place it on the hot plate. Turn on the hot plate and start the water to boil. Meanwhile, place four small candies of the same color in a large test tube and set the test tube in the test-tube rack. **CAUTION:** *Foodstuffs should never*

Name_____

be eaten in the lab. *Do not eat any of the candies.* Measure 7 mL of distilled water using a 10-mL graduated cylinder and pour it into the test tube with the candies.

 2. Add 3 drops of concentrated acetic acid to the water-candy mixture. **CAUTION:** *Concentrated acetic acid can irritate or burn your skin. If you spill any, rinse the affected area immediately with large amounts of cold water and report the spill to your teacher.*

3. As soon as the colored coating is dissolved, slowly pour, or decant, the liquid dye into a small test tube, making sure the candy or any other solid residue is left behind. Discard the candy and other solid residue.

 4. Using a stirring rod, add a 20-cm piece of woolen yarn and 3 drops of concentrated acetic acid to the liquid-dye mixture.

 5. Place the test tube that contains the yarn in the boiling water bath for about 5 minutes or until most of the dye has been absorbed by the yarn.

 6. With test-tube tongs, take the test tube out of the boiling water and place it in the test-tube rack. **CAUTION:** *Never touch hot glassware with your bare hands.* Remove the yarn from the test tube with the stirring rod. Rinse the yarn under tap water for about 1 minute. This removes the remaining acid so that the ammonia base can work completely.

 7. Measure out 5 mL of ammonia water using the graduated cylinder and pour it into a clean small test tube. **CAUTION:** *Avoid breathing the ammonia vapors.* Submerge the rinsed yarn into the ammonia water.

 8. Place the test tube with the yarn and the ammonia water in the boiling water bath for about 5 minutes or until most of the dye from the yarn has dissolved in the ammonia-water solution. The solution should turn the color of the dye. Remove the yarn with a stirring rod and rinse with water. Put the yarn in a paper towel and dispose of it in the waste basket.

 9. Use tongs to remove the test tube containing the ammonia-water-dye solution from the beaker of boiling water. Pour the dye solution into a watch glass. Set the test tube aside to cool in the test-tube rack. Place the watch glass on top of the beaker of boiling water until half of the liquid in the watch glass has evaporated, making the solution more concentrated. Turn off the hot plate, and let the liquid cool before proceeding to Part B.

 10. Dispose of the excess acid solution in a container provided by your teacher. Flush the ammonia solution down the drain. If you are not going directly on to Part B, clean up your work area and wash your hands before leaving the laboratory.

Part B

 11. Put on your goggles and lab apron. Transfer the concentrated dye to a micropipet.

Lab 6
APPLICATION

Because the dyes do not move very quickly through the paper, the students could try to do more than one chromatogram at a time. They should allow at least 30 minutes for each chromatogram to develop.

Put the data table for Question 2 of Analysis and Conclusions on the board and have students fill it in with their data.

Waste Disposal

Dispose of acetic acid by adding it to a twenty-fold excess of water while stirring. To neutralize, add sodium carbonate or sodium hydroxide until pH paper indicates neutralization. The neutralized solution can then be washed down the drain. Ammonia solution can be flushed down the drain with plenty of water. Deposit the remaining developing solution in an organic waste container and hold for commercial disposal. ∎

 12. Obtain a piece of filter paper and fold it in half. Unfold the paper and cut a 2-cm-wide wick in the paper by making two cuts from the edge to the crease in the middle. Your filter paper with wick should look like Figure 6–1. **CAUTION:** *Make sure all hot plates have been turned off and there are no flames in the laboratory before going on with this investigation. The solvent is highly flammable.*

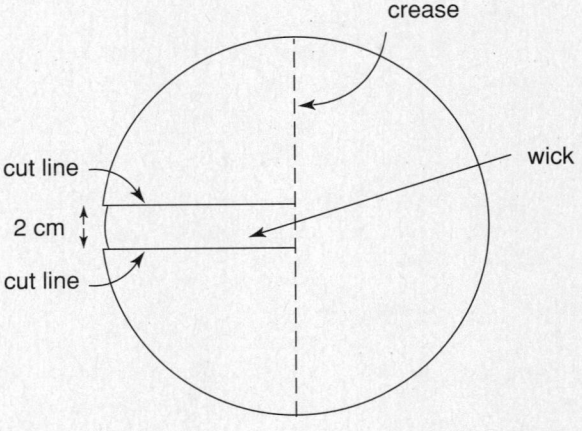

Figure 6–1

13. Transfer a few drops of the concentrated dye solution from the micropipet to a well in the well plate. Take a toothpick and crush one end by placing it on the lab bench and pushing down until the end flares slightly. Dip the crushed end of the toothpick into the dye solution and make a very small spot of dye on the creased filter paper where the wick meets the rest of the paper. Allow the spot to dry. Repeat at least ten times on the same spot to concentrate the dye on the filter paper. Make the spot as small as possible. Record the initial color of the spot.

14. Using a graduated cylinder, pour 8 mL of developing solution into the bottom half of a petri dish.

15. Cut the wick in half crosswise and bend it down to make a stand. Place it into the developing solution, as shown in Figure 6–2. Carefully place the other half of the petri dish over the filter paper, not allowing the wick to be crushed or flattened. Allow to develop undisturbed for about 35 minutes.

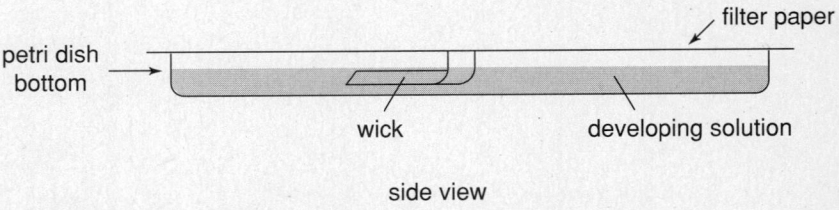

Figure 6–2

Name _____

Lab
6
APPLICATION

16. Observe how far your dye traveled from the original spot and mark the outer limit of the solvent.

17. Dispose of all your solvents as directed by your teacher. Clean up your work area and wash your hands before leaving the laboratory.

Observations (sample data)

1. Initial color of spot   Answers will vary

2. Final color of spot   See Data Table

3. Color(s) present after developing   See Data Table

4. Distance traveled by solvent   Answers will vary

5. Distance traveled by dye   Answers will vary

6. Sketch what you saw on the filter paper after the chromatography was done.

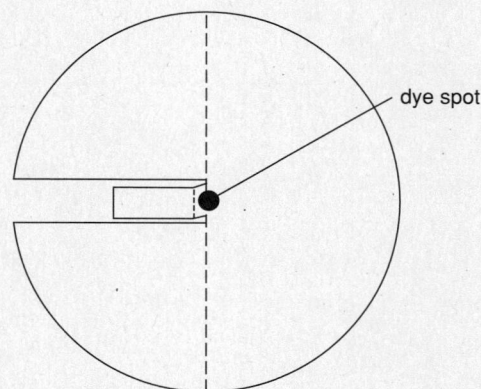

Figure 6–3

Critical Thinking: Analysis and Conclusions

1. Was the dye you tested a single compound or a mixture? Explain your answer. *(Interpreting data)* Answers will vary. See Data Table 1.

2. Complete the table on the next page by pooling your data with those of other students in the class. Are the colors of the candy all one color (dye) or are they made from a several different colors (dyes)? Are these results consistent with what you know about colors? Explain your reasoning. *(Drawing conclusions)*

© Prentice-Hall, Inc.   *Candy Coatings: Compounds or Mixtures?*   39

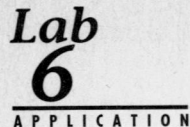

Name_____

DATA TABLE 1

Color	Component Colors	Compound or Mixture
green	blue and yellow	mixture
red	red and yellow	mixture
yellow	yellow	compound
purple	red and blue	mixture
brown	yellow, red and blue	mixture
orange	red and yellow	mixture

The green, purple, brown, and orange colors separated into component bands as expected. The red separated into red and yellow bands, which was not expected. Yellow stayed in one band as expected.

3. Why was it important to keep the spot applied to your filter paper as small as possible? *(Designing experiments)* The more concentrated spot will result in less trailing of the dyes, better separation, and a more distinct and narrower color band.

4. What would have happened if the entire filter paper, and not just the wick, had sat in the developing solution? *(Making predictions)* If the entire filter paper was wet, the dyes would just dissolve and would not separate as well.

Critical Thinking: Applications

1. What do you think would have happened if you had used an ink pen to mark the initial spot on the paper? Why? *(Applying concepts)* The ink would have traveled up the paper with the solvent and would have interfered with the results.

2. Do you think the coating of the candies you tested is made with the same type of food coloring sold in grocery stores? How could you test your hypothesis? *(Developing hypotheses)* These dyes are not the same as the food coloring available in grocery stores. Household food colorings are water soluble. If the dyes used in candy coatings were water soluble, they would be very messy to handle because they would dissolve too easily in your hand.

Going Further

1. Test the dyes in some other brands of candies and compare their intensity of color.
2. Design an experiment to see if the same chemicals are used in commercial and household food colorings.

Rutherford's Experiment

Lab 7

Text reference: **Chapter 3**

Introduction

Have you ever seen a large package and immediately thought you knew what was inside? Just as you cannot see inside a sealed package, no one can see inside an atom. How then can we describe the structure of an atom? We use indirect evidence. Indirect evidence has enabled scientists to visualize many unseeable phenomena: ancient climates, the center of the earth, as well as the structure of atoms.

In the early 1900s, the New Zealand scientist Ernest Rutherford (1871–1937) discovered that radioactive alpha particles were helium atoms with the electrons removed. Rutherford and his colleagues were curious to see what would happen if they aimed a beam of positively charged alpha particles at thin sheets of gold—one of the densest elements known. When they did the experiment, they found that most of the alpha particles passed straight through the gold foil—as if nothing were there. A very tiny fraction of the particles was reflected back from the foil, however, and Rutherford realized that something quite small, but quite massive, was scattering the alpha particles. This experiment was the first evidence for the existence of a nucleus within the atom.

In the lab investigation in Chapter 3 of your textbook, you had an opportunity to probe the contents of various sealed boxes and then open them. In this investigation, you will probe a box that cannot be opened. You will gather indirect information about the contents of a sealed box and then draw a model based on this information. You will eventually be able to compare your results with others in your class, but you will not know the real answer for certain, just as scientists do not know the real answer for certain when they publish their data.

Pre-Lab Discussion

Read the entire laboratory investigation and the relevant pages of your textbook. Then answer the questions that follow.

1. In what ways is the sealed box similar to Rutherford's gold atoms?
   It is not possible to see inside the box, and Rutherford could not see inside atoms.

2. What did Rutherford use to probe gold atoms, and what will you use to probe the inside of a sealed box? Rutherford used alpha particles. This investigation uses a steel ball.

Materials (class of 30 in pairs)
15 pairs safety goggles
15 $8\frac{1}{2}'' \times 11'' \times 2''$ shipping boxes
soft sponge or plastic foam for cutting into shapes
glue stick
tape
15 steel balls, $\frac{1}{4}''-\frac{1}{2}''$ diameter
15 ceramic "donut" type magnets
15 metric rulers

Time Required
30–40 minutes for the investigation and 30–40 minutes for the symposium.

Advance Preparation
The boxes should be as similar in size and shape as possible. Use a pattern to cut 15 identical shapes from soft plastic foam and use a glue stick to anchor the foam shapes securely in the same central position and orientation in each box. The foam shapes should be simple, such as squares or rectangles with one or two corners cut off, but not so simple that the shape can be guessed without experimentation. In an $8\frac{1}{2}'' \times 11''$ box, the foam shape should be approximately $4'' \times 6''$. Place a steel ball in each box and make sure that it rolls freely on all sides of the foam shape. Seal the boxes securely with tape.

Following the investigation, have students present their findings in a symposium. Provide plenty of chalkboard space and chalk, or large sheets of paper, such as a flip-chart pad, with markers and tape or tacks for hanging up the diagrams for

Rutherford's Experiment **41**

Lab 7

comparison and review. As an additional option, you can prepare a photocopy of an opened box, using the lightest setting. The copy may be uniformly dark gray with a slight contrast difference revealing the foam shape, looking much like an X-ray.

Introduction
Students are used to having correct answers for problems they encounter. This experiment mimics real science in having no such answer. Some students may recognize that research involves not just finding answers, but thinking of questions that one might be able to answer. In Rutherford's case, the research began with the question, "Can we find a structure within atoms?"

Safety
Make sure students wear their goggles at all times during the investigation. ■

Teaching Tips
Do not tell students whether their guesses about the contents of the box are correct, or hint at the answer at any time, despite student pleas. Simply tell students that in scientific investigations, the correct answer can only be determined from the data. Suggest to them that they work carefully and thoroughly and then they will be able to construct a good theory about the box's contents. Act as a colleague in making limited suggestions about different probing methods. Constantly remind students to record their techniques and observations. Note any collusion between student groups.

After the investigation, convene a "symposium" in which students simultaneously draw and

Name _____

3. Why would it be too difficult for you to duplicate Rutherford's alpha-scattering experiment in your chemistry laboratory? <u>Alpha particles are radioactive, and gold is expensive.</u>

4. List some of the procedures you expect will help in your investigation of the sealed box. <u>Listen for sounds that might indicate whether contents are metallic or nonmetallic; use magnet on areas where the steel ball is not present; roll ball in a systematic pattern.</u>

Problem
How can you use indirect evidence to study the nature of something you cannot see?

Materials
safety goggles   ceramic magnet
sealed box   metric ruler

Safety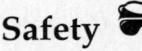
Wear your goggles at all times during the investigation.

Procedure

 1. Put on your goggles. Obtain a sealed box whose contents are to be investigated, a ceramic magnet, and a metric ruler. You should be able to hear a steel ball rolling inside the box.

2. You can investigate the contents of the box by shaking or tipping it, but you cannot open the box or make holes in it. Use the steel ball as a probe to determine the box's contents. Use the magnet on the outside of the box to guide the steel ball.

3. Probe the contents of the box. Determine as many characteristics—such the texture, size, and shape—of the contents as you can. Record each procedure you use (for example, rolling the ball in a particular direction) and what it reveals (for example, the position and size of any obstacle that is encountered). Vary your procedures to obtain as complete and exact an image of the contents of the box as possible. Use the clues you gather about the contents to draw the features and shapes of the structures inside the box.

4. Do not open the box at any time, pry up the lid, or make openings of any kind. Draw the best image you can of the box's contents using only information you gather by investigating the sealed box. Be prepared to present your methods and findings before the class. Remember that you are simulating a scientific investigation in which only student investigations can provide an answer to the problem. Your answer may or may not agree with the results of others.

 5. Clean up your work area and wash your hands before leaving the laboratory.

Lab 7

Observations (sample data)
DATA TABLE

Procedure	Results
1. Roll the ball in different directions	Determined size and position of contents
2. Listen for sounds	Object is soft and nonmetallic
3. Shake the box	Object stays in place
4. Roll the ball in a systematic pattern	Found the shape of the object
5.	

Critical Thinking: Analysis and Conclusions

1. Based on your observations, draw a picture of the contents of your box in the space below. *(Drawing conclusions)*

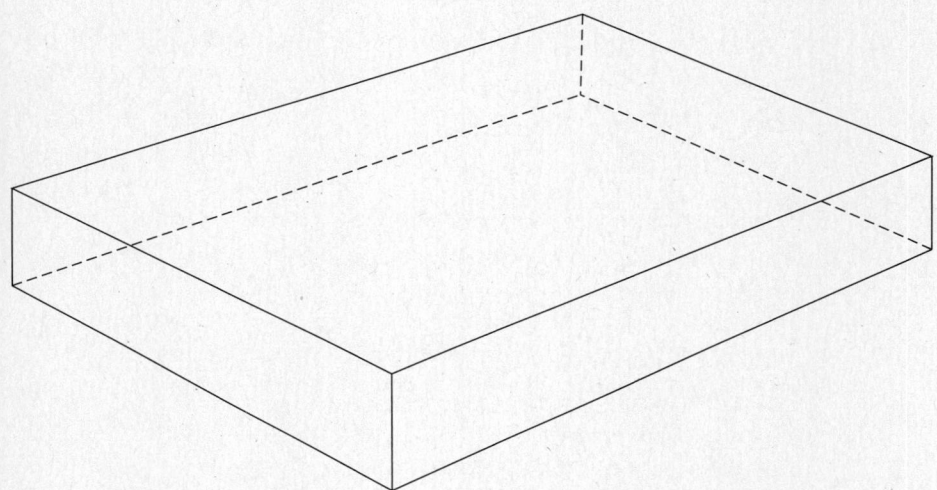

Figure 7–1

2. Compare your drawing of the contents of the box with the drawings of others in the class. How do scientists know when their experimental results are correct? *(Making comparisons)* To be considered correct, experimental results must be independently confirmed by the results of other scientists.

3. If two or three groups present images of the box contents that are very similar, what does this suggest to you about the validity of these results compared with the singular results of others? *(Making judgments)* These similar results tend to confirm their validity, provided the groups did not confer before reaching their conclusions.

---

orally describe their results on chalkboards or large sheets of paper to be displayed near each other. There are likely to be great differences, but students will notice that features like texture, approximate size, and some shape characteristics will be similar among some groups. Have students point out these "confirmed" features, and point out other areas that need more investigation. Bring up the possibility of collusion if two groups have nearly identical results, and discuss how such action can prejudice results. Coordinate the fabrication of a "best guess" for the box contents.

In order to retain the discovery-like nature of this lab, do not open a box to reveal its contents. As an option, you can use the photocopy that looks like an X-ray.

Project SERAPHIM produces a good computer simulation, "Rutherford's Experiment," available at minimal cost, which can be substituted for the boxes.

Rutherford's Experiment

Lab 7

Critical Thinking: Applications

1. In Rutherford's experiment, most of the positively charged alpha particles passed directly through the gold foil. However, a very small percentage of the alpha particles rebounded or changed course. What do these results suggest to you about the structure of gold atoms as compared to the contents of your box? *(Making comparisons)* The object in the box occupies a much larger portion of space in the box than a nucleus does in an atom.

2. In what ways could you test your model of the contents of the box? *(Developing models)* Put an object similar to the one you think is in the box into an identical box and see if it behaves in the same way. Determine the mass of this box and see if it matches that of the sealed box.

3. What other tests would you like to do if you had more equipment? *(Designing experiments)* X-rays or CAT scans—other answers may appear as well.

4. If you used some of the special instruments you mentioned in Question 3, and the results did not agree with your previous determination, what would you need to do? *(Developing hypotheses)* Redo the original experiment, making careful observations. From these observations, make new, but logical, predictions.

5. Rutherford did not rush to publish the results of the alpha-scattering experiments despite their far-reaching implications. By contrast, today the results of some scientific research are published before they are properly reviewed by other scientists. What problems, if any, do you think could occur from trying to short-cut the scientific method of validating experimental results? *(Making judgments)* Answers will vary but the expectation of quick answers, right or wrong, disrupts good research and can make all scientific research seem untrustworthy.

Going Further

1. Investigate one of the people connected with uncovering the structure of the atom. How did the person's personality or philosophy affect the scientific results? What role did history play?
2. No one has ever seen a black hole in space. Why then should people believe that black holes exist? Find out what a black hole is and what evidence there is for the existence of black holes. Share your findings with your class in a brief oral report.

Going Further
1. Some references are:
   Ferris, Tim, *Coming of Age in the Milky Way*. Anchor Books, New York, 1988.
   Gribbin, John, *In Search of Schrödinger's Cat: Quantum Physics and Reality*. Bantam Books, 1984.

Name _____ Date _____ Class _____

Finding the Charge of an Electron

Lab 8

Text reference: **Chapter 3**

Introduction

An electron is too small to see or to have its mass measured in a school laboratory, but a flow of electrons (an electric current) can produce large-scale changes in matter. An electric current in the form of a lightning bolt, for example, can incinerate a tree. On a smaller scale, you probably know from experience that the electric current in a toaster can easily make your breakfast waffle too hot to touch.

In this investigation, you will monitor a chemical change, called an electroplating reaction, produced by an electric current. In an electroplating reaction, a source of electric current is connected to two metal electrodes immersed in a solution that can conduct electricity. The solution is composed of water and a compound that dissolves into charged particles, called ions. The current causes metal atoms to leave one electrode and dissolve into the solution. At the same time, metal atoms plate out, or attach, onto the other electrode.

You will use zinc metal (Zn) for the electrodes in this investigation. At the positive electrode, zinc atoms lose two electrons each and dissolve as Zn^{2+} ions. These ions travel freely in the solution. At the negative electrode, Zn^{2+} ions from the solution gain two electrons and plate out as neutral zinc atoms. You will be able to measure the change in mass at each electrode and from these data derive the number of zinc atoms gained or lost. Since changes in each zinc atom involve two electrons, the number of electrons involved is double the number of atoms.

The electroplating reaction is driven by an external battery, which causes electrons to move through a wire toward the negative electrode and away from the positive electrode through another wire. You will measure the flow of electrons through the external wire using an ammeter. With the data you have, you can use a series of calculations to find the charge on one electron.

Pre-Lab Discussion

Read the entire laboratory investigation and the relevant pages of your textbook. Then answer the questions that follow.

1. What quantities do you need to know in order to determine the charge of the electron? <u>The change of mass at each electrode; the current flowing through the circuit; the elapsed time the current flows; the mass of a single zinc atom.</u>

Materials (class of 30 in pairs)

30 pairs chemical splash goggles
30 laboratory aprons
30 zinc (Zn) electrodes, 3 cm × 10 cm
15 pieces steel wool
15 marking pens or pencils
15 beakers, 250-mL
3 L zinc sulfate solution ($ZnSO_4$), 1.0 M
15 sets of 4 D batteries, connected in series
45 wire leads with alligator clips
15 ammeters (0–1.0 ampere)
15 stopwatches or clocks with a second hand
2 beakers, 500-mL, about two-thirds full of water
beaker, 250-mL, containing about 200 mL of denatured alcohol
15 laboratory balances

Time Required

80 minutes. To split the tasks over two or more days, have students prepare their electrodes and set up the dry apparatus on the first day. The next day students can add the electrolyte solution, run the reaction, and wash the electrodes. If necessary, let the electrodes dry overnight and have students take the final mass readings on the following day. You also can save time by setting up the external circuits (batteries and ammeters) in advance.

Advance Preparation

Prepare the 1.0 M zinc sulfate solution by dissolving 288 g of zinc sulfate septahydrate ($ZnSO_4 \cdot 7H_2O$) per liter of water until you have the volume needed for the class.

© Prentice-Hall, Inc.

Lab 8

To reduce the risks associated with the denatured alcohol, set up a single wash station in a fume hood with a 250-mL beaker containing about 200 mL of the alcohol, and have two or three 500-mL beakers of water nearby. Have students carry their electroplating cells with the electrodes to the wash area and rinse the electrodes under your supervision.

Have ready a container in which to collect the used zinc sulfate solution.

Introduction

Direct measurement of the charge on an electron, as done by Millikan, is a difficult experiment, and not a very good classroom demonstration. A Crookes tube, on the other hand, is a standard piece of physics laboratory equipment, and shows the effect of an electric or magnetic field on cathode rays quite graphically. Demonstrations of static electricity are also striking, and students may be familiar with them. If you do any of these demonstrations in class, follow up with a discussion, giving students an opportunity to speculate about the submicroscopic explanations for their macroscopic observations.

Safety

Make sure students wear their goggles and lab aprons at all times during the investigation. Instruct them not to connect the last of the wires until after you have checked their setups.

The open alcohol bath presents a risk of fire; make sure no flames are present in the laboratory. The alcohol bath also contains methanol, which is toxic. Minimize the students' exposure to and handling of the alcohol by limiting them to one rinsing beaker for the class. Have

Name _____

2. How is each quantity in Question 1 obtained? __Change in mass is measured with a balance; current flow is measured with an ammeter; time with a stopwatch or clock. Mass of the zinc atom is given.__

3. What quantity is measured by the ammeter? __Electron flow, or current.__

4. How is the total charge calculated? __Total charge is the product of average current and elapsed time (in seconds).__

5. Why must the number of zinc atoms be doubled to find the number of electrons that flowed through the circuit? __Each zinc atom loses or gains two electrons during the reaction, so the change in one zinc atom corresponds to the flow of two electrons.__

6. What hazards are present in this investigation, and what safety precautions should you follow? __The alcohol rinse is toxic and highly flammable. Wash any spills or splashes immediately with plenty of water. Be sure all flames in the laboratory are extinguished.__

Problem

How can the charge of an electron be determined?

Materials

chemical splash goggles
laboratory apron
2 zinc (Zn) electrodes
steel wool
marking pen or pencil
beaker, 250-mL
zinc sulfate solution, ($ZnSO_4$) 1.0 M
4 D batteries

3 wire leads with alligator clips
ammeter
stopwatch or clock with a second hand
beaker containing tap water
beaker containing denatured alcohol
laboratory balance

Safety

Wear your goggles and lab apron at all times during the investigation. The denatured alcohol bath contains methyl alcohol, which is poisonous and highly flammable. Wash any spills and splashes immediately with plenty of water and make sure there are no open flames in the laboratory. Use the alcohol bath only under your teacher's supervision.

Note the caution alert symbols here and with certain steps of the Procedure. Refer to page xi for the specific precautions associated with each symbol.

Name_____

Lab 8

Procedure

 1. Put on your goggles and lab apron.

 2. Rub both sides of the two zinc electrodes with steel wool to remove any dirt or grease. Use the marking pen to draw a + (positive sign) on one electrode and a − (negative sign) on the other electrode. Measure the masses of the electrodes, and record these values in Data Table 1.

3. Assemble the apparatus shown in Figure 8–1 as follows. Bend one end of each electrode so that it can rest on the rim of the 250-mL beaker. Then place the electrodes on opposite sides of the beaker and add 200 mL of the zinc sulfate solution to the beaker. **CAUTION:** *Be sure that the electrodes do not touch each other.* Connect one of the wire leads to the positive zinc electrode and the other end of that lead to the negative terminal of your ammeter. Connect a second lead to the negative zinc electrode and the other end of that lead to the negative terminal of the batteries. Do not connect the third wire yet.

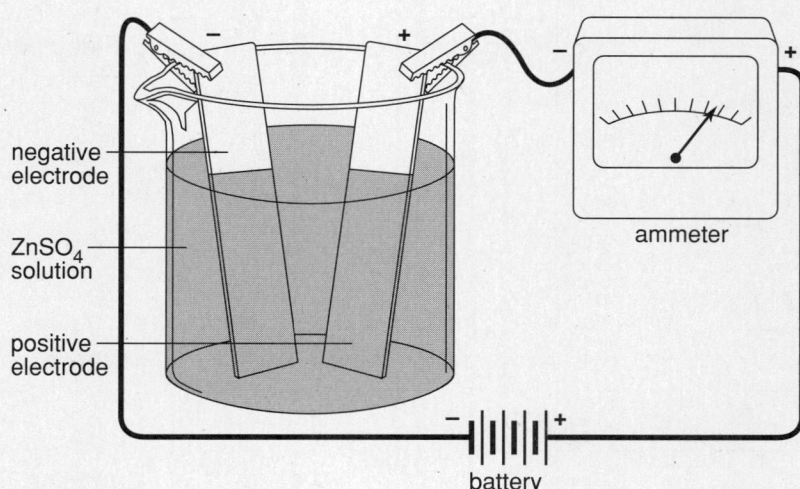

Figure 8–1

4. After your teacher has checked your apparatus, connect the third lead between the positive terminal of the ammeter and the positive terminal of the batteries. Watch the ammeter for a few moments until the current remains unchanging, and then adjust the current to between 0.70 and 0.80 amperes by moving the electrodes closer together or further apart. Do not allow the electrodes to touch.

5. In Data Table 2, record the current indicated by the ammeter. Take a reading at the beginning of each minute for 20–25 minutes. If the current varies beyond the 0.70–0.80 ampere range, readjust the positions of the electrodes. Be sure to wait until the end of a 1-minute interval to make any adjustments.

them wash their electrodes under your supervision. ■

Teaching Tips
Cleaning the electrodes before use also removes any zinc oxide that may have accumulated. Have students compare the appearance of the cleaned electrodes before and after the electroplating reaction. They should find that both electrodes are shinier. Ask them to suggest reasons for their observations. (As the zinc dissolves from the positive electrode, further dirt and impurities—including zinc oxide—are removed, exposing unreacted zinc metal. At the negative electrode, pure zinc plates out.)
  When students assemble the apparatus, have them secure the electrodes in a vertical position by attaching each alligator clip so that it holds the electrode to the rim of the beaker.
  Students may benefit from a review of how an electric circuit works. Ask them to infer from the description of the reaction in the Introduction the direction of electron flow in the circuit. (Electrons flow into the positive electrode and toward the battery as Zn atoms give up electrons and become ions. Electrons flow from the battery to the negative electrode, where positive Zn ions take up electrons and become atoms.) Most students imagine electrons racing through and completely around the circuit. They will be surprised to find out that a single electron migrates only an inch or so through the circuit during the entire reaction.
  You may wish to discuss the calculations ahead of time so that students have a clear idea of the steps they will follow and the units with which they will work.

© Prentice-Hall, Inc.   *Finding the Charge of an Electron* 47

Lab 8

Name _____

Alert students to watch for increases in current larger than the range recommended and adjust the electrodes as needed. If the current increases too much, the data may be affected by other reactions, such as the decomposition of water.

Ask students why they think an alcohol rinse is used after the water rinse. (Alcohol evaporates very quickly and will dry the electrodes before the metal oxide has a chance to form.)

Students may benefit from a discussion of Analysis and Conclusions Question 2. Point out that the data at the negative electrode are more reliable because only zinc plates out, whereas the loss of impurities from the positive electrode can produce a greater change in mass.

Waste Disposal
The zinc sulfate solution can be collected, saved, and reused from class to class and year to year. ■

6. Disconnect the wire leads from the electrodes when you have finished taking readings. Carry your beaker containing the electrodes to the washing area set up by your teacher. Holding each electrode by its dry end, rinse it very carefully by dipping it first in a large beaker of water and then in a beaker of denatured alcohol. Do not shake or swirl the electrodes in the rinse liquids, or you may dislodge pieces of zinc. **CAUTION:** *The alcohol is toxic, and its vapors are flammable. Use only under your teacher's supervision. Be sure there are no flames in the laboratory. Avoid touching the alcohol. Wash spills or splashes on your skin with plenty of water.*

7. Set the electrodes gently on a paper towel, and place them in a protected area to dry. Return the zinc sulfate solution to a container provided by your teacher.

8. Measure the mass of each electrode when it is completely dry, and record these values in Data Table 1.

9. Clean up your work area and wash your hands before leaving the laboratory.

Observations (sample data)
DATA TABLE 1

	Negative Electrode	Positive Electrode
initial mass (g)	13.79	13.11
final mass (g)	14.09	12.78
change in mass (g)	0.30	0.33

DATA TABLE 2

Time (min)	Current (amp)	Time (min)	Current (amp)
1	0.73	11	0.75
2	0.73	12	0.75
3	0.73	13	0.75
4	0.74	14	0.75
5	0.74	15	0.75
6	0.74	16	0.76
7	0.74	17	0.76
8	0.74	18	0.77
9	0.74	19	0.77
10	0.75	20	0.77

Name _____

Lab 8

 Calculations (based on sample data)

1. Find the change in mass for each electrode and write this value in Data Table 1.

$$\Delta\ mass_{neg}: 14.09\ g - 13.79\ g = 0.30\ g$$
$$\Delta\ mass_{pos}: 13.11\ g - 12.78\ g = 0.33\ g$$

2. The mass of a zinc atom is 1.09×10^{-22} g. Find the total number of zinc atoms involved at each electrode by dividing the change in mass by the mass of one atom.

$$\text{Zn atoms}_{neg}: \frac{3.0 \times 10^{-1}\ g}{1.09 \times 10^{-22}\ g/atom} = 2.8 \times 10^{21}\ \text{atoms}$$

$$\text{Zn atoms}_{pos}: \frac{3.4 \times 10^{-1}\ g}{1.09 \times 10^{-22}\ g/atom} = 3.0 \times 10^{21}\ \text{atoms}$$

3. Calculate the average current flowing through the ammeter. Then find the total charge in ampere-seconds by multiplying the average current by the time elapsed in seconds. (Remember to convert minutes to seconds.)

$$\text{average current} = \frac{14.96\ amp}{20} = 0.75\ amp$$

total charge = 0.75 amp × 20 min × 60 sec/min = 9.0×10^2 amp-sec

4. In SI units, charge is measured in coulombs. One coulomb is equal to one ampere-second. Convert your value for total charge to coulombs and calculate the charge per zinc atom involved at each electrode.

9.0×10^2 amp-sec = 9.0×10^2 coulomb

$$\text{charge per atom}_{neg} = \frac{9.0 \times 10^2\ \text{coulomb}}{2.8 \times 10^{21}\ \text{atoms}} = 3.2 \times 10^{-19}\ \text{coulomb/atom}$$

$$\text{charge per atom}_{pos} = \frac{9.0 \times 10^2\ \text{coulomb}}{3.0 \times 10^{21}\ \text{atoms}} = 3.0 \times 10^{-19}\ \text{coulomb/atom}$$

5. Find the charge per electron. (Note: Remember that for every zinc atom in the reaction, two electrons are involved.)

$$\text{charge per } e^-_{neg} = \frac{3.2 \times 10^{-19}\ \text{coulomb/atom}}{2\ e^-/\text{atom}} = 1.6 \times 10^{-19}\ \text{coulomb}/e^-$$

$$\text{charge per } e^-_{pos} = \frac{3.0 \times 10^{-19}\ \text{coulomb/atom}}{2\ e^-/\text{atom}} = 1.5 \times 10^{-19}\ \text{coulomb}/e^-$$

Critical Thinking: Analysis and Conclusions

1. How closely do your two values for the charge of an electron match the accepted value given in your textbook? *(Making comparisons)*

   Answers will vary. Students who have collected reliable data will have values close to the accepted value of 1.60×10^{-19} coulombs, especially for the calculation at the negative electrode.

© Prentice-Hall, Inc.   *Finding the Charge of an Electron* **49**

Lab 8

Name _____

2. Are the charge values you calculated for the two electrodes the same? If not, how might the discrepancy be explained? *(Making inferences)* Most students will not have two equal values. The data at the positive electrode may be less reliable due to the presence of impurities or the possible flaking of zinc metal into the solution during the electroplating reaction.

3. What source of energy caused the change in masses of the electrodes? *(Making inferences)* The flow of electric current from the batteries.

4. Are the changes in mass measured at each electrode consistent with the reactions taking place? Explain. *(Interpreting data)* Students should detect a loss in mass at the positive electrode and a gain at the negative electrode. The changes are consistent with the reaction because zinc loses electrons and dissolves from the positive electrode, and gains electrons and plates onto the negative electrode.

Critical Thinking: Applications

1. If you were to try this experiment using a different metal for the electrodes (and an appropriate conducting solution), predict whether or not you would find similar values for the charge on the electron. Explain. *(Making predictions)* The value for the charge on an electron should be the same because all electrons carry the same charge. The changes in mass and the current measured might be different.

2. How do you think the number of zinc ions in solution at the start of the reaction compares to the number at the end? Explain your reasoning. *(Developing hypotheses)* They are the same. Each time a zinc atom enters the solution as a zinc ion at the positive electrode, a zinc ion already in solution simultaneously plates out as a neutral atom at the negative electrode.

Going Further

1. Under your teacher's supervision, redo this experiment using a different metal (lead or copper are recommended). See if you arrive at the same value for the charge on an electron.

2. Look in your textbook to find the mass of an electron as calculated by Robert Millikan. Using this value and the value you found for the charge on the electron at the negative electrode, calculate the charge-to-mass ratio of an electron. Compare your answer to the charge-to-mass ratio determined by J.J. Thomson.

Going Further

1. If students repeat the experiment with copper electrodes, they will need copper screen and 1.0 *M* copper sulfate solution. A small amount (25 mL) of concentrated sulfuric acid should be added to each liter of copper sulfate solution to increase the conductivity. The reaction at the positive copper electrode may yield unreliable data due to a loss of unreacted copper particles in the solution. Have students do their calculations using data from the negative electrode only.

2. Millikan determined the mass of an electron to be 9.11×10^{-28} g. Using the sample data from the investigation, the charge-to-mass ratio is calculated as follows:

$$\frac{1.6 \times 10^{-19} \text{ coulomb}}{9.11 \times 10^{-28} \text{ g}}$$

$$= 1.8 \times 10^{8} \text{ coulomb/g}$$

Thomson's value for the charge-to-mass ratio is 1.76×10^{8} coulomb/g.

Isotopes of "Pennium"

Small Scale Lab 9 APPLICATION

Text reference: **Chapter 3**

Introduction

Unless you're a coin collector, you probably think all United States pennies are pretty much the same. To the casual observer, all the pennies in circulation do seem to be identical in size, thickness, and composition. But just as elements have one or more isotopes with different masses, the pennies in circulation have different masses. In this investigation, you are going to use pennies with different masses to represent different "isotopes" of an imaginary element called pennium, or Pe. Remember that chemical isotopes are atoms that have the same number of protons, but different numbers of neutrons. Thus, chemical isotopes have nearly identical chemical properties, but some different physical properties.

In this investigation, you will determine the relative abundance of the isotopes of pennium and the masses of each isotope. You will then use this information to determine the atomic mass of pennium. Recall that the atomic mass of an element is the weighted average of the masses of the isotopes of the element. This average is based on both the mass and the relative abundance of each isotope as it occurs in nature.

Pre-Lab Discussion

Read the entire laboratory investigation and the relevant pages of your textbook. Then answer the questions that follow.

1. What do the 20 pennies in this investigation represent? <u>The 20 pennies represent 20 atoms of the imaginary element pennium.</u>

2. What do the different masses of the pennies represent? <u>Pennies with different masses represent isotopes of pennium.</u>

3. What information do you need to calculate the average atomic mass for an element? <u>You need to know the average atomic mass of each isotope and its percent abundance.</u>

Problem

What are the masses and relative abundances of isotopes of pennium and what is the atomic mass of the element?

Materials

safety goggles
laboratory balance
20 pennies in a resealable bag

Materials (class of 30 in pairs)
- 30 pairs safety goggles
- 15 laboratory balances
- 240 pennies minted after 1982
- 60 pennies minted before 1982
- 15 small resealable plastic bags

Time Required
30–40 minutes. Allow more time if you intend to pool class data.

Advance Preparation
Gather 60 pre-1982 and 240 post-1982 pennies. Exclude 1982 pennies from the collection. Place 20 pennies in each plastic bag, using a ratio of 4 pre-1982 pennies to 16 post-1982 pennies. This combination will give a 20% abundance of pre-1982 pennies. You can change this ratio by adjusting the number of pre-1982 and post-1982 pennies.

Introduction
Discuss the concepts of isotopes and atomic mass. Demonstrate how average atomic mass is calculated, and leave the formulas on the board.

Safety
Make sure students wear their goggles at all times during the investigation. ■

Teaching Tips
Pennies minted before 1982 are copper and have an average mass of about 3.0 g while pennies minted after 1982 are made of zinc with a copper coating and have an average mass of about 2.5 g.

© Prentice-Hall, Inc.

Isotopes of "Pennium" 51

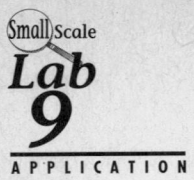

Lab 9 APPLICATION

You might suggest students write the numbers 1–20 spread out on a piece of paper, and place each penny heads up next to a number. In this way, they can easily check their work, if necessary.

Name _____

Safety

Wear your goggles at all times during the investigation.

Procedure

1. Put on your goggles. Remove the pennies from the resealable bag and count them to make sure that there are 20. Determine and record the combined mass of your 20 pennies.
2. Find the mass of each penny separately. In the Data Table, record the year the penny was minted and its mass to the nearest 0.02 g.
 3. Place the 20 pennies in the resealable bag and return the pennies and the laboratory balance to the area designated by your teacher. Clean up your work area and wash your hands before leaving the laboratory.

Observations (sample data)

Combined mass (to nearest 0.02 g) of 20 pennies 52.58 g

DATA TABLE

Penny	Year	Mass (g)
1	1981	3.10
2	1984	2.46
3	1983	2.54
4	1987	2.58
5	1989	2.52
6	1980	3.04
7	1990	2.50
8	1986	2.50
9	1991	2.48
10	1987	2.54
11	1985	2.58
12	1984	2.56
13	1976	3.02
14	1991	2.52
15	1986	2.50
16	1989	2.48
17	1966	3.10
18	1988	2.54
19	1984	2.56
20	1986	2.50

Name _____

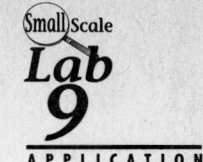

Calculations (based on sample data)

1. Inspect your data carefully. Determine the number of isotopes of Pe that are present. **There are two isotopes of pennium, as is evident by the two different groups of masses. One group is pre-1982, and the other is post-1982.**

2. Calculate the fractional abundance of each isotope in your sample.
   Fractional abundance = number of pennies for each isotope/total number of pennies
   Fractional abundance for pre-1982 = 4/20 = 0.2
   Fractional abundance for post-1982 = 16/20 = 0.8

3. Calculate the average atomic mass of each isotope.
   Average atomic mass =
      total mass of pennies of each isotope/number of pennies of that isotope
      Isotope 1 (pre-1982) = 12.22 g/4 = 3.06 g
      Isotope 2 (post-1982) = 40.36 g/16 = 2.52 g

4. Using the fractional abundance and the average atomic mass of each isotope, calculate the atomic mass of Pe.
   (average mass of isotope 1) × (fractional abundance)
     + (average mass of isotope 2) × (fractional abundance) = atomic mass
   (3.06 g)(0.2) + (2.52 g)(0.8) = 2.63 g

Critical Thinking: Analysis and Conclusions

1. Was the mass of 20 pennies equal to 20 times the mass of one penny? Explain. *(Making comparisons)* **No. The masses of the individual pennies vary and therefore the mass of 20 pennies will be different from 20 times the mass of one penny.**

2. In what year(s) did the mass of Pe change? How could you tell? *(Interpreting data)* **1982. The mass of a post-1982 penny is noticeably less than the mass of a pre-1982 penny.**

3. How can you explain the fact that there are different "isotopes" of pennium? *(Making inferences)* **Answers will vary, but may include the inference that the materials used in pennies were changed in 1982. Post-1982 pennies are made of lighter metals.**

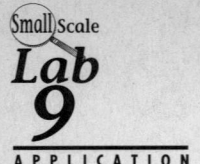

Name _____

Critical Thinking: Applications

1. Why are the atomic masses for most elements not whole numbers? *(Applying concepts)* Atomic masses of most elements are not whole numbers because atomic mass represents a weighted average of the isotope masses.

2. How are the three isotopes of hydrogen (hydrogen-1, hydrogen-2, and hydrogen-3) alike? How are they different? *(Making comparisons)* All have 1 proton and 1 electron. They have the same chemical properties. They differ in the number of neutrons, and in mass.

3. Copper has two isotopes, copper-63 and copper-65. The relative abundance of copper-63 is 69.1% and copper-65, 30.9%. Calculate the average atomic mass of copper. *(Applying concepts)*

   (63)(0.691) + (65)(0.309) = 63.618 amu

Going Further

2. Students may wish to contact the United States Mint in Washington, DC, to find out the composition of dimes and pennies.

Going Further

1. Repeat this investigation using dimes (Di). Are there different "isotopes" of dimes? Calculate the atomic mass of dimes.
2. Find out the chemical composition of pennies and dimes. How have these changed over the years?

Flame Tests

Small Scale Lab 10

Text reference: **Chapter 4**

Introduction

According to the Bohr theory of the atom, electrons may occupy only specific energy levels. When an atom absorbs sufficient energy, an electron can "jump" to a higher energy level. Higher energy levels tend to be less stable, however, and if a lower energy level is available, the electron will "fall" back, giving off energy in the process. The difference in energies between the two levels is emitted in the form of a photon of electromagnetic radiation. The energy of each photon is described by the equation $E = h\nu$, where h is Planck's constant and ν is the frequency of the radiation. If the wavelength of the released photon is between 400 and 700 nm, the energy is emitted as visible light. The color of the light depends on the specific energy change that is taking place.

White light is a continuous spectrum in which all wavelengths of visible light are present. An excited atom, however, produces one or more specific lines in its spectrum, corresponding to the specific changes in energy levels of its electrons. Because each element has a distinct electron configuration, each has a unique line spectrum.

Flame tests are a quick method of producing the characteristic colors of metallic ions. The loosely-held electrons of a metal are easily excited in the flame of a lab burner. The emission of energy in the visible portion of the spectrum as those electrons return to lower energy levels produces a colored flame. The color is a combination of the wavelengths of each transition, and may be used to determine the identity of the ion.

In this investigation you will perform flame tests on seven metallic ions, then use your results to determine the identity of several unknowns.

Pre-Lab Discussion

Read the entire laboratory investigation and the relevant pages of your textbook. Then answer the questions that follow.

1. Write out the electron configurations for each of the metallic ions to be tested in this investigation.

   Ba^{2+} _____ [Xe] or $1s^2 2s^2 2p^6 3s^2 3p^6 3d^{10} 4s^2 4p^6 4d^{10} 5s^2 5p^6$

   Cu^{2+} _____ [Ar]$3d^9$ or $1s^2 2s^2 2p^6 3s^2 3p^6 3d^9$

   Li^+ _____ [He] or $1s^2$

   K^+ _____ [Ar] or $1s^2 2s^2 2p^6 3s^2 3p^6$

   Sr^{2+} _____ [Kr] or $1s^2 2s^2 2p^6 3s^2 3p^6 3d^{10} 4s^2 4p^6$

   Ca^{2+} _____ [Ar] or $1s^2 2s^2 2p^6 3s^2 3p^6$

   Na^+ _____ [Ne] or $1s^2 2s^2 2p^6$

Materials (class of 30 in pairs)

30 pairs chemical splash goggles
30 laboratory aprons
30 pairs latex gloves
15 well plates with at least 12 wells
15 marker pens
38 brown dropper bottles with droppers
100 mL of 0.1 M solutions of each of the following:
 barium nitrate ($Ba(NO_3)_2$)
 copper nitrate ($Cu(NO_3)_2$)
 strontium nitrate ($Sr(NO_3)_2$)
 lithium nitrate ($LiNO_3$)
 potassium nitrate (KNO_3)
 sodium chloride ($NaCl$)
 calcium nitrate ($Ca(NO_3)_2$)
3 or more unknown solutions
15 nichrome wires, with loop and handle
15 beakers, 50-mL
150 mL 6.0 M HCl
15 lab burners
15 wash bottles with distilled water

Time Required

30 minutes.

Advance Preparation

For 0.1 M solutions, mix 100 mL of distilled water with each of the following:

$Ba(NO_3)_2$	2.6 g
$Cu(NO_3)_2 \cdot 6H_2O$	3.0 g
$LiNO_3$	0.7 g
KNO_3	1.0 g
$NaCl$	0.6 g
$Ca(NO_3)_2$	1.6 g
(or 2.4 g $Ca(NO_3)_2 \cdot 4H_2O$)	
$Sr(NO_3)_2$	2.1 g

For 6.0 M HCl, mix equal parts of 12.0 M HCl and distilled water, making sure to add the acid to the water.

Have available at least two sets of bottles of solutions from which students take their samples. To prepare the solution bottles, put 30 mL

© Prentice-Hall, Inc.

Flame Tests 55

Small Scale Lab 10

Name _____

into each of the bottles. Label the bottles and the dropper-tops with the name of the solution. Small beakers could also be used, but not all salt solutions are colorless. Provide a container to collect the waste solutions from the well plates at the end of the activity.

About 10 mL of 6.0 *M* HCl should be poured into each small beaker and placed at each station for cleaning the wires. Caution students not to touch or breathe fumes from the HCl.

The unknowns can be solutions of the salts by themselves or mixed together. Label the unknowns by letter. In order to see the colors of individual ions clearly, the following mixtures are recommended: Na$^+$ and Li$^+$, Ba^{2+} and K$^+$, Na$^+$ and Cu^{2+}. Simply mix 5–10 mL each of the desired solutions together in a clean dropper bottle. Li$^+$ and Sr^{2+} have similar flame tests and should not be combined.

Introduction
Demonstrate the line spectra for different elements using gas discharge tubes, diffraction gratings, or spectroscopes. Relate the line spectrum to the color of the glowing gas and to the idea of electrons gaining and losing energy. Compare the line spectra seen with the gas discharge tubes to the continuous spectra seen with incandescent and fluorescent light bulbs.

Students may wonder whether differences exist in test results of ions, salts, or metallic forms of an element. The color of the flame test is the same for all forms of the metal.

Safety
Make sure students wear their goggles and lab aprons at all times during the investigation. The 6.0 *M* HCl

2. What does a flame test indicate about the energy changes taking place among the electrons in a metallic ion? __Energy is being released as the electrons "fall" from higher to lower energy levels, producing a characteristic color.__

3. Explain why a metallic ion produces a characteristic color in a flame test, regardless of the compound used as the source of the ion. __The color is always the same for a particular ion because the transition energy is characteristic of the electron configuration of the ion.__

4. What wavelengths correspond to the visible spectrum? Which color has the shortest wavelength? The longest? __The visible spectrum ranges from about 400 nm (corresponding to violet) to 700 nm (corresponding to red).__

5. What precautions should be taken when using 6.0 *M* HCl? __Eye and clothing protection should be worn. If any acid splashes on skin, affected area should be flushed with copious amounts of water.__

6. Why is it important to use a clean nichrome wire for each test? __A clean wire prevents contamination from other sources.__

Problem
What colors are characteristic of particular metallic ions in a flame test?

Materials
chemical splash goggles
laboratory apron
latex gloves
well plate
marker pen
solutions of the following salts:
  barium nitrate (Ba(NO$_3$)$_2$)
  copper nitrate (Cu(NO$_3$)$_2$)
  strontium nitrate (Sr(NO$_3$)$_2$)
  lithium nitrate (LiNO$_3$)

potassium nitrate (KNO$_3$)
sodium chloride (NaCl)
calcium nitrate (Ca(NO$_3$)$_2$)
nichrome wire loop
beaker, 50-mL
hydrochloric acid
  (HCl), 6.0 *M*
lab burner
wash bottle with distilled water
3 unknown solutions

Safety

Wear your goggles and lab apron at all times during the investigation. The 6.0 *M* HCl is corrosive and irritating to skin, nasal passages, eyes, and clothing. The salt solutions, with the exception of NaCl, are toxic. Handle all of the solutions with care, and do not inhale their vapors. If a solution should splash on your skin, wash the affected area with large amounts of water and notify your teacher. When you work near the burner flame, tie back or cover loose hair, and secure loose or bulky clothing.

Name _____

Note the caution alert symbols here and with certain steps of the Procedure. Refer to page *xi* for the specific precautions associated with each symbol.

Procedure

1. Put on your goggles and lab apron. Obtain a well plate and use a marker to label seven wells with the names of the known solutions. Put a dropperful of each known solution into its labeled well.

2. Put on your latex gloves. Obtain a beaker with about 10 mL of 6.0 M HCl and a nichrome wire loop. Light the burner, and adjust the flame to low. **CAUTION:** *Hydrochloric acid is corrosive to skin and clothing and its vapors are irritating to lungs and eyes. Avoid contact with the solution and inhalation of its vapors. Loose hair should be tied back or covered, and bulky or loose clothing should be secured in some manner.*

3. For each test, be sure that the nichrome wire is clean, so as not to contaminate the solutions. To clean the wire, first rinse it with distilled water, using the wash bottle. Then dip it in the 6.0 M HCl solution. Place it in the burner flame for a few moments, as shown in Figure 10–1. Determine the color of the clean nichrome wire in the flame. This is the color you should see after every trial.

4. Sodium has a very strong color, which may affect your other tests, so test the sodium solution last. Dip the clean nichrome wire in one solution. Place the wire in the burner flame and observe. Record your observations on Data Table 1. Clean the wire and repeat this step with the next known solution until you have tested all seven solutions. **CAUTION:** *Do not let these* is corrosive and can cause damage to eyes and lungs. Remind students that the salt solutions, with the exception of NaCl, are poisonous and should be handled with care. If solutions should splash on skin, wash the affected area immediately with copious amounts of water.* ■

Teaching Tips

The biggest problem with this lab is cross contamination of the solutions. Make sure that students follow the cleaning procedure carefully, and that they test sodium last. For an alternative technique, use wooden splints and 1.0 M salt solutions. Dispose of the splints after each use.

Tell students that very little solution is needed to perform each test. A drop on the looped end of the nichrome wire is sufficient. It may be helpful to use a cobalt glass to view potassium, particularly in the mixed unknowns.

Copper salts in solution have a blue color, which undermines their use as an unknown. Either give out unknowns in brown bottles, or do not use copper solution as an unknown.

If there are any color-blind students, pair them with normal-vision students.

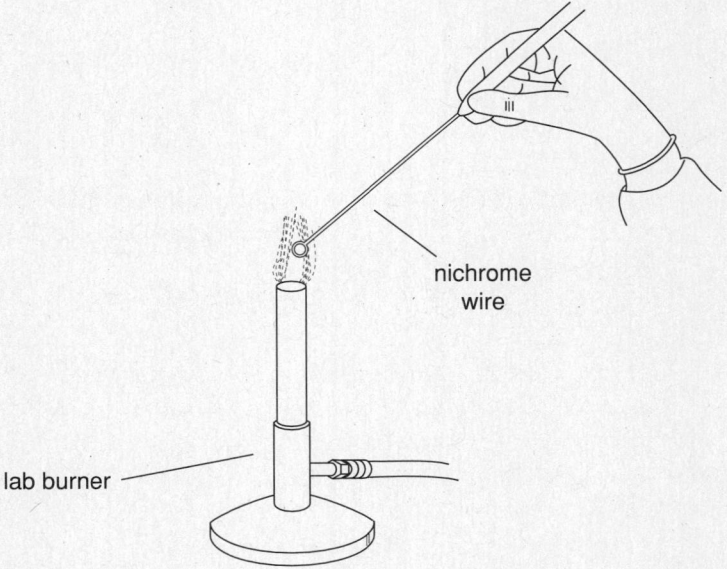

Figure 10–1

Flame Tests 57

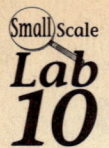

Name _____

substances come in contact with your skin. If a solution should splash on your skin, wash the affected area with large amounts of water and notify your teacher.

5. Obtain three unknowns from your teacher. Repeat Step 4 for each unknown. Record your observations on Data Table 2.

 6. Turn off the burner. Clean up your work area and wash your hands before leaving the laboratory.

Waste Disposal

The unused solutions can be capped tightly and stored for future use. Excess HCl should be neutralized, and then rinsed down the sink. Have the students use a wash bottle to rinse all the unused solutions from their well plates into the container provided. React the mixture with 100 mL of 1.0 M sodium sulfate to precipitate the barium. Filter the precipitate and store it in a solid waste container for commercial disposal or for shipment to a secure landfill. Flush the filtrate down the drain. ■

Observations (sample data)

DATA TABLE 1 Flame Tests of Known Solutions

Salt Solution	Color
$Ba(NO_3)_2$	yellowish green
$Cu(NO_3)_2$	bluish green
$LiNO_3$	deep red
KNO_3	lilac
NaCl	yellow
$Ca(NO_3)_2$	orange
$Sr(NO_3)_2$	bright red

DATA TABLE 2 Tests of Unknown Solutions

Unknown	Color
	See Data Table 1. The mixtures
	give bits of individual colors and
	some blended colors.

Critical Thinking: Analysis and Conclusions

1. What metallic ions are present in the unknown solutions? *(Drawing conclusions)* __Answers will vary according to which salt solutions were tested.__

2. Summarize the process that produces the colors seen in the flame tests. *(Applying concepts)* __The electrons of the metallic ions are excited by the heat of the flame and move to higher energy levels. When the electrons "fall" back to lower energy levels, they emit energy. Energy that is in the visible range of the electromagnetic spectrum is seen as the color of the flame test.__

3. What is the relationship of the colors you saw and the lines of the electromagnetic spectrum produced by the metals? *(Making inferences)* __The color seen is a blend of the lines that each ion produces when its electrons absorb and then emit energy.__

© Prentice-Hall, Inc.

Critical Thinking: Applications

1. When a glass rod is heated, a yellow flame is observed around the point of heating. What does this yellow flame indicate? Why is it observed when glass is heated? *(Developing hypotheses)* A yellow flame is indicative of sodium which, therefore, must be present in glass. When glass is heated, the Na$^+$ ions are excited and produce the characteristic yellow color.

2. The line spectrum of lithium has a red line at 670.8 nm. Calculate the energy of a photon with this wavelength. *(Making predictions)*
   $\lambda \nu = c$, $\nu = (3.0 \times 10^8$ m/s$)/(670.8$ nm $\times 10^{-9}$ m/nm$) = 4.47 \times 10^{14}$ s^{-1}
   $E = h\nu$, $E = (6.626 \times 10^{-34}$ J·s$)(4.47 \times 10^{14}$ s$^{-1}) = 2.96 \times 10^{-19}$ J

3. What other equipment could you use in this investigation if burners were not available? *(Designing experiments)* Spectrographs, diffusion gratings, or any heat source strong enough to excite the electrons may be used.

4. How do you think metallic salts are used in fireworks? *(Applying concepts)* The salts are a source of color in the fireworks. Metallic ions are excited by the energy of the explosion. As their electrons lose energy, they produce colors exactly like those seen in flame tests.

Going Further

1. Get some copper metal filings from your teacher. Work under your teacher's supervision. Pick up a small piece of copper filing with the wire loop, and put it in the burner flame. Is the color of copper in the flame the same as the color of copper nitrate solution?
2. Neon is a gas that has a reddish-orange emission spectrum. Find out why neon lights can display a multitude of colors.
3. The invention of the spectroscope by Robert Bunsen and Gustav Kirchoff opened up a new era of chemical investigation and research. Bunsen and Kirchoff discovered two elements through the use of their invention. Find out which elements they discovered, and how the spectroscope is now used.

Going Further

2. "Neon" lights are not all filled with neon gas. The tubes are actually filled with many other gases, including argon and helium, each of which emits its own characteristic color.
3. Biographical sketches of Robert Bunsen and accounts of spectroscopic discovery of elements are included in the following:
   Biographical Disk, *History of Chemistry Institute,* Woodrow Wilson National Fellowship Foundation, 1992.
   Davenport, Derek, "Robert Bunsen . . . More Than a Burner Design," *ChemMatters,* 1984, V.2, p. 14.
   Roberts, Royston M., *Serendipity: Accidental Discoveries in Science.* Wiley, 1989.
   Weeks, Mary E. and Leicester, Henry M. (rev), *Some Spectroscopic Discoveries, Discovery of the Elements,* Journal of Chemical Education, 1968, p. 598.

Name _____ Date _____ Class _____

Spectral Analysis of Fluorescent Lights

Lab **11**
APPLICATION

Text reference: Chapter 4

Introduction

A marine ecologist notices that many bottom-dwelling organisms are dying in a local harbor. A high school junior with an interest in boating and ecology volunteers to help the ecologist find the cause. From mud samples taken from the bottom of the harbor, the student chemically extracts metal ions. Her quest is to see if there are any toxic metals in the mud.

In the ecologist's laboratory, the student injects the metal ions into the hot flame of the atomic emission spectrometer, an instrument that can measure the wavelengths emitted by atoms. Energy from the flame excites the electrons of the metal ions and boosts them to higher energy levels from which they cascade downward in a distinctive pattern, losing their energy in the form of light. As you know from Investigation 10, each type of atom produces a specific set of colors at wavelengths characteristic of that type of atom.

The light emitted from the metal ions is observed and recorded after it passes through a diffraction grating. The diffraction grating spreads the light into a line spectrum. In samples from the upper layers of mud, the student observes a line spectrum with wavelengths of 563.1 nm and 615.0 nm, indicating the presence of tin.

The student traces the tin to a newly marketed paint used to coat the bottoms of boats. The paint proves to be lethal to almost all bottom-dwelling marine organisms and is banned from further use. So the mystery of the dying marine life is solved.

In this investigation you too will be a detective, identifying a gas by its spectral lines. First, you will see how the spectrum of visible light looks when viewed through a diffraction grating spectrometer. Then you will familiarize yourself with the line spectra of various elements, and the relationship between color and light wavelength. Finally, you will use this knowledge to identify the gas in a fluorescent light bulb.

Pre-Lab Discussion

Read the entire laboratory investigation and the relevant pages of your textbook. Then answer the questions that follow.

1. What instrument will you use to separate colors of light and analyze their wavelengths? __A diffraction grating spectrometer is used to analyze light.__

2. When atoms are heated so that they emit light, what characteristic of their light allows you to tell one atom from another? __When viewed through a spectrometer, each element is seen to produce a characteristic spectrum of lines at particular wavelengths.__

Materials (class of 30 in pairs)
30 pairs safety goggles
30 laboratory aprons
15 spectrometers
white (incandescent) light source
H_2, He, and Hg spectrum tubes with power supplies (other tubes may be substituted)
fluorescent light

Time Required
45 minutes. The actual time will vary depending on the number of spectrometers and spectrum tubes available.

Advance Preparation
Set up spectrum tubes and white light source and make sure each is labeled. An overhead- or slide-projector light narrowly focused on a white screen works well as a white light source. Check out the quality of the spectrum obtained from overhead fluorescent lights. It may be better to buy an inexpensive fluorescent tube and holder at a hardware store than to focus on ceiling lights.

You may want to make, or have students make, some calibrated spectrometers, like the one shown on page 66. Directions are provided on page 66 of the teacher's notes for this investigation.

Introduction
You may want to discuss with students how spectrometers are used in astronomy, medicine, and industry.

© Prentice-Hall, Inc.

Spectral Analysis of Fluorescent Lights **61**

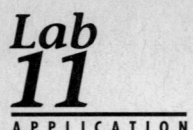

Name _____

3. Why must you avoid touching the gas spectrum tubes? Gas discharge tubes become very hot, and a high voltage shock can be delivered by the metal ends when turned on.

Problem
What gas is present in fluorescent light bulbs?

Materials
safety goggles
laboratory apron
spectrometer
white (incandescent) light source
gas spectrum tubes of:
   hydrogen (H_2)
helium (He)
mercury (Hg)
any other elements obtained
   from your teacher
fluorescent light

Safety
Wear your goggles and lab apron at all times during the investigation. Spectrometers and gas spectrum tubes are fragile, so handle them with care. Do not touch the gas spectrum tubes, because they are hot enough to burn the skin. Touching the ends of the gas spectrum tubes can cause a strong electric shock.

Note the caution alert symbols here and with certain steps of the Procedure. Refer to page *xi* for the specific precautions associated with each symbol.

Procedure
1. Put on your goggles and lab apron. View the incandescent light source with the spectrometer. **CAUTION:** *The spectrometer is fragile, so handle it with care.* In Figure 11–1 in the Observations section, sketch what you see, marking the wavelengths that define each colored region. Also mark the limits of your visual range on both ends of the spectrum. Note the regions where the colors are brightest and dimmest.

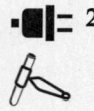
2. Use the spectrometer to observe the light from each of the labeled gas spectrum tubes. Make sure that the center of the glowing spectrum tube is very close to and directly in front of the spectrometer slit. **CAUTION:** *Do not touch the gas spectrum tubes, because they are hot and may give you an electrical shock.*

3. For each spectrum tube, carefully measure and list the observed wavelengths of the set of lines produced by the gas. Record the color of each line.

4. Now turn your spectrometer slit toward a fluorescent light fixture. Look carefully at each colored region of the light spectrum. You should see a line spectrum standing out from the full spectrum background. In addition, certain regions may be abnormally dim or missing. Measure the wavelength of the line spectrum and any dim or missing regions. If your instrument gives consistently high or low readings, take this into account.

Safety
Make sure students wear their goggles and lab aprons at all times during the investigation. Caution students not to touch spectrum tubes to avoid burns or shock. Remind students that the tubes are fragile and should be handled with care. ∎

Teaching Tips
Set the tubes up at various lab stations, and have the students rotate through each station until all the tubes have been seen. Have students take their time and make careful observations, including notes on the colors of each line. Add or substitute other gas spectrum tubes if you have them. Add reference line information for the substituted tubes to Table 11–1.

If spectrometers are in short supply, you may want to use a worksheet exercise to engage students while they wait to use the equipment. Electron configuration problems, problems related to electron energy level transitions and line spectra, and possibly calculations with Planck's constant to find the energy value of various lines might be useful.

Advanced students may wish to calculate energy

Name _____

5. Clean up your work area and wash your hands before leaving the laboratory.

TABLE 11–1   Reference Line Spectra at Visible Wavelengths (nm)

Calcium	Helium	Hydrogen	Iron	Oxygen (band)	Mercury	Sodium	Neon
393	447	410	431	686 to 688	405	589	470
397	469	434	438		436	590	535
423	502	486	467		546		585
	588	656	496		579		640
	668		527		615		694
					691		718

levels for hydrogen according to the Bohr model. The electron transitions responsible for the various spectral lines of hydrogen can be determined given the first ionization energy (E_1) and the calculated values of other energy levels ($E_1/2^2$, $E_1/3^2$ . . .), so that line energy values can be matched to energy differences between these levels.

A photograph of a full spectrum is interesting for comparison to the observed full spectrum. Many differences can be seen, including the extent of the visible range, and the width of the colored regions, especially yellow.

Observations (sample data)

1. Sketch the spectrum of incandescent white light on the blank diagram in Figure 11–1. The full spectrum should show the rapid dimming on both ends, and relative brightness of the green/yellow region.

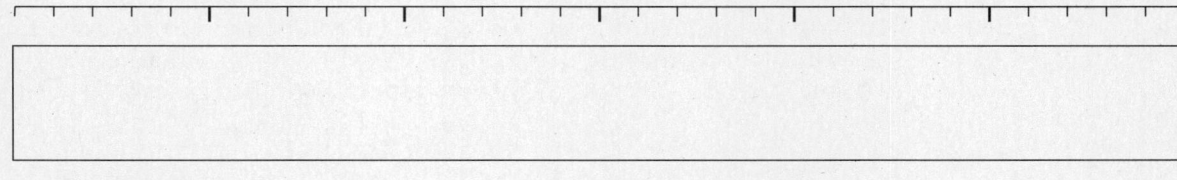

Figure 11–1

2. Enter the color, observed wavelength, and reference values from Table 11–1 for each of the known gas spectrum tubes. Remember to use the correct units of measurement.

Pair students who are color-blind with students who have normal color vision.

DATA TABLE   Line Spectra of Known Gases

Gas	Color	Observed Wavelength	Reference Values
Hydrogen	purple	440 nm	434 nm
	blue/green	490 nm	486 nm
	red	660 nm	656 nm
Mercury	purple	435 nm	436 nm
	green	550 nm	546 nm
	orange	580 nm	578 nm
Helium	blue/indigo	460 nm	470 nm
	blue	500 nm	502 nm
	yellow	590 nm	588 nm
	red	670 nm	668 nm

Cooperative Learning Strategy

In each group, one student should observe, and the other record measurements and notes. They should then switch roles to check objectively the precision of these observations and measurements.

Spectral Analysis of Fluorescent Lights

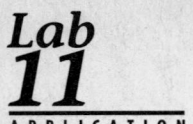

Name _____

3. Enter your line spectrum measurements for the fluorescent light, and write down any other observations you made.

435 nm

550 nm

580 nm

_____

Critical Thinking: Analysis and Conclusions

1. Compare your observed wavelengths with the reference values for various elements provided in Table 11–1. State whether your measurements tend to be consistently higher or lower than the reference values. Note the reference lines that you did not see. *(Making comparisons)* The observed readings are slightly higher than the reference values. Answers will vary as to which lines were not seen.

2. What is the gas inside the fluorescent light bulb? Support your conclusion with data from Table 11–1 and with your observations of the line spectra produced by the spectrum-tube gases. *(Drawing conclusions)* Fluorescent lights contain mercury, because the line spectrum corresponds to that of mercury.

3. In this investigation, you analyzed brightly colored line spectra. Could you still successfully complete this investigation if you were color-blind? Explain. *(Making predictions)* Yes. Each color corresponds to a wavelength that can be measured. Color does not need to to be taken into account.

4. Why do you think that some of the reference lines given for the various gases you observed were not visible to you? *(Making inferences)* Some lines may have been too faint to see, and others are just beyond the red and violet limits of what humans can see clearly.

Critical Thinking: Applications

1. Use the bright-line wavelength data in Table 11–1 to identify which gas would produce the bright-line spectrum shown in Figure 11–2. *(Applying concepts)* The line spectrum diagramed is from hydrogen.

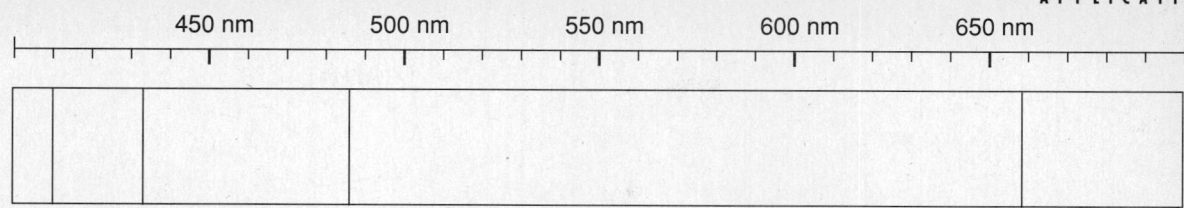

Figure 11–2

2. Now that you know more about what gases fluorescent light bulbs contain, discuss why there is concern about breakage and improper disposal of these bulbs. *(Evaluating)* Although fluorescent bulbs contain only small amounts of mercury, low levels of mercury threaten water supplies and the environment in general and are highly toxic to humans.

3. Helium was discovered in the Sun's corona during the eclipse of 1868. In 1888, traces of helium were isolated on Earth. Discuss how scientists could tell this was the same gas that had been identified in the Sun's corona. *(Drawing conclusions)* Some of the lines from the solar corona visible through a spectrometer did not match those of any known element. The new element helium, later isolated on Earth, could be identified by its distinctive line spectrum.

4. How might film or electronic light sensors, such as those in video cameras, enhance spectroscopy data? *(Applying concepts)* Film and light sensors can be used to make more permanent records. They respond to dimmer light than our eye, and can respond to a much wider range of wavelengths.

Going Further

1. Some fluorescent sources, such as energy-saver bulbs and the grow lights used on plants, contain a different gas than the one in the fluorescent light you investigated. Use your spectrometer to check for different line spectra from these fluorescent lights.
2. Spectroscopy, or spectrophotometry, is a far-reaching, versatile analytical tool. Research the different types of spectroscopy and some of its uses. Report your findings to your class in an oral presentation.
3. Find directions for making and calibrating a spectrometer, and produce one suitable for class use. Experiment with it, using a video camera or still camera to record your results. Ordinary film can record fainter images than can be seen with the eye alone.
4. If a university is nearby, visit the chemistry department and see how an atomic spectrometer operates.

Going Further
2. Encyclopedias, advanced chemistry or physics texts, and other library materials will include discussions of visible, UV, IR, Raman, NMR, and X-ray spectrophotometry.
3. Directions for producing a calibrated spectrometer are on the following page.

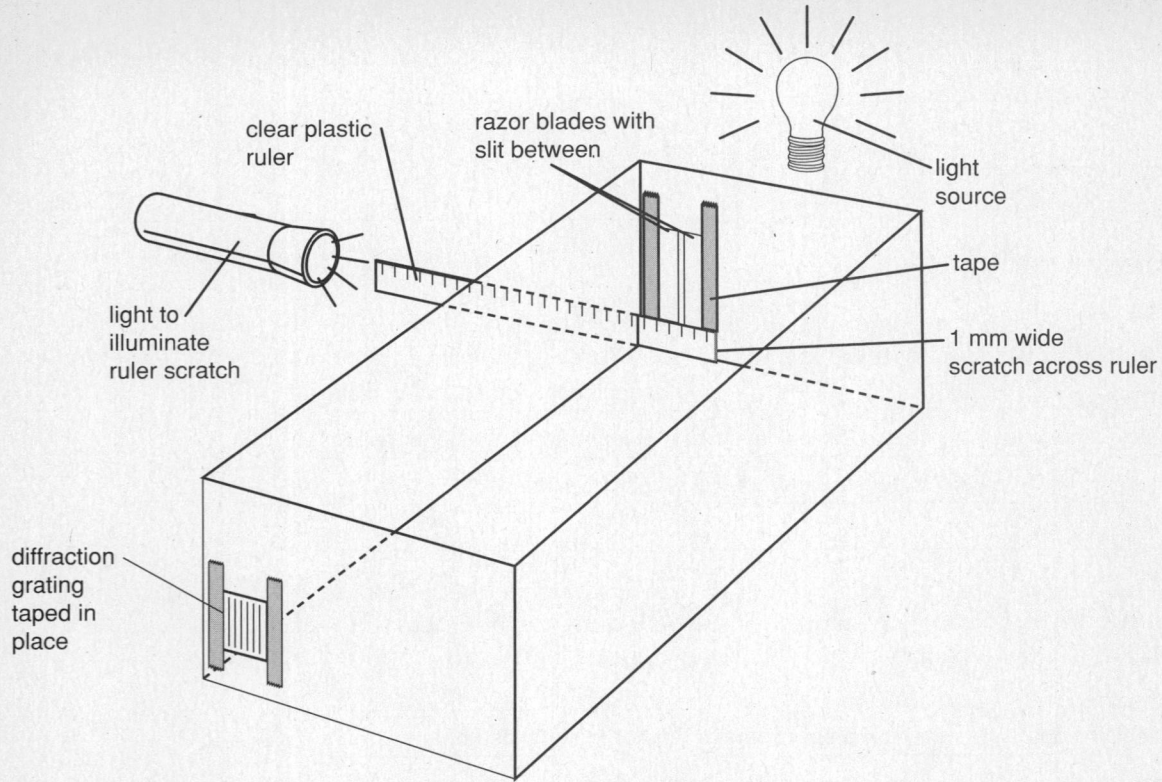

For each spectrometer, you will need a sturdy box with a cover, such as a shoe box (at least half as wide as it is long, and at least 3 inches deep), a clear plastic ruler, a razor knife, two razor blades, tape, and a strip of plastic diffraction grating. (Check your physics lab or obtain a diffraction grating from a cardboard tube spectroscope by popping out the cardboard disk eyepiece.)

One narrow end of the box will contain a slit opening, the other the diffraction grating eyepiece. About 2 cm from the left edge of one end and a ruler's width up from the bottom of the box, cut a slit opening that is 1 cm wide by 3 cm high. Inside the box, position a razor blade vertically so that it covers about half of the opening. Tape the razor blade in place. Over the opening, align the second razor blade edge with the first razor blade, leaving about a 1 mm slit between the blade edges. Tape the second blade in place. With the cover on, light should only be able to enter the box through the slit.

To make the eyepiece opening, cut a 2-cm square hole in the end of the box opposite the slit. The hole must be directly opposite and centered on the slit. Place the diffraction grating over the hole. Pointing the slit at a light source and looking through the grating should reveal a horizontal spectrum image to the right of the slit. Rotate the diffraction grating until this is seen, and tape the grating in place.

Cut a slit for the ruler in the side of the box adjacent to the corner next to the slit, and just above the box bottom. Slide the ruler into this opening. It should move only when pushed or pulled, sliding on edge across the box bottom under the slit and spectrum image. Roughen the plastic ruler in a 1-mm wide band across the width of the ruler between the 0 and 1 mm gradations. Light traveling down the length of the plastic will escape from this scratch and provide a visible marker inside the box. The scratch should face the eyepiece, and if not easily visible, the scratch may be deepened. A small light placed to shine onto the opposite end of the ruler outside the box will also brighten the scratch mark.

To calibrate the spectrometer, view a hydrogen gas spectrum tube. Push the ruler scratch mark under each line in the spectrum, and measure the distance on the ruler to the outside of the box. Graph these distances vs. the known wavelengths of the lines (red—656 nm, aqua—486 nm, violet—434 nm), connecting the points smoothly, and check that calibration graph against the 546 nm green line of mercury. Tape this reference graph to the top of the spectrometer box.

Name _____ Date _____ Class _____

Electron Distribution Using Peas

Lab 12

Text reference: **Chapter 4**

Introduction

Could you determine the exact position and momentum of a baseball as it soared through the air? Of course, you could—by taking a timed series of snapshots of the baseball as it moved. Why then can't scientists follow a similar procedure to determine the position and momentum of an electron?

You can see a moving baseball or its image because of the light bouncing off the baseball. The effect of light on either the position or the momentum of the baseball is negligible. By contrast, an electron has such an extremely small mass that light disturbs it in an unpredictable way. How then can the position and momentum of an electron be determined?

Knowledge of the behavior of electrons in the atom comes from theoretical work done in the 1920s by the German physicist Werner Heisenberg (1901–1976) and the Austrian physicist Erwin Schrodinger (1887–1961). Heisenberg postulated that it was impossible to determine exactly both the position and momentum of an electron at the same instant. Heisenberg deduced that the more precisely you know the position of an electron, the less certain you are about its momentum, and vice versa. Because its exact position and momentum can never be established at any given time, the exact path of an electron around the nucleus cannot be determined. Instead the quantum-mechanical model of the atom gives the probabilities of finding an electron in a particular region around the nucleus.

In this investigation, you will model the probable locations of electrons around the nucleus of an atom. You will use peas to represent electrons to help you visualize regions of high and low electron density.

Pre-Lab Discussion

Read the entire laboratory investigation and the relevant pages of your textbook. Then answer the questions that follow.

1. Why isn't it possible to determine the exact path of an electron in an atom? <u>To find the exact path of an electron, you must shine a light on it, thus disturbing its path.</u>

2. What does the quantum-mechanical model of the atom tell you about the location of an electron in an atom? <u>Quantum theory predicts the probability of finding electrons in a particular location. It cannot predict the precise path the electron took to get to the location.</u>

Materials (class of 30 in pairs)
30 pairs safety goggles
15 pieces of circular filter paper, 15–25 cm in diameter
15 metric rulers
15 marker pens
15 pairs scissors
15 tripod ring stands
15 compasses
15 sheets of newsprint or butcher paper
1-lb bag of dried peas
15 beakers, 150-mL
15 plastic containers

Time Required
30–50 minutes.

Advance Preparation
Physics teachers often have a roll of butcher paper. The art department usually has a supply of newsprint. Count out 100 peas, and determine an approximate volume for them. Have students measure out this volume of peas with a 150-mL beaker, so that they can count their peas from a reasonably sized sample.

Introduction
Show the class a Landsat photo that has been colored to indicate the population density of a region. Discuss the similarities between the photo and the quantum-mechanical model of the atom. No person is seen in the photo, but regions where a person is most likely to be found may be predicted.

You may wish to review the meaning of probability with your students before having them do this lab. You can also review Section 4–3 of the text dealing with Heisenberg's uncertainty principle.

© Prentice-Hall, Inc.

Electron Distribution Using Peas **67**

Name _____

3. What do the peas represent in this investigation? What setup do you use to distribute the peas around the nucleus? <u>The peas represent electrons. The number of peas per ring represents the probability of an electron being located in a specific location around the nucleus. The setup involves letting 100 peas drop through a filter-paper funnel on a ring stand and then watching the peas randomly roll to different positions on the target beneath the ring stand.</u>

4. How will you process your data to illustrate the probabilities of finding electrons in particular regions around the nucleus? <u>A graph of number of peas (electrons) in each region vs. distance from the nucleus will be drawn. The highest points or tallest bars on the graph represent the most probable locations for electrons, the highest electron densities.</u>

Problem
How can a model be used to represent the probable locations of electrons in an atom?

Materials
safety goggles
filter paper, circular
metric ruler
marker pen
scissors
tripod ring stand

compass
sheet of newsprint or butcher paper
dried peas
beaker, 150-mL
plastic container

Safety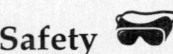
Wear your safety goggles during this investigation.

Procedure
 1. Put on your goggles. Fold the filter paper in half and then fold it again into quarters. Using the ruler, measure up 1.5 cm from the closed point of the paper and make a mark. Make a small hole in the bottom of the folded filter paper by cutting at the 1.5-cm mark with the scissors. Insert the cut filter paper into the ring of the tripod ring stand to create a funnel with the small hole at the bottom.

2. Use the compass to draw a circle with a radius of 3 cm in the center of a large sheet of paper. Then draw four more concentric circles 3 cm apart, around the first circle. Number the rings 1–5, starting from the center.

3. Mark the center of the innermost circle with a large dot. Let this dot represent the nucleus of the atom. Place the ring stand so that the hole in the filter paper is exactly above the large dot, or nucleus, as shown in Figure 12–1.

Safety
Make sure students wear their goggles at all times during this investigation. Caution students against throwing peas about the room or spilling them on the floor. ■

Name _____

Lab 12

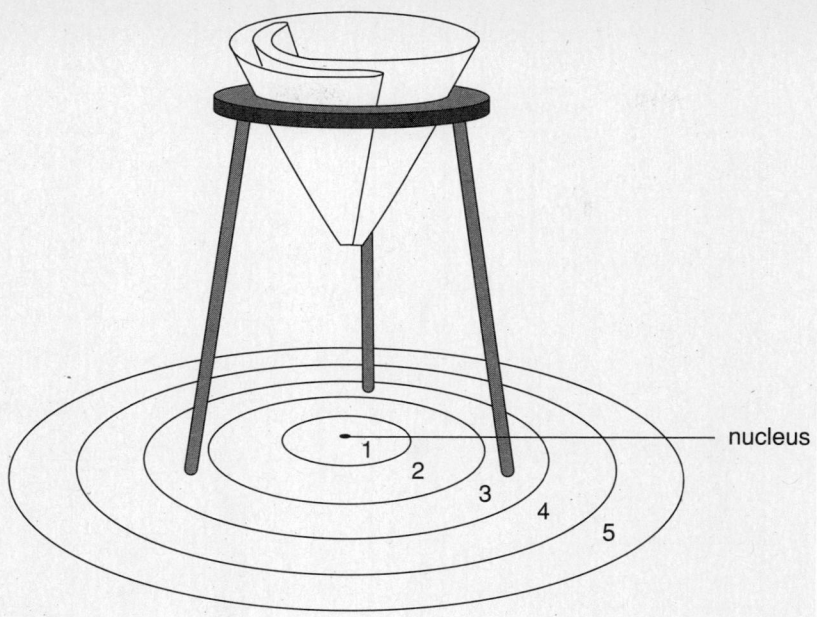

Figure 12–1

Teaching Tips

If you do not have compasses, substitute pencil and string. Students may have to use clay triangles to support the filter-paper funnels or you may wish to supply students with plastic funnels.

Students may have to adjust the size of the hole in the filter paper, depending on the rate at which peas fall or the distance they travel. If tripod stands are not available, substitute ring stands with iron rings. Make certain the iron ring is about 8 or 9 inches above the paper to avoid excess scattering of the peas. Scattering may be minimized by having the students set up the investigation on a tray. Regular paper may be substituted for filter paper. You may wish to have a student cut the paper circles before the beginning of the lab.

If time permits, pool the class data prior to graphing. This will ensure that a large enough sample is evaluated to obtain valid probabilities.

4. Count out 100 dried peas and place them in a plastic container. Pinch closed the hole at the base of the filter paper and add the 100 dried peas, or "electrons," to the filter. Let go of the filter, allowing the peas to fall through the small hole onto the target beneath the ring stand. If the peas jam up in the filter, push them gently to keep them moving.

5. Count the number of peas in each ring around the nucleus, as well as any that fall outside the rings. Record the data in the table, beginning with the innermost ring number 1.

6. Gather up the peas and place them in the plastic container. Return all equipment to the supply area. Clean up your work area and wash your hands before leaving the laboratory.

Observations (sample data)

DATA TABLE Distribution of Peas

Ring	Distance from Nucleus	Number of Peas in Ring
1	3 cm	5
2	6 cm	27
3	9 cm	22
4	12 cm	16
5	15 cm	11
outside the rings	beyond 15 cm	19

© Prentice-Hall, Inc.   *Electron Distribution Using Peas* **69**

Lab 12

Using the data in the table, graph the number of peas (vertical axis) vs. the distance from the nucleus (horizontal axis). This can be either a point average graph or a bar graph.

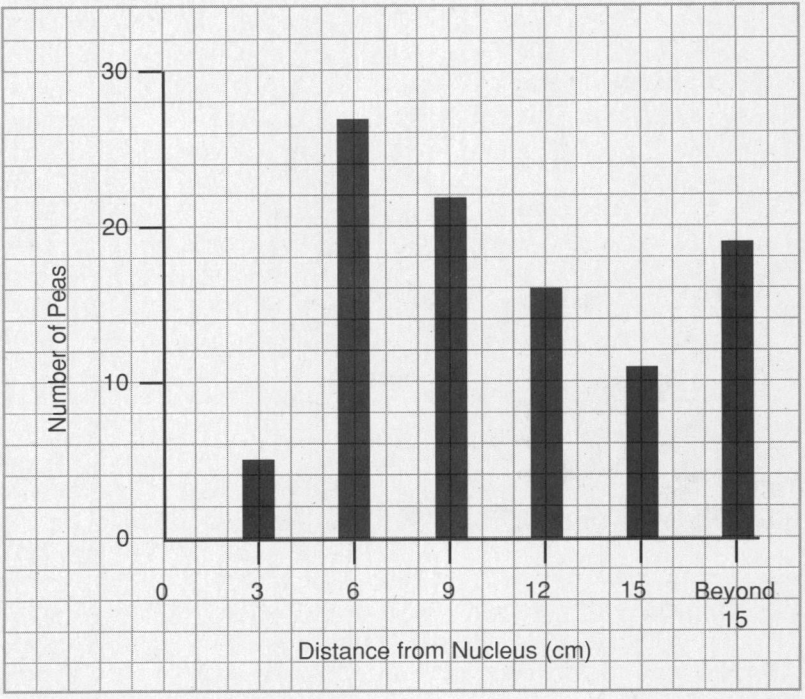

Critical Thinking: Analysis and Conclusions

1. Judging from your graph, in which region would you be most likely to find electrons? In which region would you be least likely to find electrons? *(Interpreting diagrams)* The probability of finding electrons is greatest in the regions represented by rings 2 and 3. The probability of finding electrons is least in rings 1 and 5.

2. Were you able to determine the exact path by which each pea (electron) arrived at its position on the target? How does this finding relate to the quantum theory? *(Developing models)* The exact path of each pea could not be predicted, nor could its path be determined after all the peas had dropped onto the target. This finding is in agreement with the quantum-mechanical idea that the exact path of an electron cannot be predicted or determined.

3. Which orbital do the results of this experiment best approximate? *(Making inferences)* The results look like the distribution in an *s* orbital.

Critical Thinking: Applications

1. What would your graph look like if you had used 200 peas instead of 100? *(Making predictions)* The numbers of peas would be larger, but the shape of the graph would be the same.

2. Write a brief paragraph explaining how the quantum-mechanical model of electron distribution in an atom differs from the Bohr model. *(Using the writing process)* Heisenberg postulated that the path of an electron could never be known because the precise position and momentum of an electron at any given moment cannot be determined. Therefore, you can only know the probability of an electron being at a given location. In the Bohr model, electrons travel around the nucleus in set paths—much like the planets orbiting the Sun.

3. Why do you think that many people persist in visualizing the atom according to the out-dated Bohr model as opposed to accepting the quantum-mechanical model? *(Making judgments)* The Bohr model corresponds with our knowledge of the world around us and is easy to visualize; the quantum theory is very abstract, deals with the subatomic world, and is hard to visualize.

Going Further

1. Playing darts is a popular recreational activity. Design an experiment using a dart game to model the probabilities for electron distribution within the atom. Graph the probabilities.

Going Further
1. Velcro balls and target boards are less dangerous for students to use than metal-tipped darts. Students may use spreadsheet software to display their probability data.

Mendeleev for a Day

Small Scale Lab 13

Text reference: **Chapter 5**

Introduction

As more and more elements were discovered during the 1800s, chemists began to categorize them according to similarities in chemical and physical properties. A Russian chemist, Dmitri Mendeleev (1834–1907), was more successful than most. He arranged the elements in vertical columns in order of increasing atomic mass. The columns were then arranged so that elements with similar chemical properties were placed side by side.

Mendeleev left numerous spaces in his table because there were no known elements with the appropriate properties to fill the spaces. (See Figure 13–1.) He then predicted the properties of these unknown elements based on the properties of the elements next to them on the periodic table. When these "missing elements" were discovered, they were found to have properties very similar to those predicted by Mendeleev.

Like Mendeleev, in this investigation you will group unknown compounds according to their chemical behaviors. You will see if a precipitate (solid substance) forms when two solutions are mixed together. You then will observe which precipitates are dissolved by another solution. Finally you will record any color changes that occur when two solutions are mixed together. After analyzing your data, you will place each unknown solution into a group with other solutions of similar characteristics.

Materials (class of 30 in pairs)
- 30 pairs chemical splash goggles
- 30 laboratory aprons
- 45 test tubes
- 15 marking pens
- 15 test-tube racks
- 15 graduated cylinders, 10-mL
- 100 mL of the following eleven solutions:
    - sodium bromide (NaBr), 0.5 M
    - calcium nitrate (Ca(NO$_3$)$_2$), 0.30 M
    - lithium carbonate (Li$_2$CO$_3$), 0.18 M
    - barium nitrate (Ba(NO$_3$)$_2$), 0.15 M
    - sodium iodide (NaI), 0.33 M
    - potassium carbonate (K$_2$CO$_3$), 0.50 M
    - sodium chloride (NaCl), 1.0 M
    - sodium carbonate (Na$_2$CO$_3$), 0.35 M
    - strontium nitrate (Sr(NO$_3$)$_2$), 0.75 M
    - lead nitrate (Pb(NO$_3$)$_2$), 0.23 M
    - sodium sulfate (Na$_2$SO$_4$), 1.0 M
- 4 drops hydrochloric acid (HCl), 1 M
- 1 mL phenolphthalein, 1%
- 200 mL nitric acid (HNO$_3$), 3 M
- 60 micropipets, 6-mL capacity
- 15 stirring rods

Time Required
45 minutes.

Advance Preparation
Prepare the following solutions by dissolving the specified amounts of the specified compounds in 100 mL distilled water:
solution #1: NaBr, 5.0 g
solution #2: Ca(NO$_3$)$_2$, 5.0 g

			Ti = 50	Zr = 90	? = 180.
			V = 51	Nb = 94	Ta = 182.
			Cr = 52	Mo = 96	W = 186.
			Mn = 55	Rh = 104,4	Pt = 197,4
			Fe = 56	Ru = 104,4	Ir = 198.
		Ni = Co = 59	Pd = 106,6	Os = 199.
H = 1			Cu = 63,4	Ag = 108	Hg = 200.
	Be = 9,4	Mg = 24	Zn = 65,2	Cd = 112	
	B = 11	Al = 27,4	? = 68	Ur = 116	Au = 197?
	C = 12	Si = 28	? = 70	Sn = 118	
	N = 14	P = 31	As = 75	Sb = 122	Bi = 210?
	O = 16	S = 32	Se = 79,4	Te = 128?	
	F = 19	Cl = 35,5	Br = 80	I = 127	
Li = 1	Na = 23	K = 39	Rb = 85,4	Cs = 133	Tl = 204
		Ca = 40	Sr = 87,6	Ba = 137	Pb = 207.
		? = 45	Ce = 92		
		?Er = 56	La = 94		
		?Yt = 60	Di = 95		
		?In = 75,6	Th = 118?		

Figure 13–1 *Mendeleev's Periodic Table (1869)*

Small Scale Lab 13

solution #3: Li_2CO_3, 1.25 g
solution #4: $Ba(NO_3)_2$, 4.0 g
solution #5: NaI, 4.5 g
solution #6: K_2CO_3, 7.5 g
solution #7: NaCl, 5.8 g
solution #8: Na_2CO_3, 3.75 g
solution #9: $Sr(NO_3)_2$, 16 g
test solution A: $Pb(NO_3)_2$, 7.5 g
test solution B: Na_2SO_4, 15 g

To prepare test solution C, add 4 drops of 1 M HCl to 1 mL of 1% phenolphthalein.

To prepare test solution D, slowly add 38 mL of concentrated nitric acid to 100 mL of water and then dilute to 200 mL. CAUTION: Concentrated HNO_3 is very corrosive. Avoid contact with skin or clothing. Wash spills with large amounts of water.

Unknown solutions can be placed in flasks, and the students can dispense the required amounts into the graduated cylinder. An alternative would be to place the unknown solutions in burettes. Students can dispense 3–4 mL of an unknown into one test tube and divide it into roughly equal amounts for each of three test tubes. Exact amounts are not critical.

Place the test solutions in 6-mL capacity micropipets and give each lab pair a set of four. This approach is easier than using dropper pipettes. Have ready a labeled container in which to collect waste $Pb(NO_3)_2$, $Ba(NO_3)_2$, and $SrCO_3$.

Introduction

To give students a flavor of Mendeleev's life, you may wish to show the following video the day before students do this lab: *Mendeleev: Father of the Periodic Table*, 28 minutes, color. This video is available from Films for the Humanities & Sciences, P.O. Box 2053, Princeton, NJ 08543-2053.

Safety

Make sure students wear their goggles and lab aprons at all times during the

Name _____

Pre-Lab Discussion

Read the entire laboratory investigation and the relevant pages of your textbook. Then answer the questions that follow.

1. How does Mendeleev's periodic table differ from the modern periodic table? __The modern periodic table is arranged in order of increasing atomic number, while Mendeleev's periodic table was arranged in order of increasing atomic mass. Also, the positions of some elements are different, and some elements are missing from Mendeleev's table.__

2. Why did Mendeleev leave blank spaces on his periodic table? Did later discoveries justify his predictions? __Mendeleev left blank spaces in his periodic table to accommodate as-yet undiscovered elements that were predicted by his table. Elements discovered later had properties very similar to those predicted by Mendeleev.__

3. Why is it necessary to mix any solution that does not show an immediate change? __To enhance any reaction that might occur by bringing the reactants into contact.__

4. Why is it necessary to rinse each test tube thoroughly between trials? __To prevent contamination of the results of the next reaction.__

5. Which solutions need to be disposed of in a special container? __Test solution A and unknown solutions 4 and 9.__

Problem

How can you group compounds according to their chemical behavior?

Materials

chemical splash goggles
laboratory apron
3 test tubes
marking pen
test-tube rack

graduated cylinder, 10-mL
unknown solutions 1–9
4 micropipets containing test
    solutions A, B, C, and D
stirring rod

Safety

Wear your goggles and lab apron at all times during the investigation. Since you are dealing with unknown solutions, consider them all to be corrosive and toxic, and avoid direct contact. If you spill a solution on yourself, report the spill immediately to your teacher and wash the affected area with large amounts of cold running water. Note the caution alert symbols here and with certain steps of the Procedure. Refer to page xi for the specific precautions associated with each symbol.

74 © Prentice-Hall, Inc.

Name _____

Procedure

1. Put on your goggles and lab apron.
2. Label three test tubes A, B, and C with the marking pen. Using the graduated cylinder, obtain 3 mL of solution 1. Place 1 mL into each of the three test tubes. **CAUTION:** *Some of the solutions that you will use in this investigation are corrosive. Avoid direct contact with all of them.*
3. To test tube A, add 12 drops of test solution A.
4. To test tube B, add 12 drops of test solution B.
5. To test tube C, add 12 drops of test solution C.
6. Any test tube that does not show an immediate change should be stirred for at least 10 seconds. Rinse the stirring rod after each use. Record all results in the Data Table.
7. To any test tube that contains a precipitate, add 20 drops of test solution D and stir for at least 15 seconds. Rinse the stirring rod after each use. Record all results.

8. Pour the waste materials in test tube A into a labeled container provided by your teacher. Rinse out the test tubes and graduated cylinder thoroughly for use in the next set of tests.
9. Repeat Steps 2 through 8 for each of the other solutions. When you are done testing solutions 4 and 9, pour the waste material into the labeled containers provided by your teacher.

10. Clean up your work area and wash your hands before leaving the laboratory.

Observations (sample data)

DATA TABLE   Reactions of Unknown Solutions

Unknown	A-ppt?	B-ppt?	C-Color	D-Dissolved?
1	yes	no	no	no
2	no	yes	no	yes
3	yes	no	pink	yes
4	no	yes	no	yes
5	yes, yellow	no	no	no
6	yes	no	pink	yes
7	yes	no	no	no
8	yes	no	pink	yes
9	no	yes	no	yes

investigation. Nitric acid (test solution D) is corrosive. Spills should be cleaned by flushing with large quantities of water. Lead, barium, and strontium compounds should all be considered toxic. Avoid contact with them. ■

Teaching Tips

Although students have not been introduced to chemical equations at this point, here are the reactions that they will observe:

$2NaBr(aq) + Pb(NO_3)_2(aq) \rightarrow 2NaNO_3(aq) + PbBr_2(s)$
$2NaI(aq) + Pb(NO_3)_2(aq) \rightarrow 2NaNO_3(aq) + PbI_2(s)$
$2NaCl(aq) + Pb(NO_3)_2(aq) \rightarrow 2NaNO_3(aq) + PbCl_2(s)$
$Ca(NO_3)_2(aq) + Na_2SO_4(aq) \rightarrow 2NaNO_3(aq) + CaSO_4(s)$
$Ba(NO_3)_2(aq) + Na_2SO_4(aq) \rightarrow 2NaNO_3(aq) + BaSO_4(s)$
$Sr(NO_3)_2(aq) + Na_2SO_4(aq) \rightarrow 2NaNO_3(aq) + SrSO_4(s)$
$Li_2CO_3(aq) + Pb(NO_3)_2(aq) \rightarrow 2LiNO_3(aq) + PbCO_3(s)$
$K_2CO_3(aq) + Pb(NO_3)_2(aq) \rightarrow 2KNO_3(aq) + PbCO_3(s)$
$Na_2CO_3(aq) + Pb(NO_3)_2(aq) \rightarrow 2NaNO_3(aq) + PbCO_3(s)$
$CO_3^{2-} + H_2O \rightarrow HCO_3^- + OH^-$

In Step 7 of the Procedure, you may substitute a vortex machine if you have one.

You may decide whether or not to reveal the identities of the unknown solutions. If you do reveal them, discuss with students how the elements fit into groups in the periodic table.

Waste Disposal

Solutions containing test solution A ($Pb(NO_3)_2$) unknown 4 ($Ba(NO_3)_2$), and unknown 9 ($Sr(NO_3)_2$), should be collected in separate labeled containers. Precipitate the lead with excess chloride ion and filter out the $PbCl_2$. Precipitate the barium with excess sulfate ion and filter out $BaSO_4$. Precipitate the strontium with excess

Mendeleev for a Day 75

carbonate ion, and filter out the SrCO₃. Store the precipitates separately for shipment to a secure landfill. Filtrates may be flushed down the drain with plenty of water. ■

Name _____

Critical Thinking: Analysis and Conclusions

1. Why do you think that this investigation is titled "Mendeleev for a Day"? *(Drawing conclusions)* <u>The student is grouping unknowns based on similarities in chemical properties just as Mendeleev did.</u>

2. Based on your observations, group the unknown solutions into families according to similarities in chemical behavior. Justify your answer with data from this investigation. *(Interpreting data)* <u>One group consists of unknowns #1, 5, and 7. They formed a precipitate with A that didn't dissolve with D. They had no reaction with B or C. A second group is unknowns #2, 4, and 9. They had no reaction with A or C. They formed a precipitate with B that dissolved with D. A third group is unknowns #3, 6, and 8. They formed a precipitate with A that dissolved in D. They had no reaction with B and turned pink with C.</u>

3. Why didn't all members of the same family show identical reactions? Give an example of a reaction that was similar but not identical. *(Developing hypotheses)* <u>They may have the same outer electron configurations but different core configurations. Unknown solution #5 formed a yellow precipitate with A while unknowns #1 and #7 formed white precipitates.</u>

Critical Thinking: Applications

1. Suppose you could do experiments with your unknowns in which you reacted each of them with oxygen to form an oxide, as Mendeleev did. How would this information help you determine the location of the compounds in the periodic table? *(Making predictions)* <u>Compounds with a formula of X₂O would go in Group 1 (1A). Compounds with the formula XO would go in Group 2 (2A). Compounds that did not form an oxide would go into another group</u>

2. No members of Group 8A (18) of the modern periodic table can be found on the version of Mendeleev's table shown in Figure 13–1. Suggest an explanation for their absence. *(Making inferences)* <u>Group 8A (18) contains the noble gases. Because these gases are so unreactive, they were difficult to isolate and identify. No noble gases had been discovered at that time.</u>

Going Further

1. Research the contributions that scientists other than Mendeleev have made to the development of the modern periodic table. Prepare a short oral report to present to the class.

Name _____ Date _____ Class _____

Chemical Activity of Metals

Small Scale Lab 14

Text reference: **Chapter 5**

Introduction

Have you ever noticed that some people are more active than others? Some people play a variety of physical sports while other people like to sit and read. You can think of elements in much the same way. In the case of an element, its activity level is a measure of its ability to react chemically with other elements.

Many metals will react with ions of another metal in solution. You can tell that a reaction has occurred because the metallic ions that come out of solution form a solid precipitate of that metal. At the same time, atoms of the more active metal go into solution. Chemists use the degree of activity to predict what changes will occur in certain reactions. For example, a more active metal will always replace a less active metal in a compound. This is called a single replacement reaction, which you will study in more detail in Chapter 9.

In this experiment, you will use three metals and four solutions of compounds that contain different kinds of metallic ions. You will put each metal into a separate sample of each solution and observe what happens. If a reaction occurs, you will notice a solid precipitate forming on the metal. If a particular metal reacts with the ions of many other metals, then that metal is a chemically active metal. If a metal reacts with few or none of the other metals, then it is chemically inactive. From your observations in this experiment, you will be able to arrange the four metals in the order of their chemical activity.

Materials (class of 30 in pairs)
- 30 pairs chemical splash goggles
- 30 laboratory aprons
- 15 well plates, 24-well
- 15 marking pens
- 30 pairs latex gloves
- 60 thin-stem micropipets
- 100 mL copper(II) nitrate, $(Cu(NO_3)_2)$, 0.1 M
- 100 mL magnesium nitrate, $(Mg(NO_3)_2)$, 0.1 M
- 100 mL zinc nitrate, $(Zn(NO_3)_2)$, 0.1 M
- 100 mL silver nitrate, $(AgNO_3)$, 0.1 M
- 15 eyedroppers
- 50-cm copper strip
- 50-cm magnesium ribbon
- 50-cm zinc ribbon or mossy zinc

Time Required
30 minutes.

Advance Preparation
Prepare 0.1 M solutions by adding the specified masses of the following solutes to enough water to bring the volume up to 100 mL:
- 2.41 g $Cu(NO_3)_2 \cdot 3H_2O$
- 2.56 g $Mg(NO_3)_2 \cdot 6H_2O$
- 2.97 g $Zn(NO_3)_2 \cdot 6H_2O$
- 1.70 g $AgNO_3$

Prepare and label 15 sets of four thin-stem micropipets, corresponding to each of the four solutions. You may wish to use dropper bottles for each of the solutions instead of thin-stem micropipets.

A good size for the metal strips is 3.0 cm × 0.5 cm × 0.05 cm per group, although the sizes are not critical. You may need to cut these pieces ahead of time. Have the students cut their strips of each metal into four pieces. The metal strips will react at

Pre-Lab Discussion

1. What does the term *chemical activity* mean? The term *chemical activity* refers to a substance's ability to react chemically. An active substance reacts with many other substances; an inactive substance reacts with few or none.

2. What evidence of chemical activity will you be looking for in this investigation? The formation of a precipitate.

3. What are the hazards in handling silver nitrate and what precautions should you follow? Silver nitrate is poisonous if swallowed, and will stain skin or clothing if spilled. When handling silver nitrate, gloves should be worn.

Problem

How does the chemical activity of each of four metals compare?

© Prentice-Hall, Inc.

Chemical Activity of Metals **77**

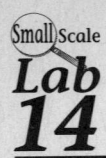

Small Scale Lab 14

Name _____

a faster rate if they are cleaned with a piece of steel wool before beginning the experiment. Have a container ready to collect the waste silver nitrate solution.

Introduction

Several days before beginning this investigation, you may want to do the following as a demonstration. In a 100-mL beaker, put a strip of zinc into a solution of copper(II) nitrate (dissolve about 10 grams of $Cu(NO_3)_2 \cdot 3H_2O$ in 80 mL of water). The blue color of the copper(II) ion in the solution will gradually fade away over several days as the zinc metal "dissolves" and replaces the copper(II) ion. Explain to the students how this demonstration relates to the reactions they will observe on the well plate.

Safety

Make sure students wear their goggles and lab aprons at all times during the investigation. Caution students to wear gloves when handling silver nitrate solution. It is toxic and will stain skin and clothing. A dilute solution of ammonia water will help remove $AgNO_3$ stains from the skin. Commercial laundry pretreatments may remove stains from clothing. ∎

Materials

chemical splash goggles
laboratory apron
well plate
marking pen
latex gloves
4 micropipets, filled with solutions of:
   copper(II) nitrate, $(Cu(NO_3)_2)$
   magnesium nitrate, $(Mg(NO_3)_2)$

zinc nitrate, $(Zn(NO_3)_2)$
silver nitrate, $(AgNO_3)$
4 pieces each of the following metals:
   copper
   magnesium
   zinc
eyedropper

Safety

Wear your goggles and lab apron at all times during the investigation. Handle all chemicals with care; avoid spills and contact with your skin. Wear gloves when handling silver nitrate solution. Note the caution alert symbols here and with certain steps of the Procedure. Refer to page xi for the specific precautions associated with each symbol.

Procedure

1. Put on your goggles and lab apron. Using the marking pen, label the wells in the well plate from left to right along the top row 1, 2, 3, and 4. Label the rows down the left side A, B, C, and D.

2. Use the micropipet labeled $Cu(NO_3)_2$ to place 8 drops of copper(II) nitrate, $Cu(NO_3)_2$, into wells A1, B1, C1, and D1. See Figure 14–1.

3. Using the micropipet labeled $Mg(NO_3)_2$, place 8 drops of magnesium nitrate, $Mg(NO_3)_2$, into wells A2, B2, C2, and D2.

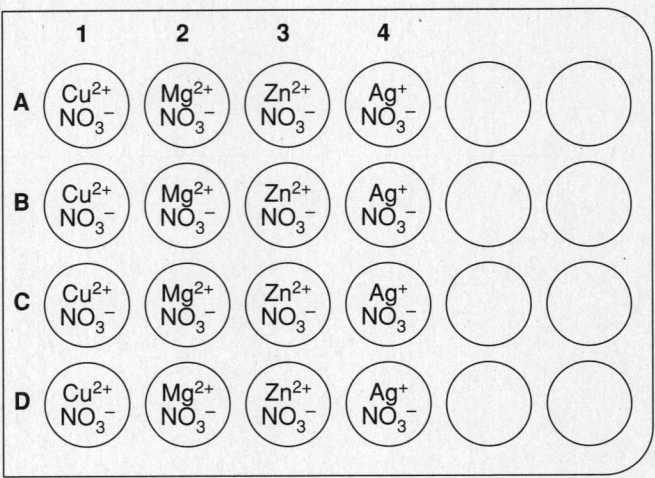

Figure 14–1

78

Name _____

Small Scale Lab 14

4. Using the micropipet labeled *Zn(NO₃)₂*, place 8 drops of zinc nitrate, $Zn(NO_3)_2$, into wells A3, B3, C3, and D3.

5. Put on latex gloves. Using the micropipet labeled *AgNO₃*, place 8 drops of silver nitrate, $AgNO_3$, into wells A4, B4, C4, and D4.
CAUTION: *Silver nitrate is poisonous if ingested. Be careful not to get it on your skin or clothing, as it will produce a stain that is hard to remove. If any spills occur, ask your teacher how to clean up safely.*

6. Place one piece of copper metal into each of the wells in row A (wells A1, A2, A3, and A4).

7. Place one piece of magnesium metal into wells B1, B2, B3, and B4.

8. Place one piece of zinc metal into wells C1, C2, C3, and C4. (Note: Strips of silver are not used because of the expense. Had silver been used, you would have been directed to put strips of it into wells D1, D2, D3, and D4. The results you would have obtained have been put into the Data Table for you.)

9. Chemical reactions will take place in some of the wells in rows A, B, and C. Placing the well plate on white paper will make it easier to observe any changes that occur. Observe what happens for five minutes. In the Data Table, record what happens to each metal. If a metal does not change, write NR for No Reaction.

10. Look at the metal samples you used. Describe the appearance of the metals on the lines provided.

11. Use an eyedropper to transfer all the silver nitrate solution from the well plate to a container provided by your teacher. Dispose of all other chemicals according to your teacher's instructions. Clean up your work area and wash your hands before leaving the laboratory.

Teaching Tips
This lab emphasizes qualitative comparisons of chemical activity. Lab 58 in Chapter 20 covers oxidation and reduction reactions in detail, using similar chemicals.

Although equation writing is not discussed until Chapter 9, you may wish to put the following equations on the board and discuss the reactions.

A4: $Cu(s) + 2AgNO_3(aq) \rightarrow 2Ag(s) + Cu(NO_3)_2(s)$
B1: $Mg(s) + Cu(NO_3)_2(aq) \rightarrow Cu(s) + Mg(NO_3)_2(s)$
B3: $Mg(s) + Zn(NO_3)_2(aq) \rightarrow Zn(s) + Mg(NO_3)_2(s)$
B4: $Mg(s) + 2AgNO_3(aq) \rightarrow 2Ag(s) + Mg(NO_3)_2(s)$
C1: $Zn(s) + Cu(NO_3)_2(aq) \rightarrow Cu(s) + Zn(NO_3)_2(s)$
C4: $Zn(s) + 2AgNO_3(aq) \rightarrow 2Ag(s) + Zn(NO_3)_2(s)$

To reduce the amount of materials used, have several groups of students share one set of labeled micropipets. These sets can be stored in boxes from cassette tapes and saved for reuse.

Waste Disposal
Silver compounds are regulated as hazardous waste (EPA waste #D011). Instruct students to use an eyedropper or micropipet to pull up the material in the Column 4 wells of their well plates and to deposit it into a clearly marked container. Similarly collect any $AgNO_3$ solution to be discarded from the micropipets. Precipitate the Ag^+ ions with excess NaCl solution. Filter out the precipitate and store for commercial disposal. Discard the filtrate. ■

Observations (sample data)
DATA TABLE

		1	2	3	4
		Cu^{2+} NO_3^-	Mg^{2+} NO_3^-	Zn^{2+} NO_3^-	Ag^+ NO_3^-
A	Cu	NR	NR	NR	Cu turns black
B	Mg	Mg turns gray	NR	Mg turns gray	Mg turns black
C	Zn	Zn turns black	NR	NR	Zn turns black
D	Ag	NR	NR	NR	NR

Appearance of metals _____

_____

_____

Chemical Activity of Metals 79

Small Scale Lab 14

Name _____

Critical Thinking: Analysis and Conclusions

1. What similarities and differences in physical properties (e.g., hardness, color, shine) did you see when you looked at the metals? *(Making comparisons)* Copper is red-orange colored. The others are silvery. Mg is brighter and shinier than zinc. All are hard and all are at least somewhat shiny.

2. Which of the four metals reacted with the greatest number of solutions? *(Interpreting data)* Magnesium. It reacted with three of the four solutions.

3. Which of the four metals reacted with the least number of solutions? *(Interpreting data)* Silver. It did not react with any of the four solutions.

4. List the metals from the most active to the least active. *(Making comparisons)* Magnesium, zinc, copper, silver.

Critical Thinking: Applications

1. The Statue of Liberty is made of copper. Use your investigation results to explain why copper is a better material for a statue than magnesium or zinc. *(Applying concepts)* Copper is less chemically active than magnesium or zinc. Hence, copper reacts less readily with substances in the environment.

2. Gold does not react with any of the solutions used in this investigation. What does this tell you about gold's chemical activity? *(Making inferences)* Like silver, gold is inactive.

3. How does the chemical activity of gold account for its use in jewelry? *(Applying concepts)* It does not readily react with other substances and therefore will keep its shiny appearance.

4. Lead is less active than zinc but more active than copper. Predict the results if lead metal is put into separate solutions of zinc nitrate and copper(II) nitrate. *(Making predictions)* Lead metal will not react with zinc nitrate solution. Lead will react with copper(II) nitrate, forming copper and lead nitrate.

Going Further

1. Research the metals that are used to make coins. Explain the choice of these coinage metals in terms of their chemical activity.
2. Visit a cookware store or department and find out what metals are used to make pots and pans. What kinds of foods react with these metals? Explain your findings in terms of the activity of metals.

Name _____ Date _____ Class _____

Relative Mass with Beans

Lab 15
APPLICATION

Text reference: **Chapter 5**

Introduction

A traveler from Honolulu, Hawaii, going to St. Paul, Minnesota, arrives at the airport in Minnesota and sees a sign displaying the local temperature as 20 degrees. At first the traveler wishes she had brought a warm coat and gloves, but she quickly realizes her mistake. A longer look at the sign tells her the temperature is 20 degrees Celsius, which is 68 degrees Fahrenheit. The moment of confusion occurred because the traveler had forgotten that temperature can be measured on more than one scale, or against different standards. A standard is a defined value or measure to which other measurements are compared. For example, the boiling point and freezing point of water are defined as 0 degrees and 100 degrees respectively on the Celsius scale. Other temperatures are measured in Celsius degrees relative to those points.

Another example of the use of a standard is the atomic mass assigned to each element in the periodic table of the elements. The standard for atomic masses is the carbon-12 atom, which is assigned a mass of exactly 12 atomic mass units (amu). The other elements are assigned masses measured by this standard, starting with 1.01 amu for hydrogen, and going above 200 amu for the heaviest elements.

It may be difficult to visualize the concept of the relative mass of atoms. The protons and neutrons in their nuclei are far too small to be counted, and atoms cannot be placed individually on a balance. One way to work with this concept on a visible scale is to use a model. In the present investigation, beans of different varieties represent atoms of different elements. Like isotopes of one element, beans of one variety have individual masses that are very similar, but not identical. Like atoms of different elements, beans of different varieties have average masses that are measurably different.

In this investigation you will measure equal numbers of different bean varieties in order to derive a standard unit for bean mass. You will then be able to assign relative masses to each bean variety based on this standard. While you will certainly be able to distinguish them, you will make no measurements with individual beans.

Pre-Lab Discussion

Read the entire laboratory investigation and the relevant pages of your textbook. Then answer the questions that follow.

1. What is the standard for comparison for the relative masses of the elements listed in the periodic table? What is the relative mass assigned to this standard? <u>The standard of comparison for relative mass is the carbon-12 atom, which is assigned a mass of exactly 12 amu.</u>

Materials (class of 30 in pairs)
30 pairs safety goggles
30 laboratory aprons
15 graduated cylinders, 50- or 100-mL
60 beakers, 150-mL
15 wax marking pencils
15 funnels
200 g (1/4 lb) navy beans
600 g (2/3 lb) kidney beans
400 g (1/2 lb) pinto beans
1200 g (1 1/4 lb) lima beans
60 paper cups
15 laboratory balances

Time Required
30 minutes. If you wish to shorten the time needed and reduce spillage of beans, prepare 15 sets of four beakers containing approximately the required amounts of each variety of bean. Allow extra time if you wish to have a class discussion about the Critical Thinking questions.

Advance Preparation
Have ready supplies of each variety of beans. There is usually a large variety of dried beans available in pound packages from the local grocery store. Biology teachers may also have a supply that you can borrow.

Introduction
Encourage students to come up with their own examples of measurements made against a standard. (Students should already be familiar with metric measures of length and mass. You might also mention the many different currency standards used by the nations of the world. Clothing sizes, while supposedly standard, are not always reliable.) Discuss how

© Prentice-Hall, Inc.

Relative Mass with Beans **81**

Lab 15
APPLICATION

different standards of measurement can affect perceptions and make comparisons difficult.

Pose students the following problem: Suppose you were in charge of purchasing 200 apples for an apple-bobbing contest. How could you accomplish your job without actually having to count apples at the grocery store? (Students eventually should reach the conclusion that they can weigh one apple, multiply by 200, and measure out that weight of apples to get their supply.) Ask students what assumptions about the apples they need to make (they are uniform in weight), and what purpose the first apple serves (it serves as a standard by which the other apples are measured).

This investigation lays the groundwork for getting students to think about measuring mass as a way of counting molecules—a concept they will need later. Focus on this idea when you discuss Pre-Lab Question 4.

Safety
Make sure students wear their goggles and lab aprons at all times during the investigation. Caution them to pick up any beans that roll onto the floor. Do not permit students to throw beans about the classroom. ■

Teaching Tips
Almost any variety of bean will show suitable variation in mass to work in this investigation. If you choose not to set up the 15 sets of beakers in advance, the beans can most easily be distributed by placing them at

Name _____

2. What will you use as the standard for comparison in determining the relative masses of the beans in this investigation? __The standard for comparison will be the smallest average bean mass of all the varieties measured.__

3. What characteristics of beans enable you to use them as models for atoms of different elements? __Each variety of bean has a range of masses, corresponding to the isotopes of an element, and the average masses of the four varieties differ, as do the atomic masses of different elements.__

4. In this investigation you will establish an average mass for each kind of bean. How could you use this average to measure out a given number of beans without actually counting them? __Multiply the number of beans desired by the average mass of one bean, and measure out that resulting mass (in beans) on the balance.__

Problem
How can the principle of relative atomic mass be modeled using beans?

Materials
safety goggles
laboratory apron
graduated cylinder, 50- or 100-mL
4 beakers, 150-mL
wax marking pencil
funnel

navy beans
kidney beans
pinto beans
lima beans
4 paper cups
laboratory balance

Safety

Wear your goggles and lab apron at all times during the investigation. If any beans spill on the floor, pick them up immediately so that no one slips on them. Note the caution alert symbols here and with certain steps of the Procedure. Refer to page xi for the specific precautions associated with each symbol.

Procedure

 1. Put on your goggles and lab apron.
 2. With the marking pencil, label each of the four beakers: *navy, kidney, pinto,* and *lima.* Using the graduated cylinder and a funnel, pour 17–20 mL of navy beans, 55–60 mL of kidney beans, 35–40 mL of pinto beans, and 110–115 mL of lima beans into the respective beakers.

82 © Prentice-Hall, Inc.

3. Label each of the four paper cups with the name of one variety of bean.

4. Measure the mass of each cup and record the value in your Data Table.

5. Count out 60 beans of each variety and place them in their respective cups.

6. Measure the masses of the cups with their contents and record these values in your Data Table.

7. Return each kind of bean to its original container.

8. Clean up your work area and wash your hands before leaving the laboratory.

Observations (sample data)

DATA TABLE Relative Mass of Beans

Bean Variety	Navy	Kidney	Pinto	Lima
Mass of Cup (g)	1.79	1.80	1.82	1.92
Mass of Cup and Beans (g)	13.39	38.88	24.71	72.87
Mass of Beans (g)	11.60	37.08	22.89	70.95
Average Mass per Bean (g)	0.1933	0.6180	0.3815	1.1825
Relative Mass of Beans (u)	1.0	3.2	2.0	6.1

Calculations (based on sample data)

1. Calculate the total mass of the 60 beans in each cup and record this value in your Data Table.

   mass of cup and navy beans − mass of cup = mass of navy beans

   13.39 g − 1.79 g = 11.60 g

2. Calculate the average mass per bean for each variety of bean and record each value in your Data Table.

   $$\frac{\text{mass of 60 pinto beans}}{60 \text{ beans}} = \text{average mass of one pinto bean}$$

   $$\frac{22.89 \text{ g}}{60 \text{ beans}} = 0.3815 \text{ g per bean}$$

stations in large labeled beakers. Mixing can be avoided by placing only one kind of bean at each station. Having more than one beaker of beans at each station will shorten the lab time. Make sure the funnels have a large opening or they will clog up—especially with the lima beans. Students can make their own funnels out of filter paper.

Remind students that the masses of individual atoms of an element vary according to what isotope they are. Isotopes differ from one another in mass, roughly speaking, by whole multiples of the hydrogen atomic mass. The masses of beans will not vary in such a stepwise manner.

Students may benefit from a discussion the next day about Analysis and Conclusions Question 5. Also discuss Applications Questions 4–7, again focusing on using mass as a way to count particles.

Waste Disposal

The dried beans may be saved from year to year. If stored in a dry, airtight container they will last indefinitely. ■

Name _____

3. Use the smallest average bean mass among the varieties measured as the standard to calculate the relative mass of each variety of bean. Assign the smallest average bean mass the relative mass of 1.0 u, where *u* stands for relative mass unit. Calculate the relative mass of each of the other varieties to the nearest tenth by using the following equation, and record the values in the data table:

$$\frac{1.0 \text{ u}}{\text{smallest average mass (g)}} = \frac{\text{u of bean variety}}{\text{average mass for bean variety (g)}}$$

$$\frac{1.0 \text{ u}}{0.1933 \text{ g}} = \frac{\text{relative mass}}{0.6180 \text{ g}}$$

relative mass of kidney bean = 3.2 u

Critical Thinking: Analysis and Conclusions

1. Which bean variety qualified as the standard for comparison? *(Interpreting data)* Navy beans.

2. How much greater is the average mass per bean of the largest variety of bean than the average mass per bean of the smallest variety of bean? *(Making comparisons)* Answers will vary. Students most probably will report that the average mass per bean of the lima beans is about 6 times greater than the average mass per bean of the navy beans.

3. If you assigned a relative mass of 1.0 u to the variety with the greatest average mass per bean, which variety would it be, and what would then be the relative masses of the other bean varieties? *(Interpreting data)* Lima beans. Navy beans would then have a relative mass of 0.16 u, kidney beans a relative mass of 0.52 u, and pinto beans a relative mass of 0.33 u.

4. What might be the drawbacks to assigning a relative mass of 1.0 u to the bean variety with the greatest average bean mass? *(Drawing conclusions)* Some major drawbacks would be that the relative masses would all be small, fractional, and more difficult to compare with each other.

5. Once you have set the standard for relative mass of beans, how can you use a chemical balance to measure out equal numbers of two varieties of beans? (Hint: Look back at your answer to Pre-Lab Question 4.) *(Applying concepts)* If you know the relative masses of the two varieties, you can measure equal numbers of beans so long as the ratio of their masses in grams is equal to the ratio of their relative masses.

Critical Thinking: Applications

1. Write a description of how your work in this investigation models the work of chemists in assigning relative atomic masses to the elements. *(Using the writing process)* The relative masses of each of the bean varieties were measured in comparison to a standard defined as part of the investigation. Chemists measure the relative atomic masses of the elements against the defined standard, which is carbon.

2. When you assign a relative mass to each variety of beans, what property of the beans do you ignore? *(Developing models)* Assigning a single relative mass ignores the variation of individual bean masses.

3. The formula for the compound methane is CH_4. One molecule of methane has one carbon atom and four hydrogen atoms bonded together. Using the relative masses of these elements given in the periodic table, calculate the relative mass of methane in amu. *(Applying concepts)* The relative mass of carbon (C) = 12.01 amu. The relative mass of hydrogen (H) is 1.01 amu. The relative mass of CH_4 = 12.01 amu + 4(1.01 amu) = 16.04 amu.

4. As stated in the periodic table, the relative mass for hydrogen is 1.01 amu. In 1.01 g of hydrogen atoms, there are 6.02×10^{23} hydrogen atoms (Avogadro's number). How many carbon atoms will be present in 12.01 g of carbon atoms? (Hint: Refer to the relative masses of carbon and hydrogen in the periodic table.) *(Applying concepts)* There are 6.02×10^{23} carbon atoms in 12.01 g of carbon atoms.

5. How many atoms of each of the following elements would be present in samples having the following masses? *(Making predictions)*

    a. 14.01 g of nitrogen atoms — 6.02×10^{23} atoms

    b. 40.08 g of calcium atoms — 6.02×10^{23} atoms

    c. 32.06 g of sulfur atoms — 6.02×10^{23} atoms

    d. 4.00 g of helium atoms — 6.02×10^{23} atoms

6. Based on your answers to Questions 4 and 5, develop a hypothesis that describes the relationship between relative mass, mass in grams, and numbers of atoms. *(Developing hypotheses)* The relative mass of an atom measured in amu is the same value as the mass in grams of a sample that contains 6.02×10^{23} atoms of that element.

7. To find how many atoms are in a sample of an element, would it be more reliable to measure the volume or the mass of the atoms? Explain your reasoning. *(Evaluating)* Mass is a more reliable means of approximating a particular number of atoms because, unlike volume, the mass will not vary as the temperature changes or the substance changes state.

Lab 15
APPLICATION

Name

Going Further

2. Chapter 10 provides the background for the mole concept. Students may need additional library resources to research the history of Avogadro's number.

Going Further

1. Research the work of John Dalton, who assigned relative masses of the elements using hydrogen as the standard. Describe the mistake he made in his assumptions and the difficulties that resulted. Find out how the mistake was discovered and what led to the use of carbon as the standard of mass.
2. The number 6.02×10^{23}, Avogadro's number, has tremendous significance and usefulness in chemistry. Find out what this number represents, how it was determined, and how it is used in chemistry.

Name _____ Date _____ Class _____

Reactivity of Alkaline Earth Metals

Text reference: **Chapter 6**

Introduction

The elements in Group 2A (2) of the periodic table are called the alkaline earth metals. Why do they have such a strange-sounding name? They were given that name because they were first isolated from compounds in which they were combined with oxygen. These were called earths by early chemists. The *alkaline* part of the name came from the fact that they formed basic, or alkaline, solutions in water. The group is composed of beryllium (Be), magnesium (Mg), calcium (Ca), strontium (Sr), barium (Ba), and radium (Ra).

All alkaline earth metals have two valence electrons, which they tend to give up rather easily, making them quite reactive. In fact, they are so reactive that they are never found uncombined in nature. In order for these shiny white metals to remain in their unreacted state, they must be protected from air and water. Magnesium and calcium, for example, are obtained in their elemental state by a chemical process called electrolysis, and then stored in airtight containers.

In this investigation, you will explore the reactivity of magnesium and calcium, two of the more common alkaline earth metals. You will then compare the reactivity of these metals with that of aluminum, which is a member of Group 3A (13).

Materials (class of 30 in pairs)
30 pairs chemical splash goggles
30 laboratory aprons
45 plastic petri dishes
15 wax marking pencils
15 pairs forceps
magnesium ribbon (Mg), 60 cm
15 small pieces of calcium metal turnings (Ca)
15 pieces aluminum foil (Al), 0.5 cm × 4 cm
1 package of steel wool
15 plastic micropipets
50 mL distilled water
15 micropipets with 1% phenolphthalein solution
15 wash bottles
15 lab burners
15 strikers or books of safety matches
15 pairs crucible tongs
15 wire gauze squares
15 microspatulas
aluminum oxide (Al_2O_3), 15.0 g

Pre-Lab Discussion

Read the entire laboratory investigation and the relevant pages of your textbook. Then answer the questions that follow.

1. What are some of the properties shared by alkaline earth metals?
   They have higher densities and melting points than the alkali metals. They
   form oxides when exposed to air. They are good conductors of electricity.

2. How many valence electrons do the alkaline earth metals have in their elemental state? Two valence electrons.

3. What are some of the hazards of working with metals that are as active as the alkaline earth metals? What precautions should you follow? They are very reactive with water, combining to form a gas that is explosive in the presence of a flame. Open flames should be avoided in Part A.
   Avoid direct contact with Group 2A (2) metals, their solutions, or their products.
   Do not look directly at the burning Mg metal because the flame is very bright.

Time Required
50–60 minutes. The time can be shortened by cutting the magnesium and aluminum strips ahead of time. The procedure can be completed in less time if the class is organized into groups of four.

Advance Preparation
Cut the magnesium and aluminum strips. Check the calcium metal turnings beforehand to make sure they have not oxidized completely to chunks of calcium oxide. Have ready a labeled container in which to collect the calcium waste.

Introduction
You may wish to show students a video or videodisc

© Prentice-Hall, Inc.

Reactivity of Alkaline Earth Metals **87**

Lab 16

clip of the reactivity of the alkali metals and then have students contrast this with the reactivity of the alkaline earth metals. Have students identify the pattern of increasing reactivity as you go from the top to the bottom of Group 1A (1) in the periodic table. Then have them see if the same pattern holds for the alkaline earth metals.

4. If a piece of metal, such as calcium or magnesium, reacts with atmospheric oxygen, would you expect the product to have a greater or lesser mass than the reacting metal? Why? The mass of the product would increase due to the additional mass of oxygen that combines with the metal.

5. What does a pink color with phenolphthalein solution indicate? The pink color indicates the presence of a basic, or alkaline, solution.

6. How should you dispose of the products of the reaction of calcium and water? They have to be rinsed into the container for calcium waste.

Problem

How do the activities of the alkaline earth metals magnesium and calcium compare to each other and to aluminum?

Materials

chemical splash goggles
laboratory apron
3 petri dishes
wax marking pencil
forceps
magnesium ribbon (Mg)
calcium metal turnings (Ca)
aluminum foil (Al)
micropipet
distilled water

micropipet with phenolphthalein solution
steel wool
wash bottle with distilled water
lab burner
striker or matches
crucible tongs
wire gauze square
aluminum oxide (Al_2O_3)
microspatula

Safety

Safety

Make sure students wear their goggles and lab aprons at all times during the investigation. Make sure that all flames are extinguished when reacting calcium metal with water. This reaction produces hydrogen gas, which is explosive. Students should carry out this reaction in a covered petri dish. Do not permit students to begin Part B until everyone has finished and cleaned up the calcium-water reaction in Part A. ∎

Wear your goggles and lab apron at all times during the investigation. Avoid touching calcium metal or calcium oxide directly. Any skin or clothing that comes into direct contact with calcium metal or its reaction products should be washed with large quantities of water. If the exposed skin feels slippery, continue to rinse it with water.

Make sure no open flames are present in the laboratory when reacting calcium with water because the gas that is produced can be explosive. Carry out this reaction in a covered petri dish.

Make sure that everyone is finished with Part A before doing Part B. Tie back hair and loose clothing to avoid any fire hazard. When you burn the magnesium, avoid looking directly at the flame, which is hot and very bright. Note the caution alert symbols here and with certain steps of the Procedure. Refer to page xi for the specific precautions associated with each symbol.

Name _____

Small Scale Lab 16

Procedure

Part A

1. Put on your goggles and lab apron. Label three petri dishes and their covers *Mg, Ca,* and *Al,* using the marking pencil.
2. Remove the covers of the petri dishes and rest them open side up on your lab table. Use the forceps to place the following metal samples in the labeled petri dish covers: a 4-cm piece of Mg ribbon, a small piece of Ca turning, and a piece of aluminum foil about the size of the Mg ribbon. **CAUTION:** *Do not touch the calcium turning with your hands. It is corrosive.* Record the appearance of each kind of metal in Data Table 1.
3. Place three micropipets of distilled water into each of the petri dishes.

4. With the forceps, move the piece of calcium turning from the petri dish cover and place it into its petri dish. Place the cover over the petri dish immediately. **CAUTION:** *The reaction products of calcium and water can cause skin irritation. Observe the reaction through the plastic cover.* Record your observations now and again in one minute.
5. If any piece of metal is unreacted, lift the cover at an angle away from you and gently squirt the metal with one more pipetful of water. Place the cover over the petri dish immediately. Repeat if necessary until there is no further reaction.
6. Open the petri dish and place a drop of phenolphthalein on the reaction products. Record the color change, if any, that occurs.
7. Obtain a bit of steel wool and use it to clean the Mg ribbon. Record the appearance of the clean Mg ribbon.
8. Using the forceps, move the piece of magnesium from its cover and place it in the water in the petri dish. You need not place the cover over this dish. Watch closely for any sign of reaction. Record your observations in Data Table 1.
9. Place a drop of phenolphthalein on the piece of metal. Record any color changes or additional signs of reactions that occur over the next three minutes.
10. Repeat Steps 8 and 9, using the piece of aluminum. Record your observations in Data Table 1.
11. Using the forceps, remove and dry the solid pieces of magnesium and aluminum for use in Part B.

12. Using the wash bottle, rinse the products of the calcium metal reaction into the container your teacher has provided for calcium waste. Pour the solutions from the other petri dishes down the drain. Wash all the petri dishes with water and dry them.

13. If you do not go directly on to Part B, clean up your work area and wash your hands before leaving the laboratory.

Part B

14. Put on your goggles and lab apron. Place three micropipets of distilled water into the petri dishes labeled *Mg* and *Al.*

Teaching Tips

The micropipets with phenolphthalein can be saved and used again. Demonstrate the burning of magnesium ahead of time. Tell students that during the metal and water reactions, they will be observing the rate of gas (bubble) formation, not just whether or not the gas is produced.

Waste Disposal

Fill a large beaker (1- or 2-L) half full with water in which to collect the pink phenolphthalein-calcium hydroxide waste. Slowly add 6 *M* HCl solution to the calcium hydroxide solution until the pink color just disappears. This indicates the solution is near neutral. It can then be flushed down the drain with plenty of water. ■

Reactivity of Alkaline Earth Metals

Small Scale Lab 16

Name _____

Cooperative Learning Strategy

If groups of four are employed, a scribe should record the observations as the procedure is carried out by the three other students. Each of these three students can carry out the procedure with one of the three metal samples. All of the students in the group should observe the reactions as they are carried out. A coordinator should be appointed to direct the activities and monitor the assigned roles. The responsibilities for Part B can be divided up and completed as a group effort. There should be sufficient time to share the data and collaborate on the write-up.

15. Light the lab burner. **CAUTION:** *The gases produced in Part A are explosive. Before lighting the burner, make sure everyone is finished with Part A.* Hold the magnesium ribbon over the flame with the crucible tongs. As soon as it lights, hold the burning magnesium over the wire gauze square. **CAUTION:** *Do not look directly at the burning magnesium, as it can damage your eyes. Keep loose hair and clothing away from the fire.* When the fire is out, examine the products of the burn and record your observations in Data Table 2.

16. Place the product of the burn into the water in the petri dish labeled *Mg* and add a drop of phenolphthalein solution. Record your observations.

17. Repeat Steps 15 and 16 with the aluminum foil. Record your observations. If attempts to burn the aluminum are unsuccessful, drop a microspatula of aluminum oxide into the water of the petri dish. Place a drop of phenolphthalein solution on the aluminum oxide and record your observations.

18. Wash the contents of the two petri dishes down the drain with excess water and dry the dishes. Clean up your work area and wash your hands before leaving the laboratory.

Observations (sample data)

DATA TABLE 1 Observations of Alkaline Earth Metals

Step	Observations
(2) unreacted Ca	covered with a white crust
(2) unreacted Mg	dull gray coating
(2) unreacted Al	shiny with a silvery luster
(4) Ca + water	gas bubbles, steam, spattering
(5) Ca + water reaction products	white pasty-looking material
(6) Ca + water + phenolphthalein	turns pink
(7) Mg after cleaning with steel wool	very shiny and silvery
(8) Mg + water	very small bubbles of gas
(9) Mg + water + phenolphthalein	slight pink color that intensifies after a minute
(10) Al + water	NR
(10) Al + water + phenolphthalein	NR

DATA TABLE 2 Comparisons of Alkaline Earth Metals

Reaction	Observations
(15) Mg burning	burns very brightly; white ash is brittle and crumbles
(16) burned Mg + phenolphthalein	turns pink
(17) Al burning	aluminum melts
(17) burned Al (or Al_2O_3) + phenolphthalein	turns slightly pink

Name _____

Small Scale Lab 16

Critical Thinking: Analysis and Conclusions

Part A

1. Elemental (unreacted) calcium and magnesium metal are shiny when they are pure. If the metals you worked with were not shiny, explain why this was so. *(Making inferences)* The dull coating on the magnesium and white crust on the calcium suggest that these metals formed oxides.

2. Would you describe the reaction of calcium in water as being exothermic (energy releasing) or endothermic (energy absorbing)? Use your observations as evidence to support your answer. *(Interpreting data)* The reaction of Ca in water was exothermic. In fact, steam could be seen on the cover of the petri dish.

3. Phenolphthalein appears pink in a basic, or alkaline, solution. Did the reactions of the alkaline earth metals with water produce alkaline solutions? Explain your answer. *(Drawing conclusions)* Yes, the solutions turned pink with phenolphthalein, so they were alkaline.

4. When a solution of calcium hydroxide, $Ca(OH)_2(aq)$, becomes saturated, a white solid, calcium hydroxide $Ca(OH)_2(s)$, appears. Did your calcium hydroxide solution become saturated? How do you know? *(Drawing conclusions)* A white pasty-looking substance was seen, indicating that the solution of calcium hydroxide was saturated.

5. Did magnesium metal react with water to form a gas and an alkaline solution? Explain your answer in light of your observations. *(Drawing conclusions)* Magnesium metal reacted with water to form a few bubbles of gas. The solution turns pink with phenolphthalein, indicating the presence of an alkaline solution.

6. Groups of metals change in reactivity from the top to the bottom of the periodic table. What evidence do you have that there was a pattern of reactivity in the alkaline earth metals? *(Making comparisons)* Calcium metal, which is below magnesium in the periodic table, reacts much faster with water than does magnesium metal. The data suggest a pattern of increasing activity from top to bottom in this group.

7. Was there any evidence that aluminum reacted with water? *(Interpreting data)* No, the aluminum did not react with water.

8. Are magnesium and calcium more reactive with oxygen in the air than is aluminum? Support your answer. *(Interpreting data)* Yes, magnesium and calcium both had layers of oxide on their surface, but aluminum did not. The magnesium burned in air, but aluminum did not.

Reactivity of Alkaline Earth Metals

Name _____

9. What can you conclude from the color of the solutions made from the magnesium and aluminum oxides when phenolphthalein was added? *(Drawing conclusions)* The pink color indicated that the solutions had become alkaline.

Critical Thinking: Applications

1. Look at strontium (Sr) in the periodic table. Would you expect it to be more or less reactive than calcium? Explain. *(Making predictions)* Strontium would be more reactive than calcium because reactivity increases as you go down the periodic table in Group 2A (2).

2. Which of the metals in this lab could you use for camera flashbulbs? Why? *(Applying concepts)* You could use magnesium because it would burn brightly when ignited.

3. Would you expect to find calcium metal used in conducting wire or structural materials? Why or why not? *(Making inferences)* No, because the metal would react with the air or water.

4. Aluminum is a metal commonly used in making conducting wires, equipment, and structural materials. Use the results of your experiment to help to explain why it is used. *(Applying concepts)* Aluminum metal is low in density, yet strong. It doesn't react extensively with the air or water as do the alkaline earth elements.

Going Further

1. Research some of the commercial uses of magnesium and calcium. Relate the properties of these metals to their uses. Write a report summarizing your findings.
2. Calcium and magnesium compounds are commonly found in living systems. Use biochemical or biological reference materials in the library to determine what role these compounds play. Use this information to create a bulletin board display.
3. Alkaline earth compounds are sometimes incinerated in order to dispose of them. Research Chapters 18 and 19 in your text, or information in other chemistry books, to determine which oxides commonly form. Find out what environmental problems these materials create when disposed of in this fashion. Report your findings to your class in a brief oral report.

Name _____ Date _____ Class _____

Exploring the Halides

Small Scale Lab 17

Text reference: **Chapter 6**

Introduction

The elements in Group 7A (17) of the periodic table are nonmetals called the halogens. The word *halogen* comes from two ancient Greek words that mean "salt" and "former." There are five members of the halogen family. They are fluorine, chlorine, bromine, iodine, and astatine. Each halogen can react with a number of different metals to form compounds called halides. For example, when sodium metal reacts with chlorine, the halide sodium chloride is formed. The first four halogens form classes of halides with easily recognizable names, as follows:

fluorides—formed from a metal and fluorine

chlorides—formed from a metal and chlorine

bromides—formed from a metal and bromine

iodides—formed from a metal and iodine

In this investigation, you will observe chemical reactions of small quantities of four halides with specific solutions, or test reagents. You will use your observations of these reactions to determine which halide is present in a solution containing one or more unknowns.

Pre-Lab Discussion

Read the entire laboratory investigation and the relevant pages of your textbook. Then answer the questions that follow.

1. What are the five halogens and what is the chemical symbol for each? The five halogens are fluorine (F), chlorine (Cl), bromine (Br), iodine (I), and astatine (At).

2. What structural characteristic is shared by the atoms of all the halogens? Each atom of the halogens has seven valence electrons.

3. What are fluorides, chlorides, bromides, and iodides? Fluorides, chlorides, bromides, and iodides are compounds formed from the four common halogens combined with a metal.

4. What method will you use to study halide reactions? Solutions of halides will be mixed with several test reagents, and the results of the reactions will be compared.

5. What safety precautions should you observe when working with bleach or ammonium hydroxide? Avoid breathing the vapors given off

Materials (class of 30 in pairs)
30 pairs chemical splash goggles
30 laboratory aprons
15 well plates, 24-well
165 micropipets
45 mL of each of the following aqueous solutions:
  sodium fluoride (NaF), 0.30 M
  sodium chloride (NaCl), 0.10 M
  sodium bromide (NaBr), 0.20 M
  sodium iodide (NaI), 0.20 M
  calcium nitrate ($Ca(NO_3)_2$), 0.50 M
  silver nitrate ($AgNO_3$), 0.10 M
  sodium thiosulfate ($Na_2S_2O_3$), 0.20 M
  ammonium hydroxide (NH_4OH), 6.0 M
  starch solution
  household bleach (NaClO)
  one or more unknown solutions
300 toothpicks
30 pairs latex gloves
15 eyedroppers

Time required
45 minutes.

Advance Preparation
CAUTION: *Wear gloves and a laboratory apron when preparing all solutions. Silver nitrate will stain skin and clothing. Ammonium hydroxide solution and its vapors are irritating to skin and nasal passages. Bleach will discolor clothing. Under no circumstances should ammonium hydroxide solution be combined with bleach.*
 Prepare the following seven solutions by adding

© Prentice-Hall, Inc.

Exploring the Halides 93

Small Scale Lab 17

Name _____

the specified masses of solutes to enough water to bring the volume up to 100 mL:
  0.30 M NaF: 1.26 g
  0.10 M NaCl: 0.58 g
  0.20 M NaBr: 2.06 g
  0.20 M NaI: 3.00 g
  0.50 M Ca(NO$_3$)$_2$·4H$_2$O: 11.81 g
  0.10 M AgNO$_3$: 1.70 g
  0.20 M Na$_2$S$_2$O$_3$·5H$_2$O: 4.96 g

Prepare 6.0 M NH$_4$OH solution by adding 42.9 mL concentrated ammonium hydroxide to 57.1 mL deionized (demineralized) water. (Demineralized water, used in steam irons, can be obtained from a supermarket.)

Prepare the starch solution by making a paste from 0.4 g of soluble starch (available from chemical supply houses) and a small amount of deionized water. Add the paste to 90 mL of boiling water. Boil for a few minutes. Then add enough deionized water to bring the volume to 100 mL. A quicker method is to spray household spray starch into water until the water acquires a blue tint.

Household bleach containing 5.25% sodium hypochlorite is adequate for Step 6.

Label 15 sets of micropipets with symbols for the above solutions, and fill them with the appropriate solutions.

Have ready a set of micropipets containing one or more solutions of unknown halides, either singly or in combinations.

Have ready a labeled container in which to collect the waste silver nitrate solution.

Safety

Make sure students wear their goggles and lab aprons at all times during the investigation and that they wear gloves when handling silver nitrate. Vapors from the ammonium hydroxide solution and bleach are by either bleach or ammonium hydroxide. Also, never mix bleach and ammonium hydroxide. Their reaction product is toxic and explosive.

6. What are the hazards in handling the silver nitrate solutions, and what precautions should you follow? __Silver nitrate is poisonous if swallowed, and will stain skin or clothing if spilled. When handling silver nitrate, gloves should be worn.__

Problem

How can you determine whether a fluoride, chloride, bromide, or iodide is present in a solution?

Materials

chemical splash goggles
laboratory apron
well plate, 24-well
11 micropipets, each filled with one of the following solutions:
  sodium fluoride (NaF)
  sodium chloride (NaCl)
  sodium bromide (NaBr)
  sodium iodide (NaI)
  calcium nitrate (Ca(NO$_3$)$_2$)

silver nitrate (AgNO$_3$)
sodium thiosulfate (Na$_2$S$_2$O$_3$)
ammonium hydroxide (NH$_4$OH)
starch solution
household bleach (NaClO)
unknown solution
20 toothpicks
latex gloves
eyedropper

Safety

Wear your goggles and lab apron at all times during the investigation. Handle all chemicals with care; avoid spills and contact with your skin. Wear gloves when handling the silver nitrate solution. Take particular care not to inhale fumes from the bleach or the ammonium hydroxide. Never mix bleach and ammonium hydroxide together. Note the caution alert symbols here and with certain steps of the Procedure. Refer to page xi for the specific precautions associated with each symbol.

Procedure

1. Put on your goggles and lab apron. Add five drops of sodium fluoride solution, NaF, to each of the first four wells in row A of your well plate. Then add five drops of the remaining three halides (sodium chloride, sodium bromide, and sodium iodide) to the wells in rows B, C, and D respectively, as shown in Figure 17–1.

2. Place two drops of calcium nitrate solution, Ca(NO$_3$)$_2$, into each of the first four wells in column 1 (wells A1, B1, C1, D1). Mix the solutions thoroughly with a clean toothpick. Record your

Name _____

Small Scale Lab 17

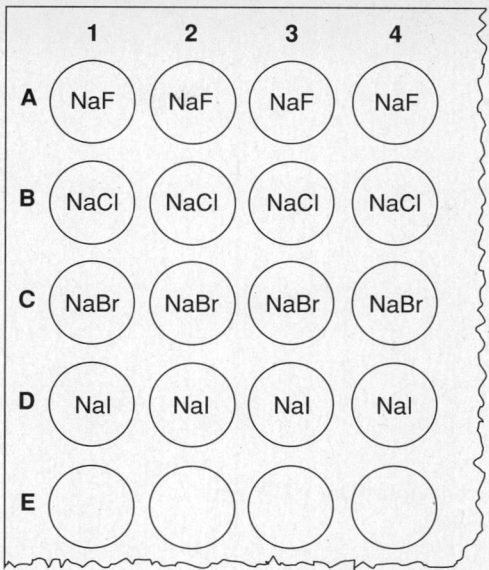

Figure 17-1

observations in the Data Table. Pay particular attention to the color of any precipitate (abbreviated *ppt*) that forms. It may help to observe the well plate first on top of a piece of white paper. If no observable change takes place, write *NR* for *no reaction*.

 3. Put on latex gloves. Into each of the column 2 wells (wells A2, B2, C2, D2), add two drops of silver nitrate, $AgNO_3$. Mix thoroughly with a clean toothpick. Observe as described in Step 2 and record your observations in the Data Table. **CAUTION:** *Silver nitrate is poisonous if ingested. Be careful not to get it on your skin or clothing, as it will produce a stain that is hard to remove. If any spills occur, tell your teacher.*

 4. Into the same column 2 wells tested in Step 3, add two drops of ammonium hydroxide solution, NH_4OH. **CAUTION:** *Avoid inhaling the ammonium hydroxide fumes.* Mix thoroughly with a clean toothpick. Observe as before and record your observations in the Data Table.

5. Following the same procedure as in Steps 3 and 4, add two drops of $AgNO_3$ solution into each of the column 3 wells (wells A3, B3, C3, and D3). Then add five drops of sodium thiosulfate solution, $Na_2S_2O_3$, and record all results.

 6. Into each of the column 4 wells (wells A4, B4, C4, and D4), place two drops of starch solution and then two drops of bleach solution. Make sure to mix the solutions thoroughly with a clean toothpick, and record your observations. **CAUTION:** *Avoid inhaling fumes from the bleach. Do not mix bleach and ammonium hydroxide solutions. The resulting vapors are toxic and explosive. Avoid spilling or splashing bleach on your skin or clothing. Wash any splashes with plenty of water.*

 7. Obtain from your teacher a solution containing one or more unknown halides. Record the solution's identification number in the

irritating to eyes, nasal passages, and lungs. Tell students to make certain not to mix ammonia and bleach, as they react to produce oxygen chloride, which is toxic and explosive. ■

Introduction

Students should recognize two concepts in this investigation. First, the solubilities of silver halides, and the reaction of the sodium halides to bleach, will show similarities in the behavior of elements of the halogen group. Second, fluorine will appear distinct from the other halogens, which in some respects it is, due to the small size of its ion and its high reactivity.

Careful observations of silver halide solubility may allow students to recognize a third concept. The solubility of silver halides decreases from fluorine to iodine. If students are able to observe this change, it will encourage them to think of silver fluoride as being at the high end of a range of solubility, rather than being distinct from the other silver halides.

Before students begin their work, have a discussion about the kinds of properties that are under investigation. Without giving the concepts away, ask students to think about and predict patterns they might find among the halides.

Teaching Tips

Caution students not to contaminate their test reagents by touching the tips of their micropipets to the solutions already in the well plates.

It may be convenient to have students place a sufficient amount of the unknown in well E5 and use this as a source of the unknown for the four (or more) tests.

The balanced equations for the reactions that involve

Exploring the Halides

Small Scale Lab 17

Name _____

precipitates in this investigation are as follows:

A1: $Ca(NO_3)_2(aq) + 2NaF(aq) \rightarrow CaF_2(s) + 2NaNO_3(aq)$

B2: $AgNO_3(aq) + NaCl(aq) \rightarrow AgCl(s) + NaNO_3(aq)$
$AgCl(s) + 2NH_4OH(aq) \rightarrow Ag(NH_3)_2^+(aq) + Cl^-(aq) + 2H_2O(l)$

B3: $AgNO_3(aq) + NaCl(aq) \rightarrow AgCl(s) + NaNO_3(aq)$
$AgCl(s) + 2Na_2S_2O_3(aq) \rightarrow Ag(S_2O_3)_2^{3-}(aq) + 4Na^+(aq) + Cl^-(aq)$

C2: $AgNO_3(aq) + NaBr(aq) \rightarrow AgBr(s) + NaNO_3(aq)$

C3: $AgNO_3(aq) + NaBr(aq) \rightarrow AgBr(s) + NaNO_3(aq)$
$AgBr(s) + 2Na_2S_2O_3(aq) \rightarrow Ag(S_2O_3)_2^{3-}(aq) + 4Na^+(aq) + Br^-(aq)$

D2: $AgNO_3(aq) + NaI(aq) \rightarrow AgI(s) + NaNO_3(aq)$

D3: $AgNO_3(aq) + NaI(aq) \rightarrow AgI(s) + NaNO_3(aq)$
$AgI(s) + 2Na_2S_2O_3(aq) \rightarrow Ag(S_2O_3)_2^{3-}(aq) + 4Na^+(aq) + I^-(aq)$

Sodium fluoride and silver nitrate may produce a very small amount of silver fluoride precipitate, but it is more likely the students will see no reaction. The variation of solubility from silver chloride to silver iodide may be difficult for students to see in the laboratory.

In the reactions with bleach, Br^- and I^- are oxidized to form Br_2 and I_2 molecules by the hypochlorite ions. The diatomic bromine and iodine form a complex with starch molecules that produces the blue color. Fluoride and chloride solutions will not produce the blue color.

A dilute solution of ammonia water will help remove silver nitrate stains from the skin. Commercial laundry pretreatments may remove stains from clothing.

Data Table. Use the test reagents and the procedure you followed in Steps 1–6 to determine which halide(s) your unknown contains. If time allows, repeat your tests to verify your results.

8. Use an eyedropper to transfer all the silver nitrate solutions from the well plate to a container provided by your teacher. Clean up your work area and wash your hands before leaving the laboratory.

Observations (sample data)
DATA TABLE

	Solution	1 $Ca(NO_3)_2$	2 $AgNO_3$ and NH_4OH	3 $AgNO_3$ and $Na_2S_2O_3$	4 Starch and Bleach
A	NaF	cloudy, some white ppt	NR	NR	NR
B	NaCl	NR	white ppt; partially dissolves	white ppt; partially dissolves	yellow color
C	NaBr	NR	yellow-tan ppt; no change	yellow-tan ppt; partially dissolves	clear; clear blue-black color
D	NaI	NR	yellow-tan ppt; no change	yellow-tan ppt; partially dissolves	clear; clear blue-black color
E	Unknown ID#				

Critical Thinking: Analysis and Conclusions

1. Describe the reactions that occurred with sodium fluoride. Did they follow the pattern you saw with the other halides? (*Making comparisons*) A white precipitate formed when sodium fluoride reacted with calcium nitrate, but no other reactions could be seen. This pattern was the opposite of what was observed with the other halides, where reactions occurred with all reagents except calcium nitrate.

2. Based on your observations, describe the precipitates formed by the reactions of the halides with silver nitrate. (*Interpreting data*) Sodium chloride, sodium bromide, and sodium iodide formed yellow or white precipitates when they reacted with silver nitrate. Sodium fluoride formed no precipitate.

3. Which of the precipitates dissolved when ammonium hydroxide was added? When sodium thiosulfate was added? (*Interpreting data*) The

© Prentice-Hall, Inc.

Name _____

sodium chloride–silver nitrate precipitate partially dissolved with ammonium hydroxide, but the other two did not. All three of the precipitates partially dissolved with the addition of sodium thiosulfate.

4. How did the halides react to the starch solution? (*Drawing conclusions*) The halides showed little, if any, reaction with the starch solution.

5. How did the halides react to the bleach solution? (*Drawing conclusions*) The lighter halides (fluorine and chlorine) did not appear to react with the bleach. The heavier halides (bromine and iodine) produced a deep blue color when bleach was added in the presence of starch.

6. Explain your reasoning in identifying the halide(s) present in your unknown. (*Interpreting data*) Answers will vary, depending on the unknown halide.

Critical Thinking: Applications

1. Chlorine is often added to drinking water to kill disease-causing organisms. Design an experiment to determine if chlorine is present in your tap water. (*Designing experiments*) Students' experiments should include the use of silver nitrate to test for chlorine.

2. How might you determine the difference between iodized salt and noniodized salt? Can you think of a reason why the results of this experiment might be inconclusive? (*Evaluating*) Students might suggest that a sample of each salt be dissolved in water and then tested with a silver nitrate solution, followed by an ammonium hydroxide solution. They might also suggest testing with the starch and bleach solutions. Iodine is present in tiny concentrations in iodized salt, so it will be difficult to detect.

Going Further

1. Look at the ingredients of several commercial products in a grocery store. Identify products in which you found halides. Make a bulletin board display based on your findings.
2. Chlorine is used to kill infectious agents, such as bacteria, in swimming pools. Find out what chlorine compounds are used and how they work. Report your findings to your class.

Waste Disposal

Silver compounds are regulated as hazardous waste (EPA waste #D011). Therefore, before students wash out their reaction plates, they should be instructed to use an eyedropper to remove the material in the column 2 and column 3 wells and to deposit the material into a clearly marked container. Collect any remaining silver nitrate solution, and precipitate the excess Ag^+ ions with excess NaCl solution. Filter out the precipitate and store in the marked container. Discard the filtrate. The toothpicks used to mix the solutions in columns 2 and 3 should also be placed in the marked container for commercial disposal. ■

Going Further

1. Student bulletin board displays may include any of the following: common table salt (NaCl); fluorides found in toothpaste and in insecticides; chlorides for preserving foods, and for dying fabrics; bromides in some kinds of medicines, including sedatives and anticonvulsants.
2. Students might begin their research by calling a swimming-pool supply company or talking with a swimming-pool maintenance person.

© Prentice-Hall, Inc.

Exploring the Halides 97

Name _____ Date _____ Class _____

Making Micro-Hindenburgs

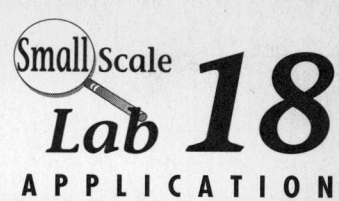

Small Scale Lab 18 APPLICATION

Text reference: **Chapter 6**

Introduction

The *Hindenburg* was the largest airship ever built. It had a record of 54 successful flights. However, what people remember most about the *Hindenburg* is its tragic end at Lakehurst, New Jersey. On May 6, 1937, the hydrogen-filled *Hindenburg* burst into flames as the pilot was attempting to land it. Thirty-six people were killed while horrified onlookers watched. The exact cause of the explosion has never been determined, but the *Hindenburg* disaster essentially ended wide-scale development and use of airships.

Why was the *Hindenburg* filled with hydrogen? Would another gas have been better? In this lab, you will make hydrogen gas and investigate its properties so that you can answer these questions.

Pre-Lab Discussion

Read the entire laboratory investigation and the relevant pages of your textbook. Then answer the questions that follow.

1. Find hydrogen in the periodic table. Why do you think it is separated from the Group 1A (1) elements? **Hydrogen is found in the upper left hand corner of the periodic table. It is separated from the other Group 1A (1) elements because it has many unique properties. Although it has only one valence electron, it is a colorless, nonmetallic gas, while the rest of the elements in Group 1A (1) are alkali metals.**

2. What chemicals are used to produce hydrogen gas in this investigation? **Zinc and hydrochloric acid (Zn and HCl).**

3. Why should you handle hydrochloric acid with extreme care? **Hydrochloric acid is corrosive, so direct contact should be avoided.**

4. What should you do if you accidentally spill some HCl? **Wash the area with plenty of water and report the spill to your teacher.**

5. What is the purpose of the bubble solution in this investigation? **The bubble solution traps the hydrogen gas in a bubble.**

6. What do you predict will happen when you hold the flame near the bubbles of gas produced in this investigation? On what information is your prediction based? **The hydrogen gas should explode like the Hindenburg since the gas is the same.**

Materials (class of 30 in pairs)
30 pairs chemical splash goggles
30 laboratory aprons
30 pairs latex gloves
15 pairs scissors
15 micropipets
15 one-hole rubber stoppers, size 0
30 g granulated zinc (Zn)
15 test tubes, 18 × 125 mm
15 test-tube racks
450 mL hydrochloric acid (HCl), 3.0 *M*
15 micropipets containing bubble solution
beaker to hold micropipets
15 boxes of matches
15 wooden splints

Time required
30 minutes.

Advance Preparation
Prepare the bubble solution by mixing 20.0 mL of liquid dish detergent, 25.0 mL of water, and 5.0 mL of glycerin. Put about 3 mL of the solution into each of 15 micropipets. Place the micropipets into a labeled beaker. Prepare 500 mL of 3.0 *M* HCl by adding 124 mL of concentrated HCl to enough water to make 500 mL of solution. CAUTION: *Wear goggles, gloves, and a lab apron.* Have ready a labeled container in which to collect the waste zinc chloride solution.

Introduction
To stimulate interest, you may wish to read an eyewitness account of the explosion of the *Hindenburg* or show a video clip of it. Also, the cover of the *Led Zeppelin I* record album has a photograph of the disaster.

© Prentice-Hall, Inc. *Making Micro-Hindenburgs* **99**

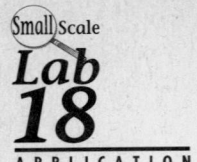

Name _____

Problem
What properties of hydrogen prevent its use in modern-day airships?

Materials
chemical splash goggles
laboratory apron
latex gloves
scissors
micropipet
one-hole rubber stopper
granulated zinc

test tube
test-tube rack
hydrochloric acid (HCl), 3.0 M
micropipet containing bubble solution
matches
wooden splint

Safety
Wear your goggles, gloves, and lab apron at all times during the investigation. Hydrochloric acid is corrosive. If you spill any acid, immediately wash the area with plenty of cold water and notify your teacher. Tie back loose hair and clothing when working with a flame. Note the caution alert symbols here and with certain steps of the Procedure. Refer to page *xi* for the specific precautions associated with each symbol.

Procedure

 1. Put on your goggles, gloves, and lab apron.

 2. Make a microfunnel, using the scissors to cut off the top of the plastic micropipet bulb. Insert the microfunnel into the one-hole rubber stopper as shown and set aside.

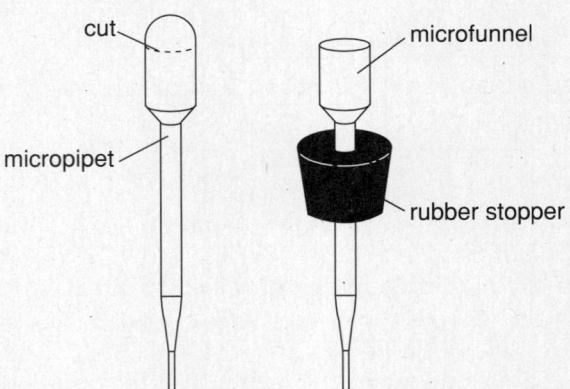

Figure 18–1

 3. Place about 2 g of granulated zinc in the test tube. Place the test tube in the test-tube rack. Then carefully pour 10 mL of 3.0 M hydrochloric acid (HCl) into the test tube. **CAUTION:** *Hydrochloric acid is corrosive. Avoid spills and splashes. If you do spill acid, immediately rinse the area with plenty of cold water and report the spill to your teacher.* Record your observations.

Safety
Make sure students wear their goggles, gloves, and lab aprons at all times during the investigation. HCl is severely corrosive to skin and eyes. Zinc chloride solution is a severe skin irritant. All solutions and chemicals should be handled with care. Splashes and spills should be rinsed immediately with plenty of water. Caution students to tie back loose hair and clothing when handling the matches and burning splints. ■

Teaching Tips
Students should have fun with this laboratory investigation. They are able to burn hydrogen in quantities that are small enough to be safe. If granulated zinc is not available, you can substitute mossy zinc, but the reaction will occur more slowly. Magnesium can also be substituted for zinc.
    Tell students the composition of the bubble solution to help them answer Question 3 of Analysis and Conclusions.

Name _____

4. Insert the rubber stopper with the microfunnel into the test tube so that no gas can escape except by way of the microfunnel. With a micropipet provided by your teacher, place 5–10 drops of bubble solution into the microfunnel, as shown in Figure 18–2. Record your observations.

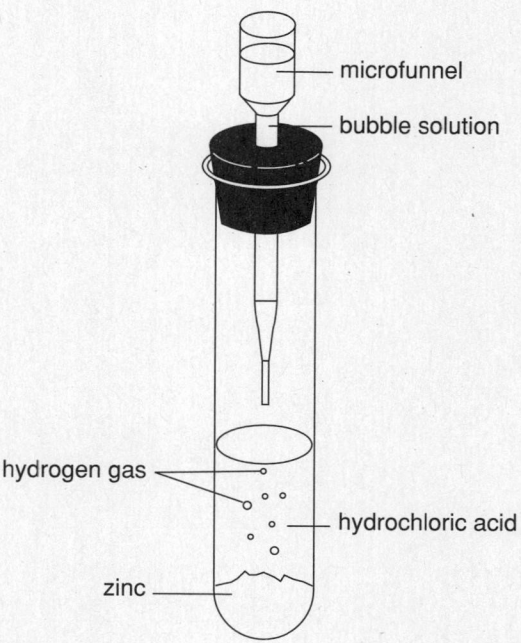

Figure 18–2

5. Light the wooden splint. **CAUTION:** *Tie back loose hair or clothing when working with the flame.* Carefully bring the flame close to the bubbles rising from the microfunnel. Record your observations. (If generation of gas slows or ceases, extinguish the flame. Remove the stopper and add more zinc and HCl. Then reinsert the microfunnel and stopper, relight the splint, and test the bubbles.)

6. Disassemble the apparatus and dispose of the reaction products in a container provided by your teacher. **CAUTION:** *The product in the test tube, zinc chloride ($ZnCl_2$), is a severe skin irritant. Avoid direct contact. If spills or splashes occur, wash the area with plenty of water.* Clean up your work area and wash your hands before leaving the laboratory.

Waste Disposal
The zinc chloride should be collected and dried by evaporation in a fume hood. It can then be safely disposed of in a landfill. Collect and wash the unused zinc. After drying, it may be used again. ∎

Observations (sample data)

zinc with hydrochloric acid	zinc dissolves; gas bubbles form in the acid
bubble solution in microfunnel	gas is trapped in bubble; bubbles float in the air
flame held near bubbles	flash of light; popping sound

© Prentice-Hall, Inc.

Making Micro-Hindenburgs

Critical Thinking: Analysis and Conclusions

1. What evidence in this investigation suggests that a chemical reaction has taken place? *(Interpreting data)* A gas was formed and the zinc metal disappeared.

2. Based upon your data, what properties of hydrogen are demonstrated in this investigation? (Hint: Why did the bubbles float in the air?) *(Making inferences)* Hydrogen is less dense than air and is explosive.

3. What purpose did the bubble solution serve? *(Making inferences)* The bubbles enclosed the hydrogen gas so it could be tested.

Critical Thinking: Applications

1. Why do you think that hydrogen gas was used to fill the *Hindenburg*? *(Evaluating)* Hydrogen is less dense than air, thus it enabled the *Hindenburg* to rise and float through the air.

2. What other gas would have been a better choice for inflating the *Hindenburg*? Explain. *(Making judgments)* Helium would have been a better choice because it too is less dense than air but it is not flammable.

3. Why do you think that this investigation is entitled "Making Micro-Hindenburgs"? *(Developing models)* The bubbles containing hydrogen gas are like tiny *Hindenburgs* because they explode on a smaller scale.

4. Why would it be dangerous to do this investigation on a larger scale where a large quantity of hydrogen is generated in a short time? *(Making predictions)* Hydrogen is highly flammable. The explosion would be frightening and hazardous.

Going Further

Going Further

3. A good starting point for students researching the use of hydrogen as a fuel source is an article entitled "Solid Progress in Hydrogen Storage" in *Technology Review*, Feb/March 1993, p. 15. Students can then contact the Florida Solar Energy Center in Cape Canaveral to get an update on this ongoing research.

1. Hydrogen is just one of several gases that can be produced in the laboratory with relative ease. Oxygen gas can be produced by mixing baker's yeast or MnO_2 with a 3% solution of hydrogen peroxide. Carbon dioxide can be produced by mixing baking soda and vinegar (acetic acid).
   Design an experiment in which you compare properties, such as the density and flammability, of hydrogen gas (H_2), oxygen gas (O_2), and carbon dioxide gas (CO_2). Under your teacher's supervision, conduct your experiment and report your results. Would either oxygen or carbon dioxide be an acceptable gas to use in an airship or blimp? Explain.

2. Research and prepare a report detailing the history of lighter-than-air craft. Find out how these craft are used today.

3. Hydrogen gas is a fuel that burns efficiently and cleanly. Research the advantages and disadvantages of using hydrogen gas as a fuel for motor vehicles. How close are scientists to overcoming the disadvantages?

Name _____ Date _____ Class _____

Formula of Lead Iodide

Small Scale Lab 19

Text reference: **Chapter 7**

Introduction

In 1808, John Dalton published *A New System of Chemical Philosophy* in which he presented his atomic theory of matter. According to Dalton's theory, chemical compounds form when atoms combine with each other. Another postulate of Dalton's atomic theory is that a given compound always has the same relative numbers and kinds of atoms.

The chemical formula of an ionic compound shows the relative number and kinds of atoms as a whole number ratio. The ratio of elements in a compound can be determined experimentally. Once the ratio is known, the formula for the compound is easily written. In this experiment, you will be reacting sodium iodide and lead nitrate together in various ratios to produce the precipitate, lead iodide. By plotting the data, you will be able to find the ratio that produces the most precipitate. This will be the correct ratio of atoms in lead iodide. From this ratio, you can determine the chemical formula of lead iodide.

Materials (class of 30 in pairs)
30 pairs chemical splash goggles
30 laboratory aprons
135 test tubes, 6 × 50 mm
15 marking pens
15 well plates
15 micropipets
100 mL distilled water
30 pairs latex gloves
25 mL sodium iodide (NaI), 0.1 M
25 mL lead nitrate ($Pb(NO_3)_2$), 0.1 M
15 metric rulers

Time Required
40 minutes.

Advance Preparation
For 0.1 M NaI, dissolve 1.50 g NaI in 100 mL of water.
For 0.1 M $Pb(NO_3)_2$, dissolve 3.31 g $Pb(NO_3)_2$ in 100 mL of water.
Have a labeled container ready in which to collect the lead waste.

Introduction
You may want to review with students the discussion of Dalton's atomic theory of matter in Chapter 3 of the textbook. Limiting reactants are discussed in Chapter 11, but you may choose to introduce the concept now in order to facilitate the students' understanding of the data.

Pre-Lab Discussion

Read the entire laboratory investigation and the relevant pages of your textbook. Then answer the questions that follow.

1. How does Dalton's atomic theory of matter apply to this investigation? _In this investigation, the formula for a compound will be deduced by studying the ratios in which the reactants combine. This procedure makes use of Dalton's postulate that a given compound always has the same relative numbers and kinds of atoms as its component elements._

2. Why should you let the reaction stand for 5 minutes before measuring the height of the precipitate in each test tube? _This allows the precipitate to settle, so that its height can be measured more accurately._

3. How will the graph help you interpret your data? _The graph will show clearly which ratio(s) yielded the most precipitate._

4. What is a subscript and what does it mean in the formula of an ionic compound? _The subscript is the small number to the lower right of the element's symbol in a chemical formula. The subscript indicates the relative numbers of atoms in an ionic compound._

© Prentice-Hall, Inc.   Formula of Lead Iodide 103

5. Why do lead compounds require caution in handling and disposal?
Lead compounds are toxic. Gloves should be worn to prevent coming into direct contact with the lead compounds, and these compounds should be disposed of in special containers provided by the teacher. Lead compounds should never be flushed down the drain.

Problem

Can you determine the chemical formula for lead iodide?

Materials

chemical splash goggles
laboratory apron
9 small test tubes
marking pen
well plate
micropipet

sodium iodide (NaI), 0.1 M
distilled water
latex gloves
lead nitrate ($Pb(NO_3)_2$), 0.1 M
metric ruler

Safety

Wear your goggles and lab apron at all times during the investigation. Lead compounds are toxic. Wear latex gloves when working with them. Do not dispose of any lead nitrate or lead iodide wastes down the drain, but place them in labeled waste containers provided by your teacher. Note the caution alert symbols here and with certain steps of the Procedure. Refer to page *xi* for the specific precautions associated with each symbol.

Procedure

1. Put on your goggles and lab apron. Label nine test tubes 1–9 with the marking pen, and place them in a well plate that will serve as a test-tube holder.

2. Fill the micropipet with 0.1 M sodium iodide (NaI) solution. Following Table 19–1 as a guide, add the indicated number of drops to each test tube. For example, place 18 drops in tube 1, 16 drops into tube 2, etc., until all nine tubes are done.

3. Put on your gloves. Rinse the micropipet four times with distilled water. Then fill it once with 0.1 M lead nitrate ($Pb(NO_3)_2$) solution and immediately discard this solution in the lead waste beaker. **CAUTION:** *Lead nitrate is toxic. Wear gloves. Do not let this substance come in contact with your skin.*

4. Fill the micropipet again with 0.1 M lead nitrate ($Pb(NO_3)_2$) solution. Following Table 19–1 as a guide, add the indicated number of drops to each test tube. For example, place 2 drops in tube 1, 4 drops into tube 2, etc., until all nine tubes are done.

Name _____

TABLE 19–1

Test Tube	Drops of NaI Solution	Drops of Pb(NO$_3$)$_2$ Solution
1	18	2
2	16	4
3	14	6
4	12	8
5	10	10
6	8	12
7	6	14
8	4	16
9	2	18

5. Allow the nine test tubes to stand for 5 minutes. If necessary, tap the test tubes gently to help the precipitates settle to the bottom.
6. With a metric ruler, measure the height of the precipitate in each test tube. Record the heights in your Data Table.

7. Dispose of all chemicals according to your teacher's instructions. Clean up your work area and wash your hands before leaving the laboratory.

Observations (sample data)

DATA TABLE

Test Tube	Height of Precipitate (mm)	Ratio of Drops Pb(NO$_3$)$_2$:NaI
1	0.6	1:9
2	1.0	1:4
3	4.0	1:2.3
4	4.0	1:1.5
5	1.2	1:1
6	1.0	1:0.67
7	0.8	1:0.43
8	0.6	1:0.25
9	0.4	1:0.11

Waste Disposal

Sodium iodide may be flushed down the drain with large quantities of water. Lead solutions should be reacted with three times their volume of 1 M sodium sulfide. Let sit, stirring occasionally, for 1 hour. Adjust the pH to neutral with sodium hydroxide. Separate the lead sulfide by filtration. Place the filter paper with the lead sulfide solid in a plastic container for disposal in an appropriate landfill. The neutral solution may be flushed down the drain with excess water. ■

Formula of Lead Iodide

Name _____

 Calculations (based on sample data)

1. Compute the ratio of drops of lead nitrate solution to drops of sodium iodide solution in each test tube and record these ratios in the data table. (Hint: Set up each ratio to give the number of drops of sodium iodide solution that would correspond to one drop of lead iodide solution.)
2. Graph your data. Plot the test tube numbers on the horizontal axis and the height of the lead iodide precipitate on the vertical axis. Beside each data point, record the drop ratios for $Pb(NO_3)_2$:NaI.

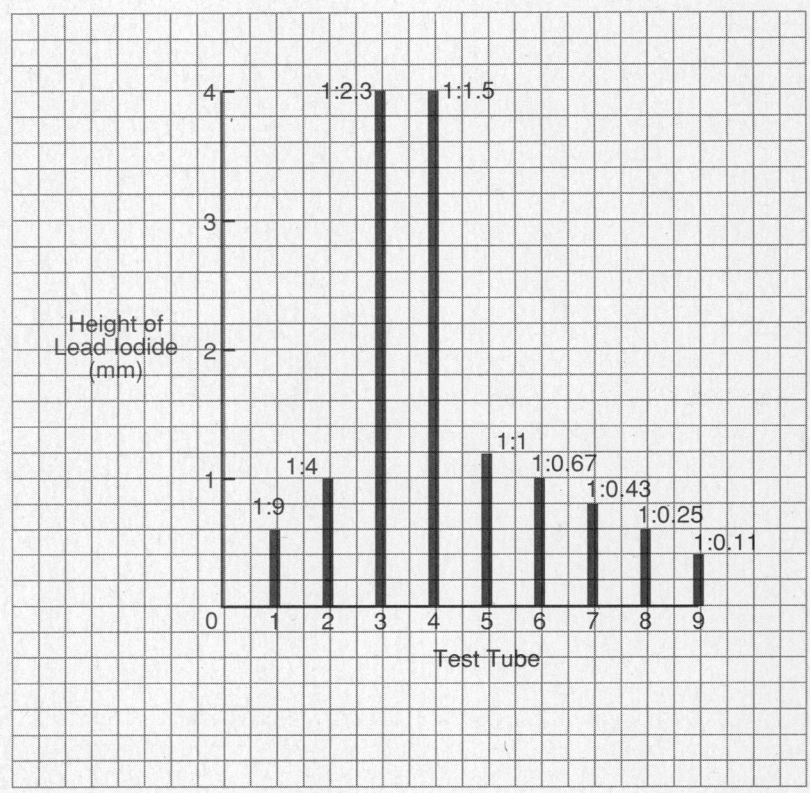

Figure 19–1

Critical Thinking: Analysis and Conclusions

1. Which reactant ratio(s) yielded the greatest amount of precipitate? *(Interpreting data)* Ratios close to 1:2 yielded the greatest amount.
2. What can you conclude from your graph of precipitate heights and reactant ratios? *(Interpreting diagrams)* Atoms will only combine in exact ratios to form a particular compound. When there is too much of one reactant, the amount made is determined by the reactant that runs out first. The most precipitate will be made when the ratio of reactants used matches the ratio of the elements in the compound.

Name _____

3. Based on the ratio that you determined in response to Question 1, what is the correct formula for lead iodide? *(Making inferences)* The formula for lead iodide is PbI_2.

4. Which reagent ran out first in tube 2? In tube 7? *(Interpreting data)* In tube 2, lead nitrate ran out. In tube 7, sodium iodide ran out.

Critical Thinking: Applications

1. Why is it important that the proper ratio be used when writing the formula of a substance? *(Evaluating)* A compound will have only one correct ratio. If a different ratio is used, it represents a different substance.

2. Would the procedure you used in this investigation work for any compound? Give an example of a type of compound for which this procedure would not work. Explain. *(Designing experiments)* No, this procedure only works when a measurable amount of precipitate is formed. The procedure would not work if the product was a liquid.

3. Making an apple pie calls for a reaction among certain ratios of ingredients. How is making an apple pie different from making lead iodide? *(Making comparisons)* An apple pie is a mixture that has a set ratio of ingredients. A compound formed in this investigation is a pure substance that has a specific chemical formula and a set ratio of reactants.

Going Further

1. Recipes indicate the ratios of ingredients that are to be used. Analyze some of your favorite recipes to see what ratios are involved. Classify the products according to whether they are compounds or mixtures. Explain why the ratios are not so critical when only mixtures are involved.

Solubility and Bond Type

Lab 20

Text reference: Chapter 7

Introduction

Compounds may contain ionic bonds, polar covalent bonds, nonpolar covalent bonds, or a combination of these bond types. Several of the investigations in this book provide clues that allow you to predict which type of bond a compound contains. Investigation 21, for example, explores the electrical conductivity of solutions of various compounds. In Investigation 23, the tendency of a liquid to rise in a narrow space is examined. Both of these behaviors depend on bond type. Another way to predict whether a substance has ionic, polar covalent, or nonpolar covalent bonds is to measure its solubility—its ability to dissolve—in different liquids. Substances with polar covalent or ionic bonds tend to dissolve in liquids that contain polar covalent bonds, while substances with nonpolar covalent bonds tend to dissolve in liquids with nonpolar covalent bonds.

In this investigation, you will compare the solubilities of sodium chloride, potassium chloride, sodium iodide, iodine, and camphor in water, ethanol, vegetable oil, and glycerol. You will also determine the solubility of the liquids in each other. Based on your data, you will then classify these substances by bond type.

Pre-Lab Discussion

Read the entire laboratory investigation and the relevant pages of your textbook. Then answer the questions that follow.

1. What are three types of chemical bonds? Do all compounds contain a single type of bond? <u>The types of bonds are ionic, polar covalent, and nonpolar covalent. Compounds may contain more than one bond type.</u>

2. What special precautions should be taken when working with iodine crystals? <u>Iodine changes directly from a solid to a vapor. The vapors are irritating. Take care to avoid breathing the fumes. All work with iodine should be performed in the fume hood. Avoid skin contact.</u>

3. Compound X dissolves in water but not in vegetable oil. Compound Y dissolves in ethanol but not in water. Which of the two more likely contains polar covalent bonds? Explain. <u>Compound X is more likely to contain polar covalent bonds since it dissolves in water, which also contains polar covalent bonds.</u>

Materials (class of 30 in pairs)

30 pairs chemical splash goggles
30 laboratory aprons
15 marking pens
60 test tubes
15 test-tube racks
15 graduated cylinders, 10-mL
tap water
750 mL ethanol (C_2H_5OH)
750 mL glycerol ($C_3H_8O_3$)
750 mL vegetable oil
15 laboratory balances
15 microspatulas
100 g of each of the following solids:
    sodium chloride (NaCl)
    potassium chloride (KCl)
    sodium iodide (NaI)
    iodine (I_2)
    camphor ($C_{10}H_{16}O$)
15 pairs forceps
60 stoppers to fit test tubes

Time Required

40 minutes. To shorten the time, have half the class test the solubility of the solids and the other half test the solubility of the liquids. Then pool the data.

Advance Preparation

Have a container ready in which to collect the waste liquids.

Introduction

Point out to the students that the properties of a compound depend, to a large extent, on the type of bond holding it together. Solubility, hardness, melting point, boiling point, electrical conductivity (studied in Investigation 21), and capillary action (studied in Investigation 23) are some examples of properties that depend on the type of bond in the molecule.

Solubility and Bond Type **109**

Lab 20

Show the students the structural formula for iodine, emphasizing its diatomic character. They should realize that all diatomic molecules comprised of two identical atoms are nonpolar due to the equal electronegativity of the two atoms.

Safety
Make sure students wear their goggles and lab aprons at all times during the investigation. Iodine and ethanol are toxic in all their forms. Skin contact with iodine is hazardous. Remind the students to use forceps when handling iodine. All procedure steps involving iodine should be done in a fume hood.
Ethanol is flammable. Be sure there are no open flames in the laboratory. ■

Teaching Tips
Have students bring in vegetable oil from home. You may want to compare results with corn oil, sunflower oil, and olive oil.
Demonstrate the procedure for determining solubility of the solids. Students need to see the results that correspond to soluble, insoluble, and partially soluble solids. Use NaCl in H_2O, I_2 in H_2O, and NaCl in glycerol, respectively.
Ethanol and glycerol are considered incompletely polar. This is because each contains one or more hydroxyl (OH) groups along with a hydrocarbon backbone. The hydroxyl

Name_____

Problem
How can a compound's solubility be used to predict the type of bonds it contains?

Materials
chemical splash goggles
laboratory apron
marking pen
4 test tubes
test-tube rack
graduated cylinder, 10-mL
tap water
ethanol (C_2H_5OH)
glycerol ($C_3H_8O_3$)
vegetable oil

laboratory balance
microspatula
sodium chloride (NaCl)
potassium chloride (KCl)
sodium iodide (NaI)
iodine (I_2)
camphor ($C_{10}H_{16}O$)
forceps
4 stoppers to fit test tubes

Safety

Wear your goggles and lab apron at all times during the investigation. Ethanol and iodine are toxic. Avoid breathing their vapors. All work with iodine should be done in a fume hood. Avoid skin contact with iodine; use forceps to handle it. If iodine does come in contact with skin, rinse the affected area with plenty of water. Ethanol is flammable; be sure there are no open flames in the laboratory. Note the caution alert symbols here and with certain steps of the Procedure. Refer to page *xi* for the specific precautions associated with each symbol.

Procedure
Part A

1. Put on your goggles and lab apron. Label four test tubes from 1–4. Place them in a test-tube rack.

 2. Put 5.0 mL of the listed liquids into separate test tubes as follows. **CAUTION:** *Ethanol is toxic as a liquid and a vapor. Avoid direct contact with it. It is also flammable. Be sure there are no open flames in the laboratory.*

    test tube 1: water   test tube 3: glycerol
    test tube 2: ethanol   test tube 4: vegetable oil

3. Measure four 0.5-g samples of sodium chloride. Using a microspatula, add a few grains of sodium chloride to test tube 1. Stopper and shake the tube. If the solid dissolves, add a few more grains. Keep adding grains until no more will dissolve or until you have used all of the sample.

4. If all the solid dissolves, write *soluble* in Data Table 1. If none of the solid dissolves, write the word *insoluble* in Data Table 1. If some of the solid dissolves, write the words *partially soluble* in Data Table 1.

110

Name _____

Lab 20

  5. Repeat Steps 3 and 4 for each of the other three test tubes.

 6. Pour the contents of the test tubes into the container provided by your teacher. Rinse and dry the test tubes and repeat the procedure, using potassium chloride instead of sodium chloride.

 7. Dispose of the materials and clean the test tubes as before. Repeat the procedure for sodium iodide, iodine, and camphor. **CAUTION:** *Iodine crystals and vapors are toxic. Do this part of the procedure in the fume hood. Avoid skin contact with the iodine. Use forceps when handling it.*

group gives these molecules a polar character, while the hydrocarbon backbone gives them a nonpolar character. Thus, ethanol dissolves in water (a polar behavior) but it is also able to dissolve iodine (a nonpolar behavior). Glycerol does not dissolve in water (a nonpolar behavior) but is able to dissolve sodium iodide (a polar behavior).

  8. Dispose of the materials and clean the test tubes. Iodine compounds should be collected in a specially marked container. If you are not going on directly to Part B, clean up your work area and wash your hands before leaving the laboratory.

Part B

 9. Put on your goggles and lab apron. Put 3.0 mL of water into each of three test tubes. Add 3.0 mL of ethanol to the water in one of the tubes. Stopper and shake the tube for about 30 seconds. Let it sit for another 30 seconds. Note the appearance of the liquid. If you can see layers, write the word *insoluble* in Data Table 2. If no layers are present, write the word *soluble*.

10. Repeat Step 9 using vegetable oil, and then glycerol, instead of ethanol. Dispose of the materials as before, and rinse out and dry all the test tubes.

11. Following the same procedure as in Step 9, test mixtures of ethanol with vegetable oil, ethanol with glycerol, and vegetable oil with glycerol. Write your observations in Data Table 2.

 12. Dispose of the liquids and solids as directed by your teacher. Clean up your work area and wash your hands before leaving the laboratory.

Waste Disposal

The iodine solutions should be collected and stored in a labeled container. Contact a licensed waste disposal company for removal. Camphor can be disposed of in a local landfill. All other substances can be flushed down the drain with plenty of water. ■

Observations (sample data)

DATA TABLE 1 Solubility of Solids

	Water	Ethanol	Vegetable oil	Glycerol
NaCl	soluble	insoluble	insoluble	partially sol.
KCl	soluble	insoluble	insoluble	partially sol.
NaI	soluble	soluble	insoluble	soluble
I_2	insoluble	partially sol.	soluble	partially sol.
camphor	insoluble	soluble	soluble	partially sol.

Solubility and Bond Type

Lab 20

Name _____

DATA TABLE 2 Solubility of Two Liquids

	Ethanol	Vegetable oil	Glycerol
water	soluble	insoluble	insoluble
ethanol	—	soluble	insoluble
vegetable oil	—	—	soluble

Critical Thinking: Analysis and Conclusions

1. Predict the type of bonds each of the solids you tested contains. Explain your reasoning. *(Classifying)* <u>NaCl, KCl, and NaI probably contain ionic or polar covalent bonds since they dissolve in water, which is polar. I_2 and camphor probably contain nonpolar covalent bonds since they dissolve in vegetable oil, which is nonpolar.</u>

2. Which of the liquids can be considered polar? Which are nonpolar? *(Drawing conclusions)* <u>Besides water, ethanol must also be polar. The vegetable oil and the glycerol did not dissolve in water and did dissolve in each other. They must be nonpolar.</u>

3. Why did NaCl not dissolve in vegetable oil? *(Drawing conclusions)* <u>NaCl is ionic and will dissolve only in polar solvents. Vegetable oil is nonpolar.</u>

4. Why did iodine dissolve in vegetable oil but not in water? *(Drawing conclusions)* <u>Vegetable oil is nonpolar and water is polar. Iodine contains nonpolar bonds and thus will dissolve in a nonpolar liquid.</u>

Critical Thinking: Applications

1. Salad dressing is a mixture of vegetable oil and vinegar (acetic acid). Why does the dressing have to be shaken before it is used? *(Developing hypotheses)* <u>The oil is nonpolar and the vinegar is polar. If the dressing is not shaken, only the oil, which would be on top, would be poured onto the salad. Shaking mixes the two liquids temporarily.</u>

2. What kind of liquid cleaning agents would be most effective at dissolving oily stains? *(Making judgments)* <u>Nonpolar liquids would be best since oil is also a nonpolar compound.</u>

Going Further

1. By washing the mixture with water, the NaCl will be removed. Then the water can be boiled off to recover the salt.

Going Further

1. You are given a mixture of iodine and NaCl powders. Suggest a method for separating the two. Design an experiment employing your method. Perform the experiment only under a teacher's supervision. Report on your results.

Name _____ Date _____ Class _____

Conductivity of Molecular and Ionic Compounds

Lab 21 APPLICATION

Text reference: **Chapter 7**

Introduction

The salt and sugar on your kitchen table both dissolve easily in water, but the solutions they form have an important difference. One of those kinds of white crystals is an ionic compound, and when it dissolves, it dissociates into ions. The ions are free to move in the solution, and that solution, therefore, conducts electricity. The other kind of crystal, however, is a molecular compound, and its molecules remain whole when they dissolve. With no ions, that solution conducts no electricity.

This investigation involves testing several different liquids that are distributed among the work areas in the laboratory. When you measure the conductivity of each liquid, you will find that some are good conductors, some are fair or poor conductors, and some are nonconductors. Using the conductivities you have measured, you will decide which solutions contain ionic compounds, and which contain molecular compounds.

After you have classified your solutions, you will examine sugar and salt from another point of view. Bonding theory generally predicts that ionic compounds should form from combinations of elements that are far apart on the periodic table, while molecular compounds should form from elements that are close together. You will see whether your findings on conductivity agree with this prediction.

Pre-Lab Discussion

Read the entire laboratory investigation and the relevant pages of your textbook. Then answer the questions that follow.

1. What are ions, and how do they form? __Ions are charged particles that form from atoms. Negative ions are formed by atoms gaining electrons, while positive ions are formed by atoms losing electrons.__

2. What is an ionic bond? __An ionic bond is an electrostatic attraction between two oppositely charged ions.__

3. What is a covalent bond? __A covalent bond forms between two atoms that share one or more pairs of electrons.__

4. How do aqueous solutions of ionic and molecular compounds differ? __Ionic compounds split into ions when they dissolve. Molecular compounds usually remain in molecular form in solution.__

5. When some ionic compounds dissolve, not all of their bonds dissociate. What kind of conductivity would you expect such a solution to have? __A solution of a compound that does not completely dissociate would be a poor or fair conductor.__

Materials (class of 30 in pairs)
- 30 pairs chemical splash goggles
- 30 laboratory aprons
- 15 conductivity testers
- 15 wash bottles with distilled water
- 15 beakers, 250-mL
- 20 test solutions, 125 mL each, of:
  - vegetable oil
  - salt water (sea water where available)
  - sugar water
  - antacid in distilled water
  - dishwasher detergent in distilled water
  - liquid hand soap in distilled water
  - borax solution
  - household bleach in distilled water
  - carbonated soft drink
  - distilled water
  - tap water
  - hydrochloric acid (HCl), 1.0 M
  - sodium hydroxide solution (NaOH), 1.0 M
  - lime water (saturated calcium hydroxide (Ca(OH)$_2$) solution)
  - aspirin in distilled water
  - baking soda in distilled water
  - vinegar
  - fruit juice
  - coffee
  - household ammonia

Time Required
40 minutes.

Advance Preparation
Set up the solutions in labeled beakers and the conductivity testers at individual laboratory stations. Choose as many solutions as there are testers available. It works best to have one conductivity tester per solution, since any ions left on the probes of the

© Prentice-Hall, Inc.

Conductivity of Molecular and Ionic Compounds **113**

Lab 21
APPLICATION

Name _____

testers will contaminate other solutions. Substitute other solutions as desired.

Time to gather the various solutions and to set up conductivity meters will depend on how many and what kinds of solutions you use. You can save preparation time by having the class set up the solutions the day before the investigation.

Concentration is not of vital importance for most of these solutions, although there will be some variation of conductivity with concentration. For those solutions with no concentration specified, 1 to 5 grams of solute (for both solids and liquids) in 250 mL of water will suffice.

The simplest conductivity tester consists of a battery and a flashlight bulb wired in series with two probes that are immersed in the solution. This type of tester distinguishes conductors and nonconductors. (A low-voltage power supply may be substituted for the battery.) Finer judgments on the brightness of the test light give good, fair, poor, and zero conductivity readings. A very compact tester consists of a light-emitting diode wired in series with a 1000-ohm resistor and a 9-volt battery.

More complex testers can be made with bulbs of different wattages wired in parallel with one another. One counts the bulbs that are lit to gauge the conductivity. These testers work most effectively with household voltage (120 V), and are more suitable for demonstrations than for student use.

It is also possible to use a voltmeter to measure the voltage between the test probes. The voltmeter will give a high voltage reading (for example, 5 volts or more with the LED tester) if the solution is a nonconductor, and a low reading (less than a volt) for a good conductor. Fair or poor conductors will give intermediate readings.

Problem

How can the conductivity of a solution help you to classify the bonds in the solute?

Materials

chemical splash goggles
laboratory apron
equipment at each work area:

conductivity tester
wash bottle with distilled water
test solution in 250-mL beaker
beaker, 250-mL

Safety

Wear your goggles and lab apron at all times during the investigation. Beware of electrical shocks. Use and dispose of chemicals as specified by your teacher, and wash your hands thoroughly before leaving the laboratory. Note the caution alert symbols here and with certain steps of the Procedure. Refer to page *xi* for the specific precautions associated with each symbol.

Procedure

1. Put on your goggles and lab apron.
2. Using the conductivity tester as described by your teacher, test the solution at your lab station. **CAUTION:** *Some of the test solutions may be corrosive, or may stain or discolor clothing. Avoid spills and splashes. If spills occur, wash with plenty of water and notify your teacher immediately. Avoid inhaling fumes from the bleach or ammonia solutions. Do not mix bleach and ammonia solutions. The resulting vapors are toxic and explosive.*
3. Note whether the test light is lit, and if so, how brightly. Record your observations in the Data Table.
4. Rinse the conductivity probes with distilled water over an empty beaker.
5. Move to the next lab station and check the conductivity of the solution at that station in the same manner. Record your observations.
6. Repeat Steps 2–5 until you have tested and recorded data for all the solutions.
7. Dispose of the solutions as instructed by your teacher.
8. Clean up your work area and wash your hands before leaving the laboratory.

Name _____

Observations (sample data)

DATA TABLE

Test Solution	Conductivity			
	Good	Fair	Poor	None
vegetable oil				X
salt water	X			
sugar water				X
antacid in water	results	will	vary	
dishwasher detergent in water	X			
liquid hand soap in water			X	
borax in water	X			
household bleach in water	X			
carbonated drink			X	
distilled water				X
tap water			X	
hydrochloric acid (HCl), 1 M	X			
sodium hydroxide solution (NaOH), 1 M	X			
lime water (Ca(OH)$_2$) solution)		X		
aspirin in water			X	
baking soda in water	X			
vinegar		X		
fruit juice		X		
coffee			X	
household ammonia		X		

Lab 21
APPLICATION

Conductivity meters (usually equipped with 9V batteries) are perhaps the easiest equipment to use in the lab. They may be purchased from a scientific supply house, and some of the less expensive meters will easily distinguish four levels of conductivity.

Introduction
The idea that a liquid can conduct electricity may be a novelty to some students. You can point out to them that they have all encountered such conductors, for household batteries and automobile batteries contain electrolytes.
Conductivity of a solution is probably best understood in terms of individual ions. When a potential difference is set up between two electrodes (the test probes, in this case), an ion will diffuse toward the appropriately charged electrode. For a given potential the net rate of diffusion will increase with the concentration of ions. The current, and therefore the conductivity of the solution, is greater with a greater concentration of ions. More current flowing through the solution means more current flowing through the test light, and it glows more brightly.
The usual analogy of electricity to water flowing in a pipe is informative when only wires are involved. In the present situation, where the current flows through a liquid, that analogy will probably confuse students.

Safety
Make sure students wear their goggles and lab aprons at all times during the investigation. Some conductivity testers can deliver electrical shocks. If any of your meters or power supplies use household voltage (120 V) you should use ground-fault current interrupt power outlets. Advise students about

Critical Thinking: Analysis and Conclusions

1. What types of bonds do you think the good conductors of electricity have? Explain your reasoning. *(Making inferences)* Good conductors of electricity have ionic bonds. Ionic compounds, if they are soluble, break up into ions in solution, and the ions conduct electricity.

2. What type of bonds do you think the nonconductors of electricity have? Explain your reasoning. *(Making inferences)* Nonconductors of electricity have covalent bonds. Molecular compounds do not form ions in solution, and therefore the solutions cannot conduct electricity.

Conductivity of Molecular and Ionic Compounds

Lab 21 APPLICATION

precautions that pertain to your type of conductivity meters.

Do not place ammonia and bleach solutions close to each other in the laboratory. They react to produce oxygen chloride, which is toxic and explosive.

Instruct students on the proper disposal of selected solutions. ■

Teaching Tips

Students have been introduced to ionic and covalent bonding, but in everyday life, most compounds are neither completely molecular nor completely ionic. This investigation uses everyday compounds, but you may select other, less common compounds as well. One exception to the rule regarding ionic and covalent bonding is HCl. Its bonding is polar-covalent, but it ionizes completely when dissolved in water.

Students will learn more about relative conductivities if they can distinguish good, fair, and poor conductors, and nonconductors. To make these classifications apparent, you may want to set up standard solutions for the classes of conductors you want to distinguish.

The physics laboratory may be a source from which to borrow power packs, voltmeters, light bulbs, and so on. If power packs are to be used, use low voltage.

Waste Disposal

Most household chemicals can be flushed down the drain with large quantities of water. The HCl and the NaOH should be neutralized before disposal. Vegetable oil can be saved and reused.

If other chemical compounds are to be used, consult a disposal manual from a chemical supply company. ■

3. How can you account for the fair and poor conductors of electricity? *(Developing hypotheses)* Answers will vary, but students may mention that some substances have polar-covalent bonds, some have a combination of bond types, or some ionic compounds dissociate more than others.

Critical Thinking: Applications

1. What kind of ions does sodium chloride (table salt) produce when it dissolves? *(Applying concepts)* Sodium chloride dissociates into negative chloride and positive sodium ions.

2. Where are sodium and chlorine found on the periodic table? (Consult the periodic table in the back of this laboratory manual, or in your textbook.) Do the relative positions of these elements in the periodic table agree with the prediction made in the Introduction about their structure? Explain. *(Evaluating)* Sodium is in Group 1A and chlorine is in Group 7A. Compounds of elements from these two groups should be ionic.

3. Look up the chemical formula for sucrose. Where are the elements that form sucrose found on the periodic table? Do the relative locations of these elements in the periodic table agree with the theoretical prediction about the kind of compound these elements should form? Explain. *(Evaluating)* The chemical formula for sucrose is $C_{12}H_{22}O_{12}$. Carbon is found in Group 4A. Hydrogen is found in Group 1A, and oxygen in Group 6A. Elements found close together in the periodic table tend to form covalent bonds, although hydrogen is an exception.

4. What conclusions can you draw from this investigation? *(Drawing conclusions)* If a compound in solution conducts electricity, it is most likely ionic. If the compound in solution does not conduct electricity, it is most likely molecular. The nature of the bonds can be predicted from the relative locations of the atoms in the periodic table.

Going Further

1. Using the electronegativity values listed for the elements in the periodic table, compute the electronegativity differences for the bonds in table salt and sugar (sucrose). Use these differences to predict what type of bonding will occur between the various atoms in these compounds. Do the predictions agree with your observations on table salt and sugar?
2. Investigate how Linus Pauling used bond energies to derive electronegativity values.

Models of Molecular Compounds

Lab 22

Text reference: **Chapter 8**

Introduction

Why should people care about the shapes of molecules? Consider that the properties of molecules, including their role in nature, depend not only on their molecular composition and structure, but their shape as well. Molecular shape determines a compound's boiling point, freezing point, viscosity, and the nature of its reactions.

The geometry of a small molecule can be predicted by examining the central atom and identifying the number of atoms bonded to it and the number of unshared electron pairs surrounding it. The shapes of molecules may be predicted using the VSEPR rule, which states that electron pairs around a central atom will position themselves to allow for the maximum amount of space between them.

Covalent bonds can be classified by comparing the difference in electronegativities of the two bonded atoms. If the difference in electronegativities is less than or equal to 0.4, the bond is called a nonpolar covalent bond. If the difference in electronegativities is between 0.5 and 1.9, a polar covalent bond exists. (If the difference in electronegativities is greater than 2.0, an ionic bond results.) In a polar covalent bond, the electrons are more attracted to the atom with the greater electronegativity, resulting in a partial negative charge on that atom. The atom with the smaller electronegativity value acquires a partial positive charge.

Molecules made up of covalently bonded atoms can be either polar or nonpolar. The geometry of the molecule determines whether it is polar or not. For example, if polar bonds are symmetrically arranged around a central atom, their charges may cancel each other out and the molecule would be nonpolar. If, on the other hand, the arrangement of the polar bonds is asymmetrical, the electrons will be attracted more to one end of the molecule and a polar molecule or dipole will result.

Ball-and-stick models can be used to demonstrate the shapes of molecules. In this experiment, you will construct models of covalent molecules and predict the geometry and polarity of each molecule.

Materials (class of 30 in pairs)
30 pairs safety goggles
15 ball-and-stick molecular model sets

Time Required
45 minutes.

Advance Preparation
Make sure you have enough complete model sets. If the sets are too small to make all of the molecules, you can put students into groups of four with one model set per group. Alternatively, have the students build half the molecules, bring them to you to check, and then take them apart and build the other half.

Introduction
You may wish to demonstrate how the polarity of a liquid affects its solubility in another liquid by mixing rubbing alcohol and water and then mixing oil and water. Discuss with students why one substance dissolves in water while the other does not.

Pre-Lab Discussion

Read the entire laboratory investigation and the relevant pages of your textbook. Then answer the questions that follow.

1. What is a covalent bond? A covalent bond is a chemical bond that is formed by the sharing of electrons between two atoms.

2. What is a dipole? A dipole has two distinct regions, or poles, of opposite electrical charge.

Lab 22

Name _____

3. What two factors determine whether a molecule is polar or not?
   Polarity is determined by the type of bonds in the molecule and the molecular geometry.

4. List the five different molecular geometries that you will be studying in this investigation. Tetrahedral, pyramidal, trigonal planar, bent, linear.

5. Calculate the electronegativity difference and predict the type of bond for the following examples: (Refer to Figure 7–19 in your text for a list of electronegativities.)
   a. Na—Cl   3.0–0.9 = 2.1 ionic
   b. C—H   2.5–2.1 = 0.4 nonpolar covalent
   c. S—O   3.5–2.5 = 1.0 polar covalent
   d. N—N   3.0–3.0 = 0 nonpolar covalent

Problem

How can the polarity of molecules be predicted from their geometry and the types of bonds they contain?

Materials

safety goggles
ball-and-stick model set

Safety

Wear your goggles at all times during the investigation. Note the caution alert symbols here and with certain steps of the Procedure. Refer to page xi for the specific precautions associated with each symbol.

Procedure

1. Put on your goggles. Construct ball-and-stick models of the following compounds:

H_2	HBr	H_2O
PH_3	CH_4	HClO
N_2	CH_3NH_2	CH_3Cl
H_2CO	C_2H_2	H_2O_2
HCOOH	HCN	

2. For each of the preceding compounds, complete the Data Table in the Observations section. As an example, the first line of the Data Table has been filled in for you.

3. When you have completed this investigation, take apart your models and return the model set to your teacher. Clean up your work area and wash your hands before leaving the laboratory.

Safety

Remind students that there should be no horseplay in the lab. Caution students not to throw or roll model parts on the floor. ■

Teaching Tips

A smaller lab, similar to this one, appears in Chapter 8 of the text. Depending on the amount of time you have, you may wish to do one or the other. If you want to have more variety in teaching the concepts, consider substituting the balloon approach described in Item 1 of Going Further.
    Demonstrate the use of the model sets. Show students how to construct multiple bonds. Review Lewis dot structures. If you substitute toothpicks and clay balls or gumdrops for model kits, remember to review bond angles and give the students protractors.

Name _____

Observations (sample data)

DATA TABLE Structure and Polarity of Molecules

Formula	Electron Dot Structure (Lewis)	Structural Formula	Shape of Molecule	Molecular Polarity
H_2	H:H	H—H	Linear	Nonpolar
HBr	H:Br:	H—Br	Linear	Polar
H_2O	H:O:H	H—O—H	Bent	Polar
PH_3	H:P:H (H)	P(H,H,H)	Pyramidal	Polar
CH_4	H:C:H (H,H)	H—C(H,H)—H	Tetrahedral	Nonpolar
HClO	H:O:Cl:	H—O—Cl	Bent	Polar
N_2	:N:::N:	N—N	Linear	Nonpolar
CH_3NH_2	H:C:N:H (H,H,H)	H—C(H,H)—N(H,H)	Tetrahedral	Polar
H_2CO	H:C::O: (H)	H,H \ C=O	Trigonal planar	Polar
C_2H_2	H:C:::C:H	H—C≡C—H	Linear	Nonpolar
CH_3Cl	H:C:Cl: (H,H)	H—C(H,H)—Cl	Tetrahedral	Polar
HCOOH	H:C:O: :O:H	H—C(=O)—OH	Trigonal planar	Polar
HCN	H:C:::N:	H—C≡N	Linear	Polar
H_2O_2	H:O:O:H	H—O—O—H	Bent	Polar

Models of Molecular Compounds   119

Lab 22

Name _____

Critical Thinking: Analysis and Conclusions

1. Explain how you used the molecular shapes to predict molecular polarity. Support your answer with examples from the results of this investigation. (*Classifying*) The molecules CH_4 and C_2H_2 contain polar bonds, but the molecules are all nonpolar because of the symmetrical arrangement of the bonds around the central atom. H_2 and N_2 are nonpolar because of equal sharing of electrons. The molecules HCN, H_2O, and PH_3 are polar because of the asymmetrical arrangement of polar bonds around the central atom.

2. List the advantages and disadvantages of using ball-and-stick models to construct molecules. (*Developing models*) An advantage is a three-dimensional view of molecules and shapes. Disadvantages are that bond strengths are not shown, and that the bond is seen as solid when it is not.

Critical Thinking: Applications

1. Based on your results, predict the type of bonding, molecular geometry, and molecular polarity of the following molecules. (*Making predictions*)
   a. HI — polar covalent, linear, polar
   b. SH_2 — polar covalent, bent, polar
   c. NH_3 — polar covalent, pyramidal, polar
   d. CO_2 — polar covalent, linear, nonpolar

2. The polarity of a substance can have a great effect on its reactivity and solubility. A rough rule of thumb for solubility is "like dissolves like." Knowing this general rule, what can you predict about the polarity of alcohol if you know that alcohol dissolves in water? Why do you think that water is not used to dissolve greasy stains and dirt at dry cleaners? (*Applying concepts*) Alcohol dissolves in water, so it must contain some polar bonds. If water is polar and it is not used to clean grease, then grease must be nonpolar and unaffected by water.

Going Further

1. Use balloons to create three-dimensional models of the five different molecular geometries discussed in this investigation.
2. Research what is meant by the term *isomer*. Give examples of molecular isomers.

Capillary Action and Polarity of Molecules

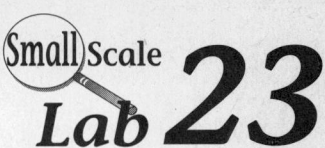

Small Scale Lab 23

Text reference: **Chapter 8**

Introduction

The tallest living things in the world are the giant redwood trees in California. These trees can reach heights of over 110 meters, equivalent to a 30-story building! How does the giant redwood supply its uppermost leaves and branches with water? Part of the answer lies in tiny (0.1-mm diameter) tube-shaped cells found in the trunk of the tree. These tube cells can move water over a great vertical distance through a process called capillary action, which is the drawing up of a liquid into a narrow tube or space.

Capillary action depends partially on the polarity of the molecules of the liquid and of the material that forms the tube or space into which the liquid rises. Polar molecules such as water are asymmetrical and have polar bonds. A polar attraction between the material of the tube and the molecules of a polar liquid causes the liquid to rise into the tube. As one molecule moves up, it attracts neighboring molecules which, in turn, attract their neighbors. Once the upward attractive force is equal to the downward force of gravity, the liquid stops rising. An extreme example of this phenomenon occurs in giant trees like the redwoods. It is estimated that these large trees move about 2000 liters of water each day from their roots to their uppermost leaves.

In this investigation, you will measure the capillary action of various liquids. By observing the height that different liquids reach in a capillary tube, you will be able to estimate the relative polarity of each liquid. Also, you will investigate how the polarity of a mixture of water and ethanol changes when the proportion of the two liquids is varied.

Pre-Lab Discussion

Read the entire laboratory investigation and the relevant pages of your textbook. Then answer the questions that follow.

1. What molecular features affect the polarity of molecules? __The presence of polar bonds and the symmetry of the molecule.__

2. How does the polarity of molecules affect the force of attractions between them? __The more polar the molecules are, the stronger are the attractions between them.__

3. Predict how the polarity of a liquid will affect the height to which that liquid can rise in a capillary tube. __The greater the polarity of the liquid, the higher will be the column of liquid in the capillary tube.__

Materials (class of 30 in pairs)
30 pairs chemical splash goggles
30 laboratory aprons
120–150 glass capillary tubes
15 well plates, 6- or 24-well
75 micropipets, 15 each containing:
  • water
  ethanol
  ethylene glycol
  propylene glycol
  glycerol
5 beakers (to hold micropipets)
15 metric rulers
paper towels
15 marking pens

Time Required
90 minutes. To shorten the investigation, decrease the number of trials or eliminate Part B.

Advance Preparation
Fill a sufficient number of micropipets with the liquids and place them in five separate labeled beakers. Have labeled containers ready in which to collect the waste liquids.

Introduction
Molecular polarity is caused by the uneven distribution of electrons within molecules, which is influenced by the electronegativity of the atoms and by molecular shape and size. In the case of water, the oxygen atom has a stronger attraction (greater electronegativity) for the electrons in the chemical bond than does the hydrogen atom. Therefore, the oxygen atom is more negative and the hydrogen atoms are more positive. Oxygen also has two pairs of unbonded electrons. According to the

© Prentice-Hall, Inc.

Capillary Action and Polarity of Molecules **121**

Small Scale Lab 23

VSEPR theory, these unbonded electrons distort the molecule, giving it a bent shape. With the negative oxygen atom at one end and the positive hydrogen atoms at the other, a water molecule is quite polar.

Capillary action is only one of the forces involved in water transport in plants. Cohesion-tension and transpiration also play important roles. Polar molecules, such as water, are attracted to one another by a cohesive force. Wherever one water molecule goes, others are attracted and tend to follow along. Transpiration occurs at the leaves of a plant when water molecules escape into the air. Other water molecules take up the empty spaces. Cohesive forces pull the chain of water molecules along, aided by capillary action.

Molecular polarities have a major influence on a wide range of material characteristics such as boiling and freezing points, vapor pressure, surface tension, stickiness, and solubility.

Safety

Make sure students wear their goggles and lab aprons at all times during the investigation. Warn students of the flammability and toxicity of the liquids. Remind students to wipe up spills and to dispose of broken capillary tubes immediately. Have available a separate container clearly marked "For Broken Glass Only." ■

Teaching Tips

Capillary tubes that are open at both ends are available from suppliers of scientific equipment. Avoid using tubes with one sealed end, as they would have to be cut, presenting unnecessary hazards.

Name _____

4. What is the main hazard in working with capillary tubes and what precautions should you follow? _Capillary tubes are made of glass and break easily. Handle them gently and dispose of broken tubes in the container provided by your teacher._

5. Why must there be no flames in the laboratory during this investigation? _Some of the liquids are flammable._

Problem

How is the polarity of a liquid related to capillary action?

Materials

chemical splash goggles
laboratory apron
well plate
8 glass capillary tubes
metric ruler
5 micropipets, each containing
   one of the following liquids:

water
ethanol
ethylene glycol
propylene glycol
glycerol
paper towels
marking pen

Safety

Wear your goggles and lab apron at all times during the investigation. Glass capillary tubes are fragile and may cause cuts when broken. Handle them very gently and dispose of broken ones in the container provided by your teacher. Ethanol, ethylene glycol, and propylene glycol are toxic. If any of these chemicals come in contact with your skin, wash with plenty of water. Ethanol is flammable. Be sure all lab burners are extinguished. Note the caution alert symbols here and with certain steps of the Procedure. Refer to page xi for the specific precautions associated with each symbol.

Procedure

Part A

  1. Put on your goggles and lab apron. Obtain a well plate, eight capillary tubes, and a micropipet containing water.

 2. Place a few drops of water into the middle of one of the wells of the well plate. With one end of a capillary tube, touch the water. **CAUTION:** *Capillary tubes are fragile and can cause cuts if broken. Handle them gently and dispose of broken tubes in the container provided by your teacher.* The top end of the tube must be open. Note that water rises inside the tube, above the outside water level. Leave the tip of the capillary tube in contact with the water in the well plate for at least 15 seconds.

Name_____

Small Scale Lab 23

3. Once the water stops rising, gently withdraw the capillary tube from the well and use a metric ruler to measure the height of the column of water. Record the value in Data Table 1.
4. Drain the capillary tube by touching its tip to a tissue or soft paper towel.
5. Repeat Steps 2–4 four more times. If air bubbles develop, use a fresh tube.

6. Repeat Steps 2–5 using each of the liquids provided. **CAUTION:** *Some of these liquids and their vapors are toxic. Care should be taken not to inhale the fumes. Do not let the liquids touch your skin.* Be sure to use a different well and a new capillary tube for each liquid. (Note: Glycerol requires more time to reach its final height than the other liquids do.)

Part B

7. Label three dry wells on the well plate with the numbers 1–3. Place the following in the appropriate well: well 1: 12 drops water and 4 drops ethanol; well 2: 8 drops water and 8 drops ethanol; well 3: 4 drops water and 12 drops ethanol. **CAUTION:** *Ethanol and its fumes are toxic. Avoid inhaling its vapors.* Be sure there are no open flames in the laboratory.
8. Repeat the procedure from Part A for the three mixtures of ethanol and water. Record the values in Data Table 2.

9. Dispose of the capillary tubes in a container provided by your teacher. Rinse excess liquids in the well plate down the drain. Clean up your work area and wash your hands before leaving the laboratory.

Use smaller diameter capillary tubes for more dramatic differences in capillary liquid height. Students should leave the capillary tubes in the liquid for the full 15 seconds in order to be certain the liquid has risen to its maximum height.

Remind students how to change from the proportions in Part B to percent water as required for the graph in Analysis and Conclusions Question 3.

You may wish to compare the behavior of water to a nonpolar liquid such as trichlorotrifluoroethane (TTE). Prepare two burets, each containing one of the liquids. Rub a balloon on a sweater or a swatch of cloth and bring it close to a stream coming from one of the burets. Repeat for the other liquid.

The attraction of water to glass can be demonstrated by placing a drop of water between two clean microscope slides. Ask one of the students to try to separate the slides.

Sandwich two glass plates together with a toothpick point between them at one end. Secure with a rubber band around the middle. Place edgewise into a petri dish containing brightly colored water. Capillary action will cause the water to rise up between the glass plates. You will notice a sweeping curve of water, showing the dependence of capillary action on the size of the space between the plates.

Observations (sample data)

DATA TABLE 1 Capillary Action of Several Liquids

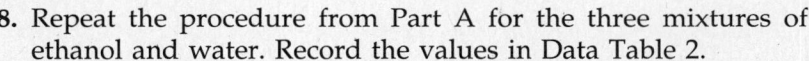

Liquid	Height of Column (mm)					
	1	2	3	4	5	Average
H_2O	21.5	23.0	22.0	23.5	22.0	22.4
ethanol	9.0	9.5	8.5	9.5	8.5	9.0
ethylene glycol	13.0	13.5	14.0	13.0	14.0	13.5
propylene glycol	12.0	10.5	11.0	11.5	10.0	11.0
glycerol	21.0	18.5	19.0	18.0	17.5	18.8

Waste Disposal

Absorb small volumes of ethylene glycol or propylene glycol from spills or well plates with paper towels and dispose of in a dry waste container. Provide a 600-mL beaker containing water for disposal of capillary tubes. Leave it in the fume hood for 1–2 days to allow the liquids to dissolve into the water.

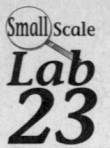

Small Scale Lab 23

Then pour the water down the drain and put the capillary tubes in the broken glass container.

Name _____

DATA TABLE 2 Capillary Action of Water/Ethanol Mixtures

Liquid	Height of Column (mm)					
	1	2	3	4	5	Average
pure water*	21.5	23.0	22.0	23.5	22.0	22.4
Mixture 1	13.0	13.5	14.5	14.0	14.5	14.0
Mixture 2	11.5	12.0	10.5	11.0	10.5	11.1
Mixture 3	9.0	9.5	10.0	9.0	10.0	9.5
pure ethanol*	9.0	9.5	8.5	9.5	8.5	9.0

*Note: Use the values for pure water and pure ethanol from Part A.

Critical Thinking: Analysis and Conclusions

1. Calculate the average heights for all the liquids tested in Part A and enter these values in Data Table 1. Based on your data, list the liquids from the most polar to the least polar. *(Making comparisons)* <u>Water, glycerol, ethylene glycol, propylene glycol, ethanol.</u>

2. Study the molecular structures of the liquids shown in Figure 23–1. Discuss how the number of oxygen atoms in the molecule might be related to the polarities of these molecules. *(Making inferences)*

Figure 23–1

<u>The more oxygen atoms that are present, the more polar the molecules tend to be. Water is an exception. Although it has only one oxygen atom, the small size of the water molecule may make it more likely to be influenced by polar forces.</u>

Name_____

3. Calculate the average heights for all the mixtures tested in Part B and enter these values in Data Table 2. Make a graph of the data from Part B with average height (mm) on the vertical axis and percent water in the water/ethanol mixture on the horizontal axis. Describe how the polarity of water appears to change when it is mixed with ethanol. *(Interpreting diagrams and data)* A curve results from the plot, showing that the relationship is not a direct proportion. However, the graph does indicate that as the concentration of water increases, the polarity of the mixture increases also.

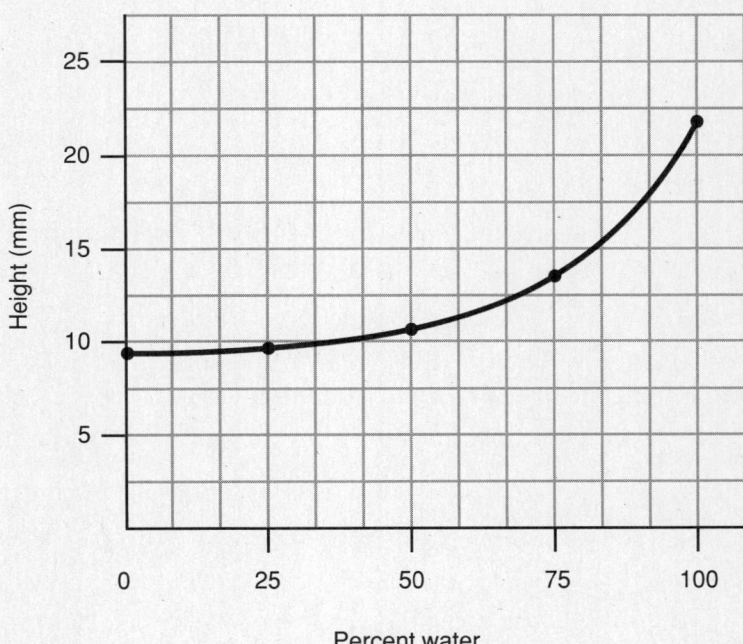

Figure 23–2

Critical Thinking: Applications

1. In addition to polarity, density affects the height a liquid may reach in a capillary tube. Heavy water containing the heavier hydrogen isotope, deuterium, is chemically identical to water, but has a higher molar mass (20.0 g/mole) and density (1.11 g/ml). How would you expect the height of heavy water in a capillary tube to compare to your data for water? *(Developing hypotheses)* The polarity of heavy water is identical to water, but since heavy water has a greater density, it will not rise as far in the capillary tube.

Capillary Action and Polarity of Molecules

2. Plastic capillary tubes are nonpolar. If plastic capillary tubes with the same diameter were substituted for the glass tubes, how would you expect the height of the liquids in the capillary tubes to be affected? Explain your answer. *(Making predictions)* The liquids would not rise as high in a plastic capillary tube due to the lack of strong polar attractions between the liquids and walls of the tube.

3. Sponges and fabrics absorb and hold water by capillary action. Some sponge materials and fabrics, like cotton, hold more water and dry more slowly than others. Relate the ability of these materials to hold water to the polarity of their molecules, and think of an example where this property is not desirable. *(Applying concepts)* Water is absorbed into microscopic spaces in polar materials to a greater extent than into nonpolar materials. Examples will vary, but bathing suits are one example where polar molecules would not be desired.

Going Further

2. Library books, chemistry texts, and periodicals such as *Scientific American* or *Science News* provide examples of how polarity and shape affect the function of biomolecules.

Going Further

1. Research the structure and chemical behavior of detergents, which facilitate the mixing of polar and nonpolar substances. Under your teacher's supervision, experiment with the effects of detergents on the capillary action of water.
2. Nerve action, the function of hemoglobin, the replication of DNA during mitosis, the resiliency of cell membranes that helps give your flesh its texture, and countless other biochemical interactions depend on the shapes and polarities of the molecules involved. Research one biochemical molecule. Find out how its shape and polarity contribute to its function.

Name _____ Date _____ Class _____

Exploring Dyes

Lab 24
APPLICATION

Text reference: **Chapter 8**

Introduction

The synthetic dye industry began with a serendipitous discovery. In 1856, eighteen-year-old William Perkin, a student at the Royal College of Chemistry in London, England, was trying to synthesize quinine, a drug used to treat malaria. What he got was a vibrant purple solution that easily colored silk. The dye was called mauve. It quickly became a commercial success and by 1870, cloth could be made in more colors than had ever been possible with dyes produced from natural sources such as flowers and vegetables.

In this investigation, you will explore the importance of molecular structure and polarity in the commercial world of dyes. Some natural fibers, such as silk and wool, are essentially protein molecules. Since proteins are made from amino acids, which have many polar sites on them, they have a strong affinity for dyes that are either polar or ionic. On the other hand, nylon has no polar sites at all except at the ends of its molecular chain (which is hundreds or even thousands of atoms long) so it is very resistant to dye. In between these extremes are fabrics such as dacron and rayon, each with only a few polar sites. As you might predict, they show intermediate attractions for dyes.

In order to dye the low-polarity fabrics, a process called mordanting can be used. The term comes from the Latin word *mordant*, which means "bite." In a sense, the dye can "bite into" the fabric. The process of mordanting alters the molecular structure of the fabric by affixing metal ions to it. These ions then bind the dye to the fabric.

In this lab, you will dye a strip made of six different fabrics with two different dyes. The fabric strip that you will use is composed of (in order) wool, orlon, dacron, nylon, cotton, and acetate rayon. You will determine the attraction of each material for dye by measuring the intensity of color—the darker the color, the stronger the attraction. From your results, you will determine which end is the wool. You will then determine the extent to which mordanting improves the dye-holding capability of the six fibers tested.

Pre-Lab Discussion

Read the entire laboratory investigation and the relevant pages of your textbook. Then answer the questions that follow.

1. What materials were used to dye fabric before synthetic dyes?
   Dyes from flowers and vegetables.

2. What is polarity? Polarity is a separation of electrical charges within a molecule.

Materials (class of 30 in pairs)
30 pairs chemical splash goggles
30 laboratory aprons
30 pairs latex gloves
30 test fabric strips
15 pairs tongs
600 mL of each of the following in 1-L beakers:
  methyl orange dye solution
  malachite green dye solution
  iron(II) sulfate mordant bath
3 hot plates per station
soap
paper towels

Time Required
50 minutes, if the work is divided up. The mordant treatment should be started right away by some students. The work can be piggybacked, so that as one fabric strip is being soaked, another fabric strip can be prepared. Alternatively, the work can be done on two separate days.

Advance Preparation
Methyl orange dye solution: add 0.7 g Na_2SO_4 and 2–3 drops concentrated H_2SO_4 to 150 mL of water; then add 0.50 g methyl orange powder to the solution.

Malachite green dye solution: dissolve 0.75 g of powdered dye in 150 mL boiling water.

Iron(II) sulfate mordant: add 4.2 g $FeSO_4 \cdot 7H_2O$ to 150 mL water.

Place the solutions in 1-L beakers on hot plates and heat in advance. Arrange hot plates with each of the three solutions at several stations about the laboratory.

© Prentice-Hall, Inc.

Exploring Dyes **127**

Lab 24 APPLICATION

Introduction

Start by explaining the role of ionic polar groups in the dyeing process. Part A, direct dyeing, is the simplest method and involves the ionic sites of the dye molecule attaching themselves to ionic sites of the fabric. In Part B, ionic sites are introduced into the synthetic fibers, so that more dye can bond.

3. Why do natural fabrics, such as wool, take up dye better than do synthetic fabrics? **Natural fabrics have many more polar and ionic sites.**

4. What is a mordant? What does a mordant do? **A mordant is a substance that "bites into" the fabrics, providing polar sites so dyes can bind onto the fabrics.**

5. Why is it necessary to use a mordant on some fabrics? **Mordants are needed on synthetic fabrics, which often do not have enough polar or ionic sites to bind the dyes sufficiently to color the fabric.**

6. Why is it necessary to wear latex gloves during this investigation? **Gloves prevent the absorption of dyes into the skin.**

7. What is meant by the term *colorfast*? **A fabric that is colorfast can be washed without losing any of its color.**

Problem

How is the polarity of a fabric related to its dye-holding capacity?

Materials

chemical splash goggles
laboratory apron
latex gloves
test fabric strips
dye baths:
   methyl orange
   malachite green

paper towels
soap
mordanting bath: iron(II) sulfate
tongs

Safety

Make sure students wear their goggles, gloves, and lab aprons at all times during the investigation. Emphasize the importance of protective clothing for this investigation. The hot plates should be placed so that they cannot be bumped by the students as they move around the hot solutions. Do not use lab burners to heat the solutions.

It would be prudent to caution students to wear old clothes suitable for painting for this investigation. The stains may be permanent. ■

Safety

Wear your goggles, gloves, and lab apron at all times during the investigation. The beakers containing the dye and mordanting baths are hot. Clean up any spills with plenty of cold water. Note the caution alert symbols here and with certain steps of the Procedure. Refer to page *xi* for the specific precautions associated with each symbol.

Procedure

Part A: Direct Dyeing

1. Put on your goggles, gloves, and lab apron. Using your tongs, immerse a strip of test cloth for seven minutes in the methyl orange dye bath set up by your teacher. Make sure the dye bath solution is near boiling temperature. **CAUTION:** *Beakers are hot. Use tongs or hot pads if you need to touch them.*

Name _____

Lab 24
APPLICATION

2. Remove the strip, allowing as much of the dye solution as possible to drain back into the bath. Rinse off excess dye with water. Place the strip on a paper towel to dry. Move fabrics carefully to avoid splashes.
3. Repeat Steps 1 and 2 with another strip of test cloth, using the malachite green dye bath. Record your observations.
4. After the fabric is dry, test it for colorfastness by cutting the strip in half and washing one half with soap. Allow the fabric to dry and compare the two halves. Staple the fabric to a sheet of paper and label the process you used on each sample.

 5. If you are not continuing on to Part B, turn off the hot plate. Clean up your work area and wash your hands before leaving the laboratory.

Part B: Mordants

 6. Put on your goggles, gloves, and lab apron. Using your tongs, soak another fabric strip in one of the mordanting baths for at least 25 minutes. **CAUTION:** *Beakers are hot. Use tongs or pads if you need to touch them.* Wring the fabric strip out over the mordanting bath.
7. Dye the strip in either malachite green or methyl orange, following the procedure in Part A. Test the fabric strip for colorfastness. Turn off the hot plates.
8. Staple the fabric to a sheet of paper and label as before. Observe and compare this strip with the untreated dyed cloths.
9. Dispose of all your solutions as directed by your teacher. Clean up your work area and wash your hands before leaving the laboratory.

Observations (sample data)
DATA TABLE

Dye Type	Observations	Colorfast?
methyl orange	Different intensities of orange. Wool has the greatest, and synthetics have the least.	Wool, cotton–yes synthetics–no
malachite green	Different intensities of green. Wool has the greatest, and the synthetics have the least.	Wool, cotton–yes synthetics–no
mordant and methyl orange	Intensities vary but are much greater in the synthetic fabrics than without mordant.	Yes
mordant and malachite green	Intensities vary but are much greater in the synthetic fabrics than without mordant.	Yes

Teaching Tips
Use several baths of each dye placed at convenient locations around the room. Assign different dyes and the combinations with mordant to different groups. This will assure that every combination is used, and will also relieve some of the crowding. Make sure that the dye and mordant baths stay close to the boiling point, but do not let them boil as they may spatter.

Test fabrics may be obtained from Testfabrics Inc., Box 118, 200 Blackford Ave, Middlesex, NJ, 08846. Order Multifiber Test Fabric 10. This has a pattern (wool, orlon, dacron, nylon, cotton, and acetate rayon) that repeats every three inches with a space at each end. The material is over 45 inches wide so 500 one-inch wide strips may be obtained from a single yard. You may also make up your own test strips with remnants.

Waste Disposal
Dye baths can be diluted with water and flushed down the sink. The mordant solution may also be flushed down the drain with large amounts of water. ■

Cooperative Learning Strategy
This lab lends itself well to the use of cooperative learning groups since it has several parts that cannot all be completed by every student within one period. If you divide the assignments, have groups pool their data at the end of the investigation.

© Prentice-Hall, Inc.

Exploring Dyes **129**

Critical Thinking: Analysis and Conclusions

1. What is the source of ions in the mordant? *(Making inferences)* Iron(II) ions from the iron(II) sulfate solution.

2. Compare your fabric strips with those of your classmates. List three variables that could account for the differences in your results. *(Interpreting data)* The amount of time the fabrics are in the hot dye bath; not allowing the strip to dry before testing it for colorfastness; and the amount of time it is in the mordant.

3. How do the colors of the mordanted fabrics compare with the colors produced without mordanting? *(Making comparisons)* The synthetic fabrics have more intense colors with mordanting than without it.

4. How did the mordanted fabrics compare to the untreated ones with respect to being colorfast? *(Making comparisons)* In general, the mordanting improves colorfastness of synthetics.

Critical Thinking: Applications

1. Why do you think it was necessary for the dye bath to be so hot? *(Developing hypotheses)* The higher temperature increases the rate of reaction, thereby lowering the time needed for the reaction.

2. During the 1970s, many of the popular clothing styles included nylon shirts that had brightly colored patterns printed on one side only. Why were the colors not dyed into the shirts? *(Applying concepts)* Nylon does not have enough polar sites to be able to get bright colors from dyeing. The process of printing colors on the fabrics yielded bright colors.

3. Silk blouses and shirts can be purchased in many intense colors. How does the nature of silk allow for a variety of intense dyes? *(Applying concepts)* Silk is a natural fiber, therefore it has many polar sites that allow the dyes to attach.

4. Washing instructions for clothing often state "wash in cold water only." What might happen if you washed this type of clothing in hot water? *(Making predictions)* The hot water would release more dye than would cold water, and the colors would run.

Going Further

1. Bring in some of your own swatches of fabric and test them under your teacher's supervision.
2. Research and report on the many dyes and mordants that are available from natural sources.

Name _____ Date _____ Class _____

Equation Writing and Predicting Products

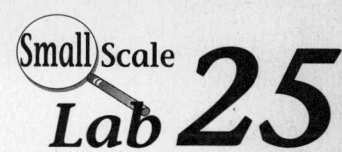

Small Scale Lab **25**

Text reference: **Chapter 9**

Introduction

If you examine a car that has been in a junkyard for a while, you will notice that it has rusted. Rusting is a slow chemical reaction of the iron in the car with oxygen gas. If sodium is put into water, a much more rapid chemical reaction occurs. Sodium reacts with water to produce sodium hydroxide and hydrogen gas. During this reaction, enough heat is liberated to ignite the hydrogen gas, causing it to explode.

Chemists observe what is happening in a chemical reaction and try to describe it in language that is simple and clear. A chemical equation uses formulas and symbols to describe the substances involved in a reaction, the physical state of the substance, the use of a catalyst (a substance that speeds up a reaction but is not used up in the process), and relative proportions. The general form of an equation is:

$$\text{Reactants} \rightarrow \text{Products}$$

In this investigation you will perform a series of reactions and make careful observations of the changes that occur. Using simple tests and your knowledge of chemistry, you will determine the identity of the products. With this information, you will write chemical equations to describe the reactions.

Pre-Lab Discussion

Read through the entire lab investigation and the relevant pages of your textbook. Then answer the questions that follow.

1. What constitutes a positive test for each of the following gases?

   a. oxygen __A glowing splint reignites and burns with a bright flame.__

   b. hydrogen __A burning splint causes the gas to ignite, producing a popping sound.__

   c. carbon dioxide __A burning splint is extinguished. Limewater turns cloudy white when CO_2 is bubbled through it.__

   d. water vapor __Cobalt chloride paper turns from blue to pink.__

   e. ammonia __Ammonia has a characteristic sharp odor.__

2. What is the proper way to smell a substance in the lab? Why should care be taken when smelling a gas such as ammonia? __Odors should be gently wafted towards the nose with the hand. Ammonia is irritating and can damage the respiratory tract.__

Materials (class of 30 in pairs)

30 pairs chemical splash goggles
30 laboratory aprons
30 pieces magnesium ribbon, 2–3 cm
15 pairs tongs
15 lab burners
15 books of matches
15 watch glasses
150 mL hydrochloric acid (HCl), 2.0 *M*
15 graduated cylinders, 10-mL
90 test tubes
15 test-tube racks
15 test-tube holders
45 wooden splints
15 pieces of copper foil, approximately 1 cm × 1 cm
15 files
15 spatulas
15 g ammonium carbonate (($NH_4)_2CO_3$)
15 pieces of cobalt chloride paper
150 mL hydrogen peroxide (H_2O_2), 3% solution
1.5 g manganese(IV) oxide (MnO_2)
15 dropper bottles of potassium iodide (KI), 0.1 *M*
15 well plates, 24-well
15 dropper bottles of lead nitrate ($Pb(NO_3)_2$), 0.1 *M*
45 g copper carbonate ($CuCO_3$)
150 mL limewater ($Ca(OH)_2$), saturated solution
15 one-hole rubber stoppers, size 0
15 glass elbows
10 mL glycerin
15 pieces of rubber tubing, 10–15 cm

Time Required

60–90 minutes. To shorten the lab, divide the reactions among the teams and have the students pool their data when finished. Have materials set up at each work

© Prentice-Hall, Inc.   Equation Writing and Predicting Products   **131**

Small Scale Lab 25

Name _____

area beforehand to save time. Alternatively, each reaction could constitute a station, and groups progress from station to station. Another suggestion to save time is to put together the rubber stopper, glass elbow, and rubber tubing assembly before the investigation begins. This assembly is used in many investigations, so it might be useful to store them already assembled.

Advance Preparation

To make limewater, place about 5 g of $Ca(OH)_2$ in a 250-mL beaker. Add 200 mL distilled water. Heat the solution while stirring for 5–10 minutes to get as much of the solid dissolved as possible. Filter the solution.

Dry the cobalt chloride paper in an oven before setting it out for students. Cut magnesium ribbons into pieces about 2–3 cm long. Cut copper into squares of 1 cm × 1 cm.

Prepare the solutions according to the following directions.

2.0 M HCl: Add 83 mL of concentrated HCl to enough water to make 500 mL of solution. CAUTION: *Wear goggles, apron, and gloves.*

0.1 M KI: Add 8.3 g KI to 500 mL of water.

0.1 M $Pb(NO_3)_2$: Add 16.6 g $Pb(NO_3)_2$ to 500 mL of water. CAUTION: *Lead compounds are toxic. Take care when working with them.*

3% H_2O_2 can be bought in a drug store.

Have labeled containers ready in which to collect the lead and copper waste solutions.

Introduction

Demonstrate the following tests for the gases produced in this investigation. Hydrogen gas will pop when in contact with a flaming splint, while carbon dioxide and ammonia will extinguish the flame. Oxygen will cause

3. What is the role of a catalyst in a reaction? How can you tell when a substance serves as a catalyst? A catalyst speeds up the rate of reaction. Catalysts are not used up in a reaction, so a substance acting as a catalyst would be regenerated when the reaction was finished.

4. One way to identify limestone ($CaCO_3$) is to drop a small amount of hydrochloric acid (HCl) on it. A positive test results in a fizz of carbon dioxide being produced. Write out in words the information represented by the following balanced chemical equation and give the molar ratio of the compounds.

$$CaCO_3(s) + 2\ HCl(aq) \rightarrow CaCl_2(aq) + H_2O(l) + CO_2(g)$$

When solid calcium carbonate reacts with aqueous hydrochloric acid, aqueous calcium chloride, liquid water, and carbon dioxide gas are produced. The molar ratios are 1:2:1:1:1.

Problem

How can chemical equations be used to describe what happens in chemical reactions?

Materials

chemical splash goggles
laboratory apron
2 pieces of magnesium ribbon
tongs
lab burner
matches
watch glass
6 test tubes
graduated cylinder
hydrochloric acid (HCl), 2.0 M
test-tube rack
test-tube holder
3 wooden splints
copper foil
file
spatula

ammonium carbonate ($(NH_4)_2CO_3$)
cobalt chloride paper
hydrogen peroxide (H_2O_2), 3% solution
manganese(IV) oxide, (MnO_2)
potassium iodide (KI), 0.1 M
well plate
lead nitrate ($Pb(NO_3)_2$), 0.1 M
copper carbonate ($CuCO_3$)
limewater ($Ca(OH)_2$ solution)
one-hole rubber stopper
glass tube elbow
glycerin
rubber tubing

Safety

Wear your goggles and lab apron at all times during the investigation. Avoid looking at the burning magnesium. The bright light could seriously damage your eyes. Tie back loose hair and clothing when working with a flame. Hydrochloric acid is corrosive. Avoid any direct contact with it. Ammonia is a skin and respiratory irritant, so avoid inhaling it deeply. Lead compounds are poisonous, so be sure to avoid contact with skin. If contact occurs with any of these chemicals, immediately wash the affected area with plenty of water and inform your teacher. Clean up all spills immediately. Lead and copper compounds should be collected in designated waste containers. Glass tubing breaks easily. Exercise caution when working with it. Note the caution alert symbols here and with certain steps of the Procedure. Refer to page *xi* for the specific precautions associated with each symbol.

Procedure

 1. Put on your goggles and lab apron. For each of the reactions, record in the Data Table observations such as the appearance of the reactants; evidence that a chemical reaction has taken place; the results of tests performed on any gases produced; the appearance of the products; and any other relevant data.

 2. Obtain a piece of magnesium ribbon. Light the lab burner. Holding the magnesium with your tongs, carefully place it in the lab burner flame. Hold the burning magnesium over a watch glass to catch any debris. **CAUTION:** *Tie back loose hair and clothing. The tongs will be hot. Do not touch them for at least 5 minutes. Do not look directly at the magnesium while it burns.* When the magnesium is finished burning, place the remains on the watch glass. Turn off the burner.

 3. Place a test tube in the test-tube rack. Have a second test tube ready in a test-tube holder. Add 5–10 mL of 3.0 M HCl to the first test tube. Drop a 2-cm piece of magnesium ribbon into the acid. **CAUTION:** *Hydrochloric acid is corrosive. Avoid spills and splashes. If you do spill acid, immediately rinse the area with plenty of cold water and report the spill to your teacher.*

 4. Invert the second test tube over the mouth of the first test tube, as shown in Figure 25–1. When the reaction appears to have ended, light a wood splint and quickly test the collected gas for flammability by holding the burning wood splint near the mouth of the second test tube. **CAUTION:** *The gas in the test tube will make a popping sound. Do not be startled.*

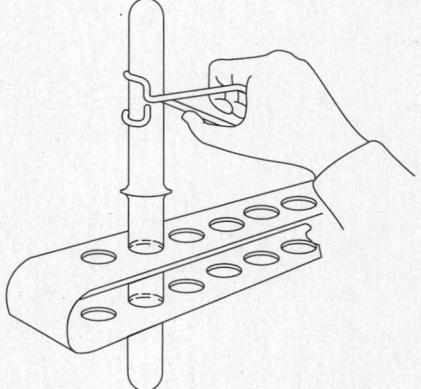

Figure 25–1

a glowing splint to reignite. Carbon dioxide will turn clear limewater cloudy. Ammonia has a distinct odor. Water vapor will change blue cobalt paper pink.

For a dramatic demonstration of a chemical reaction, put about 30 mL of 30% hydrogen peroxide (H_2O_2) in a flask and add a teaspoon of MnO_2. The heat produced by the reaction will cause the water to boil, sending a stream of steam out of the top of the flask. Point out to the students that they will be performing this reaction on a smaller scale.

Safety
Make sure students wear their goggles and lab aprons at all times during the investigation. Burning magnesium in the lab burner flame produces UV radiation. Students should be cautioned not to look directly at the light. HCl is corrosive and irritating to skin and eyes. Ammonia is a respiratory irritant at low concentrations and should not be inhaled directly. Instruct students in the proper technique to detect odors. Lead compounds are poisonous. They should be used with caution. If students spill any on their skin, they should rinse the affected area with plenty of water. ■

Teaching Tips
This is an enjoyable investigation for many students because they feel that they are doing "real" chemistry. They enjoy the color changes and like performing the tests for the different gases. Many students will have seen the tests for oxygen, hydrogen, carbon dioxide, ammonia, and water before.

Encourage students to make reasonable predictions of products based on their observations. Working in pairs or small groups is

Small Scale Lab 25

Name _____

helpful if each group has to come up with a balanced equation and be able to justify it on the basis of their observations and knowledge.

Students will need help with the equation for the decomposition of hydrogen peroxide. Manganese(IV) oxide is a catalyst and is not consumed in the reaction. All the MnO₂ can be recovered after the reaction has been completed. Students interested in this idea can be encouraged to try Going Further 2.

5. Light the lab burner. Grasp a small piece of copper foil with your tongs and heat it in the burner flame until it is red hot. Remove it from the flame and allow it to cool. Scratch the surface of the metal with a sharp object (such as a file).

6. Carefully place about one spatula of ammonium carbonate $((NH_4)_2CO_3)$ into a test tube. Holding the test tube with a test-tube holder, heat the solid gently by holding the test tube in the flame for a few seconds, then removing it for a few seconds. Continue heating in this manner for 1 minute. As you heat the solid, carefully waft the air toward your nose to detect any odor. **CAUTION:** *When heating the test tube, point the open end away from yourself and anyone nearby. The gas coming from the tube is a skin and respiratory irritant, so avoid inhaling it deeply.* Continuing to heat the solid, place a burning splint at the mouth of the test tube. Finally, as heating continues, place a piece of blue cobalt paper just inside the mouth of the test tube. Put the test tube in the rack to cool. Turn off the burner.

7. Place approximately 10–15 mL of hydrogen peroxide, H_2O_2, into a test tube. Have a wooden splint and matches ready. Add a very small amount (about the tip of a spatula) of manganese(IV) oxide, MnO_2, to the hydrogen peroxide. As the reaction occurs, light the splint and allow it to burn freely for 5 seconds. Blow the flame out and place the glowing splint halfway into the test tube.

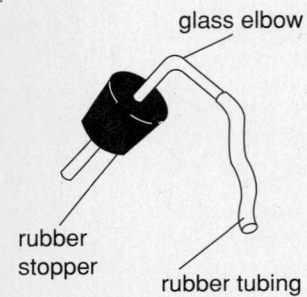

Figure 25–2

Waste Disposal

Lead compounds are regulated as hazardous waste (EPA #D008). Provide a clearly labeled container in which to collect the waste lead compounds. Hold for disposal by a qualified professional. MnO₂ can be collected, filtered, and dried for reuse. Copper foil can be collected, polished, and reused. Copper carbonate waste can be collected and stored or disposed of as solid waste. ■

8. Place a drop of potassium iodide solution, KI, in one well of a well plate. Add a drop of lead nitrate solution, $Pb(NO_3)_2$. **CAUTION:** *Lead compounds are poisonous, so be sure to avoid contact with skin. If contact occurs, immediately wash the affected area with plenty of water and inform your teacher. Clean up all spills immediately.*

9. Assemble the stopper, glass elbow, and rubber tubing as shown in Figure 25–2. Place a small amount (about one spatula) of copper carbonate, $CuCO_3$, in a test tube. **CAUTION:** *Glass tubing breaks easily. Exercise caution when working with it.* Place the stopper assembly into the test tube. Prepare another test tube with about 10–15 mL of limewater. Light the lab burner. Holding the tube containing the copper carbonate with a test-tube holder, heat the copper carbonate. As the copper carbonate is heated, push the end of the rubber tubing all the way to the bottom of the limewater in the other tube.

10. Turn off the burner. Copper and lead compounds should be disposed of in designated waste containers. Clean up your work area and wash your hands before leaving the laboratory.

Name_____

Small Scale Lab 25

Observations (sample data)

Reaction	Observations
burning Mg	shiny, grey, malleable metal before burning; flame, bright light, and smoke produced; crumbly, white residue
Mg and HCl	shiny, grey, malleable metal and a colorless, odorless liquid before mixing; colorless gas and heat produced; gas popped; some students may report a faint blue flame; clear liquid residue
heating Cu	shiny, red-brown, malleable metal before heating; surface becomes dull, black, powdery; surface easily scratched with file
heating $(NH_4)_2CO_3$	white, crystalline powder before heating; disappears while heating; colorless liquid collects at mouth of test tube; strong odor of ammonia; burning splint is extinguished; liquid turns blue cobalt chloride paper pink
H_2O_2 and MnO_2	clear liquid and black, powdery solid; colorless gas and heat produced; glowing splint reignites and burns brightly; black powder suspended in liquid
KI and $Pb(NO_3)_2$	both clear liquids before mixing; yellow precipitate suspended in clear liquid
heating $CuCO_3$	green-grey powder before heating; changes to black; colorless gas produced; limewater becomes cloudy; residue is black

Critical Thinking: Analysis and Conclusions

1. Write a balanced equation for each of the reactions performed. Include the physical state of each substance. *(Making inferences)*

    $2Mg(s) + O_2(g) \rightarrow 2MgO(s)$

    $Mg(s) + 2HCl(aq) \rightarrow MgCl_2(aq) + H_2(g)$

    $2Cu(s) + O_2(g) \rightarrow 2CuO(s)$

    $(NH_4)_2CO_3(s) \rightarrow 2NH_3(g) + CO_2(g) + H_2O(g)$

    $2H_2O_2(aq) \rightarrow 2H_2O(l) + O_2(g)$

    $2KI(aq) + Pb(NO_3)_2(aq) \rightarrow PbI_2(s) + 2KNO_3(aq)$

    $CuCO_3(s) \rightarrow CuO(s) + CO_2(g)$

2. Classify each of the reactions as direct combination, decomposition, single replacement, or double replacement. *(Classifying)* Burning Mg and heating Cu are direct combination reactions. The reactions of $(NH_4)_2CO_3$, H_2O_2, and $CuCO_3$ are decompositions. Mg and HCl is a single replacement. KI and $Pb(NO_3)_2$ is a double replacement.

3. Limewater is an aqueous solution of $Ca(OH)_2$. Speculate on the identity of the cloudy white precipitate that forms with CO_2 gas. Write a chemical equation for this reaction that is consistent with your observations. *(Making inferences)* The precipitate is calcium carbonate ($CaCO_3$). The equation is $Ca(OH)_2(aq) + CO_2(g) \rightarrow CaCO_3(s) + H_2O(l)$.

© Prentice-Hall, Inc.   *Equation Writing and Predicting Products*

4. A positive test for hydrogen was the "pop" test. What chemical reaction was occurring? Write a balanced equation representing this reaction. *(Making inferences)* Hydrogen gas reacted with oxygen gas in the air to form water. $2H_2(g) + O_2(g) \rightarrow 2H_2O(l)$

Critical Thinking: Applications

1. For each of the following situations, determine the identity of the gas produced from the information given and write a balanced chemical equation that represents the reaction. *(Applying concepts)*

    a. When potassium bromate ($KBrO_3$) is heated, it decomposes into potassium bromide (KBr) and a gas that supports the combustion of a glowing splint. Oxygen gas. $2KBrO_3(s) \rightarrow 2KBr(s) + 3O_2(g)$

    b. Sodium metal reacts violently with water to produce sodium hydroxide (NaOH) and a gas that "pops" in the presence of a burning splint. Hydrogen gas. $2Na(s) + 2H_2O(l) \rightarrow 2NaOH(aq) + H_2(g)$

    c. The recipe for the volcanic eruption used in many science projects is the reaction of baking soda ($NaHCO_3$) and vinegar (CH_3COOH). When these compounds are mixed together, the salt sodium acetate ($NaCH_3COO$) is formed as well as a gas that extinguishes a burning flame and a substance that turns blue cobalt chloride paper pink. Carbon dioxide gas.
    $NaHCO_3(s) + CH_3COOH(aq) \rightarrow NaCH_3COO(aq) + CO_2(g) + H_2O(l)$

2. Cobalt chloride is a hydrated salt used for making humidity gauges. The formula of the hydrated form is $CoCl_2 \cdot 2H_2O$. What color is associated with the hydrated form of cobalt chloride? How might it be used to predict weather changes? *(Developing models)* Hydrated cobalt chloride is pink. Increased humidity in the air would change a cobalt chloride strip from blue to pink.

Going Further

Going Further

1. A discussion of the long-term carbon cycle and its role in the evolution of Earth's climate is found in "Global Climate Change" by Dorothy K. Hall in *The Science Teacher*, Sept 1989.

1. Earth's long-term carbon cycle involves the recycling of carbon through the ecosystems over thousands of years. Many scientists believe that the cycling of carbon from carbonate rock to the atmosphere was an important factor in the development of Earth's climate. Investigate the long-term carbon cycle and its role in maintaining Earth's climate. Describe how the carbon cycle relates to the carbonate reactions in this investigation.

2. Manganese(IV) oxide (MnO_2) is considered to be a catalyst in the decomposition of hydrogen peroxide. Design an experiment to demonstrate this point. Have your teacher approve your experimental design before you begin. Perform the experiment only under a teacher's supervision.

Bags of Reactions

Lab 26
APPLICATION

Text reference: **Chapter 9**

Introduction

"Plop, plop, fizz, fizz, oh, what a relief it is," claims an old television ad for a popular antacid. Just what is in the tablet that is relieving the upset stomach? What reaction is causing the fizzing? Can you write a chemical equation for this process? With a bit of investigating, you will be able to discover answers to all these questions.

As you learned in Chapter 2, Antoine Lavoisier, in the eighteenth century, formulated the law of conservation of mass, which states that matter can neither be created nor destroyed. During a chemical reaction, the bonds of the reactants are broken and rearranged to form new substances. Because matter must be conserved, these new substances, or products, must contain the same number and type of atoms as the reactants.

In this investigation, you will first verify the law of conservation of mass. Then in the second part, you will be given some known compounds to react. You will write and balance a chemical equation for the reaction.

Materials (class of 30 in pairs)
- 30 pairs chemical splash goggles
- 30 laboratory aprons
- 15 Alka-Seltzer tablets
- 15 scoopulas or teaspoons
- 30 resealable plastic bags, 1-L
- 100 g calcium chloride ($CaCl_2$)
- 100 g sodium hydrogen carbonate ($NaHCO_3$)
- 50 mL phenol red indicator
- 15 graduated cylinders, 50-mL
- 15 laboratory balances

Time Required
40 minutes.

Advance Preparation
Prepare micropipets of phenol red indicator.

Introduction
The chemistry of Alka-Seltzer can be introduced here, although reaction equilibria will be discussed in Chapter 16. Alka-Seltzer contains sodium hydrogen carbonate, aspirin, and citric acid. What the students see in this investigation is mainly the reaction of sodium hydrogen carbonate and citric acid ($H_3C_6H_5O_7$) in water:

$H_3C_6H_5O_7(aq) + 3NaHCO_3(aq)$
$\rightleftharpoons Na_3C_6H_5O_7(aq) + 3H_2O(l) + 3CO_2(g)$

When excess acid is present in the stomach, the reaction is driven to the right, and more gas is produced (hence, the burp). Therefore, even though the pH of Alka-Seltzer in water is acidic, the compound still functions as an antacid.

Pre-Lab Discussion

Read the entire laboratory investigation and the relevant pages of your textbook. Then answer the questions that follow.

1. Define *reactants*. __Reactants are substances that react in a chemical reaction.__

2. Define *products*. __Products are substances that are produced in a chemical reaction.__

3. How can you tell when a chemical reaction has happened? __Indications of a chemical reaction include change in color, formation of a precipitate or gas, and change in temperature.__

4. What is the point of using a resealable bag? __The resealable bag is used so that all products, including gases, are retained.__

5. What is the density of water? __The density of water is 1.0 g/mL.__

6. What is the common name for sodium hydrogen carbonate? __Sodium hydrogen carbonate is commonly known as baking soda.__

Problem

Can equations be written and balanced for chemical reactions?

Lab 26 APPLICATION

Name _____

Materials

chemical splash goggles
laboratory apron
graduated cylinder, 50-mL
2 resealable plastic bags, 1-L
laboratory balance
antacid tablet

scoopula or teaspoon
calcium chloride, $CaCl_2$
sodium hydrogen carbonate, $NaHCO_3$
phenol red indicator

Safety

Wear your goggles and lab apron at all times during the investigation. Note the caution alert symbols here and with certain steps of the Procedure. Refer to page xi for the specific precautions associated with each symbol.

Safety
Make sure students wear their goggles and lab aprons at all times during the investigation. ■

Teaching Tips
If you have done the lab in Chapter 2 of the text, you may wish to skip Part A of this investigation and proceed directly to Part B.
  After rinsing, the plastic bags can be washed, turned inside out and dried for reuse. If phenol red is not available, any indicator whose color change range is 6.5–7.5, such as bromthymol blue, is acceptable.
  The baking soda can be dispensed directly from the commercial household box to reinforce the idea that it is an everyday common substance. The students might be interested in knowing that $CaCl_2$ is used to keep sidewalks and streets clear of ice during winter.

Procedure

Part A

1. Put on your goggles and lab apron. Measure 25 mL of tap water into a resealable plastic bag. Flatten the air out of the bag and seal it. Record its mass in Data Table 1.
2. Record the mass of the antacid tablet in Data Table 1.
3. Tip the bag sideways, and while holding the bag this way, add the tablet so that the tablet and water do not mix. Do not trap any extra air in the bag. Refer to Figure 26–1. Reseal the bag.

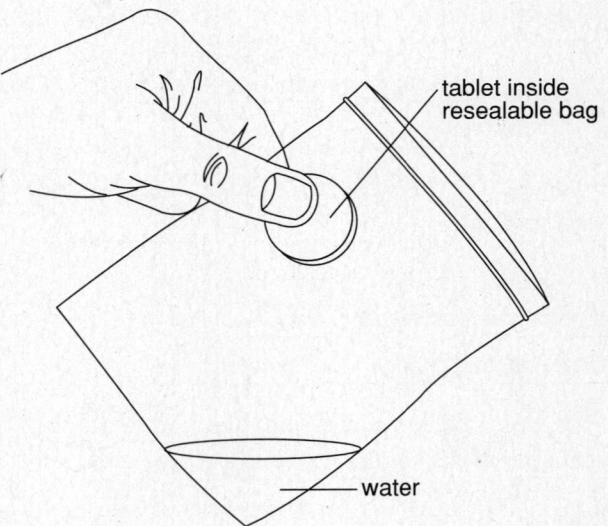

Figure 26–1

4. Let the tablet drop into the water. Observe the reaction until it comes to a complete stop. Record your observations.
5. When the reaction is complete, record the mass of the bag and its contents in Data Table 1.

138 © Prentice-Hall, Inc.

Name _____

Lab 26
APPLICATION

Part B

6. Add 2 scoops of calcium chloride, CaCl$_2$, to the second plastic bag.
7. Add 1 scoop of sodium hydrogen carbonate, NaHCO$_3$, to the bag, and shake gently to mix.
8. Determine the mass of the bag and its contents. Record this value in Data Table 2.
9. Measure 25 mL of water into the graduated cylinder. Add 5 drops of phenol red indicator to the water.
10. Tip the bag sideways, and while holding the solids in the upper part of the bag, pour the water into the bag so that the water and solids do not mix.
11. Keeping the trapped air to a minimum, reseal the bag. Hold the bag and let the liquid move from one end of the bag to the other until the contents are mixed.
12. Observe the reaction until it comes to a complete stop. Record your observations.
13. Record the mass of the unopened bag in Data Table 2. Clean up your work area and wash your hands before leaving the laboratory.

Waste Disposal
Excess phenol red indicator should be stored separately for commercial disposal or shipment to a secure landfill. All other substances can be washed down the drain. ■

Observations (sample data)

DATA TABLE 1 Antacid Tablet and Water

mass of bag and water	30.45 g	Write observations here:
mass of tablet	3.35 g	gas bubbles form, bag inflates, gets colder, hear fizzing sound
mass of bag and reactants	33.80 g	
mass of bag and products	33.79 g	

DATA TABLE 2 CaCl$_2$, NaHCO$_3$, and Water

mass of bag and dry reactants	14.45 g	Write observations here:
volume of water	25.0 mL	bag inflates greatly, bag gets hot, color changes, bubbles form
mass of water	25.0 g	
total mass of bag and reactants	39.45 g	
mass of bag and products	39.45 g	

Calculations (based on sample data)

1. Calculate the total mass of the bag and reactants in each reaction and record these values in the appropriate Data Table.
2. Using the formula for the density of water, calculate the mass of the water. Record the results in Data Table 2.

    25 mL H$_2$O (1.0 g/mL) = 25.0 g H$_2$O

© Prentice-Hall, Inc.   *Bags of Reactions*   **139**

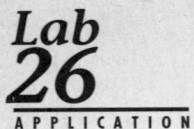

Name _____

Critical Thinking: Analysis and Conclusions

1. How do the values for total mass before and after each reaction demonstrate the law of conservation of mass? *(Interpreting data)* The mass before and after each reaction is the same.

2. What were at least five observations you made that indicated a reaction had occurred in Part A? *(Giving examples)* Student answers may vary but might include bubbles, tablet dissolved, the bag got colder, the bag inflated, the hissing sound.

3. Write an equation in words and then with formulas for the reaction that occurred in the bag in Part B. The products are sodium chloride, calcium hydroxide, and carbonic acid. *(Applying concepts)* Sodium hydrogen carbonate + calcium chloride + water yields sodium chloride + calcium hydroxide + carbonic acid.

   $2NaHCO_3(s) + CaCl_2(s) + 2H_2O(l) \rightarrow 2NaCl(aq) + Ca(OH)_2(aq) + 2H_2CO_3(aq)$

Critical Thinking: Applications

1. An indicator changes color when the acidity of a solution changes. What evidence is there that such a change occurred in Part B? *(Applying concepts)* The color of phenol red changed from red to yellow.

2. Judge whether the reaction mixture in Part B became more acidic or more basic. Explain. *(Making predictions)* Since carbonic acid formed, it should have become more acidic.

3. Carbonic acid immediately decomposes into water and carbon dioxide. Write the balanced equation for this reaction. *(Applying concepts)* $H_2CO_3(aq) \rightarrow H_2O(l) + CO_2(g)$

4. What gas was produced in Part A? *(Making predictions)* (Hint: sodium hydrogen carbonate is an active ingredient in the antacid.) Carbon dioxide.

Going Further

1. Under the supervision of your teacher, test reactions between the following pairs of reactants to determine whether they follow the law of conservation of mass. Predict the products of the reactions and balance the equations: acetic acid (vinegar) and baking soda; zinc and hydrochloric acid.

Name _____ Date _____ Class _____

Double Replacement Reactions

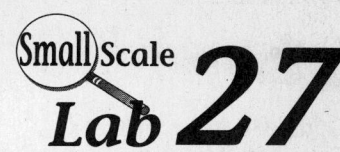

Small Scale Lab 27

Text reference: **Chapter 9**

Introduction

As you may have read in Chapter 9 of your textbook, antacid tablets contain the compound calcium carbonate, $CaCO_3$. This compound reacts with the hydrochloric acid, HCl, in your stomach in the following way:

$$CaCO_3(aq) + 2HCl(aq) \rightarrow CaCl_2(s) + H_2CO_3(aq)$$

This reaction is an everyday example of a double replacement reaction.

A double replacement reaction usually takes place between two ionic compounds that are dissolved in water. The cation of one compound replaces the cation in another compound to produce two new compounds. The new combination of cations and anions yields a product that may be a precipitate, a gas, or water. Precipitates are solids that form from the reaction between compounds that are soluble in water.

In this investigation you will mix several pairs of aqueous solutions and ionic compounds. You will observe which combinations of solutions result in the formation of a precipitate, and you will write balanced equations for the reactions.

Pre-Lab Discussion

Read the entire laboratory investigation and the relevant pages of your textbook. Then answer the questions that follow.

1. What is a double replacement reaction? __A double replacement reaction is one that takes place between two compounds dissolved in water in which the cation from one compound changes place with the cation from another compound to form two new compounds.__

2. What evidence indicates that a double replacement reaction has occurred between two dissolved compounds? __The formation of a precipitate, a gas, or water is evidence that a double replacement reaction has occurred.__

3. What type of evidence will you be looking for in this investigation? __The formation of a precipitate.__

4. What hazards are associated with using silver nitrate, and what precautions should you take in this investigation? __Silver nitrate is poisonous and can produce a stain on skin and clothing that is hard to remove. Wear gloves and avoid contact with the solutions.__

Materials (class of 30 in pairs)
30 pairs chemical splash goggles
30 laboratory aprons
30 pairs latex gloves
15 marking pens
15 well plates, 24-well
15 sheets of white paper
15 beakers to hold micropipets
105 micropipets
100 mL silver nitrate $(AgNO_3)$, 0.1 M
100 mL iron(III) nitrate $(Fe(NO_3)_3)$, 0.1 M
100 mL copper(II) nitrate $(Cu(NO_3)_2)$, 0.1 M
100 mL sodium phosphate (Na_3PO_4), 0.1 M
100 mL sodium sulfate (Na_2SO_4), 0.1 M
100 mL sodium hydroxide (NaOH), 0.1 M
100 mL sodium chloride (NaCl), 0.1 M
15 droppers

Time Required
45 minutes. Allow more time if students work individually.

Advance Preparation
Prepare 0.1 M solutions by adding the following masses of each solute to enough water to bring the volume up to 100 mL, which is enough for a class of 30 students:

1.70 g $AgNO_3$
4.04 g $Fe(NO_3)_3 \cdot 9H_2O$
2.42 g $Cu(NO_3)_2 \cdot 3H_2O$
3.80 g $Na_3PO_4 \cdot 12H_2O$
1.41 g Na_2SO_4
0.40 g NaOH
0.58 g NaCl

Have ready a labeled container in which to collect the waste silver solutions.

Introduction
The concept of a double replacement reaction may be

© Prentice-Hall, Inc.

Double Replacement Reactions **141**

Small Scale Lab 27

Name _____

hard for the students to visualize. You may want to do a demonstration using colored balls. You could even use pairs of students and make an analogy to the exchange of dance partners in some dances.

Double replacement reactions are widely used in analytical chemistry to identify cations. Since silver nitrate is one of the few soluble silver compounds, it can be used in double replacement reactions to recover silver from photographic processing wastes. Colored precipitates from double replacement reactions are sometimes used in pigments.

Safety

Make sure students wear their goggles and lab aprons at all times during the investigation. They should also wear gloves whenever handling silver nitrate solutions.

Sodium hydroxide solution is caustic, and silver nitrate can stain skin and clothing. Tell students to wash spills and splashes with plenty of water. A dilute solution of ammonia water will help remove silver nitrate stains from the skin. ■

Teaching Tips

Remind students not to let the tips of their micropipets touch the solutions in their reaction plates as it will cause contamination of the solution in the micropipet.

Refer students to Chapter 9 in their textbooks for a general discussion of double replacement reactions.

If you wish, suggest that students use colored pencils or pens to keep track of the ions as they write observations in their Data Table.

Problem

Which combinations of ionic solutions form precipitates that indicate a double replacement reaction has occurred?

Materials

chemical splash goggles
laboratory apron
latex gloves
marking pen
well plate
sheet of white paper
beaker to hold micropipets
dropper (for cleanup)

7 micropipets, each filled with one of the following 0.1 M solutions:
silver nitrate ($AgNO_3$)
iron(III) nitrate ($Fe(NO_3)_3$)
copper(II) nitrate ($Cu(NO_3)_2$)
sodium phosphate (Na_3PO_4)
sodium sulfate (Na_2SO_4)
sodium hydroxide (NaOH)
sodium chloride (NaCl)

Safety

Wear your goggles and lab apron at all times during the investigation. Wear gloves when handling silver nitrate as it is toxic and can cause stains to skin and clothing. Handle all chemicals with care; avoid spills and contact with your skin. If contact occurs, wash with plenty of cold water and tell your teacher.

Note the caution alert symbols here and with certain steps of the Procedure. Refer to page xi for the specific precautions associated with each symbol.

Procedure

1. Put on your goggles, gloves, and lab apron. Label the wells of the well plate as shown in Figure 27–1. Place the well plate on the sheet of white paper. Use a micropipet to place five drops of silver nitrate solution, $AgNO_3$, into each of wells A1 through A4. **CAUTION:** *Silver nitrate is poisonous. Be careful not to get it on your skin or clothing, as it will produce a stain that is hard to remove. If any spills occur, ask your teacher how to clean up safely.*

2. Place five drops of iron(III) nitrate solution, $Fe(NO_3)_3$, into each of wells B1 through B4. Then place five drops of copper(II) nitrate solution, $Cu(NO_3)_2$, into each of wells C1 through C4.

3. Now you will add a different ionic compound to each column of wells. To avoid contamination of the ionic solution in the micropipet, do not let its tip touch the solutions that are already in the wells. Add five drops of sodium phosphate solution, Na_3PO_4, to each of the solutions in wells A1, B1, and C1. Observe whether or not a precipitate forms in each well and record your observations in the Data Table. If a precipitate forms, record the color. If a precipitate does not form, write *NR* for *No Reaction*.

142 © Prentice-Hall, Inc.

Name_____

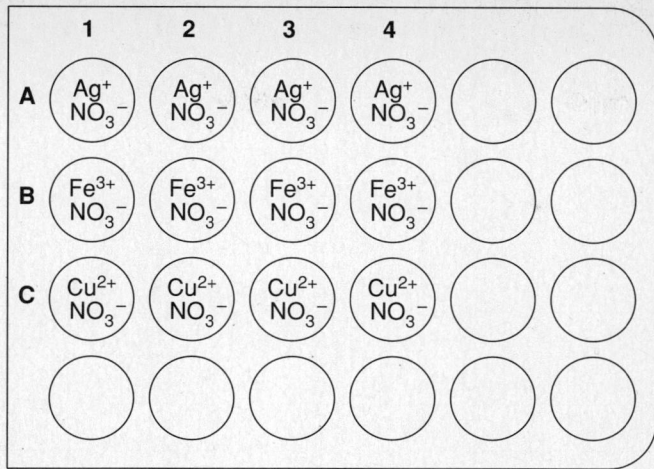

Figure 27–1

4. Add five drops of sodium sulfate solution, Na₂SO₄, to each of the solutions in wells A2, B2, and C2. Record your observations in the Data Table.

5. Add five drops of sodium hydroxide solution, NaOH, to each of the solutions in wells A3, B3, and C3 and record your observations. **CAUTION:** *Sodium hydroxide solution is caustic. Avoid spilling it on your skin or clothing. Wash spills with plenty of cold water.*

6. Add five drops of sodium chloride solution, NaCl, to the solutions in wells A4, B4, and C4 and record your observations.

7. Use a dropper to pull up the silver solutions in the row A wells of the well plate and deposit the material into the container provided by your teacher. Any silver nitrate solution left in a micropipet should be disposed of in a similar manner. Wash the sodium hydroxide down the drain with plenty of water. Clean up your work area and wash your hands before leaving the laboratory.

Waste Disposal
Silver compounds are regulated as hazardous waste (EPA waste #D011). Provide a clearly labeled container in which the students will put their waste silver compounds. Use disposal method 9. ■

Observations (sample data)
DATA TABLE

		1	2	3	4
	Ionic Solutions	Na^+ PO_4^{3-}	Na^+ SO_4^{2-}	Na^+ OH^-	Na^+ Cl^-
A	Ag^+ NO_3^-	yellow precipitate	faint white precipitate (or NR)	brown-white precipitate	white precipitate
B	Fe^{3+} NO_3^-	white precipitate	NR	orange-red precipitate	NR
C	Cu^{2+} NO_3^-	blue precipitate	NR	blue precipitate	NR

© Prentice-Hall, Inc.   *Double Replacement Reactions* **143**

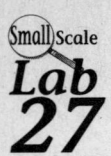

Small Scale Lab 27

Name _____

Critical Thinking: Analysis and Conclusions

1. For which combinations of solutions did no precipitate form? Based on these observations, which compounds are soluble in water? Explain. *(Drawing conclusions)* No reaction occurred when sodium sulfate was mixed with iron(III) nitrate or with copper(II) nitrate, and when sodium chloride was mixed with the same two solutions. (There may not be a visible reaction when sodium sulfate is mixed with silver nitrate.) According to these observations, the soluble compounds are sodium nitrate, iron(III) sulfate, copper(II) sulfate, iron(III) chloride, and copper(II) chloride. (Silver sulfate may also be considered soluble.)

2. Based on your observations, which positive ion reacts to form the greatest number of precipitates: Ag^+, Fe^{3+}, or Cu^{2+}? Explain. *(Interpreting data)* The silver ion reacts to form the greatest number of precipitates. Silver nitrate solution forms a precipitate when it mixes with all four of the test solutions (or three of the four solutions) used.

3. Use a solubility table to determine the identity of the precipitates that formed in the wells in column 1. Then write the balanced equation for the reactions, including the symbols for phase, *(s)* and *(aq)*. *(Interpreting data)*

   A1: $3AgNO_3(aq) + Na_3PO_4(aq) \rightarrow Ag_3PO_4(s) + 3NaNO_3(aq)$

   B1: $Fe(NO_3)_3(aq) + Na_3PO_4(aq) \rightarrow FePO_4(s) + 3NaNO_3(aq)$

   C1: $3Cu(NO_3)_2(aq) + 2Na_3PO_4(aq) \rightarrow Cu_3(PO_4)_2(s) + 6NaNO_3(aq)$

Critical Thinking: Applications

1. Write the equation for the reaction that takes place when a solution of silver nitrate is added to a solution of sodium chloride. *(Applying concepts)* $AgNO_3(aq) + NaCl(aq) \rightarrow AgCl(s) + NaNO_3(aq)$

2. Sodium hydrogen carbonate, $NaHCO_3$, and sodium chloride, $NaCl$, are both soluble in water. Will a double replacement reaction take place if a solution of sodium hydrogen carbonate is added to a solution of sodium chloride? Explain. *(Making inferences)* No double replacement reaction will occur because the only available positive ion is Na^+, which forms soluble compounds with both HCO_3^- and Cl^-.

Going Further

1. Check students' schemes and charts to ensure that they are logical.

Going Further

1. Given a solution that contains one or more of the compounds used in this investigation, explain how you could identify the unknown compound or compounds. Use a chart to show your scheme.

Molar Volume of Hydrogen Gas

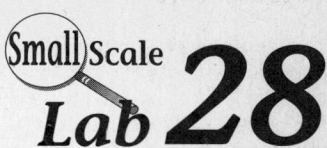

Lab 28

Text reference: **Chapter 10**

Introduction

How would you measure the mass and volume of a gas? This is actually quite a difficult problem because gases often seem to lack definitive properties. If you filled a balloon with hydrogen gas and then tried to measure the combined mass of the hydrogen and the balloon, you would obtain an inaccurate measurement because of the buoyancy of the surrounding air. You could try to measure the volume of the hydrogen, but gas volume changes with variations in temperature or pressure. If you placed hydrogen gas in a rigid container, it would expand to fill the entire volume of the container regardless of the amount of hydrogen present. Also, gases can be produced or absorbed by chemical and physical changes of solids or liquids, as in some decompositions or in evaporation and condensation.

The mystery of gas properties was a major stumbling block to the development of modern chemistry. A solution to this mystery was found when scientists discovered that the changes in gas volume caused by pressure and temperature variations could be mathematically predicted. Another pivotal discovery was the realization that the mass of a gas can be determined by measuring the change in mass of the solid or liquid that produced the gas.

In 1811, Avogadro published his hypothesis that equal volumes of different gases at a given temperature and pressure contain identical numbers of gas particles. This hypothesis led to the idea that a mole of a given gas (6.02×10^{23} particles) occupies the same volume as a mole of any other gas, as long as the temperature and pressure are the same.

In this investigation you will determine an experimental value for the molar volume of hydrogen gas. You also will see if your results confirm the accepted molar volume of 22.4 liters per mole at a temperature of 0°C and a pressure of 760 mm Hg (one atmosphere). To make your results comparable, you will keep the gas as close as possible to 0°C and do a calculation to adjust for differences in pressure.

Pre-Lab Discussion

Read the entire laboratory investigation and the relevant pages of your textbook. Then answer the questions that follow.

1. Why is this investigation carried out in a basin of ice water that is at or near 0°C? __Temperature affects gas volume. The value used for__ __comparison, 22.4 liters per mole, is determined at 0°C, which is equal or__ __close to the ice bath temperature.__

Materials (class of 30 in pairs)

30 pairs chemical splash goggles
30 laboratory aprons
30 pairs latex gloves
15 plastic basins, 2–3 L
15 L ice
tap water
15 metric rulers
15 Celsius thermometers
barometer
30 cm Mg ribbon, cut into 1-cm lengths
15 pairs scissors
15 micropipets
100 mL hydrochloric acid (HCl), 3.0 M
15 graduated cylinders, 10-mL
15 squares of plastic wrap 5 cm × 5 cm
15 rubber bands
15 pins

Time Required

20–30 minutes per trial.

Advance Preparation

Measure and record the exact length and mass of the magnesium ribbon. Divide the mass by the length to find the mass-to-length ratio to three significant figures. Then cut the magnesium ribbon into 1-cm lengths.
    Cut the squares of plastic wrap. Buy or make enough ice to supply the class.
    Prepare 3.0 M HCl by adding 25 mL of 12.0 M hydrochloric acid to enough water to make 100 mL. CAUTION: *Wear goggles, apron, and gloves.*

Introduction

Before beginning this lab, you may wish to demonstrate the size of a molar volume of carbon dioxide gas. To do this, place a molar mass of dry ice inside a large

Molar Volume of Hydrogen Gas

garbage bag or dry-cleaning bag and seal. As the dry ice sublimes, the bag will swell. The volume will not be exactly 22.4 liters because the temperature is not 0°C. You can discuss this discrepancy with your class.

Use a manometer example to explain the necessity of equalizing water levels in order to establish a pressure for the hydrogen equal to atmospheric pressure.

2. Write the balanced equation for the reaction that occurs between magnesium and hydrochloric acid. $Mg + 2HCl \rightarrow H_2 + MgCl_2$

3. How is the volume of gas collected at room temperature adjusted to standard pressure? The volume is adjusted by multiplying it by the ratio between the atmospheric pressure and the standard pressure, 760 mm Hg.

4. What happens to the acid that is placed in the graduated cylinder at the start of the experiment? How might this pose a safety hazard? Some of the acid reacts with magnesium. Some of it is diluted in the cylinder and should be handled as a dilute acid, hazardous to eyes and clothing, and an irritant to skin.

Problem

What is the molar volume of hydrogen gas?

Materials

chemical splash goggles
laboratory apron
latex gloves
plastic basin
ice
tap water
metric ruler
Celsius thermometer
barometer

magnesium strip (Mg)
scissors
plastic micropipet, long-stem
hydrochloric acid (HCl), 3.0 M
graduated cylinder, 10-mL
plastic wrap, 5 × 5 cm
rubber band
pin

Safety

Safety

Make sure students wear their goggles, gloves, and lab aprons at all times during the investigation. Caution students to avoid spills and splashes of hydrochloric acid and to wash exposed skin or clothing with plenty of cold water. ■

Teaching Tips

If you have only one barometer, leave it in one location and have each group take a reading or take the reading yourself and write it on the board.

Demonstrate the critical step of preparing the graduated cylinder for inversion in the water basin. Stress the importance of

Wear your goggles, gloves, and lab apron at all times during the investigation. The hydrochloric acid is corrosive. If you spill any, wash the affected area with lots of cold running water and report the spill immediately to your teacher. To protect your hands, be careful when rinsing out the micropipet and other equipment.

Note the caution alert symbols here and with certain steps of the Procedure. Refer to page *xi* for the specific precautions associated with each symbol.

Procedure

1. Put on your goggles, gloves, and lab apron. Fill the plastic basin one-third full of ice. Add tap water to a depth of 5–10 cm. Place a Celsius thermometer in the basin. Add more ice if necessary until the temperature is 0°C. Use a barometer to measure the atmospheric pressure in the laboratory. Record the temperature and pressure in the Data Table.

146

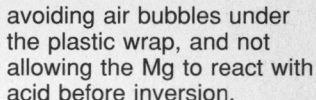

2. Obtain a strip of magnesium that is about 1.0 cm long. With scissors, trim the cut edges so that they are straight across, rather than diagonally cut. Measure the length of the strip to the nearest 0.02 cm and record the length in the Data Table.

3. Use the micropipet to dispense approximately 3 mL of 3.0 M HCl into the bottom of an empty 10-mL graduated cylinder. Insert the micropipet into the center of the cylinder to avoid getting acid on the sides of the cylinder. **CAUTION:** *Hydrochloric acid is corrosive. Avoid spills and splashes. If you do spill some, rinse the affected area with water and immediately inform your teacher.*

4. Rinse out the micropipet. Fill the rest of the graduated cylinder with tap water using the micropipet. Drip the water down the inside surface of the cylinder to prevent mixing the acid with the water. The water should overfill the cylinder top slightly to form a smooth curved surface.

5. Roll or fold the magnesium and place it carefully onto the surface of the water in the cylinder. It should float. Quickly cover the cylinder with a square of plastic wrap, stretch the plastic tight, and secure it with a rubber band. Make sure that there are no air bubbles trapped under the plastic wrap. See Figure 28–1.

avoiding air bubbles under the plastic wrap, and not allowing the Mg to react with acid before inversion.

Advise students that their hydrogen volumes may be slightly increased by evaporation of water vapor into the gas, but that this increase varies with temperature and is minimal (<1%) below 5°C. Atmospheric pressure variations are generally less than 1% of 760 mm Hg. However, during periods of very high or low pressure, or at high altitude, variations may be in excess of 2%.

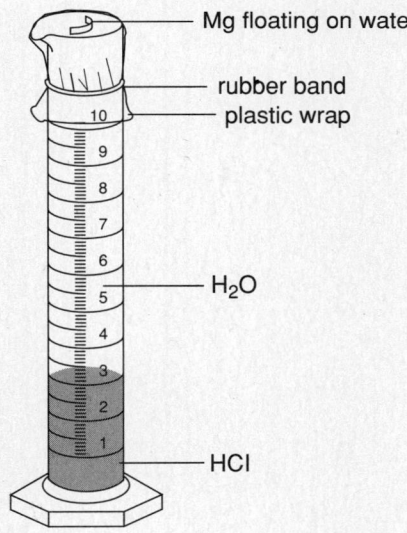

Figure 28–1

6. With a pin, poke a tiny hole in the plastic over the cylinder mouth. Holding the cylinder by the base (to avoid heating it), immediately invert it in the basin of ice water. Hold the inverted cylinder vertically with its mouth submerged. Do not block the pin hole. See Figure 28–2.

7. The magnesium will react with the acid, producing hydrogen gas that collects in the cylinder. When the reaction is complete, chill the gas by submerging the cylinder completely in the ice water for about one minute, tipping it at a slight angle if necessary.

Molar Volume of Hydrogen Gas

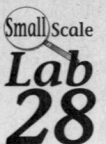

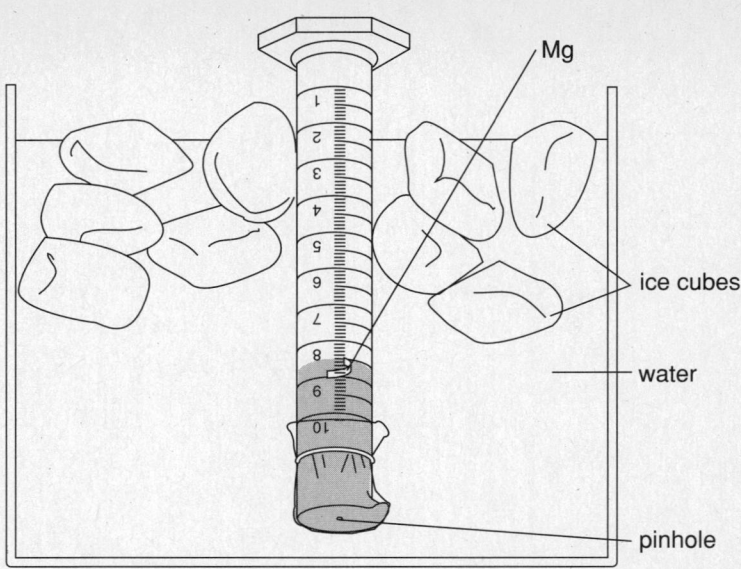

Figure 28-2

8. To read the volume of hydrogen gas in the cylinder, lift the cylinder vertically until the liquid level inside the cylinder matches the level of the water in the basin. This equalizes the gas pressure in the cylinder with the atmospheric pressure outside the cylinder. Record the volume of hydrogen gas in the Data Table.

9. If time permits, carry out a second trial by repeating Steps 2 through 8.

10. When you are finished, rinse the diluted acid in the basin down the drain. **CAUTION:** *Hydrochloric acid is corrosive. Avoid spills and splashes. If you do spill some, rinse the affected area with water and immediately inform your teacher.* Clean up your work area and wash your hands before leaving the laboratory.

Waste Disposal
Flush diluted acid down the drain with additional water. ■

Observations (sample data)
DATA TABLE

	Trial 1	Trial 2
length of Mg strip (cm)	1.30	
volume of hydrogen collected (mL)	8.9	
temperature of water in basin (°C)	1	
atmospheric pressure (mm Hg)	766	

Calculations (based on sample data)

1. Find the mass of magnesium used in each trial, using the following formula and the mass-to-length ratio provided by your teacher:

   mass (g) = mass/length ratio (g/cm) × Mg length (cm)

   (0.00734 g/cm) × (1.30 cm) = 0.00954 g Mg

Name _____

Small Scale Lab 28

2. Use the equation you wrote in Question 2 of the Pre-Lab Discussion to identify the number of moles of hydrogen produced per mole of magnesium. Then calculate the number of moles of hydrogen produced during the investigation. The equation is $Mg + 2HCl \rightarrow H_2 + MgCl_2$. Therefore one mole of magnesium produces one mole of hydrogen. Calculate the moles of Mg for each trial.

   $$\frac{0.00954 \text{ g}}{24.3 \text{ g/mol}} = 0.000393 \text{ mol Mg}$$

   0.000393 mol Mg produces 0.000393 mol H_2

3. Find the volume of hydrogen at standard pressure used in each trial, using the following formula:

   $$\text{volume} = \text{measured volume (L)} \times \frac{\text{atmospheric pressure (mm Hg)}}{760 \text{ mm Hg}}$$

   $$(0.0089 \text{ L}) \times \frac{766 \text{ mm Hg}}{760 \text{ mm Hg}} = 0.0090 \text{ L}$$

Critical Thinking: Analysis and Conclusions

1. Based on your data, calculate the molar volume of hydrogen (liters H_2/moles H_2) and compare to the accepted value of 22.4 L/mole by computing the percent error. *(Making comparisons)*

   $$\frac{0.0090 \text{ L}}{0.000393 \text{ mol}} = 22.9 \text{ L/mol}$$

   $$\text{percent error} = \frac{22.9 - 22.4}{22.4} \times 100 = 2.0\%$$

2. How would you explain the percent error for your calculation of molar volume? *(Interpreting data)* The error is mainly due to variations from standard temperature, for example, the ice water may not be at 0°C, and handling the graduated cylinder warms it. Error may also result from the small quantities being measured, water vapor, and air bubbles.

3. How would you redesign this experiment to reduce the percent error? *(Designing experiments)* Answers will vary, but should include ways of controlling variations from standard temperature and perhaps using more accurately measured quantities of materials.

4. Why do you think the graduated cylinder was inverted in the ice water bath rather than being held right side up? *(Making inferences)* The graduated cylinder was inverted so the hydrogen gas would be collected rather than escaping.

5. What type of chemical reaction—single replacement, double replacement, decomposition, or direct combination—occurred between the magnesium and the hydrochloric acid? *(Classifying)* The reaction was a single replacement reaction.

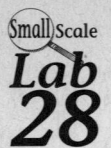

Name _____

Critical Thinking: Applications

1. How do you think each of the following factors would affect the accuracy of your results when compared with the accepted volume of 22.4 liters per mole at 0°C and 760 mm Hg? *(Making predictions)*

   a. Gas temperature higher than 0°C. <u>A higher temperature would increase the volume.</u>

   b. Evaporation of water vapor into the collected hydrogen. <u>Water vapor increases the moles of collected gas, increasing the volume.</u>

   c. Using a longer strip of magnesium. <u>With more magnesium, the volume of gas collected increases, but the number of moles also increases, so the number of liters per mole should be the same. Too much magnesium will produce hydrogen in excess of the cylinder capacity.</u>

2. Since gases change volume with changes in pressure and temperature, explain why it is not immediately obvious how much gas is in a propane gas tank. What is the minimum information you need to compare suppliers of propane gas for refilling barbecue propane tanks? *(Evaluating)* <u>Any amount of gas will expand to fill the space in the tank. Identical gas tanks can contain very different amounts of gas depending on the pressure. The minimum information needed to compare propane tanks would be the mass of gas in the tank, or the temperature, volume, and pressure of the tank when it is recharged.</u>

Going Further

1. Carbon dioxide can be produced by reacting excess vinegar with baking soda, $NaHCO_3$.

Going Further

1. Design an experiment in which you can generate and collect a measurable volume of another gas, for example carbon dioxide. Under your teacher's supervision, conduct the experiment and determine the molar volume of the gas. Analyze and report on your results.

Name _____ Date _____ Class _____

Molar Mass of Butane

Lab 29 APPLICATION

Text reference: **Chapter 10**

Introduction

Every pure substance is composed of a distinct combination of atoms and is identified by its own molecular formula. The sum of the atomic masses of the atoms in this molecular formula is the substance's formula mass. The same number, measured in grams, is the substance's molar mass.

Butane, with the molecular formula C_4H_{10}, is a gas at normal room conditions. It can be liquefied by placing it under pressure, as in a disposable butane lighter. When the valve is opened the liquid butane quickly escapes and changes into a gas. Butane also is extremely insoluble in water, so it can be bubbled through water with very little of it going into solution. Because of these properties, a refill cylinder for a butane lighter is a good source of butane gas, and water displacement is a good method of collecting a measurable sample of it.

In this investigation you will collect some butane gas in a container by means of water displacement. You will determine the volume of the gas collected and, from that volume, the number of moles of butane. The mass of the gas collected will be obtained by taking the difference between the mass of the refill cylinder before and after butane is released from it. From the mass and the number of moles of the gas collected you can then calculate the mass of one mole, or the molar mass, of butane.

Pre-Lab Discussion

Read the entire laboratory investigation and the relevant pages of your textbook. Then answer the questions that follow.

1. What is the difference between the formula mass and the molar mass of a substance? Include the appropriate units for each. The formula mass is found by adding the masses of the individual atoms that make up one formula unit of the substance. Its unit label is atomic mass units (amu). The molar mass is the mass of one mole of the substance. Its unit label is g/mol.

2. Describe the procedure known as water displacement. When is it used? Water displacement is the process of collecting a gas by bubbling it through water, thus forcing water out of a container and replacing it with the gas. It is used when the gas is not soluble in water.

3. Why should there be no flames in the laboratory when this investigation is being done? Butane gas is very flammable, and an explosion could result.

Materials (class of 30 in pairs)
30 pairs safety goggles
30 laboratory aprons
15 laboratory balances
15 butane refill cylinders
30 pieces rubber tubing, 25-cm
15 pneumatic troughs
15 flasks, 500-mL
15 glass squares

Time Required
40 minutes.

Advance Preparation
Purchase a sufficient number of butane refill cylinders. If necessary, cut the rubber tubing into 25-cm lengths. Make sure that you have tubing small enough to fit snugly over the nipple on the butane refill cylinder.

Introduction
Since students have not yet encountered the ideal gas law (see Chapter 13), you may wish to introduce them to the effects of pressure and temperature while you are discussing molar volume. The sample calculations assume that only the temperature differs from the standard, but the determination of the molar mass will be more accurate if a correction is made for barometric pressure as well. Working from the ideal gas law, the relation
$V_m = (T/273) \times (760 \text{ mm Hg}/P_{lab}) \times 22.4 \text{ L}$
determines the molar volume of a gas.
Students will probably benefit from a demonstration of how to fill the flask with water and invert it, and of how to remove the flask from

© Prentice-Hall, Inc.

Molar Mass of Butane **151**

Lab 29 APPLICATION

the pneumatic trough once it is filled with gas.

Ask students why it is safest to keep the flask of butane upright in the fume hood. They will calculate the molar mass of butane in this investigation but may not recognize that butane is about twice as dense as air. Due to its density, it will tend to stay in an upright flask and diffuse away slowly.

4. Describe the piece of equipment known as a pneumatic trough. What is its purpose during the investigation? _A pneumatic trough is a pan that holds water and has a shelf suspended in it. The pan has a drain for overflow of water, and the shelf has a hole in it so water can leave any container supported by it. The purpose of the trough in this investigation is to collect butane by water displacement._

5. Why is the insolubility of butane important in this investigation? _If butane were soluble in water some of it would dissolve, and the total volume of gas released could not be accurately measured._

6. Why is it important to make sure that the flask is filled to the very top with water before it is turned upside down? _Any air present in the flask would be measured as part of the collected gas sample and would increase the experimental error._

7. What is the volume occupied by one mole of any gas at STP? Do you think the volume would be larger or smaller at laboratory conditions? _One mole of gas occupies 22.4 L at STP. The volume at laboratory conditions would probably be larger, because the laboratory is warmer than 0°C and matter usually expands when it gets warmer._

Problem
How can you determine the molar mass of butane gas?

Materials
safety goggles
laboratory apron
laboratory balance
butane refill cylinder

2 pieces rubber tubing
pneumatic trough
flask, 500-mL
glass square

Safety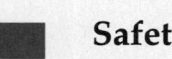

Wear your goggles and lab apron at all times during the investigation. Butane is very flammable, so make certain there are no open flames or matches in the laboratory.

Note the caution alert symbols here and with certain steps of the Procedure. Refer to page xi for the specific precautions associated with each symbol.

Safety
Make sure students wear their goggles and lab aprons at all times during the investigation. Butane is very flammable, so no open flames, matches, or electrical equipment should be used in the laboratory at any time during the investigation. Do not substitute a butane lighter, even with its flint and sparking wheel removed, for the refill cylinder in this investigation.
■

Procedure

 1. Put on your goggles and lab apron. This investigation requires you to work carefully with your partner. Decide now which one of you will handle the flask and which one will handle the butane cylinder.

Lab 29 APPLICATION

2. Determine the mass of a dry butane refill cylinder. Record the mass in your Data Table.
3. Fill the pneumatic trough with water to a level about 2 cm above the shelf. Connect one piece of rubber tubing to the overflow spout of the trough, and place the other end of it in the sink. (See Figure 29–1.)

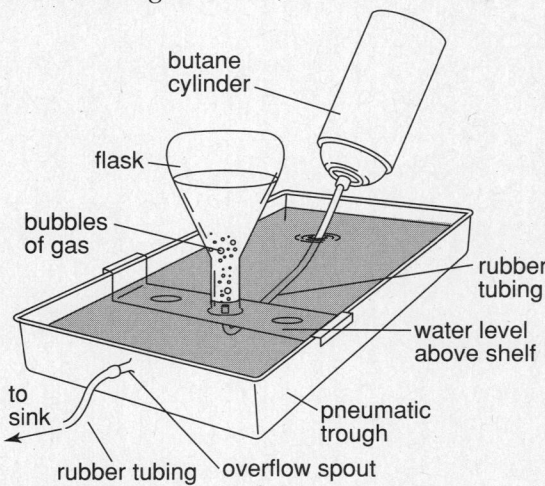

Figure 29–1

4. Fill a 500-mL flask completely (to the very top) with water. Cover the mouth of the flask with a glass square, carefully invert the flask, and place it in the trough so the mouth is under water, pointing down. Make sure that there are no air bubbles in the flask. Remove the glass square from the mouth of the flask and set the flask over one of the holes in the shelf. One student should hold the flask vertical and steady while the other handles the butane cylinder.

 5. Connect one end of the second piece of rubber tubing to the butane refill cylinder and insert the other end of the tubing a few centimeters into the neck of the flask, so that the gas will rise into the flask when the valve is opened. **CAUTION:** *Butane is highly flammable. Do not bring any flames into the laboratory, or use any electrical equipment, during this investigation.*

6. Holding the gas refill above the trough, press the valve of the cylinder to release the butane, and fill the round portion of the flask with gas exactly to the 500-mL mark. Make sure not to release any of the gas outside of the flask.

7. When the flask is filled, release the valve and carefully disconnect the rubber tubing from it.

 8. Lift the flask off the shelf in the pneumatic trough, and place the glass square over its mouth. Turn the flask right side up and carry it to the fume hood. Remove the glass square and stand the flask upright.

 9. Making sure that the butane cylinder is dry, measure its mass on the same balance used previously. Record the value in your Data Table. Clean up your work area and wash your hands before leaving the laboratory.

Teaching Tips
A correction for the partial pressure of water vapor in the flask amounts to a few percent. (At 25°C, the vapor pressure of water is 24 mm Hg.) For enrichment, point out to students that this correction to molar volume is made as follows:

$V_m = (T/273) \times$
$(760 \text{ mm Hg}/[P_{lab} - P_{wat}]) \times$
22.4 L

Another correction to the molar volume of the gas results from the column of water in the neck of the flask (it decreases the pressure on the gas). That correction is quite small, however, since atmospheric pressure is roughly equivalent to a 10-meter column of water.

To increase the accuracy of this investigation, you may wish to have students determine the actual volume of the 500-mL flasks by filling them to the 500-mL mark with water poured from graduated cylinders. The total volume poured from the graduated cylinders should then be used in the molar mass calculation. Alternatively, if your laboratory has a supply of large graduated cylinders (500-mL or 1-L), you can substitute them for the flasks described here. Students may then read the volume of gas from the markings on the graduate, instead of metering out exactly 500 mL.

Waste Disposal
Working in the fume hood, make sure that the butane cylinders are empty by holding their valves open. Empty cylinders should be stored separately for commercial disposal. Keep the used flasks in the fume hood overnight to allow the butane to dissipate. ■

Molar Mass of Butane

Name _____

Observations (sample data)

DATA TABLE

initial mass of butane cylinder	84.32 g
final mass of butane cylinder	83.09 g
mass of butane gas	1.23 g
volume of butane	500 mL

 Calculations (based on sample data)

1. Determine the mass of butane used and record it in the Data Table.

   $$84.32 \text{ g} - 83.09 \text{ g} = 1.23 \text{ g}$$

2. Using the molar volume given to you by your teacher for the conditions in your laboratory, determine the number of moles of butane gas collected.

   At 25°C and 1.0 atm (760 mm Hg) the molar volume of a gas is 24.5 L.

   $$\text{Therefore } 0.500 \text{ L} \times \frac{1 \text{ mol}}{24.5 \text{ L}} = 0.0204 \text{ mol.}$$

3. From the mass and the number of moles of butane gas collected, calculate the mass per mole of butane—its molar mass.

   $$\frac{1.23 \text{ g}}{0.0204 \text{ mol}} = 60.3 \text{ g/mol}$$

 Critical Thinking: Analysis and Conclusions

1. Calculate the formula mass of butane (C_4H_{10}) using a chart of atomic masses. *(Applying concepts)*

   $$4(12.01 \text{ g/mol}) + 10(10.01 \text{ g/mol}) = 58.1 \text{ g/mol}$$

2. Determine your percent error *(Interpreting Data)*.

   $$\% \text{ error} = \frac{|58.1 \text{ g} - 60.3 \text{ g}|}{58.1 \text{ g}} \times 100 = 3.7\%$$

3. If a small air bubble had been in the flask before you filled it with butane, how would it have affected your results? Explain. *(Making predictions)* A bubble would increase the apparent volume of the gas and consequently the mole fraction measured. The molar mass determined would therefore be lowered.

4. What other sources of experimental error might have affected your results in this investigation? How? *(Interpreting data)* Answers will vary. Some possibilities are air in the rubber tubing—smaller molar mass; errors in mass determination—larger or smaller molar mass.

5. Why were you unable to use the standard molar volume (22.4 L/mol) in this investigation? *(Making comparisons)* 22.4 L/mol is the molar volume at STP. Since this experiment was done at a temperature above 0°C, the molar volume had a different value. Some students may also cite barometric pressure differences as a factor.

Critical Thinking: Applications

1. How would you alter this investigation to determine the molar volume of a gas that is soluble in water? *(Designing experiments)* The gas could be collected by displacing some liquid other than water.

2. Propane gas tanks for barbecues are filled by weight. Can you expect a fair measurement this way? Explain. *(Making judgments)* Yes, weight (or mass) is a measure of how much matter you have.

Going Further

1. Under your teacher's supervision, determine experimentally the molar mass of another gas, for example, propane. Report your findings.

Going Further
1. Propane is available commercially in small cylinders.

Name _____ Date _____ Class _____

Water in a Hydrate

Lab 30

Text reference: **Chapter 10**

Introduction

Many compounds are formed as a result of reactions that occur in water solutions. These compounds appear to be dry, but when they are heated, large amounts of water are released. The water molecules are part of the crystalline structure and are weakly bonded to the ions or molecules that make up the compound. Such compounds are known as hydrates, meaning that they contain water. The solid that remains when the water is removed is referred to as the anhydrous salt, or anhydrate.

$$\text{Hydrate} + \text{Heat} \rightarrow \text{Anhydrate} + H_2O$$

Usually, the amount of water present in a hydrate is in a whole number molar ratio to the moles of anhydrate. An example of a hydrate is magnesium sulfate. Its formula is $MgSO_4 \cdot 7H_2O$, indicating that seven moles of water are combined with one mole of magnesium sulfate in the crystalline form.

In this investigation you will be given an unknown hydrate and asked to determine the percent of water in the compound. From this information, the molar ratio of water to anhydrous salt will be calculated. Finally, the identity of the hydrate will be determined.

Pre-Lab Discussion

Read the entire laboratory investigation and the relevant pages of your textbook. Then answer the questions that follow.

1. What is a hydrate? An anhydrate? __A hydrate is a substance that contains water as part of its crystal structure. The solid that is left when the water is removed from a hydrate is an anhydrate.__

2. Why do you think it is necessary to heat the evaporating dish before finding its mass? __To be sure the evaporating dish is completely dry.__

3. Why must the evaporating dish be cooled before finding its mass? __To avoid the possibility of burns and to minimize the effects of hot air currents affecting the apparent mass of the dish.__

4. Why must the mass of the anhydrous salt be measured immediately on cooling? __To avoid having the anhydrous salt absorb moisture from the air.__

Materials (class of 30 in pairs)
30 pairs chemical splash goggles
30 laboratory aprons
15 pipe-stem triangles
15 ring stands
15 iron rings
15 lab burners
15 books of matches
15 crucibles with covers
15 pairs crucible tongs
15 heat-resistant pads
15 laboratory balances
coded containers of the following:
   magnesium sulfate heptahydrate ($MgSO_4 \cdot 7H_2O$)
   sodium carbonate monohydrate ($Na_2CO_3 \cdot 1H_2O$)
   zinc sulfate dihydrate ($ZnSO_4 \cdot 2H_2O$)
   manganese sulfate monohydrate ($MnSO_4 \cdot 1H_2O$)
   calcium sulfate dihydrate ($CaSO_4 \cdot 2H_2O$)
   copper sulfate pentahydrate ($CuSO_4 \cdot 5H_2O$)
15 spatulas

Time Required
60 minutes. More time is required if two unknowns are tested. The investigation can be split into two shorter lab periods by stopping for the day between Steps 6 and 7.

Advance Preparation
The unknown hydrates should be placed in coded containers so that students don't know the identity of the substance they have been assigned. The amount of hydrate needed depends on the number of unknowns used, but it is helpful to have at least five grams per team of each hydrate used.

© Prentice-Hall, Inc.

Water in a Hydrate **157**

Lab 30

Provide a labeled container for disposal of waste chemicals.

Introduction

Demonstrate the rehydration of anhydrous copper sulfate. Dehydrate some copper sulfate pentahydrate by heating as in the investigation. Point out to students the white color of the compound. Add it to some water and the characteristic blue color will appear. Tell the students the blue color is the color of the hydrated form. Many hydrated salts are colorful, including nickel, chromium, and copper sulfates.

Name _____

5. Why is it necessary to handle the evaporating dish only with the crucible tongs after the initial heating? <u>To avoid the possibility of burns and to avoid adding mass from grease, dirt, or moisture that may be on the hands.</u>

6. What is the molar mass of the hydrate of magnesium sulfate described in the Introduction? <u>246.4 g/mol</u>

7. What is the molar mass of the anhydrous salt, magnesium sulfate? <u>120.4 g/mol</u>

8. What is the percent of water in $MgSO_4 \cdot 7H_2O$? <u>51.1%</u>

Problem

How can the percent of water in an unknown hydrate be determined?

Materials

chemical splash goggles
laboratory apron
pipe-stem triangle
ring stand
iron ring
lab burner
matches
crucible with cover
crucible tongs
heat-resistant pad
laboratory balance
spatula

one of the following hydrated salts:
  magnesium sulfate hepta-
    hydrate ($MgSO_4 \cdot 7H_2O$)
  sodium carbonate mono-
    hydrate ($Na_2CO_3 \cdot 1H_2O$)
  zinc sulfate dihydrate
    ($ZnSO_4 \cdot 2H_2O$)
  manganese sulfate mono-
    hydrate ($MnSO_4 \cdot 1H_2O$)
  calcium sulfate dihydrate
    ($CaSO_4 \cdot 2H_2O$)
  copper sulfate pentahydrate
    ($CuSO_4 \cdot 5H_2O$)

Safety

Wear your goggles and lab apron at all times during the investigation. The crucible and its cover are hot. Move them only with the tongs. Tie back loose hair and clothing when working with a flame. You should assume that all of the hydrates are poisonous. If they contact your skin or clothing, wash the area with plenty of water. Note the caution alert symbols here and with certain steps of the Procedure. Refer to page *xi* for the specific precautions associated with each symbol.

Safety

Make sure students wear their goggles and lab aprons at all times during the investigation. Show students how to use tongs to handle the hot crucible and cover. They should use the curved part of the tong arm to hold the crucible and the tips of the tongs to manipulate the cover. Caution students to tie back loose hair and clothing when working with lab burners. ■

Procedure

1. Put on your goggles and lab apron.
2. Prepare the setup shown in Figure 30-1.

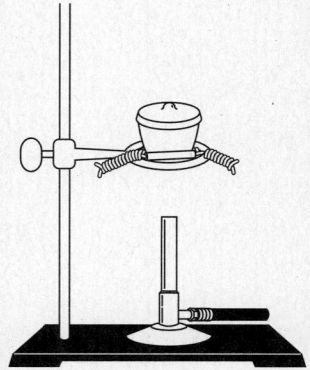

Figure 30-1

3. Light the burner and heat a clean, dry crucible with its cover in the hottest part of the flame for 3 minutes. **CAUTION:** *Tie back loose hair or clothing when working with the flame. The crucible and cover are very hot. Use tongs to move them.*
4. Remove the crucible and cover and place them on a heat-resistant pad to cool for at least 3 minutes.
5. Measure and record the mass of the cool crucible and cover to the nearest 0.01 g.

6. Add about 2 g of your unknown hydrate to the crucible. Measure and record the mass of the crucible, cover, and hydrate to the nearest 0.01 g.

7. Place the crucible, cover, and hydrate on the pipe-stem triangle. The cover should tilt slightly, which will allow water vapor to escape as it forms. See Figure 30-2. Begin heating gently, gradually increasing the heat until there is no more popping or spattering.

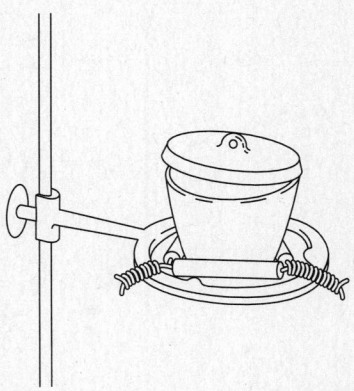

Figure 30-2

Teaching Tips

The molar masses of the anhydrous salts are:

magnesium sulfate ($MgSO_4$)
120.4 g/mol
sodium carbonate (Na_2CO_3)
106.0 g/mol
zinc sulfate ($ZnSO_4$)
161.5 g/mol
manganese sulfate ($MnSO_4$)
150.9 g/mol
calcium sulfate ($CaSO_4$)
136.1 g/mol
copper sulfate ($CuSO_4$)
159.6 g/mol

As the students heat some of the hydrates, point out the bubbling. This is the water being driven from the crystal and boiling away. This water is sometimes called the water of crystallization.

Show students how to tilt the crucible cover so water vapor can escape. They should set the cover in such a way so that, if it slips, it will be caught by an arm of the pipe-stem triangle and not fall all the way to the benchtop. Hot crucibles and covers can be set right on the metal pan of the balance if the pan is removed from its plastic holder. The crucible will cool more rapidly there than on the heat-resistant pad.

Any inaccuracy probably comes from inaccurate measurements on the balance. If possible, use an electronic balance. Emphasize to students the importance of measuring as carefully as possible.

Students will have to do some detective work for Analysis and Conclusions Question 2. Once they have determined the molar ratio of their hydrate, they can look at the Materials list to decide which compound best fits their results. There are two pairs of compounds that have the same ratios. Students can differentiate between these by comparing the molar mass you have given them to the molar mass they calculate.

Lab 30

Name _____

8. Remove the cover using the tongs and examine the material in the crucible. If the edges of the solid appear to be turning brown, reduce the heat momentarily and then begin heating again at a slower rate. Heat for 5 more minutes.

9. Remove the crucible and place it on the heat-resistant pad. **CAUTION:** *The crucible is very hot. Use tongs to move it.* Allow it to cool for at least 1 minute. Immediately measure and record the mass of the crucible, cover, and anhydrous salt.

10. Reheat the crucible, cover, and contents for a few minutes, cool and measure the mass again. The value should be within 0.02 g of the last recorded mass. If it is not, reheat and remeasure the mass until the last two measurements are within that range. Record the final mass.

11. Dispose of the reaction product as directed by your teacher. Clean up your work area and wash your hands before leaving the laboratory.

Waste Disposal
The anhydrous salts can be disposed of in qualified landfills. ■

Observations (sample data)
DATA TABLE

mass of crucible and cover	44.36 g
mass of crucible, cover, and hydrate	46.44 g
mass of crucible, cover, and anhydrate (after Step 9)	45.71 g
mass of crucible, cover, and anhydrate (after Step 10)	45.71 g

Calculations (based on sample data)

1. Calculate the initial mass of hydrate.

    46.44 g − 44.36 g = 2.08 g

2. Calculate the mass of water lost.

    46.44 g − 45.71 g = 0.73 g

3. Calculate the number of moles of water lost.

    $\dfrac{0.73 \text{ g}}{18.0 \text{ g/mol}} = 4.1 \times 10^{-2}$ mol

4. Calculate the mass of the anhydrous salt.

    45.71 g − 44.36 g = 1.35 g

Critical Thinking: Analysis and Conclusion

1. Based on the molar mass of anhydrous salt given by the teacher, calculate the moles of anhydrous salt. Determine the smallest whole number ratio of moles of water to moles of anhydrous salt. *(Interpreting data)* For CuSO$_4$: $\dfrac{1.35 \text{ g}}{159.6 \text{ g/mol}} = 8.46 \times 10^{-3}$ mol;

    $\dfrac{4.1 \times 10^{-2} \text{ mol water}}{8.46 \times 10^{-3} \text{ mol anhydrous salt}} = 4.8/1$ or $5/1$

Name _____

Lab 30

2. After consulting the list of salts in the Materials section, determine the empirical formula for your compound. *(Drawing conclusions)*
   The formula must be CuSO$_4$•5H$_2$O.

3. What is the percent water in your hydrate? What is the percent error for this investigation? *(Interpreting data)*

$$\text{Percent water} = \frac{0.73 \text{ g}}{2.08 \text{ g}} \times 100 = 35\%$$

$$\text{actual value} = 36\%; \quad \text{percent error} = \frac{|36 - 35|}{36} \times 100 = 2.8\%$$

4. The method used in this investigation is not suitable for all hydrates. Give two reasons for this. *(Making inferences)* The hydrate may decompose during the heating. The water may be held too tightly to be driven off by heating.

5. Compare your results with other members of your class with the same unknown. Are there differences? What reasons could account for these differences? *(Making comparisons)* The hydrate may not have been heated long enough. The mass may have been taken when the dish was too hot. Water may have been reabsorbed during cooling.

Critical Thinking: Applications

1. Explain what effect the following errors would have on the value for the percent water in the hydrate. *(Making predictions)*
   a. The hydrate was not heated long enough to drive off all the water. The value for the percent water would be too low since not all the water was removed from the hydrate.
   b. A damp crucible was used, and it was not dried before adding the hydrate. The mass of the water driven off would include the extra water in the dish, making the percent of water too high.
   c. The crucible and contents were allowed to cool overnight before finding their mass. The anhydrate would reabsorb water from the air. Its mass would be too high and the measured percent of water would be too low.

2. Examine some of the different hydrate crystals with a magnifying glass. Describe the shapes of the crystals. How do the crystals of one compound differ from the crystals of another? *(Making comparisons)* Answers will vary. Students should see different crystal shapes with different compounds.

Water in a Hydrate 161

Lab 30

Name _____

3. Predict what would happen if you added a few drops of distilled water to the anhydrous salt remaining at the end of this experiment. *(Making predictions)* The anhydrous salt would absorb the water and reform the hydrate. Since the original reaction was endothermic, this reaction should be exothermic.

Going Further

1. Copper sulfate and nickel sulfate make the largest crystals.

Going Further

1. Try growing your own crystals. Dissolve some of the hydrated salts in water and suspend a string in the solution. Wait about a week and examine the crystals under a magnifying glass. Compare the shape to the original crystals. Find out more about the role of water in determining the shape of crystals.
2. Dessicating agents are found in some optical equipment packages as well as some food products. What are dessicating agents? What substances are used for this purpose?

Stoichiometry Using Copper — Lab 31

Text reference: Chapter 11

Introduction

Have you ever noticed how many different uses copper has? The first things that come to mind are probably coins and electrical wires. How many others can you think of? Why is copper so useful?

Copper is widely distributed in Earth's crust. It is commonly found in sulfides, carbonates, and as uncombined metal. It is a relatively soft metal, reddish in color, and similar in many ways to another metal in Group 1B, silver. It is an excellent conductor of electricity and heat, second only to silver. Like silver, it maintains its integrity through a series of chemical reactions and has the advantage of being relatively inexpensive.

In this investigation, you will perform a series of chemical reactions involving copper and copper compounds. The equations for the reactions are listed here in unbalanced form.

$$Cu + HNO_3 \rightarrow Cu(NO_3)_2 + NO_2 + H_2O$$
$$Cu(NO_3)_2 + NaOH \rightarrow Cu(OH)_2 + NaNO_3$$
$$Cu(OH)_2 \rightarrow CuO + H_2O$$
$$CuO + H_2SO_4 \rightarrow CuSO_4 + H_2O$$
$$CuSO_4 + Zn \rightarrow Cu + ZnSO_4$$

Beginning with a sample of copper of known mass, you will perform a series of reactions, eventually recovering the copper at the end. You will then analyze your quantitative data to see what percentage of the copper was recovered.

Pre-Lab Discussion

Read the entire laboratory investigation and the relevant pages of your textbook. Then answer the questions that follow.

1. What are some properties of copper metal? <u>It is an excellent conductor of electricity and heat.</u>

2. Balance the first two equations given in the Introduction.
   <u>$Cu + 4HNO_3 \rightarrow Cu(NO_3)_2 + 2NO_2 + 2H_2O$</u>

   <u>$Cu(NO_3)_2 + 2NaOH \rightarrow Cu(OH)_2 + 2NaNO_3$</u>

3. What safety hazards are associated with dissolving copper in nitric acid? What precautions should be taken? <u>Toxic nitrogen dioxide fumes are produced. Part A must be done in a fume hood. Nitric acid is corrosive.</u>

   <u>Wear gloves, goggles, and aprons. If you splash any of the solutions on yourself, wash it off immediately and tell your teacher.</u>

Materials (class of 30 in pairs)

Part A
30 pairs chemical splash goggles
30 laboratory aprons
30 pairs latex gloves
15 laboratory balances
30 grams 18–22 gauge copper wire (cut into 15 pieces)
15 beakers, 250-mL
15 graduated cylinders, 50- or 100-mL
500 mL nitric acid (HNO_3), 6.0 M
15 watch glasses
15 beakers, 600-mL
ice
tap water
500 mL sodium hydroxide (NaOH), 6.0 M
15 rolls pH paper (wide range)

Part B
15 hot plates
15 stirring rods
15 pairs beaker tongs
1 liter sulfuric acid (H_2SO_4), 3.0 M
150 grams zinc granules, #18–22 mesh
15 evaporating dishes
weighing paper

Time Required

At least two 40–50 minute periods. Steps 9–12 may be completed on a third day if necessary. Do not stop after Step 9.

Advance Preparation

Prepare the acid and base solutions as follows. CAUTION: *Wear goggles, gloves, and a laboratory apron.*

6.0 M HNO_3: Slowly add 190 mL of concentrated HNO_3 to enough water to make 500 mL total volume.

© Prentice-Hall, Inc.

Lab 31

6.0 M NaOH: While stirring, add 120 grams of solid NaOH to enough water to make 500 mL total volume.

3.0 M H_2SO_4: Slowly add 170 mL of concentrated H_2SO_4 to enough water to make 1 liter total volume.

Determine what length of copper wire has a mass of about 2 grams. Cut the wire into 15 pieces of this length.

Introduction

To introduce this lab, you may wish to exhibit some items made out of copper.

Discuss with the students how copper atoms can become part of a series of compounds but then become elemental copper again.

Explain the difference between quantitative (numerical measurements) and qualitative (nonnumerical) data.

The students may not be familiar with the concept of pH. Explain that pH 7 is neutral, solutions below pH 7 are acidic, and solutions above pH 7 are basic. Demonstrate how the pH paper reacts to samples of acids, bases, and pure water.

Discuss the problem of recovering metals from industrial wastes. Ask the students to think about this problem as they do the investigation.

Safety

Make sure students wear their goggles, gloves, and lab aprons at all times during the investigation. Students should be instructed on the safe handling of strong acids and bases.

Part A must be performed in a fume hood to remove NO_2 vapors.

When the students are heating the mixture in Step 5, make sure that they heat it gently and stir it continuously so that it does not crack the beaker or foam out of it. ■

Name _____

4. How will copper(II) sulfate be prepared in the investigation? <u>The copper oxide precipitate will be reacted with sulfuric acid.</u>

5. In which step of this investigation is the initial copper recovered? <u>It is recovered in Step 8 when copper(II) sulfate is reacted with zinc metal.</u>

6. What method will be used to dry the final amount of copper produced? <u>A steam bath will be used to dry the copper.</u>

Problem

How is copper affected by a series of chemical reactions?

Materials

Part A

chemical splash goggles
laboratory apron
latex gloves
laboratory balance
copper wire
beaker, 250-mL
graduated cylinder,
   50- or 100-mL

nitric acid (HNO_3), 6.0 M
watch glass
beaker, 600-mL
ice
tap water
sodium hydroxide (NaOH),
   6.0 M
pH paper

Part B

hot plate
stirring rod
beaker tongs
sulfuric acid (H_2SO_4), 3.0 M

zinc granules
evaporating dish
weighing paper

Safety

Wear your goggles, gloves, and lab apron at all times during the investigation. Both 6.0 M nitric acid and 3.0 M sulfuric acid are corrosive and should be handled with care. The 6.0 M sodium hydroxide is caustic. If you spill any of these solutions on your skin, wash the spill with plenty of water and notify your teacher.

Part A must be performed in a fume hood.

Note the caution alert symbols here and with certain steps of the Procedure. Refer to page *xi* for the specific precautions associated with each symbol.

Procedure

Part A

1. Put on your goggles, gloves, and lab apron. Find the mass of the copper wire and record it in Data Table 1. Place the copper wire in a 250-mL beaker.

164   © Prentice-Hall, Inc.

2. In a fume hood, slowly add 25 mL of 6.0 M nitric acid, HNO_3, to the beaker and cover it with a watch glass. The reaction produces nitrogen dioxide, NO_2. **CAUTION:** *Do not inhale NO_2 fumes.* When the copper has completely dissolved and the reddish-brown color of NO_2 can no longer be seen, record your observations in Data Table 2.

3. Put some ice and water into a 600-mL beaker until the beaker is about half full. Place the smaller beaker in the ice bath to keep the reaction mixture cool.

4. Obtain 25 mL of 6.0 M sodium hydroxide, NaOH, in a graduated cylinder and test its pH with pH paper. Slowly add the NaOH solution to the 250 mL beaker and test the reaction mixture's pH until it is at pH 13. Record your observations in Data Table 2. If Part B will be done on another day, clean up your work area and wash your hands before leaving the laboratory.

Part B

5. Put on your goggles, gloves, and lab apron. To the reaction mixture from Part A, add 50 mL of water. Using a hot plate, gently heat the mixture to a boil. Stir while heating for approximately 5 minutes. **CAUTION:** *Stir the mixture continuously; otherwise the beaker could break or the mixture could foam out of the top.* Record your observations in Data Table 2.

6. Remove the beaker from the hot plate using beaker tongs and allow the solution to cool for approximately 5 minutes. Turn off the hot plate. Decant (pour off) the liquid from the beaker into the sink with the water running. While stirring, add 50 mL of water to the precipitate in the beaker, let it settle, and decant the liquid. Repeat this process. It is important that the precipitate remain in the beaker.

7. To the precipitate from Step 6, slowly add 50 mL of 3.0 M sulfuric acid, H_2SO_4, while stirring. Record your observations in Data Table 2.

8. Add approximately 10 grams of zinc to the solution from Step 7. Cover the beaker and swirl gently until all of the blue color disappears from the solution. Do this for a minimum of 10 minutes. Record your observations in Data Table 2.

9. Since there will be excess zinc remaining in the beaker, add 30 mL of 3.0 M H_2SO_4 and swirl. The bubbles indicate the evolution of hydrogen gas from the reaction mixture. When the evolution of gas ceases, add an additional 20 mL of H_2SO_4. When no further evidence of the evolution of gas is present, add 50 mL of water and decant the liquid.

10. Find the mass of the evaporating dish and record the value in Data Table 1. Transfer the solid remaining in the beaker to the evaporating dish. Set up a steam bath as shown in Figure 31–1 and evaporate the remaining liquid from the copper precipitate. Do not overheat the copper.

Teaching Tips

For the reaction of NaOH with $Cu(NO_3)_2$, have students use stirring rods to place a drop of reaction mixture on the pH paper. It should be at pH 13.

For the conversion of $Cu(OH)_2$ to CuO, be sure that the formation of the CuO is done carefully, with a gentle boiling for 5 minutes.

For the conversion of CuO to $CuSO_4$, be sure that the students add H_2SO_4 slowly, and that all CuO particles are converted. A small quantity of acid may need to be added to remove some small particles of CuO at the bottom of the beaker.

Removing excess zinc from the final step is critical to the experiment. Students may become impatient during the time necessary to react all of the zinc to form hydrogen gas. All bubbling of gas must be complete.

Stoichiometry Using Copper

Lab 31

Name _____

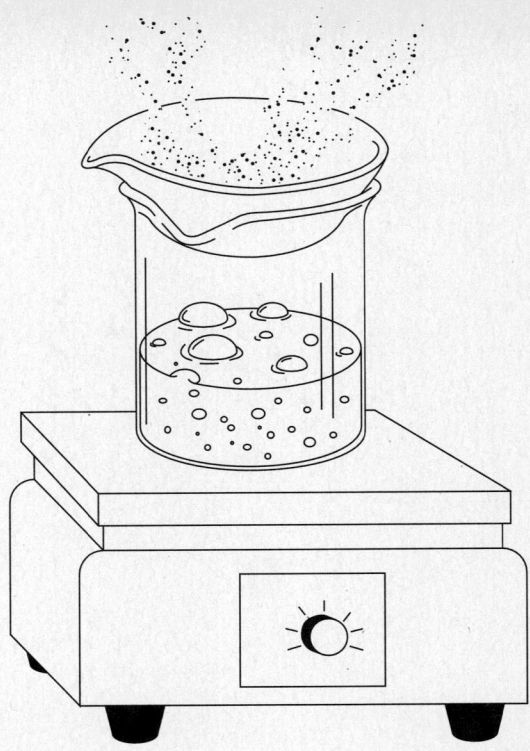

Figure 31–1

11. Remove the evaporating dish from the steam bath and let it cool. Find the combined mass of the copper and the evaporating dish and record it in Data Table 1.

 12. Dispose of the recovered copper as directed by your teacher. Clean up your work area and wash your hands before leaving the laboratory.

Waste Disposal
Decanted liquids can be safely poured into sinks with the water running.
 The recovered copper is not toxic and can be collected from the students and disposed of as solid waste. ■

Observations (sample data)

DATA TABLE 1   Quantitative Data

initial mass of copper	2.00 g
mass of evaporating dish	41.36 g
mass of evaporating dish and copper	43.21 g
mass of recovered copper	1.85 g

Name_____

Lab 31

DATA TABLE 2 Qualitative Data

Reaction	Observations
Cu + HNO$_3$	A reddish brown gas and blue solution are produced.
Cu(NO$_3$)$_2$ + NaOH	A blue precipitate is formed.
Cu(OH)$_2$	A dark brown to black precipitate is formed with clear liquid on top.
CuO + H$_2$SO$_4$	The precipitate dissolves and a blue solution remains.
CuSO$_4$ + Zn	A reddish brown precipitate forms with a clear liquid on top.
Zn + H$_2$SO$_4$	When acid is added, rapid bubbling occurs until all of the zinc has reacted.

Calculations (based on sample data)

1. Calculate the final mass of copper and record it in Data Table 1.

    $$43.21 \text{ g} - 41.36 \text{ g} = 1.85 \text{ g}$$

2. Calculate the final number of moles of copper.

    $$1.85 \text{ g Cu} \times \frac{1 \text{ mol Cu}}{63.55 \text{ g Cu}} = 0.029 \text{ mol Cu}$$

3. Calculate the initial number of moles of copper.

    $$2.00 \text{ g Cu} \times \frac{1 \text{ mol Cu}}{63.55 \text{ g Cu}} = 0.032 \text{ mol Cu}$$

4. Calculate the percentage of copper recovered.

    $$\frac{1.85 \text{ g Cu}}{2.00 \text{ g Cu}} \times 100\% = 92.5\%$$

Critical Thinking: Analysis and Conclusions

1. Why is the product of the reaction between copper and nitric acid in Step 2 placed on ice? *(Making inferences)* The reaction is exothermic (produces heat), so the mixture needs to be cooled.

2. What type of chemical reaction—single replacement, double replacement, decomposition, or direct combination—occurred in each of Steps 4, 7, and 9? *(Classifying)*

    Step 4: double replacement

    Step 7: double replacement

    Step 9: single replacement

© Prentice-Hall, Inc.   Stoichiometry Using Copper

3. The reaction of excess zinc with sulfuric acid is a critical step in this investigation. Write the balanced equation for this reaction. What problems would arise from an incomplete reaction? *(Making predictions)* $Zn + H_2SO_4 \rightarrow H_2 + ZnSO_4$. If zinc remains unreacted, then zinc particles are mixed with the copper, increasing the experimental error.

4. Account for any difference in mass between the initial amount of Cu used and the amount of Cu reclaimed. Would you expect this? *(Making inferences)* Since five reactions were done, and decanting liquids and other procedures would have inherent losses, the results should be less than 100% recovery. (If zinc was not removed, an increase in mass might have occurred.)

Critical Thinking: Applications

1. How many grams of each of the following chemicals would be formed from your initial mass of copper? *(Applying concepts)*

   a. $Cu(NO_3)_2$

   $$2.00 \text{ g Cu} \times \frac{1 \text{ mol Cu}}{63.55 \text{ g Cu}} \times \frac{1 \text{ mol Cu(NO_3)_2}}{1 \text{ mol Cu}} \times \frac{187.57 \text{ g Cu(NO_3)_2}}{1 \text{ mol Cu(NO_3)_2}}$$
   $$= 5.90 \text{ g Cu(NO_3)_2}$$

   b. $Cu(OH)_2$

   $$2.00 \text{ g Cu} \times \frac{1 \text{ mol Cu}}{63.55 \text{ g Cu}} \times \frac{1 \text{ mol Cu(OH)_2}}{1 \text{ mol Cu}} \times \frac{97.55 \text{ g Cu(OH)_2}}{1 \text{ mol Cu(OH)_2}}$$
   $$= 3.07 \text{ g Cu(OH)_2}$$

   c. $ZnSO_4$

   $$2.00 \text{ g Cu} \times \frac{1 \text{ mol Cu}}{63.55 \text{ g Cu}} \times \frac{1 \text{ mol ZnSO_4}}{1 \text{ mol Cu}} \times \frac{161.46 \text{ g ZnSO_4}}{1 \text{ mol ZnSO_4}}$$
   $$= 5.09 \text{ g ZnSO_4}$$

2. Recovery of metals from industrial processes, both from waste water and from sediments, is an important environmental issue. How does an investigation like the one just performed relate to such activities? *(Applying concepts)* If copper can be extracted by a series of chemical reactions, then it may be possible to remove other metals by similar processes.

Going Further

One thing students might discover is that copper sheets are used to extract silver from photographic waste solutions.

Going Further

1. Recycling is a focus of great environmental interest. Group 1B in the periodic table contains copper, silver, and gold. Use the library and contact photography labs and metal platers. Then write a short description of the recovery of silver from solutions.

Name _____ Date _____ Class _____

Zinc Thickness in Galvanized Iron

Lab 32
APPLICATION

Text reference: **Chapter 11**

Introduction

How much water can a rusty bucket hold? None. When a bucket gets rusty, the rust flakes off, leaving holes and leaks behind. The corrosion, or rusting, of iron has had great economic impact on the construction and automotive industries. A number of methods have been developed to prevent rust formation. The most expensive is the alloying of nickel and chromium with iron to make rust-resistant stainless steel. Other methods use a series of nonmetallic coatings to slow the formation of rust. These methods are widely used in the manufacture of automobiles. Another method that has been in use for a long time is galvanization, or coating of iron with a thin layer of zinc. Since zinc is oxidized more easily than iron, it forms zinc oxide, which stays firmly in place and continues to protect the iron for a long time. Unfortunately, even galvanized iron eventually disintegrates, so that the bucket eventually rusts and leaks despite this preventive effort.

Since zinc is more expensive than iron, it is cost effective to use the thinnest coating of zinc possible. How much zinc is involved in such a process? In this investigation, you will determine the thickness of the zinc coating on a piece of galvanized iron. You will start by determining the mass of the zinc on a piece of iron. You will then calculate the thickness of its coating.

Pre-Lab Discussion

Read the entire laboratory investigation and the relevant pages of your textbook. Then answer the questions that follow.

1. What is meant by the term corrosion of metals? __Corrosion is the oxidation of a metal.__

2. What is galvanized iron? __Iron that has been coated with zinc metal.__

3. How will the thickness of the zinc coating be determined in this experiment? __By finding the mass of the zinc, determining its volume by knowing its density, and then by dividing the volume by the total area of the zinc coating.__

4. What precautions must be taken in performing this experiment and why? __The work area must be well ventilated, since the heat of reaction will cause hydrogen chloride gas to be released. Gloves must be worn when handling 6.0 M HCl.__

Materials (class of 30 in pairs)
30 pairs chemical splash goggles
30 laboratory aprons
30 pairs latex gloves
15 rectangular pieces of galvanized iron, 2 cm × 5 cm
15 laboratory balances
15 metric rulers
15 beakers, 250-mL
500 mL hydrochloric acid (HCl), 6.0 M
tap water
15 paper towels
beaker, 1-L

Time Required
40 minutes.

Advance Preparation
Cut up pieces of galvanized sheeting in as close to rectangular shapes as possible. The industrial arts department or shop at your school may have metal cutting saws or shears for this.
Prepare 500 mL of 6 M HCl by adding 250 mL of 12 M HCl to 250 mL of distilled water. CAUTION: *Wear goggles, apron, and gloves.*

Introduction
You can introduce this lab by bringing in some steel wool a few days early. Put one piece of steel wool in water and leave one piece dry. By the time the lab starts, there will be plenty of rust on the wet piece of steel wool as a reminder of the importance of galvanization.

© Prentice-Hall, Inc.

Zinc Thickness in Galvanized Iron **169**

Lab 32 APPLICATION

Name _____

Problem

How do you determine the thickness of zinc on a piece of galvanized iron?

Materials

chemical splash goggles
laboratory apron
rectangular piece of galvanized iron
laboratory balance
metric ruler

latex gloves
beaker, 250-mL
hydrochloric acid (HCl), 6.0 M
tap water
paper towel

Safety

Wear your goggles and lab apron at all times during the investigation. Hydrochloric acid is corrosive and can give off hydrogen chloride fumes when heated. Use in a well-ventilated area, preferably under a hood. Wear gloves when using 6.0 M hydrochloric acid. Note the caution alert symbols here and with certain steps of the Procedure. Refer to page xi for the specific precautions associated with each symbol.

Procedure

1. Put on your goggles and lab apron. Determine the mass of a piece of galvanized iron and record it in the Data Table.
2. Measure the width and length of the galvanized iron and record these values in the Data Table.

3. Put on your gloves. Work in a fume hood. Place the galvanized iron in the 250-mL beaker and cover with 30 mL of 6.0 M hydrochloric acid (HCl). **CAUTION:** *Hydrochloric acid is corrosive and can give off hydrogen chloride fumes when heated.* When the rapid evolution of gas stops, add water to the beaker and then pour off the liquid into a beaker your teacher has provided. Rinse the remaining metal with tap water and dry it with a paper towel.
4. Determine the mass of the remaining metal and record it.

5. Clean up your work area and wash your hands before leaving the laboratory.

Safety

Make sure students wear their goggles and lab aprons at all times during the investigation. After they have washed the acid from the metal, they may remove their gloves. ■

Teaching Tips

Galvanized sheeting (which is more properly called steel than iron) usually comes in 4 × 8 foot sheets in .020 inch thickness and is available from metal fabricators. Often scrap pieces can be acquired for minimal or no cost. Heating contractors may have scrap available from furnace installations and duct work.

Waste Disposal

To dispose of 6.0 M hydrochloric acid, neutralize with base and flush down the drain with plenty of water. Dispose of iron in the trash. ■

Name _____

Lab 32
APPLICATION

Observations (sample data)

DATA TABLE

mass of galvanized iron (g)	5.31
mass of remaining iron (g)	4.96
mass of zinc (g)	0.35
length of metal, l (cm)	4.5
width of metal, w (cm)	2.4

Calculations (based on sample data)

1. Find the area of iron covered by zinc (remember zinc covers both sides of the piece).

   $A = l \times w \times 2 = 4.5 \text{ cm} \times 2.4 \text{ cm} \times 2 = 22 \text{ cm}^2$

2. Find the mass of the zinc coating.

   $5.31 \text{ g} - 4.96 \text{ g} = 0.35 \text{ g Zn}$

3. Given the density of zinc as 7.14 g/cm³, find the volume of zinc.

   Vol = Mass/Density; $\dfrac{0.35 \text{ g}}{7.14 \text{ g/cm}^3} = 0.049 \text{ cm}^3$

4. Find the thickness of the zinc coating.

   $\dfrac{\text{Volume of coating}}{\text{total area of coating}} = \dfrac{0.049 \text{ cm}^3}{22 \text{ cm}^2} = 0.0022 \text{ cm Zn}$

5. Given the diameter of the zinc atom as 2.66×10^{-8} cm, find the thickness of the zinc coating in atoms.

   $\dfrac{2.2 \times 10^{-3} \text{ cm}}{2.66 \times 10^{-8} \text{ cm/atom Zn}} = 8.3 \times 10^4 \text{ atoms Zn}$

6. How many moles of zinc are in the coating?

   $\dfrac{0.35 \text{ g Zn}}{65.4 \text{ g/mol Zn}} = 5.4 \times 10^{-3} \text{ moles Zn}$

Critical Thinking: Analysis and Conclusions

1. Write the balanced equation for the reaction of zinc with hydrochloric acid. *(Applying concepts)* $\text{Zn}(s) + 2 \text{ HCl}(aq) \rightarrow \text{H}_2(g) + \text{ZnCl}_2(aq)$

2. How did you know that the zinc had fully reacted with the acid? *(Interpreting data)* Zinc and HCl produced hydrogen gas vigorously. When the reaction slowed down, it indicated that the zinc had fully reacted.

Name _____

3. What are the major sources of error in this investigation? *(Drawing conclusions)* The area of the zinc coating and its mass are both measured to an accuracy of only two significant figures.

Critical Thinking: Applications

1. What does the thickness of the zinc coating indicate about the effectiveness of zinc in protecting iron? *(Drawing conclusions)* A relatively thin coating adequately prevents the oxidation of iron.

Going Further

1. Obtain from your teacher strips of metals such as aluminum, copper, magnesium and zinc. Devise an experiment to test the reactivity of these metals in acidic and basic mediums. Conduct the experiment under your teacher's supervision. Report on whether or not corrosion problems are related to the presence of acids and bases.

Name _____ Date _____ Class _____

Limiting Reactants in Brownies

Lab 33
APPLICATION

Text reference: **Chapter 11**

Introduction

Have you ever made a dip for a party and found that you were low on one ingredient you needed? Could you still make the dip? How much dip could you make? The same situation exists for chemical reactions. How do you determine how much product will come out of a chemical process? First, you have to know the balanced equation for the reaction. Then you need to know how much of each starting reactant you have. Next you need to determine which reactant is the limiting quantity, given the molar ratios of all the reactants. Finally, you must use the quantity of the limiting reactant to determine how much product you will get.

When you use recipes in the kitchen, the same process takes place. Nothing made in a chemistry lab can be eaten, so you will do this investigation at home. You will be given a list of ingredients. By comparing this list to the standard recipe, you will determine which ingredient is present in a different amount. You will calculate the quantities of materials you need based on the concept of limiting reactants, and then bake a batch of brownies according to your new recipe. It is important that you keep careful records of your procedure and the amounts of your materials. Your results will then be compared to those of your classmates.

Pre-Lab Discussion

Read the entire laboratory investigation and the relevant pages of your textbook. Then answer the questions that follow.

1. Will the results always be identical if you mix the same ingredients in exactly the same proportions every time? <u>No, other factors such as the order of mixing, length of baking time, size of pan, etc., will affect the results in the kitchen.</u>

2. What is the importance of having a procedure and following it precisely? <u>It is more likely to yield reproducible results.</u>

3. How does the quantity of a chemical in a reaction determine the outcome of an experiment in the kitchen? In the chemistry lab? <u>In the kitchen, the wrong amounts may give you a product that is too dry, doesn't rise, tastes bad, etc. In the chemistry laboratory, having limited amounts of one or more chemicals leads to an incomplete reaction.</u>

4. What safety precautions should you observe in the kitchen? <u>Handle hot pans with pot holders. Wear an apron to protect clothing.</u>

Materials (class of 30 in pairs)
- 15 index cards
- 15 kitchens, equipped with measuring cups, measuring spoons, pot holders, mixer, pan, and oven
- ingredients for brownie recipe:
  - 1/3 cup shortening
  - 2 squares unsweetened chocolate (2 oz.)
  - 1 cup sugar
  - 2 eggs
  - 1 teaspoon vanilla
  - 3/4 cup flour
  - 1/2 teaspoon baking powder
  - 1/2 teaspoon salt

Time Required
Students will need approximately 1 hour at home to prepare their brownies. They will need one class period for interviews and data collection.

Advance Preparation
Prepare index cards containing a list of ingredients in which one ingredient differs from the recipe. For example, a card could have one egg instead of two eggs, 3/4 cup sugar instead of 1 cup sugar, or other variations. Have some control groups whose ingredients are the same as the standard recipe.

Introduction
Discuss how, in the making of chemical compounds, only specific ratios of chemicals will combine and that the chemical with the smallest number of relative moles (the limiting reactant) will control the amount of the product. In the kitchen cooks can vary the ingredients—sometimes

© Prentice-Hall, Inc.

Limiting Reactants in Brownies **173**

Lab 33
APPLICATION

with favorable results, other times, not so favorable. Ask the students to share some of their cooking experiences. The use of home labs gives the students a chance to discuss chemistry with their families. Students and families will understand a little better how chemistry applies to many aspects of life.

Name _____

5. If 16.5 grams of aluminum are reacted with 39.2 grams of chlorine gas, then aluminum chloride is formed.

   a. Which reactant is the limiting reactant? __chlorine__

   $$2Al + 3Cl_2 \rightarrow 2AlCl_3$$

   $$16.5 \text{ g Al} \times \frac{1 \text{ mol Al}}{27.0 \text{ g Al}} \times \frac{2 \text{ mol AlCl}_3}{2 \text{ mol Al}} = 0.611 \text{ moles AlCl}_3$$

   $$39.2 \text{ g Cl}_2 \times \frac{1 \text{ mol Cl}_2}{71.0 \text{ g Cl}_2} \times \frac{2 \text{ mol AlCl}_3}{3 \text{ mol Cl}_2} = 0.368 \text{ moles AlCl}_3$$

   b. Calculate the mass of aluminum chloride produced.

   $$0.368 \text{ mol AlCl}_3 \times \frac{133.5 \text{ g AlCl}_3}{\text{mol AlCl}_3} = 49.1 \text{ g AlCl}_3$$

Problem

How can the concept of limiting reagents be applied to a cooking recipe?

Materials

index card with instructions
kitchen, equipped with measuring cups, measuring spoons, pot holders, mixer, oven, and pan
ingredients for brownie recipe:
  1/3 cup shortening
  2 squares unsweetened chocolate (2 oz.)

1 cup sugar
2 eggs
1 teaspoon vanilla
3/4 cup flour
1/2 teaspoon baking powder
1/2 teaspoon salt

Safety

Safety

Students working at home must have adult supervision. Make sure that each student's Safety Contract is signed by a parent or guardian. Remind students to use pot holders when taking pans out of the oven. ■

Do not work in the kitchen without adult supervision. Wash your hands with soap and water before beginning this investigation. Wear an apron. Ovens and pans are hot. Use pot holders when removing pans from the oven. Let the brownies cool before cutting them. Note the caution alert symbols here and with certain steps of the Procedure. Refer to page *xi* for the specific precautions associated with each symbol.

Procedure

Part A: At Home

1. Wash your hands with soap and water. Wear an apron. Work under adult supervision. Calculate the amount of each ingredient you will use, based upon the information on the index card you received from your teacher. List these amounts in Data Table 1.

2. Gather the ingredients and other materials you will need. Explain to your family what you are doing and how this investigation relates to what you are studying in chemistry.

Name _____

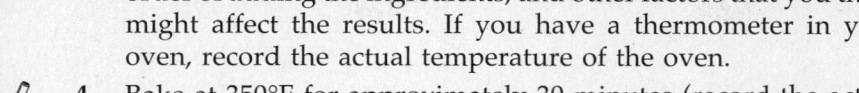

3. Mix the ingredients, making careful notes of measurements, the order of adding the ingredients, and other factors that you think might affect the results. If you have a thermometer in your oven, record the actual temperature of the oven.

4. Bake at 350°F for approximately 30 minutes (record the actual time). **CAUTION:** *Use pot holders to remove the pan from the oven.*

5. Let the pan cool completely. Cut the brownies into 30 equal-sized pieces. Clean up completely before leaving the kitchen.

Part B: In Class

6. On the day specified by your teacher, bring your experimental results to class to be tested. Arrange the experiments so that everyone can observe and then taste the brownies.

7. Make a Data Table using sample Data Table 2 as a guide. Fill in the table for dimensions, color, texture, and taste for every type of brownie.

Observations (sample data)

DATA TABLE 1

Ingredient	Amount	Order of Mixing
shortening	Answers will vary.	Answers will vary.
unsweetened chocolate		
sugar		
eggs		
vanilla		
flour		
baking powder		
salt		

DATA TABLE 2

	Brownie Ratings			
Name or Group #	Dimensions	Color	Texture	Taste

Teaching Tips

Alternatively, you could use the home economics lab and purchase ingredients yourself if you decide to do this lab at school. In either event, do the tasting part away from the lab tables or in a nonlab area. It is interesting to see the results of the students' baking experiences. Some students will mix the brownies as if they were a cake and others will use a traditional brownie-type procedure. The results will be as varied as the number of students. None of the brownies will taste bad, but some will definitely taste better. Give the students no hints on how to proceed with their baking.

The students will discuss at great lengths what they think happened. The discussions can take many directions that will give you, the teacher, the opportunity to discuss topics such as applied chemistry, measurements, procedures, good data collection, and limiting reactants.

Waste Disposal

Remind students to clean up in the kitchen. Sometimes it takes a while to get the students to take their pans home from the classroom, so you might want to suggest that they bring their brownies to school in disposable pans or on paper plates. ∎

Cooperative Learning Strategy

Let the students form working groups based on their home locations and the availability of kitchen space.

Limiting Reactants in Brownies

Name_____

Critical Thinking: Analysis and Conclusions

1. Interview the classmate who made what you consider to be the best brownie in each category (color, texture, taste). Record the order of mixing, time of baking, brand of ingredients, etc. Try to identify what factor(s) may have contributed to the success of the recipe. *(Drawing conclusions)* <u>Answers will vary. This topic can lead to a discussion on how scientists describe, explain, and measure things.</u>

2. Were all the brownies the same size? If not, what affected the size? *(Drawing conclusions)* <u>No. Every group made a different amount of brownies because of limiting reactants. Also, the sizes of the pans varied.</u>

3. Were all the brownies of the same consistency (chewy, moist, etc.)? If not, what affected the consistency? *(Making comparisons)* <u>No. Some amounts of ingredients may have been calculated incorrectly. Other brownies may have been over- or under-baked.</u>

4. Write the procedure for making what you thought was the best brownie. *(Developing models)* <u>Answers will vary.</u>

5. What effect did the lack of a written procedure have? *(Developing hypotheses)* <u>The use of different procedures led to different consistencies of the brownies.</u>

6. Why are the ratios of ingredients important in a brownie recipe? *(Drawing conclusions)* <u>To produce brownies with the best taste and texture.</u>

Critical Thinking: Applications

1. Can the amounts of the ingredients in a brownie recipe vary without ruining the product? If so, which ones do you think you could use more or less of? What would be the results if you did vary the amounts? *(Interpreting data)* <u>Less salt, sugar, or vanilla will change the taste. Less fat will affect moisture and texture. Fewer eggs—product may not rise as well and will probably be drier.</u>

2. If you wanted to make a brownie with fewer calories but good texture, what changes would you try? *(Designing experiments)* <u>Answers will vary but may include substituting applesauce for fat, using egg substitute instead of eggs, etc.</u>

Going Further

1. Look up an example of a commercial product in which limiting reactants play an important role in the manufacturing process. Prepare an oral report on this product.

Heat of Solution

Lab 34

Text reference: **Chapter 12**

Introduction

Whenever bonds are formed or broken in a chemical reaction, energy is transferred. As a solid dissolves in water, its bonds are broken, and a change in temperature is usually observed. If energy is absorbed from the solvent when a solid dissolves, the system gets colder—the reaction is endothermic, and it has a positive enthalpy change. On the other hand, if energy is released, the system gets warmer—the reaction is exothermic, and it has a negative enthalpy change.

The molar heat of solution of a compound is the heat transferred when one mole of the compound (the solute) dissolves in a solvent. That change cannot be measured in isolation, but it can be determined if the amount of solute dissolved, the amount of solvent used, and the temperature change of the solution are all known.

In this investigation, you will explore the energy changes that take place when various solids (the solutes) dissolve in water (the solvent). You will dissolve known quantities of several solids in different 100-mL samples of water and measure the temperature changes as they dissolve. From these data, the molar heat of solution for each solid will be found.

Pre-Lab Discussion

Read the entire laboratory investigation and the relevant pages of your textbook. Then answer the questions that follow.

1. What is the definition of a chemical bond? __A chemical bond is the force that holds atoms or ions together in a substance.__

2. What is the difference between heat and temperature? __Temperature is a measure of the average kinetic energy of the molecules. Heat is the transfer of energy from one object to another at a lower temperature.__

3. When the reactants get colder in an endothermic reaction, what has happened to the heat energy? __The energy comes from the thermal energy of the reactants and is stored as the energy in the chemical bonds of the product.__

4. Is the change in enthalpy positive or negative for an exothermic reaction? Explain. __In an exothermic reaction, heat is released, which means that the reactant enthalpy is greater than the product enthalpy. The change in enthalpy is negative.__

Materials (class of 30 in pairs)

30 pairs chemical splash goggles
30 laboratory aprons
15 graduated cylinders, 100-mL
distilled water, 6 L
15 large plastic foam cups
15 thermometers
15 laboratory balances
150 g sodium thiosulfate pentahydrate ($Na_2S_2O_3 \cdot 5H_2O$)
60 pieces of weighing paper
15 stirring rods
30 pairs latex gloves
60 g sodium hydroxide pellets (NaOH)
180 g ammonium chloride (NH_4Cl)
180 g calcium chloride ($CaCl_2$)

Time Required

60 minutes. To save time, students may do only two reactions and pool their data to get the full impact of this investigation.

Advance Preparation

Set out sufficient amounts of each solid in small beakers at several stations around the room to facilitate distribution of materials. Provide a spatula with each beaker.

For the sodium hydroxide, you may prepare 15 small, capped vials that contain approximately the required mass. Students can then obtain what they need from the individual vials and minimize contamination of the pellets with water.

Lab 34

Name _____

5. Why is a plastic foam cup used instead of a beaker? For what piece of equipment is this cup a substitute? A plastic foam cup is used because it will gain or lose very little heat energy, and it is a good insulator. The cup is a substitute for a calorimeter.

6. Why should you not stir the solution with the thermometer? What should be used? A thermometer might break and spill its contents (mercury or alcohol) into the reaction. A glass stirring rod should be used.

Problem

How can you measure the molar heat of solution of solids?

Materials

chemical splash goggles
laboratory apron
latex gloves
graduated cylinder, 100-mL
distilled water
large plastic foam cup
thermometer
laboratory balance

sodium thiosulfate pentahydrate ($Na_2S_2O_3 \cdot 5H_2O$)
4 pieces of weighing paper
stirring rod
sodium hydroxide pellets (NaOH)
ammonium chloride (NH_4Cl)
calcium chloride ($CaCl_2$)

Safety

Wear your goggles and lab apron at all times during the investigation. Sodium hydroxide is a very strong base and is very caustic. Wear latex gloves when working with the sodium hydroxide crystals, and do not touch them with your hands. The other solutions may also be irritating to skin. Avoid contact with them. Clean up any spills with plenty of cold water.

Note the caution alert symbols here and with certain steps of the Procedure. Refer to page *xi* for the specific precautions associated with each symbol.

Procedure

 1. Put on your goggles and lab apron. Measure 100.0 mL of distilled water at room temperature and pour it into the plastic foam cup. Record the temperature of the water in the Data Table. Do not remove the thermometer from the cup, but be careful that it does not tip the cup over.

2. Using your laboratory balance, measure out 5–10 grams of the sodium thiosulfate on a piece of paper. Record the mass used to 0.01 g. (Make sure you take the mass of the paper into account.)

Safety

Make sure students wear their goggles and lab aprons at all times during the investigation. Sodium hydroxide is a very strong base and is very caustic. Tell students to wear latex gloves when handling it. The other solutions may also be irritating to skin. Remind students to clean up any spills with plenty of cold water. ■

Teaching Tips

Explain to students that for each solid, each group should have a different amount. If each group uses different amounts of the solids, the class data as a whole will show that the amount of heat released or absorbed by each solute is proportional to the amount of solute used. The molar heats of solution found for each

3. Without removing the thermometer from the cup, shake the sodium thiosulfate from the paper into the water and stir gently with the stirring rod until the solid is completely dissolved. **CAUTION:** *All of the solutions in this investigation are irritating to skin. Avoid contact with them.*

4. Make sure that the bulb of the thermometer is fully immersed in the liquid. If the temperature rises, record the highest temperature reached by the solution. If the temperature falls, record the lowest temperature.

5. Dispose of the solution by pouring it down the drain, followed by plenty of water. Rinse and dry the cup.

6. Put on your latex gloves. Repeat Steps 1–5, using 2–4 grams of sodium hydroxide pellets as your solute. **CAUTION:** *Sodium hydroxide is a very strong base and is very caustic. Wear latex gloves when working with the sodium hydroxide pellets, and do not touch them with your hands. Clean up any spills with plenty of cold water.*

7. Repeat Steps 1–5, using 8–12 grams of ammonium chloride as your solute.

8. Repeat Steps 1–5, using 8–12 grams of calcium chloride as your solute.

9. Clean up your work area and wash your hands before leaving the laboratory.

Observations (sample data)
DATA TABLE

Solute	Solute Mass (g)	Solution Mass (g)	Initial T (°C)	Final T (°C)	ΔT (°C)
$Na_2S_2O_3 \cdot 5H_2O$	7.42	107.4	21.2	18.5	−2.7
NaOH	3.41	103.4	21.3	31.8	+10.5
NH_4Cl	11.23	111.2	21.1	13.1	−8.0
$CaCl_2$	9.16	109.2	21.3	41.2	+19.9

Calculations (based on sample data; one example given)

1. ΔT is the change from initial temperature to final temperature ($\Delta T = T_f - T_i$). Calculate ΔT for each reaction, and enter the values in the Data Table.
2. Find the total mass of solution that changed temperature in each reaction, and write the values in the Data Table. (Assume that 100.0 mL of water has a mass of 100.0 g.)
3. Calculate the energy (in joules) absorbed or released by the solution in each reaction. Use the absolute value for ΔT in the following equation.

$$\text{energy} = (\text{mass}) \times (\Delta T) \times (\text{specific heat of solution})$$

solute should be the same within reasonable experimental ranges.

The value 3.34 J/g·°C for the specific heat of the solutions is equivalent to 0.8 cal/g·°C. It is a fairly crude approximation to use the same value for all four solutions, but it does reflect the fact that the solutions have a lower heat capacity than pure water. More accurate corrections can be made for the altered heat capacities, but may not be justified, given the level of accuracy in this investigation.

Students must find the mass of the NaOH pellets as rapidly as possible to avoid having the absorption of water from the atmosphere affect their results.

To increase the accuracy of the temperature measurements, you may have students use water below room temperature for exothermic reactions. The final temperature of the solution will then be closer to room temperature, and heat loss will therefore be reduced. For endothermic reactions, students may start with water above room temperature.

If beakers of suitable size are available, you may have students nest the plastic foam cups inside them, as described in Investigation 36. The beakers provide extra thermal insulation and are more sturdy than the plastic foam cups.

Lids for plastic foam cups are available, which somewhat increase the insulating value of the cup. The lids may hinder the measurements, however, since they must be removed in order for students to read the thermometers.

Heat of Solution **179**

Lab 34

There is appreciable variation among published values of molar heats of solution for the solids used in this investigation. The best available values are given below.

$Na_2S_2O_3 \cdot 5H_2O$	+46.2 kJ/mol
NaOH	−44.5 kJ/mol
NH_4Cl	+14.8 kJ/mol
$CaCl_2$	−81.3 kJ/mol

Molar masses of the solids:

$Na_2S_2O_3 \cdot 5H_2O$	248 g/mol
NaOH	40.0 g/mol
NH_4Cl	53.5 g/mol
$CaCl_2$	111 g/mol

Waste Disposal

All of these solutions may be flushed down the drain with plenty of water. ■

The specific heat of a solution is slightly different from the specific heat of pure water. In this investigation, assume it is 3.34 J/g•°C for all of your solutions.

$$\text{energy}_{NaOH} = (103.4 \text{ g}) \times (10.5°C) \times (3.34 \text{ J/g}•°C)$$

$$\text{energy}_{NaOH} = 3630 \text{ J}$$

4. Calculate the energy per gram of solute (in J/g) for each solution.

$$\frac{3630 \text{ J}}{3.41 \text{ g}} = 1060 \text{ J/g}$$

5. Using the periodic table, calculate the molar mass of each of the solutes.

$$\text{molar mass}_{NaOH} = 23.0 \text{ g/mol} + 1.0 \text{ g/mol} + 16.0 \text{ g/mol} = 40.0 \text{ g/mol}$$

6. Calculate the molar heat of solution for each solute from the formula molar heat of solution = (energy/gram) × (gram/mole of solute).

$$\text{molar heat of solution}_{NaOH} = (1060 \text{ J/g}) \times (40 \text{ g/mol})$$
$$= 42,400 \text{ J/mol} = 42.4 \text{ kJ/mol}$$

7. Your teacher will give you the accepted values of the molar heat of solution for each of your solutes. Use those values to calculate the percent error of your experimental value, using the following equation.

$$\% \text{ error} = \frac{|\text{accepted value} - \text{experimental value}|}{\text{accepted value}} \times 100$$

$$\% \text{ error}_{NaOH} = \frac{|44.5 - 42.4|}{44.5} \times 100 = \frac{2.1}{44.5} \times 100 = 4.7\%$$

Critical Thinking: Analysis and Conclusions

1. When sodium chloride dissolves in water, the ions dissociate. The equation for this reaction is $NaCl(s) \rightarrow Na^+(aq) + Cl^-(aq)$. Write similar ionic equations to show the dissociation in water of each of the solutes used in this investigation. *(Making inferences)*

   $Na_2S_2O_3(s) \rightarrow 2Na^+(aq) + S_2O_3^{2-}(aq)$

   $NaOH(s) \rightarrow Na^+(aq) + OH^-(aq)$

   $NH_4Cl(s) \rightarrow NH_4^+(aq) + Cl^-(aq)$

   $CaCl_2(s) \rightarrow Ca^{2+}(aq) + 2Cl^-(aq)$

Name _____

Lab 34

2. Which reactions are exothermic? Which are endothermic? *(Classifying)*
   The NaOH and CaCl$_2$ reactions are exothermic, while the Na$_2$S$_2$O$_3$ and NH$_4$Cl reactions are endothermic.

3. According to your answer to the previous question, assign the proper sign to each of the molar heats of solution you calculated and write the ΔH for each reaction. *(Classifying)* Answers will vary. Some sample values:

   Na$_2$S$_2$O$_3$:   ΔH = +32 kJ/mol
   NaOH: ΔH = −42.6 kJ/mol
   NH$_4$Cl: ΔH = +14.2 kJ/mol
   CaCl$_2$:   ΔH = −88.0 kJ/mol

4. Rewrite each of the ionic equations from Question 1 showing the molar heat of solution as a reactant or a product. *(Making inferences)* Answers will vary. Some sample equations:

   Na$_2$S$_2$O$_3$(s) + 32 kJ → 2Na$^+$(aq) + S$_2$O$_3^{2-}$(aq)

   NaOH(s) → Na$^+$(aq) + OH$^-$(aq) + 42.6 kJ

   NH$_4$Cl(s) + 14.2 kJ → NH$_4^+$(aq) + Cl$^-$(aq)

   CaCl$_2$(s) → Ca^{2+}(aq) + 2Cl$^-$(aq) + 88.0 kJ

Critical Thinking: Applications

1. Suggest two uses for these solution reactions in sports injuries or camping. *(Applying concepts)* Ice packs and heat packs for sports; warming or cooling foods when camping.

2. Which solid(s) from this investigation could be used in each of your answers in the previous question? Explain your reasoning. *(Giving examples)* Dissolving Na$_2$S$_2$O$_3$ or NH$_4$Cl in water could be used for cooling because each reaction absorbs heat from the surroundings. Dissolving NaOH or CaCl$_2$ in water could be used for heating because each reaction gives off heat.

3. What other kinds of considerations should you take into account if your suggestions were to be put into use? *(Applying concepts)* The solids would have to be nontoxic and environmentally safe.

4. How could you reduce the experimental errors in this investigation? Explain your reasoning. *(Designing experiments)* Increasing the amount of water used in the calorimeter would reduce the loss of heat, allowing for a more precise measurement. Using a balance or a thermometer with a greater degree of precision would also allow for more precise measurements.

© Prentice-Hall, Inc.   Heat of Solution

Lab 34

Going Further

1. Many common salts found at home or in the chemistry stockroom can be investigated. Make certain that they pose no significant health or environmental threats.

Going Further

1. Find out what the effect is of dissolving other solids in water. Under your teacher's supervision, try sodium chloride, sodium hydrogen carbonate, or other compounds. Look up the heats of solution first, and then predict what will happen to the temperature.
2. When a solid dissolves in water, the specific heat of the solution is no longer exactly the same as the specific heat of pure water. Under the supervision of your teacher, investigate how the specific heat of water changes under these conditions.

Simulating the Flameless Ration Heater

Lab 35
APPLICATION

Text reference: Chapter 12

Introduction

Picture yourself out on military maneuvers in a desolate area. You're very hungry, but making a fire or setting up a stove would take too much time and could be very dangerous. In order to make hot meals available to its troops, the U.S. Army worked with private industry to develop the Meal Ready to Eat (MRE) and a device called a Flameless Ration Heater (FRH).

The MRE is an aluminum-foil and plastic pouch containing a main course, condiments, or dessert. The FRH consists of a long plastic sleeve containing a small, porous cardboard envelope. Inside the envelope are heat-generating chemicals that react exothermically when water is present. The food pouch is placed inside the sleeve and water is added. As the heat-generating chemicals begin to react, the MRE is heated. See Figure 35–1.

In Investigation 16, you observed the reactivity of two alkaline earth metals, magnesium and calcium. The reaction of calcium with water was both very rapid and very exothermic. The reaction of magnesium was much slower. In fact, the rate of heat release was so slow that it was difficult to tell if the reaction was even exothermic. Yet the Flameless Ration Heater uses magnesium as the major fuel to provide heat. What

Materials (class of 30 in groups of 3 or 4)
30 pairs chemical splash goggles
30 laboratory aprons
8 marking pens
40 beakers, 50-mL
8 graduated cylinders, 50-mL
8 micropipets containing phenolphthalein solution
1 beaker, 400-mL (to hold micropipets)
64 magnesium (Mg) strips, 15 cm long
8 pieces of steel wool, 5 cm × 5 cm
8 spatulas
100 g iron powder (Fe)
8 mortars and pestles
8 microspatulas
100 g sodium chloride (NaCl)
8 pairs forceps
8 FRH chemical samples, 1 cm × 1 cm
8 petri dishes
40 thermometers
8 pairs pliers
8 iron slabs
8 hammers
100 g iron (Fe) filings

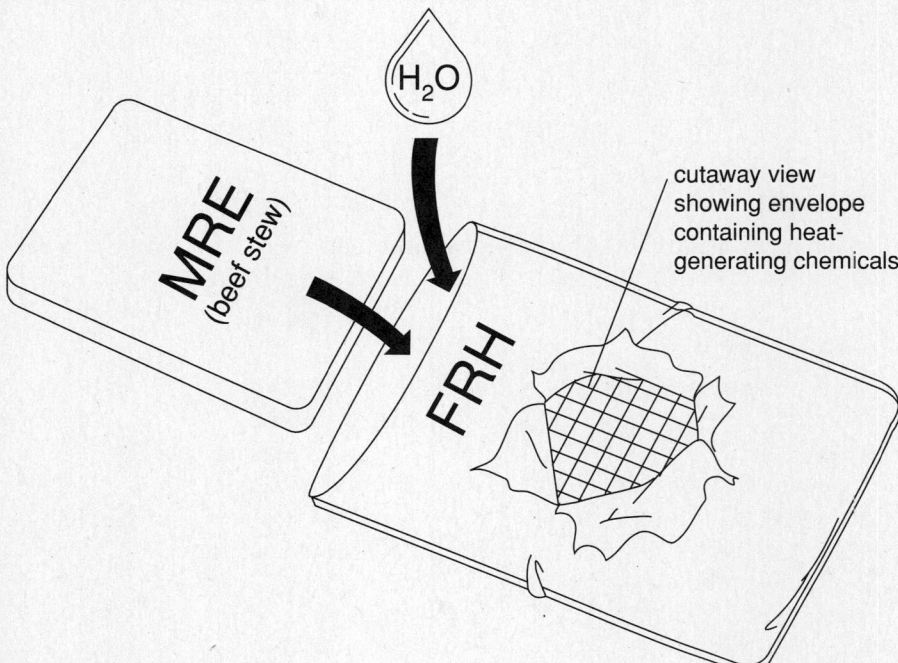

Figure 35–1

Lab 35
APPLICATION

Time Required
Each part takes about 40 minutes. To shorten the investigation, have half the class do Part A and the other half do Part B. Or, have each group of students test just one of the variables. (You will need to increase the number of beakers and thermometers if you split up the tasks.) In either case, the results can be pooled. It is also possible to do Part A one day and Part B the next.

Advance Preparation
The FRHs and MREs can be purchased from a military surplus store. You can get about 10 pieces of FRH chemical from each FRH. Chemical hand warmers are available at hardware or hunting supply stores. Cut magnesium strips into 15-cm lengths. Fill micropipets with phenolphthalein solution and place them in a labeled beaker. Point out the size difference between spatulas and microspatulas. Have ready a labeled container in which to collect the waste liquid.

Introduction
Demonstrate the function of the FRH when used to heat the MRE. Allow students to feel the heat from the FRH and to examine the food in the MRE. Pass around some hand warmers and explain that similar chemical reactions occur in these devices.

Name _____

is it about the reaction of the FRH that is different from the magnesium reaction from Investigation 16? The answer lies in the other ingredients that are present.

In this investigation, you will vary the reaction ingredients and the method of combination of the ingredients in order to determine the effect of the FRH reaction.

Pre-Lab Discussion
Read the entire laboratory investigation and the relevant pages of your textbook. Then answer the questions that follow.

1. Why isn't calcium metal used as one of the FRH heat-generating chemicals? __Calcium reacts too quickly with water, releasing potentially__ __explosive hydrogen gas. It also oxidizes quickly in air.__

2. What does the pink color of phenolphthalein indicate? __The pink__ __color indicates the presence of a base.__

3. Are the following reactions endothermic or exothermic? What is the standard change in enthalpy for each?
   a. $Mg(s) + 2H_2O(l) \rightarrow Mg(OH)_2(aq) + H_2(g) + 84$ kcal
   b. $2Fe(s) + O_2(g) \rightarrow 2FeO(s) + 130$ kcal
   c. $2Mg(s) + O_2(g) \rightarrow 2MgO(s) + 290$ kcal
   a. exothermic; -84 kcal; b. exothermic; -130 kcal; c. exothermic; -290 kcal.

4. What would be a disadvantage in using any of the reactions in Pre-Lab Question 3 as a source for heat generation? __None of these reac-__ __tions releases heat at a useful rate.__

5. What are some of the hazards associated with combining the FRH chemical or magnesium metal with water? __Hazards include the pro-__ __duction of heat and the formation of an alkaline solution.__

Problem
Under what conditions will magnesium metal react with water at a rate that generates sufficient heat to serve as an MRE heater?

Materials
chemical splash goggles
laboratory apron
marking pen
5 beakers, 50-mL
graduated cylinder, 50-mL
micropipet containing
    phenolphthalein solution
8 magnesium strips (Mg)
steel wool (Fe)
spatula
iron powder (Fe)

mortar and pestle
microspatula
sodium chloride (NaCl)
5 thermometers
forceps
FRH chemical sample
petri dish
pliers
iron slab (Fe)
hammer
iron filings (Fe)

Lab 35
APPLICATION

Name _____

Safety

Wear your goggles and lab apron at all times during the investigation. The FRH chemicals are poisonous and should be handled with the forceps. The solutions produced in this investigation are caustic and contact with your skin should be avoided. Note the caution alert symbols here and with certain steps of the Procedure. Refer to page xi for the specific precautions associated with each symbol.

Procedure

Part A

1. Put on your goggles and lab apron.
2. Using a marking pen, label five beakers 1–5. Put 25.0 mL of water, as measured in a graduated cylinder, and three or four drops of phenolphthalein solution into each beaker.
3. Polish four magnesium strips with steel wool until they are shiny. Place a spatula of iron powder into a mortar. Feed in a strip of magnesium, grinding the two metals together with the pestle. When the entire length of the magnesium strip has been ground together with the iron, turn it over and repeat the process.
4. Repeat Step 3 with another strip of magnesium. Set both strips aside.
5. To beakers 4 and 5 add a microspatula of sodium chloride (NaCl).
6. Using the thermometers, measure the temperature of the water in each beaker. Record the values in Data Table 1.

7. **CAUTION:** *The FRH chemicals are poisonous and should be handled only with the forceps.* To each beaker add the following:

   Beaker 1: FRH chemical sample
   Beaker 2: Magnesium strip
   Beaker 3: Magnesium/iron strip
   Beaker 4: Magnesium strip
   Beaker 5: Magnesium/iron strip

   Make sure the metal strips are completely submerged in the water.

8. After waiting 10–15 minutes to be sure the reactions are complete, record the final temperature, the final color, the relative rates of the reactions, and any other observations of note for each beaker.

9. Dispose of the liquid contents of the beakers by rinsing them into the labeled container provided by your teacher. The solid magnesium strips can be rinsed, dried, and cleaned, if necessary, with steel wool. Wash, rinse, and dry the beakers as well.

10. If you are not going directly on to Part B, clean up your work area and wash your hands before leaving the laboratory.

Safety

Make sure students wear their goggles and lab aprons at all times during the investigation. Although the amount of hydrogen gas produced is minimal, there should be no open flames in the laboratory. Students should be reminded to handle all of the subtances with forceps or spatulas to avoid the hazard of burns and also to keep skin oils off the reacting surfaces. The pink solution resulting from the reactions includes Mg(OH)$_2$, which is a basic substance. Although the solutions are not extremely caustic, students should be warned to dispose of them as directed. ■

Teaching Tips

Point out to students that some exothermic reactions happen so slowly that the amount of heat being released isn't sufficient to warm food efficiently. To get this point across, the question could be asked: "Does a car feel warmer while it is rusting (iron reacting with oxygen)?" Most students will realize that rusting is a slow process and that the heat from the reaction dissipates before enough accumulates to be noticed. The discussion should promote the idea that a chemical reaction used to generate heat must not only be exothermic, it must also release the heat at an appropriate rate. The iron and sodium chloride act as catalysts, speeding up the reaction.

Part B provides time for students to use some of the concepts from Part A. If you choose to split up the experiment to save time, be sure students meet with someone who did another part of the investigation.

If Part A and B are being run simultaneously, you will need more beakers and

© Prentice-Hall, Inc.   *Simulating the Flameless Ration Heater*   **185** thermometers. If there are not enough 50-mL beakers to go around, 100-mL beakers can be used.

Part B

11. Put on your goggles and lab apron. Polish four more magnesium strips with steel wool.
12. Place a spatula of iron powder in the inverted top of a petri dish and pinch the iron powder and one of the magnesium strips together with a pair of pliers. Continue for the entire length of the strip. Repeat for the other side of the strip. See Figure 35–2.

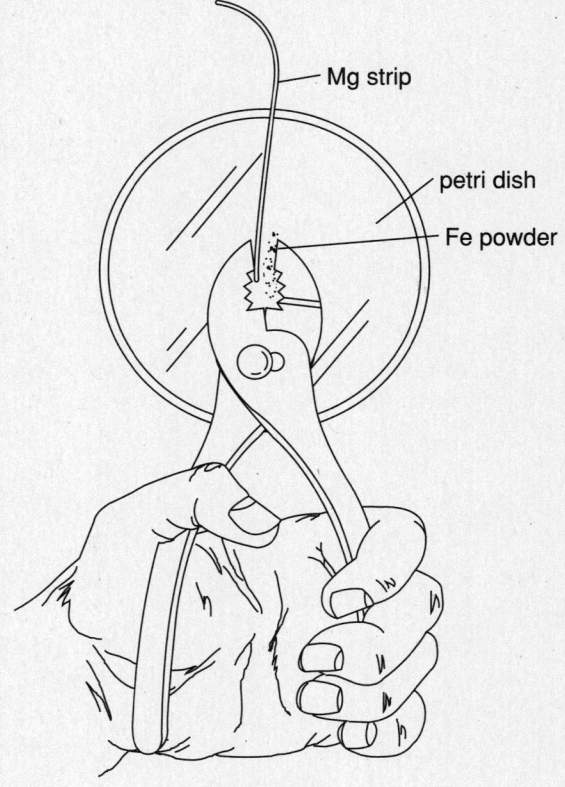

Figure 35–2

13. Place a spatula of iron powder on an iron slab, push the second magnesium strip into the powder, and strike the magnesium with a hammer as the strip is fed through the powder. Repeat for the other side of the strip.
14. Place a spatula of iron filings into a mortar. Repeat the treatment performed in Step 3.
15. Wrap a strip of magnesium with strands of steel wool. Roll the strip into a loose ball.
16. Label four beakers *1–4* and add 25.0 mL water, three or four drops of phenolphthalein, and a microspatula of sodium chloride to each.
17. In Data Table 2, record the initial temperature of the water in each beaker. To each beaker add the following:

    Beaker 1: magnesium/iron pinched with pliers
    Beaker 2: magnesium/iron hammered together

Beaker 3: magnesium/iron filings
Beaker 4: magnesium/steel wool strands

Make sure the metal strips are completely submerged in the water.

18. After waiting 10–15 minutes to be sure the reactions are complete, record the final temperature, the final color, the relative rates of the reactions, and any other observations.

19. Dispose of the liquid contents of the beakers by rinsing them into the labeled container provided by your teacher. Clean up your work area and wash your hands before leaving the laboratory.

Observations (sample data)

DATA TABLE 1

Beaker	Initial Temp. (°C)	Final Temp. (°C)	Final Color	Rate of Reaction	Other Observations
1	26	43	dark pink	1	rapid bubbling
2	26	26	light pink	5	little or no bubbling
3	26	26	light pink	4	slight bubbling
4	26	28	pink	3	moderate bubbling
5	26	39	dark pink	2	rapid bubbling

DATA TABLE 2

Beaker	Initial Temp. (°C)	Final Temp. (°C)	Final Color	Rate of Reaction	Other Observations
1	26	35	pink	1	rapid bubbling
2	26	32	light pink	2	moderate bubbling
3	26	32	light pink	3	some bubbling
4	26	31	light pink	4	some bubbling

> **Waste Disposal**
> The container with the waste solution should be placed under the hood for the disposal procedure. Stir 6.0 M HCl into the waste solution until it fails to become pink again upon sitting for 5–10 minutes. The liquid contents of the beaker can now be flushed down the drain with plenty of water. The rinsed solid that remains can be collected with a paper towel and disposed of in the solid waste. ■

Name _____

Critical Thinking: Analysis and Conclusions

1. Rank the rate of reaction for the materials in each beaker in Parts A and B on a scale of 1 to 5 with 1 being the fastest. Write your determinations in the Data Tables. *(Making comparisons)*

2. Did any of your observations suggest that the heat-generating chemical became very hot? *(Making inferences)* <u>The water emitted what looked like tiny puffs of steam when the FRH chemicals were put in it.</u>

3. What is the most likely composition of the layer of material you removed from the magnesium metal with the steel wool? Why was it important to remove this material? *(Making inferences)* <u>The layer is most likely magnesium oxide (MgO). It should be removed to expose the magnesium metal to the other reactants.</u>

4. Compare the reaction rates of the magnesium metal strips in beakers 4 and 5 of Part A. How does sodium chloride affect the rate of the reaction? *(Interpreting data)* <u>Sodium chloride increases the rate of reaction.</u>

5. Describe the conditions you observed in Part A that favored the greatest rate of reaction of magnesium metal with water. What does this indicate about the reaction ingredients? *(Interpreting data)* <u>Merging the magnesium with iron and adding sodium chloride increase the reaction rate. Therefore, they must act as catalysts.</u>

6. Did any of the beakers from Part B have a peak temperature as high as Beaker 1 from Part A? Describe the conditions that favored the highest peak temperature in Part B. *(Making comparisons)* <u>Answers will vary. Beaker 1 had the highest peak temperature, created by pinching the iron powder and magnesium strip together with pliers.</u>

Critical Thinking: Applications

1. Given the hazards associated with the FRH, would it make a good "instant hot pad" to use for applying heat to a sore or stiff body part? Explain. *(Evaluating)* <u>The FRH would not make a good hot pad. Since the bag cannot be sealed due to the hazard of trapping hydrogen gas inside, leakage of hot chemicals is likely.</u>

2. Some of the iron, magnesium, and sodium chloride will remain exposed to atmospheric oxygen when the FRH is used as directed. Give balanced chemical equations, including values for changes in enthalpy, that describe any additional reactions that could be occur-

Name _____

ring. How might these reactions affect the heat production of the FRH? *(Making predictions)* 2Fe(s) + O$_2$(g) → 2FeO(s) + 130 kcal; 2Mg(s) + O$_2$(g) → 2MgO(s) + 290 kcal. Since these reactions are both exothermic, the heat released would increase the effectiveness of the FRH.

3. Hand-warming devices are available that generate heat by exposing a package of dry, inert vermiculite particles, iron powder, and table salt to the atmosphere. No water is added to this type of warmer. State the chemical equation that describes the most likely reaction for generating the heat. Refer to the thermodynamics tables in chemistry reference material or your textbook to find the change in enthalpy for this reaction. *(Applying concepts)* The chemical reaction that is most likely to generate heat is: 2Fe(s) + O$_2$(g) → 2FeO(s) + 130 kcal.

Going Further

1. Devise an experiment with a procedure similar to the one used in this investigation that will test the heat-generating capacity of iron metal powder and salt in water without magnesium. Under your teacher's supervision, perform the experiment and report your findings to the class.
2. Devise an experiment that will test the heat-generating capacity of a commercial hand warmer. You may wish to try to simulate the efficiency of a commercial hand warmer with one that you devise. Under your teacher's supervision, perform the experiment and report your findings to the class.
3. Devise a procedure that uses a double-walled calorimeter and some FRH heat-generating chemicals to find the heat generated per gram of FRH chemicals. Under your teacher's supervision, perform the experiment and report your findings to the class.
4. Using a computer with a temperature probe, produce a temperature versus time graph of several of the beakers. Discuss the significance of any differences you observe.

Going Further
3. If the chemistry department doesn't have a double-walled calorimeter, the physics department usually does.
4. Computer temperature probes are available from many science supply companies.

Determining Heat Capacity

Lab 36 APPLICATION

Text reference: **Chapter 12**

Introduction

In the Middle Ages, defenders of a castle sometimes poured hot liquids down onto invaders who tried to storm the fortress walls. The liquid of choice was usually any available oil. What properties of oil do you think prompted this choice? This investigation will allow you to discover a chemical principle that has had many practical applications over the centuries, although today we look upon some of them as less than exemplary.

You know from experience that it takes much longer to heat a large kettle of water to boiling than it does a small pan of water. You reason that there is more water to be heated in the larger sample, and that is correct. You also know that the longer heating time involves a larger amount of heat. We say that the larger sample has a larger heat capacity. The heat capacity of anything—whether solid, liquid, or gas—depends on the amount of the material in the sample as well as its chemical composition. For example, every gram of water requires the same amount of heat on warming from room temperature to 100°C. It follows that the larger the sample, the greater is the amount of heat needed to reach the boiling point.

In this investigation you will find the heat capacity of a lead sinker. You will do this by finding the mass of the sinker, warming it to the boiling point of water, placing it in a sample of room-temperature water in a calorimeter, and measuring the temperature change of the water sample. From the data collected you will then calculate the heat lost by the sinker to the water and thus the lead sinker's heat capacity.

Pre-Lab Discussion

Read the entire laboratory investigation and the relevant pages of your textbook. Then answer the questions that follow.

1. What quantities do you need to know in order to determine the amount of heat released by the lead sinker in cooling to the final temperature? __You need to know the mass of the water sample, the change in temperature of the water, and the specific heat of water.__

2. What important assumption have you made in Question 1 in determining the amount of heat released by the lead sinker? __The assumption is that the heat gained by the water equals the heat lost by the sinker.__

Materials (class of 30 in pairs)
- 30 pairs chemical splash goggles
- 30 laboratory aprons
- 15 lead sinkers, 50-g
- 15 laboratory balances
- 15 pieces of string, 20-cm
- 15 plastic foam cups, 250-mL (8 oz.)
- 30 beakers, 250-mL
- 15 hot plates
- 15 graduated cylinders, 100-mL
- 15 thermometers
- 15 stirring rods

Time Required
45 minutes.
The lab period can be shortened by preheating the water and metal samples before class begins.

Advance Preparation
If you do not have lead sinkers in your laboratory, you may be able to obtain them from your school's physics laboratory. They may also be purchased from a science supply house or a local sporting goods store. It is even possible to use pieces of lead sheeting, which can be cut into 3-cm × 10-cm strips and loosely coiled. You should cut the string into 20-cm lengths beforehand.

Introduction
This investigation provides an opportunity to remind students that throughout history extensive use has been made of chemical and physical reactions, without benefit of our present understanding of the principles behind those reactions. This is not to suggest that one should be

© Prentice-Hall, Inc.

Determining Heat Capacity

Lab 36
APPLICATION

content with ignorance, but rather to reinforce the idea that much of the chemistry studied by today's students has been applied for centuries. For example, smelting of metals from ores, an ancient process, is a redox reaction. Moreover, producing the charcoal used to give the high temperatures needed for smelting was in itself a significant early use of a chemical process, the distillation of wood.

In this investigation students determine the heat capacity of a sample of lead, but the principles involved can be extended to several historical examples. The use of hot oil to defend castles is mentioned.

Name _____

3. How is each quantity in Question 1 obtained? The mass of the water is obtained by multiplying the volume of water in milliliters by the density of water. The change in temperature for the water can be calculated from the data, and the specific heat of water can be obtained from a table.

4. What quantities do you need to know in order to determine the heat capacity of the lead sinker? The change in temperature of the sinker and the heat lost by the sinker to the water.

5. How is each quantity in Question 4 obtained? The change in temperature is obtained by calculating the difference between the original temperature of the sinker in the hot-water bath and the final temperature of the water. The heat lost is calculated in Question 1.

6. How is the heat capacity of the lead sinker determined? The heat capacity is obtained by dividing the value for the heat lost by the sinker by the change in temperature.

7. Why should you not use the thermometer as a stirring rod? Thermometers have thin glass bulbs on the end. Stirring could make the thermometer hit the sinker, causing the bulb to break.

Problem
How can the heat capacity of a lead sinker be determined?

Materials
chemical splash goggles
laboratory apron
lead sinker
laboratory balance
string, 20-cm
plastic foam cup, 8-oz.

2 beakers, 250-mL
hot plate
graduated cylinder, 100-mL
stirring rod
thermometer

Safety
Make sure students wear their goggles and lab aprons at all times during the investigation. Alert them to the safety procedures to be followed in case of a broken thermometer. Caution students to be careful when working with hot plates and boiling water. ■

Safety
Wear your goggles and lab apron at all times during the investigation. Use caution when working with the hot plate. Never touch it with bare skin. Note the caution and alert symbols here and with certain steps of the Procedure. Refer to page xi for the specific precautions associated with each symbol.

Procedure

1. Put on your goggles and lab apron.
2. Obtain a lead sinker from your instructor and find its mass. Record the mass in the Data Table. Attach a piece of string to

the brass loop in the top of the sinker. The string is to be used in moving the sinker.

3. Place a plastic foam cup inside a 250-mL beaker. This will serve as your calorimeter.

4. On a hot plate, heat to boiling about 100 mL of water contained in another 250-mL beaker. Carefully rest the sinker in the boiling water bath and leave it there for at least three minutes. The string should be left hanging outside the beaker. **CAUTION:** *The hot plate and water are very hot. Avoid touching them with bare skin.* Measure and record the temperature of the boiling water to the nearest 0.2°C.

5. Place 50.0 mL of room-temperature water in the calorimeter. Record the temperature of the water to the nearest 0.2°C. Keep the thermometer in the calorimeter for the remainder of the investigation.

6. Carefully remove the sinker from the boiling water bath and place the sinker into the water in the calorimeter.

7. Gently stir the calorimeter water with the stirring rod while continuously observing the temperature change. Record the maximum temperature to the nearest 0.2°C.

8. When the final temperature reading has been taken, return the sinker to your instructor. Turn off the hot plate. Clean up your work area and wash your hands before leaving the laboratory.

Lab 36 APPLICATION

Teaching Tips

Nesting the cups in beakers serves two valuable purposes: it gives the cups greater stability and protects against spilling, while the trapped air between the cup and inside beaker wall provides further insulation. If you have caps or covers for the cups, using them will provide even further insulation, although they can interfere with the stirring and reading of the thermometers.

If you do not have hot plates in your laboratory and need to use a lab burner for boiling water, students should not attach strings to the sinkers. You will need to instruct them to use tongs in transferring the sinkers. When using tongs, students should hold the sinkers by the brass ring on the top. Whether tongs or attached strings are used to transfer the sinkers, remind students to be very careful when placing the sinkers in the beakers to prevent breakage.

It is possible and advisable to complete two trials of this investigation in one class period. Instruct students to keep the water boiling while the first trial is being completed. They may then quickly return the sinker to the boiling water bath for warming while measuring the new sample of water for the calorimeter.

Students should not assume that the water boils at 100°C. They should use the thermometer to determine the exact temperature. Remind them that the metal reaches the same temperature as the water.

Observations (sample data)

DATA TABLE

mass of lead sinker	49.51 g
volume of room-temperature water	50.0 mL
initial temperature of water	24.4°C
final temperature of water	27.2°C
temperature of boiling water	100.0°C

Calculations (based on sample data)

1. Determine the change in temperature of the water in the calorimeter.

$$\Delta T = T_f - T_i = 27.2°C - 24.4°C = 2.8°C$$

2. Determine the heat absorbed by the 50.0 mL of water in the calorimeter in warming to the final temperature.

$$q = 50.0 \text{ mL} \times 1 \text{ g/mL} \times 2.8°C \times 4.18 \text{ J/g·°C} = 585.2 \text{ J} = 5.9 \times 10^2 \text{ J}$$

© Prentice-Hall, Inc. *Determining Heat Capacity* **193**

3. Determine the change in temperature of the lead sinker in cooling to its final temperature.

$$\Delta T = T_i - T_f = 100.0°C - 27.2°C = 72.8°C$$

4. Calculate the amount of heat released by the lead sinker for each one-degree Celsius change in temperature. This is the heat capacity of the sinker.

$$\text{Heat Capacity} = \frac{5.9 \times 10^2 \text{ J}}{72.8°C} = 8.0 \text{ J/°C}$$

Critical Thinking: Analysis and Conclusions

1. What scientific law accounts for the assumption that the heat gained by the water in the calorimeter is equal to the heat lost by the lead sinker? *(Applying concepts)* The law of conservation of energy accounts for this assumption.

2. If you had a lead sample that was double the mass of the sinker you used in the investigation, what would be the heat capacity of the heavier sample? Give the reason for your answer. *(Making comparisons)* The heat capacity of the sample with twice the mass will be double that of the lighter sample. The heat energy needed to change the temperature of any amount of a substance by one degree depends upon the mass of the sample. Accordingly, more massive samples have greater heat capacities.

3. What is the relationship between the specific heat of a substance and the heat capacity of a sample of that substance? *(Applying concepts)* The specific heat of a substance is the amount of heat needed to change the temperature of one gram of the substance by one degree Celsius. Heat capacity is a measure of the amount of heat needed to change any given mass of the substance by one degree Celsius.

4. Given the mass of your lead sample, calculate c, the specific heat of lead. *(Applying concepts)*

$$c = \frac{8.0 \text{ J/°C}}{49.51 \text{ g}} = 0.16 \text{ J/g·°C}$$

5. Determine the percent error for the specific heat calculated in Question 4 if the accepted value for the specific heat of lead is 0.159 J/g·°C. *(Applying concepts)*

$$\text{Percent Error} = \frac{|0.159 - 0.16|}{0.159} \times 100 = 0.63\%$$

6. Predict whether or not the values for the heat capacity of the sinkers used by your classmates will be the same as the value you obtained for your sinker. *(Making predictions)* Since heat capacity depends upon the mass as well as the composition of an object, the values for each of the sinkers should differ, although the differences will be slight if all the sinkers are nearly equal in mass.

Critical Thinking: Applications

1. The specific heat of most oils is about 2 J/g·°C, compared to a value of 4.18 J/g·°C for water. Why do you now think oil, rather than water, was the liquid of choice used by castle defenders against invading forces? *(Making comparisons)* Gram for gram, the oil would require less heat, and also less time, to reach a given temperature. Oil can also be heated to a much higher temperature (about 400°C) and, at that temperature, possesses more heat energy than water at its boiling point. Another useful characteristic of oil is its viscosity, which causes it to stick to anything it contacts, such as invaders!

2. A disc of wax has several hot metal samples placed on it. The samples are of different metals. They are all at the same temperature and have the same mass and contact area with the wax. How will the heat capacity of each metal sample affect the rate at which it melts the wax? *(Making predictions)* Metals with a higher heat capacity will melt the wax at a greater rate, since the amount of heat energy released for a given temperature change is greater.

Going Further

1. The procedure used in the investigation is commonly utilized in determining the specific heat of a solid or the heat capacity of a sample of a solid. Suggest a method for determining either value for a liquid.

Going Further
1. Students may suggest heating a known mass of a liquid to a given temperature, pouring it into water in a calorimeter, and proceeding as in the investigation. The key is to devise a method to determine the amount of heat released by the sample over a known change in temperature.

Name _____ Date _____ Class _____

Boyle's Law by the Book

Lab 37

Text reference: Chapter

Introduction

Have you ever used a simple hand pump to inflate a bicycle tire? You push on the pump, and air moves into the tire. The bicycle pump operates, in part, on the principle of Boyle's law, which describes the relationship between the pressure and volume of a gas.

In this investigation, you will observe the behavior of a gas, using a device called a Boyle's law apparatus. These devices vary somewhat, but they all work in basically the same way. Observe the type of Boyle's law apparatus provided for the class. It should be much like the one shown in Figure 37–1. The apparatus consists of a graduated syringe with a movable piston. Unless there is a leak, the number of gaseous particles trapped in the syringe remains constant.

Initially, the syringe is adjusted to trap a volume of gas at the same pressure as its surroundings. The piston then does not move because the pressure exerted by the gas in the syringe equals the pressure of the atmosphere pushing on the piston. If the piston is pushed downward, it compresses the gas trapped in the syringe. If the pressure on the piston is then decreased, the pressure of the trapped gas will push the piston up.

Materials (class of 30 pairs)

30 pairs safety goggles
15 Boyle's law apparatuses
15 ring stands
15 clamps
75 chemistry or other uniformly sized textbooks
15 sets of pens or pencils in two different colors

Time Required

50 to 90 minutes. To shorten the lab, have students complete their calculations for homework. On the following day, students may need some guidance to draw the second graph and interpret the data.

Advance Preparation

Assemble the Boyle's law apparatuses and lubricate the rubber gaskets on the pistons if necessary. You may wish to use 60-mL syringes, as they are easier to read. If you do, students will need to set their initial volumes higher than 30 mL. Check to be sure the apparatuses do not leak.

The books used in the investigation should be uniform in size and have a mass comparable to a science textbook. Have the teams share their textbooks to reduce the number of additional books needed. (School storerooms that hold old or unused textbooks may be a good source for books.)

Introduction

Demonstrate the operation of a Boyle's law apparatus. You may wish to have a leaky example on hand to show students what to watch for when they test their setups in Procedure Step 3. Show

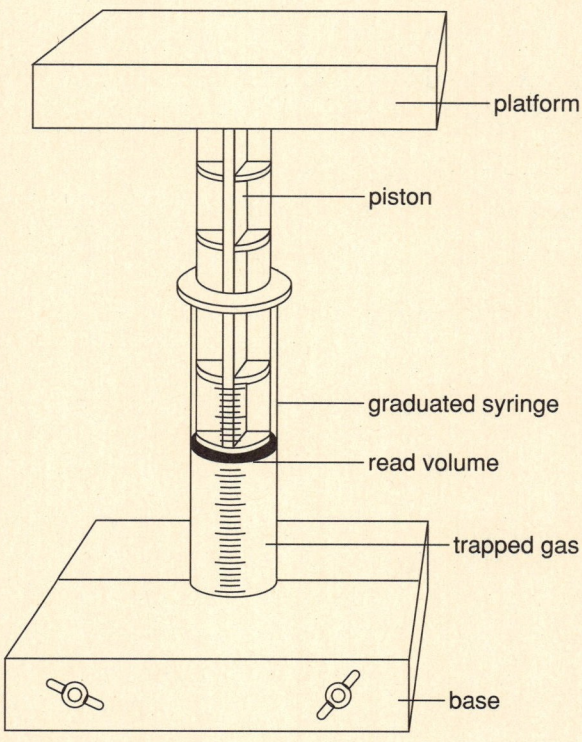

Figure 37–1

© Prentice-Hall, Inc.

Boyle's Law by the Book 197

Lab 37

students how to adjust the initial volume to atmospheric pressure. Depending on the type of apparatus, the adjustment may be done in one of two ways:
(a) If the syringe has a removable nipple on the nozzle, remove it, set the desired volume of trapped gas by adjusting the piston, and replace the nipple.
(b) If the apparatus has a small wire to adjust volume, hold the wire along the inside of the cylinder, use the wire to slide the piston to the desired volume, and remove the wire.

Advise students where on the cylinder to position the clamp so that they will have a clear view of the portion needed to measure volumes.

Name _____

In order to read the volume of trapped gas correctly, you must always read the measurement on the side of the piston that is in contact with the gas. Look again at Figure 37–1 to find this point.

In this investigation, you will use a Boyle's law apparatus to compress a sample of air. You should recognize that air actually is a mixture of gases—mostly nitrogen and oxygen—that behaves physically as a single gas. The data you obtain for the air sample may be treated as data for a single gas. As the pressure of the air changes, you will monitor and collect data on the resulting changes in volume. You can then use your data to find the atmospheric pressure and determine how closely your results agree with Boyle's law.

Pre-Lab Discussion

Read the entire laboratory investigation and the relevant pages of your textbook. Then answer the questions that follow.

1. State Boyle's law in your own words. Then write the mathematical equation for Boyle's law. __If the mass and temperature of a gas remain__ __constant, the product of the pressure times the volume has a constant__ __value. $PV = k$.__

2. When the piston in the Boyle's law apparatus is at rest, what is the relationship between the pressure of the trapped gas and the pressure on the outside of the piston? __The pressure inside the apparatus is equal__ __to the external pressure.__

3. What are the possible sources of external pressure on the piston during this investigation? __The possible sources are the atmosphere,__ __the mass of the piston, and the books.__

4. What is the benefit of collecting three sets of data in the investigation? __Collecting three sets of data reduces the effect of experimental__ __error and increases the probability that the results are reliable.__

5. In what ways can you minimize the risk of injury or damage to equipment from falling books? __The risk of injury and damage may be__ __reduced by steadying the books by hand or resting them against the ring stand.__

Problem

How does the volume of an enclosed sample of gas change as the pressure of the gas is changed?

Materials

safety goggles
Boyle's law apparatus
ring stand
clamp

5 chemistry textbooks
2 pens or pencils of different
   colors

Name_____

Lab 37

Safety

The increasing load of books on the piston of the Boyle's law apparatus may become unsteady. Falling books can injure the person measuring the gas volumes and damage the Boyle's law apparatus. Steady the books by resting them slightly against the ring stand or by nudging them into balance as you would with wooden building blocks. Additionally, one person may place his or her hands alongside the books to steady them, taking care not to lift or push down on the books. Be sure to use the Boyle's law apparatus only in the manner described by this experiment.

Note the caution alert symbols here and with certain steps of the Procedure. Refer to page *xi* for the specific precautions associated with each symbol.

Procedure

1. Work with a partner so that one person operates the apparatus while the other steadies the books and keeps track of the procedural steps. Change roles for the second and third sets of trials in Step 7.

2. Put on your safety goggles. Secure the Boyle's law apparatus with a ring stand and clamp. Adjust the initial volume (about 30 mL) to atmospheric pressure as directed by your teacher.

3. Test the apparatus by pushing down on the piston with your hand slowly and steadily until the volume of the trapped gas is reduced to 15 mL. Note whether the force you use to push the piston downward from the initial volume is the same as the force you need to compress the volume further. Release the piston and note whether it returns to the initial volume. If not, reset the apparatus to the original volume.

4. Place the apparatus on a flat, steady surface, such as a sturdy table or the floor. Record the initial volume at 0 books of pressure in the data table.

5. Place one book on the piston and record the resulting volume of trapped gas in the data table. Add a second book and record the gas volume. Continue adding books and recording the resulting volumes until all 5 books are resting on the piston. Remember to steady the books, especially when the apparatus is being read.

6. Remove all the books from the piston and reset the apparatus to the initial volume recorded in Step 2.

7. Repeat Steps 5 and 6 two more times, remembering to reset the apparatus between sets of trials.

 8. Clean up your work area and wash your hands before leaving the laboratory.

Safety

Make sure students wear their goggles and lab aprons at all times during the investigation. The floor is the best place for students to set up the apparatus in case books should fall. Remind students that in order to avoid facial injuries, they should be sure the books are steady when someone is attempting to read the volume of the cylinder. ∎

Teaching Tips

Students often have a difficult time with the concept of pressure from the trapped gas pushing on the piston inside the syringe. As students push on the piston in Procedure Step 3, ask them to explain why they have to increase the force on the piston in order to move it farther into the syringe.

To further the discussion, place the Boyle's law apparatus under a bell jar and evacuate the jar with a vacuum pump. Ask students to explain why the piston moves upward in the cylinder as the air in the bell jar is evacuated.

Review graphing concepts before students begin their calculations and analysis. Discuss with the class the characteristics of graphs of linear and inverse relationships. Students may need help with Calculation Step 5. It should be made clear to them that their graphs represent pressure values in excess of 1 atmosphere. You can use the equation $y = mx + b$ to explore this concept mathematically. The importance of including atmospheric pressure in P_{total} may also be demonstrated by having students calculate PV, using only the pressure in books, and compare the products with those they calculate in Step 7. Students may also benefit from a discussion the following day

© Prentice-Hall, Inc.

Boyle's Law by the Book **199**

Lab 37

focusing on the answers to the Critical Thinking questions. They should recognize, for example, that the product constant they calculate is specific to their sample of gas and not the same for all gases.

Cooperative Learning Strategy

Students may work in groups of three. Designate one student as the reader, one as the operator, and the third student as the recorder. The operator and reader should work together to assemble the apparatus and carry out the procedure. The recorder should make sure the data are available for all of the students to record before class is finished. Have the group members switch roles when beginning a new set of trials so that all students have an opportunity to work with the apparatus.

Name _____

Observations (sample data)

DATA TABLE

P_{books}	V_1 (mL)	V_2 (mL)	V_3 (mL)	V_{avg} (mL)	$\frac{1}{V_{avg}}$ (mL^{-1})	P_{total}	$P_{total} \times V_{avg}$
0	30.0	30.0	30.0	30.0	0.033	2.4	72
1	22.0	21.5	22.0	21.8	0.046	3.4	74
2	16.1	16.1	16.3	16.2	0.062	4.4	71
3	13.0	13.0	13.5	13.2	0.076	5.4	71
4	11.0	11.0	11.2	11.1	0.090	6.4	71
5	9.5	9.5	9.3	9.4	0.11	7.4	72

Calculations (based on sample data; examples are for $P = 1$ book)

1. Find the average of each set of three volumes and record these averages in the data table.

   $V_1 = 22.0$ mL, $V_2 = 21.5$ mL, $V_3 = 22.0$ mL

   $$V_{avg} = \frac{(22.0 \text{ mL} + 21.5 \text{ mL} + 22.0)}{3} = 21.8 \text{ mL}$$

2. On the blank graph in Figure 37–2 or on the right two thirds of a piece of graph paper, construct a graph with the pressure in books, P_{books}, on the horizontal axis and average volume, V_{avg}, on the left vertical axis. Plot the pressures versus their resulting average volumes on the graph and draw a smooth line through the points. Does

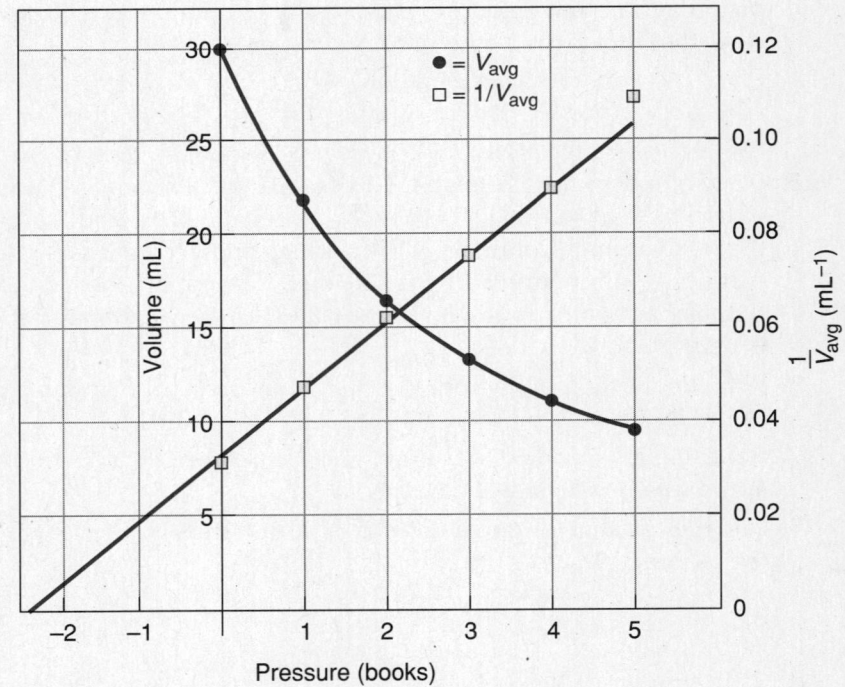

Figure 37–2

Name _____

Lab 37

the graph indicate a linear relationship (proportional relationship) between the pressures and their corresponding volumes? Explain.
No. The graph is a curve. A linear relationship would be indicated by a straight line.

3. According to Boyle's law, pressure and volume have an inversely proportional relationship. If this idea is correct, you should obtain a linear relationship (straight line) when you plot pressure versus the corresponding inverse of the average volume. Calculate the inverse, $1/V_{avg}$, of each volume and record these values in the appropriate column of the data table.

$$\frac{1}{V_{avg}} = \frac{1}{21.8 \text{ mL}} = 0.046 \text{ mL}^{-1}$$

4. Using the labels on the right vertical axis and a pen or pencil of a different color, plot the pressures versus their corresponding $1/V_{avg}$ values. Do these points suggest a linear relationship? Explain. Yes. The graph is a straight line.

5. The line obtained for the second plot crosses the vertical axis of the graph above the origin, which tells you that there is pressure on the gas even when there are no books on the piston. Consider that $1/V = 0$ only when the total pressure on the gas is zero (and the volume is infinitely large). The additional pressure is the atmospheric pressure. To find this pressure in units of books, extend the plot of P versus $1/V$ to the point where it intersects the horizontal axis. At this point, $1/V = 0$. The scale distance from this point to the origin is the atmospheric pressure measured in books. Using your graph, determine this value. __2.4 books__

6. Add the value you found for atmospheric pressure to the pressure in books for each trial and record these values of P_{total} in the table.

$P_{total} = P_{atm \text{ (from graph)}} + P_{books} = 2.4 \text{ books} + 1 \text{ books} = 3.4 \text{ books}$

7. Calculate the product of $P_{total} \times V_{avg}$ for each trial and record these values in the data table.

$P_{total} \times V_{avg} = 3.4 \text{ books} \times 21.8 \text{ mL} = 74$

Critical Thinking: Analysis and Conclusions

1. What pattern does the graph of P versus V suggest? (Interpreting diagrams) The graph illustrates that the volume of gas is reduced as pressure is applied to the piston. The volumes tend to decrease less and less as an increasing number of books are added to the piston.

2. How does your graph of P versus 1/V illustrate Boyle's law? *(Interpreting diagrams)* In general, the graph indicates a linear relationship between P and 1/V. The pressure of this gas is inversely proportional to its volume.

3. Look at the values you calculated in the last column of the data table. How do they compare? *(Making comparisons)* The values are similar.

4. What do these values mean in terms of Boyle's law? *(Making inferences)* For this sample of gas, the P × V product is constant, which means that any change in pressure results in a proportional change in volume.

Critical Thinking: Applications

1. The total external pressure on the piston when no books are present is due to the pressure of the atmosphere plus the mass of the piston. Suppose your partner says the external pressure comes exclusively from the mass of the piston. How would you disprove this idea? *(Designing experiments)* Disassemble the apparatus and find the mass of the piston. Then measure the mass of one textbook. Find the equivalent mass of the piston in units of books and compare this value to the one calculated for P_{atm}.

2. Recall the bicycle pump mentioned in the Introduction to this lab investigation. In order for the pump to work, air pressure must be greater in the pump than in the bicycle tire. Then air will move from the pump to the tire, causing inflation. How does the principle of Boyle's law come into effect in the operation of a bicycle pump? *(Applying concepts)* Pushing down on the pump decreases the volume of air in the pump and increases its pressure.

Going Further

1. Research the four-step cycle of the operation of the cylinders and pistons in an automobile engine. Find out what happens in each step of the cycle and determine when and how the principle of Boyle's law applies to the function of the engine.

Name _____ Date _____ Class _____

The Ideal Gas Constant

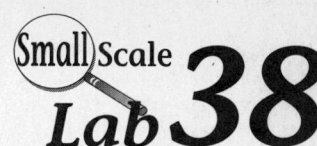

Small Scale Lab **38**

Text reference: **Chapter 13**

Introduction

The ideal gas law is represented by the formula $PV = nRT$, where R is the ideal gas constant. In this laboratory investigation you will experimentally determine the value of R. To do this, you must first determine the values of the other variables in the ideal gas equation. You will generate and collect a sample of hydrogen gas and determine its volume, temperature, pressure, and the number of moles produced under laboratory conditions.

The hydrogen gas is generated in a graduated cylinder from the reaction between magnesium and hydrochloric acid. By wrapping the magnesium ribbon in a copper wire cage, you can ensure that the magnesium will remain in the acid environment. Hydrochloric acid is in excess in the reaction so that the moles of hydrogen gas produced may be determined from the moles of magnesium that react.

Pre-Lab Discussion

Read the entire laboratory investigation and the relevant pages of your textbook. Then answer the questions that follow.

1. Describe how the values for P, V, n, and T are obtained in this investigation. <u>P is the atmospheric pressure, which is taken from a barometer. V is the volume of the hydrogen gas produced in the graduated cylinder. T is the temperature of the system, measured with a thermometer. The value for n is calculated from the reaction equation and the number of moles of magnesium used.</u>

2. Why do you think copper wire is used to make the cage for the magnesium ribbon in this reaction? <u>It probably does not react with the acid.</u>

3. When the graduated cylinder is inverted, why does the acid flow downward? <u>The acid is more dense than the water.</u>

4. Why is it important to tap the side of the graduated cylinder before reading the volume of gas collected? <u>Tapping the cylinder releases bubbles of hydrogen that may be trapped in the copper wire cage.</u>

5. How can you protect yourself from the hazards of working with 3 M HCl? <u>Wear goggles, gloves, and a lab apron. Handle the acid carefully. If spills occur, rinse with plenty of water and tell your teacher.</u>

Materials (class of 30)
30 pairs chemical splash goggles
30 laboratory aprons
30 metric rulers
30 pieces of Mg ribbon, 1.0 cm or less
30 pieces thin-gauge copper wire, 30-cm
30 graduated cylinders, 10-mL
30 one-hole rubber stoppers to fit graduated cylinder, number 0 or 1
30 beakers, 400-mL
tap water
30 pairs latex gloves
micropipet
100 mL hydrochloric acid (HCl), 3.0 M
30 wash bottles
30 thermometers
1 or more tables of vapor pressures of water

Time Required
40 minutes.

Advance Preparation
Prepare 3.0 M HCl by adding one part 12.0 M HCl to three parts distilled water. CAUTION: *Wear goggles, apron, and gloves.* Determine the mass of 100.0 cm of Mg ribbon. Cut the ribbon into pieces no longer than 1.0 cm. Pieces 0.98 cm in length work best. Cut thin-gauge copper wire into pieces approximately 30 cm long.

Introduction
Have available an example of the assembled apparatus. Discuss with students why hydrogen gas is used (it is easily generated in the laboratory in small quantities) and why it is collected by water displacement (hydrogen gas does not dissolve well in water).

© Prentice-Hall, Inc.   The Ideal Gas Constant **203**

Small Scale Lab 38

Review the concept of the ideal gas equation, and have students rearrange the equation to solve for *R*.

Problem

What is the value of the ideal gas constant?

Materials

chemical splash goggles
laboratory apron
metric ruler
1.0 cm or less of magnesium ribbon
25 cm thin-gauge copper wire
one-hole rubber stopper to fit graduated cylinder
graduated cylinder, 10-mL
beaker, 400-mL
tap water
latex gloves
micropipet
3.0 *M* hydrochloric acid (HCl)
wash bottle
thermometer
table of vapor pressures of water

Safety

Wear your goggles and lab apron at all times during the investigation. Hydrochloric acid (HCl) is corrosive. Avoid spills and contact with your skin and clothing. If HCl comes in contact with your skin or clothing, inform your teacher and flush the acid with large quantities of water. Neutralize any acid spills on the work surface with baking soda.

When inserting the stopper into the graduated cylinder, tap it down gently to avoid breaking the top of the cylinder. Note the caution alert symbols here and with certain steps of the Procedure. Refer to page *xi* for the specific precautions associated with each symbol.

Safety
Make sure students wear their goggles and lab aprons at all times during the investigation. HCl is corrosive. Because HCl is the reactant in excess, the contents of the beaker will be mildly acidic. Students should wash their hands after inverting the cylinder. ■

Teaching Tips
Instruct students to be precise in finding the length of Mg ribbon. The wire cage should be wrapped tightly around the ribbon so that no pieces float to the surface of the solution and escape the reaction. Some ribbons are thinner than others.

The cylinder must be filled to the top (not to the 10-mL mark) so that there is no air in the cylinder when the stopper is inserted. When the levels of liquid inside and outside the cylinder are the same, the gas pressure inside the cylinder will be equal to the atmospheric pressure. If there is no barometer in the laboratory, provide students with the value for the atmospheric pressure that day. Have available a table of vapor pressures of water that

Procedure

1. Put on your goggles and lab apron.
2. Using a metric ruler, measure and record the exact length of the piece of magnesium (Mg) ribbon provided by your teacher. The ribbon should be no longer than 1.0 cm.
3. Your teacher will give you the mass of 100.0 cm of Mg ribbon. Record this mass, which will be used as a conversion factor to determine the mass of your piece of Mg ribbon.
4. Wrap the copper wire around the magnesium ribbon, making a cage that surrounds the ribbon, as shown in Figure 38–1 (left). Leave a handle of copper wire approximately 6 cm long.

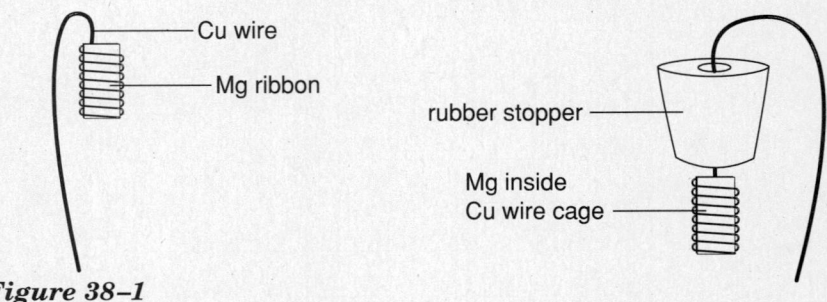

Figure 38–1

204 © Prentice-Hall, Inc.

Name _____

5. Insert the handle end of the copper wire into the one-hole rubber stopper as shown in Figure 38–1 (right). When the stopper is inserted into the graduated cylinder, the copper wire cage and Mg ribbon will be inside the cylinder.

6. Fill the 400-mL beaker or other container approximately half full with water.

7. Put on latex gloves. Use a dropper or micropipet to add approximately 3 mL of 3.0 M hydrochloric acid (HCl) to the graduated cylinder. **CAUTION:** *Hydrochloric acid is corrosive. Avoid contact with skin or clothing. Flush any spills with water and notify your teacher.*

8. Using the wash bottle, gently fill the graduated cylinder by drizzling water down the cylinder's inner side to avoid mixing. Because HCl has a greater density than water, the acid will remain at the bottom of the cylinder.

9. Insert the stopper into the graduated cylinder by tapping gently so as to avoid cracking the cylinder. The copper wire cage should be suspended at the top of the cylinder. Holding your finger over the hole in the rubber stopper, quickly invert the cylinder into the beaker of water. When the top of the cylinder is underwater you may remove your finger. Rest the cylinder in the beaker.

10. Notice the appearance of the acid solution inside the cylinder. Record any indication of a chemical reaction.

11. When the Mg ribbon is no longer reacting, tap the side of the cylinder to release any trapped bubbles.

12. Let the cylinder sit for 5 minutes. Using the thermometer, read and record the temperature in the beaker.

13. Determine and record the atmospheric pressure in the lab. Determine the water vapor pressure from a reference table.

14. Lift the graduated cylinder slightly until the levels of water inside and outside the cylinder are the same. See Figure 38–2.

students may consult to find the water vapor pressure for the temperature of the reaction system.

Cooperative Learning

This investigation is written for students working individually, but they also may work in pairs. Students can share the responsibilities of constructing and filling the apparatus. One partner then can invert the cylinder in the beaker and clean his or her hands while the other makes initial observations.

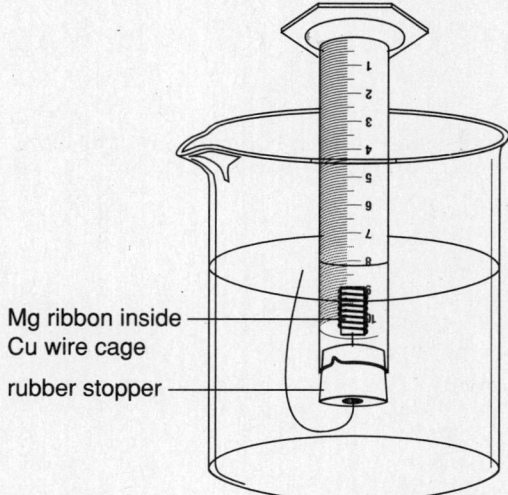

Figure 38–2

15. Read and record the volume of gas in the cylinder. Remember that you are reading an inverted cylinder.

16. After reading the volume of gas, remove the cylinder from the beaker and dispose of the contents of the beaker by pouring it down the drain. Turn the cylinder right side up, remove the stopper holding the copper cage, and dispose of any remaining liquid down the sink. Note the appearance of the copper wire.

17. Clean up your work area and wash your hands before leaving the laboratory.

Waste Disposal

Have students dilute the contents of the beaker and, with more water, pour the liquid down the drain. Then they should rinse and dry the beaker. Dispose of excess 3.0 M HCl by pouring it into a beaker of cold water and neutralizing the acid with solid sodium carbonate or bicarbonate. Pour the neutralized solution down the drain. Retain the copper wire for other use. ■

Observations (sample data)

length of Mg ribbon	0.90 cm
mass of 100.0 cm Mg ribbon	0.966 g
temperature of the reaction system	24.0° C
atmospheric pressure	754.2 mm Hg
water vapor pressure at system temperature	22.4 mm Hg
volume of gas produced	9.1 mL

Calculations (based on sample data)

1. Calculate the number of moles of Mg that reacted, using the length of Mg ribbon you used, the mass of 100.0 cm Mg ribbon provided by your teacher, and the molar mass of Mg.

   $$\text{moles Mg ribbon} = 0.90 \text{ cm Mg} \times \frac{0.966 \text{ g}}{100.0 \text{ cm}} \times \frac{1 \text{ mol Mg}}{24.3 \text{ g}} = 3.6 \times 10^{-4} \text{ mol}$$

   moles Mg = 3.6×10^{-4} mol

2. Write the balanced equation for the reaction between Mg and HCl.

   $Mg(s) + 2HCl(aq) \rightarrow H_2(g) + MgCl_2(aq)$

3. Determine the value of n. Use the balanced equation and the number of moles of Mg that reacted to calculate the moles of H_2 produced.

   $$\frac{3.6 \times 10^{-4} \text{ mol Mg} \times 1 \text{ mol H}_2}{1 \text{ mol Mg}} = 3.6 \times 10^{-4} \text{ mol H}_2$$

   $n = 3.6 \times 10^{-4}$ mol H_2

4. Determine the value of P. Calculate the pressure of the H_2 gas collected by subtracting the water vapor pressure from the atmospheric pressure. Convert your pressure units from mm Hg to atmospheres.

   pressure H_2 = 754.2 mm Hg − 22.4 mm Hg = 731.8 mm Hg

   $$\frac{731.8 \text{ mm Hg} \times 1 \text{ atm}}{760. \text{ mm Hg}} = 0.963 \text{ atm}$$

   $P = 0.963$ atm

Name _____

Small Scale Lab 38

5. Determine the value of V. Calculate the volume of gas collected in liters. Remember that you must read the bottom of the meniscus, but that the scale is inverted. Then convert the volume units from mL to L.

   volume H_2 = 9.1 mL × $\dfrac{1\ L}{1000\ mL}$ = 0.0091 L

   V = __0.0091 L__

6. Determine the value of T. Convert the temperature units of the gas collected from °C to kelvins.

   temperature = 24.0°C + 273 = 297 K

   T = __297 K__

7. Using the pressure, volume, temperature, and moles of H_2, calculate the value of the gas constant where $R = PV/nT$. Include all units in your answer.

   $R = \dfrac{PV}{nT}$

   $R = \dfrac{(0.963\ \text{atm})(0.0089\ L)}{(3.6 \times 10^{-4}\ \text{mol})(297\ K)}$ = 0.080 atm-L/mol-K

   R = __0.080 atm-L/mol-K__

Critical Thinking: Analysis and Conclusions

1. Why is it necessary to subtract the value for water vapor pressure from atmospheric pressure to determine the pressure of the H_2 gas? *(Interpreting data)* __The hydrogen gas is collected by water displacement, so there is water vapor in the cylinder that contributes to the total pressure of the gas in the cylinder.__

2. What evidence of a chemical reaction did you observe? *(Making inferences)* __Bubbles appeared, heat was generated, and the magnesium disappeared.__

3. At the end of the reaction, how did the appearance of the copper wire compare with that of the magnesium ribbon? What can you conclude about the effect of HCl on copper wire? *(Making comparisons, drawing conclusions)* __The copper wire appeared unchanged. It did not take part in the reaction. Copper does not appear to react with HCl.__

4. Using the accepted value for the ideal gas constant, determine the percent deviation of the value you calculated. Then explain the possible sources of experimental error in this investigation. *(Interpreting data)*

   $\dfrac{(0.0821\ \text{atm-L/mol-K}) - (0.080\ \text{atm-L/mol-K})}{0.0821\ \text{atm-L/mol-K}} \times 100\% = 2.6\%$

   Sources of error include the following: experimental error in the measurements of the length of the Mg ribbon or volume, temperature, and pressure of the gas; an inaccurate barometer reading of atmospheric pressure; the small sample of the gas generated; escaped pieces of magnesium that did not react.

The Ideal Gas Constant

Critical Thinking: Applications

1. What is the importance of your choice of units in expressing the value of the ideal gas constant? *(Making judgments)* The numerical value of the gas constant varies with the units of pressure and volume used.

2. Convert the pressure of dry H_2 gas to kilopascals and calculate the value of R in kPa-L/mol-K. *(Applying concepts)*

   $0.963 \text{ atm} \times \dfrac{101.3 \text{ kPa}}{1 \text{ atm}} = 97.6 \text{ kPa}$

   $R = \dfrac{(97.6 \text{ kPa})(0.0089 \text{ L})}{(3.6 \times 10^{-4} \text{ mol})(297 \text{ K})} = \dfrac{8.1 \text{ kPa-L}}{\text{mol-K}}$

3. If all other conditions remained the same, how would the value of R change if your investigation made use of a gas other than hydrogen? Explain. *(Making predictions)* The value of R would not change. It is dependent on the values of the pressure, temperature, volume, and number of moles of the gas. Under the same conditions, these variables would be the same for any gas.

4. How could you demonstrate that the copper wire did not participate in the chemical reaction? *(Designing experiments)* Find the mass of the dry copper wire before and after the investigation. If it is the same, the copper did not react.

Going Further

Going Further

1. Have students write design plans for their experiments that include safety precautions. Discuss the plans with the students before they begin work.

1. Under the supervision of your teacher, try this experiment with other metals, such as iron, aluminum, or zinc. Before you begin, find out the safety precautions you must follow.

2. Use the experimental value you found for R to calculate the molar volume of a gas at STP. Compare your calculation to the accepted value.

Diffusion of Two Gases

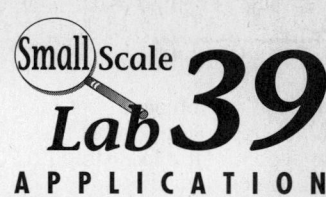

Text reference: **Chapter 13**

Introduction

Have you ever noticed how quickly a helium balloon deflates? A common latex balloon filled with helium will lose much of its gas overnight, yet the same balloon filled with air will remain inflated for several days. Why is this so? The kinetic-molecular theory states that gases consist of tiny particles in constant rapid motion. These particles have mass, and they frequently make elastic collisions with each other and the walls of their container. Different gases, however, differ in the rate at which they are able to move among each other (diffusion) or through tiny openings (effusion), such as a hole in a balloon.

Thomas Graham recognized that the different rates of movement of gas particles at constant temperature are related to the molar masses of the gases. Graham's law compares the rates of diffusion or effusion of any two gases as follows: Under constant temperature and pressure, the rate of diffusion or effusion of two gases is inversely proportional to the square roots of their molar masses. Mathematically, Graham's law may be expressed as a ratio:

$$\frac{r_a}{r_b} = \frac{\sqrt{\mathcal{M}_b}}{\sqrt{\mathcal{M}_a}}$$

In this formula, r_a is the rate of diffusion (or effusion) of a gas and r_b is the rate of diffusion (or effusion) of a second gas. Similarly, $\mathcal{M}_a$ and $\mathcal{M}_b$ are the respective molar masses of the two gases.

In this laboratory investigation, you will compare the rates of diffusion of ammonia (NH_3) gas and hydrogen chloride (HCl) gas. These two gases react chemically to form tiny white ammonium chloride (NH_4Cl) crystals that appear as an aerosol, or suspension, in the air. In Part A of the investigation, you will observe the results of the reaction between NH_3 and HCl. In Part B, you will place solutions containing these gases at different locations in a reaction tube. By measuring where in the tube the aerosol forms, you will be able to use Graham's law to find the relative rates of diffusion of the gases.

Pre-Lab Discussion

Read the entire laboratory investigation and the relevant pages of your textbook. Then answer the questions that follow.

1. In Part A, why is it important to use drops of HCl and NH_3 that are small enough to avoid drips or runs when the petri dish is inverted? __Runs or drips may result in the mixing of the solutions rather than of their gases or it may produce multiple sources of the gases, which would confuse the results.__

Materials (class of 30 in pairs)

Part A
30 pairs chemical splash goggles
30 laboratory aprons
30 micropipets
tap water
15 petri dishes
tissues
30 pairs latex gloves
15 pieces of black paper
55 mL HCl solution, 6.0 M
55 mL NH_3 solution, 6.0 M
15 wash bottles

Part B
30 chemical splash goggles
30 laboratory aprons
30 pairs latex gloves
30 clear plastic straws
15 pairs scissors
clear adhesive tape
30 cotton swabs
15 marking pens
15 small beakers, 100- or 250-mL
tap water
30 micropipets
55 mL HCl solution, 12.0 M
55 mL NH_3 solution, 14.8 M

Time Required
40 to 80 minutes.
Either part of this experiment can be accomplished within one period. To save time, Part B may be done as a teacher demonstration.

Advance Preparation
Prepare the 6.0 M HCl and NH_3 solutions for Parts A and B, and fill the pipets. Directions for making the solutions are provided in the Safety section. To avoid unwanted fumes and aerosols in the lab, prepare the solutions under a hood. Store both the concentrated and 6.0 M solutions in

Diffusion of Two Gases **209**

labeled micropipets under a fume hood. If a hood is not available in the lab, store these solutions in sealed pipets until they are needed. Have ready sealable plastic bags in which to place the pipets after they are opened and until they can be disposed of safely. Be sure each pipet is labeled with the name and concentration of the reactant it contains.

If you choose to use real balloons in the introductory discussion, fill one balloon with helium and one with air on the day before the investigation begins.

Introduction

Have one helium balloon and one air balloon that were filled a day earlier present in the laboratory. Discuss with students the differences between the balloons and ask for possible explanations for students' observations. Point out that the leakage from the balloons is an example of effusion, gas particles passing through a small opening. The formation of ammonium chloride crystals in the investigation, however, is a result of the diffusion of the reactant gases through the air in the straw tube and toward each other.

Discuss the formula for Graham's law. Review with students the relationship between distance, rate, and time, as expressed in the equation $d = r \times t$, and have students determine why it is possible to use the ratio of the distances traveled by the gases as equal to the ratio of their diffusion rates.

2. In Part A, what is the purpose of repeatedly turning the petri dish over? __Turning the dish over helps to determine if the relative positions of the drops affect where the NH₄Cl crystals form.__

3. What are the hazards of working with concentrated solutions of HCl and NH₃, and what precautions should you follow? __These solutions and their gases are corrosive to skin and clothing and irritating to eyes and nasal passages. Handle the solutions carefully and avoid inhaling their vapors. If contact occurs, flush with plenty of water. Wear gloves, goggles, and apron.__

4. How will you know when gaseous NH₃ and HCl molecules have made contact with each other? __White crystals of NH₄Cl will form.__

5. Using the molar masses of the gases and Graham's law, calculate the ratio of the diffusion rate of NH₃ to the diffusion rate of HCl that you expect to find in Part B of this investigation.

molar mass NH₃ = 14.0 g/mol + 3(1.0 g/mol) = 17.0 g/mol
molar mass HCl = 1.0 g/mol + 35.6 g/mol = 36.6 g/mol

$$\frac{r_{NH_3}}{r_{HCl}} = \frac{\sqrt{36.6 \text{ g/mol}}}{\sqrt{17.0 \text{ g/mol}}} = 1.47$$

6. Predict whether the NH₄Cl crystals will form in Part B closer to the source of NH₃ or HCl gas. __The crystal will form closer to the source of HCl gas.__

Problem

Will two gases of differing molar mass diffuse toward each other at different rates?

Materials

Part A
chemical splash goggles
laboratory apron
2 micropipets
tap water
petri dish
tissues

latex gloves
black paper
HCl solution, 6.0 M
NH₃ solution, 6.0 M
wash bottle

Part B
chemical splash goggles
laboratory apron
latex gloves
2 clear plastic straws
scissors
clear adhesive tape
2 cotton swabs

marking pen
beaker, 100- or 250-mL
tap water
micropipet containing
    concentrated HCl
micropipet containing
    concentrated NH₃

Name _____

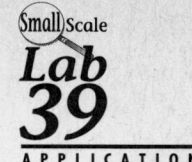

Safety

Wear your goggles and lab apron at all times in the laboratory. Gaseous ammonia (NH_3) and hydrogen chloride (HCl) molecules are irritating to skin, nasal passages, and eyes. Hydrochloric acid solution is corrosive. Wear gloves. Do not sniff these solutions. Do not let these solutions contact your skin or clothing. When the pipets containing these solutions are no longer needed, return them to the container from which they were obtained. At the end of Part A, flush these solutions from the petri dish with a stream of water from a wash bottle.

Do Part B in a fume hood. Before discarding the cotton swabs, place them in a small beaker of water to dilute the hydrochloric acid and ammonia solutions. If these solutions contact your skin or clothing, flush these areas with great quantities of water and notify your teacher.

Note the caution alert symbols here and with certain steps of the Procedure. Refer to page *xi* for the specific precautions associated with each symbol.

Procedure

Part A

 1. Put on your goggles and lab apron. Using a micropipet, place a small drop of water on the inner surface of the top plate of the petri dish. The drop needs to be small enough that it does not run or drip when the plate is turned over.

2. Practice placing one drop of water on the inside of the top plate and one on the bottom plate, closing the petri dish, and flipping it over several times until you can size the drops small enough that they remain in place. Dry the petri dish with tissue paper.

 3. Put on latex gloves. Place the petri dish on the piece of black paper. Remove the top plate and hold it open side up.

 4. Place a half drop of 6.0 *M* hydrochloric acid solution (HCl) about 1 cm from the center on the inside of the plate. Very carefully turn the plate back over without allowing the drop of acid to run. Set the top plate near the bottom half of the dish. **CAUTION:** *Hydrochloric acid is corrosive to skin and clothing and its vapors are irritating to lungs and eyes. Avoid contact with the solution and inhaling its vapors. If contact occurs, flush with plenty of cold water and notify your teacher.*

 5. Place a half drop of 6.0 *M* ammonia solution (NH_3) about 1 cm from the center of the bottom plate. **CAUTION:** *Ammonia solution is irritating to skin, lungs, and eyes. Avoid contact with the solution and inhaling its vapors. If contact occurs, flush with plenty of cold water and notify your teacher.*

6. Immediately place the top plate over the bottom plate so that the drops of solution do not line up, as shown in Figure 39–1. Observe the reaction and record your observations.

7. Without opening the petri dish, rotate the top plate slowly. Observe and record your observations.

Safety

Make sure students wear their goggles and lab aprons at all times during the investigation. Review with students all safety procedures for this investigation. Although they will be using micro quantities of the reagents, students should be cautioned about direct contact with the solutions and their fumes. Tell students they must immediately flush skin or clothing that is exposed to these solutions with water. Review with them the locations and use of the shower and eyewash facilities. To eliminate the risks associated with using concentrated reagents, you may wish to do Part B as a teacher demonstration.

CAUTION: *Concentrated HCl and its fumes are highly toxic and extremely corrosive to eyes and skin. Wear goggles, apron, and gloves. Make and store your dilutions under a fume hood. Always add acid to water. Expect considerable heat of dilution. Prepare a 1-liter volume of 6.0 M HCl solution by pouring 500 mL of 12.0 M HCl (concentrated reagent) into enough water to make 1 liter. Solid sodium bicarbonate can be sprinkled on spills to neutralize them safely and quickly.*

The vapors and solution of concentrated ammonia are toxic and extremely irritating—especially to the eyes. Make and store your dilutions under a fume hood. Prepare 6.0 *M* NH_3 by pouring 405 mL of 14.8 *M* NH_3 (*aq*) (concentrated reagent) into enough water to make 1 liter. Solid citric acid can be sprinkled on spills to neutralize them quickly and safely. ■

© Prentice-Hall, Inc.

Diffusion of Two Gases

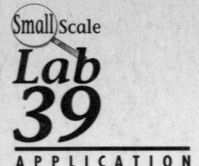

Name _____

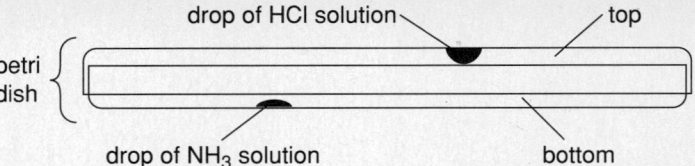

Figure 39–1

Teaching Tips

Take time to review thoroughly with students the hazards in this investigation and the safety precautions they should follow. In Part A, be certain students are sufficiently skilled at placing the drops of water to continue with Step 3.

Either part of the investigation can be accomplished independently of the other. A discussion of student observations and hypotheses in Part A serves as a good pre-lab for Part B. The ammonia molecules diffuse at a greater rate and predominate in the petri dish. The aerosol only forms at the surface of the HCl drop since few HCl molecules can escape the surface of the solution without reacting immediately with the ammonia molecules. Challenge students to explain why the aerosol does not fall from the ammonia solution when the chamber is inverted. (The NH_4Cl crystals form on what is now the bottom HCl drop and remain there.)

Part B provides quantitative evidence for the support of Graham's law. This part of the investigation is more easily done in groups of two or three students, but also may be done as a teacher demonstration. If you have difficulty getting clear straws, substitute a 30- to 40-cm length of 7-mm glass tubing.

8. Invert the closed petri dish. Note whether the relative position of the drops has any effect on the reaction.

9. Bring the petri dish back to the original position. Try to determine whether the reaction seems to occur nearer to the surface of the drop of HCl solution or the drop of NH_3 solution. Continue to turn the petri dish over and back until you have completed your observations.

10. Place the pipets containing the HCl and NH_3 solutions back in the containers where you obtained them.

11. With the wash bottle, rinse the drops of solution from the petri dish. Dry the dish with tissue paper.

Part B

 12. Put on your goggles and lab apron. Splice the two straws into one tube as follows. Using the scissors cut a small slit (about 7 mm) in the end of one straw. Push the cut end into one end of the other straw. Secure the straws together with a piece of clear adhesive tape, as shown in Figure 39–2.

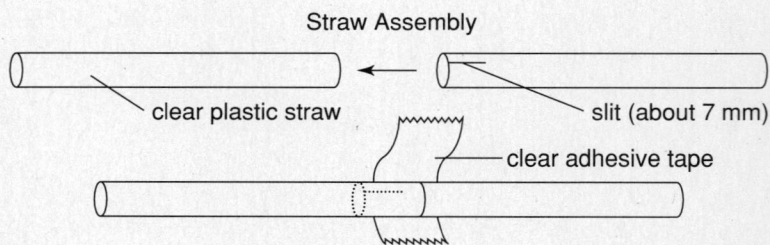

Figure 39–2

13. Place a cotton swab into each end of the straw tube. Using a marking pen, mark the tube at the points where the swabs have penetrated, as shown in Figure 39–3. These marks represent the starting points from which the gases will diffuse. Measure and record the total distance between these two marks.

14. Use the marking pen to mark one of the cotton swabs. This swab will be used for the hydrochloric acid (HCl).

15. Half fill a small beaker with water and set it aside for use in Step 19.

Name _____

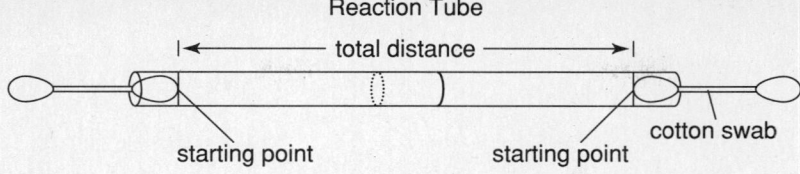

Figure 39–3

16. Put on latex gloves. Using a thin-stem or micropipet labeled "conc. HCl," place 2 drops of concentrated hydrochloric acid solution on the marked swab. Using a micropipet labeled "conc. NH_3," place 2 drops of concentrated ammonia solution on the other swab. **CAUTION:** *Work under a fume hood. Concentrated HCl and NH_3 are toxic and irritating to eyes and nasal passages. HCl is corrosive to skin and clothing. Avoid contact with the solutions and their vapors.*

17. While one person holds the straw tube steady, another person should simultaneously insert the two wet swabs in opposite ends of the tube. The swabs should penetrate to the points you previously marked.

18. Watch for the formation of a white aerosol ring inside the tube. The ring consists of tiny crystals of ammonium chloride (NH_4Cl). Measure and record the distance traveled by the HCl gas from its initial mark to the point where the ring forms. Do the same for the NH_3 gas.

19. Remove the wet swabs and immediately place them in the beaker of water you prepared in Step 15. This precaution will minimize the escape of HCl and NH_3 gases into the laboratory. It will also dilute the concentrated solutions and allow them to neutralize each other.

20. Rinse the beaker and swabs thoroughly with water and discard the swabs as directed by your teacher. Rinse the straw tube with water from the wash bottle and discard as directed by the teacher.

21. Clean up your work area and wash your hands before leaving the laboratory.

Waste Disposal

Do not add the concentrated ammonia and hydrochloric acid solutions directly to each other. First neutralize them in the following manner. Half fill a 1- or 2-liter beaker with cold water. Slowly add the ammonia solution to the water while stirring. Also add the remaining ammonia solution from the pipets. Excess 6.0 *M* HCl solution may now be added slowly to the diluted ammonia solution until pH paper indicates the solution is neutral. The resulting NH_4Cl solution may now be flushed down the drain with plenty of water. Rinse the pipets with large amounts of water and discard in the solid waste.

Dispose of additional 12.0 *M* HCl by first pouring it into a large beaker containing enough cold water to dilute the acid about 12 times. A solution of about 1 *M* sodium carbonate or sodium bicarbonate should now be added slowly until no more bubbling is visible. The resulting solution may now be flushed down the drain with plenty of water.

The used cotton swabs, which were soaked in beakers by the students, should be sufficiently diluted to rinse and discard in the solid waste. ■

Observations (sample data)

Part A
DATA TABLE

Step	Observation
6	Fine white particles form and fall from the HCl drop.
7	The stream of particles makes a trail on the bottom plate.
8	No particles fall from the NH_3 drop when it is on top.
9	The particles only form and fall from the hanging drop of HCl.

Diffusion of Two Gases

Name_____

Part B
total distance between the marks   35.6 cm
distance traveled by the HCl gas   14.2 cm
distance traveled by the NH_3 gas   21.4 cm

Critical Thinking: Analysis and Conclusions

1. Write a balanced chemical equation to describe the reaction you observed. Include the states of the reactants and products. *(Interpreting data)* $NH_3\ (g)\ +\ HCl\ (g) \rightarrow NH_4Cl\ (s)$

2. Give a possible reason for your observations of the location of the NH_4Cl crystals that formed in Part A. *(Making inferences)* The molar mass of NH_3 is less than that of HCl, so NH_3 molecules diffuse faster. The NH_4Cl crystals formed only near the HCl drop because NH_3 molecules diffused to the HCl drop.

3. Calculate the ratio (d_{NH_3}/d_{HCl}) of the distances traveled by the gases in Part B. How does your experimental ratio compare to the diffusion ratio you calculated in Pre-Lab question 5? *(Making comparisons)*

$$\frac{d_{NH_3}}{d_{HCl}} = \frac{21.4}{14.2} = 1.51$$

The experimental ratio is nearly the same as the calculated ratio.

4. Calculate the percent error of the experiment.

$$\frac{|1.47 - 1.51|}{1.47} \times 100\% = 2.72\%\text{ error}$$

5. Are the results of your investigation consistent with Graham's law? Explain. *(Drawing conclusions)* Yes. The lighter NH_3 particles diffused at a faster rate than the HCl particles, and the experimental ratio had an acceptable percent of error when compared to the theoretical ratio.

Critical Thinking: Applications

1. Suppose the distance between the solutions in the straw tube is 40.0 cm. Use Graham's law to calculate the distance the NH_3 and HCl gases would travel before they collide. *(Making predictions)*

    If NH_3 diffuses about 1.5 times faster than HCl, let $1.5x$ = the distance traveled by NH_3, and let x = the distance traveled by HCl. Then $1.5x + x = 40.0$ cm. Solving the algebraic equation for x, yields 16 cm as the distance traveled by HCl and 24 cm as the distance traveled by NH_3.

2. Consider the latex balloon described in the Introduction to this investigation. Explain why the balloon deflates more quickly if it is filled with helium than if it were filled with air. *(Developing hypotheses)* Helium has a molar mass lower than those of the most abundant gases in air. Helium, therefore, effuses more quickly out of a balloon than air does.

Name_____

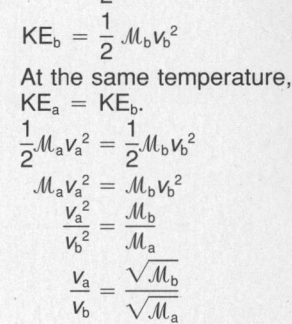

Lab 39 — APPLICATION

3. Suppose you had an unknown gas. How could you use Graham's law to design an experiment that would help you determine the identity of the gas? *(Designing experiments)* Set up an experiment in which the rate of diffusion of the unknown gas is compared to the rate of diffusion of a known gas. Use the ratio obtained and the molar mass of the known gas to solve Graham's equation for the molar mass of the unknown gas.

Going Further

1. Two gases at the same temperature have the same kinetic energy. Use the formula $KE = \frac{1}{2}Mv^2$ to derive Graham's law for two gases.
2. Research how Graham's law was applied during World War II to extract uranium-235 for use in nuclear reactions.
3. Compare the rates of loss of helium from a Mylar balloon and a latex balloon. Research possible reasons for differences you observe.

Going Further

1. $KE_a = \frac{1}{2} M_a v_a^2$

   $KE_b = \frac{1}{2} M_b v_b^2$

   At the same temperature, $KE_a = KE_b$.

   $\frac{1}{2} M_a v_a^2 = \frac{1}{2} M_b v_b^2$

   $M_a v_a^2 = M_b v_b^2$

   $\frac{v_a^2}{v_b^2} = \frac{M_b}{M_a}$

   $\frac{v_a}{v_b} = \frac{\sqrt{M_b}}{\sqrt{M_a}}$

Diffusion of Two Gases 215

How Many Drops Can You Pile on a Penny?

APPLICATION

Text Reference: **Chapter 14**

Introduction

Have you ever seen how water striders can walk across the surface of a pond, or how a mosquito can land on a puddle of water without sinking? Although the strider's weight pushes down on the water, forces within the water create a "skin" that supports the strider on the water's surface. This phenomenon is called surface tension.

The forces within water that are responsible for surface tension originate at the molecular level. As you know, a water molecule is polar. The oxygen atom has a partial negative charge, and each hydrogen atom has a partial positive charge. As a result, electrical attractions occur between the oxygen atom of one molecule and the hydrogen atom of another molecule, as illustrated in Figure 40–1. These intermolecular attractive forces are called hydrogen bonds (H-bonds).

Figure 40–1

Surface tension can be affected by substances dissolved in water. If a substance interferes with hydrogen bonding, the surface tension of water decreases. If a substance enhances hydrogen bonding, the surface tension of the water increases. In this investigation, you will observe the effects of several solutes in water. The ionic or molecular structures of the solutes you will be using are illustrated in Figure 40–2 on the next page. You will use your knowledge of molecular geometry and the behavior of molecular dipoles to make predictions about the effects of these solutes on the surface tension of water.

In Part A, you will investigate the surface tension of water by seeing how many drops of water can be piled on top of a penny. You will observe the shape and behavior of the water as surface tension holds the drops of water together. In Part B, you will design your own experiment to determine the effects of three substances on the surface tension of water: liquid detergent, sodium chloride (NaCl), and sodium carbonate (Na_2CO_3).

Materials (class of 30 in pairs)

Part A

30 chemical splash goggles
30 laboratory aprons
15 micropipets
15 clean, dry pennies
15 paper towels

Part B

45 micropipets
15 graduated cylinders, 10-mL
45 beakers, 100-mL
150 mL liquid detergent, 1% solution
150 mL saturated sodium chloride (NaCl) solution
150 mL saturated sodium carbonate (Na_2CO_3) solution
15 clean, dry pennies
tap water

Time Required

50 minutes. Part A, including discussion, should take about 20 minutes. The procedure for Part B, which may be done the next day, can usually be designed and accomplished within 30 minutes.

Advance Preparation

Prepare and label the 15 sets of three liquids for Part B. Prepare the saturated sodium chloride and sodium carbonate solutions by dissolving these solids in the desired volume of water until saturation. Care must be taken to prevent any contamination of other solutions with the detergent. Remove any remaining solids because these can confound the results.

How Many Drops Can You Pile on a Penny?

APPLICATION

It is best to have a set of pennies washed and dried for each class. Problems arise if the pennies are contaminated with grease, dirt, detergent, or other solutes.

Introduction
To introduce the lab, ask the class to guess the number of drops of water that can be added to a small glass of colored water that seems already full. As water is added to the glass, it piles up well above the rim before gravity finally pulls it over the edge.

Some students will need assistance in understanding the effect of the solutes on the surface tension of water in Part B. Students should recognize from Figure 40–2 that the polar tail of the detergent molecule will probably disrupt hydrogen bonding between water molecules and therefore reduce surface tension. If you wish, refer the students to discussions in the textbook about the hydration of ions so that they will have some idea of how ions can orient the water molecules about them. This type of organization can enhance surface tension. This lab will help students see that some ionic substances, like sodium carbonate, interfere with hydrogen bonding because they act like surfactants, while others, like sodium chloride, enhance it.

Name _____

sodium chloride (NaCl)   sodium carbonate (Na_2CO_3)

$Na^+ [:\ddot{Cl}:]^-$ $2\,Na^+ \left[\begin{array}{c} :\ddot{O}: \quad \ddot{O}. \\ \diagdown \quad \diagup \\ C \\ | \\ :\ddot{O}: \end{array} \right]^{2-}$

detergent molecule

Na^+ [... hydrocarbon chain with polar sulfonate end ...]$^-$

nonpolar end   polar, charged end

Figure 40–2

Pre-Lab Discussion

Read the entire laboratory investigation and the relevant pages of your textbook. Then answer the questions that follow.

1. Explain how the intermolecular forces between water molecules act to create the "skin" or surface tension upon which water striders can walk. <u>Hydrogen bonds exist in large numbers between water molecules. They exist across and below the surface, creating the "skin" or surface tension of water. This surface tension resists any force that would disrupt the surface.</u>

2. What causes water molecules to be polar? <u>They are polar because oxygen has a greater attraction for electrons than hydrogen. Oxygen acquires a partial negative charge and hydrogen a partial positive charge.</u>

3. Which part of a detergent molecule allows it to dissolve in water? Which part of a detergent molecule allows it to dissolve in oily substances? <u>The negatively charged end of a detergent molecule allows it to dissolve in water. The long nonpolar hydrocarbon chain on the opposite end allows detergent to dissolve in oily liquids, which are similarly nonpolar.</u>

4. Predict whether the nature of detergent molecules would increase or decrease hydrogen bonding in water. Explain. <u>The polar ends of the detergent molecules should decrease hydrogen bonding because they insert themselves between water molecules and disrupt the hydrogen bonds present.</u>

5. What is viscosity? How is viscosity related to the surface tension of a liquid? <u>Viscosity is resistance to flow. It arises because flowing requires</u>

218   © Prentice-Hall, Inc.

that intermolecular bonds be broken and reformed. Liquids that exhibit high surface tension possess intermolecular attractions and are therefore viscous.

Problem
What effects do chemicals have on the surface tension of water?

Materials

Part A
chemical splash goggles
laboratory apron
micropipet

tap water
clean, dry penny
paper towel

Part B
3 micropipets
3 beakers, 100-mL
graduated cylinder, 10-mL
10 mL liquid detergent solution
10 mL saturated sodium chloride (NaCl) solution

10 mL saturated sodium carbonate (Na_2CO_3) solution
tap water

Safety

Wear your goggles and lab apron at all times during the investigation. Sodium carbonate is irritating to the skin. Do not let this material come in contact with your skin. Note the caution alert symbols here and with certain steps of the Procedure. Refer to page *xi* for the specific precautions associated with each symbol.

Procedure

Part A

1. Put on your goggles and lab apron. Obtain one micropipet and a penny from your teacher.
2. Fill the micropipet with water.
3. Place drops of water on top of the penny. Be sure to hold the micropipet vertically. Do not touch the penny or the water that is accumulating there.
4. Count the number of drops you can add before the water flows off the penny. Record the total.
5. Dry the penny and repeat Steps 3 and 4 two more times, or until you get consistent results.

Part B
6. You will be given three solutions: sodium carbonate (Na_2CO_3), sodium chloride (NaCl), and 1% liquid detergent. Your task is

Safety
Caution students to wear their goggles and lab aprons. Care should be used with the sodium carbonate solution, which is irritating to the skin. Tell students that if any sodium carbonate gets on their skin, they should wash with plenty of water.

Teaching Tips
Demonstrate that the correct way to hold the micropipet is straight up and down, and not touching the penny.
  While students plan and execute Part B, monitor the groups. Make sure their experimental designs are logical and organized. The plans should parallel the procedure used to test tap water. Students should plan to do several trials with each solution, record data, and calculate an average number of drops used.
  If you choose to use cooperative learning groups of 3 or 4 students, adjust the quantities of materials accordingly.

© Prentice-Hall, Inc.   *How Many Drops Can You Pile on a Penny?* **219**

to design and carry out an experiment to determine their effect on the surface tension of water. Write your plans on a separate piece of paper.

7. Design a procedure for your test that includes (a) a control, (b) steps that will ensure that the results are reliable (or reproducible), and (c) your predictions of the effect of each solute.
8. Create a table that will organize your data clearly.
9. Obtain the necessary materials and run the experiment.
10. Clean up your work area and wash your hands before leaving the laboratory.

Waste Disposal
Micropipets containing the solutions for Part B may be rinsed and stored in resealable storage bags for later use. Excess solutions may be flushed down the drain with plenty of water.

Cooperative Learning Strategy
Part B provides an opportunity to use cooperative groups of three or four because there are several different solutions to explore. Students can decide how to divide the responsibilities when they plan the investigation. The group may wish to have one student act as scribe, recording the procedure as it is designed, and later recording the results as the remaining group members complete the procedure.

Observations

Part A
Number of drops of water observed:

Trial 1 _____
Trial 2 _____
Trial 3 _____
Average 25–30 drops

Critical Thinking: Analysis and Conclusions

1. Compare the average number of drops placed on your penny with the results of your classmates. What might account for any differences? *(Making comparisons)* Reasons for differences might be the size of the pipet, impurities in the water, differences in technique, or using dirty pennies.

2. What happened when the water finally flowed off the penny? Explain in terms of the chemical and physical forces involved. *(Drawing conclusions)* The chemical forces keeping the water together on the penny are hydrogen bonds. The physical force pulling the water off is gravity. When the force of gravity becomes greater than the hydrogen bond forces, the water will flow off.

3. In Part B, what were your predictions for the effect of each solute on the surface tension of water? *(Making predictions)* Accept all reasonable answers.

4. What was the control in your procedure? *(Designing experiments)* Water, as long as the same techniques were used in Parts A and B.

5. What steps did you include in your procedure to increase the reliability or reproducibility of your results? *(Designing experiments)* Students may suggest that each solution be tested several times, and washing and drying the pennies well between each trial.

Name _____

6. Do the results of your investigation agree with your hypotheses?
   (Drawing conclusions) Answers will vary. Accept all answers.

7. Is it correct to say that the addition of salts to water will always increase the surface tension of water? Explain. *(Drawing conclusions)*
   No, because one salt, sodium chloride, increased surface tension slightly, and another salt, sodium carbonate, decreased surface tension significantly.

8. What effect, if any, did the detergent have on surface tension? Why? *(Interpreting data)* The water containing detergent flowed off the penny more quickly than did plain water. Detergents decrease surface tension because their polar ends break up the hydrogen bonds of water.

Critical Thinking: Applications

1. State any questions or projects for further investigation that surfaced as a result of your investigation. *(Developing models)* Accept any reasonable answers.

2. Make judgments about the hypotheses made by the class, and be ready to discuss your opinions. *(Making judgments)* Answers will vary and should be defended.

3. People usually think of water as being wet. If water alone is used to wash clothing, however, it doesn't penetrate the fabric very well. How does the addition of detergent make water "wetter", that is, more capable of penetrating the pores of fabric? *(Applying concepts)*
   The hydrogen bonds of water tend to hold water in droplets that bead up on fabric. Adding detergent breaks down some of the hydrogen bonds and lowers its surface tension. The detergent and water solution can move or flow more easily into the small pores of the fabric.

4. There are a lot of cleaners and detergents on the market that contain sodium carbonate (Na_2CO_3). It is known that sodium carbonate neutralizes odors. Based upon the results of your experiment, does sodium carbonate play another role as well? *(Applying concepts)*
   Sodium carbonate not only neutralizes odors, it also acts to break down the surface tension of water.

5. When you read the contents of some cleaning powders or liquids, they often list anionic surfactants. Predict what these anionic surfactants might be and how they might act. *(Making predictions)* Some of these anionic surfactants are probably the detergent molecules, or anions such as carbonate that reduce the surface tension of water.

© Prentice-Hall, Inc.   *How Many Drops Can You Pile on a Penny?*

Name _____

6. Viscosity is a property described as a measure of the resistance of a liquid to flow. This resistance is affected by the same intermolecular forces as is surface tension. Which of the liquids you tested for surface tension in Part B of this investigation do you predict will exhibit the greatest relative viscosity and the least relative viscosity? *(Making predictions)* The greatest relative viscosity would probably be exhibited by the saturated sodium chloride solution. The least relative viscosity would probably be exhibited by the detergent solution.

Going Further

1. Investigate the effect of temperature on the surface tension of a liquid. First, hypothesize how varying the temperature of a liquid might affect its surface tension. Then design an experiment to test your hypothesis, taking into consideration any safety precautions you must follow. Under the supervision of your teacher, perform the experiment and present your findings to the class.

Sample Observations for Part B

Data Table

Substance	Drops (Range)	Drops (Average)
H_2O	25–30	27
NaCl	26–32	29
Na_2CO_3	15–26	21
1% detergent	15–19	17

Changes of State

Lab 41

Text reference: **Chapter 14**

Introduction

Think about a hot summer day when you have had a glass of water served with ice. You may have noticed that although the ice cubes melted slowly and steadily, your drink remained cold as long as ice was present in the glass. Only after the ice was completely melted, did the liquid begin to warm up. The reason the water stayed cold while the ice cubes melted has to do with the manner in which pure substances undergo physical changes related to temperature.

Matter can exist in one of three physical states—solid, liquid, or gas. For a pure substance, changes in state (also called phase changes) occur at a definite temperature, which is characteristic of that substance. Water, for example, changes from a solid to a liquid at 0°C. In comparison, sodium chloride liquefies at 801°C, and mercury at just under −39°C.

In a crystalline solid, the particles—either atoms, ions, or molecules—are arranged in an orderly, repeating, three-dimensional pattern. These particles vibrate and rotate around fixed positions. As the solid is heated, the kinetic energy of the particles increases, and the vibrations become more intense. Eventually, at some temperature, which is called the melting point, the vibrations become strong enough to overcome the forces of attraction holding the particles of the solid together, and the solid changes to a liquid. Once this melting begins, if the solid is pure, the temperature remains constant until the entire sample becomes a liquid. Further heating will raise the temperature of the liquid.

When a liquid is cooled, the reverse process occurs. The temperature of the liquid decreases until the freezing point is reached. Only after the liquid is completely changed to a solid will the temperature begin to decrease again. The temperature at which a substance changes between solid and liquid is one of the defining physical properties of that substance and may be used to identify it.

In this investigation, you will observe the melting and freezing behavior of lauric acid ($C_{12}H_{24}O_2$). You will measure the temperature at timed intervals as the lauric acid is heated and cooled and determine experimentally its freezing point and melting point.

Pre-Lab Discussion

Read the entire laboratory investigation and the relevant pages of your textbook. Then answer the questions that follow.

1. Define melting point and freezing point. __The melting point is the__ __temperature at which a solid changes to a liquid. The freezing point is the__ __temperature at which a liquid changes to a solid.__

Materials (class of 30 in pairs)

30 pairs chemical splash goggles
30 laboratory aprons
30 beakers, 400-mL
tap water, hot and cold
15 hot plates
30 thermometers
15 large test tubes, 20 × 180 mm
225 g lauric acid, $C_{12}H_{24}O_2$
15 test-tube holders
15 stop watches or a clock with a second hand
15 sets of pens or pencils in 2 different colors

Time Required

45 minutes.

Advance Preparation

Prepare the test tubes containing the 15-g samples of lauric acid. At the end of the experiment, collect the test tubes for use by another set of students. If hot plates are not available, provide students with the equipment to construct a ring-stand apparatus (iron ring, wire gauze, and laboratory burner) on which to heat the beaker. The test tube should be suspended in the beaker with a test-tube clamp.

Introduction

Discuss the example of the ice-and-water mixture given in the Introduction. Ask students if they can explain why the temperature of the system remains constant despite the heat from the environment. (The heat is being absorbed by the ice at a rate of 6.0 kJ/mol, the heat of fusion of water. Heat from the environment will not increase the temperature of the liquid until all the ice has

Changes of State 223

Lab 41

turned to liquid water.) Set up a small beaker with an ice-and-water mixture. Tell the students that while they conduct their investigation, you will take periodic temperature readings of the water and record them on the board. At the end of class, have students look at the data and determine if the example has verified the theory.

Safety

Caution students about using the hot plates and handling the heated test tubes. Also, remind students to stir with the thermometer gently and not force it through the lauric acid. An alternative to stirring is to have students twist the thermometer in place, stopping when it no longer moves freely. ■

Teaching Tips

You can substitute salol (phenyl salicilate) if lauric acid is not available. Salol is easy to work with and gives reliable results (accepted melting point is 41–43°C).

If your laboratory periods are long enough, have students air cool the sample or let it cool as the warm-water bath cools after the heat is turned off. By cooling the sample slowly, students will obtain a greater number of data points. You will need to advise students to expand their data tables to allow for 100 readings.

This investigation is a rare example of a case when the use of a stirring rod hinders the procedure. The careful use of a thermometer, however, will work so long as students remember not to try to stir once the solid begins to form.

This investigation lends itself nicely to computer interfacing. Temperature probes and the appropriate software are needed.

Name _____

2. Why is it necessary to have two water baths? **A warm water bath is needed to observe the solid-to-liquid phase change. A cool water bath is needed to observe the liquid-to-solid phase change.**

3. Describe what happens to the particles of a solid at its melting point. **The particles of the solid acquire enough energy to overcome the forces of attraction that hold them together, and the solid changes to a liquid.**

4. What two phase changes will you observe in this investigation? **The two phase changes are liquid to solid and solid to liquid.**

5. What is the greatest safety hazard in this investigation, and what precautions should you take? **The greatest safety hazard is burns. Avoid contact with the hot plate, and handle the test tube with a test-tube holder.**

6. Why is it necessary to stir the lauric acid as it is heated or cooled? **Stirring the lauric acid distributes the material evenly through the test tube so that it is heated or cooled uniformly, giving more accurate temperature readings.**

Problem

How can you determine the melting point and the freezing point of lauric acid?

Materials

chemical splash goggles
laboratory apron
2 beakers, 400-mL
hot and cold tap water
hot plate
2 thermometers

large test tube
lauric acid ($C_{12}H_{24}O_2$)
test-tube holder
stop watch
2 pens or pencils of different colors

Safety

Wear your goggles and lab apron at all times in the laboratory. Hot plates and heated glassware can cause burns. Avoid touching the hot plate or the heated beaker of water. Handle the heated test tube with a test-tube holder. Note the caution alert symbols here and with certain steps of the Procedure. Refer to page *xi* for the specific precautions associated with each symbol.

Procedure

Part A

 1. Put on your goggles and laboratory apron. Construct a data table similar to the one shown, leaving enough lines for about 25 time and temperature readings.

224 © Prentice-Hall, Inc.

2. Fill one 400-mL beaker about three-fourths full of tap water and heat it on the hot plate. Use a thermometer to monitor the water's temperature, and adjust the hot plate as needed to keep the temperature constant at about 60°C. **CAUTION:** *Do not touch the hot plate or beaker.*

3. Use hot and cold tap water to fill the second 400-mL beaker three-fourths full of water that is adjusted to a temperature of about 30°C.

4. Obtain a large test tube containing about 15 g of lauric acid from your teacher. Attach a test-tube holder near the top of the test tube and place the test tube in the 60°C water bath, as shown in Figure 41–1.

5. As the solid begins to melt, place a thermometer into the test tube and stir carefully. **CAUTION:** *The thermometer is fragile. Do not bang it against the sides of the test tube or force it through the lauric acid crystals.* Record the approximate temperature at which melting occurs, and continue heating the lauric acid until the temperature is about 10°C higher.

6. Using the test-tube holder, remove the test tube from the 60°C water bath and place it in the 30°C water bath. Make sure that the level of the water in the beaker is above the level of the liquid in the test tube.

7. Gently stir the liquid with the thermometer. When the temperature of the liquid decreases to 55°C, begin taking temperature readings every 30 seconds. (One lab partner should stir and read the thermometer, while the other partner watches the clock and records the temperature readings.) Record the temperature to the nearest 0.2°C.

8. When the sample is mostly solid, stop stirring. Continue to take temperature readings until the temperature of your sample has fallen to about 40°C. Record your findings in the data table.

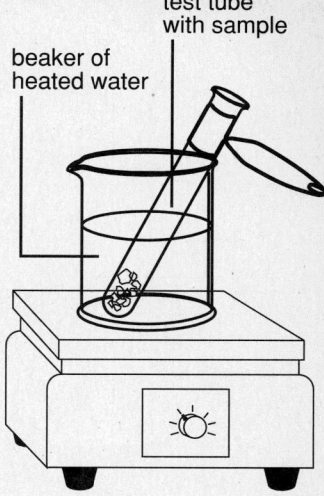

Figure 41–1

Part B

9. Check the temperature of the hot-water bath and adjust it to 60°C if necessary.

10. Remove the test tube from the 30°C water bath and place it in the beaker of water at 60°C. Immediately begin to take temperature readings every 30 seconds. Begin stirring gently as soon as you are able to move the thermometer easily. Continue to measure and record the temperature until the lauric acid is at approximately 50°C.

11. Turn off the hot plate. Carefully remove the thermometer from the sample of lauric acid and return the test tube to your teacher. Pour the water in the beakers down the drain, and clean and dry the thermometers.

12. Clean up your work area and wash your hands before leaving the laboratory.

Waste Disposal
Retain the test tubes of lauric acid for future use.

Changes of State

Lab 41

Sample Data

Time (min)	Part A Temp. (°C)	Part B Temp. (°C)
0	55.0	30.0
0.5	52.6	33.2
1.0	49.4	35.4
1.5	45.4	37.8
2.0	44.4	39.0
2.5	44.2	41.0
3.0	44.0	42.0
3.5	44.0	42.6
4.0	44.0	43.0
4.5	44.0	43.2
5.0	44.0	43.4
5.5	44.0	43.6
6.0	44.0	43.8
6.5	44.0	44.0
7.0	44.0	44.0
7.5	43.8	44.0
8.0	43.6	44.2
8.5	43.4	44.6
9.0	43.0	45.2
9.5	42.6	46.0
10.0	42.4	47.6
10.5	41.8	49.0
11.0	41.4	51.4

Observations

Approximate melting point of lauric acid   44°C

DATA TABLE Freezing and Melting of Lauric Acid

	Part A: Liquid to Solid	Part B: Solid to Liquid
Time (min)	Temperature (°C)	Temperature (°C)
See sample data.		

Critical Thinking: Analysis and Conclusions

1. Make a graph of your data from Part A. Plot time (min) on the horizontal axis and temperature (°C) on the vertical axis. Connect the points in a smooth curve. *(Interpreting data)*
2. Using a pen or pencil of a different color, plot the data from Part B on the same graph. *(Interpreting data)*

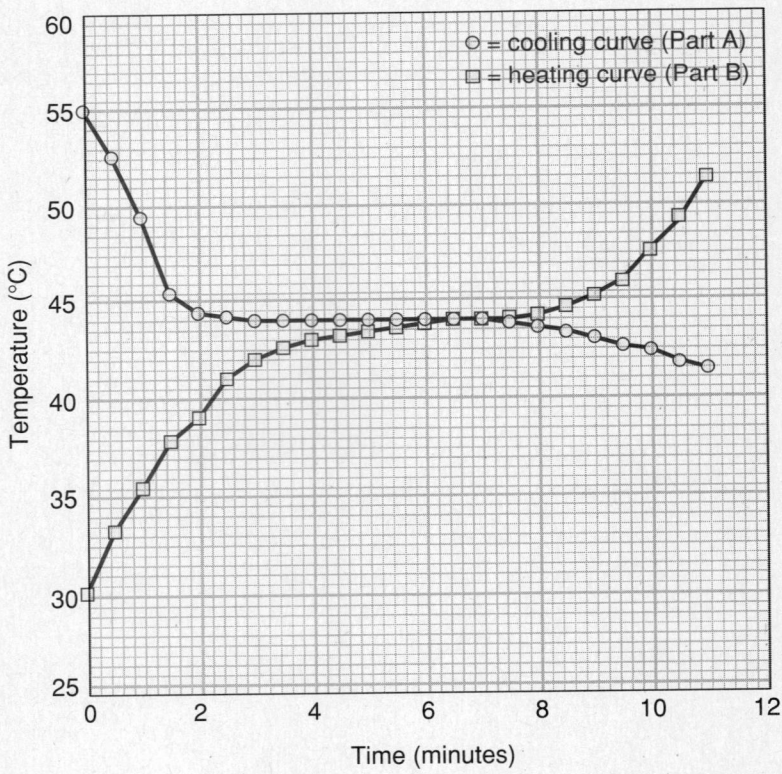

Figure 41–2

Name _____

Lab 41

3. Using your graph, determine the freezing point and melting point of lauric acid. *(Interpreting diagrams)* The melting point and freezing point should be about 44°C.

4. Does lauric acid freeze and melt at the same temperature? How do you know? *(Drawing conclusions)* Yes. The two curves partly overlap where each change of state occurs.

5. Explain the shapes of the graphs in terms of energy changes that occur as the lauric acid heats up and melts and as it cools down and freezes. *(Making inferences)* As the lauric acid is heated, its temperature increases steadily until the melting point is reached. The temperature then remains constant while the added energy enables the particles of the solid to move more freely. Once all the solid has melted, further heating raises the temperature of the liquid. As the liquid cools, its temperature decreases steadily until the freezing point is reached. The temperature then remains constant while intermolecular forces reduce the movement of the particles. Once all of the lauric acid has frozen, further cooling decreases the temperature of the solid.

6. Compare the value you obtained for the freezing point of lauric acid with the values obtained by your classmates. Account for any similarities or differences. *(Making comparisons)* The values should be similar. Experimental error will account for most differences.

Critical Thinking: Applications

1. What effect would increasing the amount of lauric acid have on the melting point? On the shape of the graph? *(Making predictions)* An increase in the amount of lauric acid would not affect the melting point, but it would increase the amount of time required for each phase change and, therefore, the horizontal part of each graph would be longer.

2. Look back at the discussion about the ice water in the Introduction to this investigation. Write a brief paragraph that explains, in terms of temperature and physical changes, what happened to the ice and liquid from the time the glass was first filled until after the ice melted. *(Using the writing process)* Initially, ice absorbs heat from the liquid, causing the liquid's temperature to decrease. This effect continues until the temperature of the system reaches the melting point of the ice. While the ice melts, the temperature remains constant. After all the ice is gone, external heat then causes the temperature of the liquid to increase.

Lab 41

Going Further

1. Students' results will depend on the initial temperatures of their samples. Hot water can freeze faster than lukewarm water that is at or above 60°C because the hot water loses more heat through vaporization, causing a faster decrease in overall temperature. If the initial temperature of the cooler sample is below 60°C, however, it will reach the freezing point and freeze faster than the hot sample, all other factors being constant.

2. Melting points and freezing points of the elements may be found in some versions of the periodic table. The data for elements, inorganic compounds, and organic compounds are contained in any edition of the *Handbook of Chemistry and Physics.* You may wish to limit the students' research of organic compounds to a selected list so that their data focus on familiar substances.

Going Further

1. Find out which freezes faster, hot or cold water. Make a prediction and devise an experiment to be conducted at home that tests your hypothesis. Remember to eliminate all variables except the initial temperature of the water. Report your experimental procedure and explain your results.

2. People tend to think of freezing and boiling in terms of water. Yet, some substances freeze at temperatures hotter than 100°C while others boil at temperatures lower than 0°C. Research the freezing points and boiling points of some elements and familiar compounds, and develop a list of substances that freeze "hot" or boil "cold."

Name _____ Date _____ Class _____

Melting Points of Common Substances

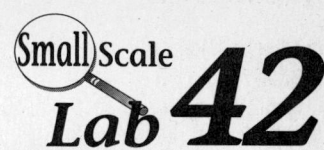

Text reference: **Chapter 14**

Introduction

A solid substance melts when it absorbs enough energy for its particles to overcome the attractive forces that lock them together. The particles then can slide around and about each other randomly, giving the substance fluid properties. Nearly all pure substances have distinct melting points that are determined by the strength of attractions between their particles. The greater the attractive forces are, the more energy is needed to overcome them.

Molecular compounds have melting points considerably lower than those of ionic compounds, which contain strong electrostatic attractions between their ions. Among molecular compounds, differences in melting points depend on the degree of intermolecular forces that occur. These forces include dipole-dipole forces, dispersion forces, and hydrogen bonding.

In this investigation, you will determine the melting points of four molecular substances by heating small amounts of each substance in capillary tubes immersed in oil. You will also compare the structural formulas of the substances and determine what factors might account for the similarities and differences in the melting points that you find.

Pre-Lab Discussion

Read the entire laboratory investigation and the relevant pages of your textbook. Then answer the questions that follow.

1. What is a polar bond? A polar molecule? A polar bond results from the unequal sharing of electrons between atoms. The atom that attracts the electrons more strongly will have a partial negative charge, while the other atom will have a partial positive charge. A polar molecule has one or more polars bonds arranged in a way that results in the molecule having a slightly positive end and a slightly negative end.

2. What causes dipole-dipole interactions? Dipole-dipole interactions occur between polar molecules. The partially negative part of one molecule is attracted to the partially positive end of another molecule.

3. What are dispersion forces and what causes them? Dispersion forces are weak attractions between nonpolar molecules. They occur as a result of temporary dipoles that form when electrons become unevenly distributed in nonpolar molecules.

Materials (class of 30 in pairs)
- 30 pairs chemical splash goggles
- 30 laboratory aprons
- 30 pairs latex gloves
- 60 capillary tubes
- 15 beaker tongs
- 15 books of matches
- 15 lab burners
- 15 spatulas
- 60 pieces of glassine paper
- 10 g benzoic acid ($C_6H_5CO_2H$)
- 10 g sulfur (S_8)
- 10 g naphthalene ($C_{10}H_8$)
- 10 g sucrose ($C_{12}H_{22}O_{11}$)
- 15 ring stands
- 15 clamps
- 15 iron rings
- 15 wire gauze squares
- 30 beakers, 150-mL
- 1.5 L mineral oil
- 60 rubber bands
- 15 thermometers, 0°–250°C, fitted with one-hole stoppers
- 15 hot pads

Time Required
90 minutes. To save time, have students do fewer of the determinations and then share their data with other lab pairs. Prepare the capillary tubes ahead of time and set them out for student use.

Advance Preparation
Fit the thermometers with the one-hole stoppers prior to class. Prepare labeled samples of each of the four substances, keeping the naphthalene under a fume hood. Provide receptacles for collecting unused portions of the student samples. Have a large heat-proof container ready to receive the hot oil as the students are done with it. The oil may be cooled and reused.

© Prentice-Hall, Inc.
Melting Points of Common Substances **229**

Small Scale Lab 42

Name _____

Introduction

Melting points are useful to a chemist because, like density, they are specific to a substance. Although color, odor, and appearance often help identify an unknown substance, melting point determination is more definitive. The melting point is also indicative of the purity of a compound. If melting occurs over a wide range, it indicates a mixture of compounds or the presence of impurities in the sample.

Discuss Pre-Lab Question 6 in class. Students may need help determining which substances are polar and which are nonpolar. Have students name elements whose atoms frequently form polar bonds. Review the effects of symmetry on a molecule that contains polar bonds.

4. How is molar mass related to the dispersion forces in a nonpolar substance? <u>The greater the molar mass of a substance, the more electrons its molecules contain and the more opportunity there is for dispersion forces to arise.</u>

5. What effect would hydrogen bonding have on the melting point of a substance? <u>Hydrogen bonding increases the intermolecular attractions between the molecules of a compound, causing it to have a higher melting point than would otherwise be expected.</u>

6. Look at the structural formulas of the substances in Figure 42–1. Determine whether they are polar or nonpolar, and predict how their melting points will compare. (Hint: Look for the presence of polar bonds arranged in such a way that their effects do not cancel out.) <u>Benzoic acid and sucrose are polar and should melt at higher temperatures than naphthalene and sulfur, which are nonpolar.</u>

7. Why must naphthalene (moth balls) be kept in a tightly capped container and stored under a fume hood? <u>Naphthalene sublimates, which means it changes directly from a solid to a gas at room temperature. Its vapors are toxic. Capping the container and storing it under a hood prevent the vapors from escaping into the room.</u>

8. Why is a mineral oil bath used instead of a water bath? <u>A mineral oil bath is used because some of the substances may melt above 100°C, which is the boiling point of water. The boiling point of mineral oil is much higher.</u>

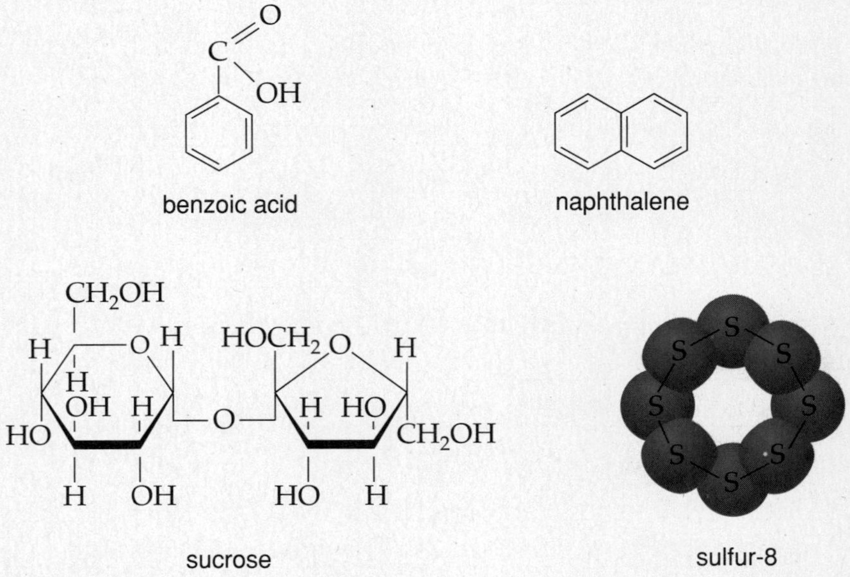

benzoic acid   naphthalene

sucrose   sulfur-8

Figure 42–1

Name_____

9. Why must the mineral oil in the beaker be changed after each determination? <u>The temperature of the oil may be higher than the melting point of the next substance to be tested.</u>

Problem
What factors affect the melting point of a molecular substance?

Materials
chemical splash goggles
laboratory apron
latex gloves
4 capillary tubes
beaker tongs
matches
lab burner
spatula
4 pieces of glassine paper
small amounts (a few crystals) of
    benzoic acid ($C_6H_5CO_2H$)
    sulfur (S_8)
    naphthalene ($C_{10}H_8$)
    sucrose ($C_{12}H_{22}O_{11}$)

ring stand
clamp
iron ring
wire gauze
beaker, 150-mL
mineral oil
4 rubber bands
thermometer, 0°–250°C, with
    one-hole stopper
hot pads

Teaching Tips
The lab will run more smoothly if the location for discarding oil is separate from where the students go to obtain materials. Remind students to take only a small part of a spatulaful of each substance. If you have not prepared the capillary tubes ahead of time, demonstrate how to seal them before the students begin. Have ready a glass disposal container in which students may discard the used capillary tubes. Capillary tubes that are already sealed at one end are also available. Using presealed tubes eliminates a safety concern and reduces the time needed for this investigation.

Safety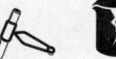

Wear your goggles and lab apron at all times while you are in the laboratory. When you seal one end of a capillary tube, hold the tube with beaker tongs, and hold the open end of the tube away from you. Wear gloves while filling the capillary tubes. Keep naphthalene and sulfur away from burner flames, as they are flammable. The vapors of naphthalene are toxic. Keep it in a tightly capped container and use only in a fume hood. Do not breathe its vapors. Use hot pads for handling the beaker of hot mineral oil.

Note the caution alert symbols here and with certain steps of the Procedure. Refer to page *xi* for the specific precautions associated with each symbol.

Safety
Naphthalene should be stored in tightly capped containers and tested under a fume hood. It should not be handled with bare hands. Remind students to use gloves while filling the capillary tubes.
  Do not allow students to insert the thermometers into the rubber stoppers because of the risk of breakage. Cutaway corks may be substituted for rubber stoppers to hold the thermometers, in which case, students may do the assembly. ■

Procedure
Part A

1. Put on your goggles and laboratory apron.

2. Light the burner. Seal one end of each of four capillary tubes by holding the end of the tube in the tip of the blue flame of a lab burner. Allow the tubes to cool. **CAUTION:** *Tie back loose hair and clothing. Capillary tubes are fragile. Handle gently. Use tongs to hold the capillary tube when heating, and point the open end of the tube away from you.* Turn off the burner.

3. Put on gloves. Using a clean spatula, obtain a small amount (a tipful) of one solid to be tested and place it on a sheet of glassine paper. Tap the open end of a capillary tube in the solid to capture a few crystals. Turn the tube over and gently tap against the counter to shake the crystals to the bottom. Continue this process until the tube has about 1 cm of crystals. Tape the tube to a sheet of paper and label it. Repeat this procedure for each of the other three compounds. **CAUTION:** *Naphthalene should be used in a fume hood. Do not breathe its vapors. Wear gloves to protect your hands from corrosive substances.*

4. Fill the beaker half full with mineral oil. Set up the apparatus as diagramed in Figure 42–2, using a ring stand, iron ring, wire gauze, clamp, and burner.

5. Secure the capillary tube to the thermometer with a rubber band so that the bulb of the thermometer is even with the sealed end of the capillary tube. Clamp the stopper that contains the thermometer to the ring stand so that the mouth of the capillary tube is above the surface of the mineral oil and the solid in the tube is completely immersed.

6. Light the burner. Heat the oil slowly so that the temperature rises only about 2–3 C° per minute. Keep a close watch on the solid in the tube. Record the temperature at which the solid is completely melted. **CAUTION:** *Keep hair and clothing away from burner flames. The oil will become very hot. Do not touch the beaker with your bare hands. Use tongs or a hot pad.*

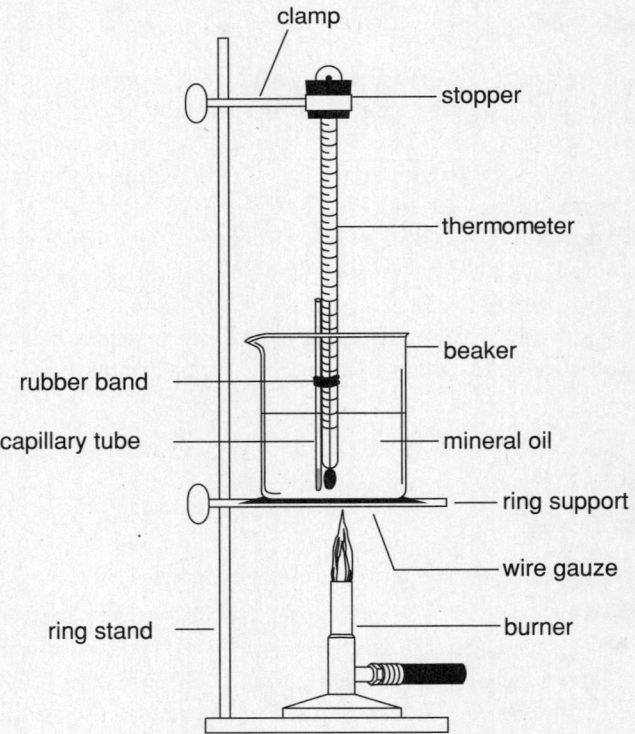

Figure 42–2

Name _____

 7. Carefully remove the beaker with the hot oil from the apparatus and pour the hot oil into a receptacle marked for this purpose. Refill the beaker with unheated oil. Discard the capillary tube in the container marked for glass disposal.

8. Repeat Steps 6 and 7 with the remaining three substances.

 9. Clean up your work area and wash your hands before leaving the laboratory.

Waste Disposal
Dilute the benzoic acid 20-fold with water. Neutralize it with sodium carbonate and then flush it down the drain. Sulfur and naphthalene should be contained and removed as solid waste. ■

Observations (sample data)

DATA TABLE 1

Substance	Melting Point (°C)	Molar Mass (g/mol)
benzoic acid	122	122
naphthalene	80	128
sucrose	185	342
sulfur	113	256

Critical Thinking: Analysis and Conclusions

1. Calculate and compare the molar masses of the substances tested. Write the values in Data Table 1. *(Making comparisons)* <u>Sucrose has the largest molar mass, followed by sulfur, naphthalene, and then benzoic acid.</u>

2. Rank the substances in order from lowest to highest melting point in the following table. Look back at your answers to Pre-Lab Question 6 and write the polarity of each substance on the appropriate line. *(Making comparisons)*

DATA TABLE 2

Substance	Melting Point (°C)	Polarity
naphthalene	80	nonpolar
sulfur	113	nonpolar
benzoic acid	122	polar
sucrose	185	polar

3. Describe the relationship between a substance's polarity and its melting point, using an example from your data. *(Drawing conclusions)* <u>The polar substances have higher melting points than the nonpolar substances. For example, benzoic acid has a higher melting point than sulfur.</u>

4. What factor could account for the conclusion you formed in Pre-Lab Question 1? *(Making inferences)* Dipole-dipole forces between the molecules of the polar compounds would cause them to have higher melting points than the nonpolar compounds.

5. What factor could account for the difference in melting points between the two nonpolar substances or between the two polar substances? Explain. *(Making inferences)* Differences in molar mass could account for the differences in melting points. Substances of greater molar mass have more electrons and, therefore, more dispersion forces among their molecules. These forces result in greater intermolecular attractions and, therefore, higher melting points.

6. How do the predictions you made in Pre-Lab Question 6 compare to the actual results of your experiment? *(Drawing conclusions)* Answers will vary depending on the predictions made. Accept all answers.

Critical Thinking: Applications

1. What is the freezing point of each substance tested in the investigation? Explain. *(Applying concepts)* The freezing point is the same as the melting point. The use of the terms *freezing point* and *melting point* relates to whether the substance is changing respectively from a liquid to a solid or from a solid to a liquid.

2. Does the nature of intermolecular forces change when a substance goes from a solid to a liquid? Explain. *(Applying concepts)* No, the nature of the forces does not change. The added heat increases the kinetic energy of the molecules, which overcomes the attractive forces enough for the molecules to slide past each other.

3. Water is polar and contains hydrogen bonds, while sulfur is nonpolar and does not contain hydrogen bonds. Explain why water melts at a temperature below the melting point of sulfur. *(Developing hypotheses)* Sulfur has a greater molar mass than water and, therefore, is subject to greater dispersion forces, which would cause its melting point to be higher.

Going Further

1. Make a list of the types of substances whose melting points could not be determined by the procedure used in this investigation. Explain why the procedure would not work, and give at least one example of each type of substance.

Going Further

1. The types of substances students might name include the following: substances with melting points too high to measure in the lab, such as table salt; mixtures that would not give a specific melting point, such as chocolate; substances that decompose before they melt, such as calcium carbonate.

T-Shirt Chromatography

Lab 43 APPLICATION

Text reference: **Chapter 15**

Introduction

Have you ever been caught in the rain on your way home from school and gotten your notebooks all wet? If your notes were written in water-soluble ink, they would be turned into a colorful blur, which would not be much help if you had a quiz scheduled for the next day. This everyday occurrence is an example of a process called chromatography.

In chromatography, solutes are distributed along a medium by a moving solvent. In this way, a liquid or gaseous mixture is separated into its components. The term *chromatography* comes from two ancient Greek words, *chroma* meaning "color" and *graphein* meaning "to write." The molecules of the solutes have different masses, and so they travel along a medium—such as paper as it becomes wet—at different rates. Lighter molecules travel faster than heavier molecules. The resulting pattern is called a chromatogram.

In this investigation, you will be separating a familiar mixture—indelible ink—into its constituent compounds. Indelible ink is a nonpolar compound and is insoluble in a polar solvent such as water. Therefore, a solvent such as 2-propanol, which is only slightly polar, must be used. Figure 43–1 shows the structure of 2-propanol, commonly known as rubbing alcohol or isopropyl alcohol. When indelible ink is placed on a medium, such as cotton cloth, and 2-propanol is added slowly, the ink separates as each component is carried along by the traveling solvent.

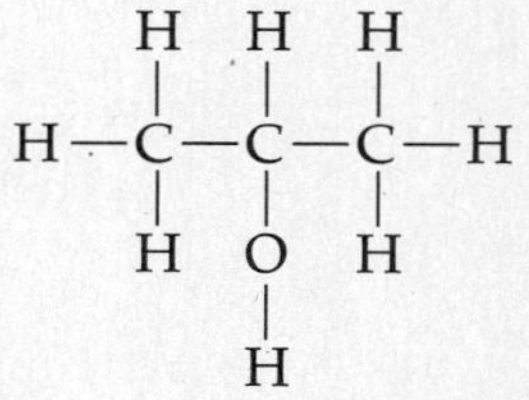

Figure 43–1

Materials (class of 30)
- 30 pairs chemical splash goggles
- 30 laboratory aprons
- 30 white cotton T-shirts, prewashed without fabric softener
- 30 large cans or jars without lids
- 30 elastic bands
- 150 permanent (not water soluble) felt-tip pens, different colors
- 1.5 L 2-propanol
- 30 droppers
- 30 large plastic bags

Time Required
45 minutes.

Advance Preparation
Make sure students wash and dry the T-shirts before bringing them into the lab. Each student can bring a washed T-shirt from home, or you can buy irregular T-shirts in bulk, and students can pay you for the cost of a T-shirt. Filter paper or coffee filters can be used instead of a shirt.

Ask the students and faculty to bring in empty large jars and coffee cans. Then store them for later use. Save them from year to year.

Dilute the 2-propanol about 50% (concentration is not critical) by volume to end with 3.0 L. CAUTION: *Wear chemical splash goggles. Keep the 2-propanol away from open flames.* Rubbing alcohol (70% 2-propanol) may be purchased at a drug store. Add water to dilute it to about 50%. If the 2-propanol is too concentrated, it will travel too quickly and the colors will not separate well.

Buy enough permanent markers (such as medium-tip

Pre-Lab Discussion

Read the entire laboratory investigation and the relevant pages of your textbook. Then answer the questions that follow.

1. How would you define *chromatography*? <u>Chromatography is the technique by which a mixture can be separated into its components by use of a solvent absorbed on a medium such as paper or cloth.</u>

2. What is a solute? What is the solute in this investigation? <u>A solute is the substance that is being dissolved. Ink is the solute in this investigation.</u>

Lab 43
APPLICATION

Sharpie pens) for the class. If each group starts with a different color and then trades pens with another group, the total number of pens needed can be reduced.

Introduction
You may wish to demonstrate how water-soluble ink separates when placed on filter paper to which water is slowly added.

3. What is a solvent? What is the solvent in this investigation? _A solvent is a substance that does the dissolving. The solvent in this investigation is 2-propanol._

4. Why is a medium necessary in chromatography? What medium is used in this investigation? _The medium is the substance through which the solute and solvent travel. The T-shirt is the medium in this investigaton._

5. Why is 2-propanol used instead of water in this investigation? _Indelible ink is a nonpolar solute and will not dissolve in water. The ink will dissolve in 2-propanol, which is only slightly polar._

6. What makes 2-propanol slightly polar? _It is fairly symmetrical and contains mostly nonpolar bonds._

7. Why should you take care not to expose the 2-propanol to heat or flames? _2-propanol is flammable._

8. Why do you think the ink will separate into its component compounds? _The ink is a mixture of several compounds, all of which have different molar masses and travel at different speeds through the medium as they dissolve in the solvent._

Problem
How can you separate a mixture using chromatography?

Materials
chemical splash goggles
laboratory apron
white cotton T-shirt, prewashed without fabric softener
large can or jar
elastic band

5 permanent felt-tip markers, different colors
2-propanol
dropper
large plastic bag

Safety
Make sure students wear their goggles and lab aprons at all times during the investigation. 2-propanol is flammable so there should be no open flames in the laboratory. ■

Teaching Tips
Make sure students do not drip the 2-propanol too quickly onto the T-shirt, or the colors will not separate well.
  This is an enjoyable activity

Safety

Wear your goggles and lab apron at all times during the investigation. Make sure there are no open flames in the lab, because 2-propanol is flammable.
  Note the caution alert symbols here and with certain steps of the Procedure. Refer to page *xi* for the specific precautions associated with each symbol.

Procedure

1. Put on your goggles and lab apron. Stretch a single thickness of cloth of the T-shirt over the open top of the can or jar. Pull the cloth taut and secure it with an elastic band placed around the outside of the can or jar. See Figure 43–2.

Name _____

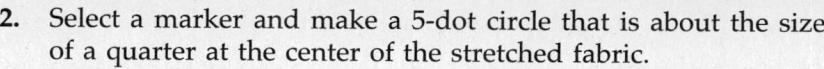

Lab 43
APPLICATION

2. Select a marker and make a 5-dot circle that is about the size of a quarter at the center of the stretched fabric.

 3. Fill a dropper with 2-propanol and slowly drip it onto the center of the circle, as shown in Figure 43–2. **CAUTION:** *Make sure there are no open flames in your lab because 2-propanol is flammable.* Continue dripping the 2-propanol onto the cloth until the solvent has spread to the edges of the can or jar.

4. Allow the wet section of the T-shirt to dry.

5. Repeat Steps 1–4 with each of the other markers, using a different color marker each time to make another set of dots or to make creative patterns. Record your observations.

6. If desired, repeat Steps 1–5 on a new section of the T-shirt.

7. After all the chromatography patterns have developed, allow the T-shirt to dry completely. Place the dry T-shirt in a plastic bag to bring home.

 8. Dispose of any excess 2-propanol as directed by your teacher. Rinse out the can or jar and the dropper with water. Clean up your work area and wash your hands before leaving the laboratory.

9. At home, you can iron the T-shirt to help set the inks. For the first machine washing, wash the T-shirt by itself in case any of the inks run.

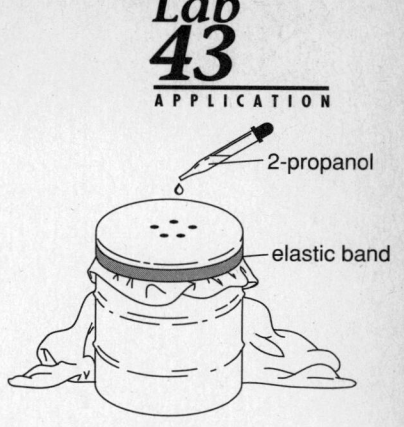

Figure 43–2

for students, and they come away with a souvenir they can keep and wear. Encourage them to use their imagination to create colorful and interesting patterns on their T-shirts.

If there are color-blind students in your class, pair them with students who have full color perception.

Waste Disposal

Any excess 2-propanol can be flushed down the drain with water or use disposal method 3. ■

Observations (sample data)
DATA TABLE

Color Trial	Observations
1	Different color inks give different sets of colors. The inks
2	move in a straight line. Yellow travels farthest.
3	
4	
5	

Critical Thinking: Analysis and Conclusions

1. Why was it necessary to stretch the cloth taut? What do you think would have happened if the cloth had remained loose? *(Making inferences)* The T-shirt must be pulled taut in order to get a good separation. A loose piece of cloth would not allow the solute molecules to move easily.

2. Which marker contained the greatest number of compounds? The fewest? How were you able to tell? *(Interpreting data)* Black markers contain the most compounds because the black ink separated into the most colors. Yellow, red, and blue did not separate into different colors.

© Prentice-Hall, Inc.   *T-Shirt Chromatography* **237**

Lab 43 APPLICATION

Name _____

3. What differences were there between your results and the predictions you made in the Pre-Lab Discussion? *(Making comparisons)* Answers will vary depending on the predictions that students made.

4. Explain how the components of each ink separate. What can you infer about the molecules making up the color that travels the greatest distance? The least distance? *(Making inferences)* The colors separate according to their molar masses. The lightest molecule travels farthest because it moves the fastest.

Critical Thinking: Applications

1. Predict what would have happened in the investigation if a polar solvent had been used. *(Making predictions)* There would have been little or no separation of colors because the nonpolar ink would not dissolve in a polar solvent.

2. Are "permanent" markers truly permanent? Explain. *(Applying concepts)* A "permanent" marker is only permanent when exposed to polar solvents such as water. It is not permanent when exposed to a slightly polar solvent such as 2-propanol.

3. Chromatography is often used to identify unknown compounds. Explain how this might be done. *(Applying concepts)* Every molecule has a distinct molar mass. Therefore, compounds in a mixture can be separated by molar mass if an appropriate solvent and a medium are used. An unknown can be identified by comparing its chromatogram with chromatograms of known compounds.

Going Further (sidebar)
1. A sampling of pieces of fabrics can easily be obtained from fabric shops. Other solvents that could be used include methanol or ethanol.
2. If water is used as the solvent, water-soluble markers could be used.

Going Further

1. Cotton was used in this investigation. Find out if other fabrics work equally well. With the approval and supervision of your teacher, try this investigation using swatches of rayon, wool, or polyester.
2. Redesign this investigation so that it works with water-soluble inks.
3. Research the uses of chromatography in measuring and monitoring pollutants in air and water. Prepare an oral report to present to your class.

Name _____ Date _____ Class _____

Boiling Points of Solutions Lab 44

Text reference: Chapter 15

Introduction

You may know that the boiling and freezing points of a solution are different from the boiling and freezing points of a pure solvent. Adding a solute to a solvent elevates the boiling point and depresses the freezing point. There are many everyday examples of this chemical principle. Antifreeze is added to the water in automobile radiators to prevent both boiling over in hot weather and freezing in cold weather. Saltwater harbors may freeze during prolonged cold spells, but only when the temperature of the salt water is much lower than 0°C. Adding table salt to cooking water is probably the most familiar example of a solute elevating the boiling point of a solution.

When antifreeze is added to a car radiator there are well-defined mixing directions to be followed. As with all other solutions, the molality of the antifreeze-water mixture determines the temperature at which the solution will boil. When one mole of particles is dissolved in one kilogram of solvent (a one molal solution), the boiling point is elevated by a precise amount depending on the solvent. If the solvent is water, the increase will be $K_b = 0.52°C$ for a one molal solution. (This figure is a constant.) For nondissociating solutes, there is no change in the number of particles as the solute dissolves, so the temperature change for the solution is determined by multiplying the molality by the solvent constant, according to the following formula:

$$\Delta T_b = K_b m$$

As ionic solids dissolve, they dissociate, resulting in at least two moles of particles in solution for each mole of crystalline solute. The molal concentration of the ions in solution increases—doubling, tripling, and so on. Accordingly, the change in temperature for a solvent's boiling point is two, three, or more times the value of the solvent constant.

In this investigation, you will find the boiling points of distilled water, a urea-water solution, and a salt-water solution. Temperature readings will be taken for the samples as each is heated from room temperature to the boiling point. The time and temperature data will be plotted on a single graph. From the graph you can compare the boiling points of the different samples. Where the boiling points of the samples differ, you can suggest reasons for the differences based on an examination of the chemical formulas of the solutes.

Pre-Lab Discussion

Read the entire laboratory investigation and the relevant pages of your textbook. Then answer the questions that follow.

Materials (class of 30 in pairs)

30 pairs chemical splash goggles
30 laboratory aprons
15 graduated cylinders, 100-mL
1 L distilled water
15 large test tubes
supply of boiling chips (60–150)
15 thermometers, −10°C to 110°C
15 #2 cork stoppers, cutaway
15 ring stands
15 rings
15 test-tube clamps
15 wire gauze squares
15 lab burners
15 watches or a clock with a second hand
40 g urea, NH_2CONH_2
15 laboratory balances
mortar and pestle
15 stirring rods
40 g sodium chloride, NaCl

Time Required
60 minutes.

Advance Preparation

Pulverize the urea using a mortar and pestle so that it will dissolve more readily in the water. You may choose to use one or more other solutes in place of, or in addition to, the two used in the investigation. The ionic solids potassium chloride (KCl) and copper sulfate (use $CuSO_4 \cdot 5H_2O$) both give favorable results. Table sugar ($C_{12}H_{22}O_{11}$) is a good substitute for urea, while all of the following nondissociating liquid solutes yield consistent results as well: glycerol, methanol, and ethanol. (If you choose to use the flammable liquids as solutes, take appropriate steps to inform students of

Lab 44

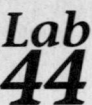

Name _____

1. What is the molality of a solution if 0.0300 moles of nonionizing solute dissolve in 15.0 mL of water?

   $m = \dfrac{0.0300 \text{ mol solute}}{0.0150 \text{ kg solvent}} = 2.00 \text{ mol/kg solvent}$

2. What is the concentration of the particles in solution in Question 1?
   The concentration of the dissolved particles is equal to the concentration of the solution, or 2.00 mol/kg.

3. Calculate the concentration of particles in solution if 0.0300 moles of an ionic solid such as $CaCl_2$ dissolve in 15.0 mL of water. The aqueous ion concentration of $CaCl_2$ is triple the solution concentration.

   $m = \dfrac{0.0300 \text{ mol CaCl}_2}{0.0150 \text{ kg solvent}} \times \dfrac{3 \text{ mol ions}}{1 \text{ mol CaCl}_2} = 6.00 \text{ mol ions/kg solvent}$

4. How many grams of urea (NH_2CONH_2) equal 0.0300 moles of urea?
   0.0300 mol urea × 60 g urea/1 mol urea = 1.80 g urea

5. How many grams of sodium chloride (NaCl) equal 0.0300 moles of sodium chloride? 0.0300 mol NaCl × 58.5 g NaCl/1 mol NaCl = 1.76 g NaCl

6. How should the test tube be heated so that the temperature increases continuously but not rapidly? The test tube should rest on the wire gauze and should be off to the side rather than directly over the flame.

7. What precautions should you take when using the burner? Tie back hair and clothing. Use the clamp to move the hot test tube.

Introduction

While students are generally aware of everyday examples of freezing points being depressed or boiling points being elevated, they commonly come to class with a wide variety of preconceptions about the reasons for these changes. Class time should be taken to elicit students' theories. Some examples of typical preconceptions about changed freezing or boiling points include: the new boiling or freezing points reflect a value somewhere between those of the solute and solvent; the changes are due to a chemical reaction between the solute and solvent; and, as a corollary to the previous idea, the solvent becomes a new substance with the introduction of the solute.

It is also helpful to demonstrate the laboratory setup and the handling of the hot test tube between trials before doing this investigation. In demonstrating the setup, show how the bottom of the test tube should just rest on the top of the wire gauze, while the inner cone of the burner flame should just touch the bottom of the test tube, and the safety precautions that must be followed. You may choose to test these liquids as a demonstration.)

If you do not have cutaway cork stoppers, they need to be prepared in advance. Using a razor blade or utility knife, cut a pie-shaped, vertical slice into the hole of a one-hole #2 cork stopper. The cutaway section allows students to insert the thermometer into the stopper with less danger of breakage. Also, the calibrations are visible over the whole temperature range, and the opening that results at the mouth of the test tube allows the expanding vapors to escape.

Problem

What effect do solutes have on the boiling point of a solvent?

Materials

chemical splash goggles
laboratory apron
graduated cylinder, 100-mL
distilled water
large test tube
boiling chips
thermometer
#2 cork stopper, cutaway
ring stand
ring

test-tube clamp
wire gauze square
lab burner
watch or clock with a second hand
urea (NH_2CONH_2)
laboratory balance
stirring rod
sodium chloride (NaCl)

Name _____

Lab 44

Safety

Wear your goggles and lab apron at all times during the investigation. Tie back loose hair and clothing to avoid any fire hazard. Always point the open end of a test tube away from yourself and others when heating a substance. Since glass retains heat without looking hot, heated glassware should be given ample time to cool before it is handled.

Note the caution alert symbols here and with certain steps of the Procedure. Refer to page *xi* for the specific precautions associated with each symbol.

Procedure

1. Put on your goggles and lab apron.
2. Precisely measure out 15.0 mL of distilled water and pour it into the test tube. Put two or three boiling chips into the test tube.
3. Carefully insert the thermometer into the cutaway cork stopper, positioning it so the calibrations are fully visible. Place the thermometer in the test tube so that the bulb of the thermometer is about 1 cm above the bottom of the test tube.
4. Set up the ring stand and attach the ring and test-tube clamp. Place the wire gauze on the ring. Adjust the height of the ring so that the burner will fit underneath it. Put the test tube into the test-tube clamp and position it so that the bottom of the test tube just rests on the wire gauze. Rotate the clamp and test tube away from the ring.
5. Light the burner and adjust the flame to a medium setting. **CAUTION:** *Tie back loose hair and clothing to avoid any fire hazard.* Move the burner underneath the wire gauze and adjust the height of the ring so the inner cone of the burner flame just hits the gauze. Readjust the position of the test tube if necessary. Preheat the wire gauze for a minute or two without the test tube in place.
6. Find the initial temperature of the water and record it in the Data Table. Turn the clamp back so the test tube again rests on the wire gauze. The test tube should be slightly off to the side rather than directly over the flame. Record time and temperature readings at 30-second intervals. Continue until the temperature remains constant for three or four readings. If necessary, change the position of the burner so the temperature of the water increases continuously but not rapidly. **CAUTION:** *Always point the open end of a test tube away from yourself and others when heating a substance.*
7. Turn off the burner. Remove the thermometer, rinse it, and set it aside for the next trial. Keeping the hot test tube in the clamp, carefully remove the clamp and test tube from the ring stand. Pour the water in the sink and rinse out the test tube. Discard the boiling chips. **CAUTION:** *Since glass retains heat without looking hot, heated glassware should be given ample time to cool before it is handled.*

wire gauze. You may want to check each team's setup before they proceed. Remind the students to rotate the test tube and clamp about one fourth of a turn away from the burner before lighting the burner and preheating the wire gauze. Another point to emphasize is the proper handling of the hot test tube. When the readings have been completed for a trial, the contents of the hot test tube are to be poured into the sink and the test tube rinsed. If the students remove the clamp and test tube together, the clamp can serve as a holder for the test tube.

Safety

Make sure students wear their goggles and lab aprons at all times during the investigation. Loose hair and clothing should be tied back to avoid any fire hazard. Since glass retains heat without looking hot, heated glassware should be given ample time to cool before it is handled. ■

Teaching Tips

Remind students to be certain that there is a clear opening at the mouth of the test tube to allow vapor to escape. If the section cut out of the stopper is too small, the opening may inadvertantly be forced closed as the stopper is put into the test tube.

While nondissociating solutes have a smaller effect on solvents than dissociating solutes, each solute has a specific effect on a given solvent; this effect can vary slightly from the accepted boiling or freezing point constants.

You may want to have the students graph all of the data on a full-size piece of graph paper.

Satisfactory results in this investigation are elusive unless great care is taken

© Prentice-Hall, Inc.   *Boiling Points of Solutions* **241**

Lab 44

throughout. Experimental results often diverge from the predicted boiling points, especially since the temperature changes for a 2-molal solution—both with nondissociating and dissociating solutes—are relatively small and difficult to measure precisely.

There are at least three common sources of error in doing this investigation:

Readings must be taken very precisely as the temperatures of the liquids approach the boiling points. (Point out to the students that it is very difficult to obtain precise data in the early stages of each trial; since the temperature often rises very rapidly, a reading to the nearest degree is probably the best that can be expected.)

The liquids must be heated with the burner flame at medium intensity. The wire gauze should be preheated. As the test tube is moved in place for each trial, the burner should not be directly beneath the test tube, but rather 1 or 2 cm off to one side. By moving the burner closer or further from the bottom of the test tube, the heat can be adjusted.

It is easy to miss the boiling plateau for the solutions if the heating is not even or is too intense. Since the temperature of the solutions will continue to increase as water evaporates, it is important that the liquids be kept at a gentle rolling boil once the temperature approaches the boiling point.

Waste Disposal
All of the solutions can be rinsed down the sink. ■

8. Using the calculations from Pre-Lab Discussion Question 4, obtain 0.0300 moles of urea and record its mass to the nearest 0.01 g. Place the urea and 15.0 mL of distilled water into the test tube. Stir gently with the stirring rod until the urea dissolves. Put two or three boiling chips into the solution.

9. Repeat Steps 3–7 for the urea-water solution.

10. Using the calculations from Pre-Lab Discussion Question 5, obtain 0.0300 moles of sodium chloride and record its mass. Place the sodium chloride and 15.0 mL of distilled water into the test tube. Stir gently with the stirring rod until the sodium chloride dissolves. Put two or three boiling chips into the solution.

11. Repeat Steps 3–7 for the sodium chloride–water solution.

12. Clean up your work area and wash your hands before leaving the laboratory.

Observations (sample data)
DATA TABLE

Time (min)	Temperature (°C)		
	Distilled Water	Urea-Water	Salt-Water
0.0	24.2	26.0	25.4
0.5	36.0	38.0	38.0
1.0	48.0	51.0	52.0
1.5	59.0	65.0	66.0
2.0	68.0	75.0	78.0
2.5	76.0	86.0	88.0
3.0	88.0	92.6	94.6
3.5	93.6	97.8	99.0
4.0	97.8	99.8	101.2
4.5	98.8	100.6	101.6
5.0	99.6	100.8	101.6
5.5	99.6	100.8	101.8
6.0	99.6	101.4	102.4
6.5	99.6	—	—

Name_____

Lab 44

Calculations

1. Predict the new boiling point for the urea-water solution.

$$\Delta T_b = K_b m = 0.52°C/m \times \frac{0.0300 \text{ mol urea}}{0.0150 \text{ kg water}} = 1.04°C$$

$$BP_f = BP_i + \Delta T_b = 100.0°C + 1.04°C = 101.0°C$$

2. Predict the new boiling point for the sodium chloride–water solution.

$$\Delta T_b = K_b m = 0.52°C/m \times \frac{0.0600 \text{ mol ions}}{0.0150 \text{ kg water}} = 2.08°C$$

$$BP_f = BP_i + \Delta T_b = 100.0°C + 2.08°C = 102.1°C$$

Critical Thinking: Analysis and Conclusions

1. Construct a boiling-point graph using only the data collected for temperatures above 80°C, plotting temperature as a function of time. Plot the data for all three samples—the distilled water, the urea-water solution, and the sodium chloride–water solution—on the same graph. Use different symbols or colors to differentiate among the data points for each of the three samples. Draw best-fit curves for all three sets of data points. *(Interpreting data)*

2. Examine the graph. Do you see any pattern in the boiling points of the two solutions compared to the boiling point of the distilled water? *(Making comparisons)* The temperature plateaus for the solutions are both higher than that for distilled water. The boiling point of the sodium chloride–water solution is higher than that of the urea-water solution.

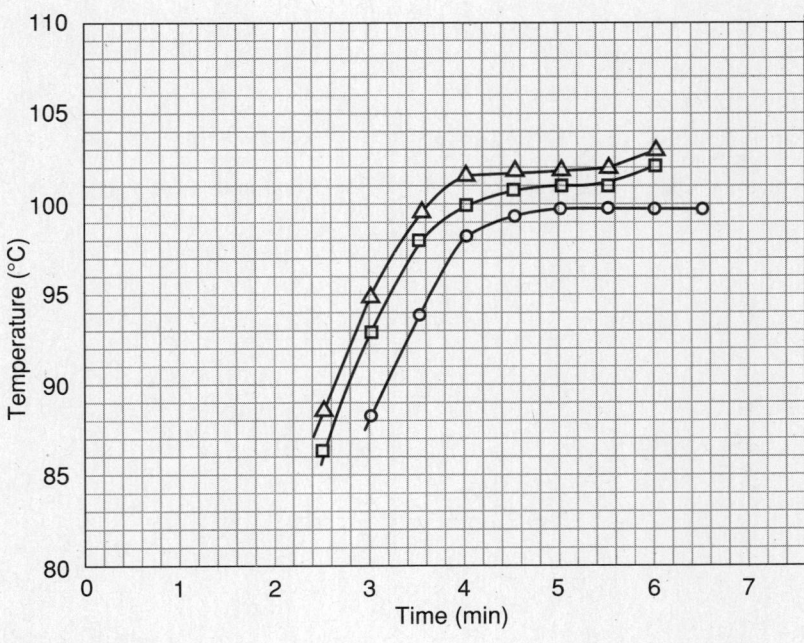

Figure 44–1

© Prentice-Hall, Inc.

Boiling Points of Solutions 243

3. Examine the formulas for the two solutes, urea (NH_2CONH_2) and sodium chloride (NaCl). What inferences can you make about the effects of each of these two solutes on the boiling point of water? *(Making inferences)* The NaCl, an ionic solid, has a greater effect on the boiling point of water than the urea, a nondissociating solid.

4. Compare the boiling points of the two solutions from your graph to the predicted values from Calculations 1 and 2. Do the experimental and predicted values match? If they differ, how might you account for the differences? *(Making comparisons)* The experimental values do not match the predicted values, but they are close and in the same order. Water boils at the lowest temperature, followed by the urea-water solution, and then the sodium chloride–water solution. Some possible reasons for the differences include inaccurate thermometers, heating the solution too intensely and missing the first plateau, and not enough solute added to make a difference.

Critical Thinking: Applications

1. What do you think would happen to the temperature of either solution if you kept heating it? Explain. *(Making predictions)* The temperature would continue to rise. As the heating continues, water evaporates from the solution, increasing the solute concentration in the solution and forcing the boiling point higher.

2. In terms of particles, explain why the boiling points of the solutions are higher than the boiling point of distilled water. *(Developing models)* There are fewer solvent particles at the surface of the solution since solute particles occupy some of the space. This lowers the rate at which solvent particles evaporate from the surface. Thus, the vapor pressure of the solution is lower, forcing the boiling point higher.

Going Further

1. Predict the boiling point for a 2.00 molal solution of aluminum chloride ($AlCl_3$). Under the supervision of your teacher, conduct an investigation to test your prediction. Report your findings.

Freezing Point Depression with Antifreeze

Lab 45 APPLICATION

Text reference: **Chapter 15**

Introduction

Have you ever wondered how antifreeze lowers the freezing point of water in the cooling systems of automobiles? In the latter part of the nineteenth century the French chemist François Raoult noted that the vapor pressure of a solvent was lowered by the addition of a solute (Raoult's Law), and that the freezing points of solutions also were lowered.

Eventually, the following mathematical expression that related freezing point depression and molality (moles of solute per kilogram of solvent) was developed.

$$\Delta T = K_f m$$

In this equation, ΔT is freezing point depression, K_f is the molal freezing point constant for the solvent, and m is the molality of the particles in solution.

As you can see from the equation, the lowering of the freezing point depends on the concentration of dissolved particles present. In the case of a nonelectrolyte, the molality of the nonelectrolyte and the molality of particles in solution are the same (a 1:1 ratio). For electrolytes, the molality of particles is equal to the molality of the electrolyte times the number of ions in the chemical formula of the compound.

Automobile manufacturers make use of the principle of freezing point depression to protect engines from freezing in cold weather. Antifreeze, a nonelectrolyte, is added to the water-filled radiator that cools the engine. Under most conditions the presence of the antifreeze molecules in the water is sufficient to keep the system from freezing.

In this investigation, you will determine the freezing point depression of antifreeze solutions by cooling them in an ice-salt bath. You will also use this information to find the molar mass of ethylene glycol.

Pre-Lab Discussion

Read the entire laboratory investigation and the relevant pages of your textbook. Then answer the questions that follow.

1. What is the mathematical relationship between freezing point depression and molality? $\Delta T = K_f m$

2. What is a colligative property? A colligative property is a property, usually of solutions, that depends on the number of solute particles but is independent of their nature.

Materials (class of 30 in pairs)

30 pairs chemical splash goggles
30 laboratory aprons
15 beakers, 600-mL
5 L crushed ice
500 g sodium chloride (NaCl)
15 stirring rods
15 thermometers, $-10°C$ to $100°C$
roll of paper towels or aluminum foil
45 large test tubes
3 L distilled water
30 beakers, 250-mL
15 marking pens
15 laboratory balances
600 mL permanent antifreeze
15 graduated cylinders, 10- or 25-mL
15 droppers
15 graduated cylinders, 100-mL

Time Required

40–50 minutes.

Advance Preparation

Purchase antifreeze (any commercial brand), crushed ice, and table salt.
Have ready a container in which to collect the waste antifreeze-water solutions.

Introduction

One of the most important practical applications of freezing point depression is the use of antifreeze in automobile cooling systems. Ask students to speculate about the problems that would result if automobiles did not contain antifreeze in their cooling systems. (The water could freeze, cracking the engine block.)
Ethylene glycol also increases the boiling point of water. (See Investigation 44.)

APPLICATION
Ask students how this property is applied to the radiator systems of automobiles. (The ethylene glycol prevents the coolant from boiling at high temperatures.)
You may want to demonstrate some other compounds that depress the freezing point of water, for example alcohol.

Name _____

3. What precautions should be taken with antifreeze when performing this investigation? Do not drink the antifreeze, since ethylene glycol is poisonous. Do not eat the ice, since it may be contaminated with ethylene glycol.

4. What is the reference point for freezing point depression in this investigation? The reference point is the experimental freezing point of distilled water.

5. Why is Calculation Step 5 necessary? The investigation uses a 0.1-kg solution. Molality, however, is measured per 1 kg of solvent. Since the molality is needed to calculate the molar mass in Step 6, the number of grams of antifreeze per kg (1000 g) must be calculated.

6. Write the mathematical expression for molality.

$$m = \frac{\text{number of moles of solute}}{1 \text{ kg solvent}}$$

7. Write the mathematical expression that relates the mass, number of moles, and molar mass of a substance.

$$\text{number of moles} = \frac{\text{mass in grams}}{\mathcal{M}}$$

8. Using these two expressions, derive an equation for calculating the molar mass of a sample if you know its mass and the freezing point depression it causes for water.

$$m = \frac{\text{mass in grams}/\mathcal{M}}{1 \text{ kg solvent}}$$

$$\mathcal{M} = \frac{\text{number of grams of solute}}{m \times 1 \text{ kg}}$$

Problem

How can you find the freezing point depression of water solutions of antifreeze and the molar mass of ethylene glycol?

Materials

chemical splash goggles
laboratory apron
beaker, 600-mL
300 mL crushed ice
sodium chloride (NaCl)
stirring rod
thermometer
paper towels or aluminum foil
3 large test tubes

distilled water
2 beakers, 250-mL
marking pen
laboratory balance
40 mL antifreeze
graduated cylinder, 10- or 25-mL
dropper
graduated cylinder, 100-mL

246

Name _____

Lab 45 APPLICATION

Safety

Wear your goggles and lab apron at all times during the investigation. Commercial antifreeze is primarily ethylene glycol, which is highly toxic. The ice used in the investigation could become contaminated with antifreeze by accident. Do not eat the ice. Note the caution alert symbols here and with certain steps of the Procedure. Refer to page *xi* for the specific precautions associated with each symbol.

Procedure

1. Put on your goggles and lab apron. Half fill a 600-mL beaker with ice and cover it with about 20 grams of sodium chloride (NaCl). Stir this ice-salt mixture with a stirring rod until it reaches a constant temperature at or below −10°C. Cover the outside of the beaker with paper toweling or aluminum foil with the reflective side in.

2. Half fill a test tube with distilled water and place it in the ice bath. Rinse the stirring rod and use it to stir the water gently until ice crystals first appear. Use a thermometer to measure the freezing point and record it in the Data Table. **CAUTION:** *Thermometers are fragile. Do not use the thermometer as a stirring rod.*

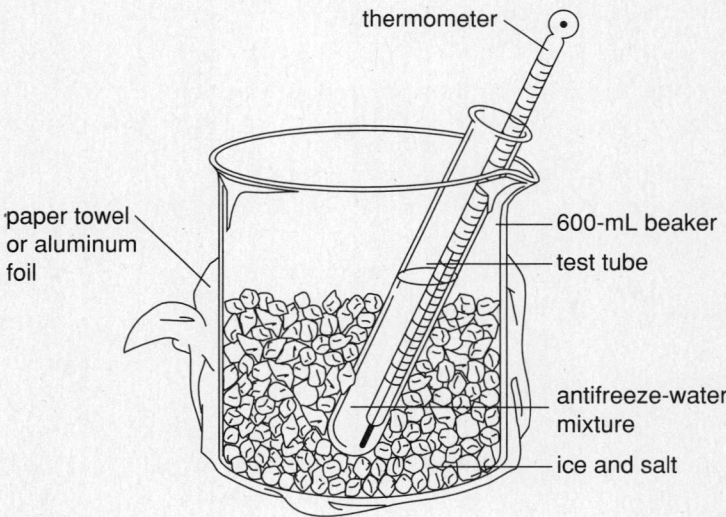

Figure 44–1

3. Find the mass of a 250-mL beaker. Leaving the beaker on the balance, set the balance for an additional 10.00 grams. Add antifreeze to the beaker carefully from a 10- or 25-mL graduated cylinder. **CAUTION:** *Antifreeze is toxic. Do not drink it. If you spill any, rinse it off with plenty of water and tell your teacher.* When the balance is close to equalization, add the final antifreeze with a dropper. Now add 100 mL of distilled water to the beaker and stir thoroughly with the stirring rod. In a similar fashion, prepare a second solution using 20.00 grams of antifreeze. Label the beakers *Solution 1* and *Solution 2*.

Safety

Make sure students wear their goggles and lab aprons at all times during the investigation. Ethylene glycol solutions are toxic. Warn the students not to drink them and to wash up spills promptly.

Warn the students not to use the thermometers as stirring rods, as they could break. ■

Teaching Tips

Temperature measurement is critical for the success of this experiment. If thermometers sensitive to 0.1°C or better are available, then the results will be more reliable. Standard student thermometers can be used, but if they do not register the freezing point of water as 0.0°C, calibrate several thermometers for reference.

Supercooling can occur with solutions. Explain to students that adding an ice chip will begin crystallization.

Additives to commercial antifreeze include corrosion inhibitors and surfactants to form more protective coverage for the copper core of the radiator. These additives can introduce errors of up to 5 percent, depending on the type and amount.

Help students to realize that the use of the ice-salt bath to cool the antifreeze mixture is based on the same concept being studied in the investigation.

Students may need help with the last few questions in the Pre-Lab Discussion. Review the mathematical concepts that form the basis for the analysis of the data.

Freezing Point Depression with Antifreeze

Lab 45 APPLICATION

4. Half fill a test tube with Solution 1 and place it in the ice/salt bath. Rinse the stirring rod and use it to stir the solution gently until the temperature is 0°C. Add a small chip of ice to the solution. (This will eliminate the possibility of supercooling.) Continue to stir until the first appearance of slush ice. Measure the temperature and record it in the Data Table.
5. Repeat Step 4 with Solution 2.
6. Dispose of the antifreeze solution in the container provided by your teacher. Clean up your work area and wash your hands before leaving the laboratory.

Waste Disposal
The waste antifreeze solutions should be collected in a labeled container and taken to an approved recycling or disposal facility or held for disposal by a licensed commercial contractor.

Observations (sample data)
DATA TABLE

freezing point of distilled water (T_{H_2O})	0.0°C
freezing point of Solution 1 (T_1)	−3.2°C
freezing point of Solution 2 (T_2)	−6.5°C

Calculations (based on sample data)

1. Determine the freezing point depression of Solution 1.
$$\Delta T = T_1 - T_{H_2O} = -3.2°C$$

2. Determine the freezing point depression of Solution 2.
$$\Delta T = T_2 - T_{H_2O} = -6.5°C$$

3. Determine the molality (m) of Solution 1. ($K_f = -1.86°C \cdot kg/mol$ for water)
$$m = \Delta T / K_f = \frac{-3.2°C}{-1.86°C \cdot kg/mol} = 1.7 \text{ mol/kg}$$

4. Determine the molality (m) of Solution 2.
$$m = \Delta T / K_f = \frac{-6.5°C}{-1.86°C \cdot kg/mol} = 3.5 \text{ mol/kg}$$

5. To find the molar mass of antifreeze, you first need to calculate the number of grams of antifreeze per 1000 grams of solvent for the solutions.

Solution 1 $\quad 1000 \text{ g H}_2\text{O} \times \dfrac{10.00 \text{ g antifreeze}}{100 \text{ g H}_2\text{O}} = 100.0 \text{ g antifreeze}$

Solution 2 $\quad 1000 \text{ g H}_2\text{O} \times \dfrac{20.00 \text{ g antifreeze}}{100 \text{ g H}_2\text{O}} = 200.0 \text{ g antifreeze}$

6. Find the molar mass of antifreeze. (Note: Review your answers to Pre-Lab Questions 6–8.)

Solution 1 $\quad \mathcal{M} = \dfrac{100.0 \text{ g antifreeze}}{1.7 \text{ mol/kg} \times 1 \text{ kg}}$
$= 58.8 \text{ g/mol}$

Solution 2 $\quad \mathcal{M} = \dfrac{200.0 \text{ g antifreeze}}{3.5 \text{ mol/kg} \times 1 \text{ kg}}$
$= 57.1 \text{ g/mol}$

Name _____

Lab 45 APPLICATION

Critical Thinking: Analysis and Conclusions

1. Permanent antifreeze is almost 100% ethylene glycol (1, 2 ethanediol, $C_2H_4(OH)_2$). Calculate its molar mass. *(Applying concepts)* __62.1 g/mol__

2. Calculate the percent error in both trials. *(Interpreting data)*

    Solution 1 $\dfrac{\text{accepted value} - \text{experimental value}}{\text{accepted value}} \times 100\% =$

    $\dfrac{62.1 \text{ g} - 58.8 \text{ g}}{62.1 \text{ g}} \times 100\% = 5.3\%$

    Solution 2 $\dfrac{\text{accepted value} - \text{experimental value}}{\text{accepted value}} \times 100\% =$

    $\dfrac{62.1 \text{ g} - 57.1 \text{ g}}{62.1 \text{ g}} \times 100\% = 8.1\%$

3. What do you think are the major sources of error in this investigation? How might some of them be reduced? *(Interpreting data)* __The thermometer probably has a precision of, at best, 0.2°C. A thermometer accurate to 0.1°C would reduce error. The antifreeze may contain additives that would affect the data.__

Critical Thinking: Applications

1. Could freezing point depression be used for substances not soluble in water? *(Making predictions)* __Yes, since there are a number of solvents that could be used for dissolving particular compounds. Each solvent must have its own K_f, from which molalities and molar masses may be determined.__

2. What effect on the freezing point depression of water would a 1 m solution of the ionic substance $(NH_4)_3PO_4$ have? *(Making predictions)* __The freezing point depression is dependent on the number of particles present. One mole of $(NH_4)_3PO_4$ would produce 4 moles of ions and theoretically depress the freezing point to $-7.44°C$.__

3. What assumption is made about the density of distilled water in this investigation? *(Making inferences)* __The density of water is assumed to be 1.0 g/mL.__

4. Would this method of molar mass determination be practical for other substances soluble in water? *(Applying concepts)* __It would be practical only for substances that are essentially nonelectrolytes.__

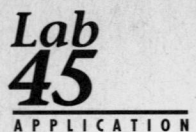

Name _____

Going Further

1. There are a number of commercial antifreezes on the market. Under your teacher's supervision, devise an investigation to test as many antifreezes as you can and make a cost comparison based on freezing point depression.
2. Since ethylene glycol is toxic, support is growing to replace it with safer substances. Research proposed alternatives to ethylene glycol and their effectiveness. Write a report on your findings.

Observing Chemical Equilibrium

Lab 46

Text reference: Chapter 16

Introduction

Some types of eyeglasses get darker when light shines on them. This is because a silver compound (AgCl) present in the lenses undergoes a chemical reaction when exposed to light. The products of the reaction (silver and chlorine atoms) are more opaque than the reactant. The reaction can be reversed by decreasing the amount of light, returning the sunglasses to a lighter tint:

$$AgCl(s) + \text{light} \rightleftharpoons Ag°(s) + Cl°(s)$$
(transparent)   (dark)

This reaction is an example of an equilibrium reaction since, assuming the amount of light remains constant, the rate of the forward reaction is equal to the rate of the reverse reaction. In this example, light energy is considered to be a reactant.

In this investigation, you will examine three other examples of equilibrium reactions. In each case, you will establish equilibrium in the system. Then you will disturb the equilibrium by changing either the concentration of a reactant, the acid/base level, or the temperature. The effects on the equilibrium of each system will be observed.

Pre-Lab Discussion

Read the entire laboratory investigation and the relevant pages of your textbook. Then answer the questions that follow.

1. What is meant by the statement "The reaction is in equilibrium"?
   The rate of the forward reaction is equal to the rate of the reverse reaction.

2. How can equilibrium be compared to passengers entering and leaving an elevator as it changes floors? If the same number of people get on and off the elevator at each floor, then the number of people on the elevator is in equilibrium.

3. What is meant by the term *dynamic equilibrium*? Although the reaction appears to have stopped, the forward and reverse rates are equal rather than zero.

4. What are some safety hazards associated with sodium hydroxide solutions? Sodium hydroxide is a strong base and is highly caustic. It should be handled with care.

Materials (class of 30 in pairs)

30 pairs chemical splash goggles
30 laboratory aprons
30 beakers, 600-mL
15 hot plates
15 graduated cylinders, 10-mL
75 g sodium chloride (NaCl)
15 laboratory balances
45 test tubes
45 stoppers to fit the test tubes
15 sets of 5 micropipets, filled with the following solutions:
    hydrochloric acid (HCl), 1.0 M
    bromthymol blue indicator
    hydrochloric acid (HCl), 0.1 M
    sodium hydroxide (NaOH), 0.1 M
    copper(II) sulfate ($CuSO_4$), 0.1 M
2 petri dishes
15 test-tube racks
15 marking pens
500 mL distilled water

Time Required

30 minutes. The lab can be shortened by having heated water already available at the beginning of class. You can assign different teams to do each of the three parts and have the class pool the data at the end.

Advance Preparation

Fill the micropipets with the solutions and set them upside down in a petri dish cover. Be sure to label the petri dishes.
    Prepare the solutions according to the following instructions.

© Prentice-Hall, Inc.   *Observing Chemical Equilibrium*

Lab 46

CAUTION: *Wear goggles, gloves, and a laboratory apron when working with 12.0 M HCl and solid NaOH.*

1.0 *M* HCl: Dissolve 8.3 mL of 12.0 *M* HCl in enough water to make 100 mL of solution.

0.1 *M* HCl: Take 10.0 mL from the 1.0 *M* HCl and dissolve it in enough water to make 100 mL of solution.

0.1 *M* NaOH: Dissolve 0.8 g NaOH in enough water to make 200 mL of solution.

Bromthymol blue: Dissolve 0.1 g bromthymol blue powder in a solution made by combining 16.0 mL of 0.01 *M* NaOH with 234 mL distilled water. If your bromthymol blue is in the form of the sodium salt, dissolve 0.1 g in 250 mL of distilled water.

0.1 *M* CuSO₄: Dissolve 2.5 g CuSO₄·5H₂O in enough water to make 100 mL of solution.

Introduction

A tug-of-war is a good example of equilibrium. Ask students to predict what would happen if two people of identical strength pulled on the rope. Then ask them to predict what would happen if someone else was added to help pull on one side. How might the effect of the additional person be counteracted? Adding another person of equal strength to the opposite side would counteract the effect of the additional person. This is similar to the idea of equilibrium and the response of systems in equilibrium to disturbances.

Safety

Make sure students wear their goggles and lab aprons at all times during the investigation. Caution students to be careful when working with hot plates and hot water. Tell them to avoid mixing the HCl solutions with the NaOH solutions. ∎

Problem

What are some of the factors that affect the equilibrium of a chemical system?

Materials

chemical splash goggles
laboratory apron
2 beakers, 600-mL
hot plate
graduated cylinder, 10-mL
sodium chloride (NaCl)
laboratory balance
3 test tubes
3 stoppers to fit the test tubes
test-tube rack
5 micropipets, containing the following solutions:

hydrochloric acid (HCl), 1.0 *M*
bromthymol blue indicator
hydrochloric acid (HCl), 0.1 *M*
sodium hydroxide (NaOH), 0.1 *M*
copper(II) sulfate (CuSO₄), 0.1 *M*
marking pen
distilled water

Safety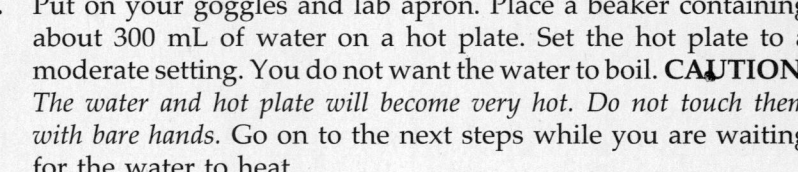

Wear your goggles and lab apron at all times during the investigation. Hot plates get very hot, so do not touch them with bare hands. Hydrochloric acid and sodium hydroxide solutions are irritating to skin and will damage clothing. If you spill any of these, immediately wash the area with plenty of cold water and notify your teacher. Copper(II) sulfate is poisonous. Avoid contact with it.

Note the caution alert symbols here and with certain steps of the Procedure. Refer to page *xi* for the specific precautions associated with each symbol.

Procedure

Part A

1. Put on your goggles and lab apron. Place a beaker containing about 300 mL of water on a hot plate. Set the hot plate to a moderate setting. You do not want the water to boil. **CAUTION:** *The water and hot plate will become very hot. Do not touch them with bare hands.* Go on to the next steps while you are waiting for the water to heat.

2. Put 10.0 mL of water into a test tube. Create a saturated solution of sodium chloride by adding 4.0 g NaCl to the test tube, inserting a stopper, and shaking. Remove the stopper, allow the solution to rest for 1 minute, and then, using a micropipet, add 1.0 *M* HCl a few drops at a time. **CAUTION:** *Hydrochloric acid is corrosive. Avoid spilling it on your skin or clothing.* Keep adding drops until you observe a change. Record your observations.

3. Rinse the contents of the tube down the drain with plenty of water. Set the tube upside down in the test-tube rack to drain.

252

Name_____

Lab 46

Part B

4. Label three test tubes *1–3*. Half-fill them with distilled water. Add three drops of bromthymol blue indicator solution to each tube. Insert stoppers into each tube and shake.

5. Add two drops of 0.1 M HCl to test tube 1. Observe and record.

6. Add two drops of 0.1 M NaOH to test tube 2. **CAUTION:** *Sodium hydroxide is caustic. Avoid spilling it on your skin or clothing.* Observe and record.

7. Add two drops of 0.1 M HCl to test tube 3. Then add two drops of 0.1 M NaOH to the test tube. Observe and record.

8. Rinse out the test tubes with plenty of water.

Part C

9. Place 3.0 mL 0.1 M copper(II) sulfate solution in each of two test tubes. Add an equal number of drops of 0.1 M NaOH to each test tube until a thick blue-white precipitate forms.

10. Place one of the tubes into the hot-water bath. After four minutes, observe and record any changes. Use the other tube for comparison.

11. Rinse the test tubes out with plenty of water. Turn off the hot plate. Clean up your work area and wash your hands before leaving the laboratory.

Teaching Tips
Alert students not to confuse the 1.0 M HCl with the 0.1 M HCl.

Waste Disposal
All the substances encountered in this investigation can be safely washed down the drain with plenty of water. ■

Observations (sample data)

HCl added to saturated NaCl solution	White precipitate forms.
0.1 M HCl added to bromthymol blue	Blue changes to yellow.
0.1 M NaOH added to bromthymol blue	No change.
0.1 M HCl then 0.1 M NaOH added to bromthymol blue	Blue to yellow to blue.
0.1 M NaOH added to 0.1 M CuSO$_4$ in hot water	Precipitate increases.

Critical Thinking: Analysis and Conclusions

1. Write a chemical equation showing solid sodium chloride in equilibrium with aqueous sodium and chloride ions. *(Making inferences)*
   NaCl(s) ⇌ Na$^+$(aq) + Cl$^-$(aq).

2. In Part A, how did the addition of HCl change the concentration of ions in solutions? Speculate on the identity of the white precipitate. *(Making inferences)* The HCl increased the concentration of H$^+$ and Cl$^-$ ions. The white precipitate was NaCl(s).

3. Write a rule that describes how the equilibrium of a system is shifted when the concentration of a substance in the reaction is increased. *(Drawing conclusions)* Increasing the concentration of a substance in the reaction shifts the equilibrium away from the side on which the substance occurs.

Observing Chemical Equilibrium

4. In Part B, does the NaOH counteract the effects of the HCl? Explain. *(Interpreting data)* The NaOH appears to counteract the effects of HCl since the original blue color is restored by the addition of NaOH.

5. Write the chemical equation showing the reaction in Part C. Include heat as a term in the equation. Is this an exothermic or endothermic reaction? *(Making inferences)* $CuSO_4(aq) + NaOH(aq) + heat \rightleftharpoons Na_2SO_4(aq) + Cu(OH)_2(s)$. Since heat is a reactant, it is an endothermic reaction.

6. Write a rule that describes how the equilibrium is shifted when the temperature of an endothermic reaction, such as this, is increased. (Hint: Look at the answer to Analysis and Conclusions Question 3.) *(Drawing conclusions)* Increasing the temperature of an endothermic reaction causes the equilibrium to shift to the side away from the heat term.

Critical Thinking: Applications

1. Write a rule that describes the effect on the equilibrium of a system when the concentration of a substance in the reaction is decreased. *(Making predictions)* Decreasing the concentration of a substance will cause a shift toward the side on which the substance occurs.

2. Are the rates of the forward and reverse reactions still equal immediately after a disturbance is introduced to a system at equilibrium? Explain. *(Applying concepts)* The rates differ since the equilibrium has been disturbed. Eventually, the equilibrium will be restored but at different forward and reverse rates of reaction.

3. Write a general rule covering all of the types of disturbances to equilibrium observed in this investigation. *(Developing hypotheses)* A system in equilibrium will respond to any disturbance of its equilibrium so as to reduce the disturbance.

Going Further

1. Investigate and report on the effect of pressure on a system in which gases are involved in a chemical reaction. Give examples of equilibrium systems that would be affected by pressure.
2. Equilibrium can be shifted by decreasing the concentration of a substance. Suggest how this might be done. Devise an experiment to test your idea. Have your teacher approve your experimental design before you begin. Perform the experiment only under your teacher's supervision.

Going Further

2. A reaction that precipitates a substance can be used to decrease its concentration. Addition of a solvent can also decrease the concentration.

Le Chatelier's Principle

Small Scale **Lab 47**

Text reference: **Chapter 16**

Introduction

Most chemical reactions that you have studied so far appear to proceed to completion or until one of the reactants is used up. For example, a piece of magnesium, ignited in oxygen, burns until all of the magnesium has reacted to form magnesium oxide. In other reactions, however, the products have enough energy to react to form the reactants again in the reverse reaction. When the rate of the forward and reverse reactions are equal, a state of equilibrium exists. Both reactions continue to occur, but there is no net change in the concentrations of reactants or products.

Le Chatelier's principle enables you to predict the effect of a stress placed on an equilibrium system. Stresses include changes in the concentrations of reactants or products, or in the temperature of the system. Le Chatelier's principle can be stated as follows: If a system in equilibrium is put under a stress, the system will respond by shifting to reduce the stress. For example, adding a reactant to a system in equilibrium will cause the system to shift to the right, thereby reducing the amount of reactant.

In this investigation, you will examine the equilibrium system represented by the following net ionic equation:

$$\underset{\text{pink}}{Co(H_2O)_6^{2+}} + 4Cl^- \rightleftharpoons \underset{\text{blue}}{CoCl_4^{2-}} + 6H_2O$$

You will subject the system to various stresses and observe the effects on the equilibrium.

Pre-Lab Discussion

Read the entire laboratory investigation and the relevant pages of your textbook. Then answer the questions that follow.

1. State Le Chatelier's principle. <u>If a system in equilibrium is put under a stress, the system will respond by shifting to reduce the stress.</u>

2. Explain what happens when equilibrium is reached. <u>The rate of the forward reaction is equal to the rate of the reverse reaction.</u>

3. List the stresses that will be studied in this experiment. <u>The stresses include increasing the chloride ion concentration by adding HCl, decreasing the chloride ion concentration by adding AgNO$_3$, increasing the concentration of water, increasing the temperature, and decreasing the temperature.</u>

Materials (class of 30 in pairs)

30 pairs chemical splash goggles
30 laboratory aprons
30 pairs latex gloves
30 beakers, 250-mL
tap water
15 hot plates
15 marking pens
15 well plates, 24-well
15 sheets of white paper
15 sets of 4 micropipets, containing the following solutions:
 200 mL cobalt chloride (CoCl$_2$), 0.2 M
 100 mL hydrochloric acid (HCl), 12.0 M
 100 mL distilled water
 100 mL silver nitrate (AgNO$_3$), 0.1 M
15 petri dishes
15 plastic toothpicks
paper towels
15 small test tubes, 10 mm × 75 mm
60 ice cubes

Time Required

45 minutes. To shorten the investigation, do the heating and cooling part as a demonstration.

Advance Preparation

Prepare the solutions as follows:
 0.2 M CoCl$_2$: Dissolve 9.4 g CoCl$_2$·6H$_2$O in enough distilled water to make 200 mL of solution.
 0.1 M AgNO$_3$: Dissolve 1.7 g AgNO$_3$ in enough distilled water to make 100 mL of solution.
CAUTION: *These solutions are poisonous, and AgNO$_3$ will stain skin and clothing. Use goggles, a lab apron, and gloves when handling them.*
 Label 15 sets of four micropipets each as follows:

© Prentice-Hall, Inc.

Le Chatelier's Principle **255**

Small Scale Lab 47

Co, HCl, H₂O, and Ag. Fill the micropipets with the appropriate solution and place them upside down in a labeled beaker. Have ready a container in which to collect the waste solutions and precipitate.

Introduction

On the blackboard, draw a picture of a submerged submarine. Point out that the submarine is in equilibrium since the downward force of gravity and the upward buoyant force are equal but opposite in direction. The submarine is not moving vertically. Compare this example to the conditions inside a test tube in which a reaction is at equilibrium. There is no net force to push the reaction in either direction, but there are two counteracting forces of equal size, so the reaction appears to be halted.

Safety

Make sure students wear their goggles and lab aprons at all times during the investigation. Caution students to wear gloves when handling silver nitrate solution and 12.0 M hydrochloric acid. AgNO₃ will stain skin and clothing and, along with CoCl₂·6H₂O, is poisonous. A dilute solution of ammonia water will help remove AgNO₃ stains from

Name _____

4. The formula for solid cobalt(II) chloride is CoCl₂·6H₂O. What is the name given to compounds such as this, which have water as part of their crystal structure? **These compounds are called hydrates.**

5. What safety precautions must be observed with hydrochloric acid (HCl)? With silver nitrate (AgNO₃)? **Hydrochloric acid is corrosive and care should be taken to avoid contact with skin or clothing. AgNO₃ is toxic and causes stains to skin and clothing. Care should be taken to avoid contact.**

6. Predict the effect on the following equilibrium system if you: (a) add HCl; (b) add H₂O; (c) add NaOH.

$$2CrO_4^{2-} + 2H^+ \rightleftharpoons Cr_2O_7^{2-} + H_2O$$

(a) Adding HCl increases the concentration of H⁺ ions, thereby shifting the equilibrium to the right; (b) adding H₂O shifts the equilibrium to the left;
(c) adding NaOH consumes H⁺ ions, causing a shift to the left.

Problem

What are the effects of stressing a system at equilibrium?

Materials

chemical splash goggles
laboratory apron
latex gloves
2 beakers, 250-mL
tap water
hot plate
marking pen
well plate, 24-well
1 sheet of white paper
4 micropipets containing the following liquids:
    cobalt chloride (CoCl₂), 0.2 M

hydrochloric acid (HCl), 12.0 M
distilled water
silver nitrate (AgNO₃), 0.1 M
petri dish
plastic toothpick
paper towel
small test tube
ice cubes

Safety

Wear your goggles and lab apron at all times during the investigation. Hot plates get very hot; use caution when working with them. Hydrochloric acid is extremely corrosive. It will irritate skin and damage clothing. Wear gloves when working with it. If you spill any acid, immediately wash the area with plenty of cold water and notify your teacher. Cobalt chloride and silver nitrate are toxic, and silver nitrate will stain skin and clothing; avoid contact with them. Do not put your fingers in your mouth at any time during the investigation. Note the caution alert symbols here and with certain steps of the Procedure. Refer to page xi for the specific precautions associated with each symbol.

Name _____

Lab 47

Procedure

1. Put on your goggles and lab apron. Place a beaker containing about 100 mL of water on a hot plate. Set the hot plate to a moderate setting; you do not want the water to boil. **CAUTION:** *The water and hot plate will become very hot.* Go on to the next steps while you are waiting for the water to heat.

2. Using the marking pen, label a well plate from left to right along the top with the numbers 1–6. Down the left side, label the rows of wells A–D. Place the well plate on a sheet of white paper.

3. Put on latex gloves. Obtain four micropipets labeled as follows: *Co* ($CoCl_2$ solution), *HCl* (hydrochloric acid), *H_2O* (distilled water), and *Ag* ($AgNO_3$ solution). Place them upside down in an inverted petri dish cover. **CAUTION:** *Be careful not to spill any $CoCl_2$, HCl, or $AgNO_3$ solution. Wear gloves when working with 12.0 M hydrochloric acid. If spillage does occur, wash with plenty of water and inform your teacher.* Use these micropipets to fill the wells of the labeled well plate as indicated in Steps 4–8.

4. Place five drops of $CoCl_2$ solution in each of the 24 wells of the labeled well plate on the white sheet of paper. **CAUTION:** *Be careful not to ingest any $CoCl_2$ or spill any on your skin.*

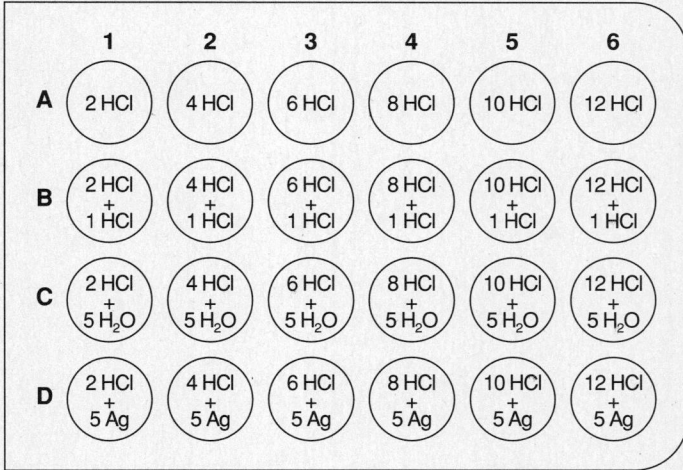

All wells contain 5 drops of $CoCl_2$ solution.

Figure 47–1

5. As shown in Figure 47–1, add two drops of HCl to the $CoCl_2$ solution in wells A1, B1, C1, and D1. Similarly, place four drops of HCl in each well in column 2, six drops in each well in column 3, eight drops in each well in column 4, ten drops in each well in column 5, and 12 drops in each well in column 6. Mix the contents of each well with the plastic toothpick. Rinse the toothpick with water and set it aside on a paper towel. **CAUTION:** *12.0 M hydrochloric acid is extremely corrosive. Avoid spilling it on your skin or clothing.* Record the color of the solution in each well of row A in the Data Table. Row A will be your control.

the skin. Some commercially available laundry pretreatments may remove stains from clothing.

Warn students that 12.0 *M* HCl is extremely corrosive. If HCl comes in contact with skin or clothes, have students wash with plenty of water. HCl can be neutralized with a solution of sodium carbonate or sodium bicarbonate. ∎

Teaching Tips

Since the reaction used in the investigation is endothermic, adding heat produces the same effect as adding a reactant. Cooling has the same effect as taking a reactant away. Heating and cooling a reaction in equilibrium is a good way to determine whether the reaction is endothermic or exothermic.

Do not allow the water on the hot plates to boil. You may want to start the water boiling about 10 minutes before class and then turn the settings on the hot plates down to low or medium as the students come into the room.

© Prentice-Hall, Inc.

Le Chatelier's Principle 257

Name _____

6. In row B, add one more drop of HCl to each well and stir thoroughly with the toothpick. Rinse the toothpick with water and set it aside on a paper towel. Record the colors of row B in the Data Table.

7. Add five drops of distilled water to each well in row C. Stir thoroughly with the toothpick. Rinse the toothpick with water and set it aside on a paper towel. Record the colors of row C in the Data Table.

8. Add five drops of AgNO$_3$ solution to each well in row D and stir thoroughly with the toothpick. Discard the toothpick. **CAUTION:** *Be careful not to ingest any AgNO$_3$ or spill any on your skin.* Record any color changes and precipitate formation in the Data Table.

9. Place 5 mL of the cobalt solution in a test tube. Add just enough distilled water to get a purple color half-way between blue and pink. Place the test tube in the beaker of hot water from Step 1 until a color change occurs. **CAUTION:** *The water and hot plate are hot. Do not touch them with bare hands.* Record your observations. Turn off the hot plate.

10. Prepare an ice bath by placing ice cubes in a 250-mL beaker and adding water. Place the test tube in the ice bath until a color change occurs. Record your observations.

11. Dispose of all chemicals according to your teacher's instructions. Clean up your work area and wash your hands before leaving the laboratory.

Observations (sample data)
DATA TABLE

	1	2	3	4	5	6
A	increasing	intensity	of blue			→
B	more	blue	than	Row A		→
C	increasing	intensity	of pink			→
D	precipitate	and	increasing	intensity	of pink	→

CoCl$_2$ at room temperature: purple

CoCl$_2$ in hot water: blue

CoCl$_2$ in cold water: pink

Waste Disposal

Silver compounds are regulated as hazardous waste (EPA waste #D011). Therefore, before students wash out their reaction plates, they should be instructed to use an eyedropper to remove the material from the wells in row D and deposit it into a clearly marked container. Collect any remaining silver solution and precipitate the Ag$^+$ ions with excess NaCl solution. Filter out the precipitate and store in the marked container. Discard the filtrate.

Cobalt compounds should be stored separately in marked containers for commercial disposal.

Dispose of 12.0 M HCl by first pouring it into a large beaker containing enough cold water to dilute the acid about 12 times. A solution of 1.0 M sodium carbonate or sodium bicarbonate should then be added slowly until no more bubbling is visible. The resulting solution may be flushed down the drain with plenty of water.

All other substances can be flushed down the drain with plenty of water. ∎

Name _____

Small Scale Lab 47

Critical Thinking: Analysis and Conclusions

1. Refer to the net ionic equation below or in the Introduction to answer the following questions. *(Interpreting data)*

$$Co(H_2O)_6^{2+} + 4Cl^- \rightleftharpoons CoCl_4^{2-} + 6H_2O$$

In what direction was the equilibrium shifted by

  a. the addition of HCl? Since the color shifted from pink to blue, the equilibrium shifted to the right.

  b. the addition of water? Since the color shifted from blue to pink, the equilibrium shifted to the left.

  c. the addition of AgNO$_3$? Since the color shifted from blue to pink, the equilibrium shifted to the left.

  d. increasing the temperature? Since the color shifted from pink to blue, the equilibrium shifted to the right.

  e. decreasing the temperature? Since the color shifted from blue to pink, the equilibrium shifted to the left.

2. How do you explain the results described in answers 1a and 1b? *(Making inferences)* Le Chatelier's principle states that a system in equilibrium will adjust to minimize any stress on the system. Adding chloride ions (reactants) or water (a product) shifts the equilibrium in opposite directions. In the case of chloride, the equilibrium was shifted to the right, and in the case of water, the equilibrium was shifted to the left.

3. Explain the results observed when AgNO$_3$ was added. *(Making inferences)* Since the color change indicated an equilibrium shift to the left, AgNO$_3$ must either increase the amount of product or decrease the amount of reactant. Since a precipitate formed, it is probable that a reaction that consumed a reactant occurred. The most likely net ionic reaction is Ag$^+$(aq) + Cl$^-$(aq) $\rightleftharpoons$ AgCl(s).

4. Is the reaction shown in the Introduction exothermic or endothermic? How do you know? *(Drawing conclusions)* It is endothermic. Adding heat causes the equilibrium to shift to the right and cooling it causes the equilibrium to shift left. This shows that heat can be considered a reactant.

5. Write the equilibrium expression for the system studied. *(Applying concepts)*

$$\frac{[CoCl_4^{2-}][H_2O]^6}{[Co(H_2O)_6^{2+}][Cl^-]^4}$$

© Prentice-Hall, Inc.

Le Chatelier's Principle

Name _____

Critical Thinking: Applications

1. Predict how the addition of sodium chloride would affect the equilibrium. Explain your prediction in terms of Le Chatelier's principle. *(Making predictions)* Sodium chloride would increase the concentration of chloride ions. The equilibrium would shift to the right, producing a blue color.

2. Rewrite the net ionic equation including the energy term where appropriate. The ΔH for this reaction is $+50$ kJ/mol. *(Applying concepts)* The equation is: $Co(H_2O)_6^{2+} + 4Cl^- + 50 \text{ kJ} \rightleftharpoons CoCl_4^{2-} + 6H_2O$.

3. Silver chloride (AgCl) is a white solid. For the equilibrium reaction

$$Ag^+(aq) + Cl^-(aq) \rightleftharpoons AgCl(s)$$

$K_{eq} = 6 \times 10^9$. At equilibrium, would you expect to have more silver and chloride ions or more solid silver chloride? Explain. *(Making predictions)* Since the equilibrium constant is greater than 1, more solid silver chloride would be expected. In fact, almost no silver and chloride ions should be present at equilibrium since the constant is much greater than 1.

Going Further

1. Design an experiment to test the hypothesis that the effects observed in row B were due to added H^+ rather than Cl^-. Under your teacher's supervision, perform the experiment and report the results to your class.
2. Use a solution of $CaCl_2$ to further verify the role of Cl^- in the changes observed in row B. Under your teacher's supervision, perform the experiment and report the results to your class.

Going Further

2. Addition of any chloride ion will shift the equilibrium to the right, resulting in an increasing blue color.

Shifting Equilibria in Plant Tissues

Lab 48 APPLICATION

Text reference: Chapter 16

Introduction

The variety and beauty of the colors of flowers have touched human emotions and sparked the imagination of poets for centuries. What makes flowers so colorful? Even the fruits and leaves of some plants appear unusually rich in colors. The reason you see such a wealth of colors in plants is that they possess a variety of pigments. Pigments are compounds that give color to the cells in leaves, stems, fruits, and flowers. Two examples of these pigments are carotenoids and anthocyanins. Carotenoids, found in such plants as carrots and tomatoes, cause plant parts to appear yellow to orangish red. Anthocyanins cause fruits and flowers to appear red, blue, violet, or creamy yellow.

Some of these pigments are sensitive to certain air pollutants and will undergo equilibrium reactions in their presence. Consider the following example. When gaseous sulfur dioxide (SO_2) invades leaves or flower petals and dissolves in the water surrounding the cells, it reacts to form sulfurous acid (H_2SO_3), which in turn dissociates into hydrogen (H^+) and hydrogen sulfite (HSO_3^-) ions.

$$SO_2(g) + H_2O(l) \rightleftharpoons H_2SO_3(aq)$$
$$H_2SO_3(aq) \rightleftharpoons H^+(aq) + HSO_3^-(aq)$$

The hydrogen sulfite ions react with pigments in the plant cells to form a colorless compound. A simplified description of the reaction is shown by the following equation, where Pgm represents a plant pigment.

$$\text{Pgm}^+ + HSO_3^- \rightleftharpoons \text{Pgm-}SO_3^- + H^+$$
$$\text{(color)} \qquad\qquad \text{(colorless)}$$

As you can tell from the equation, the presence or absence of pigment color indicates shifts in the equilibrium reaction.

In this investigation you will see Le Chatelier's principle in action. First, you will generate sulfur dioxide gas in a petri dish containing samples of plant tissue and observe the color changes. Then you will cause a shift in equilibrium by adding sulfuric acid (H_2SO_4) to the mixture. You will be able to observe and analyze the shift by the appearance or disappearance of the color in the plant tissue.

Pre-Lab Discussion

Read the entire laboratory investigation and the relevant pages of your textbook. Then answer the questions that follow.

1. How can Le Chatelier's principle help explain a shift in the equilibrium of a reversible reaction? <u>Le Chatelier's principle states that when a system in equilibrium is subjected to a change in conditions, the equilibrium will shift in the direction that counteracts the change.</u>

Materials (class of 30 in pairs)
30 pairs chemical splash goggles
30 laboratory aprons
15 plastic petri dishes with access ports
15 sheets of white paper
15 single-hole paper punches
15 pieces of red cabbage leaf
15 cotton swabs
tap water
15 pens or pencils
assortment of the following flowers:
    red petunia
    orange lily
    yellow lily
    blue hydrangea
15 pairs scissors
15 sets of 3 labeled micropipets, containing the following solutions:
    sodium sulfite (Na_2SO_3), 0.5 M
    sulfuric acid (H_2SO_4), 2.0 M
    ammonia ($NH_3(aq)$), 2.0 M
15 wash bottles
paper towels

Time Required
50 minutes.

Advance Preparation
The petri dishes can be given an access port by punching a hole with a glass capillary tube or shortened pasteur pipet that has been heated over a burner. When the glass is hot enough it will melt through the top plate easily. The hole has to be only about the size of the stem of a thin-stem pipet. As shown in Figure 48–1, make a little fold on the end of a 1-inch piece of clear tape and cover the hole with the tape, leaving the fold as

© Prentice-Hall, Inc.

Shifting Equilibria in Plant Tissues **261**

Lab 48
APPLICATION

a tab to lift the tape off the hole.

Flowers can be obtained cheaply from a local florist. With advance notice, and at little or no cost, florists will usually save flowers for you that would otherwise be thrown away.

Prepare the needed solutions as follows. CAUTION: *Wear goggles, gloves, and a laboratory apron.*

0.5 M sodium sulfite (Na_2SO_3): Add 6 grams of solid Na_2SO_3 to enough water to make 100 mL total volume.

2.0 M sulfuric acid (H_2SO_4): Slowly add 11 mL of concentrated H_2SO_4 to enough water to make 100 mL total volume.

2.0 M ammonia ($NH_3(aq)$): Add 11 mL of concentrated $NH_3(aq)$ to enough water to make 100 mL total volume.

Have ready a container into which the students can rinse the waste materials from their petri dishes.

Introduction

Introduce the investigation by discussing the problem of sulfur dioxide gas and how it affects plants. The gas is an air pollutant that contributes to acid rain. It originates when high-sulfur coal is burned at electric power plants or when metal sulfide ores are reduced. Sulfur dioxide molecules can diffuse into leaves and flowers in gaseous form and react to form HSO_3^- ions in the plant tissue. Although the chemical reaction that causes the color change is the same, the change occurs sooner with exposure to the gas than with acid rain because the gas can enter the plant tissues more quickly.

Although students have not yet studied organic chemistry, you may wish to tell them that differences in molecular structure of the carotenoids and anthocyanins account for their differing sensitivity to HSO_3^- ions. The carotenoids

Name _____

2. In this investigation, you will generate SO_2 gas by reacting a solution of sodium sulfite (Na_2SO_3) with sulfuric acid (H_2SO_4). Also formed are sodium sulfate and water. Write the balanced equation for this reaction. $Na_2SO_3(aq) + H_2SO_4(aq) \rightarrow Na_2SO_4(aq) + H_2O(l) + SO_2(g)$

3. What is the source of HSO_3^- ions in this investigation? The SO_2 gas dissolves in water to form H_2SO_3, which dissociates into H^+ and HSO_3^- ions.

4. What ions are introduced to the system by the addition of more H_2SO_4 in Step 6? (Hint: Study the equation for the dissociation of sulfurous acid (H_2SO_3) given in the Introduction.) H^+ and SO_4^{2-} ions

5. What are some of the hazards associated with the generation of sulfur dioxide gas (SO_2) in this investigation? How can you avoid these hazards? Sulfur dioxide gas will dissolve in the wet mucous membranes and eyes to produce an acid. Avoid breathing this gas— especially if allergy to sulfites is a problem. The reaction should be carried out in a covered petri dish and neutralized as directed.

6. How are the acids in the petri dish neutralized before cleanup? The acids are neutralized with the addition of ammonia.

Problem

How can the reactions of certain plant pigments serve as indicators of an equilibrium reaction?

Materials

chemical splash goggles
laboratory apron
plastic petri dish with access port
sheet of white paper
single-hole paper punch
piece of red cabbage leaf
cotton swab
tap water
pen or pencil
petals from each of the following flowers:
   red petunia
   orange lily
   yellow lily
   blue hydrangea

scissors
3 micropipets, containing the following solutions:
   sodium sulfite (Na_2SO_3), 0.5 M
   sulfuric acid (H_2SO_4), 2.0 M
   ammonia ($NH_3(aq)$), 2.0 M
wash bottle
paper towel

262   © Prentice-Hall, Inc.

Name _____

Lab 48
APPLICATION

Safety

Wear your goggles and lab apron at all times during the investigation. Sulfuric acid is corrosive. Ammonia and its fumes are caustic and irritating to eyes and nasal passages. Wash any skin or clothing that comes into contact with these substances with large quantities of water.

Sulfur dioxide gas forms a corrosive acid when it dissolves in the eyes and nasal passages. If you are allergic to sulfites, report your allergy to your teacher before the investigation. Once the reaction begins, open and close the petri dish only according to directions.

Note the caution alert symbols here and with certain steps of the Procedure. Refer to page xi for the specific precautions associated with each symbol.

Procedure

1. Put on your goggles and lab apron. Place the bottom plate of the petri dish on the white paper.

2. Using the single-hole paper punch, carefully punch two small circular pieces from the red cabbage leaf. Place what is left of the cabbage leaf aside for later color comparison.

3. Using a moistened cotton swab, pick up the circular pieces of cabbage leaf and position them opposite each other in the bottom plate of the petri dish as shown in Figure 48–1. Notice that the samples should be placed about the same distance from the center of the dish as the access port in the lid. Lift the dish and write labels on the white paper corresponding to the position of the cabbage circles in the petri dish. Replace the dish.

4. If the flower petals are sufficiently large, punch out two pieces of each of the flower types and place them opposite each other in the petri dish. If the leaf is fragile you can use scissors to cut small squares from the petal. If the petals are tiny, simply use the whole petal. As with the cabbage samples, label the flower types on the white paper. Place what is left of the flower samples aside for later color comparison. The first column of the Data Table lists the type and original color of each sample.

5. Generate SO_2 gas by placing two drops of 0.5 M Na_2SO_3 in the center of the petri dish and then adding two drops of 2.0 M H_2SO_4. Immediately cover the bottom half of the petri dish with the lid. Observe for 5 minutes and record any color changes that occur during that time. **CAUTION:** *Sulfuric acid is corrosive. If you spill any on your skin or clothing, rinse it off immediately with lots of cold water. Do not breathe the sulfur dioxide gas produced.*

6. Peel back the piece of clear adhesive tape from the access port. Rotate the lid so that the access port is over the left side of the petri dish and introduce one drop of 2.0 M H_2SO_4 onto each sample on that side of the dish. Record any color changes that occur.

all have a long linear chain of carbon atoms bonded together. The anthocyanin molecules, on the other hand, have a skeleton of carbon and oxygen atoms that are arranged in rings. In both cases, there is an alternation of double and single bonds throughout the molecules. The anthocyanins react with HSO_3^- ions as shown below.

(Red)

⇅

(Colorless)

Safety

Make sure students wear their goggles and lab aprons at all times during the investigation. Caution students to avoid contact with the sulfuric acid and ammonia solutions, and to avoid breathing ammonia vapors. Tell students to wash with large quantities of water any skin or clothing that comes into contact with these solutions.

The quantities of SO_2 gas released by lifting the lid of the petri dish are not dangerous except to someone allergic to sulfites. Students should be warned to avoid breathing these gases. Students who are allergic to sulfites may be excused from doing the investigation and given an alternative assignment. ■

Teaching Tips

The color changes that occur in the plant tissues and the time it takes for them to occur will vary greatly with the

Shifting Equilibria in Plant Tissues **263**

Lab 48 APPLICATION

Name _____

plant type, color, and even the geographic location where the plant was grown. A red rose may not fade with sulfur dioxide, and it will become slightly darker red when ammonia is added to the petri dish. Hydrangeas, petunias, and red cabbage are quite sensitive to sulfur dioxide, sulfuric acid, and ammonia.

Students may be confused about the double use of sulfuric acid. Explain that the reaction with sodium sulfite is solely to generate SO_2 gas, and the acid is consumed. The addition of the acid in Step 6 introduces H^+ ions.

This investigation actually contains several equilibrium reactions—the dissociation of sulfurous acid and the acid-base equilibrium involving ammonia are two examples. You may wish to discuss some or all of them, depending on the ability levels of your students.

The more obvious reaction is the addition of ammonia, which causes dramatic color changes in the anthocyanins. This reaction is unrelated to the presence of HSO_3^- ions, depending instead on the pH of the system. (You might mention that $NH_3(aq)$ is ammonium hydroxide.) Anthocyanins change from red to purple to blue as the concentration of H^+ ions decreases. Since students have not yet studied acids, bases, and pH in depth, you may wish to discuss briefly in class the results of Step 7 and the students' answers to Analysis and Conclusions Question 5.

Regardless of the depth to which you take the class discussions, emphasize to students that the plant pigments serve to give macroscopic evidence of reactions that are occurring at the submicroscopic level.

If there are color-blind students in your class, pair them with students who have full color perception.

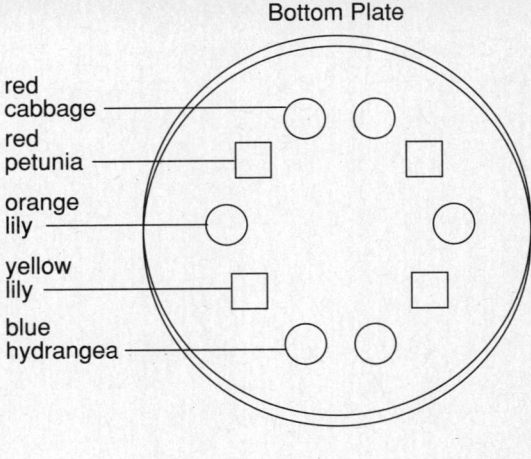

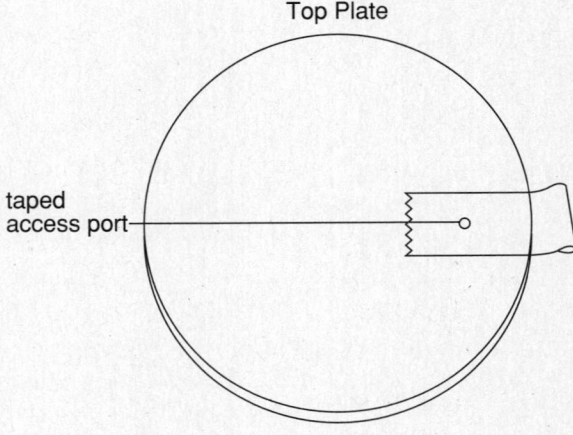

Figure 48–1 *Petri Dish with Plant Samples*

7. When all observations are completed, terminate the production of SO_2 gas by adding a few drops of 2.0 M $NH_3(aq)$ to the dish through the access port. Note the color changes that occur. **CAUTION:** *Ammonia is caustic. If you spill any on your skin, rinse it off immediately with plenty of cold water. Do not breathe the ammonia fumes.*

8. Wait about 5 minutes. Open the petri dish and use a wash bottle to flush the plant samples and solution from the bottom of the dish into the container provided by your teacher. Rinse the petri dish well with tap water and dry it with a paper towel. Clean up your work area and wash your hands before leaving the laboratory.

Name_____

Lab 48 APPLICATION

Observations (sample data)
DATA TABLE Color Changes in Plant Pigments

Plant Type and Original Color	SO_2	H_2SO_4	$NH_3(aq)$
red cabbage	fades	turns scarlet	turns green to blue
red petunia	fades	turns scarlet	turns green to blue
orange lily	fades to yellow	turns orange	turns deep orange
yellow lily	no change	no change	no change
blue hydrangea	turns red to colorless	turns scarlet	turns green to blue

Waste Disposal

The contents of the dishes will be neutralized by the students as they introduce the ammonia. The purpose of collecting the dish contents is to remove the plant solids before they find their way into the traps of the sink. Filter these solid pieces by pouring the mixture through a wire screen. The solution can be flushed down the drain with plenty of water, and the plant solids can be discarded in the solid waste. ■

Critical Thinking: Analysis and Conclusions

1. Assume that most of the yellow and orange colors in the samples are due to carotenoids. Which category of pigments appears to be most sensitive to discoloration due to SO_2 gas? (*Interpreting data*) Anthocyanins are more sensitive to bleaching by SO_2 gas. The yellow carotenoid pigments changed little or not at all.

2. Is there evidence that bleaching of the anthocyanins with the hydrogen sulfite ion is reversible? Explain. (*Interpreting data*) Bleaching of the anthocyanins is reversed by the addition of sulfuric acid, although the color that returns may differ from the original.

3. Look back at the equation for the reaction between the plant pigment and HSO_3^- ions given in the Introduction. In what direction would the equilibrium have to shift for the color to return? (*Making inferences*) The equilibrium has to shift to the left.

4. Look at the answer you wrote for Pre-Lab Discussion Question 4. Based on your data and keeping Le Chatelier's principle in mind, explain what caused the reaction to shift toward the re-formation of the red-colored anthocyanin molecule. (*Making inferences*) Adding H_2SO_4 increased the concentration of H^+ ions. According to Le Chatelier's principle, if the concentration of one of the products in an equilibrium reaction is increased, the reaction shifts toward the reactants.

5. In which direction did the addition of $NH_3(aq)$ appear to shift the equilibrium? Explain your reasoning. (*Making inferences*) $NH_3(aq)$ appeared to shift the equilibrium further to the left because the color intensified or changed. If the shift had been in the other direction, the system would have become colorless.

© Prentice-Hall, Inc.   *Shifting Equilibria in Plant Tissues*

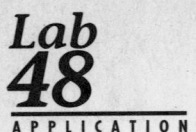

Name_____

Critical Thinking: Applications

1. Some fresh fruits and vegetables turn brown after being cut. This effect results when the pigment melanin in the plant tissue reacts with oxygen in the atmosphere. Hydrogen sulfite ions react with browned melanin to render it colorless and prevent further browning. Considering the results of your investigation, which types of fruits and vegetables are most likely to be protected from browning without affecting their natural colors? Explain. (*Making judgments*) Yellow fruits and vegetables are least likely to be bleached or faded by HSO_3^- ions. They seem to be unaffected by the reactions with SO_2 gas.

2. Suppose you were a fruit farmer or flower grower whose business was downwind of a coal-burning power plant (a source of SO_2 gas). What pollution problems would you have to deal with? Would the problem exist only when it rained? (*Applying concepts*) Non-yellow fruits and flowers grown downwind from a source of SO_2 gas would tend to be less colorful. The SO_2 gas would not have to be dissolved in rain water to cause the problem because the gas would produce HSO_3^- ions inside the plant tissue.

3. Acid-base indicators are colorful molecules that are sensitive to changes in acidity or alkalinity. They have predictably different colors at different levels of acidity values. Could anthocyanins, such as those found in red cabbage leaves, serve as indicators if they are extracted from the red cabbage tissue? Explain in light of your observations. (*Making judgments*) Anthocyanin pigments could serve as good indicators because they appear to be red in acidic solutions and violet or blue in basic solutions.

Going Further

Going Further

1. When fresh fruits and vegetables are cut with a dull knife or a serrated plastic knife, the tissues brown exceptionally fast. Fresh peaches, apricots, plums and apples are good examples of fruit to use. The yellow vegetables and fruits will be protected from browning but will not fade when exposed to sulfites.

2. Fruit Fresh is available at most grocery stores. If it is not available, a ground-up 250- or 500-mg vitamin C tablet dissolved in 100 mL of water will suffice.

1. Using the procedure from this investigation, design a controlled experiment to test whether hydrogen sulfite ions will efficiently prevent the browning of freshly cut fruit. Under the supervision of your teacher, carry out the investigation and present the results to your class.

2. Because some people are allergic to sulfites, a better method for preventing the browning of fruits is to bathe the fruits with vitamin C, ascorbic acid. This chemical is sold commercially in such products as Fruit Fresh. Design an investigation to compare the effect of bathing the fruits with a solution of Fruit Fresh (according to the directions on the package) with that of introducing hydrogen sulfite ions. Under the supervision of your teacher, carry out the investigation and report on your results.

Solubility Curve of KNO₃   Lab 49

Text reference: **Chapter 17**

Introduction

The maximum amount of solute that will dissolve in a given amount of solvent is called its solubility. What factors determine the solubility of a substance? Certainly the identity of the solute affects the amount of the substance that can dissolve. For example, sodium iodide is more soluble than sodium chloride in a given amount of water. The identity of the solvent also affects the solubility of a substance. Sodium chloride is highly soluble in water but not very soluble in ethanol. Temperature of the solvent is another factor affecting solubility. The solubility of most solids varies directly with temperature. In other words, the higher the temperature of the solvent, the more solute will dissolve—that is, the greater the solubility of the solid.

In this investigation, you will study the relationship between the solubility of potassium nitrate (KNO_3) and the temperature of the water solvent. Different amounts of KNO_3 will be dissolved in a given amount of water at a temperature close to its boiling point. You will observe each solution as it cools and note the temperature at which crystallization occurs. Crystallization indicates a saturated solution, or one that contains the maximum amount of KNO_3 in that amount of water. From this solubility data, a solubility curve for KNO_3 can be constructed.

Pre-Lab Discussion

Read the entire laboratory investigation and the relevant pages of your textbook. Then answer the questions that follow.

1. Define the following terms.

   solubility: The maximum amount of solute that will dissolve in a given amount of solvent under a given set of conditions.

   saturated solution: A solution containing the maximum amount of solute.

   unsaturated solution: A solution containing less than the maximum amount of solute.

   supersaturated solution: A solution containing more than the theoretical maximum amount of solute.

2. Determine the solubility of sodium sulfate, Na_2SO_4, in grams per 100 g of water, if 0.94 g of Na_2SO_4 in 20 g of H_2O results in a saturated solution.

$$\frac{0.94 \text{ g } Na_2SO_4}{20 \text{ g } H_2O} = \frac{x}{100 \text{ g } H_2O}$$

$$x = 4.7 \text{ g } Na_2SO_4$$

Materials (class of 30 in pairs)
- 30 pairs chemical splash goggles
- 30 laboratory aprons
- 60 test tubes, 18 mm × 150 mm
- 15 marking pens
- 15 test-tube racks
- 15 beakers, 400-mL
- 15 thermometers
- 15 hot plates
- 15 laboratory balances
- 350 g potassium nitrate (KNO_3)
- 15 graduated cylinders, 10-mL
- 300 mL distilled water
- 15 utility clamps
- 15 ring stands
- 15 stirring rods
- 15 test-tube holders

Time Required
80 minutes. To save time, you can begin heating the water before the class begins. You can assign different masses of KNO_3 to different teams for testing. The results can then be pooled.

Advance Preparation
Set out several reagent bottles containing potassium nitrate.

Introduction
Show the class some rock candy. Explain that it is made by heating water to boiling and adding a large quantity of sugar. When a string is suspended in the resulting solution and the solution is allowed to cool, crystals of sugar form around the string. This process takes advantage of the dependence of solubility on temperature.

Lab 49

3. Why is it necessary to warm the thermometer in Procedure Step 2 before placing it into the solutions? __A cool thermometer can cause premature cooling of the solution.__

4. A student stated that the solubility of potassium chloride, KCl, at 20°C was 36 g of KCl per 100 g of solution. What is wrong with this statement? __Solubility should be stated in grams of solute per 100 grams of solvent, not 100 grams of solution.__

5. How do you know when the solid is completely dissolved? __The solid is dissolved when it is no longer visible in the test tube.__

6. What special precautions should be taken while doing this investigation? __The hot plate and water will get very hot, so care should be taken to avoid contact with bare skin.__

Problem
How does the solubility of potassium nitrate depend on temperature?

Materials

chemical splash goggles
laboratory apron
4 test tubes, 18 mm × 150 mm
marking pen
test-tube rack
beaker, 400-mL
thermometer
hot plate

laboratory balance
potassium nitrate (KNO_3)
graduated cylinder, 10-mL
distilled water
utility clamp
ring stand
stirring rod
test-tube holder

Safety

Wear your goggles and lab apron at all times during the investigation. Do not touch the hot plate or heated water with your bare skin. Note the caution alert symbols here and with certain steps of the Procedure. Refer to page xi for the specific precautions associated with each symbol.

Procedure

1. Put on your goggles and lab apron. Label four test tubes 1–4 with a marking pen. Place them in a test-tube rack.

2. Fill a 400-mL beaker three-fourths full of tap water, place a thermometer in it, and heat the water on a hot plate until its temperature is about 90°C. **CAUTION:** *Do not touch the hot plate or heated water with your bare skin.* While you are waiting for the water to heat, go on to Steps 3 and 4.

Safety
Make sure students wear their goggles and lab aprons at all times during the investigation. Caution students about removing the hot test tubes from the water bath. They should do so only with test-tube holders. ■

Teaching Tips
Caution students to watch carefully for the first sign of crystallization. It usually occurs around the bottom of the test tube, especially around the bulb of the thermometer. If crystallization occurs too rapidly to observe,

3. Place the following masses of potassium nitrate (KNO₃) into the test tubes:

   2.0 g in test tube 1
   4.0 g in test tube 2
   6.0 g in test tube 3
   8.0 g in test tube 4

4. Add 5.0 mL distilled water to each test tube. Attach a utility clamp to a ring stand.

5. Place test tube 1 in the clamp and lower it into the hot water bath. Stir the KNO₃ solution with the stirring rod until the solid is completely dissolved. Remove the stirring rod and rinse it off. Loosen the utility clamp and, using a test-tube holder, remove the test tube.

6. One lab partner should place the warm thermometer from the hot water bath into test tube 1 while the other repeats Step 5 for test tube 2.

7. Watch test tube 1 for the first sign of crystallization and when it occurs record the temperature in the Data Table. Remove test tube 2 from the hot water bath and repeat Steps 6 and 7.

8. Repeat Steps 5–7 for test tubes 3 and 4.

9. Place all the test tubes back in the hot water bath and redissolve the solid. Flush the solutions down the drain with plenty of hot water. Turn off the hot plate. Clean up your work area and wash your hands before leaving the laboratory.

they can simply redissolve the KNO₃ by placing the test tube back in the water bath and repeating the step.

Waste Disposal
Potassium nitrate solutions can be safely flushed down the drain followed by plenty of warm water. ■

Observations (sample data)

DATA TABLE

Test Tube #	Temperature (°C)
1	26
2	50
3	67
4	76

Lab 49

Name _____

Calculations (based on sample data)

1. For each test tube, determine the solubility of KNO_3 in grams per 100 g H_2O.

    test tube 1: $\dfrac{2.0 \text{ g}}{5.0 \text{ g}} = \dfrac{x}{100 \text{ g}}$

    $x = 40.0 \text{ g}$

    test tube 2: $\dfrac{4.0 \text{ g}}{5.0 \text{ g}} = \dfrac{x}{100 \text{ g}}$

    $x = 80.0 \text{ g}$

    test tube 3: $\dfrac{6.0 \text{ g}}{5.0 \text{ g}} = \dfrac{x}{100 \text{ g}}$

    $x = 120.0 \text{ g}$

    test tube 4: $\dfrac{8.0 \text{ g}}{5.0 \text{ g}} = \dfrac{x}{100 \text{ g}}$

    $x = 160.0 \text{ g}$

Critical Thinking: Analysis and Conclusions

1. Construct a solubility curve for KNO_3 by graphing the mass of KNO_3 per 100 grams H_2O (solubility) versus temperature. Place temperature on the x-axis and solubility on the y-axis. Connect the points in a smooth curve. *(Interpreting data)*

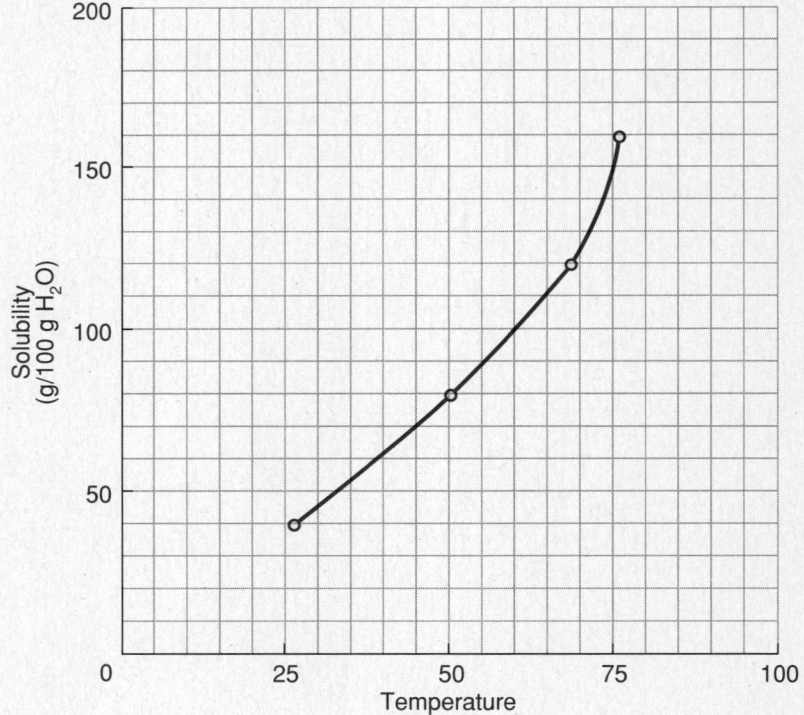

Figure 49–1

Name _____

Lab 49

2. Describe the relationship between the solubility of KNO_3 and the temperature of the solvent. *(Interpreting diagrams)* The solubility of KNO_3 varies directly with the temperature of the solvent.

3. Using your graph, determine how many grams of KNO_3 can be dissolved in 100 g of H_2O at the following temperatures: *(Interpreting diagrams)*

   35°C 54 g

   60°C 100 g

   70°C 125 g

Critical Thinking: Applications

1. Using your graph, predict whether the following solutions of KNO_3 would be considered saturated, unsaturated, or supersaturated. *(Making predictions)*

   75 g KNO_3/100 g H_2O at 40°C Supersaturated, since the plotted point is above the solubility curve.

   60 g KNO_3/100 g H_2O at 50°C Unsaturated, since the plotted point is below the solubility curve.

2. Sketch the general shape for a solubility curve for a gas. *(Applying concepts)* The graph shows an inverse relationship between the solubility of a gas and the temperature of the solvent.

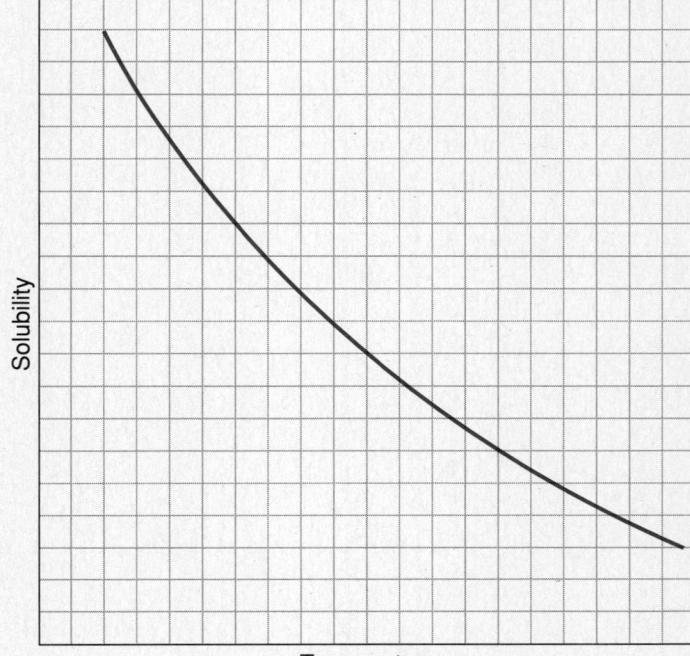

Solubility Curve of KNO_3

Lab 49

Going Further

1. A graph of the data should show an inverse relation between temperature and solubility, the opposite of the graph obtained from data in this investigation.

Going Further

1. Design a procedure to determine a solubility curve for lithium carbonate, one of the solutes whose solubility decreases with increasing temperature. With your teacher's supervision, conduct the experiment.
2. The dissolved oxygen content of water is extremely important to marine life. Investigate the solubility of oxygen in water in relation to temperature and relate that to the oxygen needs of various kinds of marine animals. Report your findings to the class.

Precipitates and Solubility Rules

Small Scale Lab 50

Text reference: **Chapter 17**

Introduction

What do geothermal vents have in common with a bathtub ring? The vents spew clouds of mineral-rich water from deep inside Earth into the ocean near mid-ocean ridges. A bathtub ring is a deposit formed from hard water and soap. Both involve the process of precipitation, the formation of insoluble or slightly soluble solids. When oppositely charged ions come in contact, they attract each other, and if that attraction is stronger than the ions' attraction to water, they form crystalline solids.

When two different ionic solutions with concentrations below their saturation points are combined and a precipitate forms, they have undergone a double replacement reaction in which one of the products is insoluble. The reaction of aqueous solutions of calcium chloride and zinc sulfate, for example, combines Ca^{2+} ions and SO_4^{2-} ions in a concentration above the saturation point of calcium sulfate. The formation of the precipitate is described by the following equation:

$$CaCl_2(aq) + ZnSO_4(aq) \rightarrow ZnCl_2(aq) + CaSO_4(s)$$

Insoluble salts can be identified by their low K_{sp} values (equilibrium dissociation constants). The identity of precipitates can also be deduced from the results of combining pairs of salt solutions, as you will do in this investigation. A comparison of the products from the combinations allows for the identification of any precipitates that form. Trends, called solubility rules, can also be found for some ions that tend to form precipitates more readily than others.

In this investigation, you will combine pairs of six given salt solutions and look for precipitates. After you write a chemical equation for each combination, you will attempt to deduce which products are precipitates, and also discover some common solubility rules.

Pre-Lab Discussion

Read the entire laboratory investigation and the relevant pages of your textbook. Then answer the questions that follow.

1. How many products are there in a double replacement reaction from which to choose the precipitate? __There are always two products from double replacement reactions.__

2. How can you recognize a precipitate when you see one? __The suspended solid precipitate that forms makes the solution cloudy.__

3. Why is it necessary to use different micropipets for different solutions? __Ions from one solution will contaminate others.__

Materials (class of 30 in pairs)
30 pairs chemical splash goggles
30 laboratory aprons
30 pairs latex gloves
90 micropipets
100 mL of each of the following 0.1 M solutions:
  sodium carbonate (Na_2CO_3)
  magnesium chloride ($MgCl_2$)
  copper(II) sulfate ($CuSO_4$)
  sodium nitrate ($NaNO_3$)
  silver nitrate ($AgNO_3$)
  potassium phosphate (K_3PO_4)
15 well plates, 24-well
15 marking pens
distilled water

Time Required
30–50 minutes. Fill the micropipets ahead of class to save time.

Advance Preparation
Make 0.1 M solutions by adding the following amounts of solutes to 100 mL distilled water:

Na_2CO_3: 1.1 g Na_2CO_3 or 1.2 g $Na_2CO_3 \cdot H_2O$
$MgCl_2$: 0.9 g
$CuSO_4$: 1.6 g $CuSO_4$ or 2.5 g $CuSO_4 \cdot 5H_2O$
$NaNO_3$: 0.9 g
$AgNO_3$: 1.7 g
K_3PO_4: 2.1 g

Have ready labeled containers in which to collect the waste silver solutions and precipitates.

Introduction
Demonstrate the appearance of a precipitate in a large test tube. $CaCl_2(aq) + Na_2CO_3(aq)$ work well. For a more spectacular and colorful demo try the following: Fill a large graduated cylinder 1/3 full of

1–2 M NaOH and dissolve in it 1–2 g of a soluble zinc salt ($ZnCl_2$ or $Zn(NO_3)_2$, etc.). Add phenol red indicator or other neutral pH indicator that gives two distinct colors. Pipet, or pour down the side, an equal volume of 0.5–1 M sulfuric acid with phenol red. The bright yellow acid floats on the more dense red base and a fluffy precipitate of amphoteric zinc hydroxide forms in the neutral partition zone. Swirling produces colorful whirlpool clouds of precipitate that dissolve as they rise or fall into the acid or base on either side of the partition zone.

Introduce precipitates by writing an equation for a double replacement reaction on the board. Ask students to suggest what makes some compounds insoluble. (They are insoluble because the individual ions can no longer be surrounded by water molecules—their attraction to each other is greater than their attraction to water.)

Safety

Make sure students wear their goggles and lab aprons at all times during the investigation. Caution students to wear gloves when handling silver nitrate solution. It is toxic and will stain skin and clothing. ■

Teaching Tips

Students will see the precipitates more easily if they keep the well plates on a dark surface.

Remind students that they need to do some detective work in analyzing the data. Without telling them what to do, ask questions that will lead them to examine the data closely for clues about which ions form soluble salts and which ones do not. They will also need to refer to Figure 17–9 in the text for the fact that potassium salts are always soluble.

Name _____

4. Why were the solutions made with distilled water? <u>Because tap water contains ions that may form precipitates.</u>

Problem
What are the precipitates that form from the reactions of salt solutions?

Materials
chemical splash goggles
laboratory apron
latex gloves
6 micropipets, containing the following 0.1 M solutions:
    sodium carbonate (Na_2CO_3)
    magnesium chloride ($MgCl_2$)

copper(II) sulfate ($CuSO_4$)
sodium nitrate ($NaNO_3$)
silver nitrate ($AgNO_3$)
potassium phosphate (K_3PO_4)
well plate
marking pen
distilled water

Safety

Wear your goggles and lab apron at all times during the investigation. Silver nitrate ($AgNO_3$) causes stains to skin and clothing. Wear gloves while handling silver nitrate. Note the caution alert symbols here and with certain steps of the Procedure. Refer to page xi for the specific precautions associated with each symbol.

Procedure

1. Put on your goggles and lab apron. Obtain micropipets of each solution and label them if necessary. Mark the well plates with the names of the six solutions in the manner shown in the Data Table.

2. Put on your gloves. In the upper left well of the well plate, combine the first pair of solutions, ten drops each, using the micropipets. Note the appearance or absence of a precipitate and record your observation in the Data Table. Write NR if there is no reaction.

3. Continue the solution combinations (15 total) until each of the solutions has been combined with all of the others. Record the results in the Data Table.

4. Dispose of any solutions containing silver compounds in a labeled container provided by your teacher.

5. Wash the well plate with soapy water, then rinse with tap water and finally distilled water. Clean up your work area and wash your hands before leaving the laboratory.

Small Scale Lab 50

Name _____

Observations (sample data)

DATA TABLE

	$AgNO_3$	$NaNO_3$	K_3PO_4	Na_2CO_3	$MgCl_2$
$CuSO_4$	PPT	NR	PPT	PPT	NR
$MgCl_2$	PPT	NR	PPT	PPT	
Na_2CO_3	PPT	NR	NR		
K_3PO_4	PPT	NR			
$NaNO_3$	NR				

Critical Thinking: Analysis and Conclusions

1. Complete the double replacement reaction equations for each combination. Leave blank spaces for the phase symbols. You will fill them in for Question 2. (*Applying concepts*)

   $CuSO_4(aq) + 2AgNO_3(aq) \rightarrow Ag_2SO_4(s) + Cu(NO_3)_2(aq)$

   $MgCl_2(aq) + 2AgNO_3(aq) \rightarrow 2AgCl(s) + Mg(NO_3)_2(aq)$

   $Na_2CO_3(aq) + 2AgNO_3(aq) \rightarrow Ag_2CO_3(s) + 2NaNO_3(aq)$

   $K_3PO_4(aq) + 3AgNO_3(aq) \rightarrow Ag_3PO_4(s) + 3KNO_3(aq)$

   $NaNO_3(aq) + AgNO_3(aq) \rightarrow$ N/A

   $CuSO_4(aq) + 2NaNO_3(aq) \rightarrow Cu(NO_3)_2(aq) + Na_2SO_4(aq)$

   $MgCl_2(aq) + 2NaNO_3(aq) \rightarrow Mg(NO_3)_2(aq) + 2NaCl(aq)$

   $Na_2CO_3(aq) + NaNO_3(aq) \rightarrow$ N/A

   $K_3PO_4(aq) + 3NaNO_3(aq) \rightarrow 3KNO_3(aq) + Na_3PO_4(aq)$

   $3CuSO_4(aq) + 2K_3PO_4(aq) \rightarrow Cu_3(PO_4)_2(s) + 3K_2SO_4(aq)$

   $3MgCl_2(aq) + 2K_3PO_4(aq) \rightarrow Mg_3(PO_4)_2(s) + 6KCl(aq)$

   $3Na_2CO_3(aq) + 2K_3PO_4(aq) \rightarrow 3K_2CO_3(aq) + 2Na_3PO_4(aq)$

   $CuSO_4(aq) + Na_2CO_3(aq) \rightarrow CuCO_3(s) + Na_2SO_4(aq)$

   $MgCl_2(aq) + Na_2CO_3(aq) \rightarrow MgCO_3(s) + 2NaCl(aq)$

   $CuSO_4(aq) + MgCl_2(aq) \rightarrow CuCl_2(aq) + MgSO_4(aq)$

2. Find those equations in Question 1 that have no precipitate in the products. The products in these equations are salts that must be soluble. Label each of these salts with (*aq*), like the reactants that are soluble. Search for these same soluble salts in the products of the reactions that did produce precipitates. Where they occur, label them (*aq*), and note that the other product must be the precipitate. Label the precipitates with the symbol (*s*) for "solid." Refer to Figure 17–9 in your text for any additional solubility rules you may need. (*Interpreting data*)

A dilute solution of ammonia water will help remove $AgNO_3$ stains from the skin. Commercially available laundry pretreatments may remove stains from clothing.

Waste Disposal

Silver compounds are regulated as hazardous waste (EPA waste #D011). Instruct students to use an eyedropper or micropipet to pull up the material in wells containing Ag^+ ions and precipitates and to deposit it into a clearly marked container. Similarly collect any $AgNO_3$ solution to be discarded from the micropipets. Precipitate the Ag^+ ions with excess NaCl solution. Filter out the precipitate and store for commercial disposal. Discard the filtrate. Recycle excess $CuSO_4$ solution by evaporating solvent from the solution in a plastic beaker to recover crystals. ■

3. There should still be equations for which no precipitate has been identified. To deduce solubility rules for use in identifying precipitates in these cases, fill in conclusions for the following list based on your lab results. (*Making predictions*)
   a. List all metal ions that are not part of any precipitate.
      Na^+ and K^+
   b. List all negative ions that are not part of any precipitate.
      NO_3^-
   c. List all metal ions that occur only in products that are precipitates.
      Ag^+
   d. List all metal ions sometimes found in a precipitate.
      Cu^{2+} and Mg^{2+}
   e. Use the list of generalities in a–d above to find which salts are the precipitates in the remaining cases.
      $Cu_3(PO_4)_2$ and $Mg_3(PO_4)_2$

Critical Thinking: Applications

1. Which metal ions of those encountered in this investigation would you expect to find contributing to precipitates formed on the ocean floor around geothermal vents? Explain your answer. (*Making predictions*) Ag^+ seems to precipitate most readily. Possibly Cu^{2+} and Mg^{2+}, if the appropriate negative ions are present.

2. Soaps often contain sodium stearate. (Stearate is a complex ion derived from fatty acids or fat.) If a precipitate forms when soap is dissolved in hard water (water containing Ca^{2+} and Mg^{2+} ions), what ion from the soap would you expect to find in the precipitate? Why? (*Making predictions*) The precipitate would contain stearate ion, because sodium salts are soluble.

Going Further

1. Check the table of K_{sp} values in a textbook or the *Handbook of Chemistry and Physics*.

Going Further

1. Look up the K_{sp} values for the precipitates in this lab and list them from the most to the least soluble.
2. Under the supervision of your teacher, prepare a saturated solution of NaCl by placing excess salt in water and stirring periodically until no more of the salt on the bottom dissolves. Adding drops of concentrated HCl to the saturated NaCl causes a precipitate to form. The precipitate has to be NaCl. Explain.

Investigating Hardness of Water

Small Scale Lab 51
APPLICATION

Text reference: **Chapter 17**

Introduction

Have you ever had trouble washing your hair or clothes because of hard water? Hard water contains calcium and magnesium ions that react with compounds in soaps and detergents to form insoluble salts. These insoluble salts may be familiar to you as "ring-around-the-tub." The ions dissolved in hard water also reduce the amount of suds made by soaps and detergents, diminishing the cleansing action of these products.

In this investigation, you will determine the amount of calcium ions present in a water sample by reacting it with $EDTA^{4-}$, or ethylenediaminetetraacetate. $EDTA^{4-}$ is a large carbon-based ion that can donate six electron pairs to form coordinate covalent bonds with calcium. In a coordinate covalent bond, one atom donates both electrons.

Figure 51–1 *Lewis Dot Diagram of $EDTA^{4-}$ Ion*

The reaction of EDTA with calcium occurs best in a basic solution. The negative ion of EDTA reacts with the positive calcium ions according to the following equation.

$$EDTA^{4-} + Ca^{2+} \rightarrow [Ca \cdot EDTA]^{2-}$$

In this reaction, the negative EDTA ion surrounds the positive calcium ion to form the complex ion $[Ca \cdot EDTA]^{2-}$ shown in Figure 51–2.

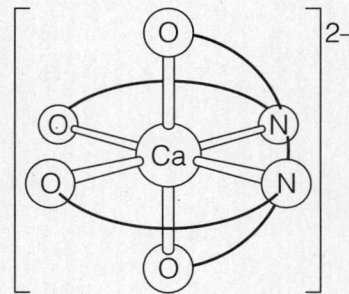

Figure 51–2 *Ball-and-Stick Model of $[Ca \cdot EDTA]^{2-}$*

Materials (class of 30 in pairs)

- 30 pairs chemical splash goggles
- 30 laboratory aprons
- 15 well plates, 24-well
- 15 marking pens
- 15 sheets of white paper
- 15 graduated cylinders, 10-mL
- 120 mL EDTA solution, 0.0030 M
- 15 sets of 6 labeled micropipets filled with the following solutions:
    - 60 mL EDTA solution, 0.0030 M
    - 30 mL distilled water
    - 60 mL tap water with Ca^{2+} ions
    - 60 mL Ca^{2+} solution, 0.0020 M
    - 30 mL buffer solution, pH 10
    - 15 mL calmagite indicator solution, 0.050%
- 15 plastic toothpicks
- 15 wash bottles with distilled water

Time Required

30 minutes.

Advance Preparation

Ca^{2+} solution: Dissolve 0.101 g dried $CaCO_3$ in 20 drops of 6 M HCl. Heat to dissolve. Dilute to 500 mL. CAUTION: *Hydrochloric acid is corrosive. Wear goggles, gloves, and an apron while working with it.*

If your tap water is not hard, add enough Ca^{2+} (0.350 g $CaCl_2 \cdot 2H_2O$/1000 mL) to make a usable solution. If well water is available, assign several different samples to students as alternate unknowns. You could also use labeled mineral waters.

Investigating Hardness of Water **277**

Lab 51 APPLICATION

Name _____

EDTA solution: Dissolve 0.560 g EDTA in 500 mL of water and add six drops of 0.10 M $Mg(NO_3)_2$ to enhance the endpoint. To make 0.10 M $Mg(NO_3)_2$, use 1.84 g magnesium nitrate dihydrate in 100 mL of solution. (A standard 0.10 M solution of EDTA can be purchased from scientific suppliers.)

The calmagite solution can be purchased from scientific suppliers as a 0.050% solution. Its blue color at pH 10 will change to red upon adding Ca^{2+} or Mg^{2+} ions.

The buffer solution of pH 10 can be made from 6.4 g NH_4Cl dissolved in 57.0 mL of aqueous ammonium hydroxide (15 M), then diluted to 100 mL. CAUTION: *Ammonium hydroxide is caustic. Wear goggles, gloves, and an apron while working with it.* Prepare the solution in an open flask in a well-ventilated area since vapors may cause splattering in a stoppered vessel. Store the buffer in a plastic bottle. A standard buffer solution of pH 10 can be purchased from scientific suppliers.

Fill the pipets. Retain excess solutions in small stock bottles from which the student pipets may be refilled.

Introduction

Depending on the geographical area, students may be familiar with the effects of hard water and may have water softeners in their homes. Discuss local conditions and compare them with those that would be characteristic of a community with a softer or harder water supply. Ask students who have had opportunities to travel to describe differences they may have noticed in other water supplies.

In a basic solution, the carboxylic acid groups of EDTA are ionized. Thus, the four carboxylate groups plus the two lone pairs of

In this investigation, you will analyze various water samples and measure the amount of EDTA required to remove all of the calcium ions from each sample. (Calmagite, a dye indicator, turns from red to blue when there are no uncombined calcium ions in a solution.) You will then be able to use your data to calculate the concentration of calcium in the water.

Pre-Lab Discussion

Read the entire laboratory investigation and the relevant pages of your textbook. Then answer the questions that follow.

1. What is the purpose of the solution in well B1? __It is used as a standard for color comparisons.__

2. Why are three trials used for each solution? __Three trials are made and the results averaged in order to reduce the effects of experimental error.__

3. How is the formation of bonds in a complex ion used to determine the concentration of calcium ions? __$EDTA^{4-}$ reacts with the calcium ions to form a complex ion. Calmagite is used as an indicator to show when all of the calcium ions have reacted. The amount of EDTA is used in a ratio that allows you to calculate the concentration of calcium ions.__

4. What is the purpose of the white paper? __The white paper makes it easier to see the color of the solution.__

5. What is a coordinate covalent bond? __It is a bond between two atoms in which one atom donates both electrons.__

Problem

How can the concentration of calcium ions in water be determined?

Materials

chemical splash goggles
laboratory apron
well plate
marking pen
sheet of white paper
6 micropipets, containing the following solutions:
    EDTA solution

distilled water
tap water with Ca^{2+} ions
Ca^{2+} solution
buffer solution
calmagite solution
plastic toothpick
wash bottle with distilled water
graduated cylinder, 10-mL

Safety

Wear your goggles and lab apron at all times during the investigation.
    If you spill EDTA or calmagite solution on your skin or clothing, rinse it off immediately with plenty of water and notify your teacher.

Name _____

Small Scale Lab 51 APPLICATION

Note the caution alert symbols here and with certain steps of the Procedure. Refer to page *xi* for the specific precautions associated with each symbol.

Procedure

1. Put on your goggles and lab apron. Using the marking pen, label the wells of the well plate from left to right along the top: 1, 2, 3, 4, 5, 6. Down the left side, label the top two rows of wells A and B. Place the well plate on a sheet of white paper.
2. Obtain micropipets containing the six solutions needed for the investigation.
3. Place 20 drops of distilled water in well B1. Throughout this investigation, be sure to count accurately the number of drops. Hold the pipets in the same vertical position whenever you are dispensing drops.
4. Test the indicator by adding four drops of buffer solution and one drop of indicator solution to well B1 and stirring with a plastic toothpick. The solution should be blue. If not, add one drop of EDTA to well B1. Rinse the toothpick with distilled water.

electrons on the nitrogen atoms make EDTA a hexadentate ligand.
Using a diagram or model, point out how coordinate covalent bonds form between $EDTA^{4-}$ and Ca^{2+}. Note that these bonds, like many other covalent bonds, are somewhat slow to form.

Safety
Make sure students wear their goggles and lab aprons at all times during the investigation. Remind students to wash spills and splashes of the Ca^{2+} and EDTA solutions with plenty of water. ■

Teaching Tips
Point out that the indicator color change is due to the reaction of the excess amount of Ca^{2+} ion with the calmagite.
You may need to remind students of the proper technique for dispensing drops.
Students may need to refill their micropipets with EDTA solution from the leftover stock.

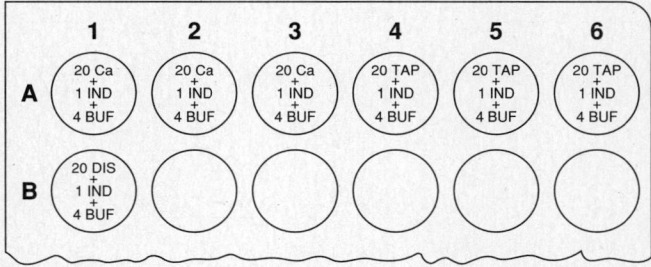

Figure 51–3

5. Place exactly 20 drops of the known Ca^{2+} solution in well A1. Record the concentration of the solution and the number of drops in Data Table 1. Then add four drops of buffer solution and one drop of indicator solution to well A1.
6. Add one drop of the EDTA solution to well A1 and stir. Continue adding EDTA one drop at a time until the solution turns the same color blue as the solution in well B1. The reaction takes time so you should add a drop, stir, and then wait a few seconds before adding another drop. In Data Table 1, record the number of drops of EDTA solution you added to well A1. Rinse the toothpick with distilled water.
7. Repeat Steps 5 and 6 using wells A2 and A3. Enter the data from these two wells in Data Table 1.
8. You will now determine the Ca^{2+} concentration in tap water. Place 20 drops of tap water in each of wells A4, A5, and A6. Record the number of drops placed in each well in Data Table 2. Add four drops of buffer solution and one drop of indicator solution to each of wells A4, A5, and A6.

© Prentice-Hall, Inc.   *Investigating Hardness of Water*   279

Name_____

9. Add the EDTA solution one drop at a time to well A4 and stir after each drop. Stop adding drops after the solution turns the same color blue as the solution in well B1. Repeat this procedure for wells A5 and A6. In Data Table 2, record the number of drops of EDTA solution added to each well.

10. Flush all of the chemicals down the drain with large amounts of water. Clean up your work area and wash your hands before leaving the laboratory.

Waste Disposal
The chemicals used in this investigation may be flushed directly down the drain with large quantities of water. ■

Observations (sample data)

DATA TABLE 1   EDTA with Known Ca^{2+} Solution

	Trial 1	Trial 2	Trial 3
Concentration of Ca^{2+} (mol/L)	2.0×10^{-3}	2.0×10^{-3}	2.0×10^{-3}
Number of drops of Ca^{2+} solution	20	20	20
Number of drops of EDTA solution	15	15	16
Ratio A	0.75	0.75	0.80

DATA TABLE 2   EDTA with Tap Water

	Trial 4	Trial 5	Trial 6
Number of drops of tap water	20	20	20
Number of drops of EDTA solution	11	10	11
Ratio B	0.55	0.50	0.55

Calculations (based on sample data)

1. For each trial, calculate the ratio of drops of EDTA solution to drops of known Ca^{2+} solution. Enter these values in Data Table 1 as Ratio A.

2. For each trial, calculate the ratio of drops of EDTA solution to drops of tap water. Enter these values in Data Table 2 as Ratio B.

3. Calculate the average ratio of drops for trials 1–3 and 4–6 respectively to obtain values for Ratio A_{avg} and Ratio B_{avg}.

   Ratio A_{avg} ___0.77___   Ratio B_{avg} ___0.53___

4. Calculate the concentration of Ca^{2+} in the tap water by using the following formula:

$$Ca^{2+}(\text{tap water}) = Ca^{2+}(\text{known solution}) \times \frac{\text{Ratio } B_{avg}}{\text{Ratio } A_{avg}}$$

$$2.0 \times 10^{-3} \text{ mol/L} \times \frac{0.53}{0.77} = 1.38 \times 10^{-3} \text{ mol/L}$$

280

Name _____

Critical Thinking: Analysis and Conclusions

1. For each trial of the solution with the known concentration of Ca^{2+} ions, calculate the percent deviation from Ratio A_{avg} using the following formula: *(Interpreting data)*

$$\text{Percent deviation} = \frac{\text{trial result} - \text{average value}}{\text{average value}} \times 100\%$$

   Trial 1 __−2.6%__   Trial 2 __−2.6%__   Trial 3 __3.9%__

2. For each trial of the solution with the unknown concentration of Ca^{2+} ions, calculate the percent deviation from Ratio B_{avg}. *(Interpreting data)*

   Trial 4 __3.8%__   Trial 5 __−5.7%__   Trial 6 __3.8%__

3. Why are there differences in results from trial to trial? *(Making inferences)* __Answers will vary. Variations could be due to technique differences.__

4. How does the hardness of the tap water compare to that of the known solution of Ca^{2+} ions? *(Making comparisons)* __Answers will vary depending on the water supply. The less EDTA needed, the softer the water.__

5. Based on your data, how is the number of drops of EDTA needed for a color change related to the hardness of water? *(Making inferences)* __The more drops of EDTA needed, the harder the water is.__

6. Why is it possible to use the formula in Calculations Step 4 to find the concentration of Ca^{2+} ions in the tap water? *(Making inferences)* __The formula works because the concentration of the EDTA is constant.__

Critical Thinking: Applications

1. Design an experiment using soap or detergent to measure the hardness of water. *(Designing experiments)* __Hard water reduces the sudsing ability of soaps and detergents. Hardness can be measured by seeing how many drops of soap or detergent it takes to produce suds that do not collapse immediately.__

2. You have probably seen advertisements for cleaning products that remove tub and tile stains caused by hard water. What type of chemicals do you think might be in the active ingredients of these cleaners? *(Making predictions)* __The cleaners would have to contain compounds that dissolve the insoluble salts.__

Name _____

Going Further

1. Find out how water softeners work to remove Ca^{2+} ions from hard water. Using the techniques you learned in this investigation, test the effectiveness of three different water softeners on a sample of hard water.
2. Research the occurrence of hard water in different regions of the country. Find out where hard water is most common and what geographical conditions contribute to the cause.

Name _____ Date _____ Class _____

Properties of Acids and Bases

Lab 52

Text reference: Chapter 18

Introduction

Acids and bases are common chemicals in everyday life. Many products—from shampoos to fruit juices, from medicines to cleaning agents—derive much of their usefulness from their activity as acids or bases. Acids can be classified as substances that ionize in aqueous solutions to produce hydronium ions, H_3O^+. Acids react with metals to produce hydrogen gas and turn litmus paper red. Bases can be classified as substances that dissociate in aqueous solutions to produce hydroxide ions, OH^-. Bases turn litmus paper blue and feel slippery. The strengths of acids and bases depend on the extent to which they ionize, or dissociate. Strong acids or bases dissociate almost completely, while weak acids or bases dissociate to a lesser degree.

In this investigation you will observe some reactions of acids and bases with each other, with other compounds, and with various indicators. From your observations, you should be able to describe some of the characteristic properties of acids and bases.

Pre-Lab Discussion

Read the entire laboratory investigation and the relevant pages of your textbook. Then answer the questions that follow.

1. What is an acid? **A substance that produces hydronium ions (H_3O^+) when dissolved in water.**

2. What is a base? **A substance that produces hydroxide ions (OH^-) when dissolved in water.**

3. What is an indicator? What indicators will you be using in this experiment? **Indicators are weak acid or base dyes whose colors are sensitive to hydronium ion concentration. Red and blue litmus paper, pH paper, and phenolphthalein are used.**

4. Write balanced chemical equations for the reactions that occur when the following solutions are mixed:

   a. $HNO_3(aq) + NaOH(aq) \rightarrow$ **$H_2O(l) + NaNO_3(aq)$**

   b. $2HCl(aq) + Ca(OH)_2(aq) \rightarrow$ **$2H_2O(l) + CaCl_2(aq)$**

5. What safety precautions need to be observed when handling acids and bases? **Wear goggles, an apron, and latex gloves. Do not allow skin or clothing to come into contact with acids or bases.**

Materials (class of 30 in pairs)
30 pairs chemical splash goggles
30 laboratory aprons
30 pairs latex gloves
15 marking pens
15 well plates, 24-well
200 mL hydrochloric acid (HCl), 3.0 M
100 mL hydrochloric acid (HCl), 1.0 M
100 mL acetic acid ($HC_2H_3O_2$), 1.0 M
100 mL sodium hydroxide (NaOH), 0.5 M
45 pieces of red litmus paper
45 pieces of blue litmus paper
75 pieces of pH paper
15 dropper bottles of phenolphthalein, 1%
15 microspatulas
15 g mossy zinc (Zn)
30 pieces of magnesium ribbon (Mg), 1-cm lengths
15 g iron filings (Fe)
15 g copper wire or sheet (Cu)
75 test tubes, 18 × 150 mm
15 test-tube racks
15 wooden splints
matches
15 1-hole rubber stoppers to fit test tubes
15 pieces of glass tubing with right-angle bends
100 mL limewater
15 g calcium carbonate ($CaCO_3$)
30 micropipets

Time Required
60–90 minutes. To shorten the investigation, assign Parts A, B, C, and D to different groups of students, and pool the data.

Advance Preparation
Prepare the right-angle glass bends and insert in rubber stoppers. CAUTION: *Wear goggles and apron while*

© Prentice-Hall, Inc.

Properties of Acids and Bases **283**

Lab 52

heating glass. Let glass cool completely before touching it.
  Prepare the solutions as follows. Be sure to add acid to water in all acid preparations. CAUTION: Wear goggles, latex gloves, and an apron. Acids are corrosive. Bases are caustic. Both can cause serious injury if they come into contact with skin or eyes. Wash spills and splashes with plenty of water.

3.0 M HCl: Mix 1 part of 12.0 M HCl to 3 parts distilled water.

1.0 M HCl: Mix 8.6 mL 12.0 M HCl and enough distilled water to make 100 mL.

1.0 M $HC_2H_3O_2$: Mix 5.7 mL of 17.0 M $HC_2H_3O_2$ (glacial acetic acid) with enough water to make 100 mL of solution.

0.5 M NaOH: Mix 2.0 g NaOH with enough water to make 100 mL.

1% phenolphthalein: purchase, or use 1.0 g per 100 mL of 50% ethanol.

Limewater: Add solid $Ca(OH)_2$ to distilled water until no more dissolves. Filter off any remaining solid. Limewater can be purchased commercially.

Acid and base solutions should be placed in dropper bottles or micropipets, one set for each lab group. Cut up the metal pieces ahead of time. Small pieces—about the size of the head of a match—are sufficient. Try to cut pieces of the same size so that surface area is not a factor affecting relative reaction rates.

Introduction
Begin with a discussion about familiar acids and bases that students have encountered as foods, cosmetics, medicines, cleaning agents, etc. Have students generate a list of properties of acids and bases derived from their experience. Review molarity, em-

6. For what gas is the reaction product being tested in Step 8? Step 10? <u>A test for the presence of hydrogen gas is done in Step 8. A test for the presence of carbon dioxide gas is done in Step 10.</u>

7. Give an example of each of these reactions from the investigation:
   a. neutralization <u>HCl + NaOH → NaCl + H_2O</u>
   b. double replacement <u>$CaCO_3$ + 2HCl → H_2CO_3 + $CaCl_2$</u>
   <u>The H_2CO_3 decomposes to produce H_2O and CO_2.</u>

Problem
How do you observe the properties of acids and bases?

Materials
chemical splash goggles
laboratory apron
latex gloves
marking pen
well plate
hydrochloric acid (HCl), 3.0 M and 1.0 M
acetic acid ($HC_2H_3O_2$), 1.0 M
sodium hydroxide (NaOH), 0.5 M
litmus paper, red and blue
pH paper
phenolphthalein
microspatula

zinc (Zn)
magnesium ribbon (Mg)
iron filings (Fe)
copper wire or sheet (Cu)
5 test tubes, 18 × 150 mm
test-tube rack
wooden splint
match
rubber stopper, 1-hole, fit with right-angle bend glass tubing
limewater
calcium carbonate ($CaCO_3$)
2 micropipets

Safety

Wear your goggles and lab apron at all times during the investigation. Acids are corrosive and bases are caustic; avoid contact with skin or clothing. Wash spills and splashes with plenty of cold water. Note the caution alert symbols here and with certain steps of the Procedure. Refer to page xi for the specific precautions associated with each symbol.

Procedure
Part A: Using Indicators

1. Put on your goggles and lab apron. Add five drops of each of the following solutions to separate labeled depressions in the well plate: 1.0 M HCl; 1.0 M $HC_2H_3O_2$; 0.5 M NaOH. **CAUTION:** Handle solutions with care. Acids are corrosive and bases are caustic. They can cause serious injury if they come into contact with skin or eyes. Wash spills and splashes with plenty of water.

2. Place a drop of each solution onto a piece of red litmus paper. Record your observations in Data Table 1. Discard the litmus paper in a solid waste container.

3. Repeat Step 2, using blue litmus paper and then pH paper. Record your observations.
4. Add one drop of phenolphthalein to each solution. Record your observations. Discard the solutions by rinsing them down the drain with plenty of water. Rinse the well plate with water and dry.

Part B: Reactions of Acids with Metals

5. To four separate, clean, labeled depressions in your well plate, add a small piece of zinc, magnesium, iron, and copper.

6. To each of these depressions, add enough 1.0 M HCl to cover the metal. Observe and compare the relative speed of reaction of the metals with the acid. Record your observations in Data Table 2.
7. Repeat Steps 5 and 6, using clean wells but substituting 1.0 M acetic acid ($HC_2H_3O_2$) for 1.0 M HCl. Compare the reactivity of each metal with $HC_2H_3O_2$ to its reactivity with HCl. Record your observations. Discard the contents of the well plate by putting the metals into a solid waste container using the microspatula and rinsing the solutions down the drain. Rinse and dry the well plate.
8. Add a small amount of zinc to a depression in your well plate. Cover the zinc with 1.0 M HCl. As the reaction proceeds, hold an inverted test tube over the zinc for about two minutes. Without turning the test tube upright, quickly insert a burning splint into the test tube. Record your observations. Discard the contents of your well plate as you did in Step 7. Clean and dry the well plate.

Part C: Reactions of Acids with Carbonates

9. Put on your latex gloves. Half fill a clean test tube with limewater solution. Into a second test tube, place a small amount of calcium carbonate ($CaCO_3$). Obtain from your teacher a rubber stopper with a right-angle bend of glass tubing.

10. Add enough 3.0 M HCl to cover the $CaCO_3$. **CAUTION:** *Acids are corrosive. They can cause serious injury if they come into contact with skin or eyes. Wash spills and splashes with plenty of water.* Insert the rubber stopper into the test tube containing $CaCO_3$ and HCl. Place the open end of the glass tubing into the limewater. Record your observations. Discard the solutions and place any leftover $CaCO_3$ into the solid waste container. Clean the test tube.

Part D: Neutralization

11. Using a micropipet, add ten drops of 1.0 M HCl to a clean test tube. Add one drop of phenolphthalein. Test with pH paper. Record your observations.
12. Using a second micropipet, add 0.5 M NaOH to the acid, one drop at a time. After the addition of each drop, swirl the test tube to thoroughly mix the contents. Count and record the total

Properties of Acids and Bases

Lab 52

Name _____

number of drops of NaOH needed to cause a permanent color change. Once the color change is observed, test the solution again with pH paper. Record your results. Pour the solution down the drain and clean the test tube.

13. Clean up your work area and wash your hands before leaving the laboratory.

Waste Disposal
Neutralize acid solutions with sodium hydrogen carbonate and then flush down the sink with water. ■

Observations (sample data)

DATA TABLE 1 Reactions with Indicators

Solution	Red litmus	Blue litmus	pH paper	Phenolphthalein
1.0 M HCl	no effect	turns red	1	colorless
1.0 M $HC_2H_3O_2$	no effect	turns red	1	colorless
0.5 M NaOH	turns blue	no effect	13	turns pink

DATA TABLE 2 Speed of Reaction with Metals

Metal	1.0 M HCl	1.0 M $HC_2H_3O_2$
zinc	fast	very slow
magnesium	very fast	slow
iron	slow	NR
copper	NR	NR

Test results with burning splint: __A loud pop occurs and drops of liquid form at the mouth of the test tube.__

Test results with limewater: __The limewater becomes cloudy.__

pH of acid solution: __1__

Number of drops of 0.5 M NaOH added: __20__

pH of neutral solution: __about 7__

Critical Thinking: Analysis and Conclusions

1. For each metal that reacted with HCl, write a balanced chemical equation. (*Interpreting data*)

   Mg(s) + 2HCl(aq) → $MgCl_2$(aq) + H_2(g)

   Zn(s) + 2HCl(aq) → $ZnCl_2$(aq) + H_2(g)

   2Fe(s) + 6HCl(aq) → 2$FeCl_3$(aq) + 3H_2(g)

2. For each metal that reacted with $HC_2H_3O_2$, write a balanced chemical equation. (*Interpreting data*)

   $Mg(s) + 2HC_2H_3O_2(aq) \rightarrow Mg(C_2H_3O_2)_2(aq) + H_2(g)$

   $Zn(s) + 2HC_2H_3O_2(aq) \rightarrow Zn(C_2H_3O_2)_2(aq) + H_2(g)$

3. List the reactivity of the metals in decreasing order (fastest to slowest). (*Making comparisons*) magnesium, zinc, iron, copper

4. Explain the difference in reaction rates of a given metal with the two different acids. (*Drawing conclusions*) Since HCl dissociates to a greater degree than $HC_2H_3O_2$, HCl produces a greater concentration of hydronium ions to react with the metal. Therefore, the reactions with HCl were more rapid than they were with $HC_2H_3O_2$.

5. Explain the differences in volumes (number of drops) of HCl and NaOH required to produce a neutral solution in Part D. (*Making comparisons*) One mole of HCl neutralizes one mole of NaOH. Because the molarity of the HCl was twice the molarity of the NaOH, twice as much NaOH was needed to neutralize the acid.

Critical Thinking: Applications

1. Describe the type of reaction that occurs between certain metals and an acid. (*Applying concepts*) A single replacement reaction occurs in which the metal replaces hydrogen in the acid.

2. What is the effect of acid rain on statues made of marble (calcium carbonate)? (*Making inferences*) The acid dissolves the marble, forming calcium salts and carbonic acid.

3. Based on your data, write a brief paragraph summarizing some properties of acids and bases. (*Using the writing process*) Acids turn litmus paper red, react with some metals to produce hydrogen gas, and neutralize bases. Bases turn litmus paper blue, turn phenolphthalein pink, and neutralize acids.

Going Further

1. Research the effects of acid rain on lakes. Find out the impact of increased acidity on living organisms in a lake. Report on how acid rain is neutralized in some lakes by natural processes or human intervention.
2. Design an experiment to test the effects of acidic and basic soils on plant growth.

Name _____ Date _____ Class _____

Comparing Acid Strengths

Small Scale Lab **53**

Text reference: **Chapter 18**

Introduction

You know from everyday experience that there are several ways to make things stronger. One way is just to use more of a material. Glass used for tables is much thicker than the glass in windows, and much stronger. A sheet of steel 0.5 cm thick is not nearly as strong as one that is 3.0 cm thick. Mixing two or more substances together is another way to increase the strength of the resulting material. Metals, such as gold for jewelry or stainless steel, are made stronger by the addition of other materials.

The strength of acids is a different matter, though. Strength depends upon how many hydrogen ions (H^+), or more properly hydronium ions (H_3O^+), are present in a liter of an acid solution. In turn, this ion concentration depends upon the degree of dissociation of the acid molecules when they dissolve in water. Strength is not a measure of the solution concentration. You will see in this investigation that two different acids, hydrochloric and acetic, can have the same solution concentration but different strengths.

In this investigation, you will work with five different concentrations of hydrochloric acid (HCl) and acetic acid (CH_3COOH, sometimes written as HAc, where "Ac" stands for the acetate ion, CH_3COO^-), ranging from 0.1 M through 0.00001 M. The first three concentrations (in decreasing order) will be provided by your teacher. You will prepare the other two solutions by further diluting some of the 0.001 M samples. When all the concentrations have been readied, you will put 1-mL samples of the acids in the wells of a well plate. In Part A, you will observe and compare the reactivity of magnesium metal and magnesium carbonate in the acid samples. In Part B, you will use some common indicators to compare the concentrations of H_3O^+ ions in the solution samples.

Pre-Lab Discussion

Read the entire laboratory investigation and the relevant pages of your textbook. Then answer the questions that follow.

1. How many moles of HCl are in 2.0 mL of 0.001 M HCl?

   mol HCl = molarity × volume = 0.001 mol/L × 0.0020 L = 2 × 10⁻⁶ mol HCl

2. If 2.0 mL of 0.001 M HCl is diluted with 18.0 mL of distilled water, what will be the molarity of the new solution?

   M HCl = mol/volume (L) = 2 × 10⁻⁶ mol HCl/0.0200 L = 0.0001 M HCl
   or
   molarity₁ × volume₁ = molarity₂ × volume₂
   0.001 mol/L × 0.0020 L = M₂ × 0.0200 L; M₂ = 0.0001 M HCl

Materials (class of 30 in pairs)
- 30 pairs chemical splash goggles
- 30 laboratory aprons
- 15 marking pens or pencils
- 90 beakers, 50-mL
- 60 micropipets
- 2 L distilled water
- 15 graduated cylinders, 25-mL
- 60 mL 0.1 M HCl
- 60 mL 0.01 M HCl
- 90 mL 0.001 M HCl
- 60 mL 0.1 M CH_3COOH
- 60 mL 0.01 M CH_3COOH
- 90 mL 0.001 M CH_3COOH
- 15 glass stirring rods
- 15 well plates, 24-well
- 15 pairs scissors
- 15 strips of magnesium (Mg), 6 cm
- 15 g magnesium carbonate ($MgCO_3$)
- 100 mL orange IV indicator
- 100 mL methyl orange indicator

Time Required

90 minutes. The time can be shortened if you group the students into teams of four and have one pair of students prepare the hydrochloric acid dilutions and the other pair prepare the acetic acid dilutions. Each team can then give half of their prepared solutions to the other for use in testing. If you use this cooperative team approach, the amounts used in the student section are sufficient for testing by both student pairs.

Advance Preparation

You will need to prepare the 0.1 M, 0.01 M, and 0.001 M dilutions for both acids. The 0.1 M HCl is made by adding 8.55 mL of concentrated HCl (12 M stock) to enough

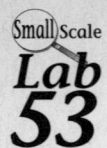

Lab 53

Name_____

distilled water to make a 1-L solution. When preparing the 0.01 M HCl solution, add 100.0 mL of the 0.1 M acid to enough distilled water to again make a 1-L solution. The same procedure can be used for preparing the 0.001 M HCl solution, if you start with 100.0 mL of the 0.01 M acid. The acetic acid solutions can be prepared the same way, but you will need to start with 5.7 mL of the concentrated CH_3COOH (17 M stock) added to enough distilled water to make 1 L for the initial 0.1 M sample. CAUTION: *Wear goggles, apron, and gloves when working with HCl and CH_3COOH.*

Cut off as many 5–6 cm lengths of magnesium ribbon as you have student pairs in your class. The students can then cut the short lengths of ribbon into the 5 mm × 5 mm pieces needed in the investigation.

Both indicators can be prepared by dissolving 0.1 g of the powdered solid in 100 mL of distilled water.

Introduction

There are numerous everyday examples of acid chemistry familiar to your students. Cleaning agents, car batteries, and tropical fish aquaria are all examples with which students may be acquainted. It is important to discuss at least one such example with your students so their ideas about acids can emerge. Students most generally perceive the difference between strong and weak acids as a matter of concentration. You might choose to explore this idea by discussing the use of vinegar in salad dressings, noting that vinegar is about 5 percent acetic acid. If spilled on a table cloth, will the salad dressing—or for that matter, pure vinegar—eat a hole in the fabric? Why or why not? What would

3. What important feature of HCl allows you to infer that the concentration of H_3O^+ ions of each HCl solution is numerically equal to the value of the concentration expression? For all practical purposes, HCl dissociates completely when it dissolves in water, which means that nearly every molecule of gaseous HCl reacts with water to form H_3O^+ ions and Cl^- ions.

4. Although the concentrations of acids in this investigation are very low, what precautions should be taken when working with them? All acids are corrosive. Care should be taken to avoid contact with the skin. Even at these low concentrations, eye damage could result if any acid splashes into the eyes.

Problem

How can the strengths of acids be determined?

Materials

chemical splash goggles
laboratory apron
marking pen or pencil
6 beakers, 50-mL
4 micropipets
distilled water
graduated cylinder, 25-mL
samples of the following
   solutions:
    0.1 M HCl
    0.01 M HCl
    0.001 M HCl

0.1 M CH_3COOH
0.01 M CH_3COOH
0.001 M CH_3COOH
glass stirring rod
well plate
scissors
strip of magnesium (Mg)
magnesium carbonate ($MgCO_3$)
orange IV indicator
methyl orange indicator

Safety

Wear your goggles and lab apron at all times during the investigation. Dilute solutions of hydrochloric and acetic acids are irritating to skin and may damage clothing. Methyl orange and orange IV may stain skin and clothing. Wash spills and splashes with plenty of cold water.

Note the caution alert symbols here and with certain steps of the Procedure. Refer to page *xi* for the specific precautions associated with each symbol.

Procedure

Part A

1. Put on your goggles and lab apron.

290   © Prentice-Hall, Inc.

2. Clean and rinse each item of glassware with a small amount of distilled water. Pour the rinse water down the drain. With the marking pencil, label three 50-mL beakers *0.001 M, 0.0001 M,* and *0.00001 M* respectively. Label two micropipets for use with the HCl and CH$_3$COOH.

3. Refer to Figure 53–1 in completing the dilutions through Step 6. Carefully pour distilled water into a 25-mL graduated cylinder until the water level is exactly 18.0 mL. Obtain 6.0 mL of 0.001 *M* hydrochloric acid (HCl) from your teacher and place it in the 50-mL beaker labeled *0.001 M.* Using the micropipet labeled *HCl,* add 0.001 *M* HCl to the distilled water in the graduated cylinder until the level of the mixture is exactly 20.0 mL. Retain the unused 0.001 *M* HCl in the beaker. Pour this new mixture, now at 0.0001 *M* concentration, into the 50-mL beaker labeled *0.0001 M,* stir, and retain. **CAUTION:** *Hydrochloric acid is corrosive. Care should be taken to avoid contact with your skin or clothing. If contact does occur, rinse with plenty of water and notify your teacher.*

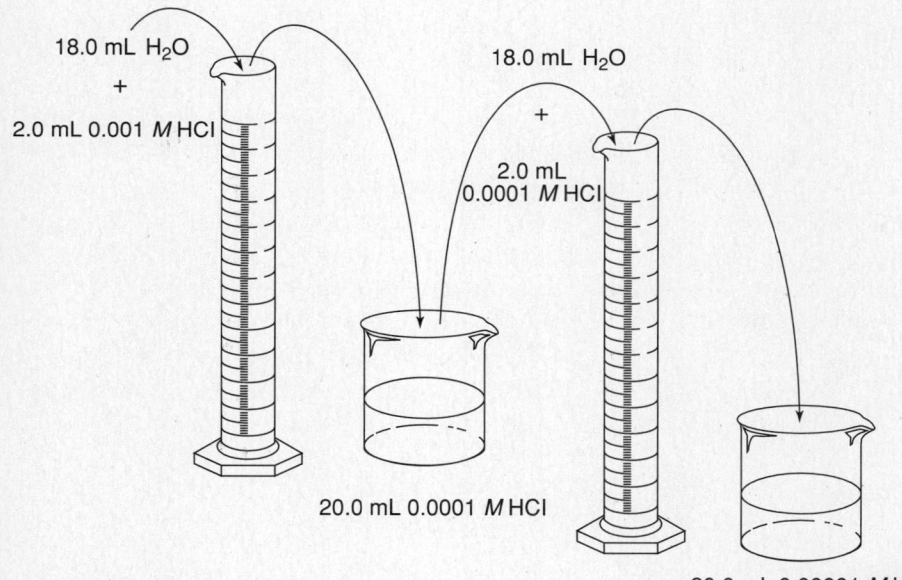

Figure 53–1

4. After rinsing the graduated cylinder, stirring rod, and micropipet, add 18.0 mL of distilled water to the graduated cylinder as you did in Step 3. Using the micropipet, add 0.0001 *M* HCl to the distilled water until the level of the mixture is exactly 20.0 mL. Retain the unused 0.0001 *M* HCl in the beaker. Pour this new mixture, now at 0.00001 *M* concentration, into the 50-mL beaker labeled *0.00001 M,* stir, and retain.

5. Obtain 4-mL samples of 0.1 *M* and 0.01 *M* HCl from your teacher and set them aside, arranged along with the beakers containing the other three samples, in decreasing order of concentration.

happen with a 5 percent HCl solution? A discussion of this type provides an opportunity for students to see that their views about acids generally need to be revised.

Safety

Make sure students wear their goggles and lab aprons at all times during the investigation. Although students will be working with dilute solutions of the acids, they should avoid spills and splashes and wash any spilled acid with cold water. ■

Teaching Tips

Demonstrate the colors of the indicators associated with particular acid strengths. Orange IV (Tropeolin 00) gives a sharp color change (red to yellow) over a pH range of 1 through 3. Methyl orange (Orange III or Tropeolin D) gives a sharp color change (red to orange-yellow) over a pH range of 3 through 4.5.

Use the block form of magnesium carbonate. Small pieces can be broken off and given to the students, who in turn can break the carbonate into smaller, match-head–sized pieces. If powdered magnesium carbonate is used, the reaction rate is often too fast for students to make comparisons.

When the students are ready to add the magnesium metal and magnesium carbonate, it is important that they do not try to do everything at once. Advise them to put the magnesium metal pieces in both the HCl and CH$_3$COOH samples as quickly as possible. They should observe the reactions, noting in particular differences between the acids, as well as differences from one concentration to the next for a given acid. After the magnesium metal reactions have stopped (or at least 2 minutes have passed), the magnesium

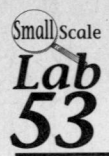

carbonate can be added to the other acid samples. There are no time constraints for the students when they use the indicators.

This investigation requires great care in carrying out the dilutions, both on the instructor's part in preparing the three stock solutions, and on the students' part in completing the final two dilutions. If the dilutions are done with precision, the observable patterns for both the reaction rates of the solids and the color changes with the indicators reveal a decrease in strength for the acids.

Since, for all practical purposes, the dissociation of hydrochloric acid is complete, a 0.1 M HCl solution has a 0.1 M concentration of hydronium ions. For the acetic acid the results are quite different. Acetic acid dissociates only slightly. For the 0.1 M sample, the dissociation is about 1.3 percent, and the pH of the solution is about 2.9. Although the percent dissociation of a weak acid actually increases as it becomes more dilute (a question of equilibrium), it is still very slight, and the pH of acetic acid remains considerably less than that of like concentrations of HCl.

With careful observations it is possible for the students to see that the rates of reaction for the magnesium metal and magnesium carbonate differ from one acid concentration to the next. If the differences between two samples are too subtle, remind the students to take a wider view. For example, the rates of reaction in both 0.1 M acid solutions are faster than in the 0.00001 M solutions. The more important observation is to compare the rates of reaction between the two different acids. It should be evident that the rate of reaction for either magnesium metal or

 6. Complete the same procedure and dilution scheme carried out in Steps 2–5 using acetic acid (CH_3COOH). **CAUTION:** *Acetic acid is corrosive. Care should be taken to avoid contact with your skin or clothing. If contact does occur, rinse with plenty of water and notify your teacher.*

7. Using the Data Tables as guides, label the well plate columns with numbers 1–5 and the rows with letters A–D. Place about 1 mL of the 0.1 M HCl in the first wells in rows A and C (wells A1 and C1). Proceed to place 1-mL samples of the remaining HCl concentrations, in decreasing order of concentration, in the other wells in rows A and C. Be certain to rinse the micropipet with distilled water when changing from one concentration to another.

8. Use the same procedure for the acetic acid, placing the designated samples in rows B and D. Be certain to use the acetic acid micropipet and to rinse it with distilled water when changing from one concentration to another.

9. From a larger piece of magnesium ribbon, cut ten pieces approximately 5 mm × 5 mm in size. Place one magnesium metal piece in each of the wells in rows A (with HCl) and B (CH_3COOH). Observe the rate of reaction of the metal in each well. Note if the rate of reaction is faster in one acid than in the other. Note as well if there is an observable pattern for the rate of reaction in the five samples of each of the acids. Observe for at least 2 minutes. Record your observations in Data Table 1.

10. Using pieces of $MgCO_3$ about the size of a match head, place one sample in each of the wells of rows C and D. Make the same observations as you did in Step 9 and record in Data Table 1.

 11. Pour the liquids down the drain and rinse the well plate and sink with running water. Be certain to recover any unreacted metal and dispose of it according to your teacher's directions.

Part B

 12. Label the two remaining micropipets for use with the orange IV and methyl orange indicators. With the well plate again clean, fill the wells in rows A–D as you did in Part A. **CAUTION:** *Hydrochloric and acetic acids are corrosive. Care should be taken to avoid contact with your skin or clothing. If contact does occur, rinse with plenty of water and notify your teacher.*

13. With the appropriately labeled micropipet, add a drop of orange IV indicator to each acid sample in rows A and B. Following the same procedure, add methyl orange indicator to the wells in rows C and D.

14. Observe the colors that result in each of the wells and record them in Data Table 2.

 15. Pour all the liquids down the drain and rinse the sink with running water. Clean up your work area and wash your hands before leaving the laboratory.

Name_____

Observations (sample data)

DATA TABLE 1 Reactions of Mg and MgCO₃ with Acid Samples

		1	2	3	4	5
		0.1 M	0.01 M	0.001 M	0.0001 M	0.00001 M
A	HCl + Mg	fastest	then	rate	decreases	→
B	HAc + Mg	moderate	then	rate	decreases	→
C	HCl + MgCO₃	fastest	then	rate	decreases	→
D	HAc + MgCO₃	moderate	then	rate	decreases	→

DATA TABLE 2 Color Changes Using Indicators

		1	2	3	4	5
		0.1 M	0.01 M	0.001 M	0.0001 M	0.00001 M
A	HCl + orange IV	reddish	turning	to yellow	→	→
B	HAc + orange IV	yellow	becoming	fainter	yellow	→
C	HCl + methyl or	dark red	turning	reddish	orange	yellow
D	HAc + methyl or	reddish	becoming	orange	yellow	→

magnesium carbonate in 0.1 M HCl is faster than in 0.1 M CH₃COOH. It will be much harder, and in fact quite subjective, to see that the rate of reaction in 0.001 M HCl is about the same as in 0.1 M CH₃COOH. There will probably be less subjectivity in comparing the color of the solutions when the indicators are added, with the 0.001 M HCl about the same color as the 0.1 M CH₃COOH.

The expression pH was introduced by the Danish chemist S.P.L. Sorensen. The p in the expression comes from the first letter of potenz, the German word for potency. The pH of an acid is then the potency (concentration) of the H⁺ ion.

Waste Disposal

All solutions may be washed down the drain with plenty of water. Remind students to first recover any unreacted pieces of metal. ■

Critical Thinking: Analysis and Conclusions

1. Did the rate of reaction of the magnesium metal appear to be faster in one acid than in the other? Explain your answer. *(Interpreting data)* The magnesium metal reacted faster in HCl. In any two samples of like concentrations of the acids, the magnesium metal reacted faster in HCl than in CH₃COOH.

2. Did the rate of reaction of the magnesium carbonate appear to be faster in one acid than in the other? Explain your answer. *(Interpreting data)* The magnesium carbonate reacted faster in HCl. In any two samples of like concentrations of the acids, the magnesium carbonate reacted faster in HCl than in CH₃COOH.

3. Based upon your results in Part A, what can you say about the strength of the acid samples in column 1, rows A–D? In subsequent columns? On what do you base your answer? *(Drawing conclusions)* The strength of the samples in column 1 is different, since both the magnesium metal and magnesium carbonate reacted more rapidly in HCl than in CH₃COOH. These reactions suggest HCl is the stronger acid.

© Prentice-Hall, Inc.

Comparing Acid Strengths

4. In terms of relative concentrations of H_3O^+ ions, describe what the colors of orange IV and methyl orange indicate. *(Making inferences)* As the H_3O^+ ion concentration decreases, the color of the indicators gets more yellow.

5. Based on your data, which of the two acids dissociates more fully in water? *(Drawing conclusions)* HCl dissociates more fully than CH_3COOH.

6. Do you have evidence indicating whether any one sample of the HCl has a strength about the same as any one sample of CH_3COOH? Explain. Yes. The color patterns with both indicators generally show a match between the 0.001 *M* (or possibly 0.0001 *M*) HCl and 0.1 *M* CH_3COOH.

Critical Thinking: Applications

1. Based on your observations, which side of the following equations are favored? Explain your reasoning. *(Applying concepts)*

$$HCl(g) \rightleftharpoons H^+(aq) + Cl^-(aq)$$

$$HAc(g) \rightleftharpoons H^+(aq) + Ac^-(aq)$$

In the first reaction the right side is favored. The observations indicated a high concentration of hydrogen ions. In the second reaction the left side is favored, since the observations indicated a low concentration of hydrogen ions.

2. Muriatic acid, a solution of HCl and water, is used to clean hearths or house sidings. Suppose a store clerk tells you that muriatic acid is perfectly safe to use because it is such a weak acid. Is the clerk correct? Write a paragraph explaining your answer. *(Using the writing process)* No. HCl is a strong acid. The clerk probably means that muriatic acid is a dilute solution, and therefore less dangerous than a more concentrated form of HCl. In all cases, however, it is important to read the label and follow the manufacturer's instructions for handling and use of the chemical.

Going Further

1. Under your teacher's supervision, conduct a similar investigation to compare the relative strengths of some other common acids, for example, nitric acid, citric acid, and oxalic acid.

Going Further

1. If you want to make available some other acids, the following dilutions can be used. Add 6.4 mL of concentrated nitric acid, HNO_3 (17 *M* stock), to water to make 1 L of total solution for a 0.1 *M* concentration. You may also add 5.6 mL of sulfuric acid, H_2SO_4 (18 *M* stock), to water in the same way to have a 0.1 *M* solution, but remember that this is a polyprotic acid, and the pH of dilute solutions is not as straightforward as with the HCl or HNO_3. Make 0.1 *M* solutions of oxalic acid by adding 12.6 g of oxalic acid to enough water to make 1 L, and 0.1 *M* citric acid solution can be made by adding 21.0 g of citric acid to water to make 1 L of solution.

Name _____ Date _____ Class _____

Making Table Salt

Lab 54
APPLICATION

Text reference: **Chapter 18**

Introduction

Table salt has been an important commodity throughout history. Its use in preserving foods for long periods of time made salt so valuable that it at times served as the basis of some economic activities and even societal customs. For example, *salarium* (Latin) is the term used to describe the money given to Roman soldiers to purchase salt. The English word *salary* comes from that expression. Seating at a royal table was based upon the relative position of the salt on the table, with people seated "above the salt" having a higher rank than people seated "below the salt."

Most of the table salt (sodium chloride) used today is obtained from underground deposits, either by mining or by pumping water into the deposits and returning the salt solution to ground level for separation. Sea salt is another source of sodium chloride. Sea salt is obtained by evaporating the water from a salt-water solution, leaving behind the precipitated solid. Even today in some parts of the world, sea salt is recovered using the heat energy of the sun and a centuries-old technique. Salt water is placed in bowl-like depressions on the surfaces of large rocks. Over a matter of days the water is evaporated, leaving behind the crystalline salt for collection.

Another way to obtain common table salt involves a process quite different from either mining or the evaporation of existing salt water. Many acid-base reactions yield salts as one of the products. In this investigation, you will react known quantities of hydrochloric acid (HCl) and solid sodium hydroxide (NaOH). The products of this reaction are sodium chloride (NaCl) and water. When the reaction ends, the water is evaporated, leaving table salt as the remaining product. You will be able to calculate the theoretical yield of NaCl and compare it to your actual yield. You also will conduct a flame test for sodium and a precipitate reaction for chlorine to give evidence that the solid product is table salt.

Pre-Lab Discussion

Read the entire laboratory investigation and the relevant pages of your textbook. Then answer the questions that follow.

1. Write the equation for the reaction between solid sodium hydroxide and hydrochloric acid.

   $NaOH(s) + H^+(aq) + Cl^-(aq) \rightarrow Na^+(aq) + Cl^-(aq) + HOH(l)$

2. How many moles of HCl are in 50.0 mL of a 1.0 M HCl solution?

   $\frac{1.0 \text{ mol}}{1 \text{ L}} \times 0.050 \text{ L} = 0.050 \text{ mol HCl}$

Materials (class of 30 in pairs)
30 pairs chemical splash goggles
30 laboratory aprons
30 pairs latex gloves
15 laboratory balances
15 beakers, 250-mL
15 marking pens or pencils
750 mL hydrochloric acid, 1.0 M
15 graduated cylinders, 100-mL
15 micropipets
15 wash bottles containing distilled water
15 pairs forceps
30 g sodium hydroxide pellets (NaOH)
15 large watch glasses
15 stirring rods
5 hot plates
15 scoopulas
15 lab burners
15 flame-test loops
15 small test tubes
15 test-tube racks
15 micropipets containing silver nitrate solution (AgNO₃), 0.1 M
beaker for the AgNO₃ micropipets

Time Required
70 minutes over two days.

Advance Preparation
Prepare the 1.0 M HCl by adding 85.5 mL of concentrated HCl to enough distilled water to make a 1-L solution. CAUTION: *Concentrated hydrochloric acid is extremely corrosive. Wear goggles, gloves, and an apron when working with it.* Prepare the 0.1 M AgNO₃ solution by adding enough distilled water to 1.70 grams AgNO₃ to make 100.0 mL of total solution. Micropipets containing about 1.0 mL of the AgNO₃ solution can then

Making Table Salt **295**

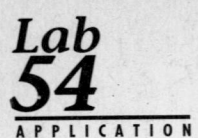

Lab 54 APPLICATION

be filled and placed upside-down in a labeled beaker. CAUTION: *Silver nitrate is toxic and stains skin and clothes. Wear gloves when working with it.* Have ready a container in which to collect the waste silver solutions.

Introduction

Place a 50-mL beaker about one-third full of 1.0 M NaOH in front of the class. Place some phenolphthalein indicator in the beaker. Tell the class the pink color indicates the presence of a base but don't tell them the identity of the base. Show the class another beaker containing 1.0 M HCl. Tell them the beaker contains an acid but don't identify the specific acid. Slowly add it to the first beaker until the color disappears. Ask your students to identify the products in the beaker. They will protest that they can't see anything in the beaker. Give them a hint by saying that whenever an acid and a base react, a salt is produced. Write the formulas of the reactants on the board. Most of them will be able to figure out the products are sodium chloride and water. Whenever an acid reacts with a base, as in this investigation, the result is water and a salt.

Safety

Make sure students wear their goggles and lab aprons at all times during the investigation. Caution students that 1.0 M HCl is an irritant and to wash spills and splashes immediately with plenty of water. Latex gloves are required when working with NaOH pellets and AgNO₃ solutions. ■

Name _____

3. How many moles of NaOH will completely react with 50.0 mL of 1.0 M HCl?

   $$0.050 \text{ mol HCL} \times \frac{1 \text{ mol NaOH}}{1 \text{ mol HCl}} = 0.050 \text{ mol NaOH}$$

4. What is the maximum mass of NaOH that will react with 50 mL of 1.0 M HCl?

   $$0.050 \text{ mol NaOH} \times \frac{40 \text{g NaOH}}{1 \text{ mol NaOH}} = 2.0 \text{ g NaOH}$$

5. Which of the two substances in this investigation, HCl or NaOH, is the limiting reactant? _The NaOH is the limiting reactant because when the reaction ends, all the NaOH will be used up, with excess HCl still present._

6. What special precautions should you take when working with the sodium hydroxide pellets? _Sodium hydroxide is caustic. The solid should be handled with gloves and forceps._

Problem

How can table salt be recovered from the reaction between sodium hydroxide and hydrochloric acid?

Materials

chemical splash goggles
laboratory apron
latex gloves
laboratory balance
beaker, 250-mL
marking pen or pencil
hydrochloric acid, 1.0 M
graduated cylinder, 100-mL
micropipet
wash bottle containing distilled water
forceps

sodium hydroxide pellets (NaOH)
large watch glass
stirring rod
scoopula
lab burner
flame-test loop
small test tube
test-tube rack
micropipet containing silver nitrate solution (AgNO₃), 0.1 M

Safety

Wear your goggles and lab apron at all times during the investigation. Sodium hydroxide pellets are very caustic and can burn skin. Silver nitrate is toxic and can stain skin and clothing. Wear latex gloves when handling these chemicals. Tie back loose hair and clothing when working with a flame. Hydrochloric acid is corrosive. It will irritate skin and damage clothing. Avoid spills and splashes. If any of these reagents contact the skin, wash with plenty of cold water and notify your teacher. Hydrochloric acid releases irritating fumes when heated. Heat HCl in the fume hood. Dispose of silver compounds according to your teacher's instructions.

Lab 54 APPLICATION

Note the caution alert symbols here and with certain steps of the Procedure. Refer to page *xi* for the specific precautions associated with each symbol.

Procedure

Part A

1. Put on your goggles and lab apron.

2. Find the mass of a 250-mL beaker. With a marking pen, mark your beaker with your team number for later identification. Record the mass in the Data Table.

3. Precisely measure 50.0 mL of 1.00 M HCl in a 100-mL graduated cylinder. Use a micropipet to add the final drops of HCl to ensure precision in the measurement of the acid. Carefully pour the acid into the beaker. Rinse the graduated cylinder two times with 2–3 mL of distilled water, adding the rinse water to the acid in the beaker. **CAUTION:** *Hydrochloric acid is corrosive. It will irritate skin and damage clothing. Avoid spills and splashes. Wash any acid that comes in contact with your skin with plenty of cold water.*

4. Put on latex gloves. In your answer to Question 4 of the Pre-Lab Discussion, you found the maximum mass of NaOH that will react with 50.0 mL of 1.0 M HCl. Using forceps, place enough sodium hydroxide pellets on the balance that the mass is in excess of this value. Remove pellets one at a time until the mass of the sodium hydroxide pellets is just below the maximum mass that would react. Find the mass of these pellets precisely. Record the mass in the Data Table. **CAUTION:** *Sodium hydroxide pellets are very caustic. Wear gloves. If any sodium hydroxide touches your skin, wash with plenty of cold water and notify your teacher.*

5. Carefully add the NaOH pellets to the HCl in the beaker. Loosely cover the beaker with a large watch glass to prevent any spattering. If the reaction appears to be completed and there is still some solid NaOH unreacted in the bottom of the beaker, gently stir the acid with a stirring rod until all the solid NaOH disappears. Rinse off the stirring rod with distilled water, allowing the rinse water to flow into the beaker. When the reaction is completed, remove the watch glass, noting first to see if there is any liquid on the underside. If liquid has collected, rinse it off with distilled water, letting the rinse water flow into the beaker.

6. Give the beaker to your teacher for drying overnight. **CAUTION:** *The beaker in the fume hood will release irritating HCl vapors. Do not breathe in the fumes. Clean up your work area and wash your hands before leaving the laobratory.*

Part B

7. Put on your goggles and lab apron. Obtain your beaker and find its new mass. Record the mass in the Data Table.

Teaching Tips

Tell students to dip the flame-test loops into distilled water if they are having trouble getting the NaCl to stick. Provide several small beakers of distilled water for this purpose. (The procedure for flame tests is introduced in Investigation 10.) Commercial laundry pre-treatment sprays may help to remove stains caused by $AgNO_3$.

The watch glass can serve two purposes in this investigation. Initially the students can use the watch glass as a weighing container when finding the mass of the NaOH. First have them find the mass of the watch glass, and then the mass of the watch glass and NaOH. Later the watch glass can be used as a cover for the beaker during the reaction. Note that it must be a large watch glass.

You may want to go through the strategy for finding the mass of the NaOH to be used in the reaction. In Question 4 of the Pre-Lab Discussion, the students calculate the maximum mass (2.00 grams) of NaOH that can react with 50.0 mL of 1.0 M HCl. In the investigation, a mass a little less than the maximum is to be used so that the limiting reactant is NaOH and not the HCl. One method for finding the mass of the NaOH is to have the students find the mass of the weighing container and then adjust the balance so it reads 2 grams heavier. If more than 2 grams of NaOH pellets are added, pellets can be removed one at a time until there are less than two grams in the weighing container. The precise mass can then be determined.

The moisture picked up by the NaOH pellets gives the appearance that the mass change due to the water will be large. In fact, the mass change is quite small.

Making Table Salt 297

Lab 54 APPLICATION

Generally it takes more than 10 minutes to have even a 1 percent increase in mass due to the absorbed water.

You should carry out the evaporation of the solution from the beakers in fume hoods (there will be a small amount of HCl fumes). Set up hot plates in the hoods. After the reactions are done, have the students place the beakers on the hot plates. Remind them to remove the watch glasses being used as covers. Check to see that each team has marked its beaker for later identification. Bring the solutions to a very gentle boil and slowly evaporate the water. It will take several hours or more. When a major portion of the liquid has been evaporated, reduce the temperature setting of the hot plates to prevent excessive spattering. After drying, set the beakers aside to be returned to the students on the following day.

Waste Disposal

Silver compounds are regulated as hazardous waste (EPA waste #D011). Collect any remaining silver solution and precipitate the Ag⁺ ions with excess NaCl solution. Filter out the precipitate and store in a marked container for commercial disposal or shipment to a secure land fill. Discard the filtrate. ∎

8. Using a scoopula, scrape some of the white solid free from the bottom of the beaker for testing. Leave it at the bottom of the beaker.

9. Light a burner and adjust the flame to a medium intensity. **CAUTION:** *Tie back loose hair and clothing when working with a flame.* Press the flame-test loop into the white solid to partially coat the loop. Move the loop to the top of the flame's inner cone and observe the resulting color. Repeat until a definite color has been identified. Record the color in the Data Table.

10. Scoop a pinch or two of the white solid into a small test tube, add distilled water, and stir with a stirring rod until the solid dissolves.

11. Put on latex gloves. Using a micropipet containing 0.1 M silver nitrate (AgNO$_3$) solution, add a small amount to the test tube and place the test tube in a test-tube rack. **CAUTION:** *Silver nitrate is toxic and can stain skin and clothing. Wear latex gloves when handling it.* Observe and record the color of the precipitate in the Data Table.

12. Discard the precipitate from the test tube according to your teacher's instructions. The remaining solid in the beaker can be dissolved in water and poured down the drain. Clean up your work area and wash your hands before leaving the laboratory.

Observations (sample data)

DATA TABLE

initial mass of beaker (g)	95.78
mass of NaOH (g)	1.81
final mass of beaker and residue (g)	98.29
flame-test color	yellow
precipitate color	white

Calculations (based on sample data)

1. Calculate the mass of the solid in the beaker.
   98.29 g − 95.78 g = 2.51 g

2. Calculate the theoretical yield of salt based upon the amount of sodium hydroxide used.

   $$1.81 \text{ g NaOH} \times \frac{1 \text{ mol NaOH}}{40 \text{ g NaOH}} \times \frac{1 \text{ mol NaCl}}{1 \text{ mol NaOH}} \times \frac{58.5 \text{ g}}{1 \text{ mol NaCl}} = 2.65 \text{ g NaCl}$$

3. Calculate the percentage yield of sodium chloride.
   $\frac{2.51 \text{ g}}{2.65 \text{ g}} \times 100 = 94.7\%$

Name _____

Lab 54 APPLICATION

Critical Thinking: Analysis and Conclusions

1. What did the result of the flame test indicate about the solid product? *(Interpreting data)* The solid produced a yellow color while burning, indicating the presence of sodium.

2. When the solid product was dissolved in water and $AgNO_3$ was added to the solution, what did the resulting precipitate indicate? *(Interpreting data)* The white precipitate was AgCl, which is highly insoluble in water. Its presence indicated the presence of chloride ions.

3. When the reaction was completed (but before the water was evaporated), do you think the remaining solution was acidic, basic, or something else? Explain. *(Making inferences)* Since the NaOH was the limiting reactant, there would have been excess HCl. The remaining solution would be acidic with a small amount of HCl left unreacted.

4. If you had used exactly 2.00 grams of NaOH and 50.0 mL of 1.00 M HCl in the reaction, how would you characterize the nature of the remaining solution? *(Drawing conclusions)* Since the reaction would be between an acid and a base in equimolar amounts, a neutral solution would have resulted.

Critical Thinking: Applications

1. Do the flame and silver precipitate tests prove the solid product is NaCl? *(Making judgments)* While the tests are consistent with NaCl, two tests alone are not conclusive. Further tests would be necessary to make a definitive identification.

2. What other tests might be conducted to prove the product is sodium chloride? *(Designing experiments)* Density, solubility in water or other liquids, and the effect on the freezing and boiling points of water are all possible tests.

3. Do you think the method employed in this investigation could be used to make very large amounts of common table salt? Explain. *(Making judgments)* There are several problems with the procedure including the need to start with large amounts of solid NaOH, the difficulty of working with large amounts of HCl, the extensive energy needed to evaporate the water, and the need to purify the NaCl.

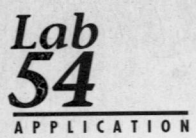

Going Further

1. Baking soda and baking powder react to produce CO_2 gas, which creates the fluffy texture. Baking powder comes mixed with its own acid while baking soda requires an acid be supplied from the food.
2. Scheele discovered ways to separate organic acids based on the solubility of their salts. In this way, he was able to isolate many organic acids, such as tartaric, lactic, citric, and oxalic acids.

Going Further

1. Baking soda ($NaHCO_3$) and baking powder (baking soda + tartaric acid) are salts used in baking to produce fluffy breads, cakes, and muffins. What is the chemical reaction that these two substances undergo? How do they produce the fluffy texture in baked goods? Take a trip to a local bakery to find out how baking soda and powders are used.
2. Research the life and work of Carl Wilhelm Scheele (1742–1786), a Swedish pharmacist and chemist. What was his contribution to the understanding of acids?

Determining the pH of an Unknown

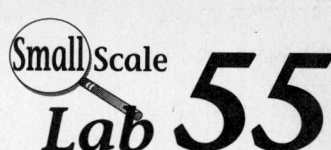

Small Scale Lab 55

Text reference: **Chapter 19**

Introduction

The pH scale uses numbers from 1 to 14 to describe how acidic or basic a solution is. A pH value of 7 is neutral (neither acidic nor basic), a pH value below 7 is acidic, and a pH value above 7 is basic. The lower the pH, the more acidic the solution. The higher the pH, the more basic the solution.

Indicators are often used to measure pH. An indicator is a weak acid (or base) that undergoes dissociation in a known pH range. In this range, the acid (or base) is a different color from its conjugate base (or acid). The three pH indicators used in this investigation are phenolphthalein, a natural indicator, and universal indicator. A natural indicator is one that is made from a material produced by a plant or an animal. A natural indicator can be made from many things, including red cabbage, grapes, and roses. Universal indicator is a mixture of several indicators, chosen so that a range of colors appears over a wide range of pH values.

In this investigation, you will observe the color changes that take place when each indicator is put into eleven solutions that have known pH values ranging from pH 2 to pH 12. You will then use your data as the basis for determining the pH of an unknown solution provided by your teacher.

Pre-Lab Discussion

Read the entire laboratory investigation and the relevant pages of your textbook. Then answer the questions that follow.

1. What is the range of pH values of an acidic solution? <u>Less than 7.</u>

2. What is the range of pH values for a basic solution? <u>>7 through 14.</u>

3. Why does an indicator change colors at different pH values?
<u>Because the ionized form has a different color than the nonionized form.</u>

4. What precautions should you take when dealing with acidic and basic solutions? <u>Wear goggles and a lab apron. Do not let the solutions come in contact with skin or clothing. Wash splashes and spills with plenty of cold water.</u>

Problem

How can the pH of an unknown solution be determined using acid-base indicators?

Materials (class of 30 in pairs)

30 pairs chemical splash goggles
30 laboratory aprons
15 sets of 11 micropipets containing about 1 mL of buffer solutions of pH 2 to 12
15 sets of micropipets containing about 1 mL of:
 phenolphthalein
 natural indicator
 universal indicator
 unknown solution
well plate, 96-well

Time Required

30 minutes.

Advance Preparation

The buffer solutions can be easily made by dissolving buffer capsules in water. Buffer capsules are sold by science supply companies.

Use the buffer solutions as the unknowns. Label them with letters other than A, B, or C or with numbers greater than 12.

Natural indicators can be made from one of a number of different foods or flowers, such as grape juice, turnip skin, plum skin, blueberries, roses, violets, and geraniums. They are red in the acidic range, and blue-green to green in the basic range. To prepare the indicator, chop up one of the foods or flowers into small pieces, add enough ethanol (ethyl alcohol) to cover the solid matter, and let sit in a fume hood overnight. Be sure no flames are in use in the laboratory. (Alternatively, the chopped-up pieces can be boiled in water for 20 minutes.) Separate the liquid from the solid matter with a

Small Scale Lab 55

Name _____

strainer or filter paper. If the indicator's color is very pale, boil away some of the liquid to concentrate the indicator.

Introduction

You can start by telling the students how you made the natural indicator they will be using. Let them know that there are many natural dyes that have properties of an indicator. You may also wish to review the concept of buffers and the role they play in the investigation. Buffers are conjugate acid-base pairs that have the capacity to maintain a constant pH when other acids or bases are added. They will be studied again in Chapter 27 (The Chemistry of Life).

Safety

Make sure students wear their goggles and lab aprons at all times during the investigation. Some solutions are toxic if ingested. This is a good time to remind students not to taste anything in the laboratory. Caution students to wash spills and splashes with plenty of cold water. ■

Teaching Tips

Remind students of the proper technique for adding solutions to the well plate. The tips of the micropipets should never touch the material in the wells. You can save on materials by having several groups of students share one set of micropipets.

Not all students will discern every color exhibited by the universal indicator. You may wish to discuss in class the data that students obtain for row C. If there are any color-blind students in the class, match them with partners who have normal color vision.

If you wish, student groups can use several different natural indicators and report the results to the class.

Materials

chemical splash goggles
laboratory apron
11 micropipets containing solutions numbered by pH
well plate

3 micropipets, containing the following:
   phenolphthalein
   universal indicator
   natural indicator
micropipet containing unknown solution

Safety

Wear your goggles and lab apron at all times during the investigation. Acids are corrosive and bases are caustic. Indicators may stain skin and clothing. Handle all chemicals with care. Avoid spills and contact with your skin. Wash spills and splashes with plenty of cold water. Note the caution alert symbols here and with certain steps of the Procedure. Refer to page *xi* for the specific precautions associated with each symbol.

Procedure

1. Put on your goggles and lab apron. Add five drops of solution 2 to the first three wells of column 2 of your well plate (wells A2, B2, and C2). For columns 3 to 12 of your well plate, repeat using solutions 3 to 12. See Figure 55–1. **CAUTION:** *Acids are corrosive and bases are caustic. Avoid spills and contact with your skin. Wash spills and splashes with plenty of cold water.*

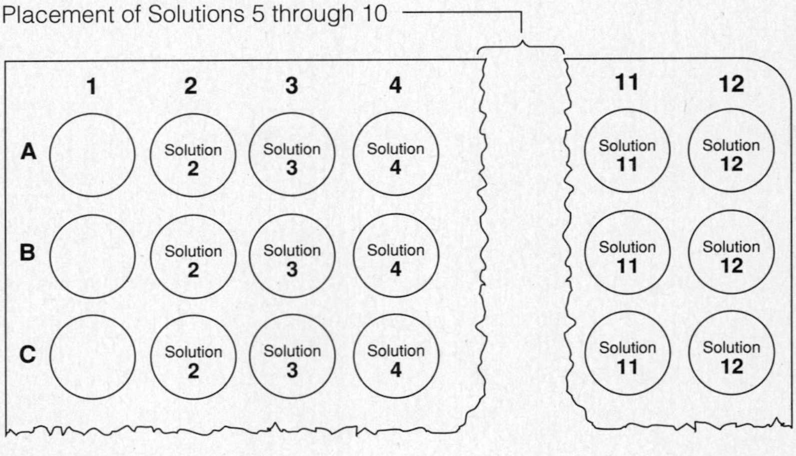

Figure 55–1

2. Add three drops of phenolphthalein indicator to wells A1 through A12. (Although well A1 is empty, a solution will be added to it in a later step.) Record in the Data Table any color changes you observe. If no color is seen, record *colorless* in the Data Table.

302

Name_____

Small Scale Lab 55

3. Add three drops of the natural indicator to wells B1 through B12. Record in the Data Table any color changes you observe.
4. Add three drops of universal indicator into well C1 through C12. Record in the Data Table any color changes you observe.
5. Obtain from your teacher a solution of unknown pH. Record the solution's identification number in the Data Table. Add five drops of the unknown to the first three wells in column 1 (wells A1, B1, and C1).
6. Compare the color of your unknown in well A1 to the colors in the other wells in row A. Similarly, compare the color of wells B1 and C1 with their respective rows. Record your observations in the Data Table.

 7. Wash all solutions in the well plate down the drain. Clean and dry the well plate. Clean up your work area and wash your hands before leaving the laboratory.

Waste Disposal
Have students rinse the liquids from their reaction plates into the sink and wash them down the drain with plenty of water. ■

Observations (sample data)
DATA TABLE

	Indicator	pH of Solution					
		2	3	4	5	6	7
A	phenol-phthalein	color-less	color-less	color-less	color-less	color-less	color-less
B	natural	red	red	red	red	red	red
C	universal	red	red-orange	orange-red	orange	yellow	yellow-green

	Indicator	pH of Solution					Un-known
		8	9	10	11	12	
A	phenol-phthalein	pink	pink	pink	pink	pink	
B	natural	green	green	green	green	green	
C	universal	green	blue-green	blue	violet	violet-red	

Critical Thinking: Analysis and Conclusions

1. What is the color of phenolphthalein in solutions with pH values ranging from 2 to 6? *(Interpreting data)* __Colorless.__

© Prentice-Hall, Inc.   *Determining the pH of an Unknown*   303

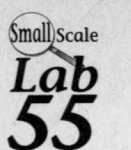

Name _____

2. What is the color of phenolphthalein in solutions with pH values ranging from 8 to 12? *(Interpreting data)* Pink.

3. Which indicator had the greatest number of colors? *(Making comparisons)* Universal indicator had several colors over the pH range of 2 to 12.

4. Which indicator used in the investigation could most precisely identify the pH of your unknown solution? Explain. *(Drawing conclusions)* Universal indicator gives the most precise indication of the pH of the unknown solution because it has the greatest number of colors corresponding to the range in pH values.

Critical Thinking: Applications

1. Give an explanation for why universal indicator has a number of different colors over the pH range used in this investigation, whereas most indicators have only two colors. *(Drawing conclusions)* Universal indicator is actually a mixture of many different acid-base indicators.

2. Soils have different acidities, affecting the growth of many plants. Some plants do well in a more acidic soil, whereas others do better in a basic soil. Describe a method for testing the acidity of the soil near your home or school. *(Designing experiments)* Dig up a small sample of soil and put it into a container. Cover the soil with water that is neutral and allow the soil to sit for a while. Filter the mixture to separate the solid from the solution. Add universal indicator to a sample of the solution. Compare that color to the colors observed in row C of the well plate.

Going Further

1. An acid-base indicator can be prepared from red cabbage, which turns a number of different colors when added to solutions with different acidities. Research how to prepare cabbage indicator and try making some under your teacher's supervision. Then use the cabbage indicator to test some familiar products such as vinegar and household ammonia. **CAUTION:** *Be careful when handling a knife or a blender and heating anything over a flame. Do not breathe household ammonia. Wear goggles and a lab apron while doing this procedure.*

Name _____ Date _____ Class _____

An Indicator for Acid Rain

Small Scale **Lab 56** APPLICATION

Text reference: **Chapter 19**

Introduction

The effects of acid rain on plants and animals in some forests, lakes, and streams are increasingly troublesome. The damage is most noticeable in areas downwind from heavy automobile traffic and industries that burn high-sulfur coal. Citizens concerned about relieving the problem need to know which polluting acids are causing the damage and how they are finding their way into the environment.

One of the pollutants, nitric acid, is formed from nitrogen monoxide, a gas produced by many industrial processes and by the internal combustion engines of cars, trucks, and buses. The nitrogen monoxide gas released from exhaust pipes reacts very quickly with oxygen to produce nitrogen dioxide gas (NO_2).

$$2NO(g) + O_2(g) \rightarrow 2NO_2(g)$$

Nitrogen dioxide gas reacts readily with water to form both nitric acid (HNO_3) and more nitrogen monoxide (NO).

$$3NO_2(g) + H_2O(l) \rightarrow 2HNO_3(aq) + NO(g)$$

Then nitrogen monoxide gas reacts again with O_2 to produce more nitrogen dioxide gas via the first equation, and the cycle is repeated. Nitric acid is a strong acid that can lower the pH of rain or snow to values well below 4.

Carbon dioxide is another gas that is present in the atmosphere. It also produces an acid when dissolved in water. Carbon dioxide is not considered to be an acid rain pollutant since it forms carbonic acid, which is a weak acid. It dissociates very little in water.

$$CO_2(g) + H_2O(l) \rightleftharpoons H_2CO_3(aq)$$
$$H_2CO_3(aq) \rightleftharpoons H^+(aq) + HCO_3^-(aq)$$

In the environment, carbon dioxide alone does not reduce the pH of rainwater below 5, so it does not cause problems for plant and animal life.

The polluting acids that do cause major damage in the environment, such as nitric, sulfurous, and sulfuric acids, are capable of lowering the pH of the water in clouds to values well below 3.9. This highly acidic rain creates problems over large areas of land and water. On land, plants become less able to extract important minerals such as calcium and magnesium from the soil. They become more susceptible to fungal infections. In water systems, animals and plants cannot develop properly when the pH of the water in lakes and rivers falls too low.

The purpose of this investigation is to find an indicator that will distinguish between the pH effects of the weak acid product of carbon dioxide and the strong acid product of nitrogen oxides. You will study the formation of nitric acid under circumstances similar to its occurrence

Materials (class of 30 in pairs)

30 pairs chemical splash goggles
30 laboratory aprons
15 petri dishes
15 sheets of white paper
15 sets of 7 micropipets filled with the following reagents:
  bromcresol green indicator
  bromthymol blue indicator
  universal indicator
  potassium nitrite (KNO_2), 0.5 M
  sulfuric acid (H_2SO_4), 2.0 M
  sodium hydrogen carbonate ($NaHCO_3$), 0.001 M
  ammonium hydroxide (NH_4OH), 2.0 M
15 drinking straws
15 wash bottles with distilled water
roll of paper towels
15 petri dishes with sealed access port
15 sheets of black construction paper
ice chips

Time Required
50 minutes.

Advance Preparation

The customized petri dish serves as a condensation chamber in this investigation. Instructions for making an access port may be found in the Advance Preparation of the Teacher's Notes for Investigation 48.

If your preparation time is short, students can quickly label the pipets and draw their own liquids into them. After 15 sets of the pipets are made by one class they can be stored in a resealable plastic bag to be used by the remaining classes.

© Prentice-Hall, Inc.

An Indicator for Acid Rain **305**

Small Scale Lab 56
APPLICATION

To prepare the 0.5 M KNO_2 solution, add 4.3 g KNO_2 to enough water to make 100 mL. To prepare the 2.0 M H_2SO_4 solution, add 11.1 mL concentrated H_2SO_4 to enough water to make 100 mL. To prepare the 0.001 M $NaHCO_3$ solution, add 8.4 g $NaHCO_3$ to 1 L water; then mix 10 mL of the resulting solution with enough water to make 1 L. To prepare the 2.0 M NH_4OH solution, add 7.0 g NH_4OH to enough water to make 100 mL.

You may wish to have color charts for universal indicator available. Have ready containers in which to collect waste H_2SO_4 and NH_4OH solutions.

Introduction
You can start with a class discussion of acid rain. Ask students what they think about the sources and causes of acid rain. What examples of acid rain have they seen? Bring in some pictures showing buildings or sculptures that have been affected by acid rain.

Discuss the chemical reaction between KNO_2 and H_2SO_4. Write the equation on the board and explain how NO_2 is generated. Students have not done redox reactions as yet, but you can go back to these reactions at a later date and use them as examples.

Name _____

in nature. You will also compare the sensitivity of three indicators to changes in pH and use your findings to identify the best indicator of acid rain formed from nitrogen oxides.

Pre-Lab Discussion
Read the entire laboratory investigation and the relevant pages of your textbook. Then answer the questions that follow.

1. What is a major source of nitric acid pollution? __Nitrogen oxides produced by internal combustion engines.__

2. Why should great care be taken to rinse the petri dish three times with distilled water before attempting each part of the procedure? __The petri dish should be rinsed well to remove acidic or basic contaminants that might affect later results.__

3. Describe the process by which you will neutralize the polluting gas and the source that generates it. __The NO_2 gas and its generating source are neutralized by the addition of two drops of 2.0 M NH_4OH solution.__

4. Write and balance the net equation for the neutralization reaction that occurs between nitric acid and sodium hydrogen carbonate in Step 11. $HCO_3^-(aq) + H_3O^+(aq) \rightarrow 2H_2O(l) + CO_2(g)$

5. Explain why carbon dioxide gas is not normally considered a pollutant that causes acid rain. __It is a weak acid that cannot reduce the pH of rain to dangerous levels (below pH 5).__

6. How does the condensed liquid you collect on the under surface of the petri dish lid simulate the cloud of acid rain? __The NO_2 gas that dissolves in the water droplets of a cloud produces nitric acid, which then is released as acid rain.__

Problem
Why is bromcresol green an excellent indicator for detecting the environmentally harmful effects of nitrogen oxides?

Materials
chemical splash goggles
laboratory apron
petri dish
white paper
7 micropipets, filled with the
  following reagents:
    bromcresol green indicator
    bromthymol blue indicator
    universal indicator
    potassium nitrite (KNO_2),
      0.5 M
    sulfuric acid (H_2SO_4), 2.0 M

sodium hydrogen carbonate
  ($NaHCO_3$), 0.001 M
ammonium hydroxide
  (NH_4OH), 2.0 M
drinking straw
wash bottle with distilled water
ice chips
petri dish with sealed access
  port
paper towels
black construction paper

Name_____

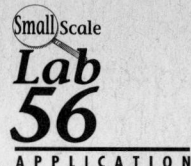

Safety

Wear your goggles and lab apron at all times during the investigation. Nitric acid and sulfuric acid are corrosive. Avoid direct contact with them. Wash spills and splashes with plenty of cold water. The NO_2 gas generated in this experiment is irritating to eyes and nasal passages. In Part B, open the petri dish only as directed.

Ammonium hydroxide (NH_4OH) and its fumes are irritating to eyes and nasal passages. Do not inhale the vapors directly. Wash any skin or clothing that comes into contact with NH_4OH solution with plenty of cold water. Note the caution alert symbols here and with certain steps of the Procedure. Refer to page *xi* for the specific precautions associated with each symbol.

Procedure

Part A: Exposure of Indicators to Carbon Dioxide

1. Put on your goggles and lab apron. Rinse both halves of the petri dish three times with distilled water. Dry the dish. Place the bottom half of the petri dish on the white paper background.
2. Place one drop each of bromcresol green, bromthymol blue, and universal indicator in the dish as illustrated in Figure 56–1.

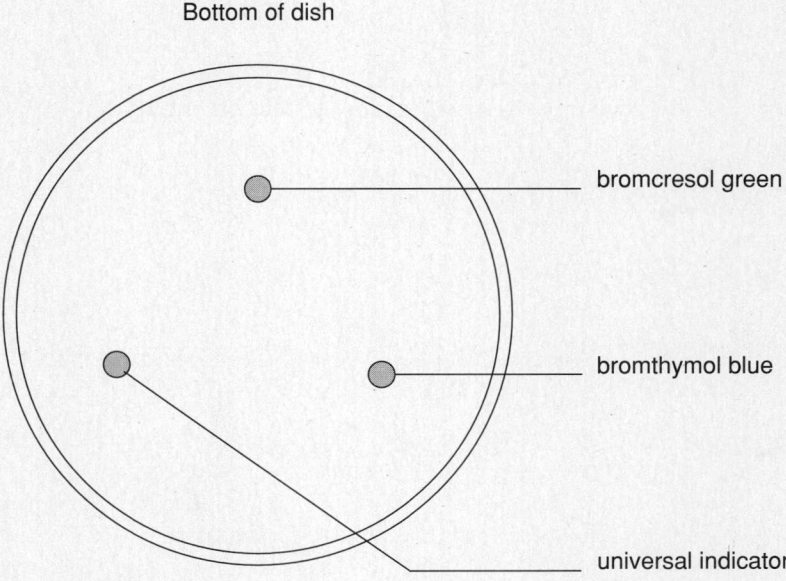

Figure 56–1

3. Expose each of the drops of indicator to carbon dioxide gas (CO_2) by blowing *gently* on the drops for about 1 minute through a clean straw. Observe any color changes that occur within the drops of each indicator during this time. Record these color changes in Data Table 1.

Safety

Make sure students wear their goggles and lab aprons at all times during the investigation. Have them wash any skin or clothing that comes into contact with any of the solutions with large quantities of water.

Even though very small quantities of NO_2 gas are generated in this investigation, students should be reminded to neutralize the gas and generating medium with NH_4OH before cleaning up. This gas can irritate the eyes and nasal passages. Caution students not to sniff the 2.0 *M* ammonium hydroxide solution directly.

Teaching Tips

The customized petri dish allows students to experiment safely with some of the nonmetal oxides that cause strong acids in rain. The concept of strong and weak acids is critical to understanding the problems associated with acid rain. In Investigation 53, students were asked to compare the hydrogen ion concentration of a strong acid to that of a weak acid. At this point, they should be able to explain why the weak acid is incapable of driving the pH of water down to lower values.

Some students believe that indicators are used to determine only if a solution is acidic, neutral, or basic. In order to explore their concept of indicators, ask them: "Why do we use different indicators?" In this lab they will use different indicators as tools to detect specific pH ranges.

In Calculation 3, an assumption is made that the volume of the droplets is about 2×10^{-6} L. If you have microliter pipets, the students can measure the actual volume and substitute this number into the calculation.

© Prentice-Hall, Inc.

An Indicator for Acid Rain 307

4. Discard the straw in the trash. Without using any detergent, wash the contents of the petri dish into the sink. Rinse the dish three times with distilled water, and dry it.

Part B: Producing Acid Rain

5. Place the bottom half of the petri dish on the white paper background. Use the micropipet to place rows of droplets of bromcresol green in the dish as illustrated in Figure 56–2.
6. Place one drop of 0.5 M KNO_2 in the middle of the dish as illustrated in Figure 56–2. Record the color in Data Table 2.
7. Cover the bottom plate of the petri dish with its lid, and move it to the black paper. Place a piece of ice about 1 cm in diameter in the middle of the top of the lid. Using distilled water from the micropipet, enlarge the puddle of melting ice to about 2 cm in diameter. Droplets of condensed water vapor should appear on the underside of the lid.

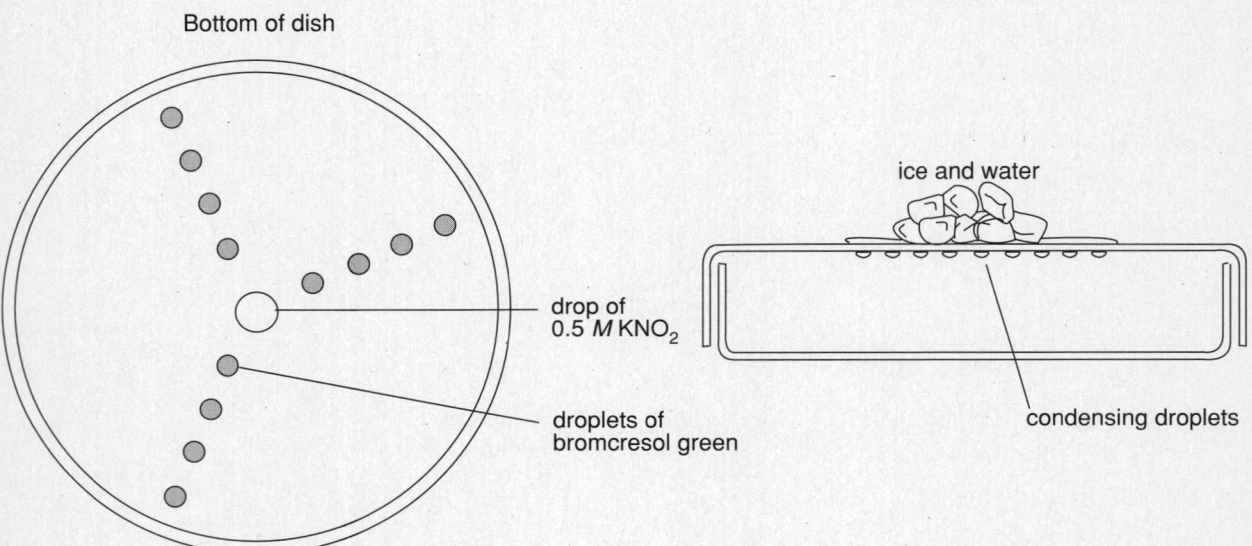

Figure 56–2

8. Carefully lift the lid without disturbing the pool of ice water. Drop two drops of 2 M H_2SO_4 into the puddle of KNO_2. *Immediately* place the lid back onto the bottom plate of the petri dish. **CAUTION:** *Sulfuric acid is corrosive. Avoid contact with the acids. Wash spills with plenty of water.* Watch the changes that occur in the indicator and record them in Data Table 2.
9. Wait 2–4 minutes. Carefully remove the lid and *immediately* replace it with the lid having the sealed access port. Set the dish with the new lid aside for now and work with the old lid. Wipe the ice water off the top side of the lid with a paper towel and place the lid upside-down on the black paper.
10. Collect the droplets in the following manner: First, add two drops of distilled water to the center of the lid. Next, collect all

Name _____

of the fine droplets by tilting and rolling the petri dish lid. Carefully slide the lid back to the white background and add one drop of bromcresol green indicator solution to the collected puddle. Record the resulting color in Data Table 2.

11. Titrate the puddle with drops of 0.001 M $NaHCO_3$. Hold the micropipet vertically as you deliver and count the drops. Gently move the dish to stir the contents. Record in Data Table 2 the number of drops of base (0.001 M $NaHCO_3$) needed to turn bromcresol green to a blue color.

12. Return to the petri dish that has the sealed access port. Raise the tape from the access port and introduce two drops of 2.0 M ammonium hydroxide solution through the port. Immediately replace the tape over the port. Wait about 5 minutes.

13. Wash the contents from the bottom plate of the petri dish into the sink. Rinse the bottom plate again with distilled water and dry it. Clean up your work area and wash your hands before leaving the laboratory.

Observations (sample data)

DATA TABLE 1 Indicators and CO_2 Gas

Indicator	Observations
bromcresol green	remains blue-green
bromthymol blue	turns yellow
universal indicator	changes from green to dark orange or red

DATA TABLE 2

Procedure	Observations
KNO_2 and bromcresol green	green
NO_2 and bromcresol green	turns yellow
water droplets and bromcresol green	yellow color
drops 0.001 M $NaHCO_3$	5 (will vary)

Calculations (based on sample data)

1. Using the equation you wrote in Question 4 of the Pre-Lab Discussion, determine the number of moles of sodium hydrogen carbonate used in the titration with nitric acid. Assume that the volume of one drop from a micropipet held vertically is 4×10^{-5} L.

   Concentration of $NaHCO_3$ × volume of $NaHCO_3$ = mol $NaHCO_3$
   (0.001 mol $NaHCO_3$/L) × (5 drops) (4 × 10^{-5} L/drop) = 2 × 10^{-7} mol $NaHCO_3$

Waste Disposal

The contents of the petri dishes can be neutralized and then washed down the drain with plenty of water. Excess potassium nitrite solution should be stored separately for commerical disposal or shipment to a secure landfill. Excess 2 M sulfuric acid should first be diluted to less than 1 M and then neutralized with 1 M Na_2CO_3 solution. Excess 2 M ammonium hydroxide solution should be disposed of under the hood by diluting it to less than 1 M and then neutralizing it by adding 1 M HCl. ∎

Cooperative Learning Strategy

If students are organized into groups of four, one should be designated as the scribe and the other three should be designated as coordinators for each of the parts of the procedure. The coordinator for part A can quickly demonstrate the effects of CO_2 on the indicators to the rest of the group. After this, the coordinator for Part B can prepare the petri dish by placing the required drops of different solutions in the bottom plate, but only up to the point of adding the sulfuric acid. When the preparations for Part B are complete, the coordinator can describe the dish contents and begin generating gas by adding the 2.0 M sulfuric acid. Everyone in the group should have an opportunity to observe the effects of the gases on the indicators and the neutralization process that follows.

Name _____

2. How many moles of nitric acid were in the acid droplets? Assume that the sodium hydrogen carbonate exactly titrated the moles of nitric acid present in the droplets.

   1:1 molar ratio, therefore there were 2×10^{-7} mol HNO_3.

3. Assume that the volume of your cloudlike droplets was 2×10^{-6} L. What was the molarity of the nitric acid in the droplets?

   2×10^{-7} mol $HNO_3/(2 \times 10^{-6}$ L$) = 0.1$ mol HNO_3/L

4. Assume that the acidic droplets you titrated in Part B contained only nitric acid. Use the concentration of nitric acid you just calculated to determine the pH.

   Nitric acid dissociates fully, so 0.1 mol HNO_3/L = 0.1 mol H^+ ions
   pH = $-\log [H^+]$ = $-\log 0.1$ = $-(-1)$ = 1

Critical Thinking: Analysis and Conclusions

1. The pH range of each indicator is given below:

   Bromthymol Blue
   ← blue ← green → yellow →
   (7.6)   (6.0)

   Bromcresol Green
   ← blue ← green → yellow →
   (5.5)   (3.8)

   Universal Indicator
   ←violet→ ←blue→ ←blue green→ ←green→ ←yellow→ ←orange→ ←red→
   (10)   (9)   (8)   (7)   (6)   (5)   (4)

   Using these ranges and the color changes observed for each indicator in Part A, state what the indicator tells you about the pH attained by exposing the solutions to carbon dioxide. *(Interpreting data)*

   a. bromthymol blue Indicates a pH of 6.0 or lower.

   b. bromcresol green Indicates a pH lower than 5.5 and higher than 3.8.

   c. universal indicator Indicates a pH of about 4.0.

2. Using the given pH ranges of the indicators and the pH you found in Calculation 5, state the color you think you would get with the nitric acid you made and the following indicators. *(Making predictions)*

   a. bromthymol blue yellow

   b. bromcresol green yellow

   c. universal indicator red

3. Why did you titrate the bromcresol green–water solution in Part B with your base until the solution turned blue? *(Applying concepts)*

   Because the titration had proceeded to the point where the pH was above 5.5,

   which is within the natural range of the pH of rainwater.

Name _____

4. Why is bromcresol green a good indicator for testing acid rain? *(Drawing conclusions)* Bromcresol green detects pH levels below 3.8, which means it will not detect the effects of CO_2 gas, but will detect the presence of stronger acids. Bromthymol blue will not distinguish CO_2 from stronger acids.

Critical Thinking: Applications

1. Some of the mountainsides near the major highways in Germany and the United States exhibit dead or dying forests. Do the results of your titration demonstrate how NO_2 from car exhaust may be a contributing factor to this damage? Explain. *(Developing hypotheses)* The titration demonstrates that NO_2 gas dissolves very well into the droplets.

   If a cloud with 0.1 M HNO_3 reaches a mountainside, significant amounts of nitric acid will be deposited on it.

2. Compare your titration results with those of other groups of students. Discuss which variables may affect the acid concentration. Would these same variables affect the concentration of the polluting acids in clouds in nature? *(Making comparisons)* Titration results will vary with the length of time the droplets were exposed to the NO_2 gas and the size of the droplets. These variables also exist in clouds.

3. Farmers often spread limestone on soil to "sweeten" the soil. The primary mineral of limestone is calcium carbonate ($CaCO_3$). Write an equation that describes the reaction of nitric acid with calcium carbonate. Then explain why soils and aquatic systems that contain limestone are protected somewhat from acid rain. *(Applying concepts)* $CaCO_3(s) + 2HNO_3(aq) \rightarrow H_2O(l) + CO_2(g) + Ca(NO_3)_2(aq)$.

   The calcium carbonate of limestone neutralizes strong acids associated with acid rain.

4. Marble is a metamorphosed form of limestone. Powdered limestone is an important ingredient in concrete. State at least one economic reason and one aesthetic reason for you to become involved in the process of preventing acid rain. *(Evaluating)* Some ancient and priceless statues are made of marble. These may be dissolved or disfigured by acid rain. Concrete is used in making buildings, bridges, and highways, which are very expensive. These may be partially dissolved or weakened by acid rain.

An Indicator for Acid Rain

Going Further

1. Various chemistry handbooks and libraries will serve as good sources of information about catalytic converters and scrubbers.

3. Limestone and marble chips are available from gravel yards and plant nurseries as well as commercial supply houses. Concrete chips are commonly available around most concrete construction sites, and portland cement is available from hardware stores.

Going Further

1. Catalytic converters are placed on automobiles to prevent the release of specific gases. Scrubbers are often placed on coal-burning stacks. Research the chemistry of the catalytic converter and scrubbers and report your findings to the class.
2. The types of smog in London and Los Angeles present lethal problems. Research these two smog types to determine their sources and their relationship to the substances that cause acid rain. Report your results to the class.
3. Design a procedure that employs the petri dish and bromcresol green to investigate the effect of acid rain on limestone, marble, and concrete. Under the supervision of your teacher, carry out the procedure and report your findings to the class.

Titration with Oxalic Acid

Lab 57

Text reference: **Chapter 19**

Introduction

Titration is a versatile analytical procedure that can be used for a wide variety of chemical analyses. For example, when your town's water supply is tested for purity, or pond water is tested for dissolved oxygen and contaminants, chances are a titration is carried out. Some tests essential for a medical diagnosis require a titration of various body fluids.

A titration makes use of a known reaction between two chemicals. A solution of unknown concentration is reacted with a precisely measured amount of another chemical. An appropriate indicator must be used to determine when chemically equivalent amounts of each chemical are combined, that is, when no excess of either reactant is present. This is known as the equivalence point. To measure solution volumes accurately, finely calibrated pipets and burets are used. Titrations are commonly used to determine the strength of acids or bases.

Acid-base titrations follow a relatively standard procedure for analysis of acid or base strength. The concentration of either an acid or a base solution can be determined. A measured amount of acid is neutralized by reaction with a base solution titrated from a buret. Consider the following example:

$$HCl + NaOH \rightarrow NaCl + H_2O$$
(known) (unknown)

The example shows that the reaction is a double replacement in which the products are a corresponding salt and water. For reactions of strong acids and bases, the equivalence point pH is 7, but for weak acids it is somewhat higher. If a graph is made of pH vs. volume of base added (see Figure 57–1), the equivalence point is always halfway along the S curve as labeled in the illustration. Note that there is a large pH change around the equivalence point with very small additions of base.

In this investigation, you will determine the concentration of two basic solutions by titration with oxalic acid, $H_2C_2O_4$, a moderately weak acid with an equivalence point pH of approximately 8. Weak acids are used to titrate bases because the equivalence point is reached more slowly, so the results are more accurate. Phenolphthalein will be used to find the endpoint because it is colorless below pH 8, but turns pink just above pH 8.

Materials (class of 30 in pairs)

- 30 pairs chemical splash goggles
- 30 laboratory aprons
- 15 erlenmeyer flasks, 250-mL
- 15 laboratory balances
- 50 g oxalic acid dihydrate ($H_2C_2O_4 \cdot 2H_2O$), granular crystals (analytical grade)
- 15 dropper bottles or micropipets filled with 1% phenolphthalein
- 15 wash bottles with distilled water
- 15 burets
- 15 buret clamps
- 15 ring stands
- 1 L sodium hydroxide solution (NaOH), about 0.5 M
- 30 beakers, 100-mL
- 15 sheets of white paper
- 1 L clear household ammonia (NH_4OH)

Time Required

60–90 minutes. To shorten the time, titrate only one base.

Advance Preparation

Purchase clear ammonia. Prepare 1 L of 0.5 M NaOH solution by dissolving 20.0 g NaOH per liter of distilled water. Place unknown solutions in beakers labeled #1 and #2. Have available soap solution and buret brushes for students to use in cleaning the burets.

Introduction

Ask students for other examples of weak acids and bases. This is a good time to review the stoichiometry of equivalence points. Point out that equivalence means molar equivalence, and not equal amounts.

Lab 57

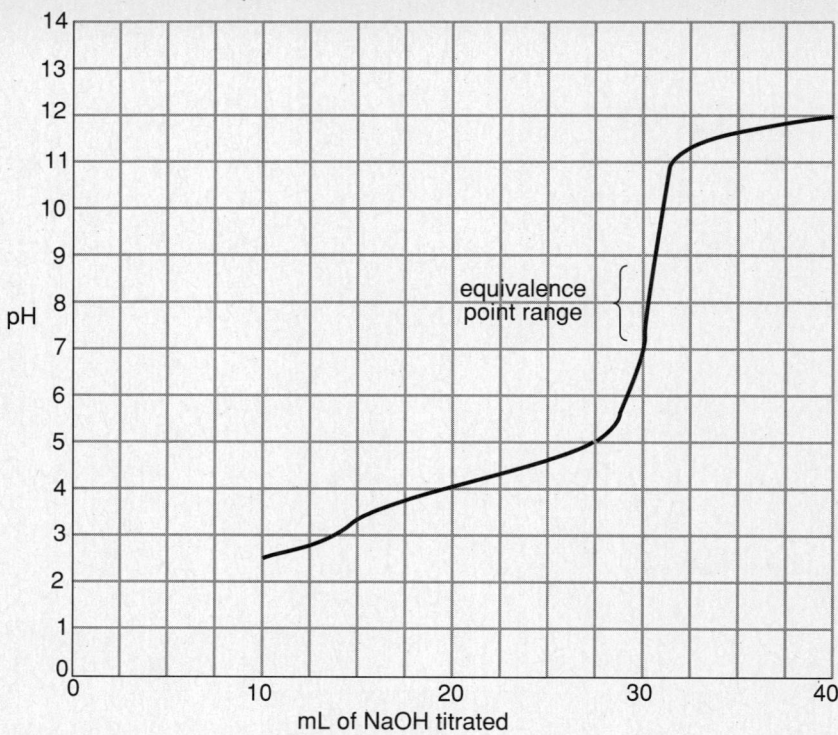

Figure 57-1 *pH curve for titration of oxalic acid*

Pre-Lab Discussion

Read the entire laboratory investigation and the relevant pages of your textbook. Then answer the questions that follow.

1. Why is it difficult to see whether you have added the pH indicator phenolphthalein to the flask of acid solution? <u>Phenolphthalein is colorless in the acid pH range, so its presence is not obvious.</u>

2. Write and balance the double replacement reaction equations for this investigation. In each case, how many moles of base are needed to neutralize one mole of acid?

    oxalic acid and sodium hydroxide:

    $$H_2C_2O_4 + 2NaOH \rightarrow Na_2C_2O_4 + 2H_2O$$

    oxalic acid and ammonium hydroxide:

    $$H_2C_2O_4 + 2NH_4OH \rightarrow (NH_4)_2C_2O_4 + 2H_2O$$

    2 moles of base in each case.

3. Why must you fill the buret only when its top is below eye level? <u>Pouring hazardous chemicals above eye level may result in spillage splashing down into the eyes or face.</u>

4. Look up the term *equivalent*. Give its root derivation, and tell how this root helps to explain the meaning of equivalence point. *Equivalent* derives from Latin, meaning "equal strength." At an equivalence point, chemicals are at equal strengths, not equal amounts.

5. Why is it better to use a weak rather than a strong acid when you titrate a base? Because the reaction proceeds more slowly around the equivalence point, so the results are more accurate.

Problem

How can you use the titration process to determine the strength of bases?

Materials

chemical splash goggles
laboratory apron
erlenmeyer flask, 250-mL
laboratory balance
oxalic acid dihydrate
 ($H_2C_2O_4 \cdot 2H_2O$)
distilled water
phenolphthalein
wash bottle

buret
buret clamp
ring stand
sodium hydroxide solution
 (NaOH), pH unknown
2 beakers, 100-mL
white paper
household ammonia (NH_4OH),
 pH unknown

Safety

Wear your goggles and lab apron at all times during the investigation. Place the top of the buret below eye level when filling it to avoid splashing the solutions into the face. Place the buret and buret stand on the floor if necessary. Acids are corrosive and bases are caustic. Wipe up spills and drips immediately with wet towels, and then dry. Wash affected skin areas with cold water after any contact and notify your teacher. Burets are cumbersome and break easily—handle them with care.

Note the caution alert symbols here and with certain steps of the Procedure. Refer to page xi for the specific precautions associated with each symbol.

Safety

Make sure students wear their goggles and lab aprons at all times during the investigation. Supervise the filling of burets, making sure no student is pouring base with the top of the buret above eye level. Point out the eye wash station. Check that spills on skin and clothing are cleaned immediately. ■

Procedure

Part A: Preparation

1. Put on your goggles and lab apron. While one lab partner prepares the oxalic acid (Steps 2 and 3), the other will prepare the buret for titration (Steps 4–8).

2. Determine the mass of a 250-mL flask to 0.01 g, then add 1.0–1.5 g oxalic acid dihydrate to the flask, and determine the mass again. **CAUTION:** *Acids are corrosive. Avoid contact with skin, eyes, and clothing. Wash spills with plenty of cold water.* Record these masses in Data Table 1.

Lab 57

Teaching Tips

Demonstrate washing and preparing the buret. Demonstrate proper titration technique and the proper appearance of the endpoint.

The most common mistake students make is to add the base too quickly and overshoot the endpoint. Remind students to follow the guidelines described in Step 10. Test student endpoints for over-titration by adding one or two drops of 0.5 M HCl to the reaction flask, which should cause the indicator color to disappear.

Oxalic acid is used rather than phthalic anhydride because it is cheaper, more stable, and it has a clearer endpoint. The type of function is the same.

3. Dissolve the acid in the flask with approximately 100 mL of distilled water. Add two or three drops of phenolphthalein indicator solution to the flask.

4. Make sure that the buret is clean. If it is not, wash the buret with detergent and a buret brush. Clean the tip by draining some detergent solution through it. **CAUTION:** *Burets are fragile. Use great care in handling them.*

5. Rinse the buret thoroughly with tap water, then rinse once with distilled water, draining final rinses through the tip. Clamp the clean buret to the support stand.

6. Obtain 50–60 mL of sodium hydroxide (NaOH) solution, unknown 1, in a 100-mL beaker. Position the buret so that the top is below your eye level and place an empty beaker under the buret tip to catch drips. **CAUTION:** *Sodium hydroxide is caustic. Keep the top of the buret below eye level when pouring sodium hydroxide. Avoid contact with skin, eyes, and clothing. Wash spills and splashes with plenty of cold water.*

7. Pour approximately 5 mL of base into the buret. Drain this through the tip to remove water and coat the inside of the buret with base. See Figure 57–2.

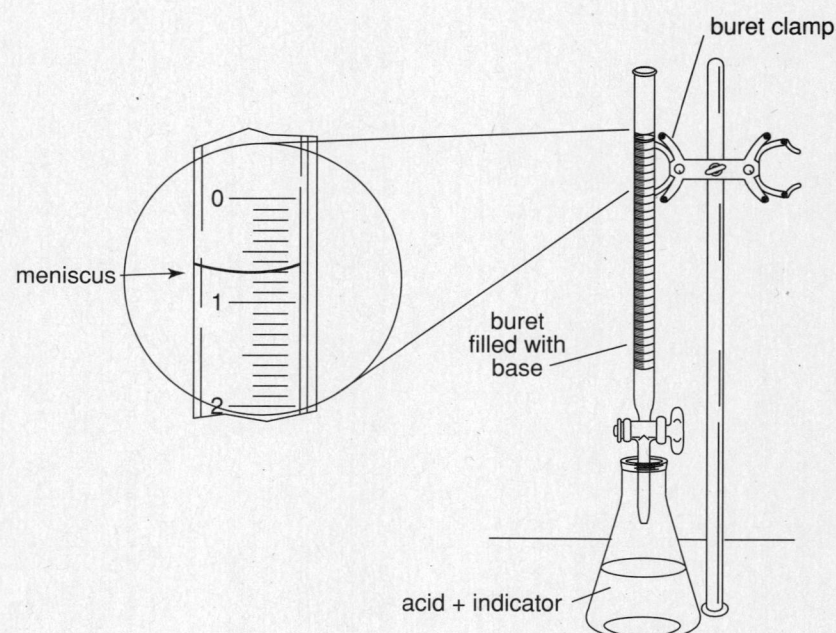

Figure 57–2

8. Now fill the buret to slightly above the zero line. Drain some base through the tip to clear the buret tip of air. Stop between 0.0 and 2.0 mL. Remove the hanging drop at the tip by touching the tip to the inside of the waste beaker. Read the initial volume in the buret and record it in Data Table 1.

Part B: Titration

9. Place the flask with acid and phenolphthalein under the buret. The buret tip should be down about 1 cm inside the mouth of the flask to avoid any outside loss of base. Place a sheet of white paper under the flask to highlight the pink indicator color.

10. Drip the base into the flask while swirling the flask. You can add base quickly at first, but as the pink color starts to last longer, slow the drip rate. When the whole flask flashes pink before turning clear again, add only one or two drops at a time and swirl until the flask is clear before adding more. Occasionally rinse down splashes on the inside of the flask using a little distilled water from a wash bottle.

11. When the faintest pink color persists, stop and record the final volume in the buret.

12. Flush all chemicals down the drain with plenty of water. Wash all beakers and the flask, and clean the buret as described in Step 4.

13. To determine the molarity of ammonia, repeat Steps 2, 3, and Steps 7–12, using clear household ammonia, NH_4OH, in the buret. Record your observations in Data Table 2. **CAUTION:** *Household ammonia is caustic and the fumes are irritating to eyes and lungs. Avoid breathing in vapors.*

14. Clean up your work area and wash your hands before leaving the laboratory.

Observations (sample data)
DATA TABLE 1   NaOH + $H_2C_2O_4$

Mass (g)		Volume of NaOH (mL)	
flask	43.25	initial	0.5
flask and oxalic acid	44.54	final	41.0
oxalic acid	1.29	titrated	40.5

DATA TABLE 2 NH_4OH + $H_2C_2O_4$

Mass (g)		Volume of NH_4OH (mL)	
flask	44.50	initial	0.0
flask and oxalic acid	45.85	final	11.5
oxalic acid	1.35	titrated	11.5

Waste Disposal
Neutralize excess solution in the burets and flush down the drain with plenty of water. ■

Cooperative Learning Strategies
Students should switch roles preparing, titrating, and recording for the second titration.
   Prepare a scatter plot of the class results. Have the class decide if any values should be excluded from an averaging of results.

Lab 57

Name _____

 Calculations (based on sample data)

1. Determine the molarity of the unknown sodium hydroxide solution as follows.

   a. Calculate the number of moles of oxalic acid used for NaOH, using the molar mass of $H_2C_2O_4 \cdot 2H_2O$.

   $$\text{mol } H_2C_2O_4 \cdot 2H_2O = \frac{1.29 \text{ g } H_2C_2O_4 \cdot 2H_2O}{126 \text{ g/mol}} = 0.0102 \text{ mol}$$

   b. Use your answer to Question 2 of the Pre-Lab Discussion to determine the number of moles of base needed to neutralize the calculated number of moles of oxalic acid.

   $$0.0102 \text{ mol } H_2C_2O_4 \times \frac{2 \text{ mol NaOH}}{1 \text{ mol } H_2C_2O_4} = 0.0204 \text{ moles NaOH}$$

   c. Calculate the molar concentration of base used.

   Molarity of base = moles of base/volume of base (L)

   Molarity of NaOH = 0.0204 mol/0.0405 L = 0.504 M

2. Determine the molarity of ammonium hydroxide, using the same method you used for sodium hydroxide.

   $$\text{mol } H_2C_2O_4 \cdot 2H_2O = \frac{1.35 \text{ g } H_2C_2O_4 \cdot 2H_2O}{126 \text{ g/mol}} = 0.0107 \text{ mol}$$

   $$H_2C_2O_4 + 2NH_4OH \rightarrow (NH_4)_2C_2O_4 + 2H_2O$$

   $$0.0107 \text{ mol } H_2C_2O_4 \times \frac{2 \text{ mol } NH_4OH}{1 \text{ mol } H_2C_2O_4} = 0.0214 \text{ mol } NH_2OH$$

   Molarity of base = moles of base/volume of base (L)

   Molarity of NH_4OH = 0.0214 mol/0.0115 L = 1.86 M

Critical Thinking: Analysis and Conclusions

1. Does the amount of water in which the oxalic acid is dissolved affect the outcome of the investigation? Why or why not? *(Applying concepts)* The amount of water used to dissolve the oxalic acid does not affect the results because the water does not change the number of moles of oxalic acid, upon which the amount of base depends.

2. Titration is capable of yielding highly reproducible results, equivalent to ±1 drop of titrant. Explain how each of the following parts of the procedure contributes to this precision. *(Drawing conclusions)*

   a. Removing drops of titrant hanging from the tip. Hanging drops have a volume already accounted for as titrated in the buret volume reading.

   b. Washing down the inside of the reaction flask with water. Splashed material on the sides may account for a drop or two of acid or base, enough to change the pH significantly near the endpoint.

   c. Rinsing the buret with the base to be used. Rinsing with base removes the rinse water in the buret that would dilute the base solution.

Name _____

Lab 57

Critical Thinking: Applications

1. Use the pH curve for titration diagramed in the Introduction to determine the effect on pH from the addition of one or two drops of base when pH = 3; when pH = 6. *(Interpreting diagrams)* When pH = 3, a small volume of base has little effect on pH. When pH = 6, a small volume of base causes pH to rise dramatically.

2. Carbonate ions, CO_3^{2-}, are contained in limestone (the major component of which is calcium carbonate, $CaCO_3$), which is used to neutralize acids in soil. Remedies sold to neutralize stomach acid contain carbonate. The equilibrium reaction that carbonate ions undergo with water is called hydrolysis. Write the reaction for this equation, and explain how carbonate neutralizes acids. *(Applying concepts)*

$$CO_3^{2-} + H_2O \rightarrow HCO_3^- + OH^-$$

Hydrolysis with carbonate produces hydroxide ions that neutralize acids.

Going Further

1. Under the supervision of your teacher, carry out a titration with a pH meter. After each milliliter of titrant is added, record the pH. Graph pH vs. volume of titrant, or enter the values into a computer spreadsheet and use a graphing option to make the graph. If the pH probe is coupled to a computer with an automatic recording option, set a slow, steady drip rate for the buret and record the pH every few seconds. Plot the pH vs. time. From the graph, find the equivalence point pH.

2. Oxalic acid is a natural organic acid present in high concentrations in some plants such as rhubarb. It is used in commercial cleansers that remove rust stains. Many biological processes depend on organic acids that also have commercial value. Research other sources and uses of oxalic acid and other naturally occurring acids.

Going Further

2. *Molecules*, by P.W. Atkins (Scientific American Library Publishers, 1987), is a great source of interesting pictures, structures, and information on many noteworthy chemicals. Acids that students identify may include hydrochloric acid (stomach acid), citric acid, ascorbic acid, salicylic acid, and DNA.

Activity Series

Small Scale Lab 58

Text reference: **Chapter 20**

Introduction

Oxidation-reduction reactions, also known as redox reactions, comprise an extremely important area of study in chemistry. These reactions provide energy in electrochemical cells and have a variety of commercial uses in batteries and solar cells. In addition, oxidation-reduction reactions are involved in rusting, cleaning agents, photography, and many other processes.

Redox reactions can be thought of as reactions in which electrons are exchanged between one species that is oxidized and another that is reduced. Reduction involves the gain of electrons, while oxidation involves the loss of electrons. A reduction reaction for a metal ion can be written in the following manner:

$$\overset{+n}{M} + ne^- \rightarrow \overset{0}{M}$$

The oxidation reaction is written:

$$\overset{0}{M} \rightarrow \overset{+n}{M} + ne^-$$

$\overset{+n}{M}$ is typically a metal with $+n$ oxidation state, and n represents the number of electrons (e^-) gained. $\overset{0}{M}$ is the metal in its reduced form.

An activity series of metals is a list that ranks metals according to their relative activity. Metals at the top of the list are oxidized most readily to their metallic ion. They tend to remain in ionic ($\overset{+n}{M}$) form. Conversely, metals at the bottom of the list are oxidized with difficulty. Their metallic ion is relatively active so they tend to be in the reduced ($\overset{0}{M}$) form. In this investigation, you will establish an activity series based on the ease with which metallic ions are reduced. The ions to be studied are Cu^{2+}, Fe^{2+}, H^+, Mg^{2+}, Ag^+, and Zn^{2+}. The metals to be studied are Zn, Cu, Mg, and Fe.

Pre-Lab Discussion

Read the entire laboratory investigation and the relevant pages of your textbook. Then answer the questions that follow.

1. Define the terms *oxidation* and *reduction*. __Oxidation is the loss of__ electrons. Reduction is the gain of electrons.

2. Are metallic ions the oxidized or reduced form of metals? Explain. Since metal ions are positively charged, they have lost electrons and are the oxidized form of the metal.

Materials (class of 30 in pairs)

- 30 pairs chemical splash goggles
- 30 laboratory aprons
- 30 pairs latex gloves
- 15 well plates, 24-well
- 15 marking pens
- 15 sets of 6 micropipets, filled with the following solutions:
    - magnesium sulfate ($MgSO_4$), 0.1 M
    - copper(II) sulfate ($CuSO_4$), 0.1 M
    - silver nitrate ($AgNO_3$), 0.1 M
    - zinc sulfate ($ZnSO_4$), 0.1 M
    - iron(II) sulfate ($FeSO_4$), 0.1 M
    - sulfuric acid (H_2SO_4), 3.0 M
- 15 pieces of steel wool
- 15 pairs tweezers
- 15 zinc strips (Zn), (0.5 × 3 cm)
- 15 copper strips (Cu), (0.5 × 3 cm)
- 15 magnesium strips (Mg), (0.5 × 3 cm)
- 15 iron strips (Fe), (0.5 × 3 cm)

Time Required
40–50 minutes.

Advance Preparation

Solutions for micropipets—add the specified masses of the following solutes to enough water to make 100 mL of each solution:
- $MgSO_4 \cdot 7H_2O$: 2.45 g
- $CuSO_4 \cdot 5H_2O$: 2.49 g
- $AgNO_3$: 1.69 g
- $ZnSO_4 \cdot 7H_2O$: 2.87 g
- $FeSO_4 \cdot 7H_2O$: 2.78 g
- H_2SO_4: 16.6 mL conc. H_2SO_4

CAUTION: *Sulfuric acid is corrosive. Silver nitrate can cause stains to skin and clothing. Wear gloves, apron,*

Activity Series **321**

Small Scale Lab 58

Name _____

and goggles when handling concentrated H_2SO_4 and $AgNO_3$. Always add acid to water. Once the solutions have been prepared and the micropipets filled, the pipets can be put in sets that can be held in small beakers or empty tape cassette holders.

Have ready a labeled container in which to collect the waste silver solutions.

Introduction

You can introduce oxidation-reduction with a demonstration. Put a strip of copper into a beaker half-filled with silver nitrate solution. After a while, the color of the solution turns blue, indicating the presence of Cu^{2+} ions. Solid pieces of silver will also appear. Ask the students what has been oxidized ($Cu(s) \rightarrow Cu^{2+} + 2e^-$) and what has been reduced ($Ag^+ + e^- \rightarrow Ag(s)$). They can then balance the combined redox equation: $Cu(s) + 2Ag^+ \rightarrow 2Ag(s) + Cu^{2+}$

Safety

Make sure students wear their goggles and lab aprons at all times during the investigation. Review the precautions for safe handling of sulfuric acid and silver nitrate solutions. Remind students to dispose of the waste silver solutions from column 4 in the labeled containers. ■

3. What safety hazards are involved in this investigation and what precautions should be followed? <u>Sulfuric acid is corrosive. Silver nitrate is poisonous if ingested and may stain skin and clothing. Wear gloves when handling sulfuric acid and silver nitrate.</u>

4. What will be the major information gained from this investigation? <u>The data will lead to a ranking of metal ions by increasing ease of reduction.</u>

5. Write an example of a typical reduction half reaction for a metal ion. <u>$Ag^+ + e^- \rightarrow Ag^0$</u>

Problem

Can an activity series for metals be developed based on the reduction of certain ions in solution?

Materials

chemical splash goggles
laboratory apron
latex gloves
well plate
marking pen
6 micropipets, filled with the following solutions:
    magnesium sulfate ($MgSO_4$), 0.1 M
    copper sulfate ($CuSO_4$), 0.1 M

silver nitrate ($AgNO_3$), 0.1 M
zinc sulfate ($ZnSO_4$), 0.1 M
iron sulfate ($FeSO_4$), 0.1 M
sulfuric acid (H_2SO_4), 3.0 M
steel wool
tweezers
zinc (Zn) strip
copper (Cu) strip
magnesium (Mg) strip
iron (Fe) strip

Safety

Wear your goggles and lab apron at all times during the investigation. Sulfuric acid is extremely corrosive. Silver nitrate is toxic if ingested. It will cause stains to skin and clothing. Wear gloves when handling silver nitrate or sulfuric acid. Wash any area of contact with plenty of cold water. Note the caution alert symbols here and with certain steps of the Procedure. Refer to page xi for the specific precautions associated with each symbol.

Procedure

 1. Put on your goggles and lab apron. Set up and label the 24-well reaction plate as shown in Figure 58–1. Place the well plate on a sheet of white paper so you can more easily view the dark precipitates.

Small Scale Lab 58

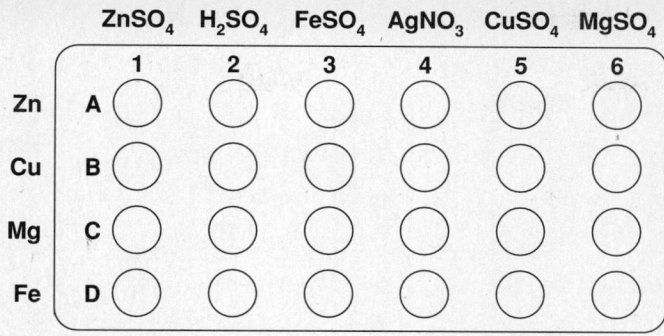

Figure 58–1

2. Put on your latex gloves. Using the appropriate micropipet, place 20 drops of 0.1 M zinc sulfate solution into the four wells in column 1. In a similar fashion, place 20 drops each of 3.0 M sulfuric acid, iron sulfate, silver nitrate, copper sulfate, and magnesium sulfate into the wells in columns 2–6 respectively.
CAUTION: *Sulfuric acid is extremely corrosive. Silver nitrate is toxic if ingested. It will stain skin and clothing. Wear gloves when handling these solutions. Wash any spills with plenty of cold water and tell your teacher.*

3. Using steel wool, clean strips of zinc, copper, magnesium, and iron. Place the strips in wells A1–D1 as shown in Figure 58-1. Wait for two minutes and check for a reaction. Record your observations in the Data Table. Rinse and dry the strips.

4. In a similar fashion, repeat the process for columns 2–6. Continue to record your observations in the Data Table.

5. Using a micropipet, dispose of the contents of the wells in column 4 in a labeled container provided by your teacher. Rinse the rest of the solutions down the drain. Clean up your work area and wash your hands before leaving the laboratory.

Observations (sample data)
DATA TABLE

		1	2	3	4	5	6
		$ZnSO_4$	H_2SO_4	$FeSO_4$	$AgNO_3$	$CuSO_4$	$MgSO_4$
A	Zn	NR	gas bubbles	turns gray	turns black	turns black	NR
B	Cu	NR	NR	NR	turns gray	NR	NR
C	Mg	turns gray	gas bubbles	turns gray	turns black	turns brown	NR
D	Fe	NR	gas–small amount	NR	turns black	turns black	NR

Teaching Tips

If you used a smaller but similar lab, Investigation 14, you may wish to point out that students will be doing an oxidation-reduction activity series in this investigation.

The preparation of solutions is straightforward. You can keep 100-mL stock bottles of solutions for 2 to 3 years. It is important that students clean the metal strips between tests. Magnesium ribbon, if used, can be cut off at the reaction point for each trial.

Waste Disposal

Silver compounds are regulated as hazardous waste (EPA waste #D011). Instruct students to use a micropipet to pull up the material from wells containing Ag^+ ions and precipitates and to deposit it into a clearly marked container. Similarly collect any $AgNO_3$ solution to be discarded from the micropipets. Precipitate the Ag^+ ions with excess NaCl solution. Filter out the precipitate and store for commercial disposal. Discard the filtrate. Other solutions can go down the drain with plenty of water. Leftover pieces of metal can be discarded as solid waste.

Activity Series

Name _____

Critical Thinking: Analysis and Conclusions

1. Which metal reacted with the largest number of solutions? *(Interpreting data)* Magnesium.
2. Which metal was the least reactive? *(Interpreting data)* Copper.
3. Which metal(s) reacted with sulfuric acid? *(Interpreting data)* Magnesium, zinc, and iron.
4. Which metal ion reacted with all metals and what is the significance of these results? *(Drawing conclusions)* Ag^+, silver ion. This ion is the most easily reduced.
5. Rank the positive ions from most easily reduced to least easily reduced and write the reduction half reactions for each. *(Making comparisons)*

Ag^+	$Ag^+ + 1e^- \rightarrow Ag^0$
Cu^{2+}	$Cu^{2+} + 2e^- \rightarrow Cu^0$
H^+	$2H^+ + 2e^- \rightarrow H_2^0$
Fe^{2+}	$Fe^{2+} + 2e^- \rightarrow Fe^0$
Zn^{2+}	$Zn^{2+} + 2e^- \rightarrow Zn^0$
Mg^{2+}	$Mg^{2+} + 2e^- \rightarrow Mg^0$

Critical Thinking: Applications

1. Magnesium blocks are often attached to iron storage tanks by a wire prior to placing these tanks underground. What is the purpose of this? *(Developing hypotheses)* Since magnesium is more reactive than iron, it reacts with any oxidizing agents and releases electrons to the iron tank, preventing the loss of electrons by iron. It protects iron from corrosion.
2. By convention, eight metals (ruthenium, rhodium, palladium, silver, osmium, iridium, platinum, and gold) have been classified as "precious." Would you expect them to be easy or difficult to oxidize? *(Making judgments)* The eight metals are not easily oxidized.
3. The element fluorine is one of the most reactive elements. Predict where it might fit in the list in Analysis and Conclusions Question 5. (Hint: it reacts with metallic silver to make silver fluoride.) *(Making predictions)* Fluorine would be first in ease of reduction in this list.

Going Further

1. There are a number of "sacrificial" metals used to protect other metals. If possible, contact boat, boat motor, and metal fabricators, find out how these metals are utilized, then do a report on the topic.

Name _____ Date _____ Class _____

Rust Marches On

Small Scale Lab 59 APPLICATION

Text reference: **Chapter 20**

Introduction

One of the most common chemical reactions involving metals is corrosion or, more precisely, spontaneous oxidation. Iron in particular oxidizes very easily, forming a compound commonly called rust. Most people are familiar with how easily rust forms despite the best efforts to prevent it. Cars, bicycles, bridges, nails—all may quickly succumb to spontaneous oxidation reactions.

Rust is actually hydrated iron(III) oxide, $Fe_2O_3 \cdot xH_2O$. When rust forms, a voltaic cell is created on the surface of the material. Iron is oxidized to its 2+ state at the anode, while oxygen is reduced in the presence of water at the cathode. Iron(II) hydroxide forms as an intermediate precipitate. Further oxidation of the iron leads to the familiar red-brown solid known as rust.

In this investigation you will look at the corrosion process, or rusting, from an electrochemical perspective. You will build an electrochemical cell on a steel plate and cause the oxidation of iron, using an indicator to determine the oxidation and reduction half reactions.

Pre-Lab Discussion

Read the entire laboratory investigation and the relevant pages of your textbook. Then answer the questions that follow.

1. What is the oxidation state of iron in $Fe_2O_3 \cdot xH_2O$? What is the significance of the "$\cdot xH_2O$"? __The oxidation state is Fe^{3+}. Rust is really a__ hydrated salt. The "$\cdot xH_2O$" means that the proportion of water associated with the salt can vary.

2. In which oxidation state is the iron in Step 1 of the Procedure? How will the presence of oxidized iron be detected? __The iron will be in__ the form of Fe^{2+}, which will be detected by using ferroxyl indicator.

3. A corroding metal is sometimes called an "unwanted voltaic cell." Briefly explain this statement. __Voltaic cells are spontaneous redox__ reactions. If a metal rusts, or corrodes, then it is spontaneously oxidizing.

4. What conditions speed up the formation of rust, for example in an automobile? __Rust formation is hastened by the presence of salts and other__ electrolytes and strains within the metal (dents, bends, and so on).

Materials (class of 30 in pairs)
- 30 pairs chemical splash goggles
- 30 laboratory aprons
- 15 well plates
- 15 pieces of white paper
- 15 sets of 3 micropipets, containing the following solutions:
  - iron(II) sulfate ($FeSO_4$), 0.1 M
  - ferroxyl indicator
  - sodium hydroxide (NaOH), 0.1 M
- 15 steel plates
- steel wool

Time Required
30 minutes.

Advance Preparation
Ferroxyl indicator solution: Dissolve 6.0 g NaCl, 0.2 g $K_3Fe(CN)_6$, and five droppersful of 1% phenolpthalein solution in 200 mL water.

0.1 M $FeSO_4$ solution: dissolve 5.6 g $FeSO_4 \cdot 7H_2O$ and ten drops concentrated sulfuric acid in 200 mL water.

0.1 M NaOH solution: Dissolve 0.80 g NaOH in 200 mL water. CAUTION: *Wear goggles and a lab apron. NaOH is caustic. Avoid its contact with skin.*

Have ready a wash bottle and a container in which to collect the waste liquids.

Introduction
One property most metals have in common is that they are easily oxidized. Let students suggest reasons for this in terms of the electron configuration of metals. If possible, demonstrate the oxidation of various metals. Iron, copper, and aluminum can be heated in a flame.

© Prentice-Hall, Inc.   Rust Marches On   **325**

Small Scale Lab 59
APPLICATION

Magnesium is easily oxidized in air, although the reaction can be dramatically speeded up in a flame. (CAUTION: *Do not look directly at burning magnesium.*) A silver spoon might be brought in (unpolished!). If possible, sodium metal may be cut with a spatula to demonstrate the oxide coating over the shiny metal. (CAUTION: *Sodium metal is highly reactive with water. Store in mineral oil and do not leave out for more than a few minutes. Do not touch the sodium metal with bare hands. Handle only with tongs or forceps.*)

Discuss the restoration of the Statue of Liberty. The Statue of Liberty was constructed in 1886 by covering a framework of about 2000 iron ribs with thin sheets of copper skin with a mass of about 90,000 kg. Cracks developed in the framework, allowing the entry of wet, salty air. The copper and iron were separated by a layer of asbestos, which wore away over time and allowed circulation of the sea air and contact between the two metals. Over the one hundred years before the statue was restored, the iron ribs lost more than half their mass through corrosion, while the copper lost very little.

The following references may be useful:

ChemMatters, Volume 3, No. 2, April 1985. It contains an article with a detailed account of the restoration of the Statue of Liberty.

Borgford, Christie and Lee Summerlin. *Chemical Activities.* American Chemical Society, 1988. Activity 63 is an investigation of the "Statue of Liberty" reaction.

Safety
Make sure the students wear their goggles and lab aprons at all times during the investigation.

Name _____

5. Compare E° for the oxidation of iron with two other common metals. Choose one that is more easily oxidized than iron, and one that is less easily oxidized. Write the equation for each half reaction.

$Cu \rightarrow Cu^{2+} + 2e^-$	$E° = 0.34$ V; less easily oxidized
$Fe \rightarrow Fe^{2+} + 2e^-$	$E° = 0.44$ V
$Al \rightarrow Al^{3+} + 3e^-$	$E° = 1.66$ V; more easily oxidized

Problem
What electrochemical processes are involved in rusting?

Materials
chemical splash goggles
laboratory apron
well plate
piece of white paper
3 micropipets, containing the following solutions:

iron(II) sulfate ($FeSO_4$), 0.1 M
ferroxyl indicator solution
sodium hydroxide (NaOH), 0.1 M
steel plate
steel wool

Safety

Wear your goggles and lab apron at all times during the investigation.
Some of the solutions used may be irritating to the skin. If any of them come into contact with skin, wash the area thoroughly with cold water and tell your teacher. Note the caution alert symbols here and with certain steps of the Procedure. Refer to page *xi* for the specific precautions associated with each symbol.

Procedure

1. Put on your goggles and lab apron. With the well plate on a white piece of paper, place two or three drops of iron(II) sulfate, $FeSO_4$, solution in one well of the well plate. Add two or three drops of the ferroxyl indicator solution. Observe the color changes. Record your observations in the Data Table.
2. In a second well, place two or three drops of sodium hydroxide, NaOH, solution. Add two or three drops of ferroxyl indicator solution. Observe and record the color changes.
3. Polish the steel plate with steel wool if necessary. Wipe it clean. Carefully place about 2 mL of ferroxyl indicator solution on the surface of the steel plate. Observe for 5–10 minutes and record your observations.

4. Use a wash bottle to rinse the solutions in the well plate and on the steel plate into the container provided by your teacher. Wash and dry the steel plate. Clean up your work area and wash your hands before leaving the laboratory.

326 © Prentice-Hall, Inc.

Name _____

Observations (sample data)
DATA TABLE

Reaction	Observations
FeSO$_4$ + ferroxyl indicator	Solution turns blue.
NaOH + ferroxyl indicator	Solution turns pink.
steel plate + ferroxyl indicator	Colorless at first; then a distinct pink outer region and a blue central region appear, with a brownish area between them.

Critical Thinking: Analysis and Conclusions

1. What ions are indicated by the color changes when ferroxyl indicator is added to the solutions in Steps 1 and 2? *(Interpreting data)* <u>Blue indicates the presence of Fe^{2+} ions. Pink indicates the presence of OH$^-$ ions.</u>

2. Based on your data, which part of the ferroxyl indicator drop on the steel plate is the anode? Explain your answer. Write the balanced chemical equation for the half reaction that is occurring there. *(Drawing conclusions)* <u>The blue region is the anode. Oxidation occurs at the anode, and the most likely candidate for oxidation in this reaction is iron, Fe. The balanced half reaction is Fe → Fe^{2+} + 2e$^-$.</u>

3. Based on your data, which part of the ferroxyl indicator drop on the steel plate is the cathode? Explain your answer. Write the balanced chemical equation for the half reaction that is occurring there. *(Drawing conclusions)* <u>The pink region is the cathode. Reduction occurs at the cathode. Since a pink color with ferroxyl indicator indicates the presence of OH$^-$ ions, OH$^-$ must be produced. The balanced half reaction is O$_2$ + 2H$_2$O → 4OH$^-$ + 4e$^-$.</u>

4. Write the balanced overall equation for the electrochemical reaction in Step 3. *(Drawing conclusions)* <u>2Fe + O$_2$ + 2H$_2$O → 2Fe^{2+} + 4OH$^-$</u>

5. How are electrons transferred from the anode to the cathode in this process? <u>Electrons are transferred from anode to cathode through the steel plate.</u>

APPLICATION

Sodium hydroxide is caustic, although 0.1 M NaOH is relatively dilute. Care should be taken to keep solutions off skin. If some should splash onto skin, instruct students to rinse the area thoroughly. ■

Teaching Tips

Students need to recognize the role of the ferroxyl indicator. If indicators have not been introduced previously, it would be helpful to demonstrate a range of indicators and their application. Ferroxyl indicator actually is two indicators, one of which is the more familiar phenolphthalein.

Students will probably have difficulty figuring out how to write the equations to get from Fe^{2+} to Fe$_2$O$_3 \cdot x$H$_2$O. Answers should demonstrate reasonable efforts.

Depending on the size of the indicator drop, there may be two brownish regions of rust. If the reaction continues long enough, visible pits in the steel may appear.

Oxidation of Fe to Fe^{2+} can be readily explained by the presence of iron in steel. Production of OH$^-$ is not so easily explained, however, until students realize that something has to be *reduced*. With some thought, students will realize that the most likely source for OH$^-$ is the reduction of oxygen in the presence of water.

A good introduction to interesting applications of spontaneous redox reactions is found in the article "Electrochemical Errors," *Journal of Chemical Education,* Vol. 62, No. 5, p. 424–425.

Waste Disposal
All solutions containing ferroxyl indicator must be stored in a sealed container for commercial disposal or shipment to a secure landfill. ■

6. In the space below, make a diagram of the ferroxyl indicator solution on the steel plate. Show where the colors appear and label the anode, cathode, and path of electrons. *(Applying concepts)*

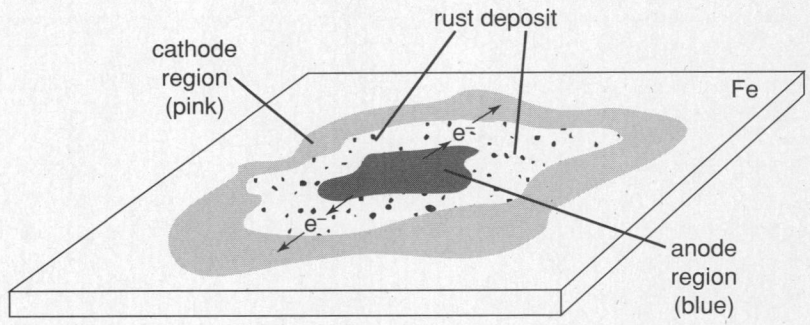

Going Further
1, 2. For each petri dish, dissolve 1 g powdered agar in 100 ml boiling water. Add three to four drops ferroxyl indicator solution. Mix well. Pour into a petri dish and cool. Nails may be pushed into the agar after it has hardened.

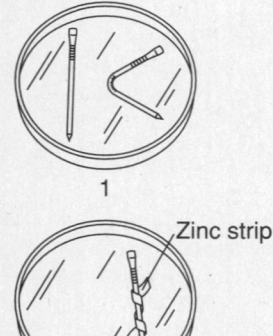

Set-ups for Going Further 1 and 2

Petrucci, Ralph, *General Chemistry*, 5th edition (MacMillan Publishing, 1989) pp. 771–772, contains a discussion of iron corrosion as outlined in this investigation, as well as illustrations of investigations with nails.

Critical Thinking: Applications

1. Speculate on a reasonable mechanism for the formation of rust. *(Developing hypotheses)* Fe was oxidized to Fe^{2+} in the presence of O_2. It is reasonable to assume that oxidation to Fe^{3+} also occurs in the presence of O_2, which is readily available.

2. Describe two practical ways of protecting iron from corrosion. For each, explain how iron is protected in electrochemical terms. Give an everyday example of each. *(Using the writing process)* Cover the surface with paint or another protective coating. This prevents oxygen from coming into contact with the metal as long as the paint remains intact. Car paint is an example. Cover the surface with another metal. If the second metal is more active than iron, it will be oxidized instead. This is the case with galvanized steel. If the metal is less active than iron, it protects the iron as long as it remains intact. An example of this is a "tin" can, where tin is electroplated on steel.

Going Further

1. Under your teacher's supervision, design and conduct an experiment to investigate factors that affect the rate of oxidation of iron nails. You may want to consider the effects of metal strain, electrolytes, or the presence of other metals.
2. Find out how galvanization protects iron and steel from rusting. Under your teacher's supervision, simulate galvanized iron by wrapping an iron nail with an appropriate metal. Report on your findings.

Quantitative Redox Titration Lab 60

Text reference: **Chapter 20**

Introduction

Earlier in this course, you performed an acid-base titration to analyze a commercial antacid. The titration methods you learned can also be used to determine the concentration of an ion in solution if the substance is easily oxidized or reduced. This method is called an oxidation-reduction, or redox, titration.

The analytical method for a redox titration is similar to that of an acid-base titration. Solutions of an oxidizing agent and a reducing agent are combined to reach an endpoint. One of these solutions is of a known concentration, and the concentration of the other solution is unknown. The purpose of the titration is to determine the concentration of the unknown, the number of moles present, or the percentage of a particular substance within a mixture. As with an acid-base titration, a balanced ionic equation must be written in order to determine the molar ratio of the reactants.

In this investigation, you will titrate standardized potassium permanganate solution, $KMnO_4$, against iron(II) sulfate solution, $FeSO_4$, of unknown concentration. In acid solution, the permanganate ion, MnO_4^-, is reduced to the manganese ion, Mn^{2+}, according to the following equation:

$$8H^+ + MnO_4^- + 5Fe^{2+} \rightarrow Mn^{2+} + 5Fe^{3+} + 4H_2O$$

At the same time, the iron(II) is oxidized to iron(III). One of the advantages of using potassium permanganate is its vivid purple color, whereas Mn^{2+} is nearly colorless. Even in very dilute solutions, permanganate ions produce a pink color. As soon as all the Fe^{2+} ions have reacted, one or two more drops of potassium permanganate will result in a persistent pink color. Once you have determined the volume of $KMnO_4$ solution needed to react completely with $FeSO_4$ solution, you can calculate the concentration of $FeSO_4$.

Pre-Lab Discussion

Read the entire laboratory investigation and the relevant pages of your textbook. Then answer the questions that follow.

1. What is the molar ratio of manganese to iron in this reaction? __1:5__

2. What is the indicator in this investigation and how does it work?
   The indicator is MnO_4^-. When the MnO_4^- is reduced by the Fe^{2+}, it loses its

   color. As soon as the Fe^{2+} ions are used up, the pink color of the MnO_4^-

   appears, indicating the endpoint.

Materials (class of 30 in pairs)

30 pairs chemical splash goggles
30 laboratory aprons
30 pairs latex gloves
30 burets, 50-mL
soap solution
15 buret brushes
6 L distilled water
1 L potassium permanganate ($KMnO_4$), 0.020 M
1 L iron(II) sulfate ($FeSO_4$), 0.20 M
30 beakers, 250-mL
15 buret clamps
15 ring stands
15 graduated cylinders, 100-mL
30 erlenmeyer flasks, 125-mL
500 mL sulfuric acid (H_2SO_4), 3.0 M

Time Required

60 minutes. If you only have 45 or 50 minutes, do only two titrations.

Advance Preparation

0.020 M $KMnO_4$ solution: Dissolve 4.7 g $KMnO_4$ in enough water to make 1.5 liters of solution and standardize the solution against sodium oxalate, $Na_2C_2O_4$.

0.20 M $FeSO_4$ solution: Dissolve 83.4 g $FeSO_4 \cdot 7H_2O$ in enough water to make 1.5 liters of solution.

3.0 M sulfuric acid: Mix 42 mL of 18 M H_2SO_4 with enough water to make 250 mL of solution.

CAUTION: $KMnO_4$ and H_2SO_4 can cause severe burns. $KMnO_4$ will stain skin and clothing. Wear goggles, gloves, and an apron while preparing these solutions and avoid contact with the chemicals. Always add acid to water.

Lab 60

Introduction
You may want to demonstrate the endpoint of the titration so students know what to look for. Also review how to read the volume on a buret.

3. What is the purpose of the solution prepared in Step 4? <u>The solution is used as a color standard for comparison with the color of the solution being titrated.</u>

4. Why is sulfuric acid added to the titration flask in Step 6? <u>The balanced equation shows H^+ as a reactant. The sulfuric acid is added to increase the hydronium ion concentration and ensure an excess of H^+ ions.</u>

5. During the redox reaction in this investigation, the MnO_4^- is changed to Mn^{2+}. How many electrons are involved? Is this change oxidation or reduction? <u>Manganese has an oxidation number of +7 in MnO_4^-. A change from +7 to +2 indicates a gain of five electrons and is reduction.</u>

6. What hazards are associated with this investigation, and what precautions should you take? <u>Sulfuric acid is corrosive. Avoid contact with skin and clothes. Potassium permanganate is a strong irritant to skin and eyes. It will stain skin and clothing. If you spill either solution, wash it off immediately with plenty of water and tell your teacher.</u>

Problem

How can you determine the concentration of an unknown solution of iron(II) sulfate?

Materials

chemical splash goggles
laboratory apron
latex gloves
2 burets, 50-mL
soap solution
buret brush
distilled water
potassium permanganate (KMnO$_4$), 0.020 M

iron(II) sulfate (FeSO$_4$) solution, unknown concentration
2 beakers, 250-mL
buret clamp
ring stand
graduated cylinder, 100-mL
2 erlenmeyer flasks, 125-mL
sulfuric acid (H$_2$SO$_4$), 3.0 M

Safety
Make sure students wear their goggles, gloves, and lab aprons at all times during the investigation. KMnO$_4$ and H$_2$SO$_4$ can cause severe burns. KMnO$_4$ will stain skin and clothing. Remind students to wear gloves and to wash off any spills immediately with plenty of water.

Safety

Wear your goggles, gloves, and lab apron at all times during the investigation. Sulfuric acid (H$_2$SO$_4$) is corrosive. Avoid contact with skin and clothes. Potassium permanganate (KMnO$_4$) is a strong irritant to skin and eyes. It will stain skin and clothing. If you spill either solution, wash it off immediately with plenty of water and tell your teacher.

Note the caution alert symbols here and with certain steps of the Procedure. Refer to page xi for the specific precautions associated with each symbol.

Name_____

Lab 60

Procedure

1. Put on your goggles, gloves, and lab apron. Clean two burets carefully, using soap solution and a buret brush. Rinse each buret several times with tap water and then with distilled water.

2. Add about 100 mL of potassium permanganate solution (0.020 M $KMnO_4$) to a 250-mL beaker. **CAUTION:** *Potassium permanganate ($KMnO_4$) is a strong irritant to skin and eyes. It will stain skin and clothing. If you spill any, rinse it off with plenty of water and tell your teacher.* Add about 100 mL of iron(II) sulfate solution ($FeSO_4$) to another 250-mL beaker.

3. Rinse one buret with about 5 mL of potassium permanganate solution and discard the rinse solution down the drain. Place the buret in the buret clamp. Fill the buret with potassium permanganate. Repeat the process with the other buret, using iron(II) sulfate. Record the initial buret readings in the Data Table.

4. Put about 50 mL of distilled water in an erlenmeyer flask and add one drop of potassium permanganate solution. This solution will be used as a color standard for the titration.

5. Measure 10.00 mL of the iron(II) sulfate solution from the buret into a clean erlenmeyer flask.

6. Add about 5 mL of sulfuric acid (H_2SO_4) to the flask in order to increase the hydronium ion concentration and immediately begin titrating with the potassium permanganate solution. **CAUTION:** *Sulfuric acid (H_2SO_4) is corrosive. Avoid contact with skin and clothes. Wear gloves. If you spill any, rinse it off thoroughly with plenty of water and inform your teacher.*

7. When the endpoint is reached, read the burets carefully and record the final readings in the Data Table. Rinse the contents of the flask down the drain with plenty of water. Rinse the flask with distilled water.

8. If time allows, repeat the titration two more times. Rinse the solutions down the drain with plenty of water. Clean up your work area and wash your hands before leaving the laboratory.

Teaching Tips
The concentration of the iron(II) sulfate will be about 0.20 M, which can easily be changed if you wish to use more than one concentration per class. If you increase the concentration, the volume used for the titration should be reduced from 20 mL to 10 or 5 mL so that you won't need an excessive amount of potassium permanganate.

Waste Disposal
All of the solutions can be washed down the drain with plenty of water. ■

Observations (sample data)

DATA TABLE   Volumes of $KMnO_4$ Titrated Against $FeSO_4$

Trial	Volume $FeSO_4$ (mL)	Initial Volume $KMnO_4$ (mL)	Final Volume $KMnO_4$ (mL)	Volume $KMnO_4$ Used (mL)
1	10.00	0.20	20.30	20.10
2	10.00	20.30	40.30	20.00
3	10.00	40.30	60.50	20.20

Lab 60

Name _____

Calculations (based on sample data)

1. Calculate the average volume of $KMnO_4$ used.

$$\frac{20.10 \text{ mL} + 20.00 \text{ mL} + 20.20 \text{ mL}}{3} = 20.10 \text{ mL}$$

2. Using the average volume you calculated in Step 1, calculate the number of moles of MnO_4^- used.

$$20.10 \text{ mL } MnO_4^- \times \frac{1 \text{ L}}{1000 \text{ mL}} \times \frac{0.020 \text{ mol } MnO_4^-}{1 \text{ L}} = 4.0 \times 10^{-4} \text{ mol } MnO_4^-$$

3. Using the molar ratio for the reactants that you listed in the Pre-Lab Discussion, calculate the number of moles of Fe^{2+} used.

$$4.0 \times 10^{-4} \text{ mol } MnO_4^- \times \frac{5 \text{ mol } Fe^{2+}}{1 \text{ mol } MnO_4^-} = 2.0 \times 10^{-3} \text{ mol } Fe^{2+}$$

4. Calculate the molarity of the $FeSO_4$ solution.

$$\frac{2.0 \times 10^{-3} \text{ mol } Fe^{2+}}{10.00 \text{ mL}} \times \frac{1000 \text{ mL}}{1 \text{ L}} = 0.20 \text{ M } FeSO_4$$

Critical Thinking: Analysis and Conclusions

1. Write the half reactions for the redox reaction in this investigation. *(Making inferences)*

   reduction: $MnO_4^- + 5e^- \rightarrow Mn^{2+} + 4O^{2-}$

   oxidation: $5Fe^{2+} \rightarrow 5Fe^{3+} + 5e^-$

2. If you did more than one titration, you probably got slightly different results each time. What are some possible sources of error? *(Interpreting data)* Possible sources of error include difficulty judging exactly when the endpoint has been reached and measurement errors.

3. If you titrated a second unknown solution of iron(II) sulfate, and less potassium permanganate was required to reach the endpoint, what could you conclude about the concentration of the second solution as compared to the first one? *(Drawing conclusions)* If less potassium permanganate was required, then there were fewer moles of iron(II) sulfate in the same volume of the second solution, therefore the concentration was lower.

Critical Thinking: Applications

1. What practical value might the titration in this investigation have? *(Evaluating)* The titration could be used to test water supplies for iron, a common contaminant. Other answers are possible.

Going Further

1. Making photographic prints and negatives depends on oxidation-reduction reactions. Investigate the process involved in black-and-white photography.

Name _____ Date _____ Class _____

Electrolysis of Water

Text reference: **Chapter 21**

Introduction

Most people studying science know that the chemical formula of water is H_2O, and that the letters H and O represent hydrogen and oxygen, the elements that comprise water. People know this because they were taught it, not because it is obvious from looking at water. For most of history, philosophers considered this clear liquid, which is an essential part of life, to be an element. In the mid-1780s, Antoine Lavoisier realized that water did not fit his new definition of elements, since it could be produced from burning hydrogen and oxygen, and it could be decomposed over high heat. In 1800, water was split into hydrogen gas and oxygen gas using electricity.

In this investigation you will use electrolysis to investigate the chemical makeup of water and the nature of the electrochemical half reactions that occur at each electrode, resulting in the decomposition of water. An electrolyte, sodium sulfate (Na_2SO_4), is used in solution to facilitate electrical conductivity because it does not itself undergo electrolysis under the given conditions.

Pre-Lab Discussion

Read the entire laboratory investigation and the relevant pages of your textbook. Then answer the questions that follow.

1. Which electrode supplies electrons to positively charged ions? __The cathode supplies electrons.__

2. At which electrode does oxidation (loss of electrons) occur? Is this electrode positively or negatively charged? __Oxidation occurs at the anode, which is positively charged.__

3. Why does the electrolysis process stop if the electrodes come in contact with each other, or short circuit? __A short circuit allows electrons to move directly from cathode to anode without causing ions to migrate toward the opposing electrodes.__

4. Why should you avoid touching the metal electrodes to each other or to your fingers while they are connected to the power source? __A short circuit may give an electrical shock, may cause the leads to become hot enough to burn skin, and may damage the power source.__

5. When should you terminate the electrolysis reaction? __When one test tube is half-filled with gas.__

Materials (class of 30 in pairs)
- 30 pairs chemical splash goggles
- 30 laboratory aprons
- 15 petri dish bottoms or covers, or other shallow containers
- distilled water
- 2 g sodium sulfate (Na_2SO_4)
- 30 platinum or stainless steel insulated electrodes
- pH indicator (phenol red or bromthymol blue)
- 15 micropipets
- 30 small test tubes
- 15 microscope-slide cover slips
- 30 sponge blocks (approximately 2 cm × 3 cm × 8 cm), notched in two places
- 15 metric rulers
- 15 9V batteries with snap-on leads, or DC power supplies with leads

Time Required
40–50 minutes.

Advance Preparation
If electrodes are not available from your lab supplies, you can make them out of either stainless steel or platinum as follows:
1. Stainless steel: Cut two 15-cm pieces of stainless steel wire. Insert each wire into a plastic micropipet stem from which the bulb has been cut off. With the wire protruding approximately 1 cm from the stem tip, pass the tip through a very low gas flame to melt and seal the plastic tip around the wire. If the plastic ignites, extinguish it immediately. Hold the cool end of the plastic stem for one minute while the melted plas-

© Prentice-Hall, Inc.

Electrolysis of Water **333**

Small Scale Lab 61

Name _____

Problem
What are the electrolysis products and half reactions for the decomposition of water?

Materials
chemical splash goggles
laboratory apron
petri dish bottom or cover
distilled water
sodium sulfate (Na_2SO_4)
2 platinum or stainless-steel insulated electrodes
pH indicator solution

micropipet
2 small test tubes
microscope-slide coverslip
2 notched sponge blocks
metric ruler
9V battery with snap-on leads, or DC power supply with leads

Safety
Wear your goggles and lab apron at all times during the investigation. To avoid possible shock or burns, do not touch bare wires from the power source or short the wire leads by touching them together. If you spill sodium sulfate or pH indicator on your skin or clothing, wash it off immediately with plenty of water and tell your teacher.

Note the caution alert symbols here and with certain steps of the Procedure. Refer to page *xi* for the specific precautions associated with each symbol.

Procedure

1. Put on your goggles and lab apron. Fill a petri dish or other shallow container nearly full of distilled water. Sprinkle the water with several grains of sodium sulfate (Na_2SO_4) and stir with one of the electrode tips to dissolve. Add a few drops of pH indicator.
2. Use a micropipet to fill two small test tubes with the solution from the dish. Overfill them slightly.
3. Place a microscope-slide cover slip over the mouth of one of the test tubes to trap the solution. Invert the test tube in the dish of electrolyte solution. Incline the filled test tube with its mouth still submerged in the dish of electrolyte solution. Rest the test tube on a notch in a block of moistened sponge placed outside the dish, as shown in Figure 61–1. Repeat the process for the second test tube.
4. Slide an electrode tip into the submerged mouth of each test tube. Rest the tops of the electrodes on notches in a second sponge block. Be careful as you move each electrode into position that you do not accidentally lift the test tube mouth above the surface. If you do, you will have to refill the test tube.

---

tic solidifies and cools. The hot melted plastic will stick to anything it touches. Visually inspect the sealed tip to ensure there are no gaps in the seal. CAUTION: *Plastic pipets are extremely flammable. Tie back long hair and loose clothing. Avoid burning plastic. Do not touch hot sticky plastic. Severe burns may result.*

High quality, stainless steel fish line (for salt water) is an inexpensive source of stainless wire that can be used in place of platinum, but some loss of oxygen is likely to result. Electrodes made in this fashion are usable anywhere in place of expensive glass-embedded electrodes, and will be virtually indestructible.

2. Platinum: Join 2 cm of platinum wire to a copper lead and seal the union inside the pipet barrel (as described above) so that no copper is exposed to the electrolyte. Platinum wire may be very fine, 22 gauge or less. It can be purchased from a jeweler's supply, or check an industrial directory under "Platinum" for manufacturers (cost approximately $35/ft.).

Cut the required sponge blocks from larger sponges and cut notches in them to support the test tubes.

Introduction
You may wish to do the following demonstration:

Fill a heavy-walled (ignition) test tube with electrolyte solution and incline it in the dish as before. Place both electrodes inside the test-tube mouth, one farther in than the other, so the metallic electrode tips do not touch. Connect the electrodes to the power source and wait for the test tube to fill with the gas mixture. Remove the gas-

Name _____

Small Scale Lab 61

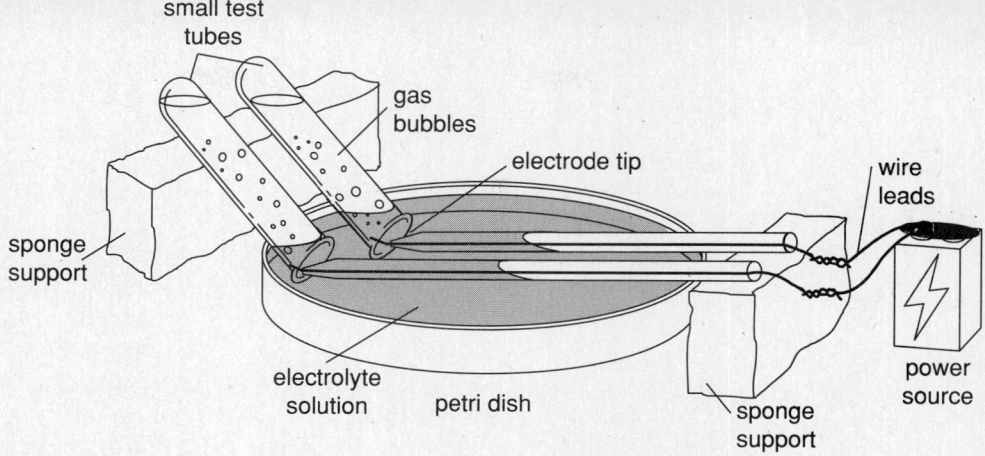

Figure 61–1

5. Connect a 9-volt battery lead, or DC power supply lead, to each electrode. Note which electrode is negative and which is positive. **CAUTION:** *Be careful not to touch the power source leads together, as this may cause the leads to become hot and may damage the battery or power supply.*

6. Soon after connection, you should see gas bubbles rising into the test tubes from each electrode. A little later, look for color changes, indicating a change in pH. Record in the Data Table the color changes at the anode and cathode, and the pH range as indicated in the following table.

TABLE 61–1 pH Ranges of Indicators

	pH < 7	pH = 7	pH > 7
phenol red	yellow	orange	red
bromthymol blue	yellow	green	blue

7. When one test tube is at least half full of gas, disconnect the electrodes, being careful not to short the leads by touching them. Remove the electrodes carefully, keeping the test-tube mouths below the surface of the solution. Holding each tube vertically in the dish, and, being careful not to lift the test-tube mouth above the surface, measure the height of gas in each tube in millimeters. Record in the Data Table the height of gas in each tube relative to the electrode at which it was produced.

8. Discard the electrolyte solution down the drain. Rinse the outside of the electrode casings and tips, the test tubes, and the dish with plenty of water. Clean up your work area and wash your hands before leaving the laboratory.

filled test tube, using a cover slip over the mouth and keeping the test-tube bottom up. Move the cover slip just enough to allow any solution to leak out of the tube. Wrap the test tube with a paper towel and bring the mouth of the test tube close to an open flame as you remove the cover slip. Be prepared for a loud report! CAUTION: *The test tube may shatter.* Allow students to inspect the walls of the test tube and discuss its appearance. (Water droplets condense on the inner walls.)

Safety
Make sure students wear their goggles and lab aprons at all times during the investigation. Demonstrate the setup with electrodes and how to avoid short circuits. ■

Teaching Tips
Demonstrate the filling and inversion of test tubes and how to recognize short circuits of power source leads or electrodes.

With respect to Analysis and Conclusions Questions 1–3, make sure the students understand that the electrode where H^+ is in excess is *not* where the H_2 forms.

In Analysis and Conclusions Question 6, it is

© Prentice-Hall, Inc.

Electrolysis of Water 335

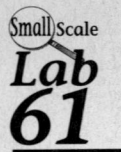

Small Scale Lab 61

Name _____

important to note that gases having the same volume under the same conditions have the same number of particles.

Waste Disposal
The electrolyte solution can be washed down the drain with plenty of water. ■

Observations (sample data)
DATA TABLE

	Anode	Cathode
pH indicator color	yellow	red or blue
indicated pH range	pH < 7	pH > 7
height of gas generated (mm)	17	38

Critical Thinking: Analysis and Conclusions

1. From the information in your text, write the half reactions that occur in this investigation. *(Interpreting data)* $2H_2O(l) \rightarrow 4H^+(aq) + O_2(g) + 4e^-$
$2H_2O(l) + 2e^- \rightarrow H_2(g) + 2OH^-(aq)$]

2. Based on pH-indicator observations, at which electrode are there excess H^+ ions? Which electrode is H^+-deficient (OH^- in excess)? *(Interpreting data)* Excess H^+ ions are present at the anode (pH < 7). The cathode is deficient in H^+ ions (pH > 7).

3. Based on your answers to Questions 1 and 2, identify the electrode at which each reaction is occurring. *(Making inferences)* The reaction that produces $O_2(g)$ occurs at the anode; the reaction that produces $H_2(g)$ occurs at the cathode.

4. Add together the two equations for the half reactions from your answer to Question 1 to obtain the overall reaction. Then write the net equation for the reaction. Explain how you reduced the terms in the net equation. *(Making inferences)*
overall reaction:
$6H_2O(l) + 4e^- \rightarrow O_2(g) + 2H_2(g) + 4H^+(aq) + 4e^- + 4OH^-(aq)$

net equation: $2H_2O(l) \rightarrow 2H_2(g) + O_2(g)$
The gain of electrons on one side of the equation is canceled by an equal loss of electrons on the other side. The $4H^+$ ions and $4OH^-$ ions on the right side are the equivalent of $4H_2O$, which cancels out all but $2H_2O$ from the left side of the equation.

5. Calculate the ratio of hydrogen gas to oxygen gas produced in the reaction. *(Interpreting data)* 38/17 = 2.2

6. What evidence do you have from the data that supports the accepted formula of water? *(Interpreting data)* The gas volume ratio (hydrogen: oxygen) is approximately 2:1. According to Avogadro's hypothesis, the mole ratio is 2:1, giving the formula H_2O.

Critical Thinking: Applications

1. If sodium chloride (NaCl) is used as an electrolyte instead of Na_2SO_4, hydrogen is produced, but at the other electrode little gas is collected. Instead, the electrolyte smells pungent like bleach. What ion from the electrolyte could account for this, and what is the half reaction that is occurring? *(Making predictions)* The chloride ion, Cl^-, is oxidized at the anode; the half reaction is $2Cl^- \rightarrow Cl_2(aq) + 2e^-$

2. How could you prove that the sodium sulfate (Na_2SO_4) electrolyte did not react in your electrolysis cell? *(Designing experiments)* Find the initial mass of the Na_2SO_4. After the reaction, evaporate the water from the electrolyte and find the mass again. There should be no mass change if the Na_2SO_4 did not react.

3. If you used concentrated hydrochloric acid as the electrolyte solution, what products would you be likely to get? In what ratio? *(Making predictions)* You would get hydrogen gas (H_2) and chlorine gas (Cl_2). The gases would occur in a 1:1 ratio.

Going Further

1. Research and describe electrolysis cells used to isolate and purify difficult-to-process metals such as aluminum, copper, and sodium.
2. Investigate commercial electroplating with metals such as chromium, silver, and gold. What base metals are suitable as cathodes, and what electrolytes are used? Obtain photographs and/or schematic diagrams of the cells.
3. Read about Michael Faraday and list some of his discoveries in the field of electrochemistry.

Going Further
2. Check the Yellow Pages under "Plating" to find local electroplating services to call or visit for information.

Name _____ Date _____ Class _____

Small-Scale Voltaic Cells

Text reference: **Chapter 21**

Introduction

From pacemakers and automatic garage door openers to portable hand-held televisions, it seems that the world runs on batteries. These batteries share some common characteristics. All of them, for example, are capable of doing work when a device is connected to their positive and negative terminals. They all derive their energy from a spontaneous chemical reaction that can be described in terms of oxidation and reduction half reactions. They can all be described as some sort of voltaic cell. A typical voltaic cell is illustrated in Figure 62–1.

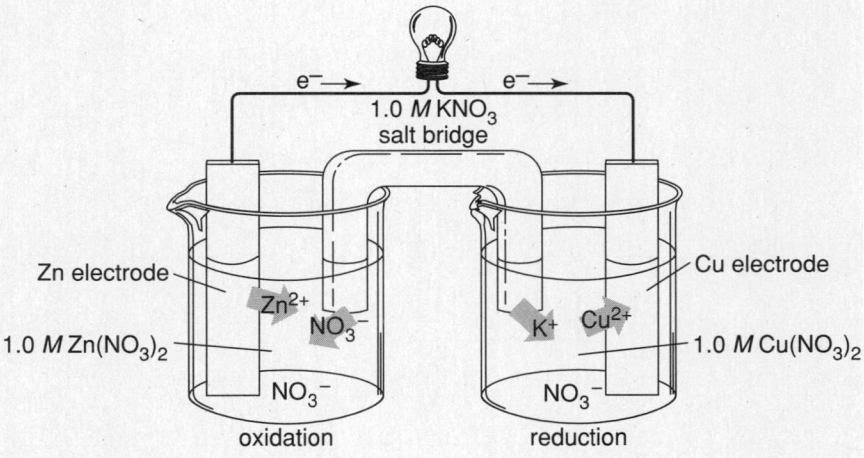

Figure 62–1

The electrons on the zinc atoms possess more chemical potential energy than the electrons on the copper atoms. This difference in potential energy creates the electromotive force, or voltage, of the voltaic cell. The amount of voltage depends on what metals are used. In this case, the voltage is 1.1 volts.

Notice in Figure 62–1 that there is a tube filled with potassium nitrate solution (KNO_3), forming a bridge between the two beakers. This tube is called a salt bridge. The salt bridge maintains the electrical neutrality of the solutions surrounding the electrodes. As the atoms of the zinc electrode lose electrons, they become positively charged ions. These ions enter the solution, causing it to become more positive. It becomes increasingly difficult for electrons to escape from the zinc side of the voltaic cell. At the same time, the atoms of the copper electrode are gaining electrons, causing it to become more negative. The electrode attracts the positive copper ions in the solution, leaving behind negative nitrate ions. This negative charge inhibits the movement of electrons onto the copper

Materials (class of 30 in pairs)
30 pairs chemical splash goggles
30 laboratory aprons
30 pairs latex gloves
75 metal samples, 1 cm × 1 cm, 15 each of the following:
 silver
 copper
 zinc
 lead
 magnesium (1-cm strips are acceptable)
15 pieces of steel wool, 5 cm × 5 cm
30 pieces of filter paper
15 pairs scissors
15 petri dishes
90 micropipets, 15 each containing the following 1.0 *M* solutions:
 50 mL silver nitrate ($AgNO_3$)
 50 mL magnesium nitrate ($Mg(NO_3)_2$)
 50 mL copper(II) nitrate ($Cu(NO_3)_2$)
 50 mL zinc nitrate ($Zn(NO_3)_2$)
 50 mL lead(II) nitrate ($Pb(NO_3)_2$)
 50 mL potassium nitrate (KNO_3)
15 multimeters with leads
30 pieces of paper towel
15 pairs forceps
tap water
distilled water

Time Required
40 minutes. To shorten the lab, have half the class do the measurements relative to the silver electrodes and the other half relative to the copper.

Advance Preparation
The physics or physical science teacher usually has a class set of multimeters.

© Prentice-Hall, Inc.

Small-Scale Voltaic Cells **339**

Small Scale Lab 62

Simple, hand-held digital multimeters are available from supply houses. Cut the metals into 1-cm² pieces ahead of time. Some supply houses offer metal samples of the appropriate size.

Dissolve the given mass of each solid in enough water to make 50 mL of solution.
CAUTION: *Wear gloves when handling silver nitrate.*
  silver nitrate ($AgNO_3$): 8.5 g
  magnesium nitrate ($Mg(NO_3)_2$): 7.4 g
  copper(II) nitrate ($Cu(NO_3)_2$): 9.4 g
  zinc nitrate ($Zn(NO_3)_2$): 9.5 g
  lead(II) nitrate ($Pb(NO_3)_2$): 16.6 g
  potassium nitrate (KNO_3): 5.1 g

Have ready labeled containers in which to collect the metal squares, used filter papers, and excess nitrate solutions.

Introduction

Students sometimes have difficulty visualizing the reaction that takes place within a voltaic cell. The changes aren't as apparent as those within electrolytic cells. It often helps to demonstrate what happens to a piece of zinc when it is placed in a copper sulfate solution over a period of time. They can see the copper metal form and become deposited on the zinc metal. They will see the solution lose its color as the copper ions are replaced by the zinc ions. If the piece is not too thick, they may also see the zinc metal disappear as it is used up in the reaction.

electrode. The salt bridge contains a solution of ions, in this case K^+ and NO_3^- ions. The negative solution surrounding the copper electrode attracts the K^+ ions, and the positive solution surrounding the zinc electrode attracts the NO_3^- ions, thereby neutralizing the electric charge of the solutions.

In this investigation, you will build an unusual apparatus that will allow you to compare the voltage created by a variety of different metallic half-cells.

Pre-Lab Discussion

Read the entire laboratory investigation and the relevant pages of your textbook. Then answer the questions that follow.

1. Write equations that describe the oxidation and reduction half reactions for the voltaic cell shown in Figure 62–1. Reduction: $Cu^{2+}(aq) + 2e^- \rightarrow Cu(s)$; oxidation: $Zn(s) \rightarrow Zn^{2+}(aq) + 2e^-$.

2. Why do the electrons only travel in one direction in the voltaic cell? Unless energy is supplied to the voltaic cell from outside, electrons must move from the electrode at which oxidation occurs to the one at which reduction occurs.

3. What is the purpose of the salt bridge in a voltaic cell? The salt bridge maintains the neutral charge of the solution surrounding the electrodes.

4. In which direction do the K^+ ions in the salt bridge in Figure 62–1 move? In which direction do the NO_3^- ions move? The K^+ ions move toward the copper electrode. The NO_3^- ions move toward the zinc electrode.

5. How are standard electrode potentials determined for the half-cells listed in the Standard Reduction Potential table found in the back of this book or in your text? The half-cells are used in a voltaic cell with a standard hydrogen half-cell.

6. Why should care be taken when working with potassium nitrate (KNO_3)? Potassium nitrate is a potentially explosive substance. It should not be heated in the presence of any organic material.

Problem

Which combination of metallic half-cells will produce a voltaic cell with the greatest potential difference?

Name _____

Small Scale Lab 62

Materials

chemical splash goggles
laboratory apron
latex gloves
metal samples, each
    1 cm × 1 cm
      silver
      copper
      zinc
      lead
      magnesium
steel wool
filter paper
scissors
petri dish

6 micropipets, containing the
  following 1.0 M solutions:
    silver nitrate ($AgNO_3$)
    magnesium nitrate
      ($Mg(NO_3)_2$)
    copper(II) nitrate
      ($Cu(NO_3)_2$)
    zinc nitrate ($Zn(NO_3)_2$)
    lead(II) nitrate ($Pb(NO_3)_2$)
    potassium nitrate (KNO_3)
multimeter with leads
paper towel
forceps
tap water
distilled water

Safety

Wear your goggles and lab apron at all times during the investigation. All the solutions are considered toxic. Silver nitrate and copper(II) nitrate are skin and tissue irritants. Silver nitrate causes stains on skin and clothes. Wear gloves when handling this solution. If any of these solutions come into contact with skin or clothing they should be washed off with plenty of water. Dispose of all the solutions according to your teacher's instructions.

Note the caution alert symbols here and with certain steps of the Procedure. Refer to page *xi* for the specific precautions associated with each symbol.

Procedure

 1. Put on your goggles and lab apron. Shine both sides of each piece of metal (the electrodes) with a piece of steel wool.

2. Hold two pieces of filter paper together and cut them so that five paper divisions extend from the center as shown in Figure 62–2 on the following page. The paper should look something like a five-petal flower.

3. Place the shaped filter papers on top of each other in the bottom plate of the petri dish.

  4. Put on latex gloves. Make a standard copper half-cell, as shown in Figure 62–2, by placing two drops of 1.0 M $Cu(NO_3)_2$ solution on one of the paper divisions and placing the shiny piece of copper on the wet spot. Repeat this process with the remaining 1.0 M metallic nitrate solutions and the corresponding metal pieces. **CAUTION:** *The solutions are all considered toxic and irritating to the skin. Wear gloves when handling them. If any of these solutions come into contact with the skin or clothing, wash them off with plenty of water and tell your teacher.*

Safety

Make sure students wear their goggles and lab aprons at all times during the investigation. When the solutions are prepared, care must be taken to avoid contact with the solid nitrates. Most of them are both strong oxidizing agents and toxic. Silver nitrate is corrosive and causes stains. Students should wear gloves when handling the solutions. Potassium nitrate is a fire and explosion hazard when heated in the presence of organic material. If skin or clothing comes into contact with any of these solids, rinse with plenty of water. ■

Teaching Tips

Students often become confused about voltaic cells after studying electrolytic cells. The key is for them to realize that voltaic cells make use of spontaneous reactions in which chemical potential energy is transformed into useful electrical energy. Electrolytic cells, on the other hand, must use electrical energy to cause a redox reaction that would not occur normally. Students already recognize the battery as a source of useful electrical energy. If the connection can

© Prentice-Hall, Inc.

Small-Scale Voltaic Cells **341**

be made that this energy is derived from a voltaic-type cell working within a battery, they may be able to mentally separate electrolytic and voltaic cells.

Students should be familiar with the operation of the multimeters. Digital meters are the best since there is no question about the scale being read. If you use analog multimeters, be sure that students have the meter on the correct voltage range and that they are reading the corresponding scale.

A dilute solution of ammonia water will help remove silver nitrate stains from the skin. Commercial laundry pretreatments may remove stains from clothing.

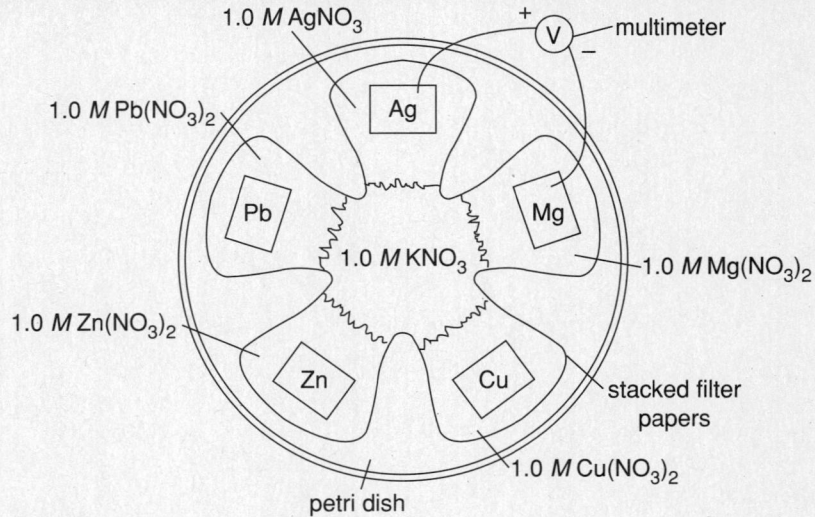

Figure 62–2

5. Make a salt bridge connecting the half-cells by placing two drops of 1.0 M KNO$_3$ solution on the center of the filter paper. The wetness of the salt bridge should run into the wetness caused by the 1.0 M salt solutions around each piece of metal.

6. Set the multimeter to measure DC voltage. If there is a scale setting, select a scale that will allow you to easily read potential differences between zero and two volts.

7. Place the positive probe (usually the red wire lead) on the piece of silver metal. This will be your reference electrode. Place the ground probe (usually the black wire lead) on the piece of magnesium metal. When the dial or digital display stabilizes, record the voltage in Data Table 1. If the voltage is a negative number, reverse the leads.

8. Keeping the positive lead on the silver piece of metal, move the ground lead to each of the remaining pieces of metal. In Data Table 1, record the potential difference that exists between the silver half-cell and each of the remaining half-cells.

9. Move the positive probe to the piece of copper metal. This will now be your reference electrode. Move the ground probe to each of the other pieces of metal. In Data Table 2, record the potential difference that exists between the copper half-cell and each of the other half-cells.

10. Switch off the multimeter.

11. Using forceps, remove the metal pieces (electrodes) from the petri dish and rinse them off with water. Place them on a paper towel to dry.

Name_____

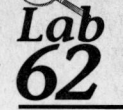

 12. Using forceps, place the wet filter paper in the labeled container provided by your teacher.

 13. Do not dispose of any of the solutions in the micropipets. Simply return them to their appropriately labeled beaker.

 14. Rinse the petri dishes with tap and distilled water. Wipe them dry with a paper towel. Clean up your work area and wash your hands before leaving the laboratory.

Waste Disposal

The pieces of used filter paper contain small quantities of all of the ions. They should be sealed inside a glass or plastic container and disposed of in a landfill that can handle chemical waste.

The unused solutions used in the experiment are stable and can be stored from year to year. If the solutions must be disposed of, they should be dehydrated in the fume hood and the residue sealed in glass or plastic bottles. They can then be disposed of in a landfill that can handle chemical waste.

Silver compounds are regulated as hazardous waste (EPA waste #D011). Collect any remaining silver solution and precipitate the Ag^+ ions with excess NaCl solution. Filter out the precipitate and store in a marked container. Discard the filtrate. ■

Observations (sample data)

DATA TABLE 1   Silver (Ag) Reference Half-Cell

Cell	Voltage (V)	Theoretical Voltage (V)	Percent Error
Ag-Mg	+2.02	+3.17	36.3%
Ag-Cu	+0.42	+0.46	8.7%
Ag-Zn	+1.41	+1.56	9.6%
Ag-Pb	+0.95	+0.93	2.2%

DATA TABLE 2   Copper (Cu) Reference Half-Cell

Cell	Voltage (V)	Theoretical Voltage (V)	Percent Error
Cu-Mg	+1.62	+2.71	40.2%
Cu-Ag	+0.42	+0.46	8.7%
Cu-Zn	+1.07	+1.10	2.7%
Cu-Pb	+0.53	+0.47	12.8%

 ## Calculations (based on sample data)

1. Calculate the theoretical potential of the cells tested, as shown in the following example for the standard Ag-Cu cell:
   a. Using a table of standard reduction potentials as a reference, determine the reduction potentials (voltages) for both half-cells.

$$Cu^{2+}(aq) + 2e^- \rightarrow Cu(s) \ (E° = +0.34 \text{ volts})$$

$$Ag^+(aq) + e^- \rightarrow Ag(s) \ (E° = +0.80 \text{ volts})$$

Small-Scale Voltaic Cells

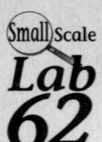

b. Reverse the sign of the potential that is the least positive (most negative) and add the two voltages. Enter the values in the appropriate Data Tables.

$$+0.80 \text{ volts} + (-0.34 \text{ volts}) = +0.46 \text{ volts}$$

Ag-Mg: $Ag^+(aq) + e^- \rightarrow Ag(s)$ (E° = +0.80 volts)
$Mg^{2+}(aq) + 2e^- \rightarrow Mg(s)$ (E° = −2.37 volts)
+0.80 volts + (+2.37 volts) = +3.17 volts

Ag-Cu: $Ag^+(aq) + e^- \rightarrow Ag(s)$ (E° = +0.80 volts)
$Cu^{2+}(aq) + 2e^- \rightarrow Cu(s)$ (E° = +0.34 volts)
+0.80 volts + (−0.34 volts) = +0.46 volts

Ag-Zn: $Ag^+(aq) + e^- \rightarrow Ag(s)$ (E° = +0.80 volts)
$Zn^{2+}(aq) + 2e^- \rightarrow Zn(s)$ (E° = −0.76 volts)
+0.80 volts + (+0.76 volts) = +1.56 volts

Ag-Pb: $Ag^+(aq) + e^- \rightarrow Ag(s)$ (E° = +0.80 volts)
$Pb^{2+}(aq) + 2e^- \rightarrow Pb(s)$ (E° = −0.13 volts)
+0.80 volts + (+0.13 volts) = +0.93 volts

Cu-Mg: $Cu^{2+}(aq) + 2e^- \rightarrow Cu(s)$ (E° = +0.34 volts)
$Mg^{2+}(aq) + 2e^- \rightarrow Mg(s)$ (E° = −2.37 volts)
+0.34 volts + (+2.37 volts) = +2.71 volts

Cu-Ag: $Cu^{2+}(aq) + 2e^- \rightarrow Cu(s)$ (E° = +0.34 volts)
$Ag^+(aq) + e^- \rightarrow Ag(s)$ (E° = +0.80 volts)
(−0.34 volts) + (+0.80 volts) = +0.46 volts

Cu-Zn: $Cu^{2+}(aq) + 2e^- \rightarrow Cu(s)$ (E° = +0.34 volts)
$Zn^{2+}(aq) + 2e^- \rightarrow Zn(s)$ (E° = −0.76 volts)
+0.34 volts + (+0.76 volts) = +1.10 volts

Cu-Pb: $Cu^{2+}(aq) + 2e^- \rightarrow Cu(s)$ (E° = +0.34 volts)
$Pb^{2+}(aq) + 2e^- \rightarrow Pb(s)$ (E° = −0.13 volts)
+0.34 volts + (+0.13 volts) = +0.47 volts

2. Calculate the percent error for the voltages measured from the cells tested. The accepted value is the theoretical standard value calculated for each cell. Enter the values in the appropriate Data Tables.

Ag-Mg: (|2.02 − 3.17|/3.17) × 100 = 36.3%   Cu-Mg: (|1.62 − 2.71|/2.71) × 100 = 40.2%
Ag-Cu: (|0.42 − 0.46|/0.46) × 100 = 8.7%   Cu-Ag: (|0.42 − 0.46|/0.46) × 100 = 8.7%
Ag-Zn: (|1.41 − 1.56|/1.56) × 100 = 9.6%   Cu-Zn: (|1.07 − 1.10|/1.10) × 100 = 2.7%
Ag-Pb: (|0.95 − 0.93|/0.93) × 100 = 2.2%   Cu-Pb: (|0.53 − 0.47|/0.47) × 100 = 12.8%

Critical Thinking: Analysis and Conclusions

1. How well do the potential differences of the cells constructed in the petri dish compare to the theoretical potential difference of the standard cells? *(Making comparisons)* The percent errors range from 2.2% to 40.2%. The largest errors occurred when measuring the potential difference between magnesium and the two reference metals. Aside from the magnesium cells, the rest of the results were within an acceptable range.

2. What variables exist within the voltaic cells that may account for the differences between the observed and theoretical values? *(Making inferences)* Some of the variables are how well the probes make contact with the metals, solution concentrations, metal purity, and temperature.

Name _____

3. Using the data obtained when silver was the reference electrode, arrange the potential differences of the cells from most positive to least positive. Does the same relative order exist when the theoretical potential differences are arranged from most positive to least positive? *(Making comparisons)* Experimental order: Ag-Mg, Ag-Zn, Ag-Pb, Ag-Cu. Theoretical order: Ag-Mg, Ag-Zn, Ag-Pb, Ag-Cu. The same order exists when the experimental and theoretical values are compared.

4. Using the data obtained when copper was the reference electrode, arrange the potential differences of the cells from most positive to least positive. Compare this to the arrangement of the potential difference found when silver was the reference electrode. Do both silver and copper have the same order of potential differences? *(Making comparisons)* Experimental order: Cu-Mg, Cu-Zn, Cu-Pb, Cu-Ag. The same order exists as with the silver reference electrode.

Critical Thinking: Applications

1. Which of the cells would be the best source of electrical energy in an electrical device? Explain. *(Making judgments)* The Ag-Mg cell would serve as the best source of electrical energy, since it has the highest potential difference.

2. What would be some practical problems in using the metals you chose for Applications Question 1 in a marketable battery? *(Applying concepts)* Silver is too expensive to use in a battery. Magnesium is too reactive and would react with air or water in the battery.

3. The copper-zinc voltaic cell shown in Figure 63–1 should theoretically have a potential difference of 1.10 volts. What would happen to this voltage if the voltaic cell was used over a period of time? Explain your answer in terms of changes that would take place in the voltaic cell. *(Making predictions)* The voltage will fall steadily as the concentration of Cu^{2+} ions decreases and Zn^{2+} ions increases. The cell will short-circuit when the Cu^{2+} ions migrate through the salt bridge and react directly with the zinc electrode. The zinc electrode could become used up if the cell is operated for a long time or if the zinc is thin.

4. In any voltaic cell, oxidation always occurs at the anode, and reduction always occurs at the cathode.
   a. Which electrode in the copper-zinc voltaic cell is the anode and which is the cathode? *(Classifying)* The zinc is the anode, and the copper is the cathode.
   b. Which electrode in the copper-silver voltaic cell is the anode and which is the cathode? *(Classifying)* The copper is the anode, and the silver is the cathode.

Small-Scale Voltaic Cells

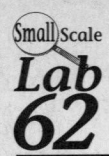

Lab 62

Name _____

Going Further

1. The internal structures of some commercial batteries are illustrated in hardware and electronics store advertisements and in popular technology magazines. Students can usually get the managers of hardware and electronics stores to give them some of these illustrations.
4. Auto parts suppliers and service centers often receive advertisements concerning car batteries. Some manufacturers and their sales representatives have technical information that is quite informative.
5. Anyone who sells car batteries also has to deal with trade-ins. They have information on both the collection part of the recycling process and how the batteries are being recycled. Some hardware and electronics stores have their own battery recovery and recycling programs.

Going Further

1. Compare the copper-zinc voltaic cell shown in Figure 63–1 to a commercial battery. Make a sketch of the internal structure of the commercial battery, illustrating some of the components common to all voltaic cells. Present your comparison to the class.
2. Research the history of the battery to determine when the earliest batteries were made, how they were constructed, and the purpose for which they were used. Present your findings to the class.
3. Research the construction of the rechargeable battery and report on how the recharging process is carried out.
4. Some name-brand car batteries are advertised to deliver 500 amps of "cranking power" at freezing temperatures. Research some of the name-brand car batteries and construct a report describing what this claim really means.
5. Prepare a report on the toxic waste problem that results from the disposal of used batteries and on some recycling solutions that are already in place.

Zinc Plating of Ornaments

Lab 63 APPLICATION

Text reference: **Chapter 21**

Introduction

You are probably familiar with gold-, silver-, or chromium-plated items such as jewelry, silverware, and chrome trim on automobiles. However, you may not be familiar with the process that produces them—electroplating.

Electroplating involves the construction of an *electrolytic cell*. In an electrolytic cell a nonspontaneous oxidation-reduction reaction is made to occur by using an external source of electrical energy, such as a battery. The battery adds electrons to the cathode and removes electrons from the anode. As a result, the cathode becomes negatively charged, while the anode becomes positively charged. At the anode the removal of electrons causes the material in the anode to be oxidized and enter the solution as cations. Simultaneously, metallic cations in the solution are attracted to the cathode. When the cations reach the cathode, they gain electrons and are reduced to the metallic state, plating out on the cathode. The concentration of cations in the solution remains constant.

In electroplating, the object to be plated is used as the cathode, and a piece of the metal that will form the plated layer is used as the anode. For example, in order to copper-plate an iron object, you would connect the iron object to the negative terminal of the battery and connect a piece of copper to the positive terminal of the battery. Figure 63–1 shows this electrolytic cell.

Materials (class of 30 in pairs)

30 pairs chemical splash goggles
30 laboratory aprons
copper sheet #22 or #30 (enough to cut 30 4-cm squares)
metal shears
electric drill with 3/32" bit *or* hammer and a small diameter nail
500 mL nitric acid (HNO_3), 2.0 M
100 g baking soda
15 pieces of steel wool
paper towels
roll of wide masking tape
15 pencils
15 single-edge razor blades or razor knives
30 cotton swabs
isopropyl alcohol
3 m bare copper wire, 16–18 gauge
1 L zinc nitrate ($Zn(NO_3)_2$), 1.0 M
10 wire leads with alligator clips
5 lantern batteries, 6-volt
5 zinc metal strips, 2.5 cm × 15 cm
5 beakers, 250-mL
can of clear acrylic spray paint

Time Required
45 minutes.

Advance Preparation

2.0 M nitric acid is made by slowly adding 62.5 mL of concentrated nitric acid to 500 mL of distilled water. CAUTION: *Nitric acid is corrosive. Wear goggles, gloves, a face shield, and an apron. Always add acid to water.*

0.1 M zinc nitrate is made by dissolving 18.9 g $Zn(NO_3)_2$ in water to produce a final volume of 1 L.

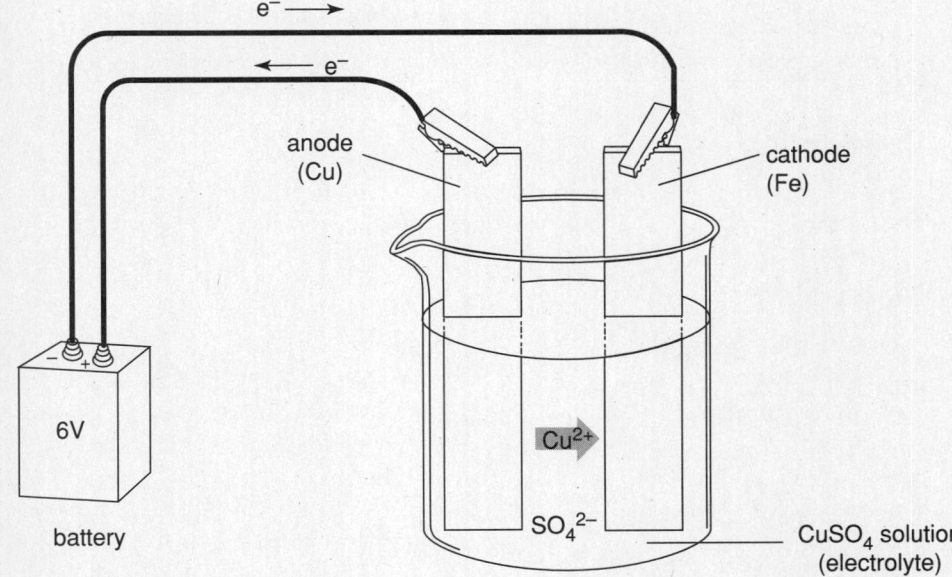

Figure 63–1

Zinc Plating of Ornaments **347**

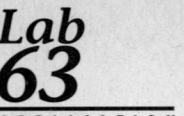

Lab 63 APPLICATION

Name _____

APPLICATION notes (teacher margin)

Purchase the copper sheeting. Copper flashing, available in building supply stores, is easy to cut.

Cut 30 4-cm squares from a sheet of copper. Drill a small hole in one corner of each square, using an electric drill or a hammer and nail.

Put the squares into a clean, dry 1-L beaker and barely cover them with 2.0 M nitric acid. Allow to stand for 2–3 minutes.

Neutralize the nitric acid with baking soda and rinse it down the drain with plenty of water. Rinse the copper squares with plenty of water and dry.

Set up five areas where the students can go to do the electroplating. Each area should have one lantern battery, two wire leads with alligator clips, one 250-mL beaker with 200 mL of the zinc nitrate solution, and one zinc strip. Alternatively, you may set up one large bath with a zinc bar at one end. Suspend a metal bar hooked up to the battery across the other end. The students can then all hang their ornaments from the bar so that they are immersed in the electrolyte.

Set up an area under the fume hood where students can spray paint their ornaments. You can suspend a string between two ring stands and cover the area with newspapers.

Have a container ready to collect the used zinc nitrate solution.

Introduction

You may wish to introduce this investigation with the following demonstration.

Place a piece of copper in a dilute zinc nitrate solution and a piece of zinc in a dilute copper(II) nitrate solution and let the students observe what happens (see Applications Question 3). Bring out the idea of spontaneous versus nonspontaneous processes.

Electrolytic cells are used to extract pure forms of metals from their ores, for example, aluminum from bauxite and sodium from halite. Impure metals such as gold and silver can be purified by electrolysis. Electrolysis can also be used to extract nonmetals such as hydrogen and oxygen from water, and chlorine from halite.

In this investigation, you will make a zinc-plated ornament and become familiar with the electroplating process. You will describe the process in terms of oxidation-reduction reactions and draw a diagram of the electrolytic cell used.

Pre-Lab Discussion

Read the entire laboratory investigation and the relevant pages of your textbook. Then answer the questions that follow.

1. Write the net ionic equations for the half reactions that are taking place at the anode and the cathode in the example given in the Introduction.

    anode: $Cu(s) \rightarrow Cu^{2+}(aq) + 2e^-$

    cathode: $Cu^{2+}(aq) + 2e^- \rightarrow Cu(s)$

2. In an electrolytic cell, does oxidation take place at the anode or the cathode? Where does reduction take place? Oxidation takes place at the anode. Reduction takes place at the cathode.

3. Why is it important that the copper square be as clean as possible before it is plated? The zinc must be able to bond directly to the copper. Oils or other coatings would prevent the solution from making close contact with the copper.

4. What are the hazards of working with acrylic paint? What safety precautions should you take? Acrylic paint is extremely toxic, and one should avoid inhaling its fumes. Use the acrylic paint under the fume hood only.

Problem

How can you use electroplating techniques to make a zinc-plated ornament?

Materials

chemical splash goggles
laboratory apron
2 copper squares
steel wool
paper towel
wide masking tape
pencil
razor blade or razor knife
cotton swab

isopropyl alcohol
bare copper wire, 10-cm
zinc nitrate $(Zn(NO_3)_2)$, 1.0 M
two wire leads with alligator clips
lantern battery
zinc metal strip
beaker, 250-mL

348   © Prentice-Hall, Inc.

Name _____

Lab 63 APPLICATION

Safety

Wear your goggles and lab apron at all times during the investigation.

The copper square and the razor blade or razor knife have sharp edges. Handle them carefully to avoid cuts. Isopropyl alcohol is flammable. Be sure there are no open flames in the laboratory. Zinc nitrate is toxic. Avoid ingestion. The acrylic spray paint is toxic. Do not inhale it. Use it under the fume hood only.

Note the caution alert symbols here and with certain steps of the Procedure. Refer to page *xi* for the specific precautions associated with each symbol.

Procedure

1. Put on your goggles and lab apron.
2. Use a piece of steel wool to polish both sides of the copper square. Rinse it with water and dry it.
3. Cover both sides of the copper square with masking tape. Be sure the tape overlaps the edges of the copper square. Trim off excess tape.
4. Sketch your desired design on one side of the square and cut its outline from the tape with a razor blade or razor knife. Remove the tape from the area you wish to have plated. Be sure the remaining tape is secure. **CAUTION:** *Be careful not to cut yourself with the razor blade or razor knife.*

5. Carefully clean the area with a cotton swab that has been dipped in isopropyl alcohol. Do not touch this area after cleaning. Let it dry. **CAUTION:** *Isopropyl alcohol is flammable. Make sure there are no open flames in the laboratory.*
6. Push a 10-cm piece of copper wire through the hole in the square and make a hook. Be sure the wire makes contact with the bare copper metal.

7. Go to one of the areas for electroplating that your teacher has designated. Using the wire leads with alligator clips, connect one wire between the negative terminal of the battery and the copper wire attached to your ornament. Connect the second wire between the positive terminal and the zinc strip. Insert the zinc strip on one side of the beaker containing the zinc nitrate, $Zn(NO_3)_2$, solution. Carefully insert your ornament into the zinc nitrate, on the side opposite from the zinc strip. Do not allow the two metals to come in contact. See Figure 63–2. Observe the electroplating of the zinc onto the surface of the copper square, and write a description of what you see. Be sure to include your observations of the zinc strip as well. Allow the reaction to continue for 1–2 minutes. **CAUTION:** *Zinc nitrate is poisonous. Do not ingest it.*

Then, connect the negative terminal of a battery to a cheap stainless steel spoon and the positive terminal to a strip of copper. Insert the copper strip and the spoon into a 1 *M* copper(II) sulfate solution. Show that the spoon becomes plated with copper. Discuss how the battery drives this nonspontaneous process. Make a diagram of this electrolytic cell.

Safety

Cuts may be produced by sharp edges on the copper square and by the razor blade or razor knife. Demonstrate how to handle the blades properly.

Zinc nitrate is toxic. Caution students to avoid ingesting it and to wash spills and splashes with plenty of cold water.

The acrylic paint is very toxic when inhaled and should only be used in a fume hood or outdoors. ■

Teaching Tips

Although students are working in pairs, let each student make an ornament if sufficient materials are available.

You may want to experiment in advance with the concentration of the zinc nitrate solution and the voltage of the power supply.

The surface of the copper must be clean and free of oils for good adherence by the zinc.

A very thin layer of zinc is plated onto the copper and can be easily rubbed off. The acrylic paint seals the surface and the ornament can then be handled. Clear nail polish can be used in place of the acrylic paint, but care must be used in brushing over the zinc plate. It also requires a longer drying time.

The color of the zinc strip may change. This is due to the oxidation of zinc as a

Zinc Plating of Ornaments **349**

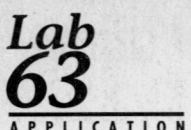

Name _____

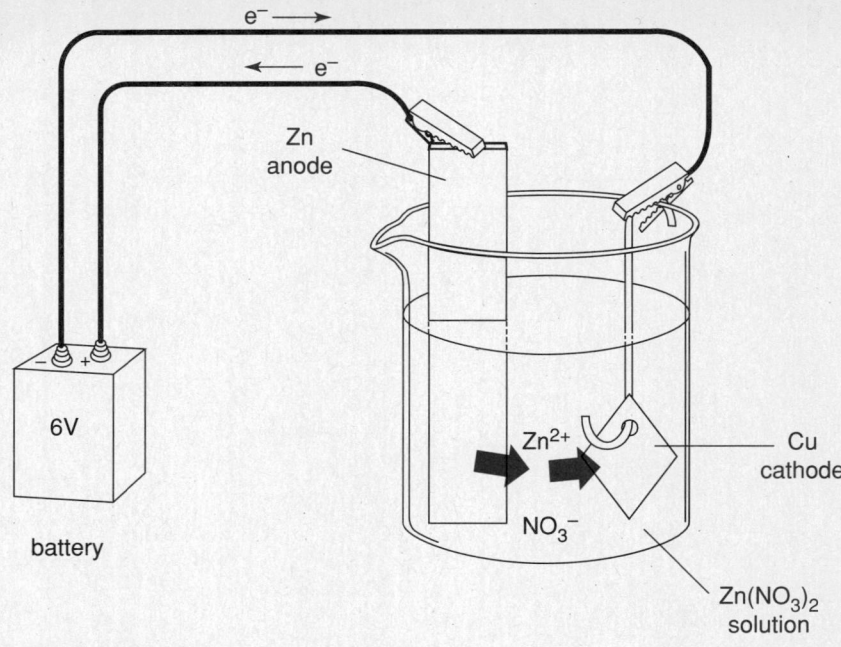

Figure 63–2

result of the decomposition of water.

In the situation described in Applications Question 1, the solution would turn blue around the copper electrode.

Waste Disposal

The zinc nitrate solution can be stored and reused. Nitric acid can be neutralized with baking soda, then poured down the drain with plenty of water. All solid waste can be disposed of in the trash. ■

8. Remove the ornament from the electroplating solution. Disconnect the wires and wash the ornament in water. Do not rub the area where zinc has been plated. Carefully remove the tape from the ornament. If any area not plated needs more polishing you can do so with steel wool. Be careful not to rub the zinc plate. Carefully pat the ornament dry with a paper towel.

9. Hang your ornament inside a designated area in the fume hood that has been protected with newspapers. Spray both sides with clear acrylic paint and let it dry. **CAUTION:** *Acrylic paint fumes are toxic. Do not breathe the fumes.*

10. Dispose of the solutions as directed by your teacher. Clean up your work area and wash your hands before leaving the laboratory.

Observations

In a very short amount of time, the copper area exposed to the zinc nitrate becomes a whitish grey. As time goes on, the area becomes a darker grey. There is no change in the solution. The zinc strip becomes lighter grey in color.

Critical Thinking: Analysis and Conclusions

1. Write the net ionic equations that show what is taking place at the anode and at the cathode during this investigation. *(Interpreting data)*

   anode: $Zn(s) \rightarrow Zn^{2+}(aq) + 2e^-$

   cathode: $Zn^{2+}(aq) + 2e^- \rightarrow Zn(s)$

Name_____

Lab 63 APPLICATION

2. Add labels to Figure 63–2, indicating the cathode, the anode, the $Zn(NO_3)_2$ solution, the direction of flow of electrons through the wire, and the direction of flow of ions in the solution. *(Making inferences)*

3. What do you think happens to the mass of the cathode over time as electroplating takes place? The mass of the anode? *(Making inferences)* The mass of the cathode (copper) increases as zinc metal plates onto it. The mass of the anode (zinc) decreases as the zinc metal is oxidized into zinc ions.

Critical Thinking: Applications

1. What would have happened in the investigation if the connections from the battery were reversed? Include reactions at the anode and the cathode. What do you think the cathode would look like if the system were allowed to run for several minutes? Explain. *(Making predictions)* The copper would be oxidized and go into solution. At first the zinc ions would be reduced at the zinc strip. These changes would not be readily visible. Then the copper ions would begin to be reduced at the zinc strip because copper has a greater reduction potential. The zinc strip would become copper plated.

    anode: $Cu(s) \rightarrow Cu^{2+}(aq) + 2e^-$
    cathode: $Zn^{2+}(aq) + 2e^- \rightarrow Zn(s)$
    $Cu^{2+}(aq) + 2e^- \rightarrow Cu(s)$

2. What would happen if the zinc strip or the zinc nitrate used in this investigation contained metallic impurities? What would determine whether the impurities would interfere or not? *(Developing hypotheses)* The metal impurities might or might not have an effect. If the reduction potential of the impurity were greater than that of the desired metal, the impurity would be electroplated and contaminate the plating process.

3. A piece of copper metal is placed in a solution of zinc nitrate and a piece of zinc metal is placed in a solution of copper(II) nitrate. What would happen to each, if anything? Explain. *(Applying concepts)* Nothing would happen to the copper metal placed in the zinc nitrate. The zinc metal would become covered with copper metal when it was placed in the copper(II) nitrate. The potential for copper(II) ions to be reduced is greater than that for zinc ions, so the reaction between the zinc and the copper(II) ions is spontaneous while the reverse reaction is not.

Lab 63 APPLICATION

Name _____

Going Further

1. The library and chemistry texts are good sources of information about the isolation and purification of aluminum. Students can also write to aluminum manufacturers.
2. The library should have information concerning electroplating of jewelry and automobile parts. Consult a telephone directory for possible industries in your area, including automobile manufacturers. If you have any of these industries in your area, you could arrange a tour.

4. If you wanted to plate a piece of iron with chromium, to which terminal of the battery would you attach the iron? The chromium? *(Applying concepts)* The iron should be connected to the negative terminal of the battery, and the chromium should be connected to the positive terminal. The iron must be made negatively charged in order to attract the chromium(III) cations. The chromium must be oxidized in order to replenish the chromium(III) ions being removed from the solution.

Going Further

1. At one time, aluminum was very rare and quite expensive. The electrolysis of bauxite, aluminum ore, provided an inexpensive means of producing aluminum. Research the means by which aluminum was extracted from ore prior to electrolysis and the electrolysis method.
2. Research the processes employed to make gold-plated jewelry and chrome-plated automobile parts.

Name _____ Date _____ Class _____

Reaction Kinetics

Small Scale Lab 64

Text reference: **Chapter 22**

Introduction

How fast do products form from reactants in a chemical reaction? The rate of a reaction depends on a number of variables: the nature of the reactants, the temperature, the concentration of the reactants, and the presence of catalysts.

In this investigation, you will determine the effect of the concentration of a reactant on the rate of a reaction that follows the sequence of chemical changes described by the following equations:

$$IO_3^-(aq) + 3HSO_3^-(aq) \rightarrow 3HSO_4^-(aq) + I^-(aq)$$

$$6H^+(aq) + IO_3^-(aq) + 5I^-(aq) \rightarrow 3I_2(aq) + 3H_2O(l)$$

$$I_2(aq) + starch(aq) \rightarrow I_2\cdot[starch](aq)$$

In this reaction, iodate ion, IO_3^-, reacts with hydrogen sulfite ion, $HSO_3^-(aq)$, in acid solution to give iodide ion, $I^-(aq)$. The iodide ion then reacts with iodate ion to give molecular iodine, $I_2(aq)$. Molecular iodine reacts instantly with starch in solution to form a complex that is blue-black in color. The colored product allows you to determine the time required to reach this point in the reaction. Because this reaction is predictable and easily observed, it is often called the "iodine-clock reaction."

Pre-Lab Discussion

Read the entire laboratory investigation and the relevant pages of your textbook. Then answer the questions that follow.

1. What are the dependent and independent variables in this investigation? What variables, if any, are held constant? __The independent variable is the concentration of iodate ion. The dependent variable is the time required to reach the formation of the I₂•[starch] complex. The hydrogen sulfite ion concentration and the temperature are variables held constant.__

2. What is the intermediate product in this reaction? __The intermediate product is I⁻.__

3. How would it affect your results if $I_2(aq)$ reacted with starch at a slower rate than the reactions that produce $I_2(aq)$? __If the time for the last step were not very small compared to the first two steps, the results would not reflect the reaction rate for the formation of I₂(aq).__

Materials (class of 30 in pairs)

30 pairs chemical splash goggles
30 laboratory aprons
15 marking pens
15 well plates, 24-well
15 sheets of white paper
15 micropipets, adapted for mixing
15 sets of 4 micropipets, containing the following solutions:
  100 mL potassium iodate (KIO_3), 0.02 M
  100 mL distilled water
  100 mL sodium hydrogen sulfite ($NaHSO_3$), 0.02 M in acid solution
  100 mL starch solution
distilled water
15 stopwatches or a clock with a second hand

Time Required

30 minutes. To save time, have the students begin the reactions at 10-second intervals and keep a running account of the time of starts and stops. This should provide time to do the procedure twice, allowing students to use the average time for the two trials. If you decide to do this, have each partner initially make up separate well plates. (You will need to increase the number of well plates.) You could also decrease the lab time by assigning different trials to different groups.

Advance Preparation

Potassium iodate: Dissolve 0.43 g of KIO_3 in 100 mL of water.
  Sodium hydrogen sulfite in acid solution: Mix 0.2 g of sodium hydrogen sulfite ($NaHSO_3$) and 0.5 mL of 1.0 M H_2SO_4 in 100 mL of

© Prentice-Hall, Inc.

Reaction Kinetics **353**

Small Scale Lab 64

water. Test this solution ahead of time. If the reaction is too fast, add 1 M NaOH drop by drop; if it is too slow, add 1 M H₂SO₄. CAUTION: *Wear goggles and an apron while preparing all solutions.*

Starch solution: Make a paste from 0.4 g of soluble starch and a small amount of deionized water. Add the paste to 90 mL of boiling water. Boil for a few minutes, then add enough deionized water to bring the volume up to 100 mL. The solution is stable for at least a week but cannot be stored indefinitely.

Label the sets of 5 pipets as follows: IO_3^- (for the potassium iodate solution), HSO_3^- (for the sodium hydrogen sulfite solution), H_2O, *Starch*, and *Mix* (for mixing). Fill the pipets with the appropriate solutions. Modify the *Mix* pipets by cutting them with a knife to produce a short stem with a fine point. CAUTION: *Use the knife with care and cut away from yourself.*

Introduction

Many students will have seen iodine solution used as a test for starch in a previous science class. Point out that this investigation uses starch as a test for iodine. Demonstrate how tincture of iodine (available in a pharmacy or from first-aid supplies) turns blue-black on white bread or a potato.

You could illustrate the "clock" feature of this reaction by doing a demonstration. Use 12 mL of $HSO_3^-(aq)$ and 12 mL of $IO_3^-(aq)$ with starch indicator in a pair of large test tubes while doing a pretimed countdown on the clock. To mix the solutions, pour them back and forth between test tubes several times.

Safety

Make sure students wear their goggles and lab aprons at all times during the investigation. The sodium

Name _____

4. What is the purpose of the mixing pipet? <u>The mixing pipet is used to transfer solutions from one well to another.</u>

5. What are the hazards associated with using NaHSO₃ solution, and what precautions should you take? <u>Handle the sodium hydrogen sulfite in acid solution with care; avoid spills and contact with your skin. If you spill any, wash it off with large amounts of water and tell your teacher.</u>

Purpose

How does changing the concentration of a reactant affect the rate of chemical reaction?

Materials

chemical splash goggles
laboratory apron
marking pen
well plate
sheet of white paper
micropipet, adapted for mixing
4 micropipets, containing the following solutions:

potassium iodate (KIO₃), 0.02 M
distilled water
sodium hydrogen sulfite (NaHSO₃), 0.02 M
starch solution
distilled water
stopwatch or clock with a second hand

Safety

Wear your goggles and lab apron at all times during the investigation. Handle the sodium hydrogen sulfite in acid solution with care; it is corrosive. Avoid spills and contact with your skin. If you spill any, wash it off with large amounts of water and tell your teacher.

Note the caution alert symbols here and with certain steps of the Procedure. Refer to page xi for the specific precautions.

Procedure

1. Put on your goggles and lab apron. Using the marking pen, label the wells from left to right along the top of the well plate 1, 2, 3, 4, 5, 6. Down the left side, label the rows of wells A, B, C, D. Place the well plate on a sheet of white paper.

2. Use the pipet labeled IO_3^- to add two drops of KIO₃ solution to well A1, four drops to well A2, six drops to well A3, eight drops to well A4, ten drops to well A5, and twelve drops to well A6. See Figure 64–1. Make sure to hold the pipet vertically to achieve a consistent drop size.

3. Use the pipet labeled H_2O to add ten drops of distilled water to well A1, eight drops to well A2, six drops to well A3, four drops to well A4, and two drops to well A5. No water should be added to well A6. See Figure 64–1.

354

Name _____

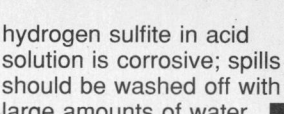

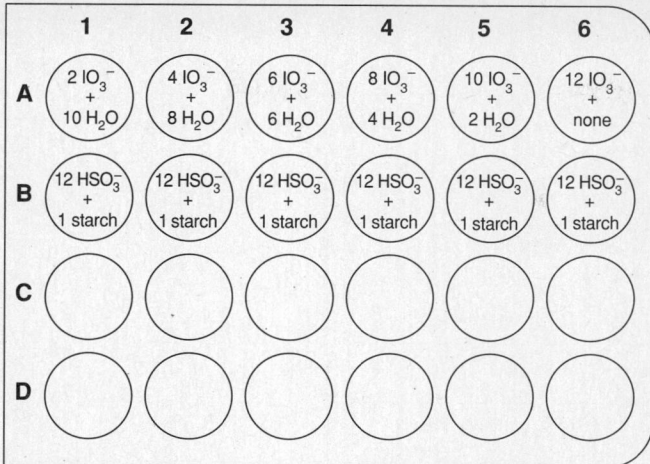

Figure 64-1

4. Use the pipet labeled HSO_3^- to add twelve drops of hydrogen sulfite solution to wells B1, B2, B3, B4, B5, and B6. Then use the pipet labeled *Starch* to add one drop of starch solution to each of the filled wells in row B. **CAUTION:** *Handle the sodium hydrogen sulfite in acid solution with extreme care. Do not allow any of the solutions to contact your skin. If you spill any of them, wash off immediately with plenty of water and notify your teacher.*

5. Use the pipet labeled *Mix* to draw up all of the hydrogen sulfite solution in well B1. Then, as rapidly and carefully as possible, transfer the contents of the pipet to well A1. The moment the two solutions come into contact, record the start time in the Data Table. Stir the solutions by gently swirling the well plate on the paper. Once you have mixed the solutions thoroughly, it is not necessary to continue moving the plate. Record the finish time in seconds when a dark blue color appears. Then clean the *Mix* pipet by flushing it three times with distilled water.

6. Repeat Step 5 by mixing solutions A2 and B2, A3 and B3, A4 and B4, A5 and B5, and A6 and B6. Record the start and finish times in the Data Table. Also record the number of drops of $HSO_3^-(aq)$ and $IO_3^-(aq)$ in the combined solutions.

7. Calculate the elapsed reaction time for each mixture by subtracting the start time from the finish time. Enter the results in the Data Table.

8. If time permits, repeat Steps 2–7 in a second trial.

9. Wash the chemicals down the sink with plenty of water. Clean up your work area and wash your hands before leaving the laboratory.

hydrogen sulfite in acid solution is corrosive; spills should be washed off with large amounts of water. ∎

Teaching Tips

A common error is to forget to add the drop of starch indicator. You may want to add the starch to the stock hydrogen sulfite solution. In this case, the solution turns a pale yellow. The addition of starch, however, limits the shelf life of any excess reagent.

Use the investigation to illustrate the principles of Section 22–3 of the text. Explain the effect of increased numbers of collisions. At higher concentrations, more collisions occur within a given time period.

The sample times given in the Data Table can vary with only small changes in technique of the experimenter, so you should do a trial run of this investigation before the students do it.

Waste Disposal

Neutralize the materials and wash them down the drain with plenty of water. ∎

Reaction Kinetics 355

Small Scale Lab 64

Name _____

Observations (sample data)
DATA TABLE

	A1/B1	A2/B2	A3/B3	A4/B4	A5/B5	A6/B6
drops IO_3^-(aq)	2	4	6	8	10	12
drops HSO_3^-(aq)	12	12	12	12	12	12
start time						
finish time						
elapsed time (s)	210	58	49	39	33	27

Critical Thinking: Analysis and Conclusions

1. Make a graph of the elapsed time versus the quantity of iodate ion on the blank graph shown in Figure 64–2. *(Interpreting data)*

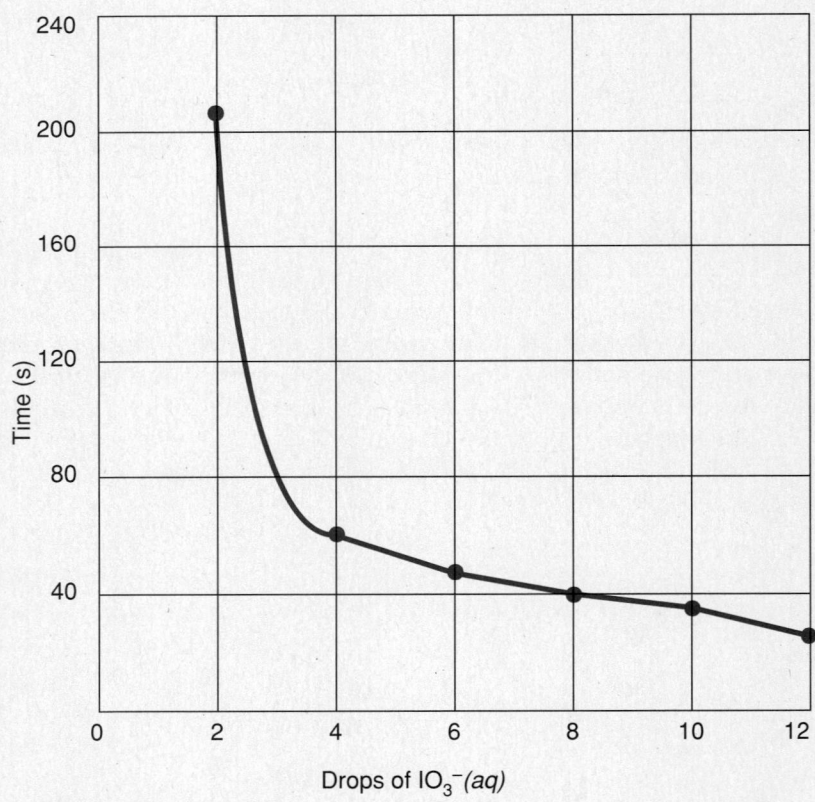

Figure 64–2

2. How does an increase in reactant concentration affect reaction time? *(Drawing conclusions)* As iodate concentration increases, the time for the reactions decreases.

Name _____

3. How does an increase in reactant concentration affect the rate of the reaction? *(Making inferences)* As iodate concentration increases, the rate of the reaction increases.

4. How is the reaction rate related to reaction time? *(Making inferences)* As reaction time increases, the rate of reaction decreases. Time and rate are inversely proportional.

Critical Thinking: Applications

1. Suppose you held the iodate ion concentration constant while varying the concentration of hydrogen sulfite ion. How would you expect the reaction rate to depend on the concentration of hydrogen sulfite ion? *(Making predictions)* As hydrogen sulfite ion concentration is increased, the reaction rate should increase.

2. What effect do you think changing the temperature would have on your results? *(Making predictions)* Heating the solutions would probably speed up the reaction. Cooling the solutions would probably slow it down.

3. Design an experiment to find an answer to the prediction you made in Question 2. *(Designing experiments)* Repeat the investigation twice, the first time using a hot water bath, and then using an ice bath.

Going Further

1. When household bleach is mixed with a solution of Fe^{3+} ions, O_2 gas is produced. Design an experiment in which the concentration of bleach is varied and the volume of O_2 gas produced each minute is monitored. Under your teacher's supervision, conduct the experiment and report on your results.

Concentration and Reaction Order

Text reference: **Chapter 22**

Introduction

Many chemists have been employed to exploit and control explosive chemical reactions for use in construction and military applications. Since explosive reactions must be exothermic as well as rapid, these chemists need to study factors affecting the rate of exothermic reactions. Temperature, concentration of reactants, gas pressure, surface area of reactants, and presence of a catalyst all affect the rate of a chemical reaction.

In this investigation, you will study how the concentration and temperature of the reactants affect the rate of the following reaction:

$$S_2O_3^{2-}(aq) + 2H^+(aq) \rightarrow S(s) + SO_2(aq) + H_2O(l)$$

The reaction is accompanied by a small net change in energy, so the temperature will remain nearly constant unless changed by an outside influence. The reaction occurs in solution and produces a suspended precipitate of sulfur. The rate can be determined by measuring the time needed to produce enough sulfur to make the solution opaque.

Pre-Lab Discussion

Read the entire laboratory investigation and the relevant pages of your textbook. Then answer the questions that follow.

1. How do you know that the reaction to be studied cannot cause an explosion? <u>The reaction is not very exothermic, and the concentrations of the reactants are low.</u>

2. If ten drops of 0.3 M HCl are mixed with ten drops of 0.3 M $Na_2S_2O_3$, what will be the concentration of each chemical in the mixture? <u>Both will have a concentration of 0.15 M.</u>

3. If the concentration of a reactant is decreased, how would you expect the rate of reaction to be affected? Are the concentration and reaction rate directly or inversely proportional? <u>The rate should decrease.</u> <u>Concentration and reaction rate are directly proportional.</u>

4. If, when mixing the chemicals to start the reaction, you dripped acid on your hands because you were not being careful, you would have to stop to wash. What negative impact on your data gathering would this interruption cause? <u>Once the chemicals have been mixed, the reaction needs to be timed. Timing could not be done as accurately.</u>

Materials (class of 30 in pairs)
- 30 pairs chemical splash goggles
- 30 laboratory aprons
- 30 sets of 3 micropipets, containing the following solutions:
  - 100 mL hydrochloric acid (HCl), 0.3 M
  - 100 mL sodium thiosulfate ($Na_2S_2O_3$), 0.3 M
  - 100 mL distilled water
- 3 beakers, 600-mL
- 15 graduated cylinders, 10-mL
- 15 pencils
- 15 pieces of paper
- 15 well plates, 24-well
- 15 marking pens
- 15 mixing micropipets
- 15 stopwatches or a clock with a second hand
- paper towels
- 15 pairs scissors
- 4–5 water baths, varying temperatures
- tap water
- ice
- 4–5 thermometers, 1 for each water bath
- 1 thermometer for room temperature
- tape

Time Required
60 minutes. Eliminate Part D to shorten time. Have half the class do Part B and the other half do Part C, then pool the class data. Do a repeat trial for Parts B and C to increase the time.

Advance Preparation
Prepare the solutions as follows:

0.3 M HCl: Mix 5.0 mL concentrated HCl with enough water to make 200 mL of solution. CAUTION: *Concentrated HCl is extremely corrosive. Use goggles, lab apron, and gloves when handling it.*

Small Scale Lab 65

0.3 M Na₂S₂O₃: Dissolve 15.0 g Na₂S₂O₃·5H₂O in enough water to make 200 mL of solution.

Place the solutions in the micropipets and have them available in labeled beakers.

Fill water-bath tubs with water and place a thermometer in each. Adjust temperatures just prior to use by adding hot or cold water or ice. Temperatures of 10° C above and below room temperature are easy to maintain. Hang a thermometer in the room so students have easy access to it or read the temperature and write it on the board.

Make the mixing micropipets by cutting their stems with a knife or razor to produce a short stem. CAUTION: *Use care when working with the knife or razor. Cut away from yourself.*

Introduction
Demonstrate the rapid oxidation of steel wool in pure oxygen. Wrap a bottle with reinforced tape used for shipping. Collect a bottle of oxygen over water by decomposing H₂O₂ with an MnO₂ catalyst or collect it directly from an oxygen tank. Cover the bottle with a glass plate when removing it from the water. Set up a shield between you and the class. Put on goggles, heat-proof gloves, and an apron. Holding a very small piece of shredded steel wool in tongs, pass it quickly through a flame, and then plunge it into the oxygen. There will be a bright flash as the steel burns. Do not hold the bottle in your hand, as it may crack.

Safety
Make sure students wear their goggles and lab aprons at all times during the investigation. Caution students that the 0.3 M HCl is an irritant, and to wipe up drips and spills immediately. ■

Problem
How is the reaction rate for the acidic decomposition of thiosulfate ion affected by the concentration and temperature of the reactants?

Materials
chemical splash goggles
laboratory apron
2 sets of 3 micropipets, containing the following solutions:
    hydrochloric acid (HCl), 0.3 M
    sodium thiosulfate (Na₂S₂O₃), 0.3 M
    distilled water
graduated cylinder, 10-mL
pencil
paper
well plate
marking pen
mixing micropipet
stopwatch or clock with a second hand
paper towels
scissors
tape

Safety

Wear your goggles and lab apron at all times during the investigation. Hydrochloric acid is corrosive. Avoid any direct contact with it. Wash spills and splashes with cold water. Note the caution alert symbols here and with certain steps of the Procedure. Refer to page *xi* for the specific precautions associated with each symbol.

Procedure

Part A

1. Put on your goggles and lab apron. Obtain one plastic micropipet containing 0.3 M HCl, another containing 0.3 M Na₂S₂O₃, and a third containing distilled water. **CAUTION:** *Hydrochloric acid is corrosive. Avoid any direct contact with it. Wash spills and splashes with cold water.*

2. Fill a 10-mL graduated cylinder with water to exactly 5.0 mL. Holding the micropipet containing HCl vertical to deliver a uniform drop size, count the number of drops of liquid needed to increase the volume to 6.0 mL, then 7.0 mL, then 8.0 mL. Be sure the drops do not hit the side of the graduated cylinder. Record in Data Table 1. Repeat with Na₂S₂O₃ and water.

3. Calculate the averages of the three sets of numbers recorded in Step 2, as shown in Calculation Step 1. Record in Data Table 1. Use this value in the Procedure to dispense exact volumes.

Part B

4. Mark an *x* on a sheet of paper. When placed under the well plate, the *x* should be clearly visible. If it is not already labeled, use a marking pen to label the well plate rows A–D and the columns 1–6. Using the number of drops calculated in Step 3, put exactly 1.0 mL of 0.3 M Na₂S₂O₃ solution into each of the six wells in Row A on the well plate.

360

5. In Row B, put 0.3 M HCl as follows. (As in Step 4, count the number of drops to obtain the exact volume required.)
   well B1: 1.0 mL; well B2: 0.8 mL; well B3: 0.7 mL
   well B4: 0.6 mL; well B5: 0.5 mL; well B6: 0.4 mL

6. Place additional drops of distilled water in each well in order to make the total volume of HCl plus water equal to 1.0 mL. For example, well B2 would require 0.2 mL additional water to make the total volume of HCl plus water equal to 1.0 mL. Note that well B1 does not require any additional water.

7. Prepare to time the reaction. Place well B1 over the x on the paper. Using the mixing micropipet to withdraw all of the solution from well A1, add it all at once but without splashing to well B1, and start timing when the solutions first come into contact. Look through the mixture at the x on the paper. In Data Table 2, record the time elapsed, in seconds, to the point when the x becomes completely obscured. Also record the volume of HCl.

8. Place each of the remaining acid wells over the x and repeat Step 7 for each.

9. Rinse the mixing micropipet with distilled water. Dispose of the well plate contents as directed by your teacher. Clean and dry the well plate.

Part C

10. Using the number of drops calculated in Step 3, put exactly 1.0 mL of 0.3 M HCl into each of the six wells in Row A on the well plate.

11. In Row B, put 0.3 M $Na_2S_2O_3$ as follows. (As in Step 4, count the number of drops to obtain the exact volume required.)
    well B1: 1.0 mL; well B2: 0.8 mL; well B3: 0.7 mL
    well B4: 0.6 mL; well B5: 0.5 mL; well B6: 0.4 mL

12. As in Step 6, place additional drops of distilled water in each well in order to make the total volume of $Na_2S_2O_3$ plus water equal to 1.0 mL. Note that well B1 does not require any additional water.

13. Prepare to time the reaction. Place well B1 over the x on the paper. Using the mixing micropipet to withdraw all of the acid from well A1, add it all at once but without splashing to well B1, and start timing when the solutions first come into contact. Look through the mixture at the x on the paper. In Data Table 3, record the time elapsed, in seconds, to the point when the x becomes completely obscured. Also record the volume of $Na_2S_2O_3$.

14. Place each of the remaining acid wells in turn over the x and repeat Step 13 for each.

15. Dispose of the well plate contents as directed by your teacher. Clean and dry the well plate.

Teaching Tips
Have students use a computer graphing routine to prepare their graphs. Many of these routines have a best-fit option for drawing a line through data points. If this option is not available, the best-fit line should be hand drawn.

Demonstrate how to hold the micropipet in order to get uniform drop sizes. The micropipet should be held as close to vertical as possible the entire time the drops are being counted. Students should be reminded to hold the micropipets in this manner whenever they are dispensing liquid throughout the investigation.

Small Scale Lab 65

Name _____

Part D

16. Cut out the *x* from the white sheet of paper and tape it under one of the wells with the *x* facing up. Put 1.0 mL of 0.3 *M* HCl into that well and 1.0 mL of 0.3 *M* $Na_2S_2O_3$ into another well.

17. Float the well tray on a water bath provided by your teacher. The water should be approximately 10°C warmer than room temperature.

18. After waiting five minutes, prepare to time the reaction. Withdraw all of the 0.3 *M* $Na_2S_2O_3$ from its well and add it to the HCl in the other well. Look through the mixture at the *x* on the paper. In Data Table 4, record the time elapsed, in seconds, to the point when the *x* becomes completely obscured.

19. Record the room temperature and the temperature of the water bath. Put these values in Data Table 4.

20. As time permits, repeat Steps 16–19, using water baths at varying temperatures.

21. Dispose of the well plate contents as directed by your teacher. Clean up your work area and wash your hands before leaving the laboratory.

Waste Disposal
Contents of well trays may be discarded in sink drains, flushed with plenty of water. ■

Observations (sample data)
DATA TABLE 1   Drops to Make 1.0 mL

Liquid	5.0–6.0 mL	6.0–7.0 mL	7.0–8.0 mL	Average
HCl	26	25	24	25
$Na_2S_2O_3$	24	25	26	25
distilled water	22	18	20	20

DATA TABLE 2   Rate with Varying HCl Concentration

Well	Reaction Time (s)	Reaction Rate (1/s)	Volume of HCl (mL)	Initial [HCl] (mol/L)	Final [HCl] (mol/L)
B1	21	0.048	1.0	0.30	0.15
B2	21	0.048	0.8	0.24	0.12
B3	22	0.045	0.7	0.21	0.11
B4	22	0.045	0.6	0.18	0.09
B5	22	0.045	0.5	0.15	0.08
B6	23	0.043	0.4	0.12	0.06

DATA TABLE 3 Rate with Varying Na₂S₂O₃ Concentration

Well	Reaction Time (s)	Reaction Rate (1/s)	Volume of Na₂S₂O₃ (mL)	Initial [Na₂S₂O₃] (mol/L)	Final [Na₂S₂O₃] (mol/L)
B1	19	0.053	1.0	0.30	0.15
B2	24	0.042	0.8	0.24	0.12
B3	27	0.037	0.7	0.21	0.11
B4	31	0.032	0.6	0.18	0.09
B5	38	0.026	0.5	0.15	0.08
B6	54	0.019	0.4	0.12	0.06

DATA TABLE 4 Rate with Varying Temperature

Temperature (°C)	Reaction Time (s)	Reaction Rate (1/s)
32	13	0.08
12	32	0.03
22	20	0.05

Calculations (based on sample data; one example shown)

1. Calculate the average number of drops of each liquid needed to obtain 1.0 mL. Enter the values in Data Table 1.

   HCl: (26 + 25 + 24)/3 = 25 drops

2. Calculate the reaction rate for each reaction. Note that the reaction rate is the inverse of the time. Enter the values in the Data Tables.

   well B1, Part B: 1/21 sec = 0.048

3. Calculate the initial concentration of each of the solutions in wells B1–B6 before the reaction. Enter the values in the Data Tables.

   well B2, Part B: 0.8 × 0.3 = 0.24 M

4. Calculate the concentration of each solution after it is mixed with the other reactant. The concentration after mixing will be half the original concentration in each well, since the volume is doubled when mixed with the other reactant. Enter the value in the Data Tables in the columns for final concentration.

   well B3, Part B: 0.24 M/2 = 0.12 M

5. Calculate the average reaction time at room temperature for well B1 from Parts B and C. Enter the value in Data Table 4.

   (19 + 21)/2 = 20 seconds

Concentration and Reaction Order

Critical Thinking: Analysis and Conclusions

1. Make a graph of reaction rate vs. HCl concentration from the data for Part B, and a graph of reaction rate vs. $Na_2S_2O_3$ concentration from the data for Part C. *(Interpreting data)*

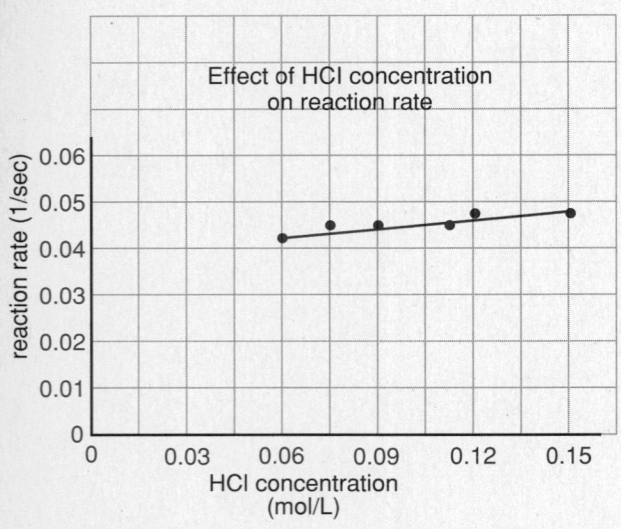
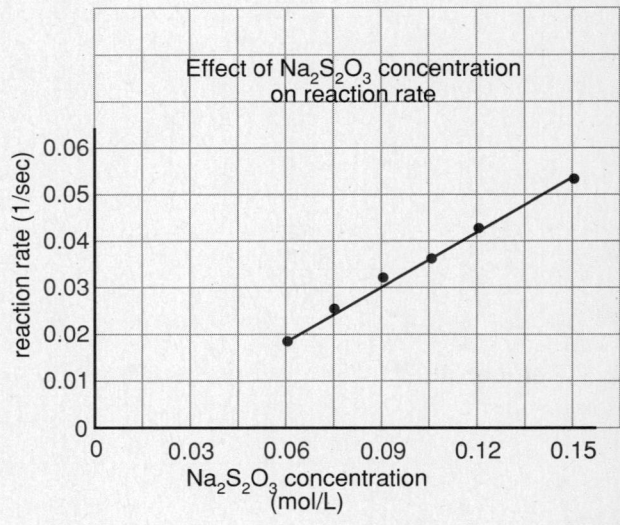

Figure 65–1

2. Decide, in each case, whether the changes in reactant concentration had a significant effect on reaction rate. Determine the reaction rate order for each reactant, using the following definitions:

   zero order—no effect on rate by changes in concentration
   first order—rate directly proportional to concentration
   second order—rate proportional to the square of the concentration
      (e.g., doubled concentration results in a four-fold increase in rate)
   third order—rate proportional to the cube of the concentration.
   (Making inferences) <u>The HCl concentration had little effect on the rate. It is</u> <u>zero order. The rate is directly proportional to the thiosulfate concentration. It</u> <u>is first order.</u>

3. Most reactions occur in a series of steps. The slowest step controls the rate of the overall reaction. Which of the reactants is involved in the slowest step of the reaction observed in this investigation? Explain. *(Drawing conclusions)* <u>Since the reaction rate is directly proportional</u> <u>to the thiosulfate concentration, the thiosulfate must be involved in the slowest</u> <u>step.</u>

4. From your data in Part D, how would you judge the validity of the rule: Changing the temperature of an intermediate-speed reaction by 10°C doubles its rate. *(Making judgments)* <u>Answers will vary but</u> <u>the rate does change significantly with a 10°C change.</u>

364 © Prentice-Hall, Inc.

Name _____

Critical Thinking: Applications

1. TNT (trinitrotoluene), an explosive, occurs naturally as an intermediate product of the decomposition of certain types of organic matter. Why does it not explode? *(Developing hypotheses)* <u>The concentration of the TNT is too low to produce energy rapidly enough.</u>

2. Propose ways to increase the rate of oxidation of iron (rusting). *(Designing experiments)* <u>The temperature can be raised. The concentration of oxygen or iron can be increased. The surface area of the iron can be increased.</u>

3. Hexane, a component of gasoline, releases more energy per mole when it combusts than does nitroglycerine when it explosively decomposes. Explain why hexane is a better fuel and nitroglycerine is a better explosive. *(Evaluating)* <u>Hexane is more useful as a fuel because it releases its energy slowly and lasts longer. Nitroglycerine releases its energy all at once, making it more useful as an explosive.</u>

Going Further

1. Do research on the decomposition rates of pesticides or pollutants in the environment. Produce graphs showing how concentrations change over time.
2. Research the life of Alfred Nobel and his work on explosives.
3. Use a computer graphing program to make a graph of the data from Analysis and Conclusions Question 1.

Going Further

1. Library periodical searches will provide information on environmental issues as well as local, state, and federal agencies with environmental missions.
2. Many books and encyclopedias contain information on Nobel.

Rates of an Antacid Reaction

Text reference: **Chapter 22**

Introduction

Many people are familiar with the "plop, plop, fizz, fizz" that takes place when antacid tablets are dropped into a glass of water. When someone takes an antacid tablet, he or she is probably more interested in gaining relief from an upset stomach than the chemistry that takes place in the glass. However, as the tablet fizzes, it demonstrates a reaction that can be timed and studied.

The ingredients in one brand of fizzing antacid tablets are listed as "aspirin 325 mg;... sodium bicarbonate 1916 mg; citric acid 1000 mg." The fizz results when citric acid ($H_3C_6H_5O_7$) reacts with the base, sodium bicarbonate ($NaHCO_3$), to give carbon dioxide, water, and a salt (sodium citrate). The balanced reaction is:

$$H_3C_6H_5O_7\,(aq) + 3NaHCO_3\,(aq) \rightarrow Na_3C_6H_5O_7\,(aq) + 3H_2O\,(l) + 3CO_2\,(g)$$

All of the ingredients for this reaction are present in the antacid tablet, but nothing happens until it is put into water. The tablet, therefore, provides you with a nice chemical package that you can use to carry out timed kinetics experiments.

Temperature is one of many factors that affect the rate at which a chemical reaction proceeds. Collision theory states that as temperature increases, the particles in a reaction move faster, resulting in a higher frequency of collisions and increased kinetic energy in each collision. Other variables affect reaction rates as well. In this investigation, you will examine the effect of temperature on the rate of reaction of an antacid tablet in water. You will also design your own investigation to determine the effect of another variable on reaction rate, choosing from among those covered in Section 22-3 of your text. After performing this investigation, you will report on how your results fit with your understanding of collision theory and rates of reaction.

Pre-Lab Discussion

Read the entire laboratory investigation and the relevant pages of your textbook. Then answer the questions that follow.

1. Would you describe the antacid tablet–water system as a heterogeneous or homogenous system? Briefly explain your answer. _The antacid tablet–water system is a heterogenous system because it contains solids, liquids, and gases._

2. List as many variables as you can that can affect the rate of a reaction. _Temperature, nature of reactants, concentration of reactants and products, surface area, and the presence of a catalyst._

Materials (class of 30 in pairs)
- 30 pairs chemical splash goggles
- 30 laboratory aprons
- 15 shallow pans or troughs
- 15 gas-collecting bottles, 500-mL
- ice
- tap water, hot and cold
- 15 thermometers
- 15 glass squares
- 150 Alka-Seltzer™-brand fizzing antacid tablets
- 15 stopwatches or clock with a second hand
- 15 glass marking pens
- 15 graduated cylinders, 100-mL

Additional materials for Part B
- 15 mortars and pestles (optional)
- 500 mL hydrochloric acid (HCl), 0.1 M
- 500 mL sodium hydroxide (NaOH), 0.1 M
- 1 L of a saturated solution of carbon dioxide and water (carbonated water).
- graph paper

Time Required
90 minutes. Students can usually complete Part A in less than 45 minutes. There is enough time for students to hypothesize about the choice of another variable and to design a procedure to test their hypothesis. They can complete Part B and present their results on the following day.

Advance Preparation
Alka-Seltzer™ tablets are usually available in bulk from drugstores. Students should be able to obtain water at 20°C, 30°C, and 40°C by

© Prentice-Hall, Inc.

Lab 66
APPLICATION

mixing different proportions of hot and cold tap water. If hot water is not available, set up hot plates with large beakers of tap water at 30°C and 40°C. For 20°C water, let tap water adjust to room temperature and readjust if necessary. Cool water to 10°C with ice.

Club soda or any other carbonated solution for use in Part B is available from the grocery store. Diet soft drinks may be substituted as long as carbonates and/or citric acid (or acids other than carbonic acids) are not listed as contents. Prepare the HCl and NaOH solutions by adding 4.2 mL concentrated HCl and 2.0 g NaOH respectively to enough water to make 500 mL of each solution.

Have plain paper and graph paper available.

Introduction

Some students have difficulty understanding the inverse relationship between the rate of the appearance of a product (or disappearance of reactant) and time. To help these students, ask them to describe the rate of some other things, such as automobile speed. As they consider additional rate measurements, they may begin to see that the time factor is commonly placed in the denominator position of the rate description. Asking "How does the length of time it takes for a reaction to take place compare to the rate of the reaction?" will encourage students to consider the correct relationship.

Safety

Make sure students wear their goggles and lab aprons at all times during the investigation. If students do Part B, remind them that the

3. How do you relate each of the variables listed in Question 2 to collision theory? __Temperature: as temperature increases, the particles in the reaction move faster, resulting in a higher frequency of collisions and increased kinetic energy in each collision. Nature of reactants: some reactants form bonds more easily than others when they collide. Concentration: the greater the concentration, the more frequently the reactants collide. Surface area: the greater the surface area, the more frequently the reactants can collide. Catalysts lower the activation energy per collision.__

4. How does the length of time it takes for a reaction to occur relate to the rate of the reaction? __As the length of time it takes for a reaction to occur increases, the rate of the reaction decreases.__

5. What role (or roles) does water play in the antacid reaction? __Water dissolves and then ionizes the reactants.__

6. Why should no one ever attempt to swallow a fizzing antacid tablet without first letting it react in water? __If you swallow a fizzing antacid tablet without first letting it react in water, a dangerously large volume of gas will be released in the stomach.__

Problem

Which factors affect the rate of the antacid reaction?

Materials

chemical splash goggles
laboratory apron
tap water, hot and cold
shallow pan or trough
gas-collecting bottles, 500-mL
ice
thermometer
glass square or piece of poster board
fizzing antacid tablets
stopwatch or clock with a second hand

glass marking pen
graduated cylinder, 100-mL

Additional materials for Part B
mortar and pestle
hydrochloric acid (HCl), 0.1 M
sodium hydroxide (NaOH), 0.1 M
saturated solution of carbon dioxide (carbonated water or club soda)
graph paper

Safety

Wear your goggles and lab apron at all times during the investigation. The 0.1 M hydrochloric acid is corrosive, and 0.1 M sodium hydroxide is caustic. If skin or clothing come into contact with these solutions they should be washed with plenty of cold water. Do not ingest the antacid tablet. Ingestion of undissolved antacid tablets causes gas pains and can lead to a herniated stomach. Handle hot water with care to avoid burns. Use hot pads or tongs when handling hot objects. Note the caution alert symbols here and with certain steps of the Procedure. Refer to page *xi* for the specific precautions associated with each symbol.

Procedure

Part A

1. Put on your goggles and lab apron. Place about 3 cm of tap water in the bottom of a pan or trough. Fill the bottle to the brim with ice-cold water. Record the temperature in the Data Table.
2. Place a glass square over the mouth of the bottle and hold it tightly. Invert the bottle, and place it mouth-down into the pan of tap water. Remove your hand and the glass square. Some water may run from the gas-collecting bottle into the pan.
3. Remove a fizzing antacid tablet from its package. Get ready to time the reaction by watching the clock or readying the stopwatch.
4. When the person who is timing gives the signal, tilt the gas-collecting bottle slightly and slip the tablet under the mouth of the bottle. Do not lift the mouth of the bottle above the surface of the water in the pan.
5. Time the reaction until the last bit of tablet stops fizzing. Record the time of reaction in the Data Table.
6. Measure the volume of gas given off as follows: Mark the gas/water line of the bottle with a glass marking pen. Remove the bottle from the pan, let the water run out, invert the bottle, and fill it with water to the mark. Measure the volume of this water using a graduated cylinder. (You may have to fill the cylinder more than once.) Record.

7. Rinse any antacid residue from the bottle. Repeat Steps 1–6 with bottles filled with water adjusted to 10°C, 20°C, 30°C, and 40°C. Adjust tap water to 10°C with ice. Make the temperature of the water 30°C and 40°C by combining hot and cold tap water. Continue to record your observations in the Data Table.

8. Flush leftover solutions down the drain with excess water. If you are not going directly on to Part B, clean up your work area and wash your hands before leaving the laboratory.

Part B: Effects of Other Variables on Reaction Rate

9. Do this section on a separate sheet of paper. Choose a variable from the list you made in Question 2 of the Pre-Lab Discussion. Write this variable on the paper. State a hypothesis that describes how you believe the variable will affect the reaction rate of the antacid in water.
10. Make a list of the materials you wish to use in your procedure. Select them from the Materials list. Seek permission from your teacher if you wish to use additional materials.

Lab 66 APPLICATION

Name _____

11. Design a procedure that tests the effect of the variable you have chosen on the rate of the reaction of antacid in water. The procedure must include controls, safety precautions, and any steps necessary for waste disposal.

12. Construct a table for organizing and recording your data.

13. Obtain your teacher's approval, and then carry out the procedure under your teacher's supervision.

14. Clean up your work area and wash your hands before leaving the laboratory.

Waste Disposal
The products of the antacid reaction can be disposed of by flushing them down the drain with plenty of water.

Cooperative Learning Strategy
To complete Part A, cooperative groups of four could be organized so that one person is designated as the scribe. They should each select temperatures at which they will prepare their bottles. They should also take turns inverting the bottles and acting as timers.

To complete Part B, the groups should first pick a coordinator. They should then decide which variable they will manipulate in their investigation. As a group, they should collaborate to design a controlled investigation. The coordinator should be responsible for organizing the efforts necessary to carry out the procedure and making sure that the disposal and cleanup are complete.

Observations (sample data)

DATA TABLE   Effect of Temperature on Reaction Rate

Temperature (°C)	Time (s)	CO_2 (cm^3)
0	118	25
10	83	50
20	38	70
30	29	125
40	26	183

Critical Thinking: Analysis and Conclusions

1. Construct separate graphs of the reaction time vs. temperature and of CO_2 volume vs. temperature. *(Interpreting data)*

2. How did the rate of reaction vary with the temperature of the water? *(Drawing conclusions)* The rate of the reaction increased as the temperature of the water increased.

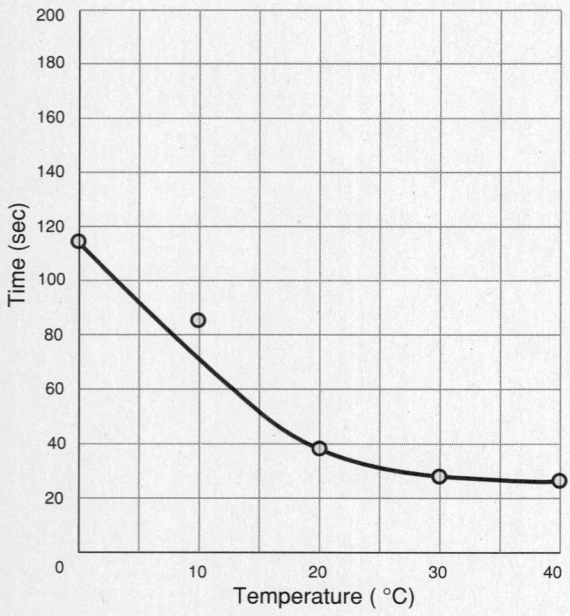
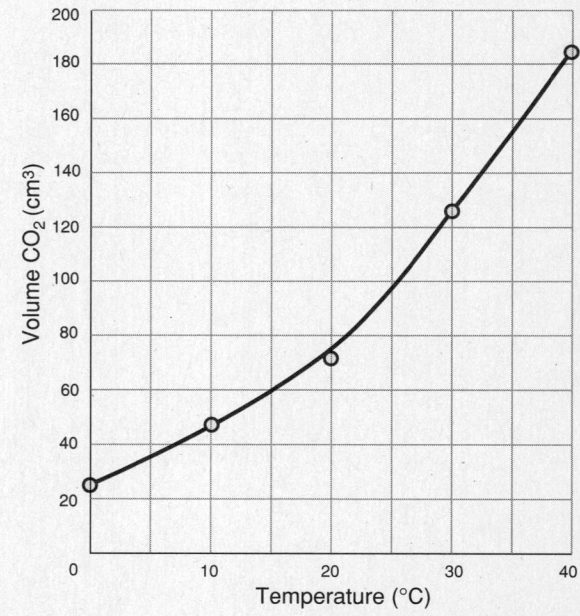

Name _____

Lab 66 APPLICATION

3. Assuming that the same amount of carbon dioxide gas is produced when each tablet reacts, and that the solutions in each gas-collecting bottle are saturated with carbon dioxide, what is the relationship between the solubility of carbon dioxide and temperature? *(Making inferences)* The solubility of carbon dioxide decreases as the temperature increases.

4. State the hypothesis you made for the variable you chose in Part B, and give the rationale you used to make it. *(Developing hypotheses)* Answers will vary.

5. State the rationale for each control you used. *(Designing experiments)* The controls selected and the rationale will vary. They should reflect the need to keep constant the other variables that might affect the rate of the reaction.

6. On a separate sheet of paper, construct any graphs relevant to your data in Part B and summarize your results. *(Interpreting data)*

7. Did your results support your hypothesis? Explain. *(Drawing conclusions)* Conclusions concerning the hypothesis will vary.

8. Compare your results to those of other groups of students who experimented with the same variable. *(Making comparisons)* The results of the experiments will vary somewhat with the procedure, but the pattern of results should be similar if the same variable was manipulated in a controlled manner.

9. Did any of the other investigations give results that you did not expect? Explain. *(Making judgments)* Critical analysis of unexpected results should be related to an examination of the controls in the investigation.

Critical Thinking: Applications

1. Refer to the equation for the reaction of citric acid and sodium bicarbonate (sodium hydrogen carbonate) given in the Introduction. The initial products of the reaction are sodium citrate and carbonic acid. The carbonic acid (H_2CO_3) immediately decomposes to water and carbon dioxide. Using sodium citrate and carbonic acid as the reaction products, write the rate law for the antacid reaction. *(Applying concepts)*

$$k = \frac{[Na_3C_6H_5O_7] \times [H_2CO_3]}{[H_3C_6H_5O_7] \times [NaHCO_3]}$$

© Prentice-Hall, Inc.

Rates of an Antacid Reaction

Lab 66
APPLICATION

Going Further

1. The chemistry of Alka-Seltzer™ in water consists of two reactions:
   a. $H_3C_6H_5O_7(aq) + 3NaHCO_3(aq) \rightleftharpoons Na_3C_6H_5O_7(aq) + 3CO_2(g) + 3H_2O(l)$
   b. $NaHCO_3(aq) +$ acetylsalicylic acid $(aq) \rightleftharpoons$ sodium acetysalicylate $(aq) + CO_2(g) + H_2O(l)$

   The initial pH of Alka-Seltzer™ in water is 6.0–7.0. There is a buffer system consisting of sodium citrate, carbon dioxide, and residual sodium hydrogen carbonate. This buffer system absorbs excess H^+ ions in the stomach. For example, sodium citrate reacts with the excess acid in your stomach to re-form citric acid.

   $C_6H_5O_7{}^{3-}(aq) + 3H_3O^+(aq) \rightleftharpoons H_3C_6H_5O_7(aq) + 3H_2O(l)$

2. Using what you know about Le Chatelier's principle, explain how the equilibrium of the antacid reaction would change with the addition of hydrochloric acid in the stomach. *(Applying concepts)*

   The equilibrium would be shifted to the right.

3. If the mass of citric acid is 1000 mg and the mass of sodium bicarbonate (sodium hydrogen carbonate) is 1916 mg, determine which of these substances is the limiting reactant, and which is in excess. *(Applying concepts)*

   Citric acid is the limiting reactant, and sodium bicarbonate is in excess:
   moles of $NaHCO_3$: 1.92 g × 1 mol/84.0 g = 0.0229 mol
   moles of $H_3C_6H_5O_7$: 1.00 g × 1 mol/192 g = 0.00521 mol

Going Further

1. Investigate further the chemistry of the antacid reaction. Write to the company that makes the tablets for product information. What is the antacid that forms as the reaction proceeds in the glass? Write a net equation that describes the reaction that occurs when the antacid reacts with the excess acid in your stomach.

2. Survey different brands of antacids in a drugstore to determine the active ingredients they contain. Design a controlled experiment to determine the relative rate at which the recommended dosage of these antacids will neutralize 50 mL of simulated stomach acid (0.1 M hydrochloric acid). Under your teacher's supervision, carry out the procedure and report your results to the rest of the class.

Name _____ Date _____ Class _____

Hess's Law

Lab 67

Text reference: **Chapter 23**

Introduction

Magnesium metal burns with a bright, extremely hot flame to produce magnesium oxide. It would be difficult to measure the heat of reaction, ΔH_r, since the reaction is rapid and occurs at a high temperature. As you learned in Chapter 12, the value of ΔH for a reaction is the same whether it occurs directly or in a series of steps. This principle, known as Hess's law, allows you to calculate the enthalpy of the magnesium reaction by performing two reactions that are easier to control.

Magnesium oxide, a white powder, reacts (exothermically) with a solution of hydrochloric acid to produce magnesium chloride, liquid water, and heat. Solid magnesium metal reacts with a solution of hydrochloric acid to produce magnesium chloride, hydrogen gas, and (since this reaction is also exothermic) heat. By using the preceding two reactions and knowing the enthalpy for the formation of water (-285.8 kilojoules per mole of water) you will be able to calculate the change in enthalpy for the burning of magnesium in oxygen.

In this investigation, you will measure the heat released by these two reactions. From this information and your knowledge of Hess's law, you will calculate the heat of reaction for magnesium burning in air.

Pre-Lab Discussion

Read the entire laboratory investigation and the relevant pages of your textbook. Then answer the questions that follow.

1. What safety procedures need to be observed when working with each of the following compounds?

   a. magnesium oxide <u>Avoid inhaling the dust from the magnesium oxide container.</u>

   b. magnesium chloride <u>Magnesium chloride is irritating to the skin. Contact should be avoided.</u>

   c. hydrochloric acid <u>Hydrochloric acid is corrosive. Wear goggles and an apron when working with it. Wash splashes immediately.</u>

2. State Hess's law in your own words. <u>If a reaction can be expressed as the sum of two or more other reactions, the corresponding enthalpy changes can also be added.</u>

Materials (class of 30 in pairs)

30 pairs chemical splash goggles
30 laboratory aprons
15 g magnesium oxide (MgO)
15 laboratory balances
15 graduated cylinders, 100-mL
1.5 L hydrochloric acid (HCl), 1.0 M
30 plastic foam cups
15 thermometers
15 cardboard covers for cups
paper towels
15 pieces of magnesium ribbon, 0.5-cm
steel wool
scissors

Time Required

50 minutes. You can divide the groups into two parts and let one half do Part A and the other half do Part B. The results can then be pooled.

Advance Preparation

Prepare 1.0 M HCl by adding 125 mL of concentrated HCl to enough water to equal 1.5 L of solution. CAUTION: *Concentrated HCl is extremely corrosive. Wear goggles, gloves, and an apron when working with it.*
  Measure out a 1-g sample of MgO to get an idea of the amount needed. Then make up 15 samples of about the same size. CAUTION: *MgO dust is toxic. Work with it should be performed in the fume hood.* Leave each sample on weighing paper in the fume hood.
  Polish the magnesium ribbon with steel wool to remove any surface contamination. It should be shiny. Then cut it into 0.5-cm pieces. Cut lids for the cups

Hess's Law **373**

Lab 67

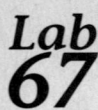

from cardboard and poke a hole in the lids with a pencil for the thermometers.

Introduction

Hold a tiny (2–3 cm) piece of magnesium ribbon in a pair of forceps and light it in front of the class. After showing the students the bright light for a moment, drop the piece into a sink or other opaque container. Discuss with them ways to determine the amount of heat being released as the magnesium burns. Point out that it is theoretically possible to use a calorimeter but the water in a calorimeter would probably extinguish the flame. Another way to approach the problem is to determine the heat evolved by two separate reactions that, when added, result in the original reaction. Then, simply adding the heats associated with the two reactions gives the heat of the original reaction.

Safety

Make sure students wear their goggles and lab aprons at all times during the investigation. MgO dust is toxic. All work with it should be performed in the fume hood. Magnesium chloride is moderately toxic if ingested. Hydrochloric acid is corrosive and should be handled with care. Tell students to flush spills immediately with large quantities of water. If hydrochloric acid is spilled on a lab table or floor, sprinkle baking soda over the area until fizzing stops and then clean up with water. ■

Name _____

3. Write the balanced chemical equations for the three reactions described in the Introduction.
   $H_2(g) + 1/2 O_2(g) \rightarrow H_2O(l)$
   $Mg(s) + 2HCl(aq) \rightarrow MgCl_2(aq) + H_2(g)$
   $MgO(s) + 2HCl(aq) \rightarrow MgCl_2(aq) + H_2O(l)$

4. What is the sign of the change in enthalpy for each of the three reactions used in this investigation? Why? The signs for all three of the reactions are negative. All are exothermic because heat is produced by the reactions.

Problem

What is the enthalpy change associated with the reaction of magnesium with oxygen to produce magnesium oxide?

Materials

chemical splash goggles
laboratory apron
magnesium oxide (MgO)
laboratory balance
graduated cylinder, 100-mL
hydrochloric acid (HCl), 1.0 M

2 plastic foam cups
thermometer
cardboard cover for cup
paper towel
piece of magnesium ribbon

Safety

Wear your goggles and lab apron at all times during the investigation. Hydrochloric acid is corrosive and should be handled with care. Wash any splashes or spills immediately with water and notify your teacher. Magnesium oxide dust is toxic if inhaled. Do all steps of the Procedure involving MgO under a fume hood. Magnesium chloride is moderately toxic if ingested. Be sure to keep your fingers and hands away from your mouth. Note the caution alert symbols here and with certain steps of the Procedure. Refer to page xi for the specific precautions associated with each symbol.

Procedure

Part A

1. Put on your goggles and lab apron. Obtain a sample of MgO from your teacher. **CAUTION**: *Magnesium oxide is toxic. Avoid inhalation of the dust. Perform all procedural steps involving MgO in a fume hood.* Measure and record the mass of the MgO to the nearest 0.01 g.

Name_____

Lab 67

2. Using a graduated cylinder, place 100.0 mL of 1.0 M HCl into a plastic foam cup. **CAUTION:** *Hydrochloric acid is corrosive. Use care when handling it. Wash spills and splashes immediately with plenty of water and notify your teacher.* Use a thermometer to measure the temperature of the HCl to the nearest 0.2°C, and record this value. Also record the volume. Place the cup inside another cup.

3. Work under a fume hood. Add the MgO to the HCl. Immediately cover the inner cup with a lid and insert a thermometer into the hole in the lid. Swirl the cup gently to mix the contents.

4. Record the highest temperature reached by the MgO/HCl mixture.

5. Dispose of the magnesium chloride solution in your cup as directed by your teacher. Rinse the cups and dry them with a paper towel.

Part B

6. Obtain a 0.5-cm piece of magnesium ribbon. Measure and record its mass to the nearest 0.01 g.

7. Using a graduated cylinder, place 100.0 mL of 1.0 M HCl into a plastic foam cup. **CAUTION:** *Hydrochloric acid is corrosive. Use care when handling it. Wash spills and splashes immediately with plenty of water and notify your teacher.* Measure and record the temperature of the HCl to the nearest 0.2°C. Also record the volume. Place the cup inside another cup.

8. Add the magnesium to the HCl. Immediately cover the inner cup with the lid and insert the thermometer into the hole in the lid. Swirl the cup gently to mix the contents.

9. Record the highest temperature reached by the Mg/HCl mixture.

10. Dispose of the magnesium chloride solution in your cup as directed by your teacher. Clean up your work area and wash your hands before leaving the laboratory.

Teaching Tips
The magnesium oxide must be fresh. Use a new container, if possible, or an unopened container if you can't get new MgO. Make sure the students in each class all take their MgO from the same container.

Waste Disposal
Magnesium chloride may be flushed down the drain with plenty of water if your drainage system flows into a water-treatment plant. If the waste flows into a septic system or ground water, the magnesium chloride should be dried, wrapped, and disposed of in a landfill certified to handle it. ■

Observations (sample data)

Part A
Mass of MgO	1.00 g
Volume of HCl	100.0 mL
Initial temperature of HCl	22.4°C
Final temperature of MgO/HCl	29.6°C

Part B
Mass of Mg	0.49 g
Volume of HCl	100.0 mL
Initial temperature of HCl	22.4°C
Final temperature of Mg/HCl	43.4°C

Hess's Law

Lab 67

Name _____

 Calculations (based on sample data)

Part A

1. Calculate the number of moles of MgO used.

$$\frac{1.00 \text{ g}}{40.3 \text{ g/mol}} = 0.0248 \text{ mol}$$

2. Calculate the mass of the HCl solution. Assume the density of the HCl solution is the same as water (1.0 g/mL).

$$100.0 \text{ mL} \times 1.0 \text{ g/mL} = 100.0 \text{ g}$$

3. Calculate the change in temperature.

$$29.6°C - 22.4°C = 7.2°C$$

4. Calculate the amount of heat released by the reaction. Ignore the heat capacity of the MgCl$_2$, and assume the specific heat of the HCl solution is the same as water (0.00418 kJ/g·°C).

$$q = mC\Delta T = 100.0 \text{ g} \times 0.00418 \text{ kJ/g·°C} \times 7.2°C = 3.0 \text{ kJ}$$

5. Calculate the heat of reaction in kilojoules per mole of MgO.

$$\frac{3.0 \text{ kJ}}{0.0248 \text{ mol}} = 120 \text{ kJ/mol}$$

Part B

6. Calculate the number of moles of Mg used.

$$\frac{0.49 \text{ g}}{24.3 \text{ g/mol}} = .020 \text{ mol}$$

7. Calculate the mass of the HCl solution. Assume the density is the same as water (1.0 g/mL).

$$100.0 \text{ mL} \times 1.0 \text{ g/mL} = 100.0 \text{ g}$$

8. Calculate the change in temperature.

$$43.4°C - 22.4°C = 21.0°C$$

9. Calculate the amount of heat released by the reaction.

$$q = mC\Delta T = 100.0 \text{ g} \times 0.00418 \text{ kJ/g·°C} \times 21.0°C = 8.8 \text{ kJ}$$

10. Calculate the heat of reaction in kilojoules per mole of Mg.

$$\frac{8.8 \text{ kJ}}{0.020 \text{ mol}} = 440 \text{ kJ/mol}$$

Critical Thinking: Analysis and Conclusions

1. Write the balanced thermochemical equation for the formation of one mole of liquid water from gaseous hydrogen and oxygen.
   (Applying concepts) $H_2(g) + 1/2 O_2(g) \rightarrow H_2O(l) + 285.8 \text{ kJ}$

2. Based on your data, write a balanced thermochemical equation for the reaction of one mole of magnesium oxide with hydrochloric acid.
   (Making inferences) $MgO(s) + 2HCl(aq) \rightarrow MgCl_2(aq) + H_2O(l) + 120 \text{ kJ}$

3. Based on your data, write a balanced thermochemical equation for the reaction of one mole of magnesium with hydrochloric acid.
   (Making inferences) $Mg(s) + 2HCl(aq) \rightarrow MgCl_2(aq) + H_2(g) + 440 \text{ kJ}$

4. Combine the three equations from Questions 1–3 so they will add to make a balanced thermochemical equation for the burning of one mole of magnesium in oxygen. You may have to reverse one or more of the equations. *(Making inferences)*

$H_2(g) + 1/2O_2(g) \rightarrow H_2O(l) + 285.8$ kJ

$Mg(s) + 2HCl(aq) \rightarrow MgCl_2(aq) + H_2(g) + 440$ kJ

$MgCl_2(aq) + H_2O(l) \rightarrow MgO(s) + 2HCl(aq) - 120$ kJ

Sum: $Mg(s) + 1/2O_2(g) \rightarrow MgO(s) + 606$ kJ

5. Based on your data, calculate the change in enthalpy for the burning of magnesium in oxygen. Use the appropriate sign on your answer. *(Drawing conclusions)* $\Delta H = -606$ kJ/mol Mg

6. Calculate the percent error for this investigation given the known heat of reaction is -601.8 kJ/mol Mg. *(Interpreting data)*

$$\frac{|-606 \text{ kJ/mol} - (-601.8 \text{ kJ/mol})|}{-601.8 \text{ kJ/mol}} \times 100 = 0.70\%$$

Critical Thinking: Applications

1. Given the following information:

   $NH_3(g) + HCl(g) \rightarrow NH_4Cl(s)$ $\Delta H = -176.0$ kJ/mol
   $N_2(g) + 3H_2(g) \rightarrow 2NH_3(g)$ $\Delta H = -92.2$ kJ/mol
   $N_2(g) + 4H_2(g) + Cl_2(g) \rightarrow 2NH_4Cl(s)$ $\Delta H = -628.9$ kJ/mol

   calculate the ΔH for the synthesis of hydrogen chloride gas from hydrogen and chlorine gas. The equation is

   $H_2(g) + Cl_2(g) \rightarrow 2HCl(g)$ *(Applying concepts)*

   Reversing the first two equations and multiplying the first by 2 yields:

   $2NH_4Cl(s) \rightarrow 2NH_3(g) + 2HCl(g)$ $\Delta H = 2(+176.0 \text{ kJ/mol}) = +352$ kJ

   $2NH_3(g) \rightarrow N_2(g) + 3H_2(g)$ $\Delta H = +92.2$ kJ/mol

   $N_2(g) + 4H_2(g) + Cl_2(g) \rightarrow 2NH_4Cl(s)$ $\Delta H = -628.9$ kJ/mol

   The sum of these reactions is the same as the desired reaction, therefore ΔH for the reaction is the sum of the separate ΔH's. $\Delta H_{total} = +352 + (+92.2) + (-628.9) = -184.7$ kJ/mol.

2. The Calorie (note the capital C) mentioned in connection with foods is actually a kilocalorie (1000 calories). If 4.18 joules are equal to 1 calorie and a cup of ice cream releases 200 kilocalories, how many cups of ice cream release the same amount of energy as the reaction producing one mole of liquid water from its constituent gases? *(Applying concepts)*

$$285.8 \text{ kJ} \times \frac{1000 \text{ J}}{1 \text{ kJ}} \times \frac{1}{4.18 \text{ joules/cal}} = 68{,}400 \text{ calories}$$

$$68{,}400 \text{ calories} \times \frac{1 \text{ cup}}{200 \text{ kcal}} \times \frac{1 \text{ kcal}}{1000 \text{ cal}} = 0.342 \text{ cups}$$

Lab 67

Going Further

1. Information on Hess might be difficult to obtain. Students might make a phone call to a college science library to ask about more sophisticated resources.

Going Further

1. Investigate the life of Germain Hess, a Swiss chemist who in 1840 proposed the law of heat additivity that came to bear his name. Write a report and present it to the class.

Name _____ Date _____ Class _____

Entropy and Enthalpy Changes

Lab 68

Text reference: **Chapter 23**

Introduction

Does your bedroom seem to get messy spontaneously? Have you ever noticed how the walls and roof of a deserted building seem to collapse on their own? Can you explain what happens to the arrangement of water molecules as ice melts?

Each of these questions is related to the concept of entropy. Entropy is a measure of the disorder of a system. Spontaneous processes are those that result in a more disordered arrangement of substances, that is, an increase in entropy. Your room gets messy because it has a natural tendency to do so. (Using entropy as an excuse to not clean your room is not recommended!) Old buildings collapse by themselves and water molecules in an ice crystal leave the crystal structure spontaneously because, in both cases, the entropy increases.

In this investigation, you will apply the principle of entropy to three related, spontaneous reactions. You will dissolve solid sodium hydroxide (NaOH) in water, react NaOH solution with hydrochloric acid (HCl), and react solid NaOH with HCl. You will then decide what change in entropy has occurred in each reaction. You will also measure the enthalpy change associated with each reaction.

Pre-Lab Discussion

Read the entire laboratory investigation and the relevant pages of your textbook. Then answer the questions that follow.

1. What is the definition of a spontaneous reaction? __A spontaneous reaction is one that proceeds by itself, without any outside intervention.__

2. How many chemical reactions will be performed in this investigation? Which of them are spontaneous? __Three chemical reactions occur in this investigation: dissolving solid NaOH in water; reacting HCl with NaOH solution; and reacting HCl with solid NaOH. All of these reactions are spontaneous.__

3. Why must you wear gloves when working with NaOH pellets? __Solid NaOH is extremely caustic. Gloves protect the skin.__

4. Characterize the following as increasing entropy or decreasing entropy:
   a. gases forming from liquids __increasing entropy__
   b. decreasing the temperature __decreasing entropy__
   c. dissolving a solid in water __increasing entropy__

Materials (class of 30 in pairs)
30 pairs chemical splash goggles
30 laboratory aprons
30 pairs latex gloves
15 graduated cylinders, 100-mL
3 L distilled water
30 plastic foam cups
30 pieces of weighing paper
15 laboratory balances
15 pairs forceps or scoopulas
100 g sodium hydroxide pellets (NaOH)
15 thermometers
15 stirring rods
paper towels
750 mL hydrochloric acid (HCl), 1.0 M
750 mL sodium hydroxide (NaOH), 1.0 M
1500 mL hydrochloric acid (HCl), 0.5 M

Time Required
50 minutes. To shorten the lab, have different groups do Parts A, B, and C and then pool the results.

Advance Preparation
Solutions should be prepared 24 hours before use, so that they come to thermal equilibrium with room conditions. Three liters of distilled water should be set aside for the same amount of time. Prepare the solutions as follows:
   1.0 M HCl: Add 129 mL of concentrated HCl to enough water to make 1500 mL of solution. CAUTION: *Wear goggles, apron, and gloves when working with concentrated HCl.*
   1.0 M NaOH: Dissolve 30 g of NaOH in enough water to make 750 mL of solution. CAUTION: *Wear goggles, apron, and gloves when*

© Prentice-Hall, Inc.   Entropy and Enthalpy Changes   **379**

Lab 68

working with NaOH.
0.5 *M* HCl: Take 750 mL of the 1.0 *M* HCl and dilute it with 750 mL of water.

Introduction
Discuss the examples in the Introduction. Students will be especially interested in the messy room example. Point out to them that a room left by itself will become disordered. Ask them how to reduce the disorder. Some may say by expending energy. None of them will say a messy room will spontaneously become clean. Tell students the universe is driven toward increasing entropy.

Many students confuse spontaneous reactions with exothermic reactions. An exothermic reaction is one in which the enthalpy decreases while a spontaneous reaction is one in which the combination of the enthalpy and entropy decreases. This combination of changes in enthalpy and changes in entropy is called Gibbs' free energy.

Some spontaneous reactions are endothermic. A good example is the melting of ice. This process absorbs heat but is spontaneous at any temperature above 0°C. This is because the entropy increase of the water molecules is greater than their enthalpy increase.

Safety
Make sure students wear their goggles and lab aprons at all times during the investigation. Sodium hydroxide is extremely caustic and the HCl solutions are corrosive. Both should be handled with care. Warn students to avoid mixing the NaOH and HCl solutions unless directed to do so. Solid NaOH should be handled with gloves and forceps. ∎

Name _____

5. In what units will the heat of reaction be expressed? __In kilojoules per mole of NaOH.__

Problem
What is the level of entropy and the thermochemical relationship of three chemical reactions?

Materials

chemical splash goggles
laboratory apron
latex gloves
graduated cylinder, 100-mL
distilled water
2 plastic foam cups
weighing paper
laboratory balance
forceps or scoopula

sodium hydroxide pellets (NaOH)
thermometer
stirring rod
paper towel
hydrochloric acid (HCl), 1.0 *M*
sodium hydroxide (NaOH), 1.0 *M*
hydrochloric acid (HCl), 0.5 *M*

Safety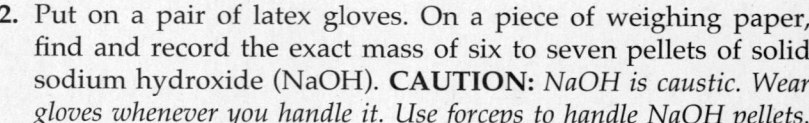

Wear your goggles and lab apron at all times during the investigation. Sodium hydroxide pellets and solutions are caustic. Gloves should be worn when handling the pellets. Hydrochloric acid is corrosive to skin and clothing. If you spill any acid, immediately wash the area with plenty of cold water and notify your teacher. Note the caution alert symbols here and with certain steps of the Procedure. Refer to page *xi* for the specific precautions associated with each symbol.

Procedure
Part A

1. Put on your goggles and lab apron. Use a graduated cylinder to put 100.0 mL of distilled water in a plastic foam cup. Record this volume.

2. Put on a pair of latex gloves. On a piece of weighing paper, find and record the exact mass of six to seven pellets of solid sodium hydroxide (NaOH). **CAUTION:** *NaOH is caustic. Wear gloves whenever you handle it. Use forceps to handle NaOH pellets.*

3. Place the cup inside another cup. Measure the temperature of the water to the nearest 0.2°C and record this value as the initial temperature (T_i). Pour the NaOH pellets into the cup and begin gently stirring with the stirring rod. Record the highest temperature reached as the final temperature (T_f).

4. Pour the solution down the sink followed by plenty of water. Rinse and dry the cups.

Lab 68

Part B

5. Place one cup inside the other. Using a graduated cylinder, put 50.0 mL of 1.0 *M* HCl into the inner cup. Rinse the graduated cylinder and put 50.0 mL of 1.0 *M* NaOH into it. Record these volumes. **CAUTION:** *NaOH solutions are caustic and HCl solutions are corrosive. Care should be taken when working with them.*

6. Measure the temperature of each solution. Be sure to rinse and dry the thermometer when changing from one solution to another. The temperatures should be within 0.2°C of each other. If not, notify your teacher. Record the HCl value as the initial temperature (T_i).

7. While gently stirring, add the NaOH to the HCl and measure the highest temperature reached. Record this value as the final temperature (T_f).

8. Pour the solution down the sink followed by plenty of water. Rinse and dry the cups.

Part C

9. Place one cup inside the other. Using a graduated cylinder, put 100.0 ml of 0.5 *M* HCl into the inner cup. Record this volume.

10. Repeat Steps 2 and 3 of Part A, using the 0.5 *M* HCl instead of distilled water.

11. Clean up your work area and wash your hands before leaving the laboratory.

Observations (sample data)

Part A
volume of H₂O	100.0 mL
mass of NaOH pellets	1.98 g
initial temperature	23.6°C
final temperature	27.4°C

Part B
volume of HCl solution	50.0 mL
volume of NaOH solution	50.0 mL
initial temperature	23.0°C
final temperature	29.2°C

Part C
volume of HCl solution	100.0 mL
mass of NaOH pellets	2.04 g
initial temperature	23.0°C
final temperature	33.8°C

Teaching Tips

It is possible to use plastic travel coffee mugs as calorimeters. They have a hole in the top for the thermometer.

To minimize contamination with water, dispense the NaOH in 15 small, capped vials. Each team can then take one of the vials. The number of NaOH pellets in the Procedure is based on about three pellets per gram. You should measure the NaOH pellets to be sure this figure agrees with the material you use. Since the amount of heat absorbed by the plastic foam cup is negligible, it is not included in calculating total heat released in the reactions.

The specific heats and densities of HCl and NaOH solutions are only slightly different from water, with the densities slightly higher and the specific heats slightly lower. The effects of assuming HCl and NaOH solutions have the same values as water tend to cancel out.

Waste Disposal

All substances used in this investigation can be flushed down the sink followed by plenty of water. ■

Entropy and Enthalpy Changes

Lab 68

Name _____

 Calculations (based on sample data)

Part A

1. Calculate the mass of the water in the cup. Assume the density of water is 1.0 g/mL.

$$100.0 \text{ mL} \times 1.0 \text{ g/mL} = 100 \text{ g}$$

2. Calculate the temperature change.

$$27.4°C - 23.6°C = 3.8°C$$

3. Calculate the moles of NaOH.

$$\frac{1.98 \text{ g}}{40.0 \text{ g/mol}} = 0.0495 \text{ mol}$$

4. Calculate the heat absorbed by the water as the NaOH dissolved. Use 0.00418 kJ/g·°C as the specific heat of water.

$$100 \text{ g} \times 0.00418 \text{ kJ/g·°C} \times 3.8°C = 1.6 \text{ kJ}$$

5. Calculate the heat released per mole of NaOH. Label this value as ΔH_A.

$$\Delta H_A = \frac{1.6 \text{ kJ}}{0.0495 \text{ mol}} = 32 \text{ kJ/mol}$$

Part B

1. Calculate the temperature change, the mass of the liquids in the cup, and the moles of NaOH as you did in the calculations for Part A. Assume the density of the HCl and NaOH solutions are the same as water.

$$\Delta T = 29.2°C - 23.0°C = 6.2°C$$
$$\text{mass (HCl + NaOH)} = 100.0 \text{ mL} \times 1.0 \text{ g/mL} = 100 \text{ g}$$
$$\text{moles NaOH} = 1.0 \text{ M} \times 0.050 \text{ L} = 0.050 \text{ mol}$$

2. Calculate the heat absorbed by the liquids as the HCl and NaOH reacted. Assume the specific heat of the solutions is the same as that of water.

$$100 \text{ g} \times 0.00418 \text{ kJ/g·°C} \times 6.2°C = 2.6 \text{ kJ}$$

3. Calculate the heat released per mole of NaOH. Label this value as ΔH_B.

$$\Delta H_B = \frac{2.6 \text{ kJ}}{0.050 \text{ mol}} = 52 \text{ kJ/mol}$$

Part C

1. Calculate the change in temperature, mass of the HCl, and moles of NaOH as before.

$$33.8° - 23.0°C = 10.8°C$$
$$100.0 \text{ mL} \times 1.0 \text{ g/mL} = 100 \text{ g}$$
$$\frac{2.04 \text{ g}}{40.0 \text{ g/mol}} = 0.051 \text{ mol}$$

2. Calculate the heat absorbed by the liquids as the HCl and NaOH reacted. Assume the liquids have the same specific heat as water.

$$100 \text{ g} \times 0.00418 \text{ kJ/g·°C} \times 10.8°C = 4.5 \text{ kJ}$$

3. Calculate the heat released per mole of NaOH. Label this value as ΔH_C.

$$\Delta H_C = \frac{4.5 \text{ kJ}}{0.051 \text{ mol}} = 88 \text{ kJ/mol}$$

Critical Thinking: Analysis and Conclusions

1. Explain what happens to the entropy in each of the three reactions. *(Making inferences)* The entropy increases for reaction A since the solid dissociates into ions. Entropy decreases for reaction B since the number of particles decreases when water forms. Students will have difficulty determining the entropy change for reaction C since the total number of particles does not change. Calculation shows that the entropy increases, but students should not be expected to make the calculation.

2. Write the equations for the reactions in Parts A, B, and C. Include the heat terms as determined in the investigation. How does the sum of A + B compare to the equation for Part C? *(Making comparisons)*
   Part A: $NaOH(s) \rightarrow Na^+(aq) + OH^-(aq) + 32$ kJ/mol NaOH
   Part B: $H^+(aq) + Cl^-(aq) + Na^+(aq) + OH^-(aq) \rightarrow Na^+(aq) + Cl^-(aq) + H_2O(l) + 52$ kJ/mol NaOH
   Part C: $NaOH(s) + H^+(aq) + Cl^-(aq) \rightarrow Na^+(aq) + Cl^-(aq) + H_2O(l) + 88$ kJ/mol NaOH. The sum of A + B is the same as the equation for Part C although the heat term is not precisely equal.

3. Which of these reactions is exothermic? How do you know? *(Interpreting data)* All of the reactions are exothermic since they are all accompanied by a release of heat to the environment.

4. Compare the sum of $\Delta H_A + \Delta H_B$ to ΔH_C. Are they different? Explain the source of any error. *(Making comparisons)* The sum of $\Delta H_A + \Delta H_B$ is 84 kJ/mol and ΔH_C is 88 kJ/mol. Most student error will derive from the measured temperature changes or from heat that escapes to the air.

5. What process is represented by ΔH_A? By ΔH_B? By ΔH_C? *(Making inferences)* ΔH_A represents the heat of solution. ΔH_B represents the heat of reaction, and ΔH_C represents both the heats of solution and reaction.

Lab 68

Name _____

Critical Thinking: Applications

1. How would changing the amount of NaOH affect the results of this investigation? *(Making predictions)* <u>Since the results are expressed in terms of kilojoules per mole, changing the amount of NaOH would not have any effect.</u>

2. Solid carbon reacts with oxygen gas to form carbon dioxide gas ($\Delta H = -393.5$ kJ/mol C). Carbon monoxide (CO) gas reacts with oxygen gas to form carbon dioxide gas ($\Delta H = -282.8$ kJ/mol CO). What is the enthalpy change for the reaction of solid carbon with oxygen gas to form carbon monoxide gas? *(Applying concepts)*
<u>Reversing the equation for the second reaction reverses the sign of its ΔH:</u>
<u>$CO_2(g) \rightarrow CO(g) + 1/2 O_2(g)$ ($\Delta H = 282.8$ kJ). Adding the equations for the two reactions yields the desired equation. The sum of their enthalpy changes gives the enthalpy change for the overall reaction.</u>
<u>-393.5 kJ/mol + 2.8 kJ/mol = -110.7 kJ/mol.</u>

Going Further

Going Further

1. Packs that produce cold usually contain an ammonium salt, while heating packs usually contain iron filings and salt. (See Investigations 4 and 35.)

1. Go to your physical education department and look at the ingredients on heat packs and cold packs. Devise an experiment that would show the amount of heat evolved or absorbed by the ingredients in the packs. Have your teacher approve your experimental design before you begin. Perform the experiment only under your teacher's supervision.

Thermodynamics of Homemade Ice Cream

Lab 69 APPLICATION

Text reference: **Chapter 23**

Introduction

It's 35°C in the shade and to cool off, you are eating an ice cream cone. As you sit there, you wonder just how ice cream is made. One area of chemistry that helps explains the making of ice cream is thermodynamics. There are three laws of thermodynamics:

1. The total amount of energy in the universe is constant.
2. The entropy of the universe is always increasing.
3. Everything with a temperature above zero kelvins has energy.

You may recognize the first law of thermodynamics as the law of conservation of energy. The second law may be more familiar to you when it is expressed in everyday language: heat always flows from a warmer object to a cooler object. In making ice cream, it is this second law that is of interest.

Another aspect of chemistry involved in producing ice cream deals with the physical properties of solutions, which differ from those of pure solvents. As you learned in Chapter 15, the presence of solute particles in a solution will raise the boiling point or lower the freezing point of the solvent, depending on the number of particles dissolved in a given mass of solvent. The latter characteristic applies to ice cream because the ice cream mixture is mainly a solution of sugar in water, and its freezing point is depressed below 0°C.

Before refrigerators were invented, ice cream was made using ice. In order to solidify by this method, the "hot" ice cream mixture has to lose energy to the "cold" ice. Since ordinary ice is only at 0°C, however, the lowest temperature that the ice cream mixture can reach is 0°C. With the system at thermal equilibrium, the ice cream mixture would still be a liquid.

To freeze the ice cream mixture, it is necessary to use "colder" ice. How do you do that? Again, what you know about colligative properties provides the answer: you make a solution. A salt-ice mixture has a lower freezing point than pure ice, so it acts as "colder" ice. The more salt added to the ice, the lower the freezing point. The ice cream mixture can then lose more energy to the salt-ice mixture and freeze before thermal equilibrium is reached.

In this investigation, you will take advantage of these principles to make homemade ice cream. You will prepare a salt-ice mixture and use it to freeze an ice cream mixture provided by your teacher. Because you should never taste anything in a chemistry laboratory, you will do this investigation in a food science (home economics) lab or nonscience room. Then, yes, you can eat your ice cream!

Materials (class of 30 in pairs)
30 aprons
15 baby-food jars with lids (4 oz. size)
ice cream mixture
15 large coffee cans with lids
30 kg crushed ice
5 kg rock salt (NaCl)
15 thermometers
15 cloth towels
30 spoons

Time Required
40 minutes.

Advance Preparation
To make the ice cream mixture, combine:
  4 eggs
  300 mL sugar
  1.0 L whole milk
  1.0 L half-and-half
  2 mL vanilla flavoring
  1 box instant pudding
  Ask students and faculty to collect baby-food jars and coffee cans with plastic lids. Cans can be washed and saved to be reused.
  Arrange to use a food science (home economics) lab or nonscience classroom for the investigation. The investigation can be done at home if you give students the recipe for the ice cream mixture, scaled to smaller proportions.
  Measure the mass of the salt and of the ice for each pair of students.

Introduction
Discuss the concept of freezing point depression with the students. Make sure they understand that the ice cream mixture and the salt-ice mixture have freezing points below 0°C for the same reason: dissolved solutes.

Lab 69 APPLICATION

Name _____

Pre-Lab Discussion

Read the entire laboratory investigation and the relevant pages of your textbook. Then answer the questions that follow.

1. How would you define the second law of thermodynamics? <u>Heat always flows from a warmer object to a cooler object.</u>

2. What is thermal equilibrium? <u>Thermal equilibrium is reached when two substances are at the same temperature.</u>

3. What is a colligative property? <u>A colligative property is one that depends on the number of moles of particles involved.</u>

4. How does adding salt to ice make ice "colder"? <u>The salt depresses the freezing point of water so that the salt-ice mixture has a lower freezing point, thereby making it "colder."</u>

5. Why is the salt-ice mixture needed to freeze the ice cream mixture? <u>The salt-ice mixture is needed because the freezing point of the ice cream mixture is lower than 0°C.</u>

6. Why must a towel be used when rolling the can? <u>The towel will protect the hands and insulate the salt-ice mixture.</u>

7. Can the ice cream mixture be rolled too long? Why? <u>No, it cannot be rolled too long because eventually it will reach thermal equilibrium.</u>

8. What would be the product if pure ice was used instead of the salt-ice mixture? Why? <u>The product would be more like a milk shake. The temperature would not get low enough to freeze the ice cream mixture.</u>

Problem

How can you lower the freezing point of water in order to freeze an ice cream mixture?

Materials

apron
clean baby-food jar with lid
ice cream mixture
coffee can with lid
2 kg crushed ice

300 g rock salt (NaCl)
thermometer
cloth towel
2 spoons

Safety

Wear an apron during this investigation. Do this investigation only in a food science (home economics) lab or a nonscience classroom. Make sure the baby food jar is tightly closed so the salt-ice mixture can't contaminate it. Use a towel when rolling the can to prevent cold burns on your hands. Wipe the baby-food jar off carefully before opening it.

Safety

Because eating in the chemistry lab is not safe, this investigation should be done in a food science (home economics) room or a nonscience classroom. If work is done in a nonscience room that has no sinks, students can wash their hands in the restrooms. Bring the ice into the room in nonlaboratory containers. Collect leftover ice and water to dispose of later. If students must work at home they should do so only under adult supervision. Make sure that the students' Safety Contracts are signed by a parent or guardian.

Do not use laboratory glassware or salt from laboratory supplies. Students should wear aprons to protect their clothing, and wash their hands before and after this investigation. Check the class for food allergies and other problems. Students who are lactose-intolerant, for example, should not eat the ice cream. Towels should be used to protect hands when rolling the cold cans. Students need to be reminded to wipe off the salt mixture before opening the baby-food jar and eating the ice cream. ∎

Note the caution alert symbols here and with certain steps of the Procedure. Refer to page *xi* for the specific precautions associated with each symbol.

Procedure

1. Work in the food science (home economics) lab or a nonscience classroom. Put on an apron and wash your hands with soap and water. Describe the ice cream mixture before you begin, and record your observations in the Data Table.
2. Use a spoon to fill a clean baby-food jar three-fourths of the way with the ice cream mixture. Seal the jar tightly with the lid. (If the jar leaks, your ice cream will be salty.)
3. Use another spoon to fill a large can about one-third full with half of the ice and half of the rock salt. Describe the salt-ice mixture. Measure and record its temperature.
4. Put the closed baby-food jar in the can and surround it with the rest of the ice and salt. Put the lid on the can. See Figure 69–1.
5. Wrap the can in a towel to insulate it and to protect your hands. Roll the can back and forth on a table, countertop, or floor for about 15 minutes. Unwrap the can and describe it.
6. Take the lid off the can and describe the salt-ice mixture. Measure and record the temperature of the salt-ice mixture. Remove and rinse the baby-food jar, open the cap, and wipe the rim free of salt.
7. Describe the appearance of the ice cream mixture. Test the product.

8. Wash the jar, can, lids, and spoons. Pour the salt-ice mixture down the drain with plenty of water. Clean up your work area and wash your hands before leaving the room.

Teaching Tips
Putting the ice cream mixture into pitchers will make it much easier to pour into the students' baby-food jars.

The observed freezing point depression depends on the amount of salt used. It is usually about −7°C to −10°C.

Figure 69–1

Waste Disposal
Excess ice can be melted and poured down the sink. Excess salt should be emptied into the waste basket. The salt-ice mixture may be flushed down the drain with plenty of water. ■

Observations (sample data)

Material	Observation
initial ice cream mixture	a fairly dense liquid
initial salt-ice mixture; temperature	looks like dirty ice −10°C
can after it is rolled	colder, icy, wet
final salt-ice mixture; temperature	some ice has melted −10°C (same as initial)
final ice cream mixture	solution is now semi-solid

Thermodynamics of Homemade Ice Cream

Name _____

 Calculations (based on sample data)

1. Calculate the theoretical freezing point depression of the ice-salt mixture used in this investigation.

$$\frac{300 \text{ g NaCl}}{53.5 \text{ g/mol}} = 5.61 \text{ mol NaCl}$$

$$\text{molality} = \frac{\text{mol solute}}{\text{kg solvent}} = \frac{5.61 \text{ mol NaCl}}{2 \text{ kg ice}} = 2.80 \, m$$

NaCl dissociates into two ions, so $i = 2$ and $k_f = -1.86°C/m$ for water, so
$\Delta T_f = k_{fw}mi = (-1.86°C/m)(2.80 \, m)(2) = -10.4°C$

2. Compare your actual freezing point to the one calculated. Determine the percent error.

$$\text{percent error} = \frac{-10.0°C - (-10.4°C)}{-10.4°C} \times 100\% = 4.1\%$$

Critical Thinking: Analysis and Conclusions

1. Discuss the reason for the heat transfer that occurs as the ice melts and the ice cream mixture freezes. *(Drawing conclusions)* The ice cream mixture is above 0°C. The salt-ice mixture is below 0°C. Heat flows from warmer to cooler objects, so the energy from the ice cream mixture flows to the salt-ice mixture. The ice cream mixture gets colder, and the salt-ice mixture begins to melt.

2. How can you account for the percent error in the investigation? *(Interpreting data)* Sources of error include built-in errors of the thermometer and balance used to measure temperature and masses, respectively, and heat absorption by the ice from the environment, which prevents the lowest temperature from being reached.

3. How could you speed up the freezing of the ice cream mixture? *(Making inferences)* Add more salt to the salt-ice mixture to lower its freezing point. Precool the ice cream mixture so that not as much energy needs to be transferred to reach the freezing point.

Critical Thinking: Applications

1. Why are ionic compounds such as salt put on sidewalks in winter? *(Applying concepts)* Ionic compounds lower the freezing point of water, causing snow and ice on sidewalks to melt.

Making a Cloud Chamber

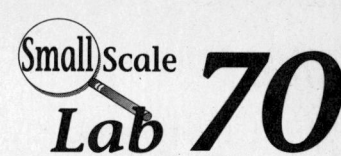

Text reference: **Chapter 24**

Introduction

Seeing the invisible radiation emitted from radioactive sources can be quite difficult without the aid of special equipment. Geiger counters can detect radiation and measure how much is being emitted, but they do not reveal the radiation itself or the path that it travels through the air. A cloud chamber is a device that allows you to see the path radiation particles travel after they are emitted from a source.

Alpha and beta radiation are known as *ionizing radiation* because when they interact with other materials, they cause the normally neutral molecules to become ionized. Geiger counters work because of this property of radiation.

In a cloud chamber the air is saturated with a volatile liquid, such as isopropyl alcohol, and cooled. When the radiation travels through this region of cooled saturated air, it ionizes some of the particles. The alcohol vapor is attracted to these ionized particles and the alcohol condenses, forming a cloud. This cloud reveals a visible track of the radiation emitted. The length of the path depends on the initial speed of the radiation, and the density of the cloud depends upon the ability of the radiation to ionize the particles in its path. Figure 70–1 shows what happens on a molecular level inside a cloud chamber.

Materials (class of 30 in pairs)

30 pairs chemical splash goggles
30 laboratory aprons
30 pairs latex gloves
15 plastic petri dishes
15 pieces of black felt
15 pairs scissors
15 bottles of glue
3 rolls of tape
wash bottles containing isopropyl alcohol
15 paper towels
15 pairs of insulated gloves or tongs for handling the dry ice
15 blocks of dry ice, 10 cm × 10 cm
15 radioactive sources
15 bright light sources

Time Required
45 minutes.

Advance Preparation
Prepare the petri dishes as follows: Separate the halves of the petri dishes and sort them so that you have pairs of tops and pairs of bottoms. Match the two halves of one of these new pairs so that they form an enclosed cylinder. Hold it together with your hands or by using small pieces of tape. Under the fume hood, heat a glass stirring rod with a burner and use the rod to melt a small hole about 1 cm in diameter in the middle of one side of the vertical cylinder walls. (An inexpensive soldering iron can be used in place of the burner and glass rod.) Let the plastic cool. Repeat this procedure for the remaining petri dish halves. CAUTION: *Keep long hair and loose clothing tied back. Melting plastic should be done only under a fume*

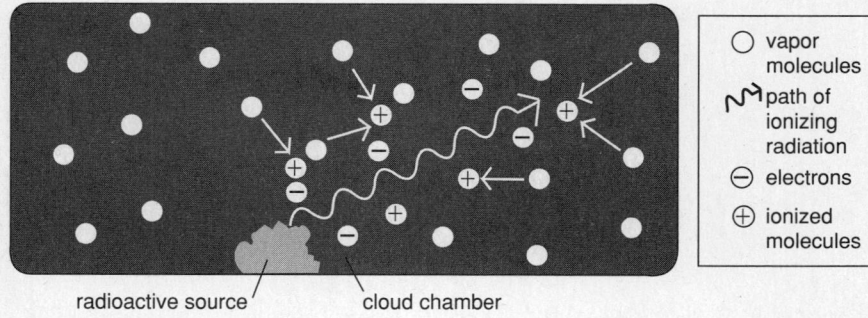

Figure 70–1

In this investigation you will construct a simple cloud chamber and use it to observe the paths formed by alpha and beta particles. The length and density of the vapor trails will tell you whether you are observing alpha particles or beta particles. Alpha particles move more slowly than beta particles, so they produce shorter trails. Alpha particles also have a greater ability to ionize matter than beta particles, so their trails are more dense.

Small Scale Lab 70

Name _____

hood. The fumes generated can be quite toxic and are noxious.
Have a plastic trash bag ready to collect students' used latex gloves.
Only a small amount of isopropyl alcohol is required. To reduce the hazards associated with using isopropyl alcohol, fill the wash bottles only one-quarter full. Have students do Step 5 in the fume hood. You can have one or two wash bottles in each fume hood.
High intensity lamps, bright flashlights, or other small but bright light sources work well. Check with your physics department.
Purchase the dry ice the night before or early in the morning. To keep the dry ice cold, put it in an ice chest with the lid on. Put this ice chest inside a second, larger ice chest. The dry ice will keep for several days depending on the original quantity. CAUTION: *Do not put the dry ice in a sealed container. The dry ice sublimes, so there must be a way for the gas to escape. If the gas cannot escape, the pressure will build up and an explosion will occur.*
The dry ice can be cut into smaller squares using a hammer and a slot screwdriver. The pieces of dry ice can be reused until gone. CAUTION: *Wear insulated gloves to protect your hands when working with the dry ice.*
There are a variety of radioactive sources that can be used. Check with your physics department or order through a catalogue. Uranium ore broken up into small pieces works well. Sources may be alpha emitters, beta emitters, or both. Make sure the sources do not produce radiation above acceptable safety levels. A level below 2 millirems per hour is unregulated.

Pre-Lab Discussion

Read the entire laboratory investigation and the relevant pages of your textbook. Then answer the questions that follow.

1. What are alpha particles? Beta particles? <u>Alpha particles are helium nuclei consisting of two protons and two neutrons. Beta particles are electrons.</u>

2. What is the mass and electrical charge of an alpha particle? A beta particle? <u>An alpha particle has a mass of 4 amu and a charge of 2+. A beta particle has a mass of 1/1836 amu and a charge of 1−.</u>

3. Briefly describe how a vapor trail forms as radiation passes through the cloud chamber. <u>As the radiation travels through the chamber, it ionizes some of the particles in the cooled air. The alcohol molecules are attracted to these ions and condense into a cloud.</u>

4. What is meant by the term *ionizing radiation*? <u>Ionizing radiation is any form of radiation that can cause a neutral molecule to become ionized.</u>

5. What are the hazards of working with the radioactive substances in this investigation? What precautions should you take? <u>Radioactive material is harmful if ingested. One should wear latex gloves when handling the radioactive sources. Gloves should be disposed of in the designated container.</u>

6. What are the hazards of working with dry ice? What precautions should you take? <u>Dry ice can cause severe tissue damage. One should wear insulated gloves or use tongs.</u>

Problem

How can you use a cloud chamber to observe the trails made by alpha and beta radiation?

Materials

chemical splash goggles
laboratory apron
latex gloves
scissors
piece of black felt
2 plastic petri dish tops or bottoms
glue
tape
wash bottle containing isopropyl alcohol
paper towel
insulated gloves or tongs for handling the dry ice
block of dry ice, 10 cm × 10 cm
radioactive sources
bright light source

Name_____

Safety

Wear your goggles and lab apron at all times during the investigation. Radioactive sources are harmful if ingested. Wear latex gloves when handling the sources. Dispose of the gloves in the container designated by your instructor. Wash your hands thoroughly with hot water and soap before leaving the laboratory. Dry ice can cause severe tissue damage due to extremely cold temperatures. Use insulated gloves or tongs to handle the dry ice. Isopropyl alcohol is toxic and flammable. Keep the alcohol away from open flames and heat sources. The light source gets very hot. Handle it with caution. Note the caution alert symbols here and with certain steps of the Procedure. Refer to page *xi* for the specific precautions associated with each symbol.

Procedure

 1. Put on your goggles and lab apron.

2. Cut a round piece of black felt so that it will cover the bottom of the petri dish. Place it in the dish. Be sure it lies flat on the bottom.

3. Using Figure 70–2 as a guide, begin assembling the cloud chamber. Cut two strips of black felt. The width of each strip should be the same as the height of the inner walls of the cloud chamber. The length of each strip should be such that the hole on one side of the assembly and about a 2-cm gap on the side opposite the hole are not covered. Secure each strip with glue.

4. Put the top on the assembly so that the cutouts for the hole align, and seal with tape. Do not cover the opening.

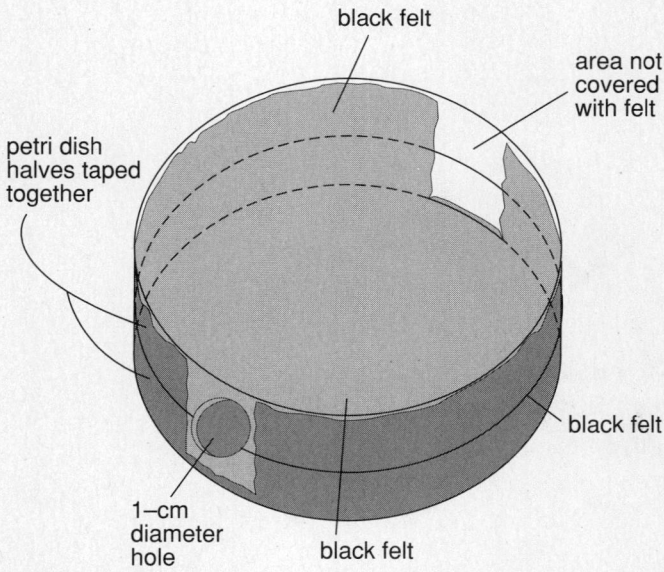

Figure 70–2

Introduction

To introduce the investigation you may want to have a Geiger counter set up near some radioactive sources at the front of the room. There are several computer interfaces that can be connected to a Geiger counter. See scientific catalogues for information.

Discuss what happens at a molecular level in the cloud chamber, as shown in Figure 70–1.

Safety

Make sure students wear their goggles and lab aprons at all times during the investigation. Dry ice can cause severe tissue damage. Caution students never to handle dry ice without protection. Insulated gloves or tongs should be used. Never store dry ice in a sealed container; explosions could result due to excessive gas pressure.

Although the radioactive sources are relatively safe, follow all safety precautions. Radiation causes tissue damage, especially if the exposure is internal. Remind students to wear latex gloves when handling the sources. The students should wash their hands thoroughly before leaving the laboratory.

Isopropyl alcohol is toxic and flammable. Have students use it in a fume hood. There should be no open flames in the laboratory. Remind students to keep the isopropyl alcohol away from the light sources, which get very hot.

Caution students that the high-intensity light sources can cause burns after being on for a while. ■

Teaching Tips

This activity can be done in larger groups to reduce the amount of materials needed, especially the amount of dry ice and the number of light sources. Groups of four or five work well.

Making a Cloud Chamber

Name _____

Do not tell the students whether their radioactive sources are alpha or beta emitters. If necessary, code the sources. If the whole class uses the same kind of source, they may have more difficulty answering Question 2 of Analysis and Conclusions.

Stress that the students should be patient.

If you do not wish to construct cloud chambers, commercial chambers are available from scientific supply houses. They may come with radiation sources.

It is important that the alcohol be cooled for at least 5 minutes. The light source will heat up the system and make it more difficult to see the vapor trails. Stress that the lights should be turned off and on at 5-minute intervals to keep the system cool.

Each group should have its chamber made and cooling before turning the room lights off.

Students may wish to try observing the cloud chamber without a source in it. They must be very patient and attentive.

There are several good resources of activities related to nuclear science, for example, *Experiments in Nuclear Science,* by Chase, Rituper, and Sulcoski (Burgess Publishing Company/ALPHA Editions, 7108 Ohms Lane, Minneapolis, Minnesota).

Waste Disposal

Radioactive sources should not be discarded. They can be reused. Leftover dry ice can be allowed to sublime. Be sure not to leave it in an area accessible to students. The cloud chambers can be saved and reused. Collect the latex gloves in a designated plastic bag. When all gloves have been collected, tie the bag closed and dispose of in the trash. ■

5. Work in a fume hood. Using the wash bottle with isopropyl alcohol, wet the sides and the bottom of the felt. The sides should be thoroughly moistened. **CAUTION:** *Isopropyl alcohol is toxic and flammable. Avoid its contact with your skin. Wash spills with plenty of water. Keep it away from open flames and heat sources.*

6. Obtain a 10-cm square of dry ice from your instructor. **CAUTION:** *Do not handle the dry ice with your bare hands. Use tongs or insulated gloves.* Set the block of dry ice on a paper towel. Set the cloud chamber on the dry ice. Let it cool for about five minutes.

7. Put on latex gloves. Obtain a radioactive source and insert it through the opening of the cloud chamber. Record the name of the source. **CAUTION:** *Radioactive sources are harmful if ingested. Wear latex gloves when handling the sources.*

8. Turn off the room lights and turn on the light source. Look for cloud trails coming from the radioactive source as alpha or beta particles are emitted. **CAUTION:** *The light source gets very hot. Handle it with caution.*

9. After about five minutes, turn off the light source and let the system cool. Then turn the light back on and observe again.

10. If more than one source is available, replace the first source with a different source and repeat Steps 7–9.

11. Dispose of the latex gloves, dry ice, and radioactive sources as directed by your teacher. Clean up your work area and wash your hands before leaving the laboratory.

Observations (sample data)

Radioactive source: _____

In the space provided, make a drawing of your cloud chamber showing the location of the source and the vapor trails formed by the radiation.

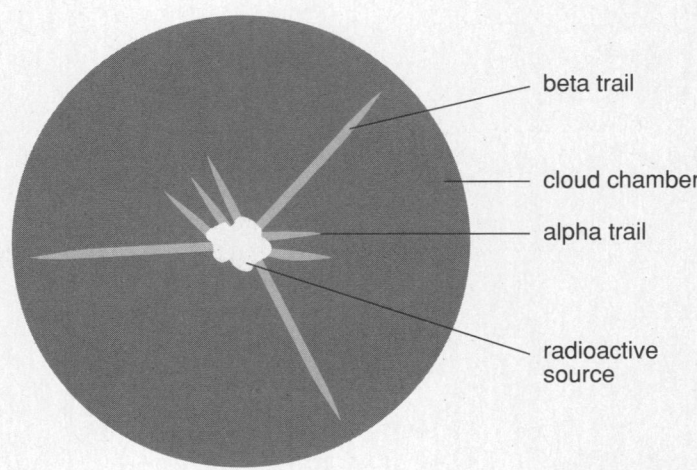

Name _____

Small Scale Lab 70

Critical Thinking: Analysis and Conclusions

1. How many different types of trails are there? *(Interpreting data)*
   There are two different types. (Answers may vary, depending on the sources used.)

2. Based on the information in the Introduction, identify the vapor trails you saw as having been made by alpha particles or beta particles. If necessary, compare your results with the results of classmates who used different sources. *(Making comparisons)* Answers will vary. Students should be able to distinguish between the shorter, denser trails of the alpha particles and the longer, thinner trails of beta particles.

3. On the drawing you made in the Observations, distinguish between the tracks made by alpha particles and those made by beta particles, and label them. *(Interpreting diagrams)*

Critical Thinking: Applications

1. Why do you think the paths of gamma rays cannot be seen in a cloud chamber? *(Applying concepts)* Gamma rays are not a form of ionizing radiation. If they do not ionize the atmosphere, a cloud cannot form.

2. Sometimes a vapor trail can be seen in the cloud chamber even though no radioactive source is in it. What do you think causes the vapor trails? *(Making predictions)* Background radiation, including cosmic radiation, will make a vapor trail.

3. Alpha particles are the least penetrating of all forms of radiation, yet they can cause serious tissue damage. Why? *(Applying concepts)* Alpha particles are highly ionizing. It is the ionization of the tissue that damages it.

Going Further

1. Research other methods used to observe the paths made by radiation, including bubble chambers and Geiger counters. Report on your findings.
2. If the light source is bright enough and you have access to a camera you may wish to attempt to photograph the particle trails made.
3. Ionizing radiation is both harmful and useful. Research the effects of ionizing radiation and the application of it to treat cancer. You might be able to visit a hospital and learn firsthand about radiotherapy.

Going Further

1. Geiger counters work on the principle of ionization of a gas by radiation. Libraries and universities are good resources. A field trip to a university lab might be possible.
2. Students interested in photography may wish to try this activity. They should use a bright light source, not a flash.
3. Libraries, universities, and hospitals should provide excellent resources. Consider arranging a field trip to a hospital.

Name _____ Date _____ Class _____

Using a Radon Test Kit

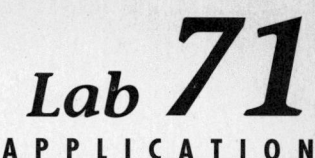

Text reference: **Chapter 24**

Introduction

Radon gas is a product in the radioactive decay series from naturally occurring uranium-238 to stable lead-206. Radon-222 is the only gas in the series and has a half-life of 3.82 days. Radon gas is released into the atmosphere through cracks in granite rock and can accumulate to dangerous levels in the basements of buildings.

Health concerns about radon gas and the study of its effects have been increasing since 1972. Environmental Protection Agency standards for measuring radon and its daughter elements, as well as suggested safe levels of radon, were established in the mid 1980s. These health concerns are not new. As early as the sixteenth century, mine workers in Germany were said to be dying from a disease called mountain sickness, which is now believed to have been caused by radon gas. Exposure to radon has more recently been identified as a cause of lung cancer.

The unit used in the detection of radiation is the pCi/L (picocuries per liter of air). A curie (Ci) is defined as 37 billion disintegrations per second, which is the rate of decay of 1 gram of radium (Ra). The threshold, or upper limit before corrective measures should be taken to reduce radon levels, is 4 pCi/L.

In this investigation you will use a radon detector to determine the radon level in the basement of a building. Three common ways to test for radon are liquid scintillation counters, alpha-track devices, and charcoal-adsorbent detectors. Most home test kits are of the charcoal-adsorbent type and must be left in place for 4–7 days. The kit is then returned to the manufacturer for evaluation. For a reliable test, there must be little or no air movement that would allow the radon to dissipate. The best places to put the test kits are quiet areas of basements. The results of your test will be reported in pCi/L by the manufacturer of the test kit.

Pre-Lab Discussion

Read the entire laboratory investigation and the relevant pages of your textbook. Then answer the questions that follow.

1. What naturally occurring element is the first precursor in the radioactive decay chain that produces radon? __Uranium-238__

2. Why is radon hazardous? __Radon can cause lung cancer.__

3. What is the basic unit used to report radon radiation levels? __The unit is picocuries per liter of air, pCi/L.__

Materials (class of 30)
1 to 4 commercial radon test kits

Time Required
30 minutes.

Advance Preparation
Purchase radon test kits. Commercial radon kits cost $20–50. This makes it expensive to run more than one test per class. Find out if some parents want to test the basements of their homes or apartment buildings and would be willing to buy kits for a take-home project. This is a good way to compare different test kits. The school board may want to purchase kits to test its buildings. If possible, use several kits from different manufacturers and compare results.

Introduction
Begin the investigation with a class discussion about radiation in the environment. Ask students what they think are possible sources of radiation (cosmic rays, building materials such as bricks and granite, radioactive decay within Earth, carbon-14 in organic matter, power plants, X-rays, residual fallout from nuclear tests). Then ask students where they could go to escape radiation and if such action is feasible or necessary. When might it be appropriate to take protective action? Get students to realize that the presence or absence of radiation is not as significant as the level of radiation under specific circumstances.

© Prentice-Hall, Inc.

Using a Radon Test Kit

Lab 71
APPLICATION

Name _____

4. Where are samples usually taken to test radon levels? Why? <u>Quiet areas in the basements of buildings are the best places to test. These locations are closest to the sources of radon and tend to have little air movement that would hasten the escape of the gas.</u>

5. What might you learn about radon test kits if your class is able to use two or more brands of kits in the investigation? <u>Results could be compared and the level of accuracy of the kits could be rated. Ease of use could also be compared.</u>

Problem

How can you determine the radon level in the basement of a building using a commercial test kit?

Materials

1 or more commercial radon test kits

Safety

Use the test kits only as directed. If the test is done at home, secure the permission of an adult responsible for the premises before proceeding.

Procedure

1. Following the directions on the test kit, place the sample collector in a quiet part of a basement 70–100 cm above ground level. For a reliable test, there must be no air movement. If more than one brand of test kit is used, place all of the kits in the same general vicinity. If additional locations are to be tested, use one or more kits at each site.
2. After the sample has been collected, follow the directions for sending in the kit for testing. The results will be returned to the school. Record the results in the Data Table.

Observations (sample data)
DATA TABLE

Kit Manufacturer	Test Site	pCi/L
test kit brand 1	school or home basement	0.4*
test kit brand 2	school or home basement	1.2

*Class data will vary with test sites, region, and local conditions.

Safety
Caution students to handle the test kits only as directed. ■

Teaching Tips
This is a whole-class project in which a quiet part of the school basement is to be tested. The sample data given are real results from samples taken in the same home basement at the same time. If the results at your site are above the threshold level, you may want to alert the appropriate parties.

If more than one test kit is used, divide students into groups and assign responsibility for one test kit to each group. If students work at home, be sure to secure permission from an adult who is responsible for the premises.

If more than one site was tested, have the students compare the radon levels for the different sites. Students should also compare data from different kits at the same sites. They may find that specific test kits produce consistently higher or lower readings than average, indicating how reliable one manufacturer's kit is compared to another's.

Critical Thinking: Analysis and Conclusions

1. What level of radon gas was shown to be present in the building tested? *(Interpreting data)* Answers will vary.

2. Calculate the average value of radon levels indicated by the kits in one location and find the percentage deviations from the average. *(Interpreting data)*

    average value = $\dfrac{0.4 \text{ pCi/L} + 1.2 \text{ pCi/L}}{2}$ = 0.8 pCi/L

    sample 1: percent deviation = $\dfrac{0.4 \text{ pCi/L} - 0.8 \text{ pCi/L}}{0.8 \text{ pCi/L}}$ = −50%

    sample 2: percent deviation = $\dfrac{1.2 \text{ pCi/L} - 0.8 \text{ pCi/L}}{0.8 \text{ pCi/L}}$ = 50%

3. Do your results suggest that action should be taken to reduce radon levels? Answers will vary. The sample data are well within the safe level, so no action would be needed in this case.

Critical Thinking: Applications

1. Cumulative effects of carcinogens create a serious threat to some people. Propose a worst-case scenario for increased lung-cancer risk. *(Making predictions)* Heavy smokers who are hard rock miners living in homes with high radon levels would have a statistically higher rate of lung cancer.

2. To save energy, many homes have been made more airtight. How could this condition increase radon levels in high-risk areas? *(Developing hypotheses)* If there is less circulation of fresh air, then there is less likelihood of radon escaping from the dwelling.

3. In some cases, the level of radon has been found to be as high as 2,700 pCi/L in one house, while a house 100 meters away has levels less than 20 pCi/L. How is this possible? *(Developing hypotheses)* Maybe one house sits on a crack in granitic rock that releases radon gas into the house in much higher volumes than in a house sitting on intact bedrock.

4. If radon decayed to polonium with a half-life of several minutes rather than 3.82 days, the health danger would be less. Explain. *(Applying concepts)* The shorter half life would mean that polonium would be produced and settle out of the air instead of entering the lungs.

Lab 71
APPLICATION

Going Further

1. One way to collect daughter elements of radon-222 is to use coffee filters taped to a vacuum cleaner intake. Experiments could run over several hours or days. A vacuum pump with a standard 47-mm Millipore type filter system could also be adapted for use.
2. Students can contact the various manufacturers and obtain literature describing the products.

Going Further

1. Devise an experiment that could, over several hours, trap daughter elements of radon-222 and test for their presence using a Geiger counter. Under your teacher's supervision, conduct the experiment. Report on your results.
2. Find out how different types of radon detectors (liquid scintillation counters, alpha-track devices, and charcoal-adsorbent detectors) work. Write a brief summary of your findings.

Name _____ Date _____ Class _____

Melting Point of an Organic Compound

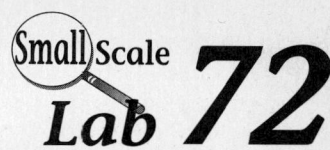

Small Scale Lab **72**

Text reference: **Chapter 25**

Introduction

The first manufacturing lab for drugs in the United States was established in 1778. Its purpose was to supply medicines to George Washington's troops. Today the Food and Drug Administration (FDA) controls legal drugs sold in the United States. Before a drug may be offered for sale, tests must prove conclusively that it is safe and pure. One method to determine the purity of a compound is the determination of its melting point. If you did Investigation 42 in this manual, you studied the effects of bond type and polarity on the melting point of pure chemicals. You learned that every compound has a characteristic melting point that is a function of its chemical structure. When impurities are present, the compound will show a melting point that is lower and possibly wider in range than that of the pure compound. A compound containing small amounts of impurities may, in fact, melt several degrees below its pure form. If the melting point is more than a few degrees off, the compound may be a different product altogether.

Many drugs, such as aspirin, can be produced in the laboratory. Aspirin is an example of a class of organic compounds called esters. You will learn more about the making of esters in the next chapter. In this investigation, you will determine the melting point of aspirin. You will then compare your results with a reference standard for this chemical product.

Materials (class of 30 in pairs)
30 pairs chemical splash goggles
30 laboratory aprons
15 spatulas
aspirin, 15g
15 glass squares or pieces of weighing paper
15 melting point tubes
15 rubber bands
15 thermometers, 150°C
15 thermometer clamps
15 one-hole stoppers or cutaway corks
15 ring stands
2 L vegetable oil
15 beakers, 250-mL
15 wire gauze squares
15 lab burners
15 iron rings
15 books of matches or strikers

Time Required
45 to 55 minutes. To save time, eliminate the waiting period between trials by having students obtain a fresh supply of cool oil.

Advance Preparation
Use canola oil, if possible. Make melting point tubes from capillary tubing if needed. Have containers ready to collect the used oil and the melting point tubes.

Introduction
You may wish to introduce the topic by showing a video on aspirin. One example, called *ASA* (acetylsalicylic acid), is part of the series, *Organic Chemistry 2*, available for purchase from:
Film for the Humanities and Sciences
P.O. Box 2053
Princeton, N.J., 08540
1-800-257-5126

Pre-Lab Discussion

Read the entire laboratory investigation and the relevant pages of your textbook. Then answer the questions that follow.

1. Aspirin is an allergen. Look up the meaning of the word *allergen* in a dictionary, and explain why it appears in a caution in the Safety section. __An allergen is any substance that causes or reveals an allergy in__ an individual. Some students may be allergic to aspirin.

2. A hot oil bath is used in the Procedure. Why doesn't the Procedure call for a hot water bath? __Water boils at 100°C, and this temperature is__ below the melting point of aspirin.

3. Why should you place the thermometer bulb and the melting point tube 3 cm above the bottom of the beaker and not on the bottom? __Because the beaker may be very hot and can damage the thermometer. Also,__ you want to record the temperature of the oil, not the beaker.

© Prentice-Hall, Inc.

Melting Point of an Organic Compound **399**

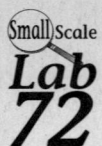

Lab 72

Name _____

4. Why will cooling the oil bath and the melting point tube allow you to repeat the Procedure and check your answer? <u>This allows the aspirin to "freeze," or become solid again.</u>

Problem
How can you use the melting point to determine the purity of an organic compound?

Materials
chemical splash goggles
laboratory apron
spatula
aspirin
glass square or weighing paper
melting point tube
rubber band
thermometer fitted with a one-hole stopper or cutaway cork

thermometer clamp
ring stand
vegetable oil
beaker, 250-mL
wire gauze square
lab burner
iron ring
matches or striker

Safety

Wear your goggles and lab apron at all times during the investigation. Acetylsalicylic acid (aspirin) is an allergen. It may cause bleeding after ingestion. Do not taste the aspirin. The oil bath and lab burner are hot. Do not touch the beaker or oil during the heating process. Tie back hair and loose clothing before lighting the burner.

Melting point tubes are fragile. Handle them with care. Note the caution alert symbols here and with certain steps of the Procedure. Refer to page *xi* for the specific precautions associated with each symbol.

Procedure

1. Put on your goggles and lab apron. Using a spatula, crush some aspirin crystals on a glass square or a piece of weighing paper. Force a small amount of crystals into the melting point tube. Invert the tube and tap it gently until the crystals fall to the bottom. Repeat the process until there is about 1 cm of crystals packed into the bottom end of the tube. **CAUTION:** *Melting point tubes are fragile. Handle them with care.*

2. Obtain a thermometer fitted with a one-hole stopper or cutaway cork. Using a rubber band, attach the melting point tube to the bottom of a thermometer. Make sure that the closed end of the tube is down. The bottom of the tube should be level with the bulb of the thermometer. Clamp the thermometer to a point near the top of a ring stand. See Figure 72–1.

Safety
Make sure students wear their goggles and lab aprons at all times during the investigation. Caution students not to touch the hot beaker or oil. If you have the students replace the oil between trials, provide hot pads or beaker tongs for them to use when disposing of the hot oil. You may wish to assign several groups of students to each setup to minimize the number of hot oil beakers in the lab. ■

Teaching Tips
Students have done an investigation using the same setup in Investigation 42. Have them review the Procedure of that lab and the diagram of the apparatus before beginning this investigation.

If you do not have melting point tubes, substitute capillary tubes with one end melted closed. Prepare these before class. You can substitute mortars and pestles for the spatulas to crush the aspirin.

Name _____

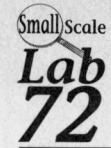

3. Set up a ring stand, ring, wire gauze square, and lab burner. Refer to Figure 42–2 in Investigation 42 in this book as a reminder of the setup of the apparatus. Pour about 100 mL of oil into a 250-mL beaker. Set the beaker on the wire gauze square. Lower the thermometer into the oil. The bulb of the thermometer should be about 3 cm from the bottom of the beaker.

4. Light the burner with the matches or striker. Heat the oil in the beaker until the temperature reaches about 110°C. Lower the burner flame to reduce the rate of heating. Continue to raise the temperature of the oil very slowly. **CAUTION:** *Tie back any hair or loose clothing that could come into contact with the flame. The heated oil is very hot. Do not touch the beaker or the hot plate with your bare hands.*

5. One partner should watch the crystals in the melting point tube closely while the other partner watches the thermometer. When the crystals melt, read the thermometer at once. Record the temperature in the Data Table.

6. Allow the oil and the melting point tube to cool to at least 120°C. Heat and observe the melting point a second time. If the temperature is not within one degree of your first reading, repeat this step.

7. Make sure your burner is shut off. Remove the thermometer from the oil bath, and allow it to cool. Put the melting point tube in the container provided by your teacher. Return the oil to a container provided by your teacher. Clean oil from your thermometer. Clean up your work area and wash your hands before leaving the laboratory.

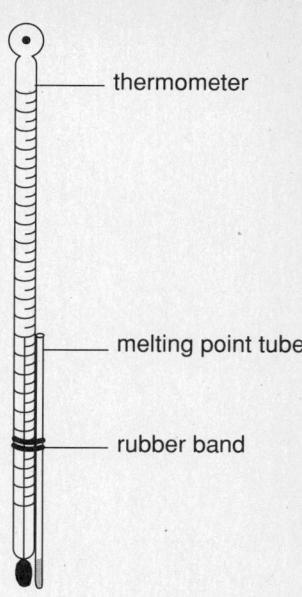

Figure 72–1

You can have some of the students test commercial aspirin (generic and name-brand varieties) and compare their results. Make sure that the commercial preparations are pure aspirin, without buffering, fillers, or other ingredients.

Other types of melting point apparatus are available. Thiele-Dennis tubes use considerably less oil. They cost $25–$30 each and are available from some scientific supply companies. The Mel-Temp Unit eliminates the oil bath altogether and costs about $375. It can be ordered from Laboratory Devices, Inc., Box 6402, Holliston, MA 01746.

Observations (sample data)

DATA TABLE   Melting Point of Aspirin

Material	Melting Point (°C)
pure aspirin reference	135
aspirin trial #1	137
aspirin trial #2	135
average of trials #1 and #2	136

Critical Thinking: Analysis and Conclusions

1. Calculate the difference between the melting point of pure aspirin and your sample. Does your compound appear to be aspirin? Why or why not? *(Interpreting data)* 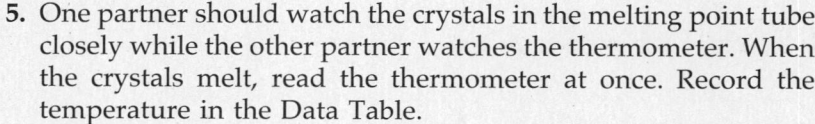 Answers will vary. If the students have measured the melting point carefully, they should obtain reasonable results and conclude that they have aspirin.

Waste Disposal

Collect the oil in a beaker or jar for use at a later date. Melting point tubes should be collected in a separate container for broken glass. ■

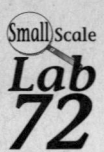

Name _____

2. If your melting point had been several degrees higher than the melting point of pure aspirin, what could you conclude? *(Drawing conclusions)* That aspirin probably was not present or that an error was made when measuring the temperature.

3. If your melting point had been 1 degree lower than the melting point of pure aspirin, what could you conclude? *(Drawing conclusions)* That the material was aspirin but may have had some impurities in it.

4. If your melting point had been 5 degrees lower than the melting point of pure aspirin, what could you conclude? *(Drawing conclusions)* That another compound was present, not aspirin.

Critical Thinking: Applications

1. What have you learned about aspirin in this investigation that can be useful to you? *(Applying concepts)* Answers can include learning about the purity of commercial aspirin and the use of melting points to determine the purity of aspirin.

2. How would your results be affected if the hot oil bath was heated more rapidly? *(Making predictions)* The temperature might rise too quickly and overshoot the actual melting point.

Going Further

1. Research the folk history of naturally occuring aspirin compounds. Find out what plants contain salicylic acid or its derivatives and how people of various cultures have used the compound. Prepare a short report for the class.
2. Research the discovery of aspirin in the laboratory and the history of its use. Report on a recent study of aspirin in the scientific literature.

Properties of an Alkyne

Small Scale Lab 73

Text reference: **Chapter 25**

Introduction

Hydrocarbons are compounds made up of only carbon and hydrogen. Hydrocarbons made of straight carbon chains are called aliphatic hydrocarbons, and include the alkanes, alkenes, and alkynes. Alkanes are saturated hydrocarbons, while alkenes and alkynes are unsaturated. In all cases, hydrocarbons with just a few carbon atoms are gaseous at room temperature and pressure. As the number of carbon atoms increases, the compounds are mostly liquids, and then solids. The number of unsaturated bonds also helps to determine whether a specific compound is a solid, liquid, or gas.

The main source of aliphatic hydrocarbons is petroleum. They are used as fuels, lubricants, waxes, and road-surfacing material, and in the production of plastics and cosmetics.

The first member of the alkynes is called ethyne, more commonly known as acetylene. Its major use is as a fuel in torches that cut and weld metals. In this investigation, you will prepare acetylene (ethyne) from a reaction of calcium carbide (CaC_2) with water and examine some of its chemical and physical properties.

Materials (class of 30 in pairs)
30 pairs chemical splash goggles
30 laboratory aprons
15 large test tubes
15 one-hole rubber stoppers, #00
15 thin-stem micropipets
15 pairs scissors
roll of clear adhesive tape
15 beakers, 600-mL
water
30 graduated micropipets
15 pairs forceps
30 pea-sized pieces of calcium carbide
15 books of matches
15 candles
15 dropper bottles of phenolphthalein indicator

Time Required
25 minutes.

Advance Preparation
Break the calcium carbide into pea-sized pieces using a hammer. Store in a dry, closed container.
Make 1% phenolphthalein solution by dissolving 1 g in 100 mL of 50% ethanol.
Have ready a container in which to collect the waste calcium carbide.

Pre-Lab Discussion

Read the entire laboratory investigation and the relevant pages of your textbook. Then answer the questions that follow.

1. Give the molecular formula and the structural formula for acetylene (ethyne).

   C_2H_2 H—C≡C—H

2. Distinguish between the term *saturated* and *unsaturated* hydrocarbons. Saturated hydrocarbons contain the greatest possible number of hydrogen atoms for their number of carbon atoms. Unsaturated hydrocarbons have fewer hydrogen atoms and instead have double or triple bonds between some carbon atoms.

3. Identify three items used by you or your family that are derived from aliphatic hydrocarbons. Possible answers include gasoline, oil, car and floor waxes, roads, anything made out of plastic, and cosmetics.

4. What do the colors of phenolphthalein indicate? Phenolphthalein indicates the presence or absence of excess hydroxide ions. If it is pink, then hydroxide ions are present; if colorless, they are not.

© Prentice-Hall, Inc.

Properties of an Alkyne **403**

Small Scale Lab 73

Introduction

There are several excellent demonstrations that illustrate the production and reactivity of acetylene. You may wish to begin the class with some of these demonstrations that students cannot easily do. Sources include *Chemical Demonstrations*, volumes 1 and 2, by Summerlin, et al., (American Chemical Society, 1988) and *Chemical Demonstrations*, volumes 1–4, by Shakhashiri (University of Wisconsin Press, 1983).

Be sure you have practiced the demonstrations prior to presenting them to the class and that you follow all safety guidelines.

Safety

Make sure students wear their goggles and lab aprons at all times during the investigation. Keep the room well ventilated. Make sure students tie back loose hair and clothing and that they do not leave the burning candles unattended. Students should not inhale the acetylene gas or the soot. Caution them not to allow the plastic collecting pipet to touch the candle flame. ∎

---

5. What safety precautions need to be taken with the candle? __Tie back loose hair and clothing. Do not leave the burning candle unattended.__

6. Why should the reaction in Procedure Step 6 be allowed to run for a short time before collecting the acetylene gas? __To expel air from the system.__

Problem

How can acetylene be produced, and what are its properties?

Materials

chemical splash goggles
laboratory apron
large test tube
one-hole rubber stopper, #00
thin-stem micropipet
scissors
clear adhesive tape
beaker, 600-mL

water
graduated micropipet
forceps
2 pieces of calcium carbide
matches
candle
phenolphthalein indicator

Safety

Wear your goggles and lab apron at all times during the investigation. Calcium carbide reacts with water to produce acetylene, a flammable gas. Keep the calcium carbide dry and away from any open flames. Tie back loose hair and clothing. Do not leave the burning candle unattended. Do not inhale the acetylene gas or the soot.

Note the caution alert symbols here and with certain steps of the Procedure. Refer to page *xi* for the specific precautions associated with each symbol.

Procedure

1. Put on your goggles and lab apron. Obtain a large test tube, a #00 rubber stopper, and a thin-stem micropipet.
2. Cut the pipet stem as shown in Figure 73–1 (top), so that a small part of the bulb remains with the stem.

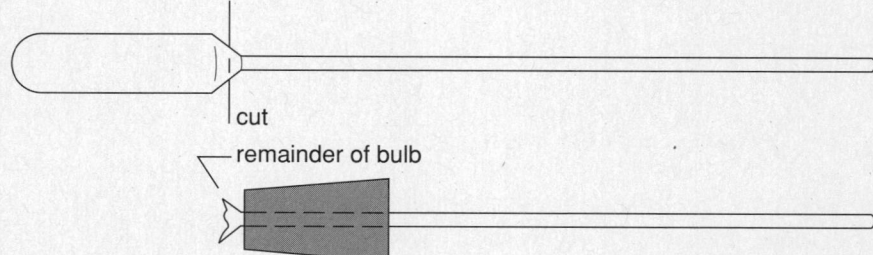

Figure 73–1 Preparing the pipet stem and stopper

3. Insert the stem through the bottom (narrow end) of the stopper and pull it through the hole so it fits snugly in the stopper. (See bottom of Figure 73–1.) If the pipet stem does not fit snugly, take it out and wrap a small piece of tape around the end.
4. Cut a graduated pipet (as shown in Figure 73–2) to be used in collecting the acetylene gas.

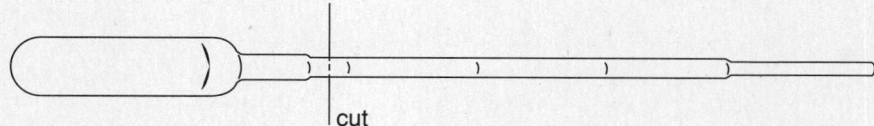

Figure 73–2 *Cutting the collecting pipet*

5. Fill the beaker three-fourths full with water. Use some of this water to completely fill the graduated pipet bulb.
6. Fill the test tube two-thirds full with water. Using the forceps, drop a pea-sized piece of calcium carbide into the test tube and insert the stopper with the pipet stem. Allow the reaction to run for 10–15 seconds.
7. Work with a partner. One person should hold the test tube and bend the pipet stem so that its end is under water in the beaker. (See Figure 73–3.) The other person should place the water-filled graduated pipet bulb over the outlet and collect the acetylene gas being generated. Once the pipet bulb is filled with gas, cover the mouth of the pipet bulb with your finger to keep the collected gas in the pipet bulb.

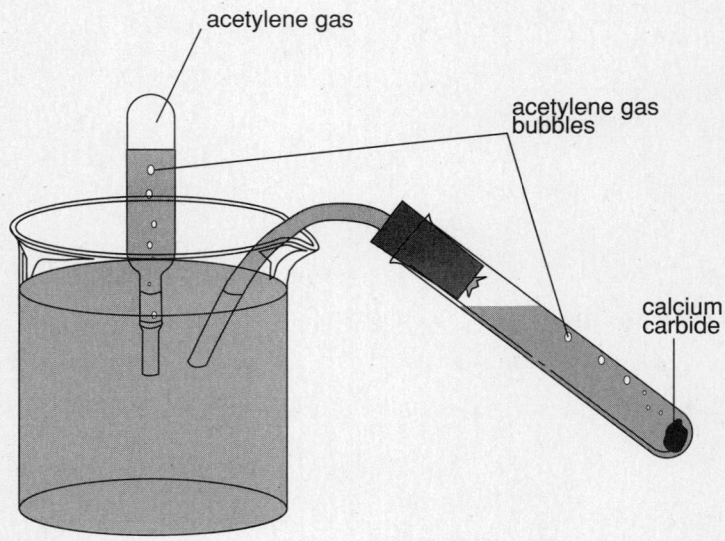

Figure 73–3

 8. Light the candle. **CAUTION:** *Tie back loose hair and clothing. Do not leave the burning candle unattended.*

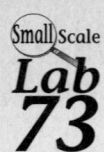

Name _____

9. Holding the pipet bulb to the side of the candle flame and about 3 cm away, quickly squeeze the collected gas into the flame. Do not allow the pipet bulb to touch the flame. Observe how well the acetylene burns and how much soot is produced. Record your observations in the Data Table. **CAUTION:** *Do not inhale the acetylene gas or the soot.*

10. Repeat Steps 5–9, except this time start with the graduated pipet bulb half full of air. With the forceps, add more calcium carbide if necessary. Once the acetylene gas has displaced the water, cover the mouth of the pipet with your finger and shake to mix the gases. Then test the mixture in the candle flame. Try smaller amounts of acetylene such as one fourth and one eighth of the graduated pipet bulb. Record your observations in the Data Table. Blow out the candle after you have finished the tests.

11. Remove the stopper from the test tube that originally contained the water and calcium carbide and add one drop of phenolphthalein indicator. Record your observations in the Data Table.

12. Put any leftover calcium carbide in the container provided by your teacher. Wash the solution in the test tube down the drain with plenty of water. Clean up your work area and wash your hands before leaving the laboratory.

Waste Disposal
Provide a container to collect the leftover calcium carbide. It can be dried out and reused. ■

Teaching Tips
Try the investigation yourself, before class, to become familiar with the results.

Demonstrate to students how to hold the collecting pipet when squeezing acetylene toward the candle flame. Warn students that the flame sometimes sucks back into the collection pipet. This may alarm the students, but it is not dangerous.

It may seem that acetylene does not burn well. However, if it is mixed with pure oxygen, as is done in acetylene torches, it produces an extremely hot flame. Such torches are widely used for cutting and welding metals.

Observations (sample data)
DATA TABLE

Test	Observation
pure acetylene	burns; large amount of soot
1:1 air-acetylene mixture	burns; amount of soot decreases as proportion of air increases
3:1 air-acetylene mixture	
7:1 air-acetylene mixture	
phenolphthalein	solution turns pink

Critical Thinking: Analysis and Conclusions

1. Describe the physical and chemical properties of acetylene. *(Interpreting data)* Acetylene is a gas at room temperature. Acetylene is combustible but produces a lot of soot unless excess oxygen is supplied.

2. What do the results of the phenolphthalein indicator test tell you? *(Interpreting data)* The pink color indicates that hydroxide ions were produced.

3. Write the balanced equation for the production of acetylene from calcium carbide. *(Making inferences)*
$CaC_2(s) + 2H_2O(l) \rightarrow Ca^{2+}(aq) + 2OH^-(aq) + C_2H_2(g)$

Name _____

Small Scale Lab 73

4. Is the burning of pure acetylene complete or incomplete combustion? What do you think the soot is? *(Interpreting data)* It is incomplete combustion. The soot is solid carbon.

5. Write the balanced equation for the incomplete combustion of acetylene. *(Making inferences)*
   A possible answer is $2C_2H_2(g) + 2O_2(g) \rightarrow 3C(s) + 2H_2O(g) + CO_2(g)$

6. Did any of the mixtures burn without producing soot? Is this complete or incomplete combustion? *(Interpreting data)* Answers will vary. Any mixtures that burned without producing soot are examples of complete combustion.

7. Write the balanced equation for the complete combustion of acetylene. *(Making inferences)*
   $2C_2H_2(g) + 5O_2(g) \rightarrow 4CO_2(g) + 2H_2O(g)$

Critical Thinking: Applications

1. Suggest some reasons why alkynes such as acetylene are not used as motor fuels. *(Applying concepts)* They do not burn completely, as shown by the amount of soot produced, and thus would foul spark plugs and cause pollution.

2. When an acetylene torch is lit, the flame is usually orange and a lot of soot is produced. When a valve on the torch is adjusted, the flame becomes blue and less soot is produced. What is the function of the valve? *(Applying concepts)* The valve mixes oxygen with the acetylene.

Going Further

1. Research the commercial methods used to obtain the various aliphatic hydrocarbons from petroleum and the uses of these compounds.
2. Hydrocarbon fuels are a blend of several different substances. The blend depends on the particular application. Fuel used in airplanes is different from fuel that would be used in a lawn mower. Research the composition and applications of various types of hydrocarbon fuels.

Going Further

1. In addition to using standard reference materials, students might contact various oil companies and associations to gather resource materials. Although it is difficult to arrange tours of refineries due to safety factors, the students conducting research might be able to arrange a guest speaker for the class.

Properties of an Alkyne

Name _____ Date _____ Class _____

Playing with Polymers

Lab 74
APPLICATION

Text reference: **Chapter 25**

Introduction

The world's great bridges are suspended on steel cables that possess the strength and flexibility to support heavy loads of traffic and changing stresses from wind. In the future, these steel cables may be replaced by cables made of spider silk, or some similar material. Spider silk is composed of a repeating pattern of monomers, or smaller molecules, linked together to create very long molecular chains, or polymers. The silk used in some spider webs is reported to be five times stronger than steel, thirty times as flexible as nylon (a synthetic polymer), and to have three times the impact resistance of Kevlar (a synthetic polymer used in bullet-proof vests).

Unfortunately, spiders are more interested in catching flies in their silk than in building bridges. Chemists and engineers, therefore, have the job of discovering how to mass-produce spider silk or similar polymers, either mechanically or by genetic engineering.

Polymers in nature give texture to living tissues. Cellulose and carbohydrates are important plant polymers made from the same monomer, glucose. Chains of amino acids, called proteins, form not only the silk of spiders and silkworms, but also skin, muscle, and hair. Even lobsters and insects are encased in a polymer, chitin.

Under certain conditions, polymer chains can become cross-linked (hydrogen bonded) to other chains and to parts of themselves, as shown in Figure 74–1. Even though the hydrogen bonds are weak by comparison to covalent bonds, more and stronger cross-linking between neighboring polymers results in greater resiliency (resistance to being deformed).

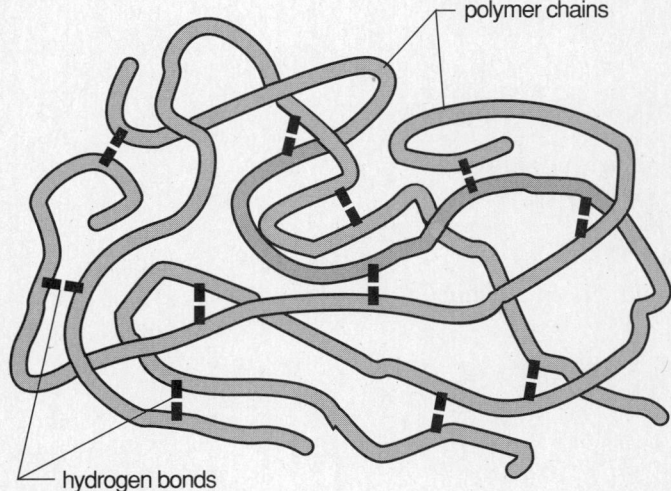

Figure 74–1

Materials (class of 30 in pairs)

30 pairs chemical splash goggles
30 laboratory aprons
30 pairs latex gloves
300 mL skim milk
30 paper medicine-dose cups
30 mL acetic acid, 6.0 M
30 wooden splints
30 filter papers
15 funnels
15 ring stands
15 iron rings
30 beakers, 100-mL
500 mL distilled water
15 hot plates
15 packages of sugar-free gelatin mix, 12 g each
warm water
15 scalpels

Time Required

30 minutes on the first day; 15 minutes on the second day.

Advance Preparation

6.0 M acetic acid: add 11 mL of glacial acetic acid (17 M) to enough water to make 30 mL of solution. CAUTION: *Glacial acetic acid is extremely corrosive. Wear chemical splash goggles, gloves, and an apron while handling it. Work under a fume hood.*

Buy the gelatin mix and skim milk. (Other types of milk do not work as well because the fat interferes with the reaction.)

Introduction

Polymer demonstrations abound in teacher resource guides. Polymer gels can be demonstrated with "grow creatures" available in novelty and toy stores. Also, sodium polyacrylate (polysorb

Playing with Polymers **409**

Lab 74
APPLICATION

Cross-linked polymers in a large amount of liquid form a colloidal suspension known as a gel. A gel, which consists of a solid dispersed in a liquid, has a structure that prevents it from flowing. Water molecules may form part of the loose irregular structure. The amount of water present can also affect the properties of the material.

In this investigation you will prepare two natural polymer gels and explore their properties.

or water lock) forms a polymer gel absorbing hundreds of milliliters of purified water per gram. Place 0.5 g in a large opaque cup. Add water while stirring, and then invert the cup, or puncture the cup bottom. None spills.

Unusual properties of polymers can be demonstrated with a ball of Silly Putty, which deforms easily if squeezed, but will bounce and keep its shape when struck with a hammer. Also, "smart and stupid" balls, available from chemical suppliers, demonstrate dramatic differences in properties for similar-feeling polymers, as one ball bounces well but the other lands with a loud thud.

Pre-Lab Discussion

Read the entire laboratory investigation and the relevant pages of your textbook. Then answer the questions that follow.

1. Are protein polymers, such as the ones in this investigation, formed by addition or condensation? **They are formed by condensation.**

2. Monomer molecules have specific molar masses, many less than 100 g/mol. Explain how these monomers become molecules with variable masses in the tens or even hundreds of thousands of grams per mole. **Monomers link together in a repeating pattern to form variable-length molecular chains, or polymers.**

3. Study the Materials list (excluding chemicals) and list the items that you believe are made of natural polymers. **Laboratory apron (cotton), paper medicine-dose cups, wooden splint, filter papers.**

4. Why is acetic acid hazardous? What safety precautions must be followed? **Acetic acid is corrosive. Be sure that materials treated with it are rinsed with water before handling. If you spill any on your skin or clothing, wash if off immediately with plenty of water and tell your teacher.**

Problem

What are the properties of some natural polymer gels?

Materials

chemical splash goggles
laboratory apron
latex gloves
skim milk
2 paper medicine-dose cups
acetic acid, 6.0 M
2 wooden splints
2 filter papers
funnel

ring stand
iron ring
2 beakers, 100-mL
distilled water
hot plate
sugar-free gelatin mix
warm water
scalpel

Name _____

Safety

Lab 74 APPLICATION

Wear your goggles, gloves, and lab apron at all times during the investigation. Polymers are difficult to remove from clothing. Acetic acid is corrosive. Rinse the milk protein gels with water before handling them. If you spill acetic acid on your skin or clothing, wash it off immediately with plenty of water and tell your teacher. The hot plate and beaker will get hot. Be careful not to touch them. Do not touch the blade of the scalpel. Under no circumstances should you taste the milk or gelatin.

Note the caution alert symbols here and with certain steps of the Procedure. Refer to page xi for the specific precautions associated with each symbol.

Procedure

Part A

1. Put on your goggles, gloves, and lab apron. Obtain 20 mL of skim milk in a paper medicine-dose cup and add 2 mL of 6.0 M acetic acid. Stir with a wooden splint and let stand for a few minutes. Do not drink the milk. **CAUTION:** *Acetic acid is corrosive. If you spill any on your skin or clothing, wash it off immediately with plenty of water and tell your teacher.*

2. Set up the ring stand and iron ring. Fold the filter paper and place it in the funnel. Put the funnel into the iron ring so that it will drain into a beaker. Filter the coagulated milk protein by pouring the acidified milk into the funnel. Pour slowly, so that the liquid does not rise above the edge of the filter paper in the funnel. It will take several minutes for the clear filtrate to drain from the protein complex.

3. While you wait, turn on a hot plate and boil 20 mL of distilled water in a 100-mL beaker. Reduce the heat and add a package of sugar-free gelatin. Stir with a wooden splint. **CAUTION:** *The hot plate and beaker will get very hot. Be careful not to burn yourself.*

4. Gently heat the gelatin in the beaker while stirring in order to completely hydrate the gelatin protein. Turn off the hot plate.

5. Carefully pour the hot gelatin into a medicine-dose cup and let it cool. Do not taste the gelatin.

6. Return to the milk protein. When the liquid stops draining, rinse the filtered protein with 10 mL of distilled water. Let the water drain through the filter.

7. Remove the filter from the funnel, gather the top edge, and gently squeeze the filter to remove additional water. Be careful not to break the filter paper.

8. Open the filter and use your fingers to push the protein complex into a pile in the middle of the filter paper. Gather the edge of the filter paper with the protein enclosed and twist the paper gently, forcing the protein into a ball inside the paper. If the paper rips, replace with a second piece.

Safety
Make sure students wear their goggles, gloves, and lab aprons at all times during the investigation. Polymers are difficult to remove from clothing. Excess acid should be rinsed from milk protein before handling. Caution students to be careful not to burn themselves on the hot plate or beaker or cut themselves with the scalpel. Make sure that students do not taste the milk or gelatin. ∎

Teaching Tips
The chemical principles in this investigation are essentially the same as those explored in Investigation 76. This Investigation focuses on natural polymers, while Investigation 76 examines synthetic compounds.

To reduce the risk of spills, you might want to have only one bottle of acetic acid and dispense it yourself.

If the students have not done a filtration for a while, you might want to review the technique and the method for folding the filter paper.

Letting the polymer gels dry overnight makes a noticeable difference in their properties.

© Prentice-Hall, Inc.

Playing with Polymers **411**

Lab 74 APPLICATION

Name _____

9. Observe the gelatin and the milk protein. Record your observations in the Data Table. Leave the polymer gels to dry overnight. Clean up your work area and wash your hands before leaving the laboratory.

Part B

10. Put on your goggles, gloves, and lab apron. Remove the gelatin from the cup by heating the cup in warm water and scraping out the gelatin, or by cutting the cup. Shape the gelatin block into a ball by slicing it with a scalpel and then smoothing it with warm water. **CAUTION:** *Be careful not to cut yourself with the scalpel.*

11. Describe the gelatin ball. Investigate its resiliency and cohesiveness. Try to bounce it, squash it, pull it apart, and so on. How easy is it to deform and/or separate into pieces—processes that require neighboring polymer molecules to slip past each other? Try to deform the polymer slowly, and then rapidly. Record your observations in the Data Table.

12. Remove the milk protein polymer ball and test it as you did the gelatin ball. Record your observations in the Data Table.

13. The polymer gels may be disposed of in the dry waste container. Flush excess liquids down the drain with lots of water. Clean up your work area and wash your hands before leaving the laboratory.

Waste Disposal
The polymer gels may be disposed of in the dry waste container. Excess fluids should be flushed down the drain with plenty of water. ■

Observations (sample data)
DATA TABLE

Polymer Gel	Day 1	Day 2
gelatin	thick liquid	resembles hard gelatin dessert; bouncy/springy; deforms but is elastic
milk protein	resembles very soft cheese	more solid; doesn't bounce; offers little resistance to slow deformation; tears if deformed quickly

Critical Thinking: Analysis and Conclusions

1. Which polymer gel do you think has more cross-linking? Which one has less? Explain. *(Drawing conclusions)* The gelatin polymer gel has more cross-linking, the milk protein polymer gel less. The gelatin has much greater resiliency.

2. What difference did leaving the polymer gel balls out overnight make? *(Making comparisons)* The gels became stiffer.

3. What role do you think water plays in keeping the gel flexible? *(Making inferences)* The more water, the more flexible the gel. The less water, the stiffer the gel.

Critical Thinking: Applications

1. In wood, strong polymer chains of cellulose and lignin are aligned in rows and layers and held in place by hydrogen bonds. What property of wood results from this structure? *(Applying concepts)* Wood is much easier to split or break along the grain than it is to split or break across the grain.

2. The latex polymer used to make natural rubber is a primary component of the sap of rubber trees, dandelions, milkweed, and other plants. Suggest how you would attempt to make a polymer gel from the liquid sap. *(Designing experiments)* You could try adding acid to the sap, heating it, or allowing it to dry out.

3. When water is added to flour and kneaded, a dough is formed. More kneading makes the dough tougher. Which of the following do you think explains what happens when dough is formed? Explain your answer. *(Applying concepts)*
   a. A chemical reaction occurs, and a new compound is formed.
   b. Monomer molecules form a polymer molecule.
   c. Cross-linking bonds form between polymer molecules.
   Answer c. There is little evidence that a new compound has been formed. The process of mixing water in is similar to that involved in making polymer gels.

Going Further

1. Compile a list of the common names of as many polymers as you can find. For each one, include the structural formula of the monomer(s) from which it is constructed and a list of its uses.

Going Further
1. Information on polymers and their uses can be found in textbooks and encyclopedias, and in books of general interest, including *Mega Molecules*, by Elias Hans-Georg (Springer-Verlag, 1987) and *Molecules by* P. W. Atkins (New York: Scientific American Library, 1987).

Observing Fermentation

Lab 75 APPLICATION

Text reference: Chapter 26

Introduction

Imagine a group of chemicals that possess a "life force"—the ability to generate life. In the early 1800s, such chemicals were thought to exist, and were called "organic" chemicals. These chemicals seemed to be the essential difference between living (organic) and nonliving (inorganic) things. But by the middle of the 1800s, some organic chemicals had been synthesized without the use of living tissue. Chemists today can make nearly any organic chemical, including pieces of DNA, in the lab, but it is still cheaper and easier to extract many organic chemicals from living organisms.

In this investigation, you will produce ethanol (ethyl alcohol) from sugars by fermentation with yeast. This is the same biochemical process that occurs in bread making and in the brewing process. Today most ethanol is produced by fermentation, just as it was in ancient times. In the last century and a half, though, notions of magical chemicals have been replaced by a better understanding of the organic chemistry involved in fermentation. Still, the series of complex chemical reactions that the yeast performs in order to convert sugar to alcohol are no less remarkable. The overall reaction for glucose fermentation to ethanol is:

$$C_6H_{12}O_6(aq) \xrightarrow{\text{yeast enzymes}} 2CO_2(g) + 2C_2H_5OH(l)$$

Ethanol has a variety of uses. It is used widely as an industrial solvent, as an ingredient in many household products and medications, and as a starting chemical from which a large variety of other chemicals are produced.

In this investigation, you will observe the reaction of a mixture of yeast and molasses. The yeast uses the dissolved sugar as an energy source to grow and reproduce. Ethanol and carbon dioxide are its waste products, and the ethanol eventually kills the yeast before all the sugar is reacted. You will run the reaction at several temperatures and identify the temperature at which the reaction proceeds most efficiently.

Pre-Lab Discussion

Read the entire laboratory investigation and the relevant pages of your textbook. Then answer the questions that follow.

1. What functional group identifies ethanol as an alcohol? __The hydroxy group (—OH).__

Materials (class of 30 in pairs)

30 pairs chemical splash goggles
30 laboratory aprons
15 erlenmeyer flasks, 50-mL
600 mL molasses fermentation mixture, 10% by volume
100 mL activated yeast suspension
15 one-hole stoppers fitted with micropipet stems
water tubs, one per team or shared
hot and cold tap water
15 thermometers
15 watches or a clock with a second hand
distillation apparatus (for optional demonstration):
  2 ring stands
  condenser with connecting parts
  distillation flask
  thermometer
  hot plate

Time Required

60–90 minutes. To shorten the time, have each team test the fermentation rate at a different temperature.

Advance Preparation

Snip approximately 4 cm from the tips of 15 plastic micropipets and insert the points into one-holed flask stoppers so that 1–2 cm protrudes through the top of the stoppers.

Obtain molasses without preservatives, and prepare a mixture of 10 percent by volume molasses in water.

Activate the yeast 15–30 minutes before the start of class by mixing 1 tablespoon (1 package) dry yeast with 100 mL lukewarm water (about 37°C). Check the home economics and/or

Observing Fermentation **415**

Lab 75 APPLICATION

biology department for the availability of yeast. Add the activated (bubbling) yeast to the molasses solution just prior to class. Fermentation will start more quickly if the suspension is lukewarm. Overheating kills the yeast. Have available several clean marbles for Step 2.

Introduction
You can start with a discussion of the fermentation process, which is used in brewing and bread making. Point out that the reason these processes are considered an art as much as a science is that they involve living organisms, which are very sensitive to minute changes in ingredients and temperature. Then review various products that are made by distillation, such as automobile fuel and butane. Also, ask the students for the connection between ethanol production and the bread-making process.

Safety
Make sure students wear their goggles and lab aprons at all times during the investigation. Caution them not to taste the mixture or the product of the reaction. In the demonstration, do not use open flames for distilling alcohol. A vapor flash may result. To avoid a pressure rupture, do not store the fermenting mixture in a closed container. ■

Name _____

2. Predict how raising the temperature will affect the rate of the fermentation reaction. _Students may expect an increase in reaction rate with temperature. However, rate will increase only to the optimal temperature, then decrease rapidly._

Problem
What is the optimal temperature for yeast to grow and ferment sugar?

Materials
chemical splash goggles
laboratory apron
erlenmeyer flask, 50-mL
molasses and yeast fermentation mixture
one-hole stopper fitted with a micropipet stem

water tub
hot and cold tap water
thermometer
clock or watch with a second hand

Safety

Wear your goggles and lab apron at all times during the investigation. The fermenting mixture is toxic; do not drink it. Do not store the mixture in an airtight container; high pressure may rupture the container. Note the caution alert symbols here and with certain steps of the Procedure. Refer to page *xi* for the specific precautions associated with each symbol.

Procedure

1. Put on your goggles and lab apron. Obtain 30–40 mL of molasses and yeast fermentation mixture in a 50-mL flask. Stopper the flask with a one-hole stopper that has a plastic micropipet stem in the hole. Be sure that the stem is above the surface of the liquid in the flask.

2. Fill a plastic tub with warm tap water. Adjust the temperature to 20–25°C and immerse the flask with the fermentation mixture completely in the water so the whole stem is below the surface. There should be enough fluid in the flask so that it sinks. (Add a marble or two if needed to submerge the flask.) You should observe bubbles of carbon dioxide gas escaping from the flask through the stem.

3. With the flask immersed, allow the fermentation to proceed for about 15 minutes, or until the bubbling rate has become constant. When bubbling appears to be at a constant rate, count the bubbles produced in one minute. Record the bubble rate and the water bath temperature in the Data Table.

Name _____

 4. Repeat Step 3 using the same fermentation mixture, but with water-bath temperatures of about 30–35°C, 40–45°C, 50–55°C, and 60–65°C. Adjust the water temperature by adding hot or cold water to the bath. In each case, immerse the flask and wait a few minutes to allow the fermentation rate (bubble rate) to become constant. Then count the number of bubbles produced in one minute. Record the number of bubbles per minute and the temperature of the water bath in the Data Table.

 5. Give your flask to your teacher, who will arrange for the fermentation to continue overnight. It may be necessary to first add a few milliliters of fermentation mixture to the flask to restart the process. Clean up your work area and wash your hands before leaving the laboratory.

 6. The next day, put on your goggles and lab apron. Retrieve your flask and check to see if fermentation has stopped (no bubbles seen). **CAUTION:** *The contents of the flask may be toxic. Do not ingest them.* Open the flask and note the odor. Return the flask with its contents to your teacher who may distill the combined contents to produce ethanol. Clean up your work area and wash your hands before leaving the laboratory.

Teaching Tips
Fermentation flasks should be filled enough so that they sink in the water bath, but not so much that foaming reaches the tube tip at the stopper. At the higher temperature ranges the yeast starts to die. A few milliliters of fermentation mixture can be added to restart the ferment.

You may wish to do a distillation as a demonstration using a standard condenser setup. Use of a reflux column will allow a much purer alcohol fraction to be obtained.

Waste Disposal
All liquids may be flushed down the drain. ■

Observations (sample data)

DATA TABLE   Fermentation Reaction Rate

Temperature (°C)	Reaction Rate (bubbles/min)
23	17
31	31
40	70
55	10
60	2

Critical Thinking: Analysis and Conclusions

1. Using Figure 75–1, make a graph of temperature vs. reaction rate (bubbles/min) from your data. *(Interpreting data)*

2. What was the optimal temperature for the reaction? Does your graph support your prediction about reaction rate change given in Question 2 of the Pre-Lab Discussion? *(Interpreting diagrams)* __Student answers will vary, but many may have expected the reaction rate to increase continuously with temperature. Instead, rate increases until the optimum temperature, then decreases rapidly, as their graphs will show.__

3. What causes the bubbling in the fermentation mixture during fermentation? *(Making inferences)* __CO_2 gas is produced during fermentation.__

© Prentice-Hall, Inc.

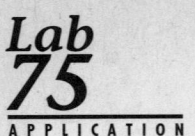

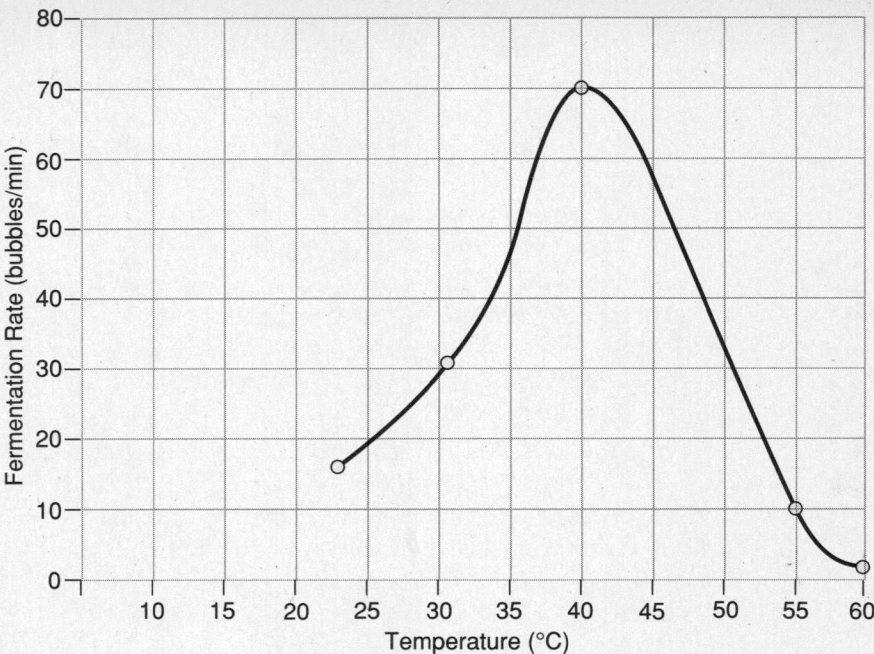

Figure 75–1

4. Suggest a reason that the reaction slowed down as the temperature was increased past the optimal point. *(Developing hypotheses)* The enzymes were inactivated by the heat.

Critical Thinking: Applications

1. Part of the art of bread making involves determining the temperature at which the dough is set to rise, and the amount of sugar and salt in the dough. Explain. *(Evaluating)* Yeast is a living organism, and optimal gas production varies with the conditions under which it is grown.

2. What happens to the ethanol when the bread is baked? *(Developing hypotheses)* It is released as a gas in quantities too small to be harmful.

Going Further

1. Make bread with yeast and observe the rising action. Try to relate the rising of the bread and the aroma to your observations in this investigation.
2. Do library research to investigate the effects of ethanol on the human nervous system and on other organisms. In particular, try to find out how ethanol acts chemically to cause intoxication.

Going Further
1. Yeast bread recipes are available in many cookbooks.
2. A good, concise account with excellent illustrations is contained in *Molecules*, by P. W. Atkins (New York: Scientific American Library, Div. of HPHLP, 1987).

Name _____ Date _____ Class _____

Making Slime

Lab 76 APPLICATION

Text reference: **Chapter 26**

Introduction

As you learned from doing Investigation 74, polymer chains can be linked together to form substances with a variety of properties. While the polymer chains are held together by strong covalent bonds, they are linked to each other by weak hydrogen bonds. The amount of cross-linking determines how resilient the gels or plastics are, that is, how much they can be deformed. Such substances include materials as soft as gelatin and as strong as Kevlar.

Chemists and engineers have invented and produced many varied polymers. Many are called plastics because they can be shaped or molded, usually with heat. Most are formed from repeating units called monomers that are derived from petroleum. Depending on the monomer molecules used and the technique used to join, or polymerize, them, polymers of vastly different properties may result. From fabrics to surface coatings to the objects of everyday life, synthetic polymers seemingly envelop the modern world.

Polyvinyl alcohol has the formula $[-CH_2-CH(OH)-]_n$. The structures of the vinyl alcohol monomer (which does not exist in isolation) and polyvinyl alcohol are shown in Figure 76-1.

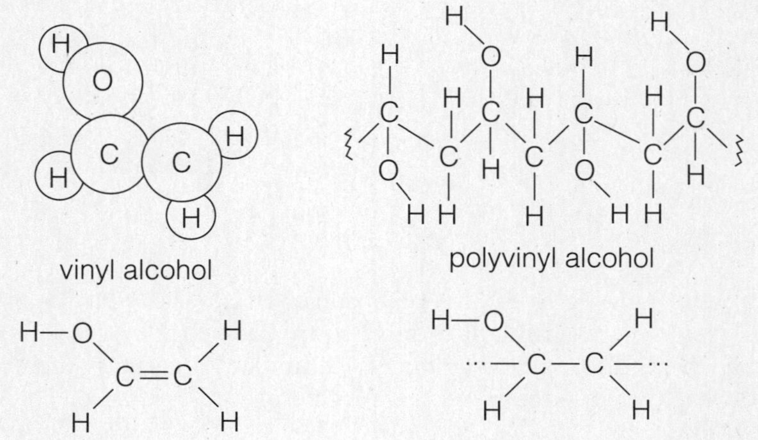

Figure 76–1

Sodium tetraborate dissociates in solution to form the borate ion, $B(OH)_4^-$. Borate ions form hydrogen bonds with the hydroxyl groups of polyvinyl alcohol, linking chains of polyvinyl alcohol to each other.

In this investigation you will make two synthetic polymers, one from polyvinyl alcohol and the other from polyvinyl acetate. After producing the polymers, you will observe and compare some of their properties.

Materials (class of 30 in pairs)
30 pairs chemical splash goggles
30 laboratory aprons
30 pairs latex gloves
15 graduated cylinders, 25-mL
400 mL polyvinyl alcohol (4% solution)
30 paper medicine-dose cups
30 wooden splints
food coloring (optional)
100 mL sodium tetraborate (4% solution)
200 mL white glue (such as Elmer's or other similar brands that contain polyvinyl acetate)

Time Required
30 minutes. You can save time by making only one slime gel.

Advance Preparation
4% polyvinyl alcohol: Heat 400 mL distilled water in a 600-mL beaker to 80–90°C and then slowly add 16.0 g polyvinyl alcohol powder while stirring. Continue stirring until the solution clears. A magnetic stirrer is recommended, as this may take some time. CAUTION: *When preparing polyvinyl alcohol solution, avoid contact with the dust, which irritates eyes and mucous membranes. Wear goggles, gloves, and an apron.*

4% sodium tetraborate (borax) solution. Dissolve 7.6 g of $Na_2B_4O_7 \cdot 10H_2O$ in 100 mL distilled water.

White glue: Buy Elmer's glue, or a similar brand, and dilute 200 mL of it with 200 mL of water.

Introduction
The chemical principles in this investigation are

© Prentice-Hall, Inc.

Making Slime **419**

Lab 76
APPLICATION

Name_____

Pre-Lab Discussion

Read the entire laboratory investigation and the relevant pages of your textbook. Then answer the questions that follow.

1. Are the polymers in this investigation formed by addition or condensation? <u>They are formed by addition.</u>

2. Study the materials list (excluding chemicals) and list the item(s) that you believe are made of synthetic polymers. <u>chemical splash goggles, latex gloves; possibly apron, graduated cylinder</u>

3. In each of the comparisons below, say which substance you think has the most cross-linking, and explain why.

    a. liquid epoxy glue/hardened epoxy glue <u>Hardened epoxy glue, since the cross-linking prevents fluid movement.</u>

    b. Silly Putty/ a superball <u>The superball, since it deforms much less easily than the Silly Putty, and cannot be pulled apart easily.</u>

    c. Kevlar/rubber band <u>The Kevlar, since the rubber band can be stretched and does not completely return to its original shape.</u>

Problem

How does cross-linking change the properties of a polymer?

Materials

chemical splash goggles
laboratory apron
latex gloves
graduated cylinder, 25-mL
polyvinyl alcohol (4% solution)

2 paper medicine-dose cups
food coloring (optional)
2 wooden splints
sodium tetraborate (4% solution)
diluted white glue containing polyvinyl acetate

Safety

Wear your goggles, gloves, and lab apron at all times during the investigation. Polymers are difficult to remove from clothing.

Note the caution alert symbols here and with certain steps of the Procedure. Refer to page *xi* for the specific precautions associated with each symbol.

Procedure

Part A

1. Put on your goggles, gloves, and lab apron. Measure 25 mL of 4% polyvinyl alcohol solution in the graduated cylinder and pour it into a paper medicine-dose cup. Add food coloring if you wish, and stir with a wooden splint until the color is evenly mixed.

Sidebar (left column):

essentially the same as those explored in Investigation 74. If the students have done that investigation, you may want to review what they learned before beginning this one. This investigation focuses on artificial rather than natural polymers.

Here are a few demonstrations you could use to introduce the investigation:

The production of polyurethane foam from monomer molecules and a "blowing" agent is utterly amazing when carried out in a latex glove. About 35 mL of each of the two reactants (available in kit form from suppliers) are enough to demonstrate polymerization and foam injection molding.

A large plastic foam (polystyrene) cup can be dissolved in an interesting demonstration by setting it down in a petri dish containing a thin layer of acetone.

Safety

Make sure students wear their goggles, gloves, and lab aprons at all times during the investigation. Polymers are difficult to remove from clothing. ■

Teaching Tips

The polymer gel formed from glue (polyvinyl acetate) is similar to the one formed from polyvinyl alcohol. However, it will show the students that chemistry involves everyday materials, not just chemicals gotten from a laboratory shelf.

Name_____

Lab 76
APPLICATION

2. Add 2 mL of 4% sodium tetraborate solution to the medicine-dose cup. Stir the two solutions together until the liquid becomes thick and pulls away from the sides of the cup.
3. Remove the polymer gel from the cup. Squeeze excess fluid from the gel as you shape it into a ball.
4. Set the ball aside to dry overnight.

5. Repeat Steps 1–4, substituting diluted white glue for the polyvinyl alcohol solution. Flush excess liquid down the drain with lots of water. Clean up your work area and wash your hands before leaving the laboratory.

Part B

6. Put on your goggles, gloves, and lab apron. Test each polymer for resiliency and cohesiveness. Try to bounce it, squash it, pull it apart, and so on. Check the polymer gel shear strength. How easy is it to deform and/or separate into pieces, which requires neighboring polymer molecules to slip past each other? Try to deform the polymer slowly, and then rapidly. Record your observations.

7. The polymer gels may be disposed of in the dry waste container. Clean up your work area and wash your hands before leaving the laboratory.

Waste Disposal
Polymer gels can be disposed of in the dry waste container. Excess fluids can be washed down the drain with plenty of water. ■

Observations (sample data)

Polyvinyl polymer gels flow slowly on their own, but feel resilient after handling.

They can be reshaped slowly but will tear rather than deform if a sudden force is

applied. They bounce well, especially after they are dried. There is very little

difference between the two polymer gels.

Critical Thinking: Analysis and Conclusions

1. What is the physical effect of cross-linking a polymer? *(Interpreting data)* The polymer takes a new form with different properties.

2. Are the substances produced in this reaction solids or liquids? Explain your answer. *(Drawing conclusions)* The substances have some properties of both. However, since they will flow to take the shape of a container, they are considered to be liquids.

Making Slime **421**

Lab 76 APPLICATION

Name _____

3. What happens when you try to deform the polymers? What do you think this tells you about their structures? (*Drawing conclusions*)
The polymers can be reshaped slowly but will tear rather than deform if a sudden force is applied. Slow deformation allows the cross-linking bonds to break and reform. A sudden force breaks the bonds but does not give new ones a chance to form.

Critical Thinking: Applications

1. Modern life depends on the use of polymers, but there is an environmental cost. Write at least a paragraph about how this statement pertains to the question asked at nearly every grocery checkout counter today, "Paper or plastic?" (*Using the writing process*)
Students may refer to the choice as "polymer or polymer," or as forest instead of petroleum depletion, or as biodegradable versus nondegradable trash.

2. In some plastics, most of the polymer molecules are aligned in one direction. How does this explain why plastic such as food wrap and tape are easier to tear lengthwise than across? (*Applying concepts*)
Tearing the plastic crossways requires breaking mostly strong covalent bonds, but tearing it lengthwise requires tearing mainly the weaker hydrogen bonds.

3. Plasticizers are substances often added to polymer plastics, such as polyvinyl chloride, to reduce the number of cross-links between polymer chains. How do you think the addition of plasticizers helps explain the properties of easily torn vinyl sheeting (as used for raincoats), flexible vinyl siding, and rigid PVC pipes? (*Applying concepts*) Since plasticizers prevent cross-linking, they make plastic more flexible. Vinyl sheeting has the most plasticizer, PVC pipe the least.

Going Further (sidebar)

1. Students can make several more polymers in the laboratory. The students doing the research can perform these as demonstrations for the rest of the class. Polymers that are easily made include natural rubber, polyurethane, nylon, polysilicon rubber, and Silly Putty. Chemical supply vendors carry the necessary chemicals and information on how to make the various polymers. Also, you can find numerous laboratory preparations in laboratory and chemistry demonstration texts.

Going Further

1. One of the major uses of alkenes and some alkynes is the production of plastics by the process of polymerization. Research these polymerization processes. Under the supervision of your teacher, try one or more of these processes in class.
2. Using a reference book, find the names and properties of other cross-linked polymers. Research and report on their uses.

Name _____ Date _____ Class _____

Analyzing Commercial Aspirin

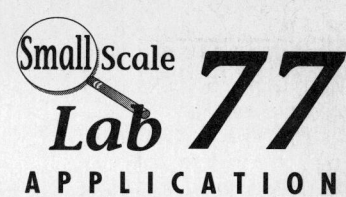

Small Scale Lab 77
APPLICATION

Text reference: Chapter 26

Introduction

Aspirin is one of the most commonly used medications in the world. It has been used for almost 100 years to treat pain, inflammation, and fever. The chemical name for aspirin is acetylsalicylic acid, or simply ASA. It can be prepared in the laboratory by the reaction between salicylic acid and acetic acid, as shown in Figure 77–1.

Salicylic acid   Acetic acid   Acetylsalicylic acid

Figure 77–1

You may have detected the vinegarlike smell of acetic acid upon opening an old bottle of aspirin. This odor often is evidence of hydrolysis, or the reaction of aspirin with water from the environment. In this process, some ASA is lost as salicylic acid and acetic acid are formed. The tablets are then partly ASA and partly salicylic acid.

In this investigation, you will determine the quantity of salicylic acid that is present in one or more commercial aspirin products. You will first prepare a set of solutions of increasing known concentrations of salicylic acid. Then you will test the solutions, using iron(III) ion solution as an indicator. The substance formed by the reaction between iron(III) ions and salicylic acid gives the solution a violet color. The intensity of the color is a measure of the concentration of salicylic acid. You will then similarly prepare and test a solution made from an ASA tablet. By comparing the color of the unknown solution to the colors of the known solutions you can determine the concentration of salicylic acid in the ASA tablet.

Pre-Lab Discussion

Read the entire laboratory investigation and the relevant pages of your textbook. Then answer the questions that follow.

1. How is aspirin made? <u>It is made by a reaction between salicylic acid and acetic acid.</u>

Materials (class of 30 in pairs)
30 pairs chemical splash goggles
30 laboratory aprons
15 marking pens
15 well plates, 24-well
15 sheets of white paper
15 sets of 3 micropipets, containing the following:
  50 mL salicylic acid solution, standardized
  50 mL distilled water
  15 mL iron(III) nitrate solution ($Fe(NO_3)_3$), 0.1 M
15 commercial aspirin tablets
15 mortars and pestles
15 beakers, 50-mL
400 mL water-ethanol solution
15 graduated cylinders, 25-mL
15 stirring rods
15 empty micropipets

Time Required
30 minutes. You can save time by making up the aspirin solution yourself (one tablet in 25 mL of water-ethanol solution). Label and fill a fourth pipet for each set and tell the students what the claimed mass of aspirin is. Have students skip Steps 5 and 6 of the Procedure.

Advance Preparation
Water-ethanol solution: Mix 250 mL distilled water with 250 mL denatured ethanol. CAUTION: *Wear chemical splash goggles during preparation of the solutions. Ethanol is flammable and toxic. Be sure there are no open flames present. Do not ingest. Wash spills and splashes with water.*
  Salicylic acid solution (3.0 mg/mL): Dissolve 150 mg of salicylic acid in

© Prentice-Hall, Inc.   Analyzing Commercial Aspirin   **423**

Lab 77 APPLICATION

50 mL of a 50/50 water-ethanol solution.

0.1 M Fe^{3+} solution: Dissolve 600 mg of $Fe(NO_3)_3 \cdot 9H_2O$ in 15 mL of 0.5 M HCl solution. CAUTION: *0.5 M HCl is irritating to skin and may damage clothing. Wear goggles and an apron. Wash spills and splashes with water.*

Label and fill the three pipets of each set with the appropriate solutions.

Introduction

Begin the investigation with a class discussion of the importance of chemical analysis. Chemical analysis is used to test the purity and consistency of products and to identify the components of experimental drugs. Pharmaceutical manufacturers regularly use the technique employed in this investigation. Ask students in what other industries or areas similar techniques might be used (food science, environmental chemistry). The procedure of matching the color of a product in an experiment to a set of standard colors is a common analytical technique in all of these fields. Ask students to recall lab investigations they have done earlier in this course that employ color comparisons.

The purpose of this investigation is to determine the amount of salicylic acid in aspirin, which may be due to the hydrolysis of aspirin or to the incomplete removal of salicylic acid during the manufacturing process.

The reaction that occurs during this investigation is the formation of a violet-colored complex of salicylic acid and Fe^{3+} ions.

Safety

Make sure students wear their goggles and lab aprons at all times during the investigation. Caution

---

Name _____

2. What safety precautions should be taken with the iron(III) ion solution? <u>Avoid spills and contact with your skin. If you spill the solution, wash it off with plenty of water and tell your teacher.</u>

3. What is the purpose of the ten solutions in rows A and B? <u>The solutions in these rows are used as color standards of known concentration for comparison with the unknown solution.</u>

4. What class of organic compounds does acetic acid belong to? <u>Acetic acid is a carboxylic acid.</u>

Problem

How can you determine the quantity of uncombined salicyclic acid in a commercial aspirin product?

Materials

chemical splash goggles
laboratory apron
marking pen
well plate
sheet of white paper
commercial aspirin tablet
mortar and pestle
beaker, 50-mL
25 mL water-ethanol solution

3 micropipets, each containing one of the following:
 distilled water
 salicylic acid solution, standardized
 iron(III) ion solution
stirring rod
graduated cylinder, 25-mL
empty micropipet

Safety

Wear your goggles and lab apron at all times during the investigation. The iron(III) ion solution contains acid and is corrosive. The water-ethanol solution contains methanol and is toxic if ingested. Handle both solutions with care. Avoid spills and contact with your skin. If you spill either solution, wash it off with plenty of water and tell your teacher.

Note the caution alert symbols here and with certain steps of the Procedure. Refer to page *xi* for the specific precautions associated with each symbol.

Procedure

1. Put on your goggles and lab apron. Using the marking pen, number the wells of the well plate from left to right along the top: *1, 2, 3, 4, 5*. Down the left side, label the rows of wells: *A, B, C*. Place the well plate on a sheet of white paper. See Figure 77–2.

Name _____

Small Scale Lab 77
APPLICATION

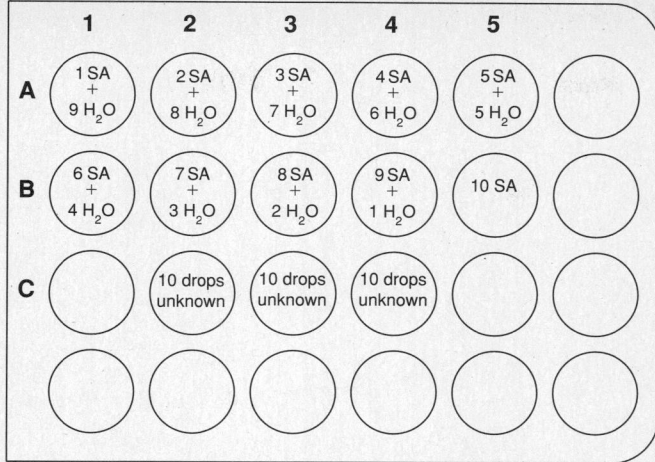

Figure 77–2

2. Use the pipet containing the standard salicylic acid solution to add 1 drop of solution to well A1, 2 drops to well A2, 3 drops to well A3, 4 drops to well A4, and 5 drops to well A5. Moving to row B, add 6 drops of standard salicylic acid to well B1, 7 drops to B2, 8 drops to B3, 9 drops to B4, and 10 drops to B5. Always hold the pipets vertically and count the number of drops carefully.

3. Use the pipet containing water to add 9 drops of water to well A1, 8 drops to A2, 7 drops to A3, 6 drops to A4, and 5 drops to A5. Moving to row B, add 4 drops of water to well B1, 3 drops to B2, 2 drops to B3, and 1 drop to B4.

 4. Use the pipet containing iron(III) ion solution to add 1 drop of solution to each well in rows A and B. **CAUTION:** *Handle the iron(III) ion solution with care. It contains acid and is corrosive. If you spill any on your skin or clothes, wash it off with plenty of water and tell your teacher.* Record your observations of the colors that appear.

5. Examine the label of an aspirin container to find the mass of ASA in one tablet as stated by the manufacturer. Record this amount. Remove one tablet from the container and crush it into a fine powder with the mortar and pestle.

 6. Use the graduated cylinder to transfer 25 mL of the water-ethanol solution into the beaker. **CAUTION:** *Handle the water-ethanol solution with care; it is toxic if ingested.* Add the powdered aspirin and stir, allowing the starch or other binder in the aspirin to settle to the bottom of the beaker. The acetylsalicylic acid (aspirin) and any salicylic acid should now be dissolved in the water-ethanol solution.

7. Use the empty pipet to transfer 10 drops of the dissolved aspirin solution into well C2. Use the pipet containing iron(III) ion solution to add 1 drop of iron(III) ion solution to this well.

students that the iron(III) ion solution is corrosive and that the water-ethanol solution is toxic if ingested. Students should avoid contact of their skin with these solutions and wash spills and splashes with water. ■

Teaching Tips
Students may work individually or in pairs. Color comparison can be a somewhat subjective basis for observations, however, so students may find it helpful to work in pairs. If any of your students are colorblind, pair them with partners who have full color vision.

If mortars and pestles are not available, aspirin tablets can be crushed inside a small bag with the blunt end of a pen.

Use of the water-ethanol solvent provides an opportunity to review the principles of solubility. Water is a more polar solvent than ethanol, but the two are totally miscible. The addition of alcohol to water permits the dissolving of some substances that are not very soluble in water alone. Be sure that the students understand that the hydrolysis of ASA occurs before the investigation is begun, not during the dissolving of the ASA tablet.

The number of drops from the pipets may vary from 25 drops/mL to 32 drops/mL or more, depending on the identity of the solution. However, this variation will not have an effect large enough to necessitate having the students calibrate the drops per milliliter for each solution or convert from drops to milliliters to do Step 1 of the Calculation.

You may want to give a prepared solution of salicylic acid to the students as an unknown sample if you want to ensure a positive test.

If all students use the same solution or aspirin from

Analyzing Commercial Aspirin 425

Small Scale Lab 77 APPLICATION

the same bottle, you may choose to collect class data. Assign students to determine average results and percent error.

Waste Disposal

Dispose of the materials by flushing them directly down the drain with large quantities of water. ■

8. Compare the color of the aspirin solution in well C2 to the standard solutions you previously prepared in rows A and B. If necessary, hold the wells up to a strong light source to determine which well provides the best color match to well C2. Record your results.

9. Repeat Steps 7 and 8 using wells C3 and C4. Record your results.

10. Dispose of all chemicals by flushing them down the drain with plenty of water. Clean up your work area and wash your hands before leaving the laboratory.

Observations (sample data)

Color of test solutions A1–B5	The violet color increases from well A1 through well B5.
Mass of ASA in tablet	375 mg
Best match to C2	A4
Best match to C3	A4
Best match to C4	A4

Calculations (based on sample data)

1. The stock solution of salicylic acid contains 3.0 mg of salicylic acid per mL. Calculate the concentration of salicylic acid for each of the wells in rows A and B. Record these values in the Data Table. (Assume all of the solutions require equal numbers of drops to make 1 mL.)

$$\text{Concentration} = \frac{\text{drops of standard solution}}{\text{total drops in well}} \times 3.0 \text{ mg/mL salicyclic acid}$$

(sample calculation)

Well A1: Concentration = $\frac{1 \text{ drop}}{10 \text{ drops}} \times 3.0 \text{ mg/mL} = 0.3 \text{ mg/mL}$

DATA TABLE Salicylic Acid Concentration (mg/mL)

	1	2	3	4	5
A	0.3	0.6	0.9	1.2	1.5
B	1.8	2.1	2.4	2.7	3.0

2. If the molar mass of ASA is 180.2 g/mol, how many moles of ASA were stated by the manufacturer to be present in the tablet you tested?

$375 \text{ mg} \times \frac{1 \text{ g}}{1000 \text{ mg}} \times \frac{1 \text{ mol ASA}}{180.2 \text{ g}} = 2.1 \times 10^{-3} \text{ mol ASA}$

426 © Prentice-Hall, Inc.

Name_____

Critical Thinking: Analysis and Conclusions

1. Referring to the color match obtained in Step 8 of the Procedure and the values calculated above, state the concentration of salicylic acid in mg/mL for the tablet that you tested. *(Interpreting data)* If the unknown matches the color in well A4, the concentration of salicylic acid in the unknown would be 1.2 mg/mL.

2. Using this concentration, calculate the mass of salicylic acid that was present in the tablet. (Recall that you used 25 mL of solution to dissolve all the soluble materials in the tablet you tested.) *(Drawing conclusions)*

    mass of salicylic acid = 25 mL × 1.2 mg/mL = 30 mg

3. If the molar mass of salicylic acid is 138.1 g/mol, how many moles of salicylic acid were in the tablet you tested? *(Interpreting data)*

    $30 \text{ mg} \times \dfrac{1 \text{ g}}{1000 \text{ mg}} \times \dfrac{1 \text{ mol SA}}{138.1 \text{ g}} = 2.2 \times 10^{-4}$ mol SA

4. If all the salicylic acid present was formed from the decomposition of ASA, what percentage of the ASA in the tablet you tested had decomposed in storage? *(Interpreting data)*

    $\dfrac{2.2 \times 10^{-4}}{2.1 \times 10^{-3}} \times 100\% = 10\%$

Critical Thinking: Applications

1. In this investigation, it was proposed that all the salicylic acid observed was the result of the decomposition of ASA from exposure to water vapor in the environment. Suggest another source of salicylic acid that may be related to the manufacturing process. *(Developing hypotheses)* If the separation of the product during the manufacturing process is less than 100% efficient, then salicylic acid may be left over.

2. What additional measurement would you need to obtain in order to determine the percentage of ASA by mass in a commercial aspirin tablet? *(Applying concepts)* The mass of the entire aspirin tablet would be needed.

3. If ASA is produced in an equilibrium reaction system, what procedure (other than adding more of one reactant) could be used to increase the percent yield of ASA? *(Designing experiments)* Dehydration or removal of ASA product would increase the percent yield.

Going Further

1. Construct models of salicylic acid, acetic acid, and ASA using materials supplied by your teacher.
2. A medication that is in competition with aspirin is acetaminophen, a distant chemical relative that contains no salicylates. Find its formula in a reference book. Construct a model of this molecule.
3. Currently many physicians advise against the use of aspirin by certain patients. Do some library research to determine why. As part of your research, define and discuss the contraindications of aspirin.

Making Sauerkraut

Lab 78 APPLICATION

Text reference: **Chapter 27**

Introduction

Fermented cabbage, or sauerkraut, has been produced for at least 2000 years. It has played a role in the cooking of many countries where cabbage is grown. Chinese manuscripts tell of its use to feed laborers working on the Great Wall of China. Since the Middle Ages, it has been part of the table fare in Germany and Austria. The word *sauerkraut* is German for "sour cabbage."

Making sauerkraut involves adding salt and water to shredded cabbage. The salt causes water and glucose in the cabbage cells to migrate into solution through the cell walls. The next step depends on the action of bacteria.

Normal cellular respiration consists of the oxidation—or breaking down in the presence of oxygen—of nutrients to produce energy for the cell. For organisms that live without oxygen, the biochemical pathway to produce energy is through fermentation. Anaerobic bacteria live naturally on the surface of the cabbage. Enzymes from these bacteria act on the glucose to produce lactic acid, which gives the sauerkraut its sour taste. The reaction is:

$$C_6H_{12}O_6 \rightarrow 2CH_3CH(OH)COOH$$
$$\text{glucose} \qquad \text{lactic acid}$$

In this investigation you will prepare sauerkraut and test it for the presence of lactic acid.

Pre-Lab Discussion

Read the entire laboratory investigation and the relevant pages of your textbook. Then answer the questions that follow.

1. Where is sauerkraut commonly produced? __Sauerkraut is produced in areas where cabbage is grown, for example, China and Germany.__

2. What is the basic process for making sauerkraut? __Shredded cabbage is allowed to ferment in a slightly saline solution.__

3. What is accomplished by the process of fermentation in this investigation? __Water and glucose are drawn out of plant cells. The glucose is turned into lactic acid by bacterial enzymes.__

4. What does the term *anaerobic* mean? __Anaerobic means "able to live without oxygen."__

Materials (class of 30 in pairs)
30 aprons
3 kg cabbage (about 6.5 lbs., or 3 heads)
15 kitchen scales
15 cutting boards
15 shredders or knives
15 pint jars with lids
15 bowls
15 spoons
75 g table salt (NaCl)
2 rolls wide-range or acid-range pH paper

Time Required
20 minutes. You can save time by chopping the cabbage yourself in a food processor.

Advance Preparation
Purchase cabbage and salt. If desired, chop the cabbage up in a food processor.
Collect jars. Ask students and/or faculty to save and bring them to school. The jars can be washed and saved to be reused.
Arrange to use a food science (home economics) lab or nonscience classroom for the investigation. The investigation can be done at home if you go over the instructions with students.
Find a place (not in the science classroom) where the jars can be stored where they cannot be tampered with.

Introduction
This experiment affords the opportunity for interdisciplinary applications. Not only can the food science (home economics) department be involved, but here is an excellent chance to call on biology teachers to give further background on lactic

© Prentice-Hall, Inc.

Making Sauerkraut

5. Why is the fermentation process important to the survival of living organisms? _Anaerobic bacteria use fermentation as a pathway to produce energy._

6. What test will indicate when the reaction is almost complete? _Wide-range or acid-range pH paper will be used to test the acidity._

Problem

How can you use the making of sauerkraut to study fermentation?

Materials

apron
200 g cabbage
kitchen scale
cutting board
shredder or knife
pint jar with lid

bowl
spoon
table salt (NaCl)
wide-range or acid-range pH paper

Safety

Wear an apron during this investigation. Wash your hands with soap and water before beginning your work. Do this investigation only in a food science (home economics) lab or a nonscience classroom. Be careful not to cut yourself with the knife or shredder. Make sure that the lid on the jar is loose, otherwise pressure could build up, breaking the jar.

Note the caution alert symbols here and with certain steps of the Procedure. Refer to page *xi* for the specific precautions associated with each symbol.

Procedure

Part A

1. Work in the food science (home economics) lab or a nonscience classroom. Put on an apron and wash your hands with soap and water.

2. Using the kitchen scale, measure approximately 200 grams of cabbage. On a cutting board, use a shredder or knife to chop the cabbage into pieces about 5 millimeters wide. **CAUTION:** *Be careful not to cut yourself with the knife or shredder.*

3. Pack the cabbage into the pint jar and add about 5 grams of table salt. Carefully fill the jar with water until the cabbage is covered. Tap the sides of the jar to get rid of air bubbles.

4. Use the spoon to remove some of the cabbage water. Test its pH with pH paper. Record your results in the Data Table.

Name _____

Lab 78
APPLICATION

5. Cover the jar loosely so that gases can escape. Put the jar in the bowl (in case it overflows) and set it aside for 2 to 4 weeks. This allows for the natural fermentation of the cabbage. **CAUTION:** *Make sure that the jar lid is loose, otherwise pressure could build up, breaking the jar.*

6. Clean up your work area and wash your hands before leaving the room.

Part B

7. Test the pH of the cabbage water every 5 days until a pH of 4 or lower is obtained. Record your results in the Data Table.

8. If you wish, drain the liquid from your sauerkraut, place it in a saucepan with fresh water, bring to a boil, and serve it with your favorite hot dog.

9. Wash the jar and spoon. Clean up your work area and wash your hands before leaving the room.

Teaching Tips
Store the students' jars in a secure location, and make the jars available only for testing pH.

If the students perform this investigation at home, instruct them in the use of pH paper or have them bring samples of the liquid for testing to school in jars.

The carbon dioxide that may be produced is a result of an alternate anaerobic fermentation reaction that yields small amounts of carbon dioxide and alcohol instead of lactic acid.

Once the process is complete, allow students to take home their sauerkraut for consumption.

Waste Disposal
Excess cabbage and salt should be emptied into the wastebasket. ∎

Observations (sample data)
DATA TABLE

Day	pH
start	7
5	6–7
10	5–6
15	4–5
20	4–5
25	3–4

Critical Thinking: Analysis and Conclusions

1. What changes in pH were noted during the course of this investigation? *(Interpreting data)* There is a gradual change from pH 7 to pH 3–4 over twenty days.

2. How long did the fermentation process take? *(Interpreting data)* The fermentation process took 2 to 4 weeks.

3. By slowly filling the jar and then tapping it, air was kept out of the cabbage-water-salt mixture. Why is this important? *(Making inferences)* The necessary enzymes are produced by anaerobic bacteria. Air would slow down their activity.

4. Your sauerkraut does not contain any artificial preservatives. What do you think keeps it from spoiling? *(Making inferences)* Both the salt and the lactic acid act as natural preservatives.

© Prentice-Hall, Inc.   *Making Sauerkraut* **431**

Lab 78 APPLICATION

Name _____

Critical Thinking: Applications

1. What other fermentation processes are of economic importance? *(Giving an example)* Wine production is the fermentation of the sugars in grapes. Ethanol for use in gasohol is produced from corn and grains. The carbon dioxide that causes bread to rise is produced by the fermentation of sugars by yeast. Beer is produced by the fermentation of roasted barley. Sour cream, yogurt, and other dairy products are made by fermentation. Other answers are possible.

2. Osmotic pressure is important in the transfer of water in and out of the cells in living systems. How does osmosis work in the production of sauerkraut? *(Applying concepts)* Differences in osmotic pressure pull water from the cells in the cabbage and dilute the salt water concentration, which in turn causes glucose to diffuse out of the cells. Once outside the cells, glucose ferments to lactic acid.

Going Further

1. Investigate the production of such foods as half-sour pickles, half-sour green tomatoes, and kimchi. Under the supervision of your teacher, try one or more of these processes.

Name _____ Date _____ Class _____

Organic and Inorganic Catalysts

Lab 79

Text reference: **Chapter 27**

Introduction

A catalyst is a substance that can increase the rate of a chemical reaction without being consumed in the reaction. Enzymes are substances that function as catalysts in living organisms. They are proteins that regulate almost all of the biochemical reactions in plants, animals, and microorganisms.

Enzymes were first discovered in the mid-nineteenth century by scientists studying metabolic processes, and the importance of these chemicals to biochemical reactions was quickly realized. Among the first enzymes to be classified were amylase, which converts starch into sugar, and pepsin, one of the digestive juices present in the stomach.

In this investigation, you will compare the effects of several organic catalysts and two inorganic catalysts on the decomposition of hydrogen peroxide. You will also investigate the effect of high temperatures on the catalytic ability of both organic and inorganic catalysts.

Pre-Lab Discussion

Read the entire laboratory investigation and the relevant pages of your textbook. Then answer the questions that follow.

1. What qualitative observations must you make in order to determine the best catalyst for the decomposition of hydrogen peroxide? __The relative number of gas bubbles produced in each test tube and the speed with which the bubbles are produced should be observed.__

2. Which are the inorganic catalysts you will be testing? __The inorganic catalysts are iron(III) chloride and manganese dioxide.__

3. Which are the organic catalysts you will be testing? __The organic catalysts are chemicals in blood, pineapples, potatoes, apples, and bananas.__

4. What are some dangers involved in using hydrogen peroxide? What precautions should be taken? __Hydrogen peroxide can burn the skin and eyes if it comes in contact with them. If it comes in contact with your skin, wash with plenty of water.__

5. Enzymes are well known for their specificity. Explain one of the accepted models for the observation that enzymes are specific to the substrate. __Students may describe either the lock-and-key or induced fit models.__

Materials (class of 30 in pairs)
30 pairs chemical splash goggles
30 laboratory aprons
120 test tubes
15 marking pens
15 test-tube racks
15 test-tube holders
1.5 L hydrogen peroxide (H_2O_2), 6%
15 microspatulas
manganese dioxide (MnO_2), 5 g
iron(III) chloride ($FeCl_3$), 5g
1 banana
1 potato
1 fresh pineapple
1 apple
1 piece of liver or 50 mL of blood from calf liver
15 beakers, 600-mL
15 hot plates

Time Required
45 minutes. To shorten the time, have some students start the water bath and test the heated catalysts while others are testing the unheated catalysts. Pool the data.

Advance Preparation
Cut the fruit into pieces. Fill 15 micropipets with a few mL of blood each. Have ready a container in which to collect the waste MnO_2 solutions.

Introduction
Before doing this investigation, you may want to review the function of catalysts and the structure and function of enzymes specifically. You may also want to discuss the importance of enzymes in maintaining health, as well as the importance of enzymes in various industrial applications. Such applications

© Prentice-Hall, Inc.

Organic and Inorganic Catalysts **433**

Lab 79

include uses in the production of baked goods, beer, wine, syrup, alcohol, paper, textiles, cheese, pharmaceuticals, detergents, chocolate, leather, and many other products.

Note that the protease that prevents the formation of gelatin, bromelain, is not the same enzyme as the catalases that break down hydrogen peroxide.

Safety
Make sure students wear their goggles and lab aprons at all times during the investigation. Caution students about avoiding burns from the boiling water bath and hot test tubes. The students should be instructed not to heat the hydrogen peroxide in the boiling water bath. ■

Teaching Tips
This activity is fairly straightforward and works well. Make sure the fruit is fresh. You may use other fresh fruits and other inorganic compounds as catalysts. If you use liver, you may use chicken or calf liver. The calf liver usually contains more blood than chicken liver and does not need to be processed in a blender. A small chunk of it works very well. Other fresh meat can be substituted. You can often get fresh animal blood from the meat department of your local grocery store.

Help the students estimate 5 mL in the test tubes.

The hydrogen peroxide used in this activity is stronger than that which can be purchased over the counter. It can be obtained from chemical supply houses.

Problem
How do organic and inorganic catalysts compare in their ability to catalyze the decomposition of hydrogen peroxide?

Materials
chemical splash goggles
laboratory apron
8 test tubes
marking pencil
test-tube rack
hydrogen peroxide (H_2O_2), 6%
microspatula
manganese dioxide (MnO_2)
iron(III) chloride ($FeCl_3$)

small piece of each of the following:
banana
potato
fresh pineapple
apple
liver or the blood from calf liver
beaker, 600-mL
hot plate
test-tube holder

Safety
Wear your goggles and lab apron at all times during the investigation. Use caution when heating objects. Hydrogen peroxide is a strong oxidizing agent and may cause burns to eyes or skin. Avoid contact with your eyes and hands. Iron(III) chloride is irritating to skin. Avoid direct contact with it. If either of these solutions makes contact with your skin, wash with plenty of cold water. Do not eat any of the foods.

Note the caution alert symbols here and with certain steps of the Procedure. Refer to page xi for the specific precautions associated with each symbol.

Procedure

1. Put on your goggles and lab apron. Number the test tubes 1–8. Place approximately 5 mL of H_2O_2 in each of the eight test tubes. **CAUTION:** *Hydrogen peroxide is a strong oxidizing agent and may cause burns to eyes or skin. Wash spills or splashes with plenty of water.*
2. Leave test tube 1 as a control by adding nothing to it. Observe the rate at which oxygen gas bubbles are produced. Record your observations in Data Table 1.
3. To test tube 2, use a microspatula to add a small amount of MnO_2 and observe. Record your observations in Data Table 1.

4. To test tube 3, add a similar amount of $FeCl_3$. Observe and record. **CAUTION:** *Iron(III) chloride is irritating to skin. Avoid direct contact with it. If it makes contact with your skin, wash with plenty of cold water.*
5. Add a small piece of banana to test tube 4, a small piece of potato to test tube 5, a small piece of pineapple to test tube 6, and a small piece of apple to test tube 7. Observe and record after each addition.

Name _____

Lab 79

6. To test tube 8, add a few drops of blood or a small piece of liver. Observe and record.

 7. Dispose of the contents of your test tubes as follows. Empty the contents of test tube 2 into a container provided by your teacher. Pour the liquids in the remaining test tubes down the drain. Place all solid pieces of fruit in the garbage can. Then wash and dry your test tubes.

 8. Set up a boiling water bath on a hot plate, using a 600-mL beaker about one-third full. **CAUTION:** *Do not touch hot objects with your bare hands.*

9. Into empty test tubes 2–8, place the same amount of each catalyst as was used in that test tube during Steps 2–6. **CAUTION:** *Do not add the hydrogen peroxide yet.*

 10. Heat all of the test tubes in the boiling water bath for about 6 minutes. Using the tongs, remove the test tubes from the water bath and allow them to cool in the test-tube rack to about room temperature.

11. Add approximately 5 mL of hydrogen peroxide to each of the eight test tubes and again observe the rate of oxygen gas produced. Record your observations in Data Table 2.

 12. Dispose of the contents of your test tubes and wash them as before. Clean up your work area and wash your hands before leaving the laboratory.

Waste Disposal

Collect the waste MnO_2 solution in a separate beaker. It can be reused when the water has evaporated. All other liquids may be poured down drain. Solids may be thrown away in the garbage can. If any $FeCl_3$ remains in solid form, it can be dissolved and poured down the drain. ■

Observations (sample data)

DATA TABLE 1 Catalysis Before Heating

Test Tube	Catalyst	Observations
1	none	no bubbles
2	MnO_2	vigorous bubbling, warm, black color
3	$FeCl_3$	vigorous bubbling, red-brown color
4	banana	bubbles form, foamy
5	potato	bubbles form, foamy
6	pineapple	bubbles form slowly
7	apple	bubbles form very slowly
8	liver	bubbles form vigorously

© Prentice-Hall, Inc.   *Organic and Inorganic Catalysts* **435**

Lab 79

Name _____

DATA TABLE 2 Catalysis After Heating

Test Tube	Catalyst	Observations
1	none	NR
2	MnO$_2$	very vigorous bubbling, warm, black color
3	FeCl$_3$	vigorous bubbling, red-brown color
4	banana	NR
5	potato	NR
6	pineapple	NR
7	apple	NR
8	liver	NR

Critical Thinking: Analysis and Conclusions

1. On the basis of your observations, which catalyst accelerated the decomposition of hydrogen peroxide the most effectively? How could you tell? *(Making comparisons)* Answers may vary due to amounts used, but most students will find the MnO$_2$ to be the best catalyst. It produced the most bubbles and acted the fastest.

2. Which of the organic catalysts accelerated the reaction most effectively? *(Making comparisons)* Answers may vary, but usually the liver is most effective.

3. How were the inorganic catalysts affected by heating them to 100°C? *(Interpreting data)* There was no change in their effectiveness.

4. How were the organic catalysts (enzymes) affected by heating them to 100°C? *(Interpreting data)* The organic catalysts no longer catalyzed the reaction after being heated.

Critical Thinking: Applications

1. Write a balanced chemical equation for the decomposition of hydrogen peroxide. *(Making inferences)* $2H_2O_2 \rightarrow 2H_2O + O_2$

2. What does it mean to denature a protein? *(Applying concepts)* An enzyme that is denatured is biologically inactive because something has changed its shape or structure.

Name _____

Lab 79

3. Could you use canned pineapple rather than fresh pineapple and obtain the same results for this activity? Why or why not? *(Developing hypotheses)* Canned pineapple would not work as a catalyst because it is heat treated in the canning process and its enzymes would be denatured.

4. After completing this investigation, suggest a reason that fresh pineapple cannot be used to make fruit gelatin. Fresh pineapple contains an active enzyme that prevents the formation of the gelatin structure. Canned pineapple works well in gelatin because that enzyme has been denatured.

Going Further

1. Investigate the reason that 3% hydrogen peroxide is effective on cuts and bruises.
2. Test pineapple and other fruits, fresh and canned, to see if they affect the formation of gelatin.
3. Under your teacher's supervision, determine the approximate temperature at which enzymes are inactivated. Take fresh pineapple juice and heat portions of it to 30°C, 35°C, 40°C, 45°C, etc. Test the heated juice with hydrogen peroxide and determine the temperature above which no reaction occurs.

Organic and Inorganic Catalysts

Analysis of Commercial Vitamin C

Small Scale Lab 80 APPLICATION

Text reference: **Chapter 27**

Introduction

Vitamin C occurs naturally in many fruits and vegetables, including oranges, kiwis, kumquats, papayas, potatoes, and hot green chilies. Chemically, vitamin C is known as ascorbic acid, $H_2C_6H_6O_6$. Its structure is shown in Figure 80–1.

Figure 80–1 *Ascorbic Acid (Vitamin C)*

Vitamin C is an important nutrient in your diet. It is essential in the formation of collagen, a protein found in the connective tissue of your ligaments and tendons. It is involved in the metabolism of several amino acids and in the absorption of iron. It aids in the healing of wounds. It also acts as an antioxidant because it prevents the oxidation of other vitamins, such as A and E.

The recommended daily allowance of vitamin C is 60 mg. Some people claim that much larger amounts—1000 to 3000 mg per day—may help prevent diseases such as the common cold, cancer, and heart attacks. Large doses, however, are toxic in 2 to 5 percent of the population. Therefore, anyone considering taking large doses of vitamin C should first consult a physician. If you eat three to five servings of fruit and two to four servings of vegetables each day, you should be getting adequate amounts of vitamin C.

In this investigation, you will employ analytical methods to determine the amount of vitamin C in a commercially produced vitamin tablet. You will conduct an acid-base neutralization reaction using sodium hydroxide to neutralize the ascorbic acid in the tablet. Phenolphthalein, an acid-base indicator, will change from colorless to pink when the neutralization is complete. By employing principles of stoichiometry, you then will be able to calculate the amount of vitamin C in the tablet and compare this amount with the amount claimed by the manufacturer.

Materials (class of 30 in pairs)

30 pairs chemical splash goggles
30 laboratory aprons
15 vitamin C tablets, 500-mg
15 laboratory balances
15 graduated cylinders, 50-mL
15 beakers, 100-mL
distilled water
15 glass stirring rods
phenolphthalein solution, 1%
300 mL standardized sodium hydroxide (NaOH), 0.1 *M*
15 beakers, 50-mL
30 micropipets
15 graduated cylinders, 10-mL
15 well plates, 12-well
box of toothpicks

Time Required

45 minutes.

Advance Preparation

To prepare the NaOH solution, measure 4.0 g of NaOH and place in a 1000-mL volumetric flask. CAUTION: *NaOH is caustic. Avoid splashes and spills.* Dissolve in distilled water and fill to the 1000-mL line. Standardize the NaOH solution by carrying out the following procedure:

1. Take a clean, dry 125-mL erlenmeyer flask and record the mass.
2. Add between 0.5 and 1.0 g of potassium biphthalate and record the mass again.
3. Add 25 to 40 mL distilled water and dissolve the potassium biphthalate.
4. Add three to four drops of phenolphthalein indicator.
5. Rinse and fill a titration buret with the NaOH solution.

Analysis of Commercial Vitamin C **439**

Name _____

6. Titrate the potassium biphthalate solution with the NaOH solution until a faint pink color remains. Note the volume of sodium hydroxide used and record.
7. Calculate the molarity of the sodium hydroxide solution using the following equation:

$$\text{\# g KHP} \times \frac{1 \text{ mol KHP}}{204.23 \text{ g}}$$
$$\times \frac{1 \text{ mol NaOH}}{1 \text{ mol KHP}}$$
$$\times \frac{1}{\text{\# mL NaOH}} \times \frac{1000 \text{ mL}}{1 \text{ L}}$$
$$= M \text{ NaOH}$$

8. Write the exact molarity on the board.
9. Keep the NaOH solution tightly sealed so that the carbon dioxide in the air will not react with it.

Introduction

Bring in some labels of various products that contain vitamin C. Discuss the percentage of the US RDA of vitamin C that each product claims to supply. Ask students how they might check to see if the claims made on the labels are correct.

You may wish to review mole/molarity calculations (Chapter 15) and acid-base neutralization (Chapter 19).

Pre-Lab Discussion

Read the entire laboratory investigation and the relevant pages of your textbook. Then answer the questions that follow.

1. What is the molar mass of ascorbic acid?
   2(1) + 6(12) + 6(1) + 6(16) = 176 g/mol

2. Write a balanced equation for the reaction of sodium hydroxide with ascorbic acid. NOTE: Only one of the hydrogen atoms of the ascorbic acid is replaced in this reaction.
   $NaOH + H_2C_6H_6O_6 \rightarrow NaHC_6H_6O_6 + H_2O$

3. What hazards are involved in working with the sodium hydroxide solution and what safety precautions should you take? Sodium hydroxide is caustic. Wear goggles at all times. If contact with sodium hydroxide occurs, wash with plenty of cold water and inform your teacher.

4. What is phenolphthalein and what is its function in this experiment? Phenolphthalein is an acid-base indicator. It is colorless in acidic solutions and pink in alkaline solutions. When the solution turns pink, you know to stop adding NaOH.

5. In what position should the pipet be held while delivering drops of sodium hydroxide? Why? The pipet should be held vertically. This ensures a uniform drop size. If held at an angle, the adhesion to the pipet would create a larger drop volume.

Problem

How can titration techniques be used to determine the amount of ascorbic acid in a commercial vitamin C tablet?

Materials

chemical splash goggles
laboratory apron
vitamin C tablet, 500-mg
laboratory balance
graduated cylinder, 50-mL
beaker, 100-mL
distilled water
stirring rod

phenolphthalein solution, 1%
standardized sodium hydroxide (NaOH) solution
beaker, 50-mL
2 micropipets
graduated cylinder, 10-mL
well plate
4 toothpicks

Name _____

Safety

Wear your goggles and lab apron at all times during the investigation. Sodium hydroxide is caustic and can cause permanent eye damage, so avoid direct contact with it. If contact occurs, immediately wash the affected area with plenty of cold water and inform your teacher. Clean up all spills immediately. Note the caution alert symbols here and with certain steps of the Procedure. Refer to page *xi* for the specific precautions associated with each symbol.

Procedure

1. Put on your goggles and lab apron. Find the mass of the vitamin C tablet and record this value.
2. Place the tablet in the 100-mL beaker and add 50 mL of distilled water.
3. Dissolve the tablet in the distilled water. The binder that holds the tablet together will not completely dissolve, so use the stirring rod to break up the undissolved part of the tablet into very small pieces.
4. Add three drops of phenolphthalein indicator to the vitamin C solution. Set the solution aside for use later.

5. Obtain 15 mL of standardized sodium hydroxide solution in a clean, dry 50-mL beaker. Note and record the exact molarity of this solution. Fill a micropipet with some of this solution. **CAUTION:** *NaOH is caustic; take care not to come into direct contact with it. If you spill any, wash the area with plenty of cold water, and inform your teacher.*
6. Calibrate a micropipet for use with sodium hydroxide solution as follows: Fill a 10-mL graduated cylinder with sodium hydroxide to exactly 5.0 mL. Then count and record how many drops are needed to increase the volume to 6.0 mL, then 7.0 mL, then 8.0 mL. Calculate the average number of drops per mL from these values. Record the numbers in the Observations section. Hold the pipet vertically while counting the drops. If you tilt the pipet, the NaOH will adhere to the sides of the pipet and the drops will be too large. Do not allow the drops to touch the sides of the cylinder. Be sure to read the volume by sighting the bottom of the meniscus at eye level.
7. Return all the NaOH solution in the graduated cylinder to the beaker. Rinse the cylinder first with tap water and then with distilled water. Using the procedure in Step 6, calibrate the second pipet for use with vitamin C solution, and calculate the number of drops of vitamin C per mL. Double this number to determine the number of drops in 2 mL.
8. Using the number of drops you just calculated, add 2 mL of the vitamin C solution to each of four wells of a 12-well plate. Touch the tip of the pipet to the side of the well to remove the last drop of solution from the pipet.

© Prentice-Hall, Inc.   *Analysis of Commercial Vitamin C*   **441**

Small Scale Lab 80 APPLICATION

Name _____

9. Titrate the vitamin C solution in the first well with the sodium hydroxide solution as follows: Use the micropipet to add sodium hydroxide one drop at a time, stirring with a toothpick after each drop, until the solution remains a faint pink color. Count and record the total number of drops needed to do this. Be sure to hold the pipet in a vertical position. Repeat this process for the remaining three wells containing vitamin C solution.

Waste Disposal
Waste materials can be flushed down the drain with plenty of water. ■

10. Discard the waste chemicals in the sink, flushed with plenty of water. Wash all equipment, rinsing the well plates and the pipets with distilled water. Clean up your work area and wash your hands before leaving the laboratory.

Observations (sample data)

Mass of vitamin C tablet		0.62 g	
Molarity of NaOH solution		0.0864 M	
Number of drops of NaOH/mL (3 trials)	40	36	39
Average number of drops of NaOH/mL		38.3 drops/mL	
Number of drops of vit. C/mL (3 trials)	35	32	30
Average number of drops of vit. C/mL		32.3 drops/mL	

Number of drops of NaOH solution used to turn the solution faint pink:

Trial 1	56
Trial 2	57
Trial 3	56
Trial 4	59

Calculations (based on sample data)

1. From the data, determine the average volume of one drop of the sodium hydroxide solution delivered by the pipet.

   1 ÷ (38.3 drops/mL) = 0.0261 mL/drop

2. Determine the average number of drops of sodium hydroxide solution necessary to react with the ascorbic acid in 2 mL of vitamin C solution. Convert the average number of drops to mL.

   Average drops = (57 + 56 + 56 + 59) ÷ 4 = 57.0 drops
   57.0 drops × 0.0261 mL/drop = 1.49 mL

3. Determine the volume of sodium hydroxide that would have been necessary to react all the vitamin C in the entire 50 mL of vitamin C solution (VC).

   $$\frac{1.49 \text{ mL NaOH}}{2.00 \text{ mL VC}} \times 50 \text{ mL VC} = 37.2 \text{ mL NaOH}$$

4. Determine the number of moles of vitamin C in the 50 mL of solution.

   $$37.2 \text{ mL NaOH} \times 0.0864 \text{ } M \text{ NaOH} \times \frac{1 \text{ mol VC}}{1 \text{ mol NaOH}} = 3.21 \times 10^{-3} \text{ mol VC}$$

Name _____

5. Using the molar mass you determined in Pre-Lab Question 1, determine the number of milligrams of vitamin C in the 50 mL of solution. (This is the number of milligrams present in the entire tablet.)

   3.21×10^{-3} mol VC $\times$ 1.76 mg/(mol $\times 10^{-3}$) = 566 mg VC

Critical Thinking: Analysis and Conclusions

1. How does your experimental result compare to the manufacturer's claim of 500 mg of vitamin C in each tablet? Are you within experimental limits or not? Explain. *(Making comparisons)* <u>Most students will obtain a value that is greater than 500 mg. This could be the result of the second proton in ascorbic acid reacting with the NaOH.</u>

2. A vitamin C tablet consists of ascorbic acid and binders that hold the tablet together. Using your experimental results for the amount of ascorbic acid in one tablet, determine the percentage of vitamin C and the percentage of binder in the tablet. *(Interpreting data)*

   $\dfrac{566 \text{ mg VC}}{620 \text{ mg tablet}} \times 100 = 91\%$ VC

   $100\% - 91\% = 9\%$ binder

3. Being as specific as possible, predict the effect of each of the following scenarios on the experimental result for the amount of vitamin C in the tablet. *(Making predictions)*

   a. The binders reacted with the sodium hydroxide solution. <u>The tablet would consume more sodium hydroxide than necessary. There would appear to be a greater amount of ascorbic acid in the tablet.</u>

   b. The pipet was not held vertically for each drop delivered. <u>Larger drops, and therefore a smaller number of drops, of sodium hydroxide would be added. There would appear to be less acid.</u>

   c. One drop more of sodium hydroxide was added than was necessary. <u>If one excess drop was added, it would indicate a greater amount of ascorbic acid than was actually present.</u>

Critical Thinking: Applications

1. This experiment was based on the assumption that only one of the protons in ascorbic acid reacted with the sodium hydroxide. If both protons reacted with the NaOH, how would you change the calculations to obtain an accurate analysis of the amount of vitamin C in the tablet? *(Making predictions)*

   In Step 4, replace $\dfrac{1 \text{ mol VC}}{1 \text{ mol NaOH}}$ with $\dfrac{1 \text{ mol VC}}{2 \text{ mol NaOH}}$.

Going Further

1. For a sample vinegar analysis lab, see *Chemistry in Microscale*, by John Mauch and David Ehrenkranz, Kendall/Hunt Publishing Company.

2. The initial pH can be used to determine the [H^+] concentration, which will equal the [$HC_6H_6O_6^-$] concentration. The total number of moles of ascorbic acid divided by the number of mL of ascorbic acid solution will result in the total ascorbic acid concentration [$H_2C_6H_6O_6$]. From this, one can calculate K_a = [H^+][$HC_6H_6O_6^-$]/[$H_2C_6H_6O_6$]. The graph of pH versus mL of NaOH can be used to determine the equivalence point by constructing tangent lines, as shown in the diagram below, and measuring the midpoint of the center line. The number of mL of NaOH needed to reach the equivalence point can then be read from the graph, and the number of moles of the ascorbic acid can be calculated. Computer interface programs will construct the graph as the data are collected and are a great time-saver for the student.

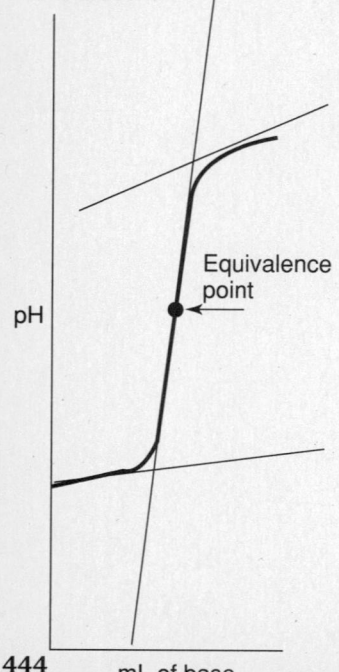

Name_____

2. Cranberries contain quinic acid, $HC_7H_{11}O_6$. Suppose you titrated 20.00 g of cranberry juice with 0.1123 M sodium hydroxide solution until all the acid was neutralized. In the process, you used 39.9 mL of sodium hydroxide. What percentage of the cranberry juice was quinic acid? *(Applying concepts)*

NaOH + $HC_7H_{11}O_6$ → $NaC_7H_{11}O_6$ + H_2O
(39.9 mL NaOH × 0.1123 M NaOH) × (1 mol $HC_7H_{11}O_6$/1 mol NaOH)
  × (192 g $HC_7H_{11}O_6$/1 mol) = 860 mg
860 mg $HC_7H_{11}O_6$ × 1 g/(1000 mg) × 1/(20.00 g juice) × 100 = 4.3% acid

3. Why will the method used in this investigation not work for the analysis of the amount of vitamin C in orange juice? Design an experiment that would allow you to measure the amount of vitamin C in orange juice. *(Designing experiments)* <u>In addition to ascorbic acid, orange juice contains citric acid. The vitamin C would have to be isolated before analysis.</u>

Going Further

1. The method used in this investigation can be applied to find the acid content of a variety of commercial products. Under the supervision of your teacher, try this method to determine the amount of acetic acid in vinegar.

2. With your teacher's help, obtain a computer interface that uses a pH probe or a standard pH meter. Use this instrumentation to analyze a vitamin C solution. You can determine the ionization constant, K_a, by first measuring the pH of the initial vitamin C solution and then titrating the 50 mL of vitamin C solution with standardized sodium hydroxide. Measure and record the pH after adding each 1.0 mL of sodium hydroxide. Make a graph of pH versus the number of mL NaOH used in order to determine the equivalence point. Then calculate the total moles of ascorbic acid and the ionization constant. This method will work with most fruit juices, with vinegar, and with other acid-containing products.

3. Health-food stores do not come under Food and Drug Administration guidelines and are allowed to sell "natural vitamins" without warnings or guarantees of actual content of vitamins. There is a move by some organizations to have these products fall under government regulations. Research this controversy. You may find Food and Drug Administration publications helpful.

APPENDICES

The Chemical Elements *447*

Formulas of Common Ions *448*

Important Formulas, Equations, and Constants *449*

Standard Reduction Potentials *450*

Vapor Pressures of Water *451*

The Chemical Elements

THE CHEMICAL ELEMENTS WITH THEIR SYMBOLS, ATOMIC NUMBERS, AND ATOMIC MASSES

Element	Symbol	Atomic Number	Atomic Mass
Actinium	Ac	89	227.0278
Aluminum	Al	13	26.98154
Americium	Am	95	(243)[a]
Antimony	Sb	51	121.157
Argon	Ar	18	39.948
Arsenic	As	33	74.9216
Astatine	At	85	(210)
Barium	Ba	56	137.33
Berkelium	Bk	97	(247)
Beryllium	Be	4	9.01218
Bismuth	Bi	83	208.9804
Boron	B	5	10.81
Bromine	Br	35	79.904
Cadmium	Cd	48	112.41
Calcium	Ca	20	40.078
Californium	Cf	98	(251)
Carbon	C	6	12.011
Cerium	Ce	58	140.12
Cesium	Cs	55	132.9054
Chlorine	Cl	17	35.453
Chromium	Cr	24	51.996
Cobalt	Co	27	58.9332
Copper	Cu	29	63.546
Curium	Cm	96	(247)
Dysprosium	Dy	66	162.50
Einsteinium	Es	99	(252)
Erbium	Er	68	167.26
Europium	Eu	63	151.96
Fermium	Fm	100	(257)
Fluorine	F	9	18.998403
Francium	Fr	87	(223)
Gadolinium	Gd	64	157.25
Gallium	Ga	31	69.72
Germanium	Ge	32	72.61
Gold	Au	79	196.9665
Hafnium	Hf	72	178.49
Helium	He	2	4.00260
Holmium	Ho	67	164.9304
Hydrogen	H	1	1.00794
Indium	In	49	114.82
Iodine	I	53	126.9045
Iridium	Ir	77	192.22
Iron	Fe	26	55.847
Krypton	Kr	36	83.80
Lanthanum	La	57	138.9055
Lawrencium	Lr	103	(260)
Lead	Pb	82	207.2
Lithium	Li	3	6.941
Lutetium	Lu	71	174.967
Magnesium	Mg	12	24.305
Manganese	Mn	25	54.9380
Mendelevium	Md	101	(258)
Mercury	Hg	80	200.59
Molybdenum	Mo	42	95.94
Neodymium	Nd	60	144.24
Neon	Ne	10	20.1797
Neptunium	Np	93	237.048
Nickel	Ni	28	58.69
Niobium	Nb	41	92.9064
Nitrogen	N	7	14.0067
Nobelium	No	102	(259)
Osmium	Os	76	190.2
Oxygen	O	8	15.9994
Palladium	Pd	46	106.42
Phosphorus	P	15	30.97376
Platinum	Pt	78	195.08
Plutonium	Pu	94	(244)
Polonium	Po	84	(209)
Potassium	K	19	39.0983
Praseodymium	Pr	59	140.9077
Promethium	Pm	61	(145)
Protactinium	Pa	91	231.0359
Radium	Ra	88	226.0254
Radon	Rn	86	(222)
Rhenium	Re	75	186.207
Rhodium	Rh	45	102.9055
Rubidium	Rb	37	85.4678
Ruthenium	Ru	44	101.07
Samarium	Sm	62	150.36
Scandium	Sc	21	44.9559
Seaborgium[b]	Sg	106	(263)
Selenium	Se	34	78.96
Silicon	Si	14	28.0855
Silver	Ag	47	107.8682
Sodium	Na	11	22.98977
Strontium	Sr	38	87.62
Sulfur	S	16	32.066
Tantalum	Ta	73	180.9479
Technetium	Tc	43	(98)
Tellurium	Te	52	127.60
Terbium	Tb	65	158.9254
Thallium	Tl	81	204.383
Thorium	Th	90	232.0381
Thulium	Tm	69	168.9342
Tin	Sn	50	118.710
Titanium	Ti	22	47.88
Tungsten	W	74	183.85
Unnilennium	Une	109	(266)
Unniloctium	Uno	108	(265)
Unnilpentium	Unp	105	(262)
Unnilquadium	Unq	104	(261)
Unnilseptium	Uns	107	(262)
Uranium	U	92	238.0289
Vanadium	V	23	50.9415
Xenon	Xe	54	131.29
Ytterbium	Yb	70	173.04
Yttrium	Y	39	88.9059
Zinc	Zn	30	65.39
Zirconium	Zr	40	91.224

[a] Approximate values for radioactive elements are listed in parentheses.
[b] The name of Element 106 has not yet been certified.

© Prentice-Hall, Inc.

Formulas of Common Ions

Positive Ions (Cations)

aluminum	Al^{3+}
ammonium	NH_4^+
barium	Ba^{2+}
calcium	Ca^{2+}
cobalt	Co^{2+}
copper(I)	Cu^+
copper(II)	Cu^{2+}
hydrogen, hydronium	H^+, H_3O^+
iron(II)	Fe^{2+}
iron(III)	Fe^{3+}
lead(II)	Pb^{2+}
lithium	Li^+
magnesium	Mg^{2+}
manganese(II)	Mn^{2+}
potassium	K^+
silver	Ag^+
sodium	Na^+
strontium	Sr^{2+}
zinc	Zn^{2+}

Negative Ions (Anions)

acetate	CH_3COO^- or $C_2H_3O_2^-$
bromide	Br^-
carbonate	CO_3^{2-}
hydrogen carbonate	HCO_3^-
chlorate	ClO_3^-
chloride	Cl^-
fluoride	F^-
hydroxide	OH^-
hypochlorite	ClO^-
iodate	IO_3^-
iodide	I^-
nitrate	NO_3^-
nitrite	NO_2^-
oxalate	$C_2O_4^{2-}$
oxide	O^{2-}
permanganate	MnO_4^-
phosphate	PO_4^{3-}
monohydrogen phosphate	HPO_4^{2-}
dihydrogen phosphate	$H_2PO_4^-$
sulfate	SO_4^{2-}
hydrogen sulfate	HSO_4^-
sulfide	S^{2-}
hydrogen sulfide	HS^-
sulfite	SO_3^{2-}
hydrogen sulfite	HSO_3^-

Important Formulas, Equations, and Constants

Density (d)
density = $\dfrac{\text{mass}}{\text{volume}}$ $d = \dfrac{m}{V}$

Percent Error
percent error = $\dfrac{\text{measured value} - \text{accepted value}}{\text{accepted value}} \times 100\%$

Percent Yield
percent yield = $\dfrac{\text{actual yield}}{\text{expected yield}} \times 100\%$

Percentage Composition
percentage composition by mass = $\dfrac{\text{mass of element}}{\text{mass of compound}} \times 100\%$

Planck's Equation
$E = h\nu$
where h is Planck's constant, E is energy, and ν is frequency

Kinetic Energy (KE)
kinetic energy = $\dfrac{\text{mass} \times \text{velocity}^2}{2}$
$KE = \dfrac{mv^2}{2}$

Gravitational Potential Energy (GPE)
gravitational potential energy = mass × acceleration due to gravity × height
$GPE = mgh$

Amount of Gas (n) in a Sample
$n = \dfrac{\text{mass}}{\text{molar mass}} = \dfrac{m \text{ (g)}}{\mathcal{M} \text{ (g/mol)}}$

Boyle's Law
$P_1 V_1 = P_2 V_2$

Charles's Law
$V_1 T_2 = V_2 T_1$

Avogadro's Law
$V = k_3 n$
where k_3 is Avogadro's law constant and n is the number of moles

Dalton's Law of Partial Pressures
$P_T = p_a + p_b + p_c + \cdots$

Ideal Gas Law
$PV = nRT$

Molarity (M)
molarity = $\dfrac{\text{moles of solute}}{\text{liters of solution}}$

Molality (m)
molality = $\dfrac{\text{moles of solute}}{\text{kilograms of solvent}}$

Mole Fraction (χ)
mole fraction = $\dfrac{\text{moles of solute or solvent}}{\text{total moles of solution}}$

Boiling Point Elevation
$\Delta T_b = K_b m$
where K_b is the molal boiling point elevation constant

Freezing Point Depression
$\Delta T_f = K_f m$
where K_f is the molal freezing point depression constant

Rate of Reaction
rate = $k[A]^x[B]^y$
where $[A]$ and $[B]$ are molar concentrations of reactants and k is a rate constant

Entropy Change
$\Delta S = S_{\text{products}} - S_{\text{reactants}}$

Gibbs Free Energy
$\Delta G = \Delta H - T\Delta S$

Avogadro's number	6.02×10^{23}
Speed of light in a vacuum	3.00×10^8 m/s
Atomic mass unit (amu)	1.66054×10^{-27} kg
Charge of an electron	1.60×10^{-19} C
Mass of an electron	9.11×10^{-31} kg
	0.0006 amu
Mass of a proton	1.0073 amu
	1.6726×10^{-27} kg
Mass of a neutron	1.0087 amu
	1.6749×10^{-27} kg
Planck's constant (h)	6.6262×10^{-34} J-s
Gas constant (R)	0.08206 atm-L/mol-K
	8.314 Pa-m³/mol-K
	8.314 J/mol-K
Molar volume of a gas at STP	22.4 L

Standard Reduction Potentials

(Ionic Concentrations 1 M Water at 298 K and 101.3 kPa)

Half Reaction	$E°$ (volts)
$F_2(g) + 2e^- \rightarrow 2\,F^-$	+2.87
$8\,H^+ + MnO_4^- + 5e^- \rightarrow Mn^{2+} + 4\,H_2O$	+1.51
$Au^{3+} + 3e^- \rightarrow Au(s)$	+1.50
$Cl_2(g) + 2e^- \rightarrow 2\,Cl^-$	+1.36
$14\,H^+ + Cr_2O_7^{2-} + 6e^- \rightarrow 2\,Cr^{3+} + 7\,H_2O$	+1.23
$4\,H^+ + O_2(g) + 4e^- \rightarrow 2\,H_2O$	+1.23
$4\,H^+ + MnO_2(s) + 2e^- \rightarrow Mn^{2+} + 2\,H_2O$	+1.22
$Br_2(l) + 2e^- \rightarrow 2\,Br^-$	+1.09
$Hg^{2+} + 2e^- \rightarrow Hg(l)$	+0.85
$Ag^+ + e^- \rightarrow Ag(s)$	+0.80
$Hg_2^{2+} + 2e^- \rightarrow 2\,Hg(l)$	+0.80
$Fe^{3+} + e^- \rightarrow Fe^{2+}$	+0.77
$I_2(s) + 2e^- \rightarrow 2\,I^-$	+0.54
$Cu^+ + e^- \rightarrow Cu(s)$	+0.52
$Cu^{2+} + 2e^- \rightarrow Cu(s)$	+0.34
$4\,H^+ + SO_4^{2-} + 2e^- \rightarrow SO_2(aq) + 2\,H_2O$	+0.17
$Sn^{4+} + 2e^- \rightarrow Sn^{2+}$	+0.15
$2\,H^+ + 2e^- \rightarrow H_2(g)$	0.00
$Pb^{2+} + 2e^- \rightarrow Pb(s)$	−0.13
$Sn^{2+} + 2e^- \rightarrow Sn(s)$	−0.14
$Ni^{2+} + 2e^- \rightarrow Ni(s)$	−0.26
$Co^{2+} + 2e^- \rightarrow Co(s)$	−0.28
$Fe^{2+} + 2e^- \rightarrow Fe(s)$	−0.45
$Cr^{3+} + 3e^- \rightarrow Cr(s)$	−0.74
$Zn^{2+} + 2e^- \rightarrow Zn(s)$	−0.76
$2\,H_2O + 2e^- \rightarrow 2\,OH^- + H_2(g)$	−0.83
$Mn^{2+} + 2e^- \rightarrow Mn(s)$	−1.19
$Al^{3+} + 3e^- \rightarrow Al(s)$	−1.66
$Mg^{2+} + 2e^- \rightarrow Mg(s)$	−2.37
$Na^+ + e^- \rightarrow Na(s)$	−2.71
$Ca^{2+} + 2e^- \rightarrow Ca(s)$	−2.87
$Sr^{2+} + 2e^- \rightarrow Sr(s)$	−2.89
$Ba^{2+} + 2e^- \rightarrow Ba(s)$	−2.91
$Cs^+ + e^- \rightarrow Cs(s)$	−2.92
$K^+ + e^- \rightarrow K(s)$	−2.93
$Rb^+ + e^- \rightarrow Rb(s)$	−2.98
$Li^+ + e^- \rightarrow Li(s)$	−3.04

Vapor Pressures of Water

Temperature (°C)	Pressure (mm Hg)	Temperature (°C)	Pressure (mm Hg)
0	4.6	33	37.7
2.5	5.5	34	39.9
5	6.5	35	42.2
7.5	7.8	36	44.6
10	9.2	37	47.1
11	9.8	38	49.7
12	10.5	39	52.4
13	11.2	40	55.3
14	12.0	41	58.3
15	12.8	42	61.5
16	13.6	43	64.8
17	14.5	44	68.3
18	15.5	45	71.9
19	16.5	46	75.6
20	17.5	47	79.6
21	18.7	48	83.7
22	19.8	49	88.0
23	21.1	50	92.5
24	22.4	60	149.4
25	23.8	65	187.5
26	25.2	70	233.7
27	26.7	75	289.1
28	28.3	80	355.1
29	30.0	85	433.6
30	31.8	90	525.8
31	33.7	95	633.9
32	35.7	100	760.0

© Prentice-Hall, Inc.

Name _____ Date _____ Class _____

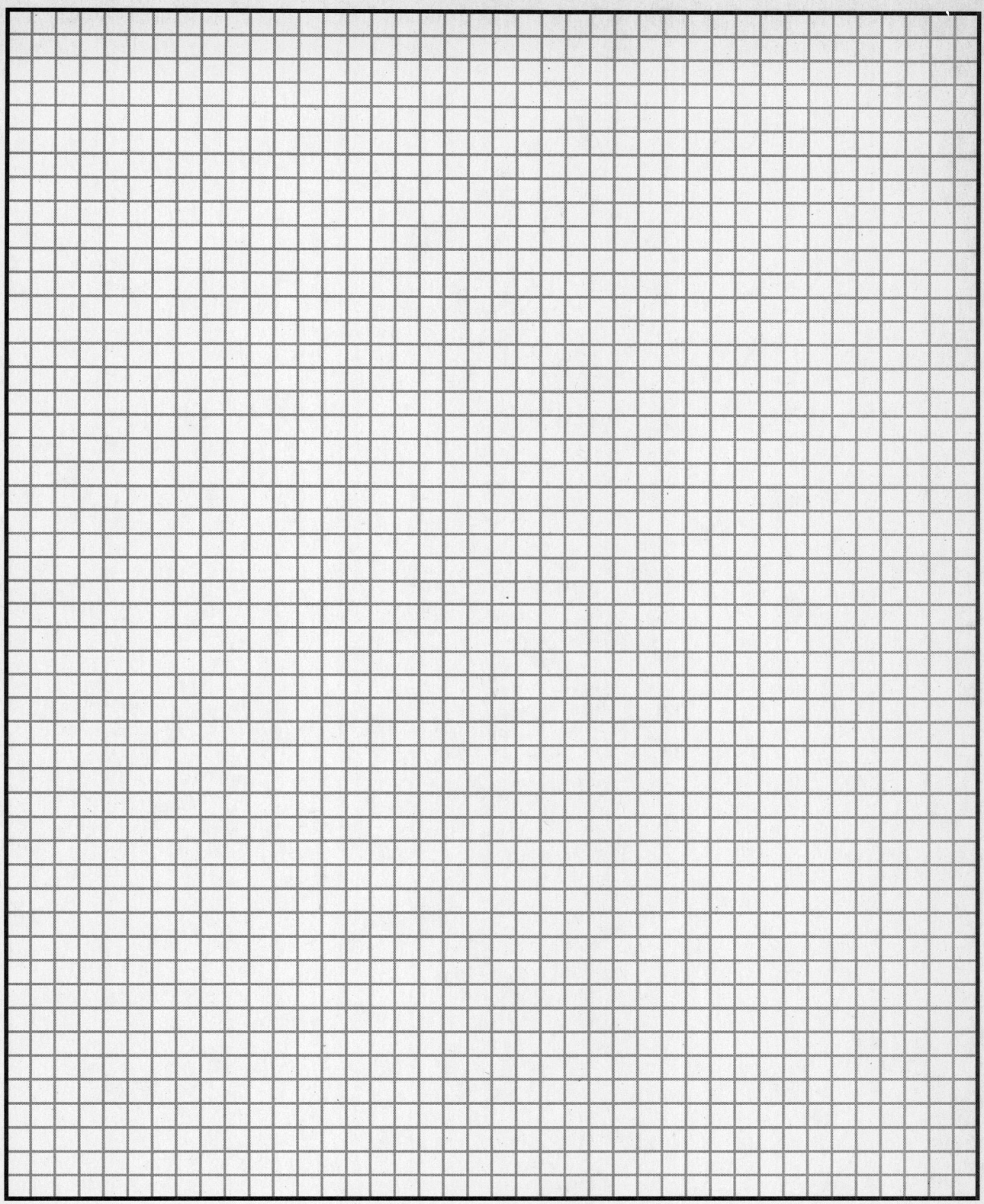

Name _____ Date _____ Class _____

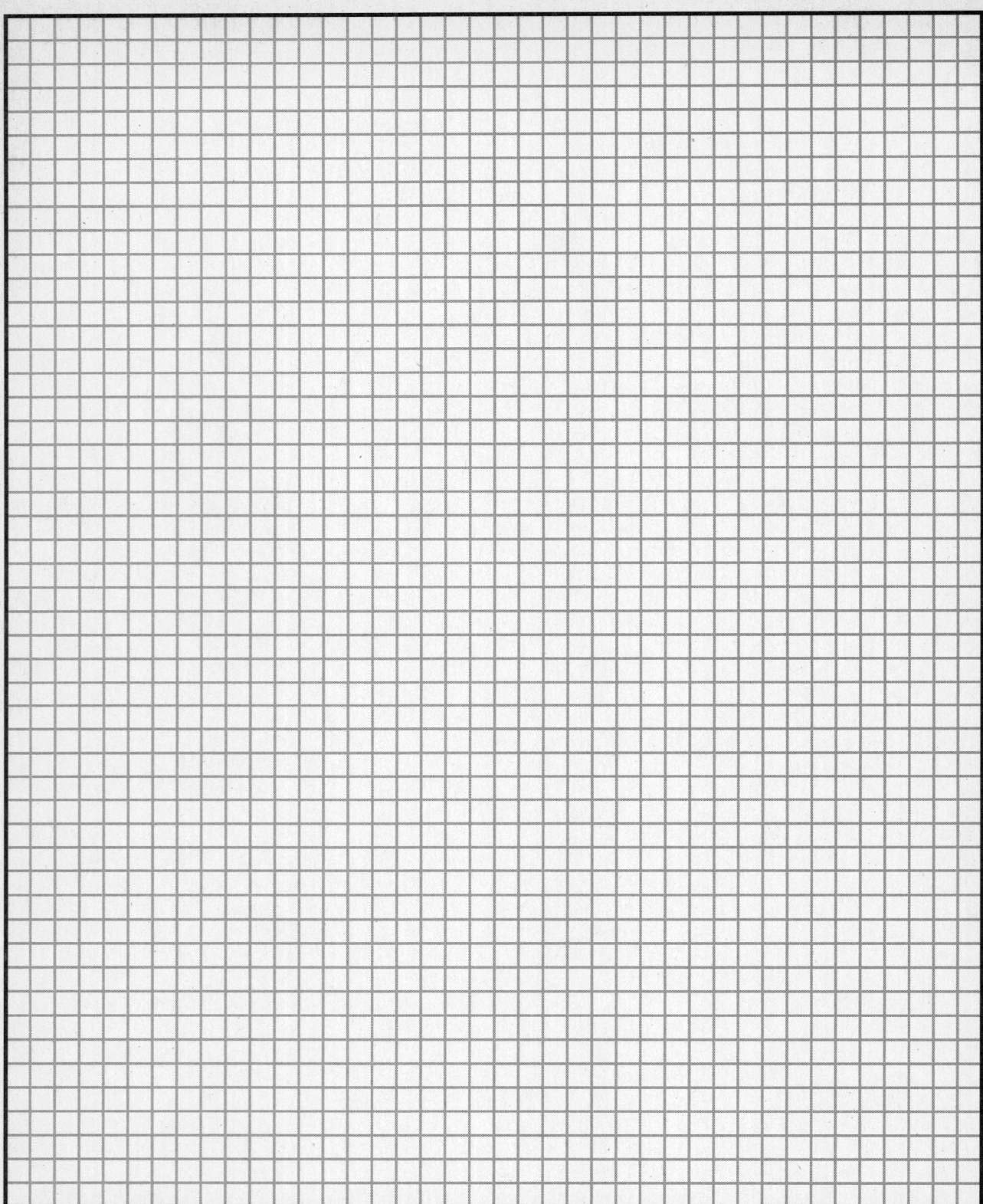

Name _____ Date _____ Class _____

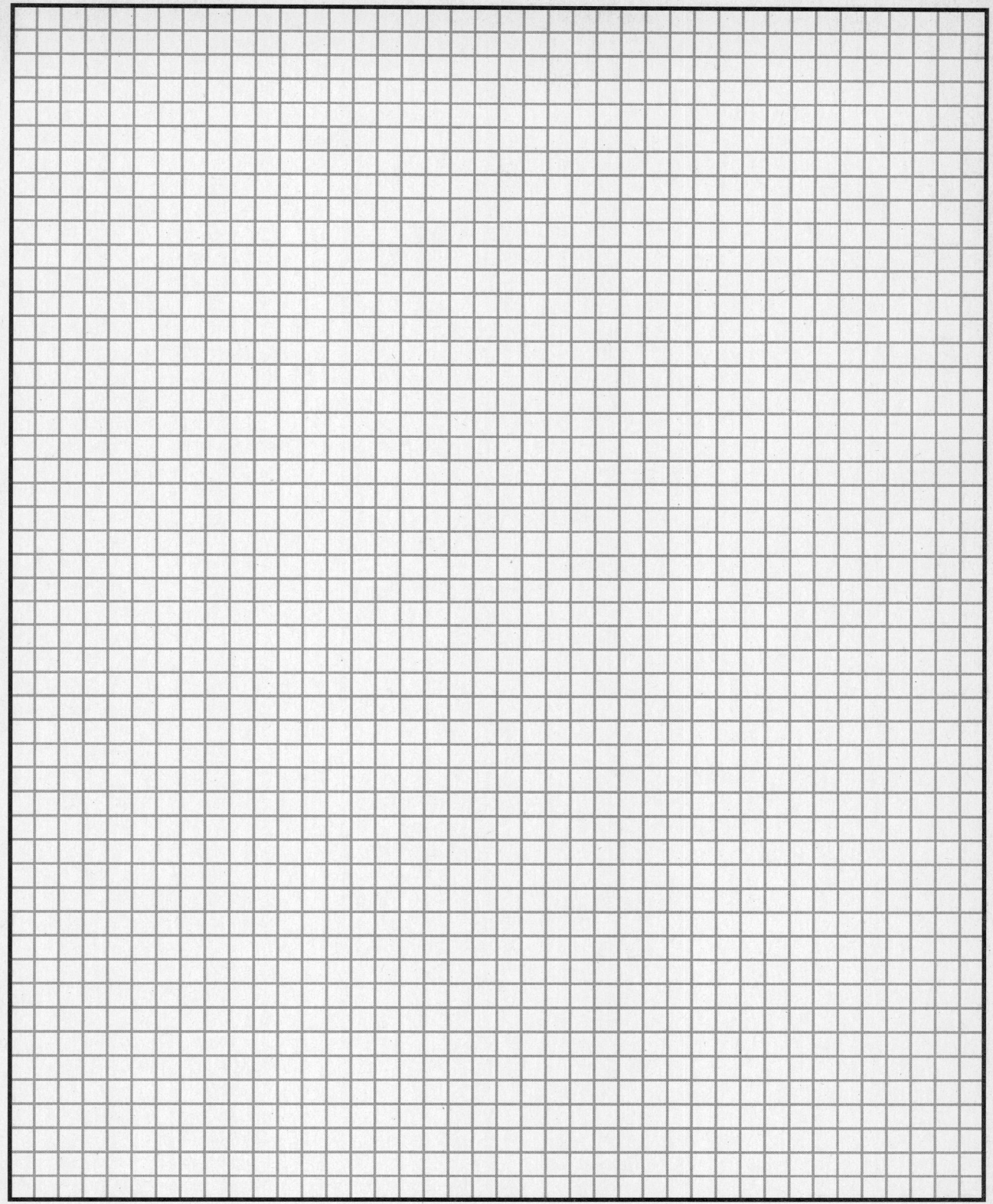

Name_____ Date_____ Class_____

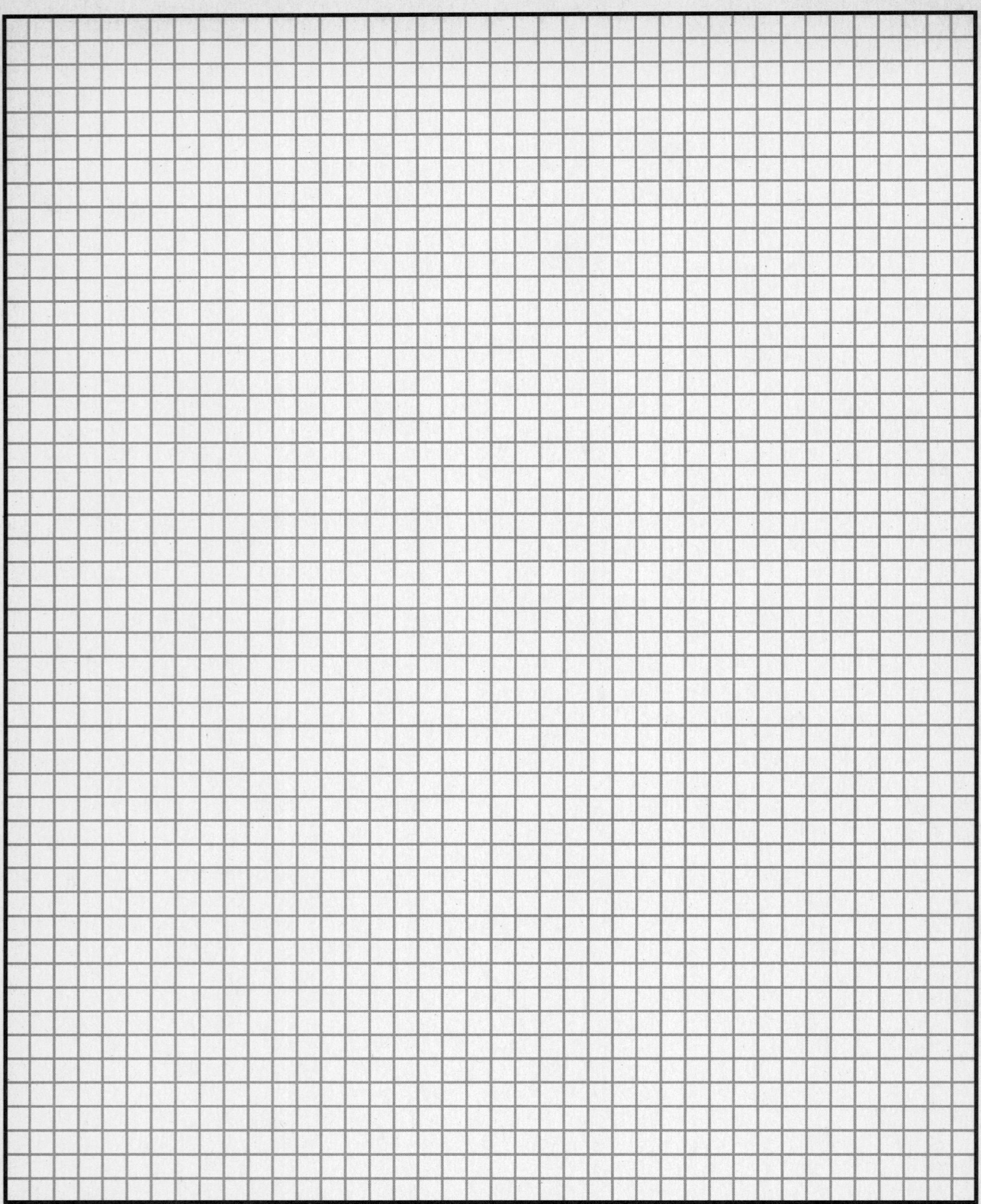

Name_____ Date_____ Class_____

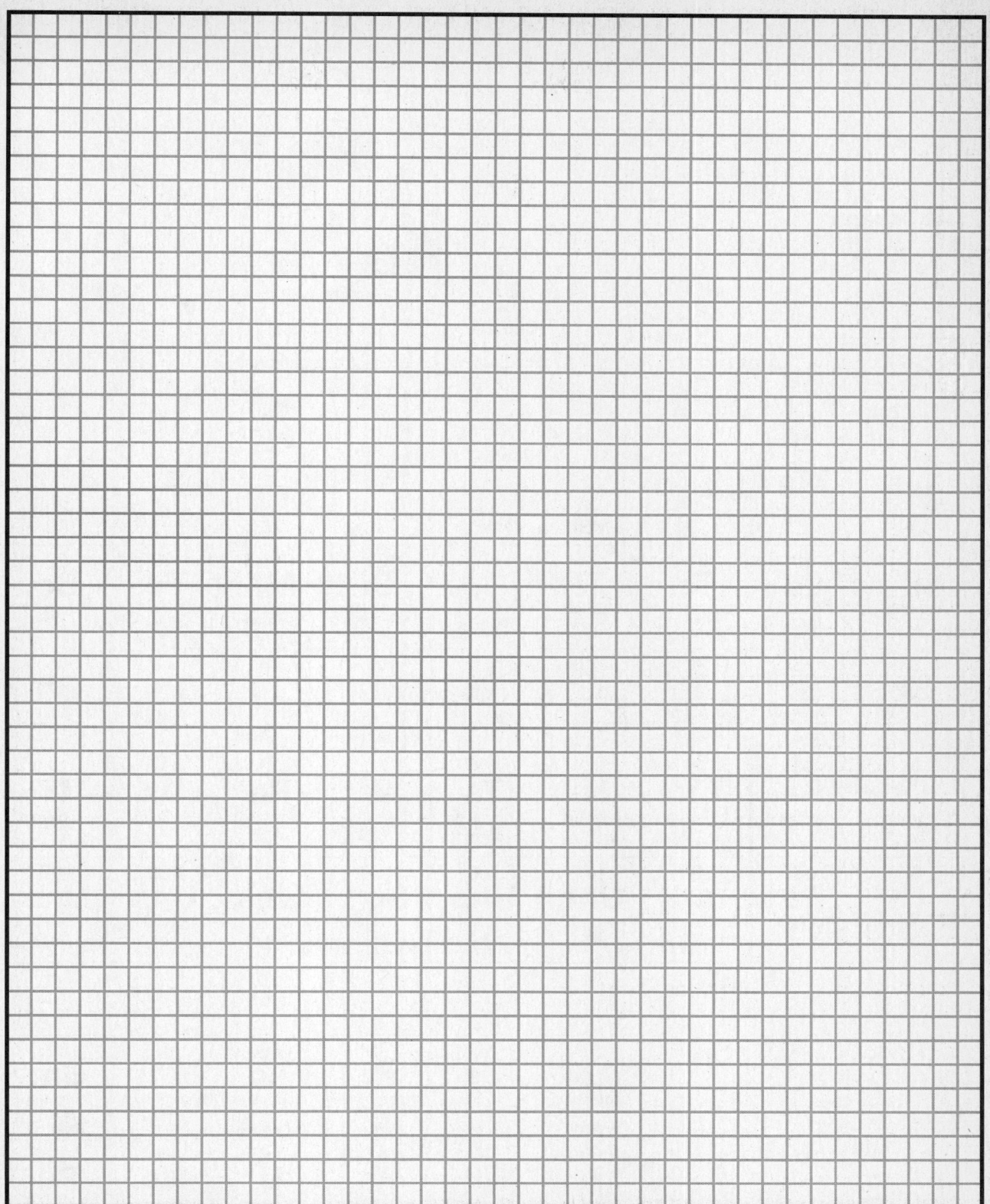

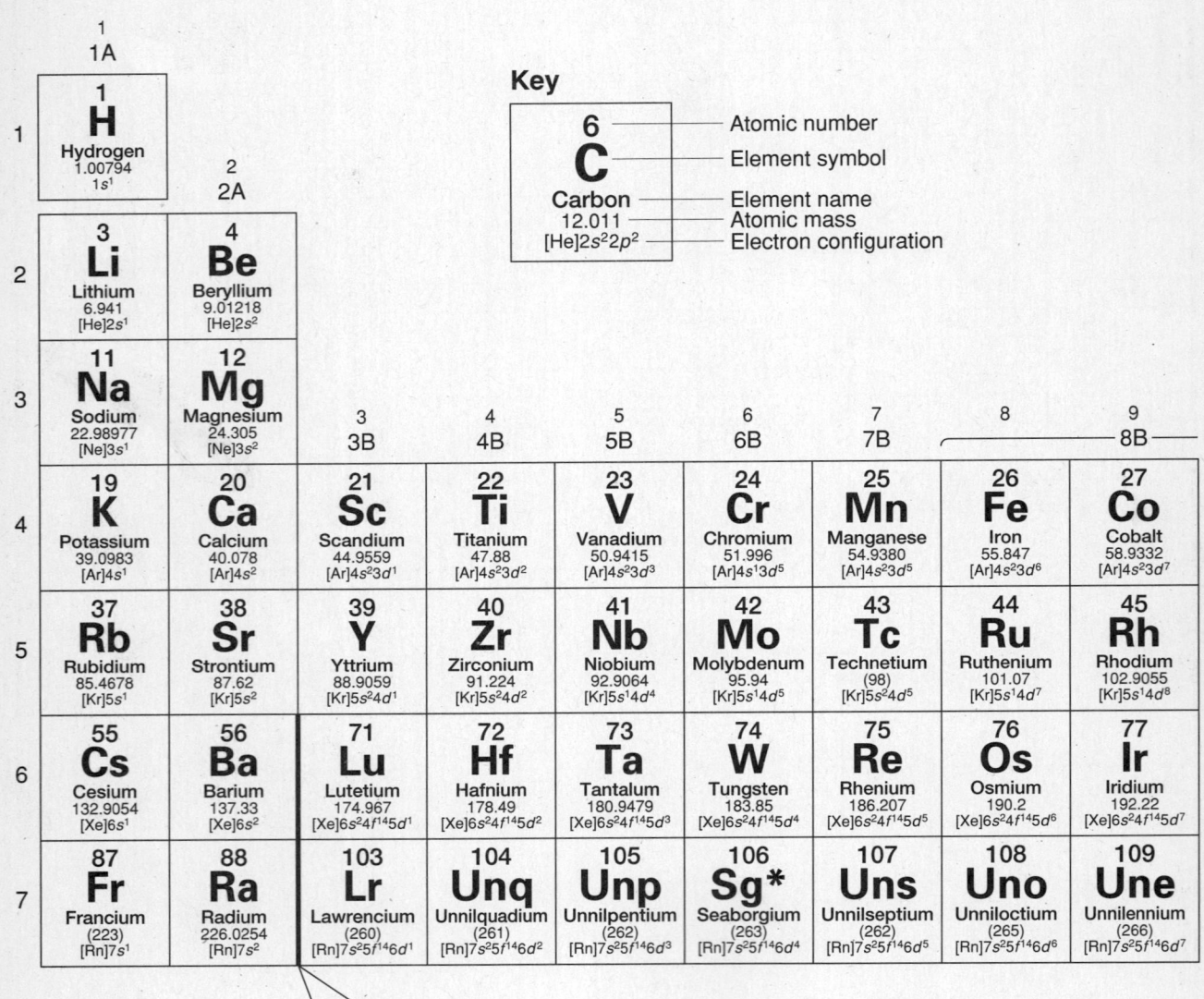